# FOOD & WINE

## an entire year of recipes 2006

## FOOD & WINE ANNUAL COOKBOOK 2006

EDITOR **Kate Heddings**
SENIOR EDITOR **Rachael Philipps Shapiro**
ASSISTANT FOOD EDITOR **Melissa Rubel**
COPY EDITOR **Lisa Leventer**
EDITORIAL ASSISTANT **Kristin Donnelly**

ART DIRECTOR **Patricia Sanchez**
DESIGNER **Nancy Blumberg**

SENIOR VICE PRESIDENT, CHIEF MARKETING OFFICER **Mark V. Stanich**
VICE PRESIDENT, BOOKS AND PRODUCTS **Marshall Corey**
SENIOR MARKETING MANAGER **Bruce Spanier**
CORPORATE PRODUCTION MANAGER **Stuart Handelman**
SENIOR OPERATIONS MANAGER **Phil Black**
BUSINESS MANAGER **Tom Noonan**

### FRONT COVER

Gingery Chicken Satay with Peanut Sauce, p. 108
PHOTOGRAPH BY Tina Rupp
FOOD STYLING BY Alison Attenborough

### BACK COVER

PHOTOGRAPHS (LAMB, SPAGHETTI) BY Quentin Bacon
FOOD STYLING (LAMB, SPAGHETTI) BY Susie Theodorou
PHOTOGRAPH (SANDWICHES) BY Tina Rupp
FOOD STYLING (SANDWICHES) BY Jee Levin

### FLAP PHOTOGRAPHS

DANA COWIN PORTRAIT BY Andrew French
KATE HEDDINGS PORTRAIT BY Andrew French

### AMERICAN EXPRESS PUBLISHING CORPORATION

ISBN 1-932624-09-0
ISSN 1097-1564

Published by American Express Publishing Corporation
1120 Avenue of the Americas, New York, New York 10036

Manufactured in the United States of America

## FOOD & WINE MAGAZINE

VICE PRESIDENT/EDITOR IN CHIEF **Dana Cowin**
CREATIVE DIRECTOR **Stephen Scoble**
MANAGING EDITOR **Mary Ellen Ward**
EXECUTIVE EDITOR **Pamela Kaufman**
EXECUTIVE FOOD EDITOR **Tina Ujlaki**
EXECUTIVE WINE EDITOR **Lettie Teague**

### FEATURES

FEATURES EDITOR **Michelle Shih**
TRAVEL EDITOR **Salma Abdelnour**
SENIOR EDITORS **Ray Isle, Kate Krader**
ASSISTANT EDITOR **Ratha Tep**
EDITORIAL ASSISTANT **Jessica Tzerman**

### FOOD

SENIOR EDITORS **Lily Barberio, Kate Heddings, Jane Sigal**
TEST KITCHEN SUPERVISOR **Marcia Kiesel**
SENIOR TEST KITCHEN ASSOCIATE **Grace Parisi**
TEST KITCHEN ASSOCIATE **Melissa Rubel**

### ART

ART DIRECTOR **Patricia Sanchez**

### PHOTO

PHOTO EDITOR **Fredrika Stjärne**
DEPUTY PHOTO EDITOR **Lucy Schaeffer**
ASSISTANT PHOTO EDITOR **Lisa S. Kim**

### PRODUCTION

ASSISTANT MANAGING EDITOR **Christine Quinlan**
PRODUCTION MANAGER **Matt Carson**

### COPY & RESEARCH

COPY CHIEF **Robert Firpo-Cappiello**
COPY EDITOR **Ann Lien**
RESEARCH EDITOR **Stacey Nield**
ASSISTANT EDITOR **Jen Murphy**

EDITORIAL BUSINESS ASSISTANT **Kalina Mazur**

# FOOD & WINE

## an entire year of recipes
## 2006

American Express Publishing Corporation, New York

**FOOD & WINE**
BOOKS

Tyler Florence created a fantastic Asian-inspired dinner party in the September issue, serving dishes like Skirt Steak with Shiso-Shallot Butter (P. 126).

# contents

The February issue featured a family lunch in Spain's Andalucía, with dishes like Fried Parsley-Flecked Shrimp Cakes (P. 203) and Garlicky Wild Mushroom Sauté (P. 224).

# foreword

Pulling together the 600-plus recipes for this annual cookbook has let us reminisce about a year's worth of extraordinary cooking and eating. F&W published an incredible variety of recipes that took us all over the world. We devoted an entire issue to Spain, gathering more than 40 recipes for dishes like Stuffed Piquillo Peppers with Idiazábal Cheese Sauce. Another issue reflected on the growing importance of Asian food in America, featuring recipes such as Skirt Steak with Shiso-Shallot Butter.

This 2006 collection also notes the trend of serious chefs using high-quality prepared foods as shortcuts. Ferran Adrià, the avant-garde genius behind El Bulli in Rosas, Spain, used supermarket ingredients like rotisserie chicken and potato chips to create stellar, fast meals. Nancy Silverton, who co-founded La Brea Bakery and Campanile restaurant in Los Angeles, shared her recipe for an antipasto salad with *bocconcini* and green olive tapenade from a jar. Dishes like these show that people who love food won't stop cooking—thank goodness—despite their need for speed.

New to the collection this year is the inclusion of 57 recipes previously published exclusively on our Web site, foodandwine.com. You'll also see more photographs of the people and places behind our recipes—a cooking class in Los Angeles, say, or a village on the Turkish coast. And we've added a glossary of pan sizes and ingredient substitutions.

Anyone looking for wine advice will find plenty of it here, with pairing notes throughout the book and a brand-new wine section by our wonderful senior editor Ray Isle. He's written clear, compelling descriptions of the key varietals, and for each category he's suggested affordable, easy-to-find bottles.

We'd love your feedback. Write us at cookbookcomments@foodandwine.com.


Dana Cowin
Editor in Chief
FOOD&WINE Magazine

Kate Heddings
Editor
FOOD&WINE Cookbooks

In the July issue, chef Nancy Silverton threw an antipasto party in Los Angeles, serving juicy little Lamb Meatballs with Red Pepper and Chickpea Sauce (P. 32).

8

# starters

**FRIED PARSNIP RIBBONS**

**SPICY RED PEPPER AND WALNUT DIP**

## Fried Parsnip Ribbons

**TOTAL: 30 MIN**

**10 SERVINGS** ● ● ●

At Little Giant restaurant in New York City, Julie Taras and Tasha Garcia usually top stewy dishes with these earthy vegetable chips for a bit of crunch. They also serve them at the bar as a salty snack.

- **2 quarts canola or vegetable oil**
- **4 large parsnips (about 1¾ pounds)**

**Kosher salt**

**1.** Place a wire rack on a large rimmed baking sheet and line the rack with 2 layers of paper towels. Heat the oil in a large saucepan until it registers 325° on a deep-fry thermometer. Meanwhile, using a sturdy Y-shaped vegetable peeler, shave the parsnips lengthwise into ribbons, moving around on all sides of the vegetable, stopping when you reach the tough inner cores of the parsnips.

**2.** Working in 5 or 6 batches, carefully drop handfuls of the ribbons into the hot oil and cook over moderately high heat, stirring occasionally with a wooden spoon, until the ribbons turn a deep honey color, about 1 minute. Using a slotted spoon or Chinese wire-and-bamboo skimmer, transfer to the paper towels and sprinkle with salt. Let cool completely, then transfer to a large platter. —*Julie Taras and Tasha Garcia*

**MAKE AHEAD** The parsnip ribbons can be fried 2 hours in advance.

## Spicy Red Pepper and Walnut Dip

**TOTAL: 30 MIN**

**4 SERVINGS** ● ● ● ●

- **1 tablespoon fresh lemon juice**
- **2 teaspoons sherry vinegar**
- **1 cup small, crustless, stale white bread cubes**
- **½ cup coarsely chopped walnuts**

- **¼ cup extra-virgin olive oil**
- **3 red bell peppers, cut into thin strips**
- **2 tablespoons water**
- **1 large garlic clove, smashed**
- **1 small dried red chile**

**Salt**

**Toasted pita wedges, for serving**

**1.** Preheat the oven to 350°. In a small bowl, mix the lemon juice and vinegar. Add the bread cubes and toss to coat; let the bread soak up the liquid.

**2.** Spread the walnuts in a pie plate and bake until lightly toasted, 5 minutes.

**3.** In a large skillet, heat 2 tablespoons of the olive oil. Add the bell peppers, water, garlic and chile; season with salt. Cover and cook over low heat, stirring occasionally, until the peppers are tender, 10 minutes. Uncover and cook over high heat, shaking the skillet, until all the liquid has evaporated, 1 minute; discard the chile.

**4.** Transfer the peppers to a food processor and let cool until warm. Add the soaked bread and pulse to a thick, coarse paste. Add the walnuts; pulse just until coarsely ground. Scrape the dip into a bowl and season with salt. Drizzle the red pepper and walnut dip with the remaining 2 tablespoons of olive oil and serve with toasted pita wedges. —*Alex Raij*

**MAKE AHEAD** The red pepper and walnut dip can be kept at room temperature for up to 4 hours.

### "Terra" Chips

**TOTAL: 45 MIN**

**8 SERVINGS** ●

The name of this recipe is a play on Hiro Sone and Lissa Doumani's Napa Valley restaurant, Terra, as well as the Terra Chips that are available nationwide.

Vegetable oil, for frying
1  large baking potato—peeled, sliced paper-thin on a mandoline and patted dry
1  medium red beet—peeled, sliced paper-thin on a mandoline and patted dry
1  small parsnip—peeled, sliced paper-thin with a vegetable peeler and patted dry
1  small lotus root—peeled, sliced paper-thin on a mandoline and patted dry
1  taro root—peeled, sliced paper-thin on a mandoline and patted dry
Kosher salt

In a large pot, heat 2 inches of vegetable oil to 310°. Working in small batches, fry each vegetable separately, stirring a few times, until they are golden, about 3 minutes. Using a slotted spoon, transfer the chips to paper towels to drain. Sprinkle the chips with salt and serve.
—*Hiro Sone*

**MAKE AHEAD** The chips can be stored overnight in an airtight container.

### Fava Bean Puree with Dill and Lemon

**ACTIVE: 30 MIN; TOTAL: 1 HR 30 MIN**
**PLUS OVERNIGHT SOAKING**

**6 SERVINGS** ● ●

¼  cup plus 2 tablespoons extra-virgin olive oil
2  medium onions, finely chopped
½  pound split, dried fava beans (1¼ cups), soaked overnight and drained
1  medium Yukon Gold potato, peeled and cut into ⅓-inch dice
2½  cups water
1  teaspoon sugar
¼  cup plus 2 tablespoons fresh lemon juice
Salt
¼  cup finely chopped dill
Warmed pita, for serving

**1.** In a large saucepan, heat 2 tablespoons of the olive oil until shimmering. Add the onions and cook over moderately high heat, stirring, until softened, about 5 minutes. Add the drained fava beans, potato, water, sugar, 2 tablespoons of the lemon juice and 1 teaspoon of salt and bring to a boil. Cover partially and cook over moderately low heat until the fava beans and potato are broken down and the liquid is nearly absorbed, about 1 hour.

**2.** Transfer the mixture to a food processor and pulse until coarsely pureed. Season with salt, add 2 tablespoons of the dill and stir until incorporated. Transfer the fava bean puree to a serving bowl and let cool to room temperature.

**3.** Meanwhile, in a small bowl, whisk together the remaining ¼ cup of olive oil, ¼ cup of lemon juice and 2 tablespoons of dill. Season the dressing with salt and pour over the fava bean puree. Serve with the pita. —*Eveline Zoutendijk*

**MAKE AHEAD** The fava puree can be refrigerated for up to 3 days. Bring to room temperature and top with the dill dressing just before serving.

### Potato Chips with Blue Cheese

**TOTAL: 15 MIN**

**4 TO 6 SERVINGS** ●

2  tablespoons unsalted butter
1  medium onion, finely chopped
2  tablespoons all-purpose flour
2  cups milk
½  pound blue cheese, such as Maytag Blue, crumbled (2 cups)
Kosher salt
¼  teaspoon cayenne pepper
One 6-ounce bag thick-cut potato chips

**1.** In a medium saucepan, melt the butter. Add the chopped onion to the saucepan and cook over moderate heat, stirring, for about 7 minutes. Whisk the flour into the chopped onion and cook for 1 minute longer. Slowly whisk the milk into the onion mixture and cook the sauce over moderate heat, whisking, until it is thickened, about 5 minutes. Off the heat, whisk the blue cheese into the chopped onion and season the blue cheese sauce with salt and the cayenne.

**2.** Put half of the potato chips in a large, shallow bowl and drizzle them with half of the blue cheese sauce. Add the remaining potato chips and blue cheese sauce to make another layer. Serve the potato chips and blue cheese sauce immediately. —*Bobby Flay*

# health
### RED BELL PEPPERS

The red bell peppers in the spicy dip recipe on the opposite page are loaded with **vitamin A,** 10 times as much as a yellow bell pepper. And one large red bell pepper contains all the **vitamin C** you need in a day, more than twice the vitamin C of a green bell pepper and about as much as two and a half grapefruit.

# starters

## Yogurt Dip with Mint and Garlic

**ACTIVE: 5 MIN; TOTAL: 2 HR**

**2 SERVINGS** ●

This thick yogurt dip is a wonderfully tangy and refreshing complement to spicy Turkish dishes. Depending on the dish it accompanies, other fresh herbs such as cilantro or parsley could stand in for the mint; grated carrots or chopped dried apricots can also be added.

- 1 cup plain full-fat Greek or Bulgarian yogurt
- 1 garlic clove, chopped

Salt

- 2 tablespoons finely chopped mint, plus mint leaves for garnish

Warm pita bread, for serving

**1.** Line a strainer with a coffee filter or a double layer of moistened cheesecloth and spoon in the yogurt. Set the strainer over a bowl and let the yogurt drain until it is fairly firm, about 2 hours.

**2.** Using the side of a chef's knife, mash the garlic to a paste with a large pinch of salt. In a bowl, mix the garlic paste with the drained yogurt and chopped mint. Sprinkle with the mint leaves and serve with warm pita. —*Eveline Zoutendijk*

**MAKE AHEAD** The dip can be refrigerated for up to 2 days.

## Spicy Spinach Dip with Pine Nuts

**ACTIVE: 15 MIN; TOTAL: 30 MIN**

**4 SERVINGS** ● ● ●

- 1½ cups plain nonfat yogurt
- 2 tablespoons extra-virgin olive oil
- ¼ cup pine nuts
- ½ small sweet onion, minced
- ½ teaspoon ground cumin
- ½ teaspoon ground coriander
- ½ teaspoon pure chile powder

Pinch of cayenne

One 10-ounce package frozen whole-leaf spinach, thawed

Salt

**1.** Scoop the yogurt into a paper towel–lined strainer set over a bowl. Let stand at room temperature for 30 minutes. You should end up with 1 cup of yogurt.

**2.** Meanwhile, heat the olive oil in a small skillet. Add the pine nuts and onion and cook over high heat, stirring frequently, until the onion is softened and lightly browned and the pine nuts are golden, 4 to 5 minutes. Add the cumin, coriander, chile powder and cayenne and cook, stirring, for 1 minute. Scrape into a bowl.

**3.** Using your hands or a potato ricer, squeeze the spinach until very dry, then coarsely chop it and discard any stringy pieces. Add the spinach and the drained yogurt to the onion mixture, season with salt and stir well. —*Grace Parisi*

**SERVE WITH** Toasted baguette slices or crudités. Or use as a condiment for curries, steaks or roasted chicken.

**MAKE AHEAD** The spinach dip can be refrigerated overnight.

## Warm Olives with Rosemary, Garlic and Lemon

**TOTAL: 25 MIN**

**8 SERVINGS** ● ● ●

- ¼ cup extra-virgin olive oil

Strips of zest from 1 small lemon

- 1 small rosemary sprig
- 2 small garlic cloves, thickly sliced
- 1 pound mixed oil- and brine-cured olives, such as Calamata, Niçoise, Moroccan, cracked green Sicilian and Cerignola (3 cups)

In a medium saucepan, combine the olive oil, lemon zest, rosemary and garlic and cook over moderate heat until the garlic just begins to brown, about 6 minutes. Remove from the heat, stir in the mixed olives and let stand for at least 15 minutes. —*Marc Murphy*

**MAKE AHEAD** The olives can be prepared up to 3 days ahead and refrigerated; warm gently before serving.

## Sweet Pepper and Fig Peperonata

**ACTIVE: 25 MIN; TOTAL: 45 MIN**

**4 SERVINGS** ● ●

At the tiny tapas bar Tía Pol in New York City, chef Alex Raij takes liberties with bell peppers, offering a Spanish version of the Italian *peperonata*.

- 12 dried black Mission figs, halved lengthwise
- 2 tablespoons balsamic vinegar
- ¼ cup extra-virgin olive oil
- 4 assorted bell peppers, sliced ½ inch thick
- 1 red onion, sliced ¼ inch thick
- 1 large garlic clove, smashed
- 1 cinnamon stick, broken in half

One 2-inch strip of lemon zest

Salt

- ¼ cup dry white wine
- ¼ cup water
- 1 thyme sprig
- 2 tablespoons chopped basil
- 1 teaspoon coarsely chopped marjoram

**1.** In a shallow bowl, toss the halved black Mission figs with 1 tablespoon of the balsamic vinegar.

**2.** In a large saucepan, heat 2 tablespoons of the olive oil. Add the bell peppers, onion, garlic, cinnamon stick and lemon zest, season with salt and cook over moderately high heat for 3 minutes. Add the white wine and cook for 1 minute. Add the water and thyme sprig, cover and cook until the bell peppers are tender, about 10 minutes. Add the black Mission figs and cook for 2 minutes longer. Remove the *peperonata* from the heat. Discard the garlic, cinnamon stick, lemon zest and thyme. Transfer the *peperonata* to a bowl and let cool slightly, then stir in the basil, marjoram and the remaining 1 tablespoon of balsamic vinegar and 2 tablespoons of olive oil. Season the *peperonata* with salt. Serve warm or at room temperature. —*Alex Raij*

**MAKE AHEAD** The *peperonata* can be kept at room temperature for up to 4 hours.

SWEET PEPPER AND
FIG PEPERONATA

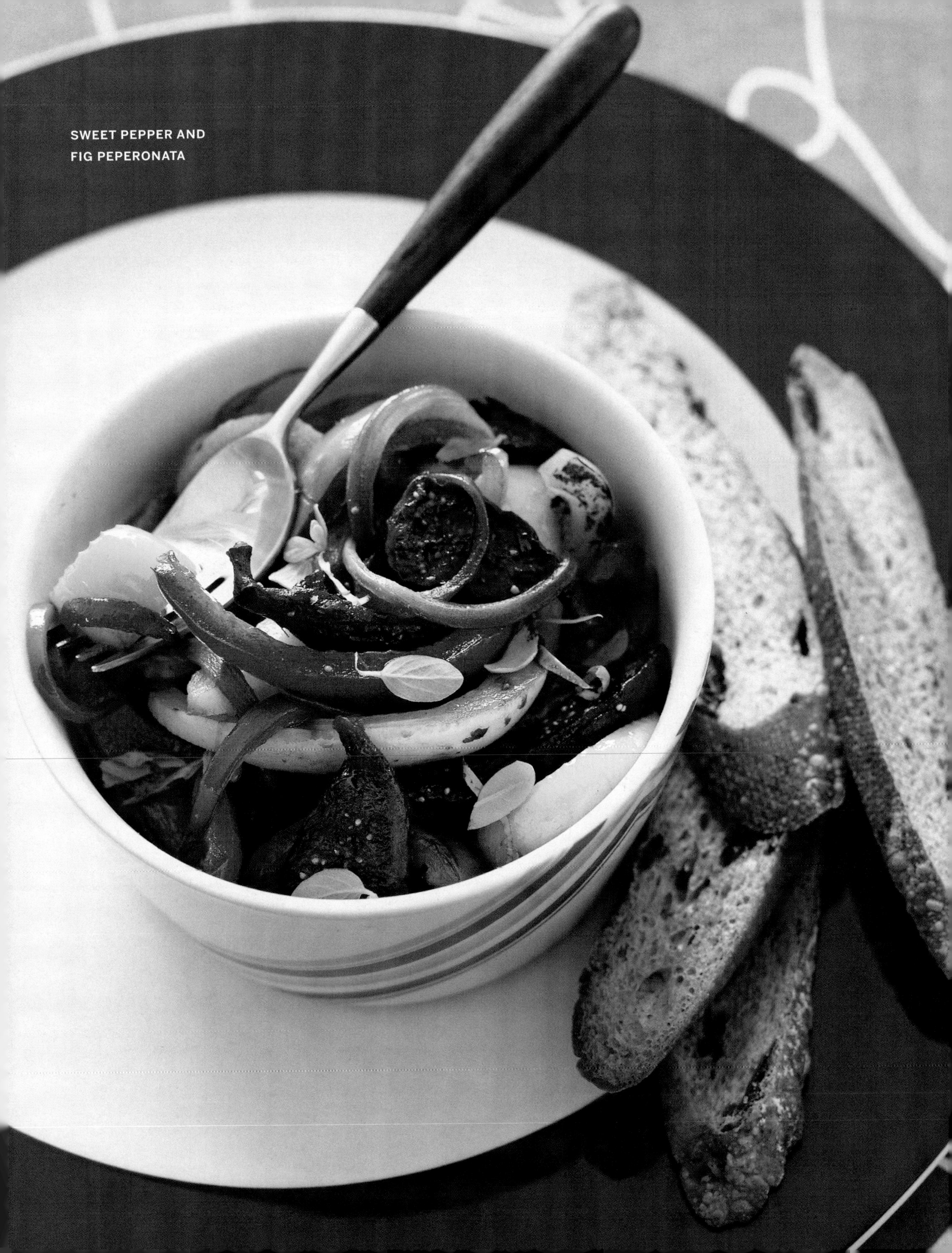

RED PEPPER JELLY WITH GRISSINI
AND MONTASIO CHEESE

## Red Pepper Jelly with Grissini and Montasio Cheese

**ACTIVE: 1 HR; TOTAL: 2 HR 30 MIN**

**8 TO 10 SERVINGS** ●

*Grissini* are Italian breadsticks—not the typical stubby, sesame-coated ones but svelte, supercrunchy ones. Lachlan Mackinnon-Patterson of Frasca Food and Wine in Boulder, Colorado, serves them with a sweet-tart red pepper jelly (a recipe handed down from his grandmother) and slices of Montasio cheese.

**JELLY**

- 3 medium red bell peppers— stemmed, seeded and quartered
- 4 cups sugar
- ¾ cup plus 2 tablespoons white wine vinegar
- 1 packet liquid pectin (¼ cup plus 2 tablespoons)

**GRISSINI**

- 1 cup milk
- 2 envelopes active dry yeast (4 teaspoons)
- 1 tablespoon sugar
- 3 cups bread flour (1 pound), plus more for kneading and rolling
- 6 tablespoons unsalted butter, softened
- 1 tablespoon salt
- 2 tablespoons extra-virgin olive oil, plus more for brushing

Coarse sea salt, for sprinkling

- ¾ pound Montasio cheese, cut into slices, for serving

**1. MAKE THE JELLY:** In a blender or food processor, pulse the red peppers until coarsely pureed. You should have 2 cups. Transfer to a large saucepan. Add the sugar and vinegar and bring to a simmer over moderate heat, stirring, until the sugar dissolves. Continue to cook over moderate heat, stirring constantly, until slightly reduced, about 8 minutes. Remove from the heat and stir in the pectin. Bring to a boil and stir constantly for 1 minute. Pour the jelly into 5 sterilized 8-ounce jars and cover tightly. Let cool completely, then refrigerate the jars.

**2. MAKE THE GRISSINI:** In a medium saucepan, warm the milk. Add the yeast and sugar and let stand until slightly foamy, about 5 minutes. Pour the milk into a large bowl. Add the 3 cups of bread flour, the butter, salt and 2 tablespoons of olive oil and stir until a stiff, raggy dough forms. Turn the dough out onto a lightly floured work surface and knead until smooth and elastic, about 5 minutes. Lightly oil the bowl and return the dough to it, turning to coat. Cover with a kitchen towel and let rest for 1 hour, or until doubled in volume.

**3.** Preheat the oven to 350°. Line 2 baking sheets with parchment paper. Turn the dough out onto a lightly floured work surface and press it down. Cut the dough into 5 pieces. Working with 2 pieces of dough at a time, roll each piece to a 10-inch square. Brush the dough lightly with olive oil and sprinkle with coarse salt. Using a ruler and a pastry wheel or pizza cutter, cut the dough into ⅓-inch-wide strips. Transfer the strips to the prepared baking sheet.

**4.** Bake the *grissini* for 12 minutes, until golden and crisp, shifting the pans from top to bottom and front to back for even browning. Repeat with the remaining dough. Let cool completely. Serve the *grissini* with the red pepper jelly and the Montasio cheese.
—*Lachlan Mackinnon-Patterson*

**MAKE AHEAD** The *grissini* can be stored in an airtight container for up to 2 days. The jelly can be refrigerated for 2 weeks.

## Falafel-Spiced Pecans

**TOTAL: 15 MIN**

**6 SERVINGS** ● ● ●

Toasting nuts briefly in the oven makes them crispy, but tossing them with falafel mix first makes them even crunchier. You can substitute walnuts in place of the pecans here.

- 2 cups pecan halves
- 2 tablespoons unsalted butter, melted
- ¼ cup falafel mix
- 1 tablespoon sugar
- ½ teaspoon cayenne pepper

Preheat the oven to 350°. In a medium bowl, toss the pecans with the butter until evenly coated. In a small bowl, combine the falafel mix with the sugar and cayenne. Pour the spice mix over the pecans and toss to coat. Spread the spiced nuts on a lightly greased baking sheet and toast for about 9 minutes, stirring once or twice, until golden. Let cool. —*Grace Parisi*

## Spicy Cashew Crunch with Ginger

**ACTIVE: 30 MIN; TOTAL: 1 HR**

**4 SERVINGS** ● ● ●

Vegetable oil

- 1 tablespoon granulated sugar
- 1 tablespoon hot water
- 2 teaspoons soy sauce
- 4 garlic cloves, very thinly sliced
- 2 cups roasted, salted cashews, split lengthwise
- 1 tablespoon coarsely grated fresh ginger, squeezed dry
- 2 teaspoons crushed red pepper
- 1 teaspoon grated lime zest
- 2 tablespoons raw sugar

Salt

**1.** Preheat the oven to 325°. Lightly oil a large baking sheet. In a small bowl, dissolve the granulated sugar in the hot water. Stir in 1 teaspoon of the soy sauce.

**2.** In a pan of boiling water, blanch the garlic for 10 seconds. Drain and pat dry. Transfer to a bowl. Add the remaining soy sauce and the cashews, ginger, red pepper and zest and toss well. Add the soy syrup and toss, then add the raw sugar and toss again.

**3.** Spread the nuts on the baking sheet; season with salt. Bake for 25 minutes, until golden. Let cool until warm but pliable. Using a metal spatula, loosen the nuts from the sheet and cool. —*Marcia Kiesel*

## Smashed Cannellini Bean Crostini with Feta Salsa Verde

**TOTAL: 50 MIN**

12 SERVINGS ● ●

- 1 baguette, cut on the diagonal into thirty-six ¼-inch-thick slices
- ½ cup extra-virgin olive oil
- 1 small rosemary sprig
- 1 dried árbol chile or other dried red chile, stemmed and coarsely crumbled
- ½ small onion, finely chopped
- 2 tablespoons minced shallot
- 1 garlic clove, minced
- 1 tablespoon thyme leaves

Two 19-ounce cans cannellini beans, drained and rinsed

- ¼ cup chicken stock or low-sodium broth

Kosher salt and freshly ground pepper
Feta Salsa Verde (recipe follows)

**1.** Preheat the oven to 375°. Brush both sides of each baguette slice with ¼ cup of the olive oil. Arrange the slices on a baking sheet and toast for about 10 minutes, until golden and the edges are crisp; let cool.
**2.** In a medium saucepan, heat the remaining ¼ cup of olive oil. Add the rosemary and chile and cook over moderately high heat until sizzling, about 1 minute. Add the onion, shallot, garlic and thyme and cook, stirring occasionally, until softened, about 2 minutes. Add the cannellini beans and cook for 3 minutes, stirring to coat well. Discard the rosemary sprig. Add the stock, season with salt and pepper and remove from the heat. Coarsely mash the beans with a fork.
**3.** Spread the cannellini puree on the toasts and arrange the crostini on platters. Spoon the Feta Salsa Verde on each crostini and serve. —*Suzanne Goin*

**MAKE AHEAD** The baguette toasts can be kept overnight in an airtight container. The puree can be refrigerated overnight; let it return to room temperature before serving. The crostini can be assembled 1 hour ahead; cover with plastic wrap.

### FETA SALSA VERDE

**TOTAL: 15 MIN**

MAKES 1¼ CUPS ● ● ●

- 1 cup chopped flat-leaf parsley
- ¼ cup coarsely chopped mint
- 1 teaspoon oregano leaves
- ¾ cup extra-virgin olive oil
- 1 small garlic clove, smashed
- 1 anchovy, preferably salt-packed, rinsed
- 1 tablespoon drained capers

Juice of ½ lemon

- 4 ounces feta cheese, crumbled

In a mortar, working in batches, pound the parsley, mint and oregano. Work in 2 tablespoons of the oil; transfer to a bowl. Pound the garlic with the anchovy and add to the bowl. Gently pound the capers and add to the bowl. Stir in the remaining olive oil and the lemon juice. Gently stir in the feta and serve. —*S.G.*

## Fried Gorgonzola Bites

**TOTAL: 1 HR PLUS 3 HR 30 MIN CHILLING**

MAKES ABOUT 5 DOZEN
BITE-SIZE CROQUETTES

Writer Jeff Koehler adapted this recipe by the young Catalan genius Sergi Arola. Arola makes these light, golden croquettes with warm, silky Gorgonzola cheese centers for his eponymous restaurant in Barcelona's Hotel Arts.

- 6 tablespoons unsalted butter
- 1¾ cups all-purpose flour
- 2 cups whole milk
- ¼ pound Gorgonzola dolce, cut into small pieces

Pinch of freshly grated nutmeg
Salt and freshly ground pepper

- 3 large eggs, beaten
- 2 cups dry bread crumbs

About 1 quart pure olive oil, for frying

**1.** Line an 8-inch square baking dish with plastic wrap and spray with vegetable oil spray. In a medium saucepan, melt the butter. Add ¾ cup of the flour and cook for 1 minute, whisking constantly. Whisk in the milk and cook over moderately high heat, whisking constantly, until thick, about 5 minutes. Reduce the heat to low and whisk in the Gorgonzola until completely melted, about 2 minutes. Add the nutmeg and season with salt and pepper. Scrape the mixture into the lined baking dish. Smooth the top and coat lightly with vegetable oil spray. Press a sheet of plastic wrap directly onto the mixture and freeze until firm but still soft enough to cut, about 3 hours.
**2.** Line a baking sheet with wax paper. Spoon the remaining 1 cup of flour into a shallow bowl. Put the beaten eggs and bread crumbs in separate shallow bowls. Invert the set cheese mixture onto a cutting board and remove the plastic wrap. Using a floured knife, cut the cheese mixture into 1-inch cubes, wiping the blade between slices. Working with 5 or 6 pieces at a time and keeping the rest refrigerated, dredge the cubes in flour, then in the egg and bread crumbs. Transfer the croquettes to the baking sheet and refrigerate for 30 minutes.
**3.** Place a wire rack over a baking sheet and line the rack with paper towels. Pour 1½ inches of oil into a medium saucepan and heat to 365°. Add 4 or 5 croquettes to the hot oil and fry until golden and crisp, about 1 minute. Using a slotted spoon, transfer the croquettes to the paper towel–lined rack to drain. Repeat with the remaining croquettes and serve. —*Jeff Koehler*

## Oven-Fried Rice Balls with Gruyère

**ACTIVE: 30 MIN; TOTAL: 1 HR**

MAKES ABOUT 30 RICE BALLS

Flecked with cracked black pepper and Gruyère cheese, these crusty rice balls are irresistible hors d'oeuvres.

- 1 tablespoon extra-virgin olive oil
- 1 medium shallot, minced
- 1 garlic clove, minced
- 1 cup arborio rice
- 2 cups water
- ¾ cup shredded Gruyère cheese (2½ ounces)

½ cup freshly grated Parmesan cheese (1½ ounces)

¼ cup mixed chopped herbs, such as thyme, basil and oregano

Salt and cracked black pepper

2 large egg whites

½ cup *panko* (Japanese bread crumbs)

1. Preheat the oven to 450°. Lightly oil a large rimmed baking sheet. Heat the olive oil in a medium saucepan. Add the shallot and garlic and cook over moderate heat until softened, about 4 minutes. Add the rice and cook, stirring, for 30 seconds. Stir in the water and bring to a boil. Cover and simmer over moderately low heat, stirring occasionally, until the water has been completely absorbed, about 10 minutes. Scrape the rice into a bowl and let cool to room temperature.

2. Stir the Gruyère, ¼ cup of the Parmesan and all of the chopped herbs into the rice. Season the rice with salt and generously season with cracked pepper.

3. In a stainless steel bowl, beat the egg whites with a pinch of salt until firm peaks form. Stir one-fourth of the whites into the rice to loosen it, then stir in the remaining whites. Roll the rice into 1½-inch balls.

4. In a shallow bowl, toss the *panko* with the remaining ¼ cup of Parmesan. Dredge the rice balls in the *panko* and transfer to the prepared baking sheet. Bake the rice balls in the upper third of the oven for 25 minutes, or until golden and crisp. Let stand for 5 minutes, then transfer to a platter and serve. —*Marcia Kiesel*

## Turkey Liver Mousse Toasts with Pickled Shallots

ACTIVE: 50 MIN; TOTAL: 2 HR PLUS 4 HR CHILLING

10 SERVINGS ● ● ●

MOUSSE

1 pound turkey or chicken livers, trimmed

1 cup milk

2 tablespoons extra-virgin olive oil

½ sweet red apple, cored and chopped

1 large shallot, chopped

1 garlic clove, chopped

1 sage leaf

¼ teaspoon ground cinnamon

¼ teaspoon freshly ground pepper

2 teaspoons kosher salt

1 tablespoon bourbon

⅓ cup heavy cream

1 baguette, sliced ⅓ inch thick on the diagonal

PICKLED SHALLOTS

½ cup sugar

½ cup cider vinegar

4 large shallots (½ pound), thinly sliced

1 teaspoon kosher salt

¼ teaspoon freshly ground pepper

1 thyme sprig

1. MAKE THE MOUSSE: In a bowl, cover the livers with the milk; refrigerate for 1 hour.

2. In a large skillet, heat the olive oil. Add the apple, shallot, garlic, sage, cinnamon, pepper and 1 teaspoon of the salt. Cook over moderate heat until the shallot is softened, about 4 minutes. Drain the livers and pat dry. Add them to the skillet and cook until just pink inside, 5 to 7 minutes. Add the bourbon and simmer for 1 minute.

3. Transfer the contents of the skillet to a food processor. Add the cream and the remaining 1 teaspoon of salt and puree until smooth. Scrape the mousse into a small bowl and refrigerate until firm enough to spread, at least 4 hours.

4. MEANWHILE, MAKE THE PICKLED SHALLOTS: In a small saucepan, combine the sugar with the vinegar and simmer over moderate heat until the sugar dissolves. Add the shallots, salt, pepper and thyme and simmer over moderately low heat, stirring occasionally, until the shallots are softened, about 8 minutes. Remove from the heat and let the shallots pickle for 10 minutes. Using a slotted spoon, remove

the shallots from the brine and spread on a plate to cool. Discard the thyme sprig. Transfer the shallots to a serving bowl.

5. ASSEMBLE THE TOASTS: Preheat the oven to 350°. Spread the bread on baking sheets; toast for about 7 minutes per side, until lightly browned. Serve the mousse with the toasts and pickled shallots. —*Allison Vines-Rushing and Slade Rushing*

## Gruyère Cheese Puffs

ACTIVE: 25 MIN; TOTAL: 1 HR

MAKES ABOUT 3 DOZEN PUFFS ● ●

This is a free-form version of gougères, the rich pastries served in Burgundy. Simply spoon the batter onto a baking sheet instead of fussing with a piping bag.

1 cup water

5 tablespoons unsalted butter, cut into tablespoons

½ teaspoon salt

¾ cup all-purpose flour

3 large eggs

2½ ounces Gruyère cheese, cut into ¼-inch dice (about ⅔ cup)

½ teaspoon freshly ground pepper

1. Preheat the oven to 400°. Line 2 large rimmed baking sheets with parchment. In a medium saucepan, combine the water, butter and salt and bring to a boil over moderate heat. Reduce the heat to low, add the flour all at once and beat with a wooden spoon until the batter is smooth and pulls away from the side of the pan. Beat for 1 minute longer over the heat to dry out the batter. Remove from the heat and let the batter cool for 5 minutes. Beat in 1 egg at a time, beating well between additions. Stir in the cheese and pepper.

2. Drop tablespoons of the batter onto the prepared baking sheets and bake for about 30 minutes, or until puffed and golden. Transfer to a rack to cool. Serve warm or at room temperature. —*Jane Martin*

MAKE AHEAD The baked puffs can be frozen for up to 1 month. Thaw and reheat in a 350° oven for 5 minutes.

# starters

## Coconut-Crab Cocktail

**TOTAL: 20 MIN**

4 TO 6 SERVINGS ●

Morsels of sweet crab are combined here with Asian flavors—lush coconut milk, piquant lime juice and aromatic cilantro—and then served with salty chips.

- 1 can (13½ ounces) unsweetened coconut milk
- ¼ cup fresh lime juice
- 2 tablespoons habanero hot sauce

Kosher salt and freshly ground pepper

- 1½ pounds lump crabmeat, picked over
- ¼ cup chopped cilantro

One 7-ounce bag plantain chips or tortilla chips

**1.** In a bowl, whisk the coconut milk with the lime juice and hot sauce and season with salt and pepper. Gently fold in the crabmeat. Let stand for 15 minutes.

**2.** Using a slotted spoon, transfer the crabmeat to shallow bowls and garnish with the cilantro. Serve the chips on the side. —*Bobby Flay*

## Crispy Chicken and Vegetable Croquettes

**ACTIVE: 1 HR; TOTAL: 2 HR 30 MIN**

MAKES ABOUT 35 CROQUETTES

Chef Ismael Prados prepares these delicately spiced snacks at the tapas bar La Vinya del Senyor in Barcelona.

- 4 skinless, boneless chicken thighs
- 1 small onion, coarsely chopped
- 1 leek, white and light green part only, cut into 1-inch lengths
- 1 carrot, cut into 1-inch chunks
- 1 garlic clove
- 1 tablespoon olive oil
- 1 tablespoon Madras curry powder

Salt and freshly ground pepper

- 2 cups whole milk
- 1 stick (4 ounces) unsalted butter
- ¾ cup all-purpose flour, plus more for dusting

About 1 quart vegetable oil, for frying

- 2 large eggs
- 1 cup dry bread crumbs

**1.** Preheat the oven to 375°. In a small roasting pan, toss the chicken thighs with the onion, leek, carrot and garlic. Add the olive oil and 1½ teaspoons of the Madras curry powder and season with salt and pepper. Roast, turning once, until the chicken thighs are cooked through and the vegetables are tender, about 35 minutes. Let the chicken and vegetables cool.

**2.** Meanwhile, in a medium saucepan, bring the milk to a simmer with the remaining 1½ teaspoons of Madras curry powder over moderately high heat. Remove from the heat and let cool.

**3.** In a food processor, pulse the chicken thighs with the roasted vegetables until a puree forms. Season the puree generously with salt and pepper.

**4.** Melt the butter in a large skillet. Add the ¾ cup of flour and cook over moderately low heat, stirring constantly, until lightly browned. Stir in the chicken and vegetable puree. Gradually add the milk, little by little at first and whisking constantly until it has all been added. Cook over low heat, stirring constantly, until the mixture is no longer sticky, about 15 minutes. Season the croquette mixture with salt and pepper and let cool to room temperature, about 1 hour.

**5.** In a large saucepan, heat 1½ inches of vegetable oil to 350°. On a lightly floured work surface, roll the croquette mixture into ¾-inch-thick ropes. Cut the ropes into 1½-inch pieces.

**6.** In a shallow bowl, beat the eggs. Spread the bread crumbs in another shallow bowl. Dip the croquettes in the egg, then coat all over with the bread crumbs. Add the croquettes to the hot oil in batches, taking care not to crowd the pan, and fry until golden brown, about 1 minute. Transfer the croquettes to paper towels to drain and serve piping hot. —*Jeff Koehler*

**MAKE AHEAD** The chicken and vegetable croquette recipe can be prepared through Step 5 and refrigerated overnight.

## Zucchini Latkes with Red Pepper Jam and Smoked Trout

**TOTAL: 40 MIN**

MAKES ABOUT 4 DOZEN

1½-INCH LATKES ●

- 1 medium zucchini (1 pound)
- 1 large baking potato (¾ pound), peeled
- 1 small onion (4 ounces), peeled
- ½ cup matzo meal
- 1 large egg, lightly beaten
- 1 teaspoon fresh lemon juice
- 1½ teaspoons salt
- ½ teaspoon freshly ground pepper

Vegetable oil, for frying

- ½ cup sour cream
- ½ cup store-bought or homemade Red Pepper Jam (recipe follows)
- 3 ounces skinless smoked trout fillet, coarsely chopped
- 2 ounces golden trout roe (see Note)
- 3 scallions, green parts only, thinly sliced

**1.** Halve the zucchini crosswise. Cut the zucchini flesh off the seedy center and coarsely grate it in a food processor. Or grate it on a box grater until you reach the seedy center. Discard the center. In a food processor or on a box grater, coarsely grate the potato and onion. Transfer the grated zucchini, potato and onion to a colander and squeeze dry. Let stand for 2 minutes, then squeeze again. Transfer the vegetable mixture to a large bowl. Add the matzo meal, egg, lemon juice, salt and pepper and stir to combine.

**2.** In a medium skillet, heat 2 tablespoons of vegetable oil until shimmering. Drop packed teaspoons of the zucchini mixture into the skillet and flatten them with the back of a spoon. Cook the latkes over moderately high heat until the edges are golden, about 1½ minutes; flip and cook until golden on the bottom, about 1 minute. Drain on paper towels. Repeat with the remaining zucchini mixture, adding more oil to the skillet as needed.

**3.** Arrange the latkes on a platter and top each one with a dollop of sour cream and a little red pepper jam, smoked trout and golden trout roe; sprinkle with the scallion greens. Serve warm. —*Rachel Klein*

**NOTE** Golden trout roe is available at specialty food stores.

**MAKE AHEAD** The fried latkes can be kept at room temperature for up to 4 hours. Reheat them on a dark baking sheet in a 375° oven for about 5 minutes, or until warmed through and crisp.

## RED PEPPER JAM

**ACTIVE: 30 MIN; TOTAL: 1 HR 30 MIN**

**MAKES ABOUT 4 CUPS** ●

- 6  large store-bought roasted red bell peppers
- 4  cups sugar
- ¾  cup cider vinegar
- 3  tablespoons fresh lemon juice
- 1  teaspoon cayenne pepper
- 1  packet liquid pectin (¼ cup plus 2 tablespoons)

In a blender or food processor, puree the red peppers. Transfer the puree to a large saucepan. Add the sugar, vinegar, lemon juice and cayenne. Bring to a simmer over moderately high heat and stir until the sugar dissolves, about 8 minutes. Reduce the heat to moderately low and simmer for 10 minutes, stirring occasionally. Remove from the heat and stir in the pectin. Bring to a boil and stir constantly for 1 minute. Pour the jam into 4 sterilized 8-ounce jars. Cover tightly and let cool for 45 minutes, then refrigerate. —*R.K.*

**MAKE AHEAD** The jam can be refrigerated for up to 1 week

CRISPY CHICKEN AND VEGETABLE CROQUETTES

ZUCCHINI LATKES WITH RED PEPPER JAM AND TROUT

### Potato Croquettes with Tonkatsu Sauce

**ACTIVE: 35 MIN; TOTAL: 1 HR 15 MIN**
MAKES 32 CROQUETTES

An Asian version of Tater Tots, these crunchy croquettes are coated with *panko,* Japanese bread crumbs, and served with intensely flavored *tonkatsu* steak sauce.

- **2 pounds baking potatoes**
- **Kosher salt and freshly ground pepper**
- **1 cup all-purpose flour**
- **2 large eggs, beaten**
- **2 cups *panko* (see Note)**
- **Vegetable oil, for deep-frying**
- **¾ cup *tonkatsu* sauce (see Note)**

**1.** Preheat the oven to 400°. Wrap the potatoes individually in foil; bake for 45 minutes, until fork-tender. Remove the foil. When the potatoes are cool enough to handle, peel with a paring knife. Trim off the rounded sides and cut the potatoes into 1-inch cubes. Season with salt and pepper.
**2.** Put the flour, eggs and *panko* in 3 shallow bowls. Dredge the potato cubes in the flour, shaking off any excess, then dip them in the egg and coat thoroughly with the *panko.* Spread the cubes on a baking sheet.
**3.** In a large, heavy pot, heat 2 inches of oil to 360°. Line a plate with paper towels. Working in batches, fry the potatoes until golden, about 2 minutes. With a slotted spoon, transfer the potatoes to the paper towel–lined plate to drain. Serve with the *tonkatsu* sauce for dipping. —*Hiro Sone*
**NOTE** Panko and *tonkatsu* sauce can be found at Asian groceries.

### Potato Latkes with Gravlax, Crème Fraîche and Caviar

**TOTAL: 40 MIN**
MAKES ABOUT 4 DOZEN
1½-INCH LATKES ●

Rachel Klein, executive chef at Om restaurant in Cambridge, Massachusetts, treats rustic potato latkes like regal blinis, serving them with paddlefish roe (a less expensive alternative to caviar) and crème fraîche.

- **1 large baking potato (1 pound), peeled**
- **1 small onion (4 ounces), peeled**
- **¼ cup all-purpose flour**
- **1 tablespoon matzo meal**
- **1 large egg, lightly beaten**
- **1½ teaspoons salt**
- **½ teaspoon freshly ground black pepper**
- **Vegetable oil, for frying**
- **½ cup crème fraîche**
- **6 ounces store-bought or homemade thinly sliced gravlax (recipe follows), cut into 2-by-½-inch strips**
- **2 ounces paddlefish roe (see Note)**

**1.** In a food processor or on a box grater, coarsely shred the potato and onion. Transfer to a colander and squeeze dry. Let stand for 2 minutes, then squeeze dry again. Transfer the potato mixture to a large bowl. Add the flour, matzo meal, egg, salt and pepper and stir to combine.
**2.** In a medium skillet, heat 2 tablespoons of vegetable oil until shimmering. Drop packed teaspoons of the potato mixture into the skillet and flatten them with the back of a spoon. Cook the latkes over moderately high heat until the edges are golden, about 1½ minutes; flip and cook until golden on the bottom, about 1 minute. Drain on paper towels. Repeat with the remaining potato mixture, adding more oil to the skillet as needed.
**3.** Arrange the latkes on a serving platter and top each one with a dollop of crème fraîche, some gravlax and some roe. Serve warm. —*Rachel Klein*
**NOTE** Paddlefish is a relative of sturgeon. Its roe is available at specialty food stores.
**MAKE AHEAD** The fried latkes can be kept at room temperature for up to 4 hours. Reheat them on a dark baking sheet in a 375° oven for about 5 minutes, or until warmed through and crisp.

### JUNIPER-AND-VODKA-CURED GRAVLAX

**TOTAL: 30 MIN PLUS 2 DAYS CURING**
MAKES ABOUT 1 POUND ● ●

- **One 1-pound center-cut salmon fillet with skin, halved crosswise**
- **½ cup light brown sugar**
- **½ cup granulated sugar**
- **½ cup chopped dill**
- **10 juniper berries, crushed**
- **1 teaspoon freshly ground white pepper**
- **¼ cup vodka**

**1.** Line a shallow baking dish with plastic wrap, leaving a 4-inch overhang all around. Lay the salmon skin side down in the dish.
**2.** In a small bowl, mix the brown sugar with the granulated sugar, dill, juniper berries and white pepper. Coat the flesh side of the salmon with the sugar mixture. Drizzle the vodka over the salmon. Sandwich the salmon, flesh side to flesh side, and wrap in the plastic. Set a plate on the salmon and weight it down with a heavy can. Refrigerate for 48 hours.
**3.** Scrape the seasonings off the salmon. Rinse under cold running water and pat dry. Transfer to a cutting board. Holding a knife horizontally against a fillet, thinly slice the gravlax and serve. —*R.K.*
**MAKE AHEAD** Once rinse and dried, the cured gravlax can be wrapped in plastic and refrigerated for up to 2 days.

### Potato Latkes with Caramelized Onion and Applesauce

**ACTIVE: 1 HR 30 MIN;**
**TOTAL: 2 HR 15 MIN**
MAKES ABOUT 4 DOZEN
1½-INCH LATKES ●

Sour cream and applesauce are the traditional latke toppings. Onion relish adds a sweet and tart kick.

- **4 large Granny Smith apples (2 pounds)—peeled, cored and cut into ¼-inch chunks**
- **¼ cup water**

1 thin lemon slice

2 tablespoons sugar

Pinch of cinnamon

Pinch of freshly grated nutmeg

1 tablespoon unsalted butter

Vegetable oil

1 large onion (¾ pound), thinly sliced, plus 1 small onion

Salt and freshly ground pepper

1 tablespoon cider vinegar

½ tablespoon light brown sugar

1 large baking potato (1 pound), peeled

¼ cup all-purpose flour

1 tablespoon matzo meal

1 large egg, lightly beaten

½ cup sour cream

1. In a medium saucepan, combine the apple chunks with the water and lemon slice. Bring to a simmer over high heat, then reduce the heat to moderate and cook, stirring occasionally, until the apple chunks are softened, about 10 minutes. Remove the lemon slice. Transfer the applesauce to a bowl. Stir in the sugar, cinnamon and nutmeg.

2. In a large saucepan, melt the butter in ½ tablespoon of vegetable oil over moderately high heat. Add the sliced onion and season with salt and pepper. Reduce the heat to moderately low and cook, stirring occasionally, until golden, about 1 hour. Stir in the vinegar and brown sugar and continue cooking until the onion is browned and almost dry, about 10 minutes longer. Remove from the heat; let cool.

3. Meanwhile, in a food processor or on a box grater, coarsely shred the small onion and the potato. Transfer to a colander and squeeze dry. Let stand for 2 minutes, then squeeze dry again. Transfer the potato mixture to a large bowl. Add the flour, matzo meal, egg, ¼ teaspoon of salt and ⅛ teaspoon of pepper and stir to combine.

4. In a medium skillet, heat 2 tablespoons of vegetable oil until shimmering. Drop packed teaspoons of the potato mixture into the skillet and flatten them with the back of a spoon. Cook the latkes over moderately high heat until the edges are golden, about 1½ minutes; flip and cook until golden on the bottom, about 1 minute. Drain on paper towels. Repeat with the remaining potato mixture, adding more oil to the skillet as needed.

5. Arrange the latkes on a platter. Top each latke with caramelized onion, applesauce and sour cream. Serve warm.
—*Rachel Klein*

**MAKE AHEAD** The fried latkes can be kept at room temperature for up to 4 hours. Reheat them on a dark baking sheet in a 375° oven for about 5 minutes, or until warmed through and crisp. The applesauce and caramelized onion can be refrigerated for up to 2 days. Serve warm or at room temperature.

## Sweet Potato Latkes with Wasabi and Wasabi Tobiko

**TOTAL: 45 MIN**

**MAKES ABOUT 4 DOZEN**

**1½-INCH LATKES** ● ●

Sweet and spicy flavors meld in this whimsical recipe. Pungent wasabi cream tops slightly sweet latkes, which are then garnished with wasabi *tobiko* (flying-fish roe) and peppery radish sprouts.

1 large sweet potato (1 pound), peeled

½ cup matzo meal

1 tablespoon sugar

2 teaspoons all-purpose flour

1½ teaspoons salt

1 teaspoon baking powder

¼ teaspoon cayenne pepper

⅛ teaspoon freshly ground black pepper

1 large egg, lightly beaten

1 large egg white, lightly beaten

½ cup milk

Vegetable oil, for frying

½ cup crème fraîche

1¼ teaspoons wasabi paste

1¼ teaspoons rice vinegar

¼ teaspoon salt

½ cup peppery sprouts, such as radish sprouts

2 ounces wasabi *tobiko* (see Note)

1. In a food processor or on a box grater, coarsely grate the sweet potato. In a large bowl, combine the matzo meal with the sugar, flour, salt, baking powder, cayenne and black pepper, then stir in the egg, egg white and milk. Stir in the sweet potato.

2. In a medium skillet, heat 2 tablespoons of vegetable oil until shimmering. Drop packed teaspoons of the sweet potato mixture into the skillet and flatten them with the back of a spoon. Cook the latkes over moderately high heat until the edges are golden, about 1½ minutes; flip and cook until golden on the bottom, about 1 minute. Drain on paper towels. Repeat with the remaining sweet potato mixture, adding more oil as needed.

3. In a small bowl, mix the crème fraîche with the wasabi paste, rice vinegar and salt. Arrange the latkes on a platter and top each one with the wasabi cream, a pinch of sprouts and a little *tobiko*. Serve warm.
—*Rachel Klein*

**NOTE** Wasabi *tobiko* (wasabi-flavored flying fish roe) is available from Wild Edibles (877-295-3474 or wildedibles.com).

# pairing
## NEW VODKAS FOR LATKES

**IMPERIA**

Made from Russian wheat; distilled eight times and blended with glacial water ($35).

**GREEN MOUNTAIN SUNSHINE VODKA**

Distilled from 100 percent organic corn and blended with springwater from Vermont ($22).

**42 BELOW**

A New Zealand vodka filtered through 35 layers of charcoal ($29).

CABRALES PHYLLO ROLLS WITH SHERRY DIPPING SAUCE

CREAMY PARMESAN CUSTARDS

## Cabrales Phyllo Rolls with Sherry Dipping Sauce

**TOTAL: 45 MIN**

MAKES 32 ROLLS

These flaky cheese-and-leek pastries were adapted from a dish served at El Faro, a restaurant in Cadiz, Spain.

- 1 tablespoon extra-virgin olive oil, plus ½ cup for brushing and frying
- 1 medium leek, halved lengthwise and thinly sliced crosswise
- ½ pound cream cheese
- 2 ounces Cabrales or other blue cheese

Salt and freshly ground pepper

- ¼ cup sweet sherry
- ¼ cup beef broth
- ¼ cup golden raisins
- ¼ teaspoon cornstarch dissolved in 1 teaspoon water
- 8 sheets of phyllo dough

**1.** In a skillet, heat the 1 tablespoon of olive oil until shimmering. Add the leek and cook over moderate heat, stirring, until softened, about 5 minutes. Remove from the heat, add the cream cheese and Cabrales and stir until melted. Season with salt and pepper. Scrape into a bowl; let cool.

**2.** In a small saucepan, combine the sherry, broth and raisins and simmer over moderate heat until the liquid is reduced by half, 8 minutes. Stir the cornstarch mixture, whisk it into the sauce and cook until slightly thickened, about 2 minutes.

**3.** On a clean, flat work surface, stack the phyllo sheets and cut them crosswise into 4 strips, each 4 inches wide by 12 inches long. Arrange 4 strips on a work surface with the short sides facing you; keep the remaining phyllo covered with plastic wrap to prevent it from drying out. Brush the strips lightly with olive oil. Spoon 1 table-spoon of the cheese filling at one end of each strip and roll them up, making about 3 turns to create small cylinders, then fold in the sides. Brush the folded sides with olive oil and continue to roll up the cylinders. Set the rolls on a plate. Repeat with the remaining phyllo and filling.

**4.** Place a wire rack on a large baking sheet and cover with paper towels. In a large skillet, heat ¼ inch of olive oil until shimmering. Add 10 to 12 of the rolls and fry over moderately high heat, turning once, until golden, about 1½ minutes. Transfer to the paper towel–lined rack to drain while you fry the rest, adding more olive oil as needed. Transfer the rolls to a platter and serve with the sherry dipping sauce. —*Jeff Koehler*

**MAKE AHEAD** The phyllo rolls can be prepared through Step 3 and refrigerated overnight. Fry directly from the refrigerator. The sauce can be refrigerated overnight.

## Creamy Parmesan Custards

ACTIVE: 25 MIN; TOTAL: 2 HR

12 SERVINGS ●

½ cup heavy cream
½ cup milk
¼ cup freshly grated
 Parmesan cheese
⅛ teaspoon salt
Pinch of white pepper
1 large egg
1 large egg yolk
Boiling water
2 ounces thinly sliced store-bought
 or homemade gravlax (p. 20), cut
 into 2-by-½-inch strips
¼ cup julienned arugula

1. In a small saucepan, combine the cream, milk, cheese, salt and pepper and cook over moderately high heat until bubbles appear around the edge. Remove from the heat, cover the pan and let the cream steep for about 30 minutes.

2. Preheat the oven to 250°. Pour the cream into a measuring cup and slowly whisk in the egg and yolk. Pour the custard into twelve 1-ounce ovenproof egg cups.

3. Set the cups in a roasting pan. Pour enough boiling water into the pan to reach halfway up the sides of the cups. Transfer the pan to the oven and bake the custards for 1 hour, or until set. Remove the pan from the oven and let the custards cool in the water bath for 5 minutes. Remove the custards from the pan. Top them with gravlax and arugula and serve warm.
—*Rachel Klein*

MAKE AHEAD The custards can be baked up to 4 hours ahead. Reheat in a water bath until heated through.

## Savory Ricotta-Squash Tart

ACTIVE: 40 MIN; TOTAL: 1 HR 15 MIN

MAKES TWO 11-INCH TARTS ● ●

Instead of appearing in a soup, squash gets cut into rings, caramelized and baked in a tart that can be served with a salad as a starter, or as an unusual side dish.

2 large eggs
14 ounces frozen all-butter
 puff pastry, thawed but chilled
All-purpose flour, for rolling
Two 11-ounce organic acorn squash,
 rinsed and dried
1 tablespoon plus 1 teaspoon
 extra-virgin olive oil
2 teaspoons unsalted
 butter, melted
1 teaspoon honey
Kosher salt and freshly ground pepper
1 pound fresh ricotta cheese
1 tablespoon heavy cream
½ cup thinly sliced shallots (2 large)
½ teaspoon sugar
Toasted pumpkin seeds, for garnish

1. In a small bowl, beat 1 of the eggs. Cut the puff pastry in half crosswise. On a lightly floured work surface, roll out 1 piece of puff pastry to a 12-inch square. Cut a ½-inch strip from each edge of the pastry. Brush the edges of the pastry square with some of the beaten egg. Place the strips around the edges to make a raised border. Chill for 30 minutes. Repeat with the second piece of puff pastry.

2. Meanwhile, preheat the oven to 450°. Using a large, sharp knife, cut off the ends of the squash until you reach the seeds. Scoop out and discard the seeds. Carefully slice the acorn squash crosswise into ¼-inch-thick rings. Arrange the rings on 2 rimmed baking sheets. Mix 2 teaspoons of the olive oil with the butter and honey and brush on the squash rings; season with salt and pepper. Bake for 15 minutes, or until the rings are browned on the bottom. Reduce the oven temperature to 375°.

3. In a medium bowl, mix the ricotta with the remaining egg and the heavy cream. Season with ¾ teaspoon of kosher salt and a generous pinch of pepper. In a medium skillet, heat the remaining 2 teaspoons of olive oil. Add the shallots and cook over moderately high heat, stirring occasionally, until golden. Stir in the sugar.

4. Brush the raised pastry borders with some of the beaten egg. Spread the ricotta filling in the pastry squares. Arrange the squash rings on top, browned side up. Scatter the shallots over the tarts and bake for 30 minutes, or until the pastry is golden brown. Sprinkle the tarts with toasted pumpkin seeds and serve warm.
—*Susan Spungen*

MAKE AHEAD The tarts can be baked early in the day; they can also be frozen for up to 1 week and reheated in a 375° oven.

## Red Curry–Lime Chicken Wings

ACTIVE: 20 MIN; TOTAL: 50 MIN

8 SERVINGS

TV chef and cookbook author Tyler Florence transforms basic chicken wings by baking them until they're crispy, then tossing them in a butter flavored with lime juice, honey and hot Thai red curry paste.

4 pounds chicken wings, tips
 discarded, wings separated
 into 2 pieces
Extra-virgin olive oil, for drizzling
Salt and freshly ground pepper
6 tablespoons unsalted
 butter, softened
1 tablespoon Thai red curry paste
1 tablespoon honey
Juice and finely grated zest of 1 lime
1 teaspoon soy sauce

1. Preheat the oven to 475°. Spread the wings on 2 large rimmed baking sheets. Drizzle with olive oil, season with salt and pepper and toss. Bake the wings for about 40 minutes, or until browned and crisp.

2. Meanwhile, in a large bowl, blend the butter with the curry paste, honey, lime juice and zest and soy sauce. When the wings are done, transfer them to the bowl and toss with the butter until well coated. Transfer the wings to a platter and serve.
—*Tyler Florence*

MAKE AHEAD The flavored butter can be refrigerated overnight or frozen for up to 1 month.

## Silky Red Peppers with White Anchovies and Watercress

**ACTIVE: 30 MIN; TOTAL: 1 HR 10 MIN**

4 SERVINGS ●

4 red bell peppers, stemmed and seeded
½ cup extra-virgin olive oil, plus more for brushing
4 garlic cloves, thinly sliced
1½ teaspoons sherry vinegar
Salt
8 white or marinated anchovies
2 ounces small watercress sprigs (2 cups)
20 roasted, salted almonds

**1.** Preheat the oven to 425°. Put the bell peppers on a rimmed baking sheet. Brush lightly with olive oil and roast for about 25 minutes, or until blistered but not collapsed. When cool enough to handle, peel the peppers and halve them lengthwise.

**2.** Layer the peppers in an 8-inch skillet. Scatter the garlic on top, pour the ½ cup of oil on top and bring to a simmer. Reduce the heat to low; cook until the peppers are very soft and the garlic is tender, 15 minutes. With a slotted spoon, transfer to a plate.

**3.** In a small bowl, whisk 1½ tablespoons of the pepper oil with the vinegar; season the dressing with salt.

**4.** Spread 2 pepper halves on each plate, peeled side up, and sprinkle with salt. Top each half with an anchovy. Add the watercress to the dressing and toss. Mound the watercress on the peppers, garnish with the almonds and serve. —*Alex Raij*

## Shrimp and Jicama Rolls with Chili-Peanut Sauce

**TOTAL: 1 HR 15 MIN**

MAKES 15 ROLLS ● ●

At grade school in Vietnam, chef Charles Phan of the Slanted Door in San Francisco would buy these chewy rice-paper rolls filled with crunchy jicama and sweet shrimp from enterprising street vendors who set up stalls in the playground.

½ pound large shrimp—shelled, deveined and quartered crosswise
¼ cup plus 2 tablespoons canola oil
Kosher salt
1 large shallot, thinly sliced
1 large garlic clove, minced
6 ounces jicama, peeled and cut into 2-by-¼-inch matchsticks
2 tablespoons Chinese cooking wine, sake or water
½ cup chicken stock
1 tablespoon Asian fish sauce
1 teaspoon Asian sesame oil
Fifteen 6-inch rice-paper rounds
½ head red leaf lettuce, ribs discarded, leaves torn into 4-inch pieces
15 large basil leaves
Chili-Peanut Sauce (recipe follows)
2 tablespoons dry-roasted, salted peanuts, chopped

**1.** In a medium bowl, toss the shrimp with 2 tablespoons of the canola oil and ½ teaspoon of kosher salt. In a large skillet or a wok, heat 2 tablespoons of the canola oil until small puffs of smoke begin to appear. Add the shrimp and stir-fry over high heat until just pink, about 1 minute. Transfer the shrimp to a medium bowl.

**2.** Add the remaining 2 tablespoons of canola oil to the skillet. Add the shallot and garlic and stir-fry until softened and fragrant, about 30 seconds. Add the jicama and cook, stirring, until crisp-tender, about 3 minutes. Add the wine and cook until slightly reduced, about 1 minute. Add the stock, fish sauce and sesame oil and bring to a boil. Simmer over moderate heat until the jicama is tender but still slightly crunchy, about 4 minutes longer. Drain and add to the shrimp. Let cool.

**3.** Fill a glass pie plate with hot tap water. Working with 1 at a time, soak each rice-paper round in the water until pliable, 1 minute; transfer the round to a work surface and blot any excess water with paper towels. Set a piece of lettuce on

the bottom third of the rice-paper round, followed by 1 basil leaf, a rounded tablespoon of the Chili-Peanut Sauce and a few chopped peanuts. Top with 4 to 5 pieces of jicama and 4 pieces of shrimp. Fold up the bottom as tightly as possible, then fold in the sides and roll up the package, forming a tight cylinder. Set the roll on a platter and cover with a damp paper towel and plastic wrap. Repeat with the remaining ingredients and serve with extra Chili-Peanut Sauce on the side for dipping, if you like. —*Charles Phan*

## CHILI-PEANUT SAUCE

**TOTAL: 30 MIN**

MAKES ABOUT 1 CUP ● ●

This recipe makes just enough creamy, spicy sauce to fill the rolls. Double the recipe if you want extra sauce for dipping.

½ cup cooked jasmine rice
1 tablespoon white or dark miso
¼ cup dry-roasted, salted peanuts, coarsely chopped
1 small jalapeño, seeded and chopped
1 garlic clove
1 tablespoon ketchup
1 tablespoon oyster sauce
1 tablespoon hoisin sauce
1 tablespoon sugar
1½ teaspoons Asian chili sauce
1 teaspoon fresh lemon juice
¼ teaspoon Asian sesame oil
1 teaspoon unseasoned rice vinegar
¼ cup water, plus more if needed

In a mini food processor, combine the cooked rice with the miso, peanuts, jalapeño, garlic, ketchup, oyster sauce, hoisin sauce, sugar, chili sauce, lemon juice, sesame oil and rice vinegar. Process until just combined. Add 2 tablespoons of water and process until a coarse paste forms. Add 2 more tablespoons of water and process until the sauce has a smooth consistency similar to mayonnaise. Add more water if the sauce is too thick. —*C.P.*

SHRIMP AND JICAMA ROLLS
WITH CHILI-PEANUT SAUCE

# starters

## Garlic Chive Dumplings Wrapped in Napa Cabbage

**TOTAL: 1 HR**

**MAKES 32 DUMPLINGS** ● ●

Garlic chives, similar to plain chives but with more garlic flavor, add their distinctive pungent taste to many Chinese and Korean dishes. The buds can be sautéed like a vegetable, and the flat leaves can be used like an herb, as in these mushroomy dumplings, which are wrapped in soft, crunchy napa cabbage leaves.

**SAUCE**

- ¼ cup mushroom soy sauce (see Note)
- 1 tablespoon unseasoned rice vinegar
- 1 tablespoon vegetable oil
- 1 scallion, thinly sliced

Freshly ground pepper

**DUMPLINGS**

- 1 small head napa cabbage

Kosher salt

- 1 tablespoon vegetable oil
- ½ pound shiitake mushrooms, stems discarded, caps cut into ¼-inch dice

Freshly ground pepper

- 3 tablespoons oyster sauce
- 3 scallions, thinly sliced
- 1 garlic clove, minced
- ½ teaspoon minced fresh ginger
- 1½ cups garlic chives or plain chives, finely chopped
- 4 ounces firm tofu, chopped
- 1 large egg plus 1 egg yolk, beaten

**1. MAKE THE SAUCE:** In a bowl, combine the mushroom soy sauce, vinegar, oil and scallion. Grind pepper over the sauce.

**2. MAKE THE DUMPLINGS:** Bring a medium saucepan of water to a boil. Remove 20 large outer leaves from the head of cabbage and blanch them in the boiling water for 1 minute. Drain and dry on paper towels. Trim and discard the thick stems. Cut the leaves into 4-inch squares, so you have about 32 cabbage squares for filling.

**3.** Finely chop enough of the unblanched cabbage to yield 2 cups. Transfer to a small colander and toss with ½ teaspoon of salt. Let stand until wilted, 10 minutes. Firmly squeeze to remove any moisture.

**4.** In a medium skillet, heat the oil. Add the shiitake, season with salt and pepper and cook over moderate heat, stirring, until lightly browned, about 4 minutes.

**5.** In a large bowl, stir the oyster sauce, scallions, garlic and ginger. Add the garlic chives, tofu, beaten egg and egg yolk, salted cabbage, sautéed shiitake and ¼ teaspoon of pepper; combine thoroughly.

**6.** Lay out the cabbage leaf squares on a work surface. Spoon 1 slightly rounded tablespoon of filling onto each square. Fold in the ends to enclose the filling neatly.

**7.** Fill a wok or a very large skillet with 1 inch of water and bring to a boil. Arrange the dumplings in a double-tiered bamboo steamer and set it over the boiling water. Cover and steam the dumplings until firm, 7 minutes. Serve right away, passing the dipping sauce at the table. *—Anita Lo*

**NOTE** Mushroom soy sauce is dark soy flavored with mushrooms. It's thick, meaty and salty. If it's unavailable, substitute regular soy sauce.

## Crispy Pork and Kimchi Pot Stickers

**TOTAL: 1 HR**

**MAKES 3 DOZEN DUMPLINGS** ●

**SAUCE**

- 1 teaspoon sesame seeds
- ⅓ cup soy sauce
- ¼ cup unseasoned rice vinegar
- 2 tablespoons water
- 1 garlic clove, minced
- 1 scallion, thinly sliced

**DUMPLINGS**

- ½ pound ground pork
- ½ pound kimchi, drained and finely chopped
- 4 scallions, green parts only, thinly sliced

- 1 large egg, beaten
- 2 teaspoons cornstarch
- ½ tablespoon sugar
- ½ tablespoon soy sauce
- ½ teaspoon kosher salt
- ¼ teaspoon freshly ground pepper
- 36 gyoza wrappers
- 2 tablespoons vegetable oil
- 1 cup water

**1. MAKE THE SAUCE.** In a small skillet, toast the sesame seeds over moderately high heat for 30 seconds, shaking the pan, until lightly browned. In a small bowl, stir the soy sauce with the vinegar, water, garlic, scallion and toasted sesame seeds.

**2. MAKE THE DUMPLINGS:** Line a large baking sheet with parchment paper. In a large bowl, combine the pork, kimchi, scallions, egg, cornstarch, sugar, soy sauce, salt and pepper. Using your hands, mix the dumpling ingredients thoroughly.

**3.** Place 4 gyoza wrappers on a work surface; keep the rest covered with plastic wrap. Lightly moisten the edges of the wrappers with water. Place a level tablespoon of the pork and kimchi filling on one side of each wrapper and fold in half to form half-moons. Press the edges of the wrapper firmly to seal, making pleats for decoration. Lift each dumpling by the pleated edge, transfer it to the baking sheet and press down lightly to flatten the bottom; the dumpling should be standing with the pleat side up on the baking sheet. Repeat with the remaining gyoza wrappers and pork and kimchi filling.

**4.** In a large nonstick skillet, heat 1 tablespoon of the oil. Add half of the pot stickers to the skillet, flattened side down. Pour in ½ cup of the water, cover and cook over moderately high heat until the water has evaporated, the filling is cooked through and the bottoms are browned, 8 to 10 minutes. Transfer to a serving platter and keep warm. Wipe out the skillet and repeat with the remaining oil, pot stickers and water. Serve with the dipping sauce. *—Anita Lo*

### Spinach and Tofu Dumplings

**TOTAL: 1 HR**

MAKES ABOUT 45 DUMPLINGS ● ●

DUMPLINGS

- 5 ounces baby spinach (5 packed cups)
- 5 ounces firm tofu, cut into ¼-inch dice
- 2½ tablespoons cornstarch
- 2 small jalapeños, seeded and minced
- 1½ tablespoons soy sauce
- 1½ teaspoons Asian sesame oil
- Salt and freshly ground pepper
- About 45 square wonton wrappers (from 1 package)

DIPPING SAUCE

- ¼ cup plus 2 tablespoons soy sauce
- 2 tablespoons unseasoned rice vinegar
- 1 teaspoon honey

**1. MAKE THE DUMPLINGS:** Bring a large saucepan of water to a boil. Add the spinach and cook for 20 seconds. Using a slotted spoon, transfer the spinach to a colander. When the spinach is cool enough to handle, squeeze it dry, then coarsely chop. Keep the water hot.

**2.** Transfer the spinach to a bowl. Stir in the tofu, cornstarch, jalapeños, soy sauce and sesame oil. Season with salt and pepper.

**3.** Working with 4 wonton wrappers at a time, dampen the edges and mound 1½ teaspoons of filling in the center of each. Fold 1 corner of each up over the filling and seal to make triangles. Repeat with the remaining wrappers and filling.

**4. MAKE THE DIPPING SAUCE:** In a small serving bowl, stir the soy sauce with the vinegar and honey.

**5.** Return the water to a boil. Add the dumplings and simmer over moderate heat, stirring gently, until the edges are al dente, about 3 minutes. Carefully drain in a colander and transfer to a platter. Serve with the dipping sauce.

—*Shaun Danyel Hergatt*

**CRISPY PORK AND KIMCHI POT STICKERS**

**SPINACH AND TOFU DUMPLINGS**

## Salmon Skin Sushi Rolls

**TOTAL: 1 HR 15 MIN**

4 SERVINGS ● ●

- 1¼ cups short-grain sushi rice
- 1⅓ cups water
- 2 tablespoons unseasoned rice vinegar
- 1½ tablespoons sugar
- Kosher salt
- 2 teaspoons sesame seeds, preferably unhulled
- 1 tablespoon wasabi powder
- 1 tablespoon hot water
- Vegetable oil, for frying
- Four 9-ounce salmon fillets with skin
- Freshly ground pepper
- All-purpose flour, for dusting
- Four 8-inch square nori sheets
- 1 medium cucumber—peeled, seeded, halved crosswise and cut lengthwise into thin strips
- Soy sauce, for serving

1. Put the rice in a medium saucepan, rinse well and drain it thoroughly. Add the water and bring to a boil. Cover and cook over low heat for 12 minutes. Remove from the heat and let the rice stand, covered, for 10 minutes.

2. In a small bowl, stir the vinegar with the sugar and ¾ teaspoon of salt until dissolved. Spread the hot rice on a large rimmed baking sheet in an even layer. Sprinkle the vinegar mixture evenly over the rice. With a wooden spoon or a pastry scraper in one hand and a simple paper fan in the other, lightly stir and toss the rice while fanning it until glossy and cool.

3. In a small dry skillet, cook the sesame seeds over moderately high heat until toasted, about 1 minute. In a small bowl, mix together the wasabi powder and hot water to make a paste; keep covered.

4. In a medium saucepan, heat ½ inch of oil to 325°. With a long, sharp knife, cut the skin from the salmon fillets, leaving ¼ inch of flesh on the skin. Season the salmon skin with salt and pepper and dust with flour. Fry 1 at a time over moderately high heat, turning once, until browned and crisp, about 3 minutes. Drain the skin on paper towels and repeat with the rest.

5. Put a nori sheet on a bamboo sushi mat, shiny side down. With moist hands, pat ¾ cup of the rice on the nori in an even layer, leaving a 1-inch border all around. Sprinkle ½ teaspoon of the toasted sesame seeds over the rice, then spread ¼ teaspoon of the wasabi paste in a thin line across the rice. Lay a salmon skin on the rice nearest you and top with one-fourth of the cucumber strips. Lift the bamboo mat end nearest you up and over, pressing to tuck the skin and cucumber into a cylinder. Tightly roll up the fillings in the rice and nori. Repeat to form the remaining 3 rolls. Cut each roll into 6 pieces and transfer to a platter. Serve with a small bowl of soy sauce and extra wasabi, if desired. —Marcia Kiesel

**MAKE AHEAD** The rice can stand at room temperature, covered, for up to 4 hours. The fried salmon skin can be prepared earlier in the day. Reheat in a 400° oven for 3 minutes.

## Lemony Shrimp Dumplings

**TOTAL: 1 HR**

MAKES 45 DUMPLINGS ●

Use thin, round gyoza wrappers for these dumplings rather than thick, square won-ton wrappers. If you can't find gyoza wrappers at the supermarket, look for thin, round dumpling wrappers.

SAUCE

- 3 tablespoons soy sauce
- 3 tablespoons water
- 2 tablespoons fresh lemon juice
- 1 tablespoon Asian fish sauce
- 1 scallion, thinly sliced

DUMPLINGS

- 1½ pounds medium shrimp, shelled and deveined
- 1½ tablespoons cornstarch, plus more for dusting
- 2 tablespoons soy sauce
- 1 tablespoon fresh lemon juice
- 1 large egg, beaten
- 1 teaspoon finely grated lemon zest
- 1 teaspoon kosher salt
- ¼ teaspoon freshly ground pepper
- ½ cup peeled, diced jicama (¼-inch)
- 2 scallions, thinly sliced
- 45 gyoza wrappers
- Green leaf lettuce leaves, for steaming

1. MAKE THE SAUCE: In a small bowl, combine the soy sauce with the water, lemon juice, fish sauce and scallion.

2. MAKE THE DUMPLINGS: Very coarsely chop two-thirds of the shrimp and transfer to a food processor. Add the 1½ tablespoons of cornstarch, the soy sauce, lemon juice, egg, lemon zest, salt and pepper and process until very finely chopped. Scrape into a large bowl. Cut the remaining shrimp into ⅓-inch pieces and add to the bowl. Mix in the jicama and scallions.

3. Dust a baking sheet with cornstarch. Lay 4 gyoza wrappers on a work surface; keep the rest covered with plastic wrap. Moisten the edges of the wrappers with water. Place a level tablespoon of filling on one side of each wrapper and fold in half to form half-moons. Press all around the filling to release any air pockets and to seal. Lift each dumpling by the sealed edge, transfer it to the baking sheet and press down lightly to flatten the bottom; the dumpling should be standing with the sealed side up on the baking sheet. Repeat with the remaining wrappers and filling.

4. Fill a wok or very large skillet with 2 inches of water and bring to a boil. Line a double-tiered bamboo steamer with lettuce and arrange half of the dumplings in the steamer without crowding. Cover and steam over moderate heat until firm and cooked through, about 12 minutes. Steam the remaining dumplings. Serve right away, passing the sauce at the table. —Anita Lo

## Plump Turkey-Stuffed Tofu Dumplings

**TOTAL: 1 HR**

**MAKES 3 DOZEN DUMPLINGS** ● ●

SAUCE

⅓ cup soy sauce

¼ cup unseasoned rice vinegar

2 tablespoons Chinese chili-bean paste

2 large scallions, white parts only, thinly sliced

DUMPLINGS

2¼ pounds firm tofu, cut into thirty-six 1½-inch cubes

1 pound ground turkey

4 large scallions, green parts only, thinly sliced

3 tablespoons soy sauce

1 tablespoon Chinese chili-bean paste

1 tablespoon fermented black beans, rinsed and finely chopped

1 tablespoon cornstarch

1 garlic clove, minced

1 large egg, beaten

½ teaspoon kosher salt

¼ teaspoon freshly ground pepper

**1. MAKE THE SAUCE:** In a small bowl, combine the soy sauce, vinegar, chili-bean paste and scallions.

**2. MAKE THE DUMPLINGS:** With a small melon baller, hollow out the tofu cubes and reserve the hollowed-out cubes. Put the tofu balls in a large bowl and add the remaining ingredients. Using your hands, mix thoroughly. Carefully stuff each hollowed-out tofu cube with 1 level tablespoon of the filling, mounding it.

**3.** In a wok or a very large skillet, bring 2 inches of water to a boil. Arrange the dumplings in a double-tiered bamboo steamer; set the steamer over the boiling water. Cover and steam until the filling is firm and cooked through, about 10 minutes. Serve the dumplings with the sauce. *—Anita Lo*

## Chicken and Coconut Shumai

**TOTAL: 1 HR**

**MAKES 40 DUMPLINGS** ●

*Shumai* are open-topped dumplings filled with ground meat, then steamed.

1 pound ground chicken

¼ cup unsweetened coconut milk

¼ cup coarsely shredded carrot

2 Thai chiles, minced

2 tablespoons chopped basil

2 tablespoons Asian fish sauce

2 tablespoons sugar

2 teaspoons fresh lime juice

1 garlic clove, minced

1 large egg, beaten

1 small shallot, minced

½ teaspoon minced fresh ginger

½ teaspoon kosher salt

¼ teaspoon freshly ground pepper

40 wonton wrappers

Green leaf lettuce leaves, for steaming

Sriracha chili sauce, for serving

**1.** In a large bowl, combine the ground chicken with the coconut milk, carrot, chiles, basil, fish sauce, sugar, lime juice, garlic, egg, shallot, ginger, salt and pepper. Using your hands, mix the filling ingredients thoroughly.

**2.** Hold a wonton wrapper in the palm of your hand; keep the rest covered with plastic wrap. Place a rounded tablespoon of filling in the center of the wonton wrapper and pinch the edges all around to form a cup that is open about 1 inch at the top. Keep the *shumai* covered with plastic wrap. Repeat with the remaining wonton wrappers and filling.

**3.** In a wok or a very large skillet, bring 2 inches of water to a boil. Line a double-tiered bamboo steamer with the lettuce leaves and arrange the *shumai* in the steamer without crowding. Cover and steam over moderate heat until cooked through, about 10 minutes. Repeat with the remaining *shumai.* Serve right away, passing the chili sauce at the table. *—Anita Lo*

## Ginger Pork with Kimchi

**TOTAL: 20 MIN**

**8 SERVINGS** ● ●

This fast and easy take on a traditional Korean dish uses quickly cooked pork loin instead of pork belly. The meat should be sliced very thin before it's boiled; to make slicing easier, freeze the loin for an hour first. The kimchi, a spicy Korean pickled cabbage sold at Asian groceries and at many supermarkets, should be cut into manageable pieces that are smaller than the pork slices.

⅓ cup pine nuts

3 quarts water

2 tablespoons kosher salt

2 pounds pork loin, sliced ⅛ inch thick

1 tablespoon peeled, finely grated fresh ginger

2 heads Boston lettuce, leaves separated

½ pound kimchi (1 cup), drained and finely chopped

**1.** In a small dry skillet, toast the pine nuts over low heat, stirring the nuts frequently, until they are fragrant and lightly browned, about 3 minutes. Transfer the pine nuts to a small bowl and let cool.

**2.** In a large saucepan, combine the water with the salt and bring to a boil over high heat. Add the pork slices to the saucepan and cook, stirring, until the pork is white, about 1½ minutes. Drain the pork in a colander, then transfer it to a serving bowl and toss with the finely grated ginger.

**3.** Spread the Boston lettuce leaves in a basket and spoon the chopped kimchi into a small bowl. Have guests serve themselves, filling the lettuce leaves with the slices of ginger pork, kimchi and pine nuts. *—Hiro Sone*

● FAST  ● HEALTHY  ● MAKE AHEAD  ● STAFF FAVORITE

## Artichoke and Ricotta Dumplings with Preserved-Lemon Sauce

**ACTIVE: 1 HR; TOTAL: 2 HR**

4 SERVINGS

These delicate artichoke-studded ricotta dumplings are crisp on the outside and warm and cheesy inside. They're excellent with the slightly sour sauce of preserved lemon, olives and herbs. Use the creamiest, thickest, freshest ricotta you can find.

- ½ lemon, plus 1 tablespoon fresh lemon juice
- 2 globe artichokes
- 1 cup fresh ricotta cheese
- 2 tablespoons freshly grated Parmesan cheese
- 1 tablespoon all-purpose flour, plus more for dusting
- Salt and freshly ground pepper
- 1 large egg yolk
- ½ small red bell pepper
- ½ small yellow bell pepper
- ¼ cup plus 2 teaspoons extra-virgin olive oil
- 2 tablespoons water
- 1 tablespoon plus 1 teaspoon Champagne vinegar
- ¼ preserved lemon, flesh discarded, rind very thinly sliced (see Note)
- 2 tablespoons cold unsalted butter, cut into pieces
- 2 tablespoons very finely chopped shallots
- 2 tablespoons chopped pitted Niçoise olives
- 1 tablespoon chopped parsley
- 1 tablespoon minced chives
- 1 teaspoon chopped tarragon
- Vegetable oil, for frying
- 2 packed cups baby arugula

**1.** Fill a small bowl with water and squeeze the lemon half into it. Working with 1 artichoke at a time, snap off the outer leaves. Using a sharp knife, trim the stem and base of the artichoke and cut off the top two-thirds of the leaves. With a spoon or melon baller, scrape out the furry choke. Rub the artichoke heart all over with the lemon half and drop it in the bowl of water. Repeat with the remaining artichoke.

**2.** Bring a small saucepan of water to a boil. Add the artichoke hearts and simmer over moderately high heat until tender, 12 minutes. Drain and cut into ¼-inch dice.

**3.** Bring a medium saucepan of salted water to a simmer. In a large bowl, mix the ricotta with the Parmesan and the 1 tablespoon of flour; season with salt and pepper. Stir in the egg yolk and the diced artichoke hearts. Using 2 large serving spoons, form the mixture into 12 oval dumplings. Add the dumplings to the simmering water and cook gently until they start to rise to the surface, about 1 minute. Using a slotted spoon, transfer the dumplings to a large rimmed baking sheet. Pat dry with paper towels and refrigerate until very cold, about 1 hour.

**4.** Roast the pepper halves over a gas flame or under the broiler, skin side up, until nicely charred. Transfer to a bowl, cover with plastic and let cool. Peel the peppers and cut them into ¼-inch dice.

**5.** In a small saucepan, combine ¼ cup of the olive oil with the lemon juice, water, 1 tablespoon of the vinegar and the preserved lemon rind; boil over moderately high heat until reduced by half, about 3 minutes. Remove from the heat and whisk in the butter, 1 piece at a time. Stir in the shallots, olives, parsley, chives, tarragon and roasted peppers and season with salt and pepper. Keep the sauce warm.

**6.** In a large skillet, heat ¼ inch of vegetable oil until shimmering. Lightly dust the dumplings with flour, add them to the hot oil and cook over moderately high heat until golden brown all over, about 4½ minutes. Transfer to paper towels to drain.

**7.** In a medium bowl, combine the remaining 2 teaspoons of olive oil and 1 teaspoon of vinegar and season with salt and pepper. Add the arugula and toss. Spoon the lemon sauce into 4 shallow bowls. Arrange 3 dumplings in each bowl, mound the arugula alongside and serve. —*Eric Ziebold*

**NOTE** Preserved lemons are lemons that have been cured in a lemon-salt mixture. They have a strong, pungent flavor. Look for them at specialty food shops.

## Vietnamese Tuna Seviche

**TOTAL: 1 HR**

4 SERVINGS ●

- 3 tablespoons Asian fish sauce
- 2½ tablespoons sugar, plus more for sprinkling
- 1½ tablespoons water
- 1 tablespoon fresh lemon juice
- 1 tablespoon fresh lime juice
- 1 small garlic clove, minced
- ½ teaspoon minced fresh ginger
- 1 serrano or Thai chile, thinly sliced, with seeds
- 1 cup yellow cherry tomatoes, halved
- 1 tablespoon soy sauce
- 1 tablespoon rice vinegar
- ½ pound cold sushi-grade tuna, cut into ½-inch cubes
- ½ pound yellow seedless watermelon, cut into ½-inch cubes
- 2 tablespoons *tobiko* (flying-fish roe)
- 2 tablespoons torn purple or green basil leaves

**1.** In a small bowl, stir the fish sauce, 2½ tablespoons of sugar, water, lemon juice, lime juice, garlic, ginger and chile.

**2.** In another small bowl, toss the tomatoes with the soy sauce, vinegar and a pinch of sugar and let stand for 5 minutes.

**3.** In a medium bowl, gently toss the tuna and watermelon with the dressing. Using a slotted spoon, transfer the salad to plates, allowing as much dressing as possible to drain back into the bowl. Using the slotted spoon, arrange the tomatoes on the plates. Garnish the salads with the *tobiko* and basil and serve. —*Tyson Cole*

## VIETNAMESE TUNA SEVICHE

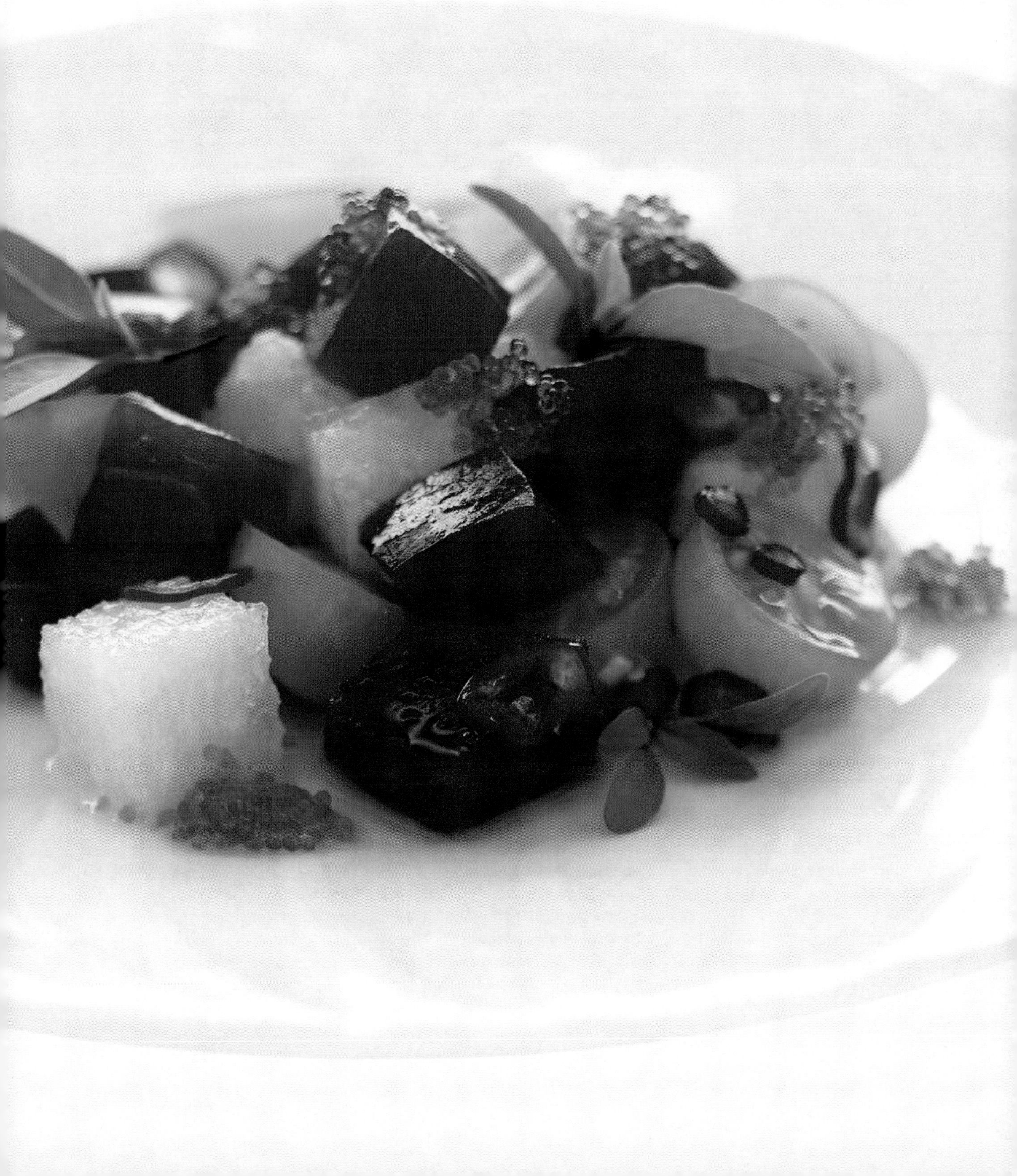

## Grilled Tuna Bruschetta with Chipotle Crème Fraîche

**TOTAL: 45 MIN**

8 SERVINGS

Chef Cornelius Gallagher of Oceana in New York City is a fish genius. For this bruschetta, he quickly marinates the fish in apple cider and olive oil, then grills it until it's slightly charred. He tops it with a luscious, smoky, spicy crème fraîche sauce that's not only wonderful with grilled tuna, but also with smoked trout or bluefish, grilled shrimp or even a chicken sandwich or burger.

- ¼ cup apple cider
- 2 tablespoons extra-virgin olive oil, plus more for brushing
- Two 8-ounce tuna steaks (¾ inch thick)
- 1 cup crème fraîche
- 2 chipotle chiles in adobo sauce— drained, seeded and minced

## F&W taste test
### CHIPOTLE CHILES

Chipotle peppers in adobo sauce add smoke and a little bit of spice to starters like the bruschetta above. These brands are F&W's favorites.

**La Costeña** $2 for 7 ounces.

**Casa Fiesta** $3 for 7 ounces.

**Goya** $2 for 7 ounces.

---

- 1 small garlic clove, minced
- 1 tablespoon chopped basil, plus 24 small basil leaves for garnish
- ½ Granny Smith apple, peeled and cut into ⅛-inch dice
- Salt and freshly ground pepper
- 24 thin slices of ciabatta or peasant bread

1. In a large, shallow dish, combine the apple cider with the 2 tablespoons of olive oil. Add the tuna steaks and turn to coat. Let the tuna steaks stand for 15 minutes, turning once.

2. Meanwhile, light a grill. In a medium bowl, stir the crème fraîche with the minced chipotles, garlic, chopped basil and diced apple and season the chipotle crème fraîche with salt and pepper.

3. Season the tuna steaks with salt and pepper. Grill the steaks over high heat, turning once, until they are lightly charred on the outside and rare inside, about 6 minutes. Transfer the tuna steaks to a platter. Brush both sides of the ciabatta slices with olive oil and grill them over high heat until toasted on both sides.

4. Cut the tuna steaks into ⅓-inch-thick slices and arrange them on the ciabatta toasts. Top each bruschetta with a dollop of chipotle crème fraîche and a basil leaf and serve. —*Cornelius Gallagher*

**MAKE AHEAD** The crème fraîche sauce can be refrigerated overnight.

## Stuffed Piquillo Peppers with Idiazábal Cheese Sauce

**TOTAL: 30 MIN**

4 SERVINGS ●

F&W's Marcia Kiesel stuffs piquillo peppers with chewy pasta and toasted almonds—an alternative to the classic filling of codfish and mashed potatoes. The pasta soaks up the bright, nutty Idiazábal sauce beautifully. Kiesel prefers using unsmoked varieties of the Spanish cheeses Idiazábal or Manchego because the piquillos already have so much woodsy flavor.

---

- 2 ounces spaghetti
- 1 tablespoon extra-virgin olive oil
- 1 small garlic clove, minced
- 6 roasted almonds, coarsely chopped
- Salt and freshly ground pepper
- 12 piquillo peppers from a 7.6-ounce jar
- 1⅓ cups heavy cream
- 1 cup finely shredded unsmoked Idiazábal or other unsmoked piquant and nutty sheep's-milk cheese (4 ounces)
- Splash of dry sherry

1. Preheat the oven to 425°. In a medium saucepan of boiling salted water, cook the spaghetti until it is al dente, then drain the pasta well. Toss the spaghetti with the olive oil, garlic and almonds and season with salt and pepper.

2. Gently stuff the piquillo peppers with the spaghetti mixture and set the peppers in a medium glass or ceramic baking dish. Pour ⅓ cup of the heavy cream over the piquillo peppers and bake them for about 5 minutes, or until they are heated through and bubbling.

3. Meanwhile, in a small saucepan, bring the remaining 1 cup of cream to a boil. Add the Idiazábal cheese and simmer over moderately low heat, stirring constantly, until melted. Remove the sauce from the heat and stir in the sherry. Season lightly with salt. Pour the sauce over the piquillos and serve at once. —*Marcia Kiesel*

**MAKE AHEAD** The piquillos can be stuffed and refrigerated earlier in the day.

## Lamb Meatballs with Red Pepper and Chickpea Sauce

**TOTAL: 40 MIN**

8 SERVINGS ●

- ½ cup roasted red peppers from a jar (4 ounces), preferably piquillo
- 2 cups low-sodium vegetable or chicken broth

½ cup whole milk yogurt, preferably Greek, plus more for serving

2 pounds ground lamb

2 large eggs, lightly beaten

1 tablespoon plus 1 teaspoon minced garlic

¼ cup minced flat-leaf parsley, plus more for garnish

1 tablespoon thyme leaves

2 teaspoons smoked paprika

4 teaspoons kosher salt, plus more for seasoning

¼ cup vegetable oil

1¾ cups chickpeas from a jar or can, drained

1. In a mini food processor, puree the roasted red peppers. Transfer the pepper puree to a bowl and whisk in the vegetable broth and ½ cup of the yogurt.

2. In a large bowl, combine the ground lamb, lightly beaten eggs, minced garlic, ¼ cup of minced parsley, thyme leaves and smoked paprika. Add the 4 teaspoons of kosher salt. Using your hands, gently mix the ingredients, then roll the mixture into sixteen 2-inch meatballs.

3. In a very large skillet, heat the vegetable oil until it is shimmering. Add the lamb meatballs to the skillet and cook them over moderately high heat until they are browned all over, about 8 minutes. Slide the meatballs to one side of the pan. Add the red pepper sauce and the chickpeas and bring just to a boil. Simmer the meatballs over moderately low heat, stirring and turning them occasionally in the sauce, until the sauce reduces slightly, about 10 minutes. Season the meatballs and red pepper sauce with salt. Transfer the meatballs and chickpeas to a platter, spoon the red pepper sauce on top, garnish with parsley and serve with yogurt. —*Nancy Silverton*

**MAKE AHEAD** The meatballs can be refrigerated overnight. Reheat the meatballs gently to serve.

## Roasted Quail with Cabbage and Raisins

**TOTAL: 30 MIN**

**4 SERVINGS** ● ●

For something so elegant, these petite quail stuffed with Madeira-soaked raisins are supersimple to make.

1½ tablespoons canola oil

¼ cup Madeira

½ cup golden raisins

1 tablespoon finely chopped sage, plus whole sage sprigs for garnish

Salt and freshly ground pepper

4 semiboneless quail

1 small onion, thinly sliced

4 cups finely shredded green cabbage (about 14 ounces)

½ teaspoon caraway seeds

1 bay leaf

1. Preheat the oven to 400°. Coat the bottom of a medium ovenproof skillet with ½ tablespoon of the oil. In a microwavable bowl, pour the Madeira over the raisins. Microwave at high power for 1 minute, or until the raisins are plump. Let cool, then drain the raisins, reserving the Madeira. Combine the raisins with the chopped sage and a pinch each of salt and pepper. Stuff the quail with the raisins and season with salt and pepper. Transfer the quail to the skillet and turn to coat them with oil. Roast the stuffed quail for 15 minutes.

2. Meanwhile, heat the remaining 1 tablespoon of oil in a large skillet. Add the onion and cook over moderately high heat, stirring, until lightly browned, about 5 minutes. Add the cabbage, caraway seeds and bay leaf and cook, stirring frequently, until the cabbage is tender, about 8 minutes longer. Stir in the reserved Madeira and any accumulated juices from the quail and cook until evaporated, about 1 minute. Discard the bay leaf. Spoon the cabbage onto plates and top with the quail. Garnish with the sage sprigs and serve. —*Kevin Graham*

## Warm Melon and Prosciutto Salad

**TOTAL: 30 MIN**

**4 SERVINGS** ●

This fast and easy recipe is from chef Aaron Whitcomb of Denver's Table 6 restaurant, who has created a menu full of clever little surprises that work fantastically well on the plate. In this case, a pungent pink-peppercorn vinaigrette and peppery greens invigorate a traditional pairing of prosciutto and melon.

2 tablespoons white wine vinegar

1 teaspoon pink peppercorns, lightly crushed

1 teaspoon Dijon mustard

½ medium shallot, thinly sliced

¼ cup vegetable oil

1 tablespoon heavy cream

Salt and freshly ground black pepper

1 tablespoon unsalted butter

½ cantaloupe, peeled and cut into 1-inch cubes

One 6-ounce bunch watercress, thick stems discarded

1½ ounces baby spinach (2 cups)

3 ounces thinly sliced prosciutto ham

2 tablespoons pine nuts, lightly toasted

Aged balsamic vinegar and toasted, buttered brioche, for serving

1. In a blender, puree the white wine vinegar, pink peppercorns, Dijon mustard and sliced shallot. Blend in the vegetable oil and the heavy cream; season the dressing with salt and pepper.

2. Melt the butter in a nonstick skillet. Add the cantaloupe cubes and toss them until they are hot. Toss the watercress and baby spinach with the dressing, then mound the greens on plates. Top the salad with the melon, ham and pine nuts; serve at once, with the balsamic vinegar and brioche. —*Aaron Whitcomb*

In the June issue, chef Seen Lippert plundered her extraordinary garden to get ingredients for this anchovy-rich Spring Vegetable Bagna Cauda (P. 42).

# salads

**MIXED GREENS WITH BALSAMIC**

**FENNEL AND ARUGULA SALAD WITH PECORINO TOSCANO**

## Mixed Greens with Balsamic

**ACTIVE: 20 MIN; TOTAL: 1 HR 20 MIN**

**4 SERVINGS** ●

- 2 pounds mixed young greens—such as spinach, watercress, radish sprouts, nettles, dandelion and arugula—coarsely chopped
- 4 teaspoons coarse salt
- ¼ cup extra-virgin olive oil
- 2 garlic cloves, minced
- 2 tablespoons balsamic vinegar

Freshly ground pepper

**1.** In a colander, toss the greens and salt; let stand for 1 hour. Rinse and squeeze dry.

**2.** In a large, deep skillet, heat the olive oil. Add the greens by the handful and cook over moderately high heat, tossing, until softened. Stir in the garlic and vinegar, then cover and cook until the greens are tender, about 2 minutes. Season with pepper and serve hot or warm. —*Paula Wolfert*

## Fennel and Arugula Salad with Pecorino Toscano

**TOTAL: 30 MIN**

**6 SERVINGS** ● ●

Six ½-inch-thick baguette slices

- 4 tablespoons extra-virgin olive oil
- 2 tablespoons fresh lemon juice
- 2 fennel bulbs, very thinly sliced
- 1 large bunch arugula, stemmed
- ¼ cup thinly sliced red onion
- ¼ pound Pecorino Toscano cheese, shredded (1 cup)

Salt and freshly ground pepper

**1.** Preheat the oven to 350°. Brush the bread with 1 tablespoon of olive oil, transfer to a baking sheet and toast until golden. Let cool, then break into ¾-inch pieces.

**2.** In a bowl, combine the remaining oil and the lemon juice. Add the fennel, arugula, onion, cheese, croutons and salt and pepper. Toss and serve. —*Laurent Tourondel*

## Spicy Caesar Salad

**TOTAL: 20 MIN**

**6 SERVINGS** ●

- ½ baguette, sliced ⅓ inch thick
- ¼ cup extra-virgin olive oil, plus more for brushing
- ½ cup mayonnaise
- 4 oil-packed anchovy fillets, preferably spicy, drained and chopped
- 2 tablespoons fresh lemon juice
- 2 large garlic cloves, coarsely chopped
- 1 teaspoon Dijon mustard

Freshly ground pepper

- 6 slices of lean bacon (3 ounces)
- 1½ pounds romaine lettuce, torn into large bite-size pieces
- 1 long red chile, seeded and thinly sliced crosswise
- ¼ cup freshly grated Parmesan

**1.** Preheat the oven to 400°. Spread the bread slices on a baking sheet and lightly brush both sides with olive oil. Bake for 5 minutes, or until golden. Let the toasts cool, then break them into large pieces.

**2.** In a mini food processor, combine the mayonnaise, anchovies, lemon juice, garlic and mustard and blend until smooth. With the processor on, slowly pour in the ¼ cup of olive oil; season with pepper.

**3.** In a large skillet, cook the bacon over moderate heat until browned and crisp, about 3 minutes per side. Drain and slice crosswise 1 inch thick.

**4.** In a large bowl, toss the romaine with the sliced chile, croutons and the bacon. Add the dressing and toss. Sprinkle the Parmesan over the salad, toss again and serve right away. —*Marcia Kiesel*

**MAKE AHEAD** The dressing can be refrigerated overnight.

## Two-Olive Caesar Salad

**TOTAL: 45 MIN**

10 SERVINGS

"Everything that goes into a Caesar salad tastes good with olives—the grated Parmesan, the anchovies, the garlicky croutons," says Michael Mina, chef at Michael Mina restaurant in San Francisco. That's why he purees Niçoise olives for the dressing and dabs aromatic green olive tapenade on the greens.

- 4 cups stale baguette cubes (¾-inch cubes)
- ¾ cup extra-virgin olive oil
- 3 garlic cloves, 2 minced
- 1 tablespoon snipped chives
- 2 tablespoons finely chopped flat-leaf parsley

Kosher salt and freshly ground pepper

- ½ cup store-bought green olive tapenade (4 ounces)
- 3 tablespoons fresh lemon juice
- 1 teaspoon grated lemon zest

- 2 large eggs
- ¼ cup pitted Niçoise olives (1 ounce)
- 1½ teaspoons Worcestershire sauce
- 1½ teaspoons Dijon mustard
- ¾ cup canola oil
- 2¼ pounds romaine hearts (about 6), cut crosswise 1 inch thick
- 1 cup freshly grated Parmesan cheese (4 ounces)
- 6 ounces white anchovy fillets (see Note)

**1.** Preheat the oven to 350°. In a large bowl, toss the baguette cubes with ½ cup of the olive oil, the minced garlic, the chives and 1 tablespoon of the parsley. Season with salt and pepper. Spread the cubes on a baking sheet and toast for about 12 minutes, stirring occasionally. Let cool.

**2.** In a small bowl, mix the tapenade with the remaining ¼ cup of olive oil and 1 tablespoon of parsley. Add 1 tablespoon of the lemon juice and the lemon zest and season with salt and pepper.

**3.** Bring a medium saucepan of water to a boil. Add the eggs and cook until softboiled, about 4 minutes. Cool the eggs slightly under cold running water. Carefully peel the eggs. Add the egg yolks to a blender along with the olives, the remaining 2 tablespoons of lemon juice, the whole garlic clove, Worcestershire sauce and mustard and blend to combine. With the machine on, add the canola oil in a thin stream and blend until incorporated. Season the dressing with salt and pepper.

**4.** Toss the romaine with the croutons, ⅔ cup of the Parmesan, three-fourths of the anchovies and the dressing. Mound the salad on a platter and garnish with the remaining anchovies, Parmesan and the tapenade. —*Michael Mina*

**NOTE** White anchovies, sold at specialty food stores, are anchovy fillets that have been marinated in white vinegar.

**MAKE AHEAD** The croutons can be stored in an airtight container for up to 3 days. The dressing can be refrigerated overnight.

## Garlicky Caesar Salad

**TOTAL: 40 MIN**

4 SERVINGS

Kimball Jones, chef at the Carneros Inn in Napa Valley, makes the garlicky dressing for this salad with a raw egg yolk.

- 1 large egg yolk
- 1 tablespoon plus 1 teaspoon white wine vinegar
- 1 tablespoon plus 1 teaspoon fresh lemon juice
- 1½ teaspoons Dijon mustard
- 1 large anchovy fillet

Dash of Worcestershire sauce

Dash of Tabasco

- 2 large garlic cloves, 1 thinly sliced
- ½ cup plus 3 tablespoons extra-virgin olive oil

Kosher salt and freshly ground pepper

- 2 cups whole wheat bread cubes (½-inch cubes)
- 3 romaine lettuce hearts, torn into bite-size pieces
- 2 ounces aged Vella Jack or Parmesan cheese, freshly grated

**1.** In a blender, puree the egg yolk with the vinegar, lemon juice, mustard, anchovy, Worcestershire sauce, Tabasco and the whole garlic clove. With the machine on, slowly add ½ cup of the olive oil. The dressing should be the consistency of thin, creamy mayonnaise; if it seems too thick, add 2 teaspoons of water. Season with salt and pepper and refrigerate.

**2.** Preheat the oven to 350°. In a skillet, heat the remaining olive oil. Add the sliced garlic. Cook over moderate heat, stirring, until light golden, 2 minutes. Remove from the heat and let cool for 10 minutes. Pick the garlic out of the oil and discard.

**3.** On a large baking sheet, toss the bread cubes with the garlic oil and a pinch each of salt and pepper. Bake for 12 minutes, stirring halfway through, or until toasted.

**4.** In a large bowl, toss the romaine with the dressing. Top with the croutons and cheese and serve. —*Kimball Jones*

# salads

## Spinach Caesar Salad

**TOTAL: 30 MIN**

6 SERVINGS ●

- 1 large egg
- 3 anchovy fillets, rinsed
- 2 tablespoons fresh lemon juice
- 2 garlic cloves, 1 minced
- 1 tablespoon Dijon mustard
- ½ cup plus 1 tablespoon extra-virgin olive oil
- 10 ounces Parmesan cheese, 3 ounces finely grated, 7 ounces coarsely shredded

Salt and freshly ground pepper

- ½ baguette, cut into ½-inch cubes (4 cups)
- 1 teaspoon paprika
- 8 ounces baby spinach (12 loosely packed cups)

**1.** Preheat the oven to 350°. Bring a small saucepan of water to a boil. Add the egg and cook for 5 minutes, until it is soft-boiled. Remove the egg with a slotted spoon and crack it into a blender, using a small spoon to scoop out all of the egg yolk and white. Add the anchovy fillets, lemon juice, whole garlic clove and Dijon mustard and blend until the dressing is smooth. With the machine on, add ¼ cup plus 2 tablespoons of the olive oil in a thin stream. Add two-thirds of the finely grated Parmesan cheese and season the dressing with salt and pepper.

**2.** In a large bowl, toss the baguette cubes with the remaining 3 tablespoons of olive oil. Add the remaining finely grated Parmesan cheese along with the paprika and minced garlic and toss to coat the bread cubes. Spread the bread cubes on a rimmed baking sheet and toast for about 8 minutes, or until the bread cubes are crisp and golden. Let cool slightly.

**3.** In the same large bowl, toss the spinach with the dressing, croutons and the shredded Parmesan; season with salt and pepper. Transfer the spinach salad to plates and serve. —*Laurent Tourondel*

## Warm Spinach Salad with Soft-Poached Eggs

**TOTAL: 20 MIN**

4 SERVINGS ● ●

This salad by Peter Berley, a talented cook and the author of *Fresh Food Fast,* is not only vegetarian and quick, but it's also decidedly healthy. That's because it features spinach, a leafy green that provides a huge amount of nutrients, especially vitamin A and vitamin K.

Salt

- 4 large eggs
- 1 pound baby spinach
- 5 tablespoons extra-virgin olive oil
- ¼ cup sherry vinegar
- 2 tablespoons balsamic vinegar
- 2 large shallots, thinly sliced
- 2 teaspoons coarsely chopped thyme

Freshly ground pepper

**1.** In a small saucepan, bring 1 quart of water to a boil. Add 1 teaspoon of salt and the eggs and simmer over moderately high heat for 5 minutes. Using a slotted spoon, transfer the eggs to a bowl of cold water and let stand for 3 to 4 minutes to stop the cooking. Keep the pan of hot water on the stove over low heat.

**2.** Meanwhile, put the baby spinach in a large bowl. In a medium skillet, combine the olive oil with the sherry vinegar, balsamic vinegar, sliced shallots and chopped thyme and boil for 1 minute.

**3.** Crack the egg shells all over and gently peel the eggs under warm running water, being careful to keep the eggs whole. Using a slotted spoon, slip the peeled eggs into the pan of hot water on the stove for 30 seconds to warm them.

**4.** In the large bowl, pour the warm dressing over the spinach, season the salad with salt and pepper and toss. Mound the salad on individual serving plates, top each serving with an egg and serve at once. —*Peter Berley*

## Mixed Citrus and Arugula Salad

**TOTAL: 20 MIN**

4 SERVINGS ● ●

A trio of readily available citrus fruits that includes navel oranges, which are meaty and slightly acidic, is the heart of this salad. Feel free to try other less-well-known varieties of citrus fruits, such as Cara Caras, a type of navel orange that has a lovely pink flesh and delicate flavor.

- 2 navel oranges
- 2 tangerines
- 3 clementines
- 1 large shallot, sliced paper-thin
- 3 tablespoons chopped mint leaves
- 1 tablespoon fresh lime juice
- 1 tablespoon walnut oil
- 1 tablespoon crème fraîche or sour cream
- 2 bunches arugula (¼ pound each), thick stems discarded

Salt and freshly ground pepper

**1.** Using a sharp knife, peel the navel oranges, tangerines and clementines, removing all the bitter white pith. Slice the clementines crosswise ½ inch thick and remove the pits. Transfer the clementines to a medium bowl. Working over the bowl, cut between the membranes of the navel oranges and the tangerines, releasing the citrus sections into the bowl. Add the shallot and mint to the citrus fruit.

**2.** In a large bowl, whisk the lime juice with the walnut oil and crème fraîche. Add the arugula to the bowl, season the salad with salt and pepper and toss gently. Using tongs, transfer the dressed arugula to plates. Add the citrus fruits to the remaining dressing, season the citrus with salt and pepper and toss to coat. Top the arugula salad with the citrus and serve at once. —*Grace Parisi*

**MAKE AHEAD** The citrus and arugula salad can be prepared through Step 1 and refrigerated for up to 2 hours.

MIXED CITRUS AND
ARUGULA SALAD

# salads

### Sweet Corn Salad with Green Beans and Hazelnuts

**TOTAL: 45 MIN**

**8 SERVINGS** ●

A late-summer salad like this one can be made almost entirely from produce from the farmers' market. The combination of flavors is clean and crisp: sweet corn, juicy tomatoes, snappy green beans and toasted hazelnuts.

- ½  cup hazelnuts
- 9  ears of corn, shucked
- 1  pound green beans
- ¼  cup plus 2½ tablespoons extra-virgin olive oil
- 2½ tablespoons white wine vinegar

Salt and freshly ground pepper

- 1  pound cherry tomatoes (3 cups), halved
- 2  scallions, thinly sliced

1. Preheat the oven to 350°. Put the hazelnuts in a pie plate and toast them in the oven for 8 minutes, or until they are golden brown. Let the nuts cool, then rub them together in a kitchen towel to remove the skins. Transfer the hazelnuts to a work surface and coarsely chop them.
2. Bring a large pot of water to a boil. Add the ears of corn and boil them over moderately high heat until they are just tender, about 4 minutes. With tongs, transfer the corn to a rimmed baking sheet. When the corn is cool enough to handle, cut the kernels from the cobs.
3. Add the green beans to the large pot and boil until they are crisp-tender, about 3 minutes. Drain and rinse the beans under cold water. Pat the beans dry and cut them into 1-inch lengths.
4. In a large bowl, combine the olive oil with the vinegar; season the dressing with salt and pepper. Add the tomatoes, scallions, corn kernels and green beans and toss to combine. Sprinkle the salad with the toasted hazelnuts and serve.
—*Jeremy Jackson*

### Watercress Salad with Prosciutto, Tangerines and Hazelnuts

**TOTAL: 45 MIN**

**8 SERVINGS** ●

This salad is an intriguing mix of strong flavors—sweet, peppery, earthy. The hazelnuts add richness, says chef Govind Armstrong of Table 8 in Los Angeles, plus they "do their job as the texture police."

- ½  cup hazelnuts
- 4  tangerines or 2 navel oranges
- 2  tablespoons sherry vinegar
- 1  tablespoon white balsamic vinegar
- 1½ teaspoons honey
- 1  small shallot, minced
- ¼  teaspoon finely chopped thyme
- ¼  cup extra-virgin olive oil
- 2  tablespoons hazelnut oil
- ¼  teaspoon truffle oil (optional)

Salt and freshly ground pepper

- 3  large bunches watercress, thick stems discarded
- 1¾ cups loosely packed flat-leaf parsley leaves (from ½ bunch)
- ¾  pound thinly sliced prosciutto, preferably duck prosciutto

1. Preheat the oven to 350°. Spread the hazelnuts in a pie plate and toast for about 10 minutes, or until fragrant. Let the nuts cool slightly, then coarsely chop them.
2. Meanwhile, peel the tangerines, removing all the bitter white pith. If you are using oranges, peel with a sharp knife. Working over a large bowl, cut in between the membranes to release the citrus sections.
3. In a bowl, whisk the sherry vinegar with the balsamic vinegar, honey, shallot and thyme. Whisk in the olive oil, hazelnut oil and truffle oil in a slow stream. Season the dressing with salt and pepper.
4. Add the watercress and parsley to the tangerine sections and toss. Add ⅓ cup of the dressing and toss well. Arrange the salad on a large platter, then arrange the prosciutto decoratively on top. Sprinkle with the hazelnuts and serve with the remaining dressing. —*Govind Armstrong*

**MAKE AHEAD** The recipe can be prepared a day ahead through Step 3. Keep the hazelnuts at room temperature; refrigerate the oranges and dressing separately.

### Serrano Ham and Arugula Salad with Pomegranate Salsa

**TOTAL: 30 MIN**

**12 SERVINGS** ● ●

This vibrant dish, layered with arugula, bright white slices of ricotta salata and thin strips of salty serrano ham, is the sort of composed salad that Suzanne Goin, chef at Lucques in Los Angeles, uses to showcase seasonal ingredients. Another of her favorite winter salads is made with blood oranges, dates and Parmesan cheese.

- 1  large shallot, minced
- 2  teaspoons fresh lemon juice

Kosher salt

- 2  tablespoons pomegranate molasses (see Note)
- ½  cup extra-virgin olive oil

Seeds from 1 small pomegranate

- 2  tablespoons chopped parsley

Freshly ground pepper

- ½  pound arugula, thick stems discarded
- 6  ounces thinly sliced serrano ham
- ½  pound ricotta salata cheese, cut into 12 thin slices

1. In a medium bowl, mix the shallot with the lemon juice and ½ teaspoon of salt; let stand for 5 minutes. Whisk in the pomegranate molasses and the olive oil. Stir in the pomegranate seeds and the parsley and season with salt and pepper.
2. Arrange the arugula on a large platter and top with the serrano ham and ricotta salata. Spoon the pomegranate salsa over the salad and serve. —*Suzanne Goin*

**NOTE** Sweet and tangy pomegranate molasses is available at specialty food stores and Middle Eastern markets.

**MAKE AHEAD** The pomegranate salsa can be refrigerated overnight.

Most specialty food shops sell a wide variety of vinegars. It's worth investing in the best you can get, which may be produced from better-quality wine or fruit juices and aged in wooden barrels to mature and mellow for anywhere from six months to 100 years.

**VINEGAR COOKING TIPS**

**To improve the flavor** of cheap balsamic vinegar, pour it into a nonreactive saucepan and simmer over moderate heat until the liquid is reduced by half.

**To prevent vinegar from losing its intensity,** add it right at the end of cooking; it loses flavor when heated.

**Substitute good-quality vinegar for salt** in salads or dishes made with vegetables, meat, fish or poultry.

**If you've accidentally oversweetened** a savory dish or sauce, stirring in ½ to 1 teaspoon of vinegar can help counterbalance the sweetness.

**Use white vinegar for pickling** or making acidulated water; this vinegar, made from distilled ethyl alcohol, has a harsh, aggressive taste. Vinegar is a natural antibacterial and a good cleaning agent. Prepare a dilution of one part vinegar to four parts hot water for cleaning kitchen surfaces.

● FAST　● HEALTHY　● MAKE AHEAD　● STAFF FAVORITE

# salads

## Spring Vegetable Bagna Cauda

**TOTAL: 45 MIN**

**10 TO 12 SERVINGS**

This bagna cauda includes butter, which makes the dish's flavor fuller and richer.

**Three** 2-ounce cans oil-packed flat anchovies, drained and rinsed

**10** garlic cloves, thinly sliced

**1½** cups extra-virgin olive oil

**4** tablespoons cold unsalted butter

**1** teaspoon fresh lemon juice

**1** pound asparagus

**1** pound fava beans or edamame, shelled (about 4 ounces)

**1** bunch watercress, thick stems discarded

**2** medium fennel bulbs— halved, cored and thinly sliced lengthwise

**2** bunches red radishes, trimmed

**1** pound baby carrots, halved

**10** large hard-cooked eggs, peeled and quartered

**1.** In a saucepan, combine the anchovies, garlic and oil. Simmer over moderately low heat until the garlic is very soft but not colored, about 30 minutes. Transfer the mixture to a blender and let cool for 10 minutes. Add the butter and lemon juice and puree until the bagna cauda is smooth.

**2.** Meanwhile, bring a large saucepan of water to a boil. Add the asparagus and cook until crisp-tender, about 3 minutes. Using a slotted spoon, transfer the asparagus to a plate and let cool. Add the shelled fava beans to the boiling water and cook for 5 minutes. Drain and cool under cold running water, then pat dry. If using favas, peel off the beans' tough outer skins.

**3.** Mound the watercress on a large platter. Arrange the fennel, radishes, carrots, eggs, asparagus and fava beans on top in separate piles and drizzle with some of the bagna cauda. Pour the remaining bagna cauda into a small bowl and serve with the vegetable platter. —*Seen Lippert*

## Knife and Fork Grilled Vegetable Salad

**TOTAL: 35 MIN**

**4 SERVINGS** ●

**1** garlic clove, halved

Kosher salt

**3** tablespoons extra-virgin olive oil, plus more for brushing

**1** tablespoon fresh lemon juice

**¼** cup pine nuts

**1** large onion, sliced ½ inch thick

**2** small eggplants, sliced crosswise ½ inch thick

**Two** 6-ounce zucchini, sliced crosswise ½ inch thick

**Two** 6-ounce yellow squash, sliced crosswise ½ inch thick

Freshly ground pepper

**1** red bell pepper

**1** yellow bell pepper

**1** large head romaine lettuce (1¼ pounds), quartered lengthwise

**4** ounces fresh goat cheese, crumbled (1 cup)

**1.** Light a grill. In a mortar, pound the halved garlic to a paste with 1 teaspoon of salt. Stir in the 3 tablespoons of olive oil and the lemon juice.

**2.** In a small skillet, cook the pine nuts over moderate heat until they are toasted, about 3 minutes.

**3.** Thread the onion slices onto 2 parallel 10-inch skewers. Put the eggplant, zucchini and yellow squash slices on 2 large rimmed baking sheets; brush both sides with olive oil and season with salt and pepper. Brush the bell peppers and lettuce with olive oil. Grill the vegetables over moderately high heat, turning occasionally, until lightly charred and just tender. The onions will take about 5 minutes per side; the eggplant, zucchini and squash will all take about 3 minutes per side; the peppers, 3 minutes on each of four sides; the lettuce wedges, about 1 minute per side. Scrape the charred skin from the peppers, discard the stems and seeds and cut into strips.

**4.** Put a romaine lettuce wedge on each plate. Mound the grilled vegetables on the lettuce and sprinkle with the crumbled goat cheese and toasted pine nuts. Pass the lemon vinaigrette at the table.
—*Karen Adler and Judith Fertig*

## Chipotle-Corn Salad

**TOTAL: 20 MIN**

**4 TO 6 SERVINGS** ● ● ● ●

F&W's Grace Parisi has been making this fresh-corn salad—with grilled sweet Vidalia onions, tart lime juice and chipotle chiles—as a summer picnic staple ever since she discovered canned chipotles in adobo sauce years ago at her neighborhood Latin grocery store. Now these chipotles are available in the Latin section of big supermarkets all around the country as well.

**5** ears of corn

**½** medium Vidalia or Walla Walla onion, thickly sliced crosswise

**1** tablespoon extra-virgin olive oil

**¼** cup plus 2 tablespoons sour cream

**2** tablespoons fresh lime juice

**2** chipotle chiles in adobo sauce, seeded and finely chopped

**1** scallion, thinly sliced

Salt and freshly ground pepper

**1.** Light a grill or preheat a grill pan. Brush the corn and onion slices with the olive oil and grill over moderately high heat until charred in spots but still slightly crisp, about 7 minutes. Let the vegetables cool slightly, then cut the kernels from the cobs and coarsely chop the onion.

**2.** In a medium bowl, combine the sour cream with the lime juice, chipotle chiles and scallion, then stir in the charred corn and onions. Season the corn salad with salt and pepper and serve immediately.
—*Grace Parisi*

**MAKE AHEAD** The corn salad can be refrigerated overnight. Let the salad stand for 20 minutes at room temperature before serving.

**CHIPOTLE-CORN SALAD**

**SUMMER VEGETABLE AND POTATO SALAD**

## Summer Vegetable and Potato Salad

**TOTAL: 40 MIN**

4 SERVINGS ●

- 4 ounces yellow wax beans
- 4 ounces thin green beans
- 6 garlic cloves
- 2 bay leaves
- 1 thyme sprig
- 1 rosemary sprig
- ½ teaspoon black peppercorns
- 12 small fingerling potatoes, scrubbed but not peeled
- 2 oil-packed anchovy fillets
- ¼ cup milk
- ¼ cup extra-virgin olive oil
- 2 tablespoons red wine vinegar

Salt and freshly ground pepper

- 1 tablespoon chopped parsley
- ½ teaspoon chopped marjoram
- 12 cherry tomatoes, halved

**1.** In a saucepan of boiling salted water, cook the yellow beans until they are just tender, about 3 minutes. Using a slotted spoon, transfer the yellow beans to a baking sheet and let cool. Add the green beans to the boiling water and cook until they are just tender, about 2 minutes. Using the slotted spoon, add the green beans to the baking sheet. Let the yellow and green beans cool, then pat dry.

**2.** Add the garlic, bay leaves, thyme, rosemary and peppercorns to the boiling water. Add the potatoes and simmer them over moderately high heat until they are tender, about 20 minutes. Drain the cooked potatoes, reserving the garlic cloves. Discard all of the other seasonings.

**3.** Meanwhile, in a small bowl, soak the anchovy fillets in the milk for 10 minutes. Drain the anchovies, then coarsely chop them and transfer to a blender. Add the olive oil and the reserved garlic to the blender and puree the anchovies and garlic. With the machine on, slowly add the vinegar. Scrape the anchovy dressing into a bowl, season it with salt and pepper and stir the chopped parsley and marjoram into the vinaigrette.

**4.** Cut the boiled fingerling potatoes into ¼-inch-thick slices and put them in a large bowl. Add half of the anchovy dressing to the potatoes and toss gently. Add the yellow and green beans, the cherry tomatoes and the remaining dressing and toss gently. Serve the salad in the bowl it was tossed in, or arrange the beans and potatoes on a large platter before serving.

*—Jonathan Benno*

**MAKE AHEAD** The recipe can be prepared through Step 3 earlier in the day. Refrigerate the beans and vinaigrette separately. Keep the potatoes at room temperature.

●FAST    ●HEALTHY    ●MAKE AHEAD    ●STAFF FAVORITE

# salads

## Sweet Roasted Pepper Salad with Anchovies and Garlic

**ACTIVE: 30 MIN; TOTAL: 2 HR**

8 SERVINGS ● ●

Hunks of crusty bread are terrific with this garlicky pepper salad, with bits of salty anchovies and chopped fresh herbs. The salad is also excellent when spread on sandwiches, mixed into pasta, paired with fresh mozzarella or even pureed as a sauce for roasted fish.

- 4 large red bell peppers
- 4 large yellow bell peppers
- ¾ cup extra-virgin olive oil, plus more for rubbing
- 4 large garlic cloves, thinly sliced
- 4 large anchovy fillets, rinsed and chopped
- 2 tablespoons coarsely chopped basil
- 2 tablespoons finely chopped flat-leaf parsley

Salt and freshly ground pepper

1. Preheat the oven to 450°. Rub the red and yellow bell peppers with olive oil, arrange them on a baking sheet and roast them for about 35 minutes, turning occasionally, until the peppers are softened and blackened. Transfer the bell peppers to a medium bowl, cover the bowl with plastic wrap and let cool.

2. Peel and seed the cooled red and yellow bell peppers and pat them dry. Cut the bell peppers into thick strips and transfer them to a medium bowl. Add the garlic, anchovies, basil, parsley and the ¾ cup of olive oil to the bell peppers and toss to coat them completely. Season the bell peppers with salt and pepper and let them stand at room temperature for at least 1 hour or for up to 6 hours.

—*Paul Bartolotta*

**SERVE WITH** Crusty bread.

**MAKE AHEAD** The roasted pepper salad can be refrigerated for up to 1 week. Let the roasted bell peppers return to room temperature before serving.

## Cauliflower and Roasted Beet Salad with Rich Herb Dressing

**ACTIVE: 30 MIN; TOTAL: 1 HR 30 MIN**

6 SERVINGS ●

- 6 medium beets (about 1½ pounds)
- Salt
- ¼ cup plus 3 tablespoons extra-virgin olive oil
- 3 tablespoons red wine vinegar
- Freshly ground pepper
- 3 large eggs
- One 2½-pound head cauliflower, cored and cut into 1-inch florets
- 1 tablespoon fresh lemon juice
- 1 large shallot, thinly sliced
- ¼ cup chopped flat-leaf parsley
- 2 tablespoons chopped mint

1. Preheat the oven to 400°. Put the beets in a small roasting pan, add salt and ¼ inch of water and tightly cover with foil. Bake the beets for 1 hour, or until tender. Drain and cool, then peel the beets and slice ¼ inch thick. In the roasting pan, toss the beets with 1 tablespoon each of the oil and vinegar. Season with salt and pepper.

2. In a saucepan, cover the eggs with water and bring to a gentle boil. Reduce the heat to low and simmer for 8 minutes. Pour off the water and shake the eggs against the sides of the pan to crack the shells. Cover the eggs with cold water; soak for 5 minutes, then pat dry, peel and finely chop.

3. In a large saucepan of boiling salted water, cook the cauliflower until just tender, about 3 minutes. Drain well. Transfer the florets to a large bowl and toss with 1 tablespoon of the olive oil and the lemon juice. Season with salt and pepper.

4. In a medium bowl, soak the shallot in the remaining 2 tablespoons of vinegar for 5 minutes. Add the parsley, mint and the remaining 5 tablespoons of olive oil. Fold in the chopped eggs and season with salt and pepper. Arrange the sliced beets on a large platter and scatter the cauliflower florets over them. Spoon the dressing over the salad and serve. —*Cal Peternell*

**MAKE AHEAD** The cooked beets, eggs and cauliflower can be refrigerated separately overnight. Bring to room temperature before proceeding.

## Salad of Mixed Greens with Grilled Peaches and Cabrales Cheese

**TOTAL: 30 MIN**

8 SERVINGS ● ●

Chef Bradford Thompson of Mary Elaine's at The Phoenician in Scottsdale, Arizona, combines Spanish blue cheese, toasted walnuts and sweet, drippy peaches with frisée for a delicious salad.

- ½ cup walnuts
- 4 firm, ripe freestone peaches, halved and pitted
- 2½ tablespoons extra-virgin olive oil
- Salt and freshly ground pepper
- 1 tablespoon sherry vinegar
- 3 ounces arugula, thick stems discarded
- One 5-ounce head frisée, torn into bite-size pieces (4 cups)
- 3 ounces Cabrales cheese, crumbled (1 cup)

1. Preheat the oven to 350°. Light a grill. Put the walnuts in a pie plate and toast in the oven for 7 minutes, or until they are golden brown. Transfer the walnuts to a plate and let cool, then coarsely chop.

2. In a medium bowl, toss the peach halves with ½ tablespoon of the olive oil and season with salt and pepper. Grill the peaches over moderately high heat until softened and lightly browned, about 5 minutes per side. Transfer the peaches to a work surface and cut each half in half.

3. In a medium bowl, mix the vinegar with the remaining 2 tablespoons of olive oil and season with salt and pepper. Add the arugula and frisée and toss well. Transfer the salad to a platter and scatter the Cabrales and toasted walnuts on top. Arrange the peaches around the salad and serve.

—*Bradford Thompson*

## Italian Tuna Salad with White Beans and Arugula

**TOTAL: 25 MIN**

8 SERVINGS ● ●

Three 7-ounce cans Italian or
    Spanish tuna in olive oil,
    drained and lightly flaked
One 19-ounce can cannellini beans,
    drained and rinsed
  1  cup cherry tomatoes, quartered
  1  small red onion, sliced lengthwise
  ½  cup extra-virgin olive oil
Salt and freshly ground pepper
  2  bunches arugula, thick stems
    discarded, leaves torn into pieces

In a large bowl, toss the tuna with the beans, tomatoes, onion and olive oil and season with salt and pepper. Just before serving, fold in the arugula.
—*Paul Bartolotta*

## Country Ham and Mango Salad

**TOTAL: 20 MIN**

4 SERVINGS ●

At his Bar Americain in New York City, Bobby Flay serves a sampler of country hams from Kentucky, Texas and Virginia. Incredible on their own, country hams are also great in a salad with juicy mangoes.

  2  tablespoons balsamic vinegar
  1  teaspoon Dijon mustard
  1  teaspoon molasses
Salt and freshly ground pepper
  ¼  cup extra-virgin olive oil
  4  ounces mesclun (8 cups)
  2  ripe mangoes, thinly sliced
  4  ounces thinly sliced country
    ham or prosciutto

**1.** In a small bowl, whisk the vinegar, mustard and molasses; season with salt and pepper. Add the olive oil in a thin stream, whisking until emulsified.
**2.** In a large bowl, toss the mesclun and mangoes with two-thirds of the dressing. Transfer the salad to a platter and top with the ham. Drizzle the remaining dressing over the ham and serve. —*Bobby Flay*

## Toasted Panzanella with Tomato and Fennel

**ACTIVE: 25 MIN; TOTAL: 50 MIN**

6 SERVINGS ● ●

Traditional *panzanella* is made by soaking rock-hard pieces of stale bread in ice water and squeezing them dry, then tossing them with chunks of tomato in a vinaigrette. Instead, chef Michael Romano of New York City's Union Square Cafe creates a crouton-based version by cutting day-old bread into cubes, coating them with olive oil and toasting them. The bread goes from wonderfully crisp to satisfyingly chewy as it soaks up the succulent juices and tangy dressing.

  8  ounces day-old sourdough
    bread with crust, cut
    into ¾-inch cubes (4 cups)
  ½  cup plus 2 tablespoons
    extra-virgin olive oil
  1  tablespoon pine nuts
  1  red bell pepper
  2  large tomatoes, seeded and cut
    into ¾-inch dice
  1  small fennel bulb, tops trimmed,
    bulb very thinly sliced
  1  small red onion, halved and
    thinly sliced
  ¼  cup brined black olives, such as
    Gaeta or Calamata, pitted and
    coarsely chopped
  ¼  cup loosely packed
    shredded basil
  2  tablespoons balsamic vinegar
Salt and freshly ground pepper

**1.** Preheat the oven to 350°. In a large bowl, toss the bread cubes with 2 tablespoons of the olive oil. Spread the cubes out on a baking sheet and bake for 12 minutes, or until nicely toasted. Let the bread cool, then return it to the bowl. Put the pine nuts on the baking sheet and bake for 3 minutes, or until golden; add them to the croutons.
**2.** Roast the bell pepper over a gas flame or under the broiler until charred all over. Transfer the pepper to a small bowl, cover with plastic wrap and let cool slightly. Peel and seed the pepper and cut it into ¾-inch dice. Add the diced bell pepper to the croutons along with the tomatoes, fennel, onion, olives and basil.
**3.** In a small bowl, whisk the vinegar with the remaining ½ cup of olive oil. Season the vinaigrette with salt and pepper and pour it over the salad. Toss and let stand for 5 minutes, then serve.
—*Michael Romano*

**MAKE AHEAD** The tossed salad can be covered with plastic wrap and kept at room temperature for up to 2 hours.

# F&W taste test
**CANNED TUNA**

F&W tasted almost 30 canned tunas—domestic packed in water, domestic packed in olive oil and Imported—and selected a favorite from each category.

**DOMESTIC WATER-PACKED**
**Chicken of the Sea Solid White Albacore** Chicken of the Sea is named for the white tuna the company first canned in 1914.
**STAFF COMMENT** "Flaky and tasty."

**DOMESTIC OIL-PACKED**
**Cento Solid Pack Light Tuna** Cento sells 100-plus products, but only one tuna.
**STAFF COMMENT** "Good, clean flavor, and just salty enough."

**IMPORTED**
**A's do Mar Tuna in Olive Oil** Line-caught Spanish tuna.
**STAFF COMMENT** "Mild and yummy."

# salads

## Heirloom-Tomato Salad with Anchovies

**TOTAL: 20 MIN**
**8 SERVINGS** ●●

¼ cup extra-virgin olive oil
2 tablespoons fresh lime juice
2 teaspoons Asian fish sauce
2 teaspoons minced peeled ginger
3 pounds assorted heirloom tomatoes, large tomatoes sliced, cherry tomatoes halved
Salt and freshly ground pepper
2 scallions, thinly sliced crosswise
2 tablespoons cilantro leaves
32 marinated white anchovy fillets or 16 canned skinless, boneless sardine fillets, drizzled with white wine vinegar (see Note)

In a bowl, whisk the olive oil with the lime juice, fish sauce and ginger. Arrange the sliced tomatoes on a platter, drizzle with the dressing and season with salt and pepper. Scatter the scallions, cilantro and anchovies over the salad and serve.
—*Michael Cimarusti*

**NOTE** Marinated white anchovies are available at specialty markets.

## Tomato, Gruyère and Red Onion Salad

**TOTAL: 15 MIN**
**6 SERVINGS** ●

Neutral-tasting sunflower oil has a way of making the other flavors more vibrant. This salad can be served year-round, but in winter you'll want to substitute grape tomatoes for the beefsteak here.

2 beefsteak tomatoes (1 pound), thickly sliced
Salt and freshly ground pepper
¾ pound Gruyère cheese, shredded (3 cups)
¼ cup sunflower or other mild oil
2 tablespoons Melfor vinegar (see Note) or apple cider vinegar
¼ cup finely chopped red onion
2 tablespoons chopped parsley

Arrange the tomatoes on a platter; sprinkle lightly with salt and pepper. Mound the cheese on top and drizzle with the oil and vinegar. Garnish with the onion and parsley and serve. —*Jean-Georges Vongerichten*

**SERVE WITH** In Alsace this salad is served with chunks of *cervelas,* a knockwurstlike sausage that's eaten cold.

**NOTE** Melfor vinegar, an Alsatian condiment seasoned with honey and infused with herbs, is available at melfor.com.

## Bacon and Tomato Salad

**TOTAL: 30 MIN**
**6 SERVINGS** ●

3 pounds tomatoes, cut into ½-inch pieces
12 basil leaves, torn
1 small red onion, coarsely chopped
¼ cup extra-virgin olive oil
2 tablespoons sherry vinegar
Salt and freshly ground pepper
¾ pound sliced bacon
½ cup mayonnaise
1½ teaspoons Dijon mustard
½ teaspoon curry powder
¾ teaspoon Cajun spice mix
1½ teaspoons fresh lemon juice
1 small garlic clove, minced
Dash of hot sauce
Crusty bread, for serving

**1.** Preheat the oven to 450°. In a bowl, toss the tomatoes, basil, onion, olive oil and vinegar and season with salt and pepper. Let stand for 15 minutes.
**2.** Set a rack on a baking sheet and arrange the bacon on it in a single layer. Bake the bacon in the upper third of the oven for 15 minutes, turning once, until it is golden and crisp-chewy. Cool, then break the bacon into small pieces.
**3.** In a small bowl, whisk the mayonnaise with the mustard, curry powder, spice mix, lemon juice, garlic and hot sauce.
**4.** Sprinkle the bacon over the tomato salad and serve the spicy mayonnaise and bread on the side. —*Laurent Tourondel*

## Tomato Salad with Mint Dressing

**TOTAL: 10 MIN**
**8 SERVINGS** ●●

¼ cup plus 1 tablespoon extra-virgin olive oil
2 tablespoons red wine vinegar
1 tablespoon fresh lemon juice
1 large garlic clove, finely chopped
Salt
½ cup coarsely chopped mint, plus mint leaves for garnish
2½ pounds ripe tomatoes, cut into wedges

In a small bowl, whisk the olive oil, vinegar, lemon juice and garlic and season with salt. Stir in the chopped mint. Arrange the tomatoes in a salad bowl. Drizzle with the dressing, garnish with mint leaves and serve. —*Victoria Amory*

## Fregola Tabbouleh

**TOTAL: 30 MIN**
**8 SERVINGS** ●●●

*Fregola sarda* is a chewy mini Italian pasta from Sardinia. Because its size is similar to bulgur wheat's, it's used here in a fun riff on tabbouleh.

1 cup *fregola sarda* (7 ounces)
¼ cup extra-virgin olive oil
2 tablespoons fresh lemon juice
1 cup minced flat-leaf parsley
¼ cup minced mint
1 Persian or kirby cucumber, thinly sliced
1 large garlic clove, minced
1 pint cherry tomatoes, halved
Kosher salt

**1.** In a large saucepan of boiling salted water, cook the *fregola sarda* until al dente, about 10 minutes. Drain, then spread on a plate to cool.
**2.** In a medium bowl, whisk the olive oil with the lemon juice. Add the parsley, mint, cucumber and garlic and toss. Add the *fregola* and tomatoes and toss again. Season with salt and serve at room temperature. —*Nancy Silverton*

**FRESH BUTTERNUT
SQUASH SALAD**

## Fresh Butternut Squash Salad

**TOTAL: 30 MIN**

**4 SERVINGS** ●

Paper-thin slices of raw butternut squash are mixed with prosciutto, Parmesan cheese and walnuts in this unusual salad. If the squash isn't completely fresh, blanch the ribbons in boiling water for 2 minutes to soften them slightly and bring out their flavor.

- 1 **medium butternut squash (about 2 pounds), peeled**
- 1 **cup walnut halves (3 ounces)**
- 2 **tablespoons red wine vinegar**

**Salt and freshly ground pepper**

- ¼ **cup extra-virgin olive oil**
- 2 **ounces thinly sliced prosciutto, cut into 2-inch strips**
- 2 **ounces Parmesan cheese, shaved (1 cup)**

**1.** Preheat the oven to 350°. Cut off the bulbous portion of the squash and reserve for another use. Using a mandoline adjusted to the thinnest setting, slice the neck of the squash lengthwise into long, thin ribbons. **2.** Spread the walnuts in a pie plate and toast for about 6 minutes, until fragrant. Let cool slightly, then coarsely chop. Transfer the squash to a bowl, toss with the vinegar and season with salt and pepper. Lightly stir in the olive oil, prosciutto and walnuts, garnish with the Parmesan and serve. —*Marc Meyer*

## Dandelion and Fig Salad with Serrano Ham and Grated Almonds

**TOTAL: 25 MIN**

**8 SERVINGS** ● ●

This salad is a brilliant combination of ingredients, from bitter dandelion greens and smoky paprika to sweet and chewy figs and ham. The most unusual touch is the finely grated almonds; the flecks imbue every bite of the salad with an intense nutty flavor. A microplane grater is the best tool to use here; to avoid cutting your fingers, discard the nub rather than grating each almond all the way down.

- ¼ **cup plus 2½ tablespoons sherry vinegar**
- 1 **teaspoon turbinado or raw sugar**
- ½ **teaspoon smoked sweet paprika**
- 1 **tablespoon honey**
- ½ **cup extra-virgin olive oil**

**Salt and freshly ground pepper**

- ¾ **cup blanched, roasted almonds (3 ounces), preferably Marcona**
- 3 **ounces tender dandelion greens, large leaves torn into bite-size pieces**
- 12 **black or green fresh figs, halved or quartered if large**
- 12 **thin slices of serrano ham (about 4½ ounces)**

**1.** In a small saucepan, combine ¼ cup of the sherry vinegar with the sugar and simmer over moderate heat until the mixture is syrupy and reduced to 1 tablespoon, about 8 minutes. **2.** In another small saucepan, warm the paprika over moderate heat until fragrant, 15 seconds. Stir in the honey and the remaining 2½ tablespoons of vinegar and scrape into a bowl. Whisk in the olive oil. Season with salt and pepper. **3.** Using a microplane grater, finely grate ¼ cup of the almonds over a sheet of wax paper. In a large bowl, toss the dandelion greens with ¼ cup of the salad dressing and transfer to a platter. Add the figs to the bowl and toss with 1 tablespoon of the dressing, then arrange on the platter. Drape the serrano ham over the greens and scatter the whole almonds around the platter. Sprinkle the grated almonds over the serrano and drizzle with the sherry vinegar syrup. Serve the salad, passing the remaining dressing at the table. —*Michael Cimarusti*

**MAKE AHEAD** The recipe can be prepared through Step 2 and refrigerated overnight. Let the syrup and dressing return to room temperature before proceeding.

## Snow Pea and Enoki Mushroom Salad with Tofu-Tamari Dressing

**TOTAL: 20 MIN**

**4 SERVINGS** ● ●

Many people confuse tamari with ordinary soy sauce because both are made from soybeans. But tamari has a richer, cleaner and mellower flavor that comes out in the silky dressing on this light salad. It is also a boon for people with wheat allergies because, unlike soy sauce, the soybeans used in authentic tamari are not fermented with toasted wheat.

- ¼ **cup plus 2 tablespoons silken tofu**
- 2 **teaspoons extra-virgin olive oil**
- 1½ **teaspoons tamari or soy sauce**
- 1 **teaspoon unseasoned rice vinegar**
- 1 **teaspoon fresh lemon juice**
- 1 **teaspoon finely grated, peeled fresh ginger**
- ¼ **teaspoon Asian sesame oil**

**Salt**

- 3 **ounces snow peas (1 cup)**
- 4 **ounces mesclun (8 cups loosely packed)**
- ¼ **cup cut chives (in 1-inch lengths)**
- 2 **ounces enoki mushrooms**
- 2 **tablespoons chopped chervil or flat-leaf parsley**
- 2 **tablespoons chopped basil**

**1.** In a blender, puree the tofu with the olive oil, tamari, rice vinegar, lemon juice, ginger and sesame oil. Scrape the dressing into a bowl and season with salt. **2.** In a small saucepan of boiling salted water, blanch the snow peas for 30 seconds. Drain and pat dry, then slice lengthwise into thin strips. **3.** In a large bowl, toss the mesclun with the snow peas, chives, enoki mushrooms, chervil and basil. Add the tofu dressing and toss again. Transfer to plates and serve. —*Josh DeChellis*

**MAKE AHEAD** The tofu-tamari dressing can be refrigerated for up to 3 days. Stir the dressing before using.

# salads

## Crunchy Winter Vegetable Salad with Olives and Capers

**TOTAL: 1 HR 15 MIN**

8 TO 10 SERVINGS ● ●

This substantial salad makes a bold statement: It's piquant and refreshing, plus it's supercharged with vegetables.

- ½ head broccoli (1¼ pounds), cut into bite-size florets
- ½ head cauliflower (1 pound), cut into bite-size florets
- ½ fennel bulb, some feathery fronds reserved and coarsely chopped
- ½ cup pitted Calamata olives, plus 1 tablespoon chopped olives
- 1 tablespoon whole drained capers, plus 1 teaspoon chopped capers
- 1 teaspoon lemon zest
- 1 tablespoon Dijon mustard
- ¼ teaspoon minced garlic
- ⅓ cup white wine vinegar
- ¾ cup extra-virgin olive oil

Salt and freshly ground pepper

- 1 head endive, sliced ½ inch thick
- 1¼ pounds jicama, peeled and julienned
- 1 small head radicchio—halved, cored and cut into ¼-inch strips
- 1 head escarole, inner leaves only, torn into bite-size pieces
- 4 celery ribs, thinly sliced on the diagonal

**1.** Bring a large pot of salted water to a boil. Add the broccoli florets and blanch just until crisp-tender, about 3 minutes; drain, plunge into a bowl of ice water and drain well. Pat the broccoli thoroughly dry. Repeat with the cauliflower florets. Using a mandoline, slice the fennel paper-thin.

**2.** In a small bowl, combine the 1 tablespoon of chopped olives and 1 teaspoon of chopped capers with the lemon zest, mustard and garlic. Add the vinegar, then whisk in the olive oil. Season the dressing with salt and pepper.

**3.** Pour half of the dressing into a large bowl. Add the cauliflower, broccoli, whole olives and capers and toss; let stand for 5 minutes. Add all of the remaining vegetables, season with salt and pepper and toss. Add more dressing if desired and toss again. Garnish the salad with the fennel fronds and serve, passing the remaining dressing at the table. —*Susan Spungen*
**MAKE AHEAD** The salad can be prepared 1 day ahead; refrigerate the vegetables and dressing separately.

## Hearts of Palm and Cress Salad

**TOTAL: 25 MIN**

4 SERVINGS ●

Hearts of palm, which are popular in Latin cooking, are tangy and tender, with a pleasant crunch. Here the hearts of palm are tossed in a salad with watercress, tomatoes, salty olives and juicy navel oranges.

- 2 large navel oranges
- 1 tablespoon fresh lemon juice
- ¼ cup extra-virgin olive oil

Kosher salt and freshly ground pepper

- ¾ pound watercress (2 bunches), tough stems discarded
- 3 plum tomatoes, each cut into 6 wedges

One 14-ounce can hearts of palm, drained and cut on the diagonal into ½-inch slices

- ½ cup pitted Calamata olives

**1.** Using a sharp knife, peel the oranges, taking care to remove all of the bitter white pith; working over a bowl, cut in between the membranes to release the sections. Squeeze the membranes to get ¼ cup of the orange juice. Save the remaining orange juice for another use.

**2.** In a large bowl, whisk the orange juice and lemon juice with the olive oil; season with salt and pepper. Add the orange sections, watercress, tomatoes, hearts of palm and olives and toss well. Serve immediately. —*Daisy Martinez*

## Antipasto Salad with Bocconcini and Green Olive Tapenade

**TOTAL: 25 MIN**

8 SERVINGS ● ●

Inspired by antipasti in Italian-American restaurants, chef and restaurateur Nancy Silverton developed a sophisticated version for Jar in Los Angeles. It features shredded, vinaigrette-dressed iceberg lettuce and salami mixed with petite mozzarella balls (*bocconcini*), which she loves because each one is a perfect little bite.

- 3 tablespoons green olive tapenade from a jar
- ¼ cup peperoncini—stemmed, seeded and finely chopped
- ½ cup extra-virgin olive oil
- 1½ cups *bocconcini* (about 9 ounces)
- 1 tablespoon plus 1 teaspoon fresh lemon juice
- 1 tablespoon plus 1 teaspoon red wine vinegar
- 1 tablespoon plus 1 teaspoon minced garlic
- 1 teaspoon dried oregano

Salt and freshly ground pepper

- 1 small head iceberg lettuce, halved, cored and finely shredded (4 cups)
- 6 ounces thinly sliced Genoa salami, cut into thin strips (1½ cups)
- 6 small basil leaves
- ½ cup green olives, such as Lucques or Picholine

**1.** In a medium bowl, mix the tapenade with the peperoncini and ¼ cup of the olive oil. Add the *bocconcini* and toss.

**2.** In a small bowl, whisk the lemon juice with the vinegar, garlic and oregano. Whisk in the remaining ¼ cup of olive oil and season the dressing with salt and pepper.

**3.** In a bowl, combine the shredded lettuce and salami. Add the *bocconcini* and half of the dressing; toss well. Transfer the salad to a platter. Top with the basil and olives, drizzle the remaining dressing around the salad and serve. —*Nancy Silverton*

ANTIPASTO SALAD WITH BOCCONCINI AND OLIVE TAPENADE

SHAVED ZUCCHINI WITH MISO VINAIGRETTE

## Shaved Zucchini with Miso Vinaigrette

**TOTAL: 25 MIN**

8 TO 10 SERVINGS ●

Be sure to serve this salad as soon as it's ready because it can get watery if it sits.

- 1½ tablespoons black or white sesame seeds
- 3 tablespoons white miso paste
- 2 tablespoons soy sauce
- 2 scallions, chopped
- 1 tablespoon rice vinegar
- 1 tablespoon fresh lemon juice
- 1 teaspoon sugar
- 1 Thai chile, very thinly sliced
- ¼ cup extra-virgin olive oil
- ¼ cup chopped cilantro

Salt and freshly ground pepper

- 6 firm medium zucchini
- 1 sheet of nori, julienned with scissors

**1.** If using white sesame seeds, in a small skillet, toast them over moderate heat until golden, 3 minutes. Cool on a plate.

**2.** In a bowl, whisk together the miso, soy sauce, scallions, vinegar, lemon juice, sugar and chile. Whisk in the oil and stir in the cilantro; season with salt and pepper.

**3.** Using a mandoline, cut the zucchini lengthwise into paper-thin slices. In a very large bowl, toss the zucchini with the vinaigrette. Transfer to a platter. Scatter the nori and sesame seeds on top and serve right away. —*Tyler Florence*

## Tangy Roasted Beet Salad

**ACTIVE: 10 MIN; TOTAL: 1 HR 40 MIN**

6 SERVINGS ● ●

Roasting beets concentrates their flavor. Rather than wrapping each beet individually, you can spread them in a cake pan or on a baking sheet and cover it with foil.

- 3 pounds medium beets
- 3 tablespoons fresh lemon juice
- 1 tablespoon extra-virgin olive oil
- ¾ teaspoon sweet paprika
- ¼ teaspoon ground cumin

Coarse sea salt

**1.** Preheat the oven to 350°. Spread the beets in a cake pan and cover with aluminum foil. Bake the beets until they are tender, about 1½ hours. Let the beets cool slightly, then peel and cut them into ¼-inch-thick strips.

**2.** In a large bowl, combine the lemon juice, olive oil, paprika and cumin. Add the beets and toss to coat. Season the salad with salt and toss again. Serve the salad at room temperature or slightly chilled.
—*Dar Liqama Cooking School*

**MAKE AHEAD** The salad can be refrigerated for 2 days. Let stand at room temperature for 20 minutes before serving.

# salads

## Edamame Salad with Baby Beets and Greens

TOTAL: 25 MIN

4 SERVINGS ● ● ●

    4  small beets (1 ounce each),
       trimmed, ½ cup greens reserved
    2  cups shelled edamame (½ pound)
    1  tablespoon rice vinegar
    2  teaspoons soy sauce
 1½  teaspoons Asian sesame oil
    1  teaspoon finely grated fresh ginger
    2  scallions, finely chopped
    1  tablespoon julienned basil

1. In a large saucepan, set a steamer basket over ½ inch of water and bring to a boil. Add the beets, cover and cook over moderate heat until tender, about 20 minutes. Check the water level in the pan halfway through steaming and add more as needed. Transfer the beets to a plate. Steam the edamame in the same steamer basket until tender, about 5 minutes. Rinse the edamame in cold water to cool, then pat dry with paper towels. Peel and cut the beets into wedges.

2. In a medium bowl, stir the vinegar with the soy sauce, oil and ginger. Add the edamame, beets, scallions and beet greens and toss to coat. Sprinkle the basil on top before serving. —Melissa Clark

## ingredient
### EXOTIC VINEGAR

Lush and fruity **O Cassis** from the O Olive company is made with wild black currants and aged Champagne vinegar. Try it drizzled over a beet and goat cheese salad or use it to brighten soups and stews. **DETAILS** $10 for 6.8 fluid ounces; ooliveoil.com.

## Cellophane Noodle and Vegetable Salad

TOTAL: 45 MIN

6 SERVINGS ●

Four 1.75-ounce packages dried
       cellophane noodles
    2  tablespoons white sesame seeds
   ¼  cup plus 2 tablespoons
       soy sauce
    3  tablespoons honey
    3  tablespoons Asian sesame oil
    6  ounces jicama, peeled and
       julienned
    2  medium carrots, julienned
    2  scallions, thinly sliced
    1  medium cucumber—peeled,
       seeded and cut into ⅓-inch dice
    1  jalapeño, seeded and minced
    1  cup mung bean sprouts
Salt and freshly ground pepper
   ½  cup chopped roasted, salted
       peanuts

1. Bring a large pot of water to a boil. Meanwhile, put the cellophane noodles in a large bowl and cover them with warm water. Let the noodles stand until pliable, about 20 minutes; drain. Using scissors, cut the noodles into 6-inch lengths.

2. In a small skillet, toast the sesame seeds over moderately high heat, stirring, until they are golden, about 1 minute. Transfer the toasted sesame seeds to a plate. In a small bowl, whisk the soy sauce with the honey and sesame oil.

3. Add the noodles to the boiling water and cook until al dente, about 3 minutes; drain. Return the noodles to the pot, fill it with cold water, then drain again. Transfer the cellophane noodles to a large bowl. Add the jicama, carrots, scallions, cucumber, jalapeño and mung bean sprouts and toss. Add the soy sauce dressing to the noodle salad and toss again to coat. Season with salt and pepper and transfer to a platter. Sprinkle the salad with the peanuts and toasted sesame seeds and serve at once. —Shaun Danyel Hergatt

## Mesclun, Tofu and Nori Salad with Citrus Dressing

TOTAL: 20 MIN

4 SERVINGS ● ● ●

This salad combines crisp baby greens, crunchy rice crackers and smooth tofu cubes in a fantastic lime, orange and soy dressing.

    1  medium white turnip
   ¼  cup vegetable oil
    2  tablespoons minced onion
    2  tablespoons fresh orange juice,
       plus ½ teaspoon finely grated
       orange zest
 1½  tablespoons fresh lime
       juice, plus ½ teaspoon finely
       grated lime zest
    1  tablespoon plus 1 teaspoon
       soy sauce
Salt and freshly ground pepper
    4  ounces mesclun (8 cups
       loosely packed)
    8  plain Japanese rice crackers,
       coarsely crushed
    6  cherry tomatoes, halved
  10  ounces firm tofu, cut into
       ½-inch cubes
    1  sheet of nori, julienned
       with scissors

1. Put the white turnip in a small saucepan, cover it with water and bring to a boil. Reduce the heat to moderately high and simmer the turnip for 5 minutes. Drain and refresh under cold running water, then peel the turnip and slice it paper-thin using a mandoline.

2. In a food processor, combine the vegetable oil with the minced onion, orange juice and orange zest, lime juice and lime zest and soy sauce. Season the citrus dressing with salt and pepper.

3. In a large salad bowl, toss the mesclun with the crushed rice crackers, cherry tomatoes, tofu, sliced turnip and the citrus dressing. Top the mesclun salad with the julienned nori and serve at once. —Yasuhiro Honma

## Marinated Carrot Salad with Ginger and Sesame Oil

**TOTAL: 25 MIN**

6 SERVINGS ● ● ●

The sesame oil, ginger juice and cilantro add vibrancy to sweet, crunchy carrots.

- 1  pound carrots, peeled and shredded
- 1  garlic clove, minced
- 2  tablespoons sherry vinegar
- 1  cup coarsely chopped cilantro
- ½  cup grapeseed oil

Salt and freshly ground pepper

- ⅓  cup fresh carrot juice
- 2  tablespoons mayonnaise
- 1½  teaspoons Asian sesame oil
- ¾  teaspoon fresh ginger juice, squeezed from 2 teaspoons finely grated fresh ginger

**1.** In a medium bowl, toss the carrots with the garlic, vinegar, ½ cup of the cilantro and ¼ cup of the grapeseed oil. Season the carrots with salt and pepper and let stand for 15 minutes, then drain well.

**2.** In a small saucepan, boil the carrot juice over moderate heat until it is reduced by half, about 5 minutes. Let the reduced carrot juice cool slightly, then transfer to a bowl. Whisk in the mayonnaise, sesame oil, ginger juice and the remaining ¼ cup of grapeseed oil. Season the carrot dressing generously with salt and pepper.

**3.** Add the carrot dressing and the remaining ½ cup of cilantro to the carrots and toss the salad well. Transfer the carrot salad to a shallow bowl and serve.

*—Laurent Tourondel*

## Avocado and Frisée Salad with Cheese-Filled Eggplant Rolls

**TOTAL: 45 MIN**

4 SERVINGS

A salad served at Ibiza, a Basque restaurant in New Haven, Connecticut, was the inspiration for this recipe. The contrast of soft textures is lovely—buttery avocado, tender roasted eggplant and oozy cheese.

- 1  narrow 1½-pound eggplant, cut lengthwise into eight ½-inch-thick slices
- 3  tablespoons extra-virgin olive oil, plus more for brushing

Salt and freshly ground pepper

- 5  ounces La Serena or other soft, ripe sheep's-milk or cow's-milk cheese, such as Edel de Cléron, rind removed and cheese cut into 8 pieces
- 2  tablespoons fresh lemon juice
- 1  Hass avocado
- 3  ounces frisée, torn into bite-size pieces
- 2  tablespoons pine nuts, toasted

Balsamic vinegar

**1.** Preheat the oven to 400°. Lightly brush both sides of the eggplant slices with olive oil and arrange the slices on a large baking sheet. Season the slices with salt and pepper and bake the eggplant for 15 minutes, or until tender.

**2.** With a spatula, carefully loosen the eggplant slices from the baking sheet. Set 1 piece of cheese at the wider end of each slice and roll the slices up neatly. Arrange the rolls seam side down and bake them for about 3 minutes, or until the cheese begins to melt. Halve the eggplant rolls crosswise and keep them warm.

**3.** Meanwhile, in a small bowl, whisk the lemon juice with the 3 tablespoons of olive oil. Season the vinaigrette dressing with salt and pepper.

**4.** Halve and peel the avocado. Cut each half crosswise, then slice the halves lengthwise ⅓ inch thick. In a medium bowl, toss the frisée with 1 tablespoon of the dressing and transfer to a platter. Top with the avocado slices and the eggplant rolls. Drizzle the salad with the remaining dressing and sprinkle with the pine nuts. Pour drops of balsamic vinegar around the salad and serve. *—Marcia Kiesel*

## Warm Artichoke and Chicken Liver Salad

**TOTAL: 40 MIN**

4 SERVINGS ● ●

- 3  medium artichokes
- ½  lemon
- ¼  cup plus 1 tablespoon extra-virgin olive oil
- 2  tablespoons very finely chopped shallots
- 2  tablespoons sherry vinegar
- 2  teaspoons finely grated orange zest
- 1  teaspoon chopped thyme
- ½  teaspoon Dijon mustard

Salt and freshly ground pepper

- ¾  pound chicken livers, trimmed

All-purpose flour, for dusting

- 4  ounces mâche or baby spinach (4 cups)

**1.** Bring a small saucepan of water to a boil. Snap off the outer leaves of each of the artichokes. Cut off the stems and the remaining leaves, then peel the artichoke bottoms and scrape out the furry chokes. Rub the bottoms all over with the lemon half to prevent their browning. Add the artichoke bottoms to the pan and cook them until they are tender, about 15 minutes. Drain and quarter the hearts.

**2.** Meanwhile, whisk 3 tablespoons of the olive oil with the shallots, vinegar, orange zest, thyme and mustard. Season the dressing with salt and pepper.

**3.** In a large nonstick skillet, heat the remaining 2 tablespoons of olive oil. Season the chicken livers with salt and pepper and lightly dust with flour. Cook the livers for about 4 minutes over moderately high heat; they should still be pink inside. Transfer the livers to a plate. Discard the oil, add the artichokes to the pan and heat through. Stir the livers and vinaigrette into the artichokes. Serve the artichoke and liver mixture on the mâche. *—Jeff Tunks*

# salads

## Greek Kale Salad

**TOTAL: 25 MIN**
**4 SERVINGS** ●●

1¾  pounds kale, thick stems
     discarded (¾ pound leaves)
  2  whole wheat pita breads
  ¼  cup extra-virgin olive oil,
     plus more for brushing
  2  tablespoons fresh lemon juice
  ¼  teaspoon crushed red pepper
Salt and freshly ground pepper

## superfast
### DRESSINGS

**CHICKPEA VINAIGRETTE**
Mix coarsely mashed chickpeas
with sherry vinegar, minced shallots,
chopped chives and parsley, extra-
virgin olive oil, salt and pepper.

**LEMON-PARMESAN DRESSING**
Mix fresh lemon juice and freshly
grated Parmesan cheese with
mayonnaise, minced garlic, extra-
virgin olive oil, salt and pepper.

**ROASTED RED PEPPER VINAIGRETTE**
Mix chopped roasted red pepper
with white wine vinegar, minced
garlic, chopped flat-leaf parsley,
extra-virgin olive oil, salt and pepper.

**PESTO VINAIGRETTE**
Mix pesto with white wine vinegar,
extra-virgin olive oil, salt and pepper.

---

  ½  cup grape tomatoes, halved
  ⅓  cup slivered pitted Calamata olives
  2  ounces feta cheese, preferably
     French, crumbled (⅔ cup)

1. Preheat the oven to 400°. In a large pot
of boiling water, cook the kale until just tender, 5 minutes. Drain and rinse under cold
water to cool; transfer to a clean kitchen
towel and squeeze dry. Fluff the leaves,
coarsely chop and transfer to a bowl.
2. Brush both sides of the pita breads with
olive oil and bake for about 8 minutes, or
until crisp. Cut the pita into wedges.
3. In a bowl, combine the ¼ cup of olive
oil with the lemon juice and crushed red
pepper; season with salt and pepper. Add
the grape tomatoes, olives and crumbled
feta to the kale and toss. Add the dressing
and toss to coat. Serve the kale salad with
the toasted pita wedges. —*Melissa Clark*

## Warm Leek, Asparagus and Potato Salad

**TOTAL: 25 MIN**
**6 SERVINGS** ●●●

  2  tablespoons Dijon mustard
  1  tablespoon red wine vinegar
  ¼  cup canola oil
Salt and freshly ground pepper
  ¾  pound small fingerling potatoes
  1  pound asparagus, cut into
     2-inch lengths
  2  medium leeks, white and tender
     green parts, split lengthwise and
     cut crosswise into 1-inch pieces
  ¼  cup snipped chives

1. In a large bowl, whisk the mustard with
the vinegar. Whisk in the oil in a thin stream
and season with salt and pepper.
2. Boil 2 saucepans of salted water. Add the
potatoes to one; cook for 20 minutes. Cook
the asparagus and leeks in the other pan
for 5 minutes; drain, pat dry and add to the
dressing. Drain the potatoes, slice ½ inch
thick and add to the bowl. Add the chives,
season with salt and pepper and gently
toss. Serve warm. —*Laurent Tourondel*

---

## Papaya, Cashew and Frisée Salad

**TOTAL: 45 MIN**
**4 SERVINGS** ●

  1  tablespoon vegetable oil
  3  garlic cloves, thinly sliced
  1  medium shallot, thinly sliced
  1  small carrot, finely diced
  1  small red bell pepper, finely diced
  1  red Thai chile, thinly sliced
  ¼  cup fresh lime juice
  3  tablespoons unseasoned
     rice vinegar
  2  tablespoons light brown sugar
  2  tablespoons granulated sugar
  ½  teaspoon chili oil
Salt
  1  teaspoon white sesame seeds
4½  ounces frisée lettuce (3 cups
     packed), torn into bite-size pieces
  2  ripe ¾-pound papayas—peeled,
     seeded and cut into 1-inch cubes
  6  canned whole water chestnuts,
     drained and cut into thin rounds,
     or 2 ounces jicama, peeled and
     cut into 1-by-1¼-inch slices
  ¼  cup roasted, salted cashews
  2  tablespoons finely julienned
     fresh ginger

1. Heat the vegetable oil in a medium skillet. Add the garlic and cook over low heat
until golden, about 1 minute. Add the shallot, carrot, bell pepper and chile and cook
over moderate heat, stirring occasionally,
until the carrot is softened, about 7 minutes. Add the lime juice, vinegar, brown and
granulated sugars and chili oil and bring to
a boil. Remove from the heat and let cool
slightly. Transfer the contents of the skillet
to a blender and puree. Season with salt.
2. In a skillet, toast the sesame seeds
over moderately high heat until golden,
40 seconds; let cool. In a bowl, toss the
frisée, papayas, water chestnuts, cashews
and ginger. Add about ⅓ cup of the dressing and toss to coat. Mound the salad on
plates, sprinkle with the sesame seeds and
serve. —*Jean-Georges Vongerichten*

**PAPAYA, CASHEW AND FRISÉE SALAD**

**DILLED CELERY AND TROUT SALAD**

## Dilled Celery and Trout Salad

**TOTAL: 30 MIN**

4 SERVINGS ● ●

½ cup walnuts
2 tablespoons sherry vinegar
1 tablespoon whole-grain mustard
3 tablespoons extra-virgin olive oil
2 tablespoons walnut oil
Kosher salt and freshly ground pepper
8 celery ribs, thinly sliced (3 cups)
1 cup flat-leaf parsley leaves
¼ cup chopped dill
¼ cup dried currants
2 smoked trout fillets (½ pound)

**1.** Preheat the oven to 350°. Spread the walnuts in a pie plate and toast until fragrant and golden, about 7 minutes. Let cool slightly, then break into small pieces.

**2.** In a large bowl, whisk the vinegar with the mustard. Slowly whisk in the olive oil and walnut oil and season with salt and pepper. Add the celery, parsley, dill and currants. Skin and flake the trout and add to the salad; toss gently. Add the walnuts, toss gently and serve. —*Jerry Traunfeld*

## Chicken Salad with Green Goddess Dressing

**TOTAL: 20 MIN**

6 SERVINGS ● ●

1 Hass avocado, coarsely chopped
⅓ cup buttermilk
¼ cup chopped flat-leaf parsley
2 tablespoons low-fat mayonnaise
2 tablespoons low-fat sour cream
2 tablespoons minced chives
1 tablespoon chopped tarragon
1 anchovy fillet, chopped
3½ teaspoons Champagne vinegar
Salt and freshly ground pepper
18 ounces cooked chicken breast without skin, chopped (4 cups)

1 tablespoon extra-virgin olive oil
2 medium cucumbers—peeled, seeded and cut into ½-inch dice
1 tomato, cut into ½-inch dice
2 ounces baby arugula (4 cups)

**1.** In a blender, puree the avocado with the buttermilk, parsley, mayonnaise, sour cream, chives, tarragon, anchovy and 1½ teaspoons of the Champagne vinegar. Scrape the dressing into a bowl and season with salt and pepper. Add the chopped chicken breast and toss to coat.

**2.** In another bowl, whisk the olive oil with the remaining 2 teaspoons of Champagne vinegar. Stir in the diced cucumbers and tomato and season the salad to taste with salt and pepper.

**3.** Mound the baby arugula on plates. Pile the chicken salad on the arugula. Spoon the cucumber and tomato salad alongside and serve right away. —*Nancy Oakes*

● FAST  ● HEALTHY  ● MAKE AHEAD  ● STAFF FAVORITE

David Ansel (a.k.a. the Soup Peddler) made this delicious Hunter's Stew with Braised Beef and Wild Rice (P. 75) for the November issue.

# soups

ZUPPA CAPRESE

GAZPACHO ON FIRE

## Zuppa Caprese

ACTIVE: 30 MIN; TOTAL: 2 HR 30 MIN

6 SERVINGS

Buffalo mozzarella has an exquisite tangy edge. Chef Shea Gallante of New York City's Cru restaurant ingeniously turns the cheese into a soup, liquefying it in a blender with the water it comes packed in and some fruity olive oil.

- **3 medium tomatoes, cored and coarsely chopped**
- **Salt**
- **Sugar**
- **¼ cup plus 2 tablespoons fruity extra-virgin olive oil**
- **Freshly ground white pepper**
- **2 balls of packaged buffalo mozzarella with their liquid, at room temperature (see Note)**
- **2 scallions, white and tender green parts only, julienned**
- **2 apricots—halved, pitted and thinly sliced**
- **1 tablespoon fresh lime juice**
- **2 tablespoons finely shredded basil**
- **1 teaspoon *vin cotto, saba* or aged balsamic vinegar**

**1.** In a blender or food processor, puree the chopped tomatoes with a pinch each of salt and sugar. Line a strainer with 2 layers of cheesecloth and set the strainer over a medium bowl. Pour the tomato puree into the strainer, gather the ends of the cheesecloth and tie with a string. Let the tomato juices drain into the bowl for 2 hours. You should have about ½ cup of tomato water. If not, gently squeeze the cheesecloth to extract a little more of the tomato water. Whisk in 2 tablespoons of the olive oil and season the tomato water with salt and white pepper.

**2.** Rinse out the blender. Pour in the mozzarella liquid—there should be ¾ cup. Cut each mozzarella ball into 6 pieces and add the pieces to the blender. Blend at low speed for 1 minute, then increase the speed to high and puree until smooth. Add the remaining ¼ cup of olive oil and puree until creamy and smooth. Season the soup with white pepper.

**3.** In a medium bowl, toss the scallions and apricots with the lime juice and season with salt and pepper. Pour ½ cup of the mozzarella soup into each of 6 small bowls. Spoon the apricot mixture on top and garnish with the basil. Drizzle a few drops of the tomato water and the *vin cotto* on top and serve right away. —*Shea Gallante*

**NOTE** Look for imported Italian buffalo mozzarella, which comes packed in water in 500-gram plastic containers, at specialty markets and at cheese shops.

## Gazpacho on Fire

**TOTAL: 30 MIN PLUS 1 HR CHILLING**

4 SERVINGS ● ●

- 3 garlic cloves, unpeeled
- 3 large tomatoes (1½ pounds)
- 1 medium cucumber
- 1 green bell pepper
- 1 red bell pepper
- 1 medium sweet onion, unpeeled
- ¼ cup extra-virgin olive oil,
  plus more for drizzling
- 2 tablespoons red wine vinegar
- ¼ cup chopped mixed herbs,
  plus more for garnish
- 1 cup cold water

Salt and freshly ground pepper

**1.** Light a grill. Wrap the garlic in foil. Grill the tomatoes, cucumber, bell peppers, onion and garlic package over moderately high heat, turning occasionally, until the vegetables are charred all over and almost softened, about 8 minutes for the tomatoes, cucumber and peppers, 10 minutes for the garlic and 15 minutes for the onion. When cool enough to handle, remove the charred skins as well as any stems and seeds and chop the vegetables coarsely.

**2.** Transfer all of the vegetables, including the peeled garlic, to a food processor and puree. With the machine on, gradually add the ¼ cup of olive oil, then blend in the vinegar. Add the ¼ cup of herbs, then transfer the mixture to a bowl. Stir in the water and season with salt and pepper. Refrigerate until chilled. Ladle the gazpacho into bowls, drizzle with olive oil, sprinkle with herbs and serve.
—*Steven Raichlen*

## Tangy Tomato Soup with Tarragon Croutons

**TOTAL: 45 MIN**

8 SERVINGS ●

Tarragon flavors the crispy croutons for this velvety, fresh-tasting tomato soup (basil or sage would also be delicious). The soup is terrific served hot or chilled.

- 4 pounds tomatoes
- ¼ cup plus 3 tablespoons
  extra-virgin olive oil
- 1 small onion, finely chopped
- 1 small carrot, finely chopped
- 1 celery rib, finely chopped
- 3 thyme sprigs
- 1 bay leaf
- 2 cups chicken stock or
  low-sodium broth

Pinch of sugar

Salt and freshly ground pepper

- 4 crustless slices of peasant bread
  (¾ inch thick), cut into cubes
- ¼ cup chopped tarragon
- ½ cup heavy cream

**1.** Preheat the oven to 350°. Bring a pot of water to a boil; fill a large bowl with ice water. Make a shallow X in the bottom of each tomato. Plunge the tomatoes into the boiling water for 30 seconds, or just until the skins begin to curl. Transfer the tomatoes to the ice water to cool. Drain the tomatoes and pat dry, then peel.

**2.** Halve the tomatoes crosswise. Set a strainer over a medium bowl. Scoop the seeds from the tomato halves into the strainer and press to extract the juices. Coarsely chop the tomatoes and add them to the bowl; discard the seeds.

**3.** In a saucepan, heat 3 tablespoons of the olive oil until shimmering. Add the onion, carrot, celery, thyme and bay leaf and cook over moderate heat, stirring occasionally, until softened, about 8 minutes. Add the tomatoes and their juices, the stock and sugar, season with salt and pepper and bring to a boil. Simmer over moderately low heat until the tomatoes are completely broken down, about 20 minutes.

**4.** Meanwhile, in a medium bowl, toss the bread cubes with the remaining ¼ cup of olive oil and the tarragon and season lightly with salt and pepper. Spread the bread cubes on a baking sheet and toast for about 10 minutes, stirring once, until golden and crisp.

**5.** Using a slotted spoon, transfer the solids from the saucepan to a blender. Discard the thyme and bay leaf. Add the cream and puree until smooth. Pour the soup back into the pan; stir well. Rewarm over moderately low heat and season with salt and pepper. Serve the soup with the croutons on the side. Alternatively, serve the soup lightly chilled. —*Carrie Dove*
**MAKE AHEAD** The soup can be refrigerated overnight and the croutons can be stored in an airtight container for up to 2 days.

## Basil-Spiked Zucchini and Tomato Soup

**TOTAL: 35 MIN**

8 SERVINGS ● ●

- ⅓ cup sliced almonds
- 4 tablespoons unsalted butter
- 1 large onion, finely chopped
- 2 pounds zucchini, halved
  lengthwise and thinly sliced
  into half-moons
- 1 quart chicken stock
- 1 cup pureed tomatoes
- ¼ cup chopped basil

Salt and freshly ground pepper

**1.** Preheat the oven to 350°. Spread the sliced almonds in a pie plate and bake for 4 minutes, or until lightly browned.

**2.** In a large saucepan, melt the butter. Add the onion and cook over moderately low heat, stirring occasionally, until softened, about 8 minutes. Add the zucchini and cook over moderate heat until softened, about 3 minutes. Add the chicken stock and bring to a boil. Simmer over moderate heat until the zucchini is tender, about 5 minutes.

**3.** Working in batches, puree the soup in a food processor. Return the soup to the saucepan. Stir in the tomatoes and bring to a simmer. Stir in the basil and season with salt and pepper. Ladle the soup into shallow bowls and garnish each serving with the toasted almonds. —*Sergi Millet*
**MAKE AHEAD** The soup can be refrigerated overnight. Stir in the basil before serving.

# soups

## Summer Squash Soup with Basil

**ACTIVE: 35 MIN; TOTAL: 1 HR**

6 SERVINGS ● ●

For this soothing soup, Michael Romano, the chef at Union Square Cafe in New York City, prefers using dense-textured *cucuzza,* which is sometimes called snake squash. He and his siblings used to transform the twisty, coil-shaped gourd into make-believe crowns and bracelets when they were kids. You can substitute any type of summer squash for the *cucuzza.*

- ¼ cup extra-virgin olive oil
- 1 medium onion, coarsely chopped
- 3 large tomatoes—peeled, seeded and chopped
- 1 garlic clove, minced
- ¼ teaspoon crushed red pepper
- 2 pounds *cucuzza*—peeled, seeded and thinly sliced crosswise—or zucchini, quartered lengthwise and thinly sliced crosswise
- 1 large baking potato—peeled, quartered lengthwise and thinly sliced crosswise
- 4 cups chicken stock or low-sodium broth
- ¼ cup shredded basil

Salt and freshly ground pepper

Heat the olive oil in a large soup pot. Add the onion and cook over moderate heat, stirring occasionally, until softened but not browned, about 6 minutes. Increase the heat to moderately high. Add the tomatoes, garlic and crushed red pepper and cook, stirring, until the tomatoes start to break down, about 5 minutes. Add the squash and potato and cook, stirring, for 2 minutes. Stir in the chicken stock and bring to a boil. Add the basil and season with salt and pepper. Cover and cook over low heat until the vegetables are tender, about 25 minutes. —*Michael Romano*

**SERVE WITH** Garlic crostini and freshly grated Parmesan cheese.

**MAKE AHEAD** The soup can be covered and refrigerated overnight. Reheat gently.

## Garden Pea Soup with Morel Cream

**TOTAL: 45 MIN**

4 SERVINGS

At his San Francisco restaurant, Campton Place, Daniel Humm serves his wonderful sweet pea soup "cappuccino-style," with a topping of morel cream that's been frothed with an immersion blender. The recipe here simply calls for swirling the cream into the soup. Indeed, the cream is so intensely mushroomy, you may be tempted to eat it on its own.

- ½ ounce dried morel mushrooms
- ½ cup very hot water
- 1 tablespoon plus 1 teaspoon unsalted butter
- 2 medium shallots, very thinly sliced
- 2 tablespoons dry white wine
- 3½ cups chicken stock or low-sodium broth
- ½ cup heavy cream

Salt

Cayenne pepper

- 2 tablespoons extra-virgin olive oil, plus more for drizzling
- 5 cups frozen peas (1½ pounds), thawed
- 1½ tablespoons chopped mint, plus 8 small leaves for garnish

**1.** In a small bowl, cover the dried morels with the hot water and set aside until the morels are softened, about 15 minutes. With a slotted spoon, carefully lift the morels out of the soaking liquid and gently rinse them under running water to remove any grit. Pick out 8 whole morels to set aside for the garnish; they should be small but pretty. Coarsely chop the remaining morels. Reserve the morel soaking liquid.

**2.** In a small saucepan, melt 1 tablespoon of the butter. Add the chopped morels and half of the shallots and cook over moderately high heat until the shallots are lightly browned, about 4 minutes. Add the wine and cook until the wine has evaporated, about 2 minutes. Add ½ cup of the chicken stock and the reserved mushroom soaking liquid, stopping when you reach the grit at the bottom of the bowl. Boil the mushroom broth until it is reduced by half, about 5 minutes. Add the heavy cream to the broth and simmer over moderately low heat until it has thickened, about 5 minutes. Season the morel cream with salt and cayenne and remove from the heat.

**3.** Transfer the morel cream to a blender and puree until smooth. Return the morel cream to the saucepan and keep warm. Rinse out the blender.

**4.** In a large saucepan, heat the 2 tablespoons of olive oil. Add the remaining half of the sliced shallots and cook over moderate heat until they are softened, about 3 minutes. Add the remaining 3 cups of chicken stock and bring the soup to a boil over high heat. Add all but ¼ cup of the peas. Add 1 tablespoon of the chopped mint and simmer the soup over moderate heat until the peas are just tender, about 4 minutes.

**5.** Working in batches, puree the pea soup in the blender and then pass it through a coarse sieve set over a heatproof bowl, pressing on the solids with the back of a wooden spoon or a plastic spatula. Return the soup to the pot, reheat it gently and season it with salt and cayenne.

**6.** In a small skillet, melt the remaining 1 teaspoon of butter. Add the reserved 8 whole morels and ¼ cup of peas and season with salt. Cook over moderately high heat until hot, about 1 minute.

**7.** Ladle the hot pea soup into 4 shallow bowls. Swirl in the warm morel cream, drizzle lightly with olive oil and scatter the hot whole morels and peas over the soup. Garnish the pea soup with the remaining ½ tablespoon of chopped mint and the mint leaves and serve immediately. —*Daniel Humm*

**MAKE AHEAD** The morel cream can be refrigerated overnight. Reheat gently over low heat before serving.

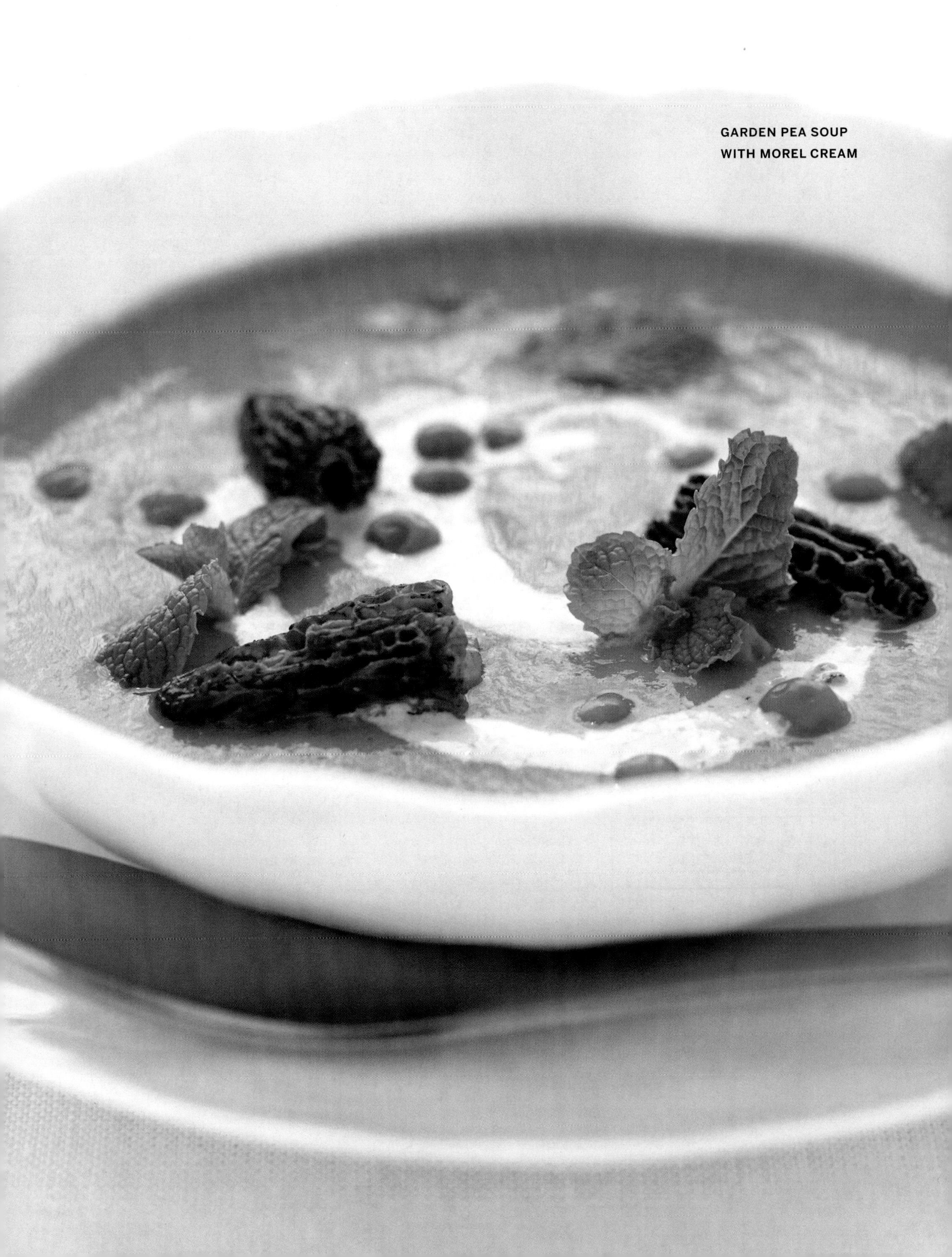

GARDEN PEA SOUP
WITH MOREL CREAM

## Yellow Split Pea Soup with Crispy Garlic

**ACTIVE: 20 MIN; TOTAL: 1 HR 10 MIN**

**8 SERVINGS** ● ●

- ¼ cup extra-virgin olive oil
- 1 medium onion, finely chopped
- 3 carrots, finely chopped
- 3 celery ribs, thinly sliced
- Kosher salt
- 2 teaspoons dry mustard powder
- ⅛ teaspoon ground cloves
- 1 pound yellow split peas, picked over and rinsed
- 8 cups vegetable stock or low-sodium broth
- Freshly ground pepper
- 4 garlic cloves, thinly sliced

**1.** In a soup pot, heat 2 tablespoons of the olive oil. Add the onion, carrots, celery and a pinch of salt. Cover and cook over moderate heat, stirring occasionally, until the vegetables are softened, about 6 minutes. Stir in the dry mustard and cloves and cook for 1 minute. Add the split peas and stock and season with salt and pepper. Cover the soup and simmer, stirring occasionally, until the split peas have broken down, about 1 hour.

## equipment
**DOUBLE-DUTY POT**

The flexible, innovative **Flame-Top ceramic** line from Emile Henry can be used on the stovetop, in the oven and in the microwave. **DETAILS** $70 from emilehenry.com.

**2.** Meanwhile, in a small skillet, heat the remaining 2 tablespoons of olive oil. Add the garlic and cook over moderately high heat until golden and crisp, about 3 minutes. Transfer to a plate to cool.

**3.** Season the soup with salt and pepper. Ladle the soup into bowls, top with the crispy garlic and serve. —*David Ansel*

**MAKE AHEAD** The soup can be refrigerated for up to 3 days.

## Sweet Pea Soup with Majorero Cream and Cheese Crisps

**TOTAL: 40 MIN**

**4 SERVINGS** ●

This vividly colored sweet pea puree is ideal for entertaining because it is delicious both warm and at room temperature; the soup and crisps can be made entirely ahead, and the tart Majorero (goat's-milk cheese) cream can be melted just before serving.

- 3 tablespoons extra-virgin olive oil
- 1 large shallot, thinly sliced
- 1 thyme sprig
- ⅓ cup dry white wine
- 3 cups water
- 5 cups frozen peas (1½ pounds)
- Salt
- ½ cup chopped flat-leaf parsley
- ½ cup coarsely shredded Roncal or semi-aged sheep's-milk cheese
- ¼ cup heavy cream
- ⅓ cup coarsely shredded Majorero or other mild, buttery, semi-aged goat's-milk cheese

**1.** Heat the olive oil in a saucepan. Add the shallot and thyme and cook over moderately low heat until the shallot is softened, 5 minutes. Add the wine and simmer over moderately high heat until reduced by half, 3 minutes. Add the water and all but 1 cup of the peas and bring to a boil. Add a pinch of salt, cover and simmer over moderately low heat until the peas are tender, about 8 minutes. Add the remaining peas and simmer for 1 minute; remove from the heat. Discard the thyme. Stir in the parsley.

**2.** Working in batches, puree the soup in a blender. Strain the soup through a coarse sieve set over another large saucepan. Season the soup with salt and keep warm.

**3.** Set a medium nonstick skillet over moderate heat. Spread four 1-tablespoon mounds of the Roncal in the skillet and flatten slightly. Cook the cheese over moderate heat until bubbling and set on the bottom, about 3 minutes; do not brown. Using a spatula, transfer the crisps to paper towels. Let cool until firm. Repeat with the remaining cheese.

**4.** In a small glass bowl, heat the heavy cream in a microwave at high power until boiling, about 30 seconds. Add the Majorero and heat until the cheese is just melted, about 20 seconds. Stir until blended.

**5.** Ladle the soup into small bowls. Swirl in the Majorero cream and serve with the Roncal crisps. —*Marcia Kiesel*

**MAKE AHEAD** The soup can be refrigerated overnight. The crisps can be made earlier in the day and reheated in a 325° oven for 1 minute.

## Wild Mushroom Soup with Parmesan Toasts

**TOTAL: 30 MIN**

**6 SERVINGS** ● ●

- 6 slices of bread, cut from a long country or sourdough loaf
- Extra-virgin olive oil
- ¼ cup freshly grated Parmesan
- Paprika
- Wild Mushroom Ragout (recipe follows)
- 1 quart chicken stock
- 1 cup frozen baby peas
- Salt and freshly ground pepper
- 1 tablespoon snipped chives

**1.** Preheat the broiler. Lightly brush both sides of each slice of bread with olive oil and arrange on a baking sheet. Broil for 1 minute, until toasted. Flip the bread, sprinkle with the Parmesan and a pinch of paprika and broil for 1 minute longer, until the cheese is melted and the bread is toasted.

2. Meanwhile, puree 1 cup of the mushroom ragout in a blender until the ragout is smooth. Transfer the mushroom puree to a medium saucepan. Add the remaining mushroom ragout, the chicken stock and the peas and bring the soup to a boil over moderately high heat. Season the mushroom soup with salt and pepper and transfer to shallow soup bowls. Garnish the soup with the snipped chives and serve with the Parmesan toasts.
—*Grace Parisi*

**MAKE AHEAD** The mushroom soup can be refrigerated overnight.

### WILD MUSHROOM RAGOUT
**TOTAL: 20 MIN**
**MAKES ABOUT 2 CUPS** ● ●

Nearly any variety or combination of wild mushrooms, such as shiitake, oyster mushrooms or chanterelles, will be terrific here; cultivated cremini and portobellos are great too. If you choose portobellos, use a small spoon to scrape away the dark brown gills, since they impart an inky color and murky flavor.

1 teaspoon extra-virgin olive oil
¼ pound thinly sliced pancetta, coarsely chopped
1¼ pounds mixed mushrooms, such as shiitake and oyster, stemmed and thinly sliced
1 large shallot, finely chopped
1 teaspoon finely chopped thyme
¼ cup Madeira or Marsala
¾ cup heavy cream
Salt and freshly ground pepper

1. In a large, deep skillet, heat the olive oil. Add the sliced pancetta and cook over moderately high heat, stirring, until it is golden, about 5 minutes. Using a slotted spoon, transfer the pancetta to a plate and set aside; leave the fat in the skillet.
2. Add the mushrooms to the skillet and cook over moderately high heat, stirring occasionally, until they are lightly browned and softened, about 8 minutes. Add the shallot and thyme and cook, stirring, until the shallot is softened. Add the Madeira and cook until it has evaporated, scraping up any browned bits from the bottom of the skillet. Stir in the heavy cream, season with salt and pepper and simmer until the ragout is slightly thickened, 2 to 3 minutes. Just before serving the ragout, stir in the pancetta. —*G.P.*

**VARIATIONS** The Wild Mushroom Ragout can be stirred into pasta or risotto, folded into omelets, spooned onto crostini or poured over polenta.

**MAKE AHEAD** The Wild Mushroom Ragout can be refrigerated overnight.

## Creamy Mushroom Soup with Thyme Croutons
**TOTAL: 50 MIN**
**8 SERVINGS** ●

2 ounces dried porcini mushrooms
1¾ cups hot water
1 tablespoon extra-virgin olive oil
1 medium onion, coarsely chopped
1 pound white mushrooms, thinly sliced
1 tablespoon dark brown sugar
1 teaspoon finely chopped thyme leaves
1 cup dry white wine
3 tablespoons unsalted butter
¼ cup all-purpose flour
2 cups half-and-half
6 cups chicken stock or low-sodium broth
1 cup heavy cream
2 tablespoons dry sherry
Salt and freshly ground pepper
Thyme Croutons (recipe follows)

1. In a medium bowl, cover the dried porcini mushrooms with the hot water and set aside to stand until softened, about 20 minutes. Strain the mushrooms and reserve the porcini soaking liquid.

2. Meanwhile, in a large enameled cast-iron casserole or soup pot, heat the olive oil. Add the onion and cook over moderate heat, stirring occasionally, until softened, about 5 minutes. Add the white mushrooms, brown sugar and thyme, cover and cook over moderately high heat until the mushrooms soften, about 3 minutes longer. Add the wine and cook over high heat until reduced to ⅓ cup, about 5 minutes.
3. In a medium saucepan, melt the butter over moderate heat. Whisk in the flour and cook for 3 minutes, whisking. Whisk in the half-and-half and bring to a simmer over moderate heat; whisk constantly until thickened, about 2 minutes. Stir the half-and-half mixture into the white mushrooms along with the porcini and their strained soaking liquid. Working in batches, puree the mixture until smooth, adding some of the chicken stock if necessary.
4. Return the soup to the casserole. Add the remaining chicken stock and simmer over moderate heat for 5 minutes. Stir in the heavy cream and sherry and heat through. Season the soup with salt and pepper and ladle into bowls. Top with the croutons and serve. —*David Ansel*

**MAKE AHEAD** The soup can be refrigerated for 2 days. Reheat gently before serving.

### THYME CROUTONS
**TOTAL: 30 MIN**
**MAKES 5 CUPS** ● ●

½ medium baguette, cut into ½-inch cubes
¼ cup extra-virgin olive oil
Salt and freshly ground pepper
1½ tablespoons finely chopped thyme leaves

Preheat the oven to 375°. On a large baking sheet, toss the bread cubes with the olive oil and season with salt and pepper. Bake the bread cubes for 6 minutes, then toss with the thyme leaves. Bake for about 6 minutes longer, until the croutons are golden and crisp. —*D.A.*

# soups

## Cream of Cauliflower Soup

TOTAL: 30 MIN

4 SERVINGS ● ● ●

- 2 tablespoons extra-virgin olive oil
- 1 medium onion, finely chopped
- 5 cups cauliflower florets (½ medium head)
- ½ teaspoon ground coriander
- 2 cups vegetable stock
- 1 cup low-fat milk
- Salt and freshly ground pepper
- 2 tablespoons snipped chives

1. In a large saucepan, heat the olive oil. Add the onion and cook over moderately high heat until lightly browned, 5 to 6 minutes. Add the cauliflower florets and the coriander and cook, stirring, for 1 minute. Add the vegetable stock and the milk and bring to a boil. Cover and cook over moderately low heat until the cauliflower is tender, about 15 minutes.

2. Strain the broth into a heatproof bowl. Puree the cauliflower in a blender with 1 cup of broth until smooth and silky. Return the broth to the pan; stir in the puree. Season with salt and pepper, stir in the chives and serve in deep bowls. —Chef Bobo

MAKE AHEAD The soup can be refrigerated for up to 1 day.

## Fines Herbes Soup

TOTAL: 30 MIN

4 SERVINGS ●

- 2 tablespoons unsalted butter
- 3 medium leeks, white and tender green parts only, halved lengthwise and thinly sliced crosswise
- 3 cups low-sodium chicken broth
- 1 tablespoon long-grain white rice
- 2 cups loosely packed flat-leaf parsley leaves
- ½ cup tarragon leaves
- ½ cup snipped chives
- 1 large egg plus 1 large egg yolk
- 3 tablespoons heavy cream
- Salt and freshly ground pepper

1. In a saucepan, melt the butter. Add the leeks and cook over moderate heat, stirring, until softened, 3 minutes. Add the broth and rice, cover and cook until the leeks and rice are tender, 15 minutes. Stir in the parsley, tarragon and chives; bring to a boil.

2. Put the egg, egg yolk and cream in a blender. At low speed, carefully pour in the soup, blending until smooth. Return the soup to the saucepan, season with salt and pepper and heat just until warm. Transfer to bowls and serve. —Jerry Traunfeld

MAKE AHEAD The soup can be refrigerated for up to 1 day.

## Truffle-Infused French Onion Soup

ACTIVE: 30 MIN; TOTAL: 2 HR 30 MIN

10 SERVINGS ●

Chef Michael Mina of Michael Mina restaurant in San Francisco invented this soup in the early days of Aqua, the San Francisco restaurant where he rose to fame in the '90s. He started playing with the combination of black truffles and caramelized onions and went crazy for the mix of earthiness and sweetness. This version of the soup calls for truffle-infused pecorino cheese (sold in any good cheese shop), which is melted to form a marvelously gooey topping for the oniony broth.

- 4 tablespoons unsalted butter
- 3 pounds sweet onions, sliced ¼ inch thick
- 2 bay leaves
- ½ cup water
- ¼ cup all-purpose flour
- 1 cup dry red wine
- 3 quarts beef stock, preferably homemade
- 10 thyme sprigs, tied with cotton string
- Kosher salt and freshly ground pepper
- 1 baguette, sliced ⅓ inch thick
- ¼ cup extra-virgin olive oil
- 10 ounces truffled pecorino cheese, coarsely shredded (3 cups)

1. Melt the butter in a large, heavy casserole. Add the onions and bay leaves, cover and cook over moderately high heat, stirring occasionally, until the onions are very soft, about 15 minutes. Uncover and cook over moderate heat, stirring occasionally, until the onions are deeply browned, about 1½ hours longer. Add water by the tablespoon as needed if the onions dry out.

2. Add the flour to the onions and cook, stirring, for 2 minutes. Add the wine and cook, stirring constantly, until nearly evaporated, about 2 minutes longer. Add the beef stock and thyme sprig bundle and simmer over moderately low heat until the beef stock is reduced to 10 cups, about 35 minutes. Discard the thyme bundle and the bay leaves and season the soup with salt and pepper.

3. Preheat the oven to 350°. Brush the baguette slices with the olive oil, arrange the bread on a baking sheet and toast it for about 12 minutes, or until the slices are golden and crisp.

4. Preheat the broiler. Ladle the hot soup into 10 heatproof bowls. Float 3 baguette toasts in each bowl and scatter the shredded pecorino cheese on top. Set the bowls on a sturdy baking sheet and broil about 4 inches from the heat source for about 2 minutes, or until the cheese has melted. Serve the onion soup at once.

—Michael Mina

MAKE AHEAD The onion soup can be refrigerated for up to 4 days.

## Butternut Squash Soup with Coconut and Ginger

ACTIVE: 30 MIN; TOTAL: 1 HR 50 MIN

6 TO 8 SERVINGS ●

Jeanette Peabody, the chef of Hamiltons' at First & Main in Charlottesville, Virginia, makes this luscious, slightly sweet butternut squash soup with coconut milk instead of heavy cream. The coconut milk gives the soup a silky texture and a hint of exotic nuttiness.

64

2 large butternut squash
(5 pounds total)—
halved lengthwise, peeled
and seeded
4 tablespoons unsalted butter
Salt and freshly ground pepper
1 tablespoon extra-virgin olive oil
1 medium onion, finely chopped
1 leek, white and tender
green part only, thinly sliced
1 shallot, finely chopped
2 tablespoons minced
fresh ginger
1 teaspoon curry powder
½ cup dry white wine
6 cups water
1 cup unsweetened
coconut milk
1 thyme sprig
Coconut shavings, for garnish
(optional)

**1.** Preheat the oven to 350°. Set the squash cut side up on a baking sheet. Fill each squash cavity with ½ tablespoon of the butter. Season the squash halves with salt and pepper. Roast the squash for about 1 hour and 20 minutes, or until they are tender; cut into large pieces.

**2.** Meanwhile, in a large soup pot, melt the remaining 2 tablespoons of butter in the olive oil. Add the onion, leek, shallot, ginger and curry powder and cook over moderate heat until lightly browned. Add the wine and cook until evaporated.

**3.** Add the cooked squash, water, coconut milk and thyme sprig. Simmer over moderately low heat for 15 minutes.

**4.** Discard the thyme sprig. Working in batches, puree the squash soup in a blender until smooth; season with salt and pepper. Ladle the soup into bowls, garnish with the coconut shavings and serve.
—*Jeanette Peabody*

**MAKE AHEAD** The soup can be refrigerated for up to 2 days. Reheat the soup gently and garnish with coconut shavings just before serving.

**TRUFFLE-INFUSED FRENCH ONION SOUP**

**BUTTERNUT SQUASH SOUP WITH COCONUT AND GINGER**

# soups

## Almond Soup with Saffron and Apples

**TOTAL: 30 MIN**
**4 SERVINGS** ●

- ¼ cup extra-virgin olive oil
- 1 cup blanched whole almonds (3½ ounces)
- 2 large garlic cloves
- 6 slices of country bread (6 ounces), crusts trimmed, bread cut into chunks
- ¼ teaspoon saffron threads
- Pinch of dried thyme
- 5 cups chicken stock or low-sodium broth
- 1 tablespoon sherry vinegar
- Salt and freshly ground pepper
- ½ Granny Smith apple, peeled and finely diced
- 1 tablespoon minced flat-leaf parsley

1. In a large saucepan, heat the olive oil until shimmering. Add the blanched almonds and the garlic and cook over moderately high heat, stirring constantly, until golden, about 5 minutes. Using a slotted spoon, transfer the almonds and garlic to a plate. Add the country bread to the saucepan and cook, turning occasionally, until the bread chunks are golden and crisp, about 4 minutes. Set aside a third of the bread.

2. In a food processor, combine the other two-thirds of the bread with the almonds, garlic, saffron and thyme and process until finely ground. Add 1 cup of the chicken stock and process until smooth.

3. Return the almond mixture to the saucepan. Add the remaining 4 cups of chicken stock and bring to a boil. Simmer over moderate heat until the soup is slightly thickened, about 15 minutes. Stir the vinegar into the soup and season with salt and pepper.

4. Meanwhile, finely dice the remaining fried bread. Serve the soup in shallow bowls, garnished with the diced bread, apples and parsley. —*Janet Mendel*

## Creamy Lentil Soup with Serrano Ham

**ACTIVE: 30 MIN; TOTAL: 1 HR 15 MIN**
**8 SERVINGS** ●

Though this is a basic recipe—you sauté the aromatic vegetables, add the stock and lentils and simmer until the soup is done—pureeing it adds elegance. You can top the soup with crunchy croutons or even dress it up with a dice of foie gras.

- 1 tablespoon unsalted butter, plus 1 tablespoon melted butter
- 1 tablespoon extra-virgin olive oil
- 5 ounces serrano ham or lean bacon, cut into ½-inch dice
- 1 large onion, finely chopped
- 1 medium leek, white and tender green part only, finely chopped
- 1 large carrot, finely chopped
- 2 quarts plus ½ cup chicken stock
- 2 cups brown lentils (14 ounces), rinsed and picked over
- 2 cups ½-inch pieces of firm-textured white bread
- ½ cup heavy cream
- Salt and freshly ground pepper

1. Preheat the oven to 350°. In a large saucepan, melt the 1 tablespoon of butter in the olive oil. Add the serrano ham, onion, leek and carrot and cook over moderate heat, stirring occasionally, until softened, about 8 minutes. Add the stock and lentils and bring to a boil over moderately high heat. Simmer the soup over low heat, stirring occasionally, until the lentils are tender, about 45 minutes.

2. Meanwhile, on a baking sheet, toss the bread pieces with the melted butter and bake for 8 minutes, or until browned.

3. In a blender, puree the soup in batches. Return it to the saucepan. Add the cream, bring to a simmer and season with salt and pepper. Serve the soup in bowls, garnished with the croutons. —*Victoria Amory*

**MAKE AHEAD** The soup can be refrigerated for up to 3 days. The croutons can be kept in an airtight container overnight.

## Lamb and Chickpea Soup with Lentils

**ACTIVE: 20 MIN; TOTAL: 1 HR 30 MIN**
**6 SERVINGS** ● ● ●

Rich and soothing soups like this one are famous in Morocco. Muslims traditionally eat them to break their daily fast during the holy month of Ramadan. Usually thickened with flour or rice, these *hariras* are also often served as supper throughout the year. It's smart to make a double batch because although *hariras* are very good the day you make them, they are exceptional the next day, after the flavors have melded.

- 3 quarts water
- 2 pounds tomatoes, coarsely chopped, or one 28-ounce can peeled Italian plum tomatoes, chopped, juices reserved
- 1 large Spanish onion, grated
- 1 pound well-trimmed boneless lamb leg, cut into ½-inch cubes
- One 19-ounce can chickpeas, drained and rinsed
- ½ cup brown or green lentils (3½ ounces)
- ¼ cup extra-virgin olive oil
- 3 tablespoons tomato paste
- 1 teaspoon ground cumin
- ⅓ cup rice
- ⅓ cup all-purpose flour
- ¼ cup chopped flat-leaf parsley
- ¼ cup chopped cilantro
- Salt and freshly ground pepper

1. In a large, heavy pot, combine the water, tomatoes, onion, lamb, chickpeas, lentils, olive oil, tomato paste and cumin and bring to a boil, stirring to dissolve the tomato paste. Reduce the heat to low and simmer for 45 minutes, stirring occasionally.

2. Add the rice and simmer for 10 minutes. In a bowl, whisk 1 cup of soup into the flour, then whisk the slurry into the soup and simmer until thickened, about 15 minutes. Stir in the parsley and cilantro, season the soup with salt and pepper and serve. —*Dar Liqama Cooking School*

### Lentil and Garlic-Sausage Soup

**ACTIVE: 20 MIN; TOTAL: 1 HR 50 MIN**

**6 SERVINGS** ●

The inspiration for this garlicky lentil soup is the traditional *cotechino* sausage from the Emilia-Romagna region of Italy. *Cotechino* is cooked slowly until it's moist and almost sticky, then served over creamy lentils.

- ¼ cup extra-virgin olive oil, plus more for drizzling
- ¾ pound garlic sausage, cut into 1-inch cubes
- 3 large carrots, cut into ½-inch dice
- 3 garlic cloves, minced
- 1 large onion, coarsely chopped
- 1 medium fennel bulb, cut into ½-inch dice
- 1 bay leaf
- 1 cup dry white wine
- 3 cups French green lentils (1 pound plus 5 ounces)
- 2 quarts chicken broth
- 1 quart water
- 1 teaspoon chopped rosemary
- Salt and freshly ground pepper
- 2½ ounces Manchego cheese, shredded (¾ cup)

**1.** Heat the ¼ cup of olive oil in a large saucepan. Add the sausage and cook over moderately low heat until it starts to brown, about 7 minutes. Add the carrots, garlic, onion, fennel and bay leaf and cook over moderate heat until softened, about 8 minutes. Add the wine and boil over moderately high heat until the pan is almost dry, about 5 minutes. Stir in the lentils, broth and water and bring to a boil. Simmer, stirring occasionally, until the lentils are tender, 1 hour. Discard the bay leaf.

**2.** Stir the rosemary into the soup and season with salt and pepper. Ladle the soup into bowls. Sprinkle with the cheese, then drizzle with olive oil and serve.
—*Tom Fundaro*

**MAKE AHEAD** The soup can be refrigerated overnight. Stir in the parsley and cilantro just before serving.

### Chunky White Bean Soup with Pan-Fried Salami

**ACTIVE: 45 MIN; TOTAL: 1 HR 20 MIN**

**PLUS OVERNIGHT SOAKING**

**8 SERVINGS** ● ●

- 1 pound dried cannellini beans, soaked overnight and drained
- 2 tablespoons herbes de Provence
- 6 garlic cloves, 3 smashed, 3 thinly sliced
- Kosher salt
- 2 tablespoons extra-virgin olive oil
- ½ pound spicy salami, such as Calabrese, cut into ½-inch dice
- 1 medium onion, finely chopped
- 2 carrots, finely chopped
- 2 celery ribs, finely chopped
- 6 cups chicken stock
- ¾ pound kale, stems discarded, leaves finely chopped
- Freshly ground pepper
- ½ cup chopped flat-leaf parsley

**1.** In a saucepan, combine the beans with 1 tablespoon of the herbes de Provence and the smashed garlic. Add water to cover by 1 inch and bring to a boil. Simmer over moderately low heat until the beans begin to soften, 25 minutes. Add 1 tablespoon of salt and simmer until the beans are tender, 20 minutes longer; drain.

**2.** In a large enameled cast-iron casserole, heat the olive oil. Add the salami and cook over high heat until crisp, about 5 minutes. Transfer to a plate. Add the onion, carrots, celery, the sliced garlic and the remaining 1 tablespoon of herbes de Provence. Season with salt and cook over moderate heat for 2 minutes, then cover and cook until softened, about 10 minutes.

**3.** Add the beans and stock to the vegetables. Pulse half of the soup in a blender until the beans are coarsely chopped; return the soup to the casserole. Add the kale and simmer until tender, 15 minutes. Stir in the reserved salami; season with salt and pepper. Ladle the soup into bowls and garnish with the parsley. —*David Ansel*

### Corn and Bacon Chowder

**TOTAL: 45 MIN**

**4 SERVINGS** ●

This simple chowder combines pureed fresh sweet corn with sautéed corn kernels for crunch and a heady infusion of lean smoked bacon.

- 6 medium ears of corn, kernels cut off, corncobs halved crosswise
- 2 cups milk
- 1¼ cups heavy cream
- 2½ tablespoons unsalted butter
- 4 thick slices of lean smoked bacon (4 ounces), cut into ½-inch dice
- 2 celery ribs, finely diced
- 1 medium onion, finely diced
- Small pinch of saffron threads
- 1 tablespoon chopped tarragon
- Salt and freshly ground pepper

**1.** In a large saucepan, cover the corncobs with the milk and cream and bring to a simmer over moderate heat. Remove from the heat, cover and let stand for about 10 minutes. Discard the corncobs.

**2.** Meanwhile, in a large saucepan, melt 2 tablespoons of the butter. Add half of the corn kernels and cook over moderately low heat, stirring occasionally, until they are just tender, about 10 minutes. Working in batches, add the corn kernels to a blender along with the milk and cream and puree until smooth.

**3.** Melt the remaining ½ tablespoon of butter in the saucepan. Add the bacon and cook over moderate heat until lightly browned, about 5 minutes. Add the celery, onion, saffron and the remaining corn kernels, cover partially and cook, stirring occasionally, until the celery and onions are tender, about 10 minutes. Add the corn puree and the tarragon and season with salt and pepper. Ladle the chowder into bowls and serve.
—*Jonathan Benno*

**MAKE AHEAD** The chowder can be refrigerated overnight.

# soups

## Littleneck Clam Soup with Butter Beans and Saffron

**TOTAL: 30 MIN**

**4 SERVINGS** ● ● ●

- 3 tablespoons extra-virgin olive oil
- 1 small onion, finely chopped
- ⅓ cup finely diced serrano ham or prosciutto (2 ounces)
- 2 large garlic cloves, finely chopped
- 1 tablespoon fine dry bread crumbs

Two 15-ounce cans butter beans with their liquid

Pinch of dried thyme

- 1 bay leaf

Large pinch of saffron threads

- 2 tablespoons water

Freshly ground pepper

- 3 dozen littleneck clams, scrubbed and shucked, liquor reserved
- 2 tablespoons minced parsley

**1.** In a large, deep skillet, heat the oil until shimmering. Add the onion and cook over moderately high heat until softened, 3 minutes. Add the ham and garlic and cook for 1 minute. Stir in the crumbs, then add the beans and their liquid along with the thyme and bay leaf and bring to a boil.

**2.** In a small bowl, crush the saffron threads into the water. Add to the beans and season with pepper. Simmer the soup over low heat for 15 minutes. Increase the heat to high, add the clams and their reserved liquor and cook for 3 minutes. Discard the bay leaf. Sprinkle the soup with the parsley and serve. —*Janet Mendel*

**SERVE WITH** Garlic-rubbed toasts.

## Shrimp Bisque with Brandy and Sherry

**ACTIVE: 40 MIN; TOTAL: 1 HR**

**8 SERVINGS** ● ●

- 1 pound large shrimp, shelled and deveined, shells reserved
- 3 cups water
- 2 tablespoons extra-virgin olive oil
- 4 garlic cloves, thinly sliced
- 1 medium onion, chopped
- ¼ teaspoon cayenne pepper
- ¼ cup brandy
- 2 tablespoons chopped basil, plus 8 leaves thinly sliced
- ¼ cup dry sherry
- 4 tablespoons unsalted butter
- ½ cup all-purpose flour
- 5 cups fish stock or 2½ cups bottled clam juice mixed with 2½ cups water
- ⅓ cup tomato paste
- 1 cup heavy cream
- 3 tablespoons fresh lemon juice

Kosher salt and freshly ground black pepper

**1.** In a small saucepan, cover the shrimp shells with the water and bring to a boil. Simmer for 20 minutes, then strain the shrimp stock into a bowl.

**2.** Meanwhile, in a large skillet, heat the olive oil. Add the shrimp, garlic, onion and cayenne and cook over high heat until the shrimp begin to turn pink, about 3 minutes. Add the brandy and boil until reduced by half, about 2 minutes. Add the chopped basil and the sherry and simmer until the shrimp are just cooked through, about 2 minutes. Transfer the shrimp to a food processor, add the shrimp stock and puree until smooth.

**3.** In a medium saucepan, melt the butter over moderate heat. Whisk in the flour and cook, whisking, until smooth, about 1 minute. Slowly whisk in the half-and-half and cook, whisking, until the roux is very thick, about 2 minutes.

**4.** In a soup pot, combine the fish stock with the tomato paste and the shrimp puree and bring to a simmer over high heat. Slowly whisk in the roux and the heavy cream. Reduce the heat to moderately low and simmer until thick and creamy, about 20 minutes. Add the lemon juice and season with salt and black pepper. Ladle the bisque into bowls, garnish with the sliced basil and serve. —*David Ansel*

## Carrot-Ginger Soup with Coconut-Roasted Shrimp

**TOTAL: 45 MIN**

**6 SERVINGS** ●

- 2 tablespoons extra-virgin olive oil
- 1 medium onion, coarsely chopped
- 4 large carrots (¾ pound), chopped
- 1 tablespoon finely grated ginger
- ½ teaspoon crushed red pepper
- 3 cups low-sodium chicken broth
- 3 tablespoons soy sauce
- 2 tablespoons fresh lime juice
- 2 tablespoons light brown sugar
- 1 tablespoon smooth peanut butter
- 1 teaspoon Asian sesame oil
- 1 cup skim milk
- ¼ cup light coconut milk

Kosher salt and freshly ground black pepper

- 16 large shrimp, shelled
- 1½ tablespoons shredded coconut

Pinch of cayenne pepper

**1.** Preheat the oven to 425°. In a large saucepan, heat 1 tablespoon of the olive oil. Add the onion and cook over moderate heat until softened, about 4 minutes. Add the carrots, ginger and crushed red pepper and cook for 6 minutes. Add the broth and bring to a boil, then simmer until the carrots are very tender, about 15 minutes. Remove from the heat and stir in the soy sauce, lime juice, brown sugar, peanut butter and sesame oil.

**2.** In a blender, puree the soup until smooth. Return it to the saucepan and stir in the skim milk and coconut milk. Season the carrot-ginger soup with salt and black pepper and keep warm.

**3.** Toss the shrimp with the coconut, cayenne and the remaining 1 tablespoon of olive oil, then season with salt and black pepper. Spread the shrimp on a parchment-lined baking sheet and roast for 8 minutes, or until they are pink. Ladle the carrot-ginger soup into warmed bowls and garnish with the coconut shrimp. —*Corbin Evans*

CARROT-GINGER SOUP WITH
COCONUT-ROASTED SHRIMP

# soups

## Pumpkin Soup with Creole Lobster

**ACTIVE: 1 HR 15 MIN; TOTAL: 2 HR 45 MIN**

10 SERVINGS

- 4 sugar pumpkins or 2 medium butternut squash (about 5 pounds total), halved and seeded
- 6 tablespoons extra-virgin olive oil

Kosher salt and freshly ground black pepper

Five 1-pound lobsters

- 1 stick (4 ounces) unsalted butter
- 1 large white onion, chopped
- 2 garlic cloves
- 1 thyme sprig
- 1 rosemary sprig
- 1 bay leaf
- 1 cup medium-dry white wine
- ½ cup crème fraîche
- 1½ teaspoons garlic powder
- 1½ teaspoons onion powder
- 1 teaspoon cayenne pepper
- 1 teaspoon dry mustard
- ½ teaspoon ground cumin
- ¼ teaspoon freshly grated nutmeg
- ¼ teaspoon cinnamon
- ¼ teaspoon ground cloves

**1.** Preheat the oven to 350°. Drizzle the pumpkin halves with 2 tablespoons of the olive oil and season generously with salt and black pepper. Wrap each half tightly in foil and bake on a large cookie sheet for 1 hour and 15 minutes, or until tender. Let the pumpkins cool slightly, then scoop the flesh into a bowl.

**2.** Bring a stockpot of water to a boil. Prepare a large bowl of ice water. Salt the boiling water and add the lobsters. Cover and cook over high heat for 3 minutes. Using tongs, carefully transfer the lobsters to the ice water and let cool. Twist off the heads and reserve. Crack the claws and remove the meat in one piece. Using a heavy knife, halve the tails lengthwise, cutting through the meat and shells. Remove the veins from the tails. Transfer the lobster tails and the claw meat to a large baking sheet and refrigerate them.

**3.** Clean out the lobster heads with a spoon and return the shells to the stockpot. Simmer the shells for 30 minutes, skimming frequently. Strain the lobster stock through a fine sieve and reserve 8 cups.

**4.** In a soup pot, melt 4 tablespoons of the butter. Add the onion, garlic, thyme, rosemary and bay leaf. Cook over moderate heat, stirring occasionally, until the onion is softened, about 8 minutes. Add the cooked pumpkin and the wine and simmer until the wine has reduced by half, about 5 minutes. Add 6 cups of the lobster stock and simmer for 30 minutes. Remove and discard the herb sprigs and bay leaf.

**5.** In a food processor or blender, puree the soup with the crème fraîche. Return it to a clean pot. Add enough of the remaining 2 cups of lobster stock to make the soup velvety; season with salt and pepper.

**6.** In a small bowl, combine 1 tablespoon of salt with 2 teaspoons of black pepper and the garlic powder, onion powder, cayenne, dry mustard, cumin, nutmeg, cinnamon and cloves.

**7.** In a very large skillet, heat the remaining ¼ cup of olive oil. Add the lobster tails, cut side down, and cook over high heat until the shells begin to brown, 3 minutes. Reduce the heat to moderate, turn the tails and add the remaining 4 tablespoons of butter and the spice mixture. Cook the tails for 2 minutes, basting them with the spice butter. Transfer the tails to a plate and remove the meat from the shells. Add the lobster claw meat to the skillet and baste with the spice butter for 2 minutes per side. Add the claw meat to the tail meat on the plate.

**8.** Bring the pumpkin soup to a simmer. Ladle into warmed bowls and garnish each serving with a lobster tail half and a claw.

*—Allison Vines-Rushing and Slade Rushing*

**MAKE AHEAD** The soup and lobster can be prepared through Step 6 and refrigerated for up to 2 days.

## Seafood Chowder with Sherry and Serrano Ham

**TOTAL: 30 MIN**

4 SERVINGS ●●

This creamy-tasting *gazpachuelo* from Málaga, Spain, has no cream in it. Instead, the soup's luscious texture comes from a mayonnaise-like blend of egg and olive oil that gets beaten into the hot chowder. This recipe is from Janet Mendel, the author of the forthcoming *Food of La Mancha*. An American expatriate who cooks like a born-and-bred Spaniard, Mendel has come up with a version of this soup that is not only authentic, but healthy and fast.

- 3 cups bottled clam broth
- 2 cups water

Pinch of dried thyme

- 1 large Yukon Gold potato, peeled and cut into ½-inch dice
- 1 large egg
- ½ cup extra-virgin olive oil
- 3 tablespoons fresh lemon juice

Salt and freshly ground pepper

- 1 pound well-trimmed monkfish fillets, cut into 1½-inch pieces
- ⅓ cup frozen peas
- ¼ cup finely diced serrano ham or prosciutto (1½ ounces)
- 2 tablespoons finely chopped piquillo pepper or roasted red pepper
- ½ pound shelled and deveined medium shrimp
- 2 tablespoons dry sherry

**1.** In a large saucepan, combine the clam broth, water and thyme and bring to a boil over moderately high heat. Add the potato and cook until almost tender when pierced, about 10 minutes.

**2.** Meanwhile, in a blender, beat the egg. With the machine on, gradually beat in the olive oil and then the lemon juice. Gradually add ½ cup of the hot clam broth and blend until emulsified. Season the sauce with salt and pepper.

**3.** Add the monkfish, frozen peas, serrano ham and piquillo pepper to the broth in the saucepan and cook for 2½ minutes. Add the shrimp and simmer until they are pink and curled, about 2 minutes. Add the sherry. Remove the chowder from the heat and stir in the egg mixture. Season the soup with salt and pepper and serve.
—*Janet Mendel*

### Red Snapper Soup with Fresh Bean Sprouts and Garlic Oil

ACTIVE: 45 MIN; TOTAL: 2 HR

6 TO 8 SERVINGS ●

Charles Phan, chef and owner of the Slanted Door in San Francisco, recalls eating numerous versions of this slightly sweet and pleasantly tangy fish soup while growing up in Vietnam. Some included only chopped tomato, while others were made with a colorful mix of vegetables. Here, Phan uses freshly squeezed lime juice for a hit of sourness instead of the more traditional tamarind pulp. Bean sprouts add a refreshing crunch.

- 3 quarts cold water
- Two 2-pound red snappers, filleted and skinned, heads and bones reserved
- ¼ cup plus 1 tablespoon Asian fish sauce
- 2 stalks of lemongrass, cut into 5-inch lengths and lightly crushed
- One 1¼-inch piece of fresh ginger, sliced into ¼-inch-thick rounds
- 1 small onion, quartered
- Kosher salt
- ½ cup canola oil
- 3 large garlic cloves, very finely chopped
- ½ pound white mushrooms, thinly sliced
- 6 ounces mung bean sprouts
- 4 scallions, thinly sliced
- Thinly sliced serrano chiles and lime wedges, for serving

**1.** Pour the water into a large stockpot. Add the reserved red snapper heads and bones, 3 tablespoons of the fish sauce and the lemongrass, ginger, quartered onion and 2 teaspoons of salt. Bring to a boil. Reduce the heat to moderately low and simmer for 1 hour.

**2.** Meanwhile, cut the snapper fillets into 1½-inch pieces and transfer them to a medium bowl. Add 2 tablespoons of the oil to the bowl, the remaining 2 tablespoons of fish sauce and toss to coat the fish. Refrigerate the fish for 1 hour.

**3.** Heat the remaining 6 tablespoons of oil in a small skillet. Add the chopped garlic and cook over high heat, stirring, until it is fragrant and lightly golden, about 30 seconds. Pour the garlic oil into a bowl and set aside to cool.

**4.** Strain the soup through a fine sieve, pressing hard on the solids. Wipe out the pot. Return the fish soup to the pot and bring it to a boil. Add the mushrooms and simmer the soup over moderate heat until they are just tender, about 1 minute. Add the marinated snapper and cook just until opaque, about 2 minutes. Season the soup with salt. Add the bean sprouts and scallions and stir in the garlic oil. Serve right away, with sliced chiles and lime wedges.
—*Charles Phan*

MAKE AHEAD The snapper fillets can be marinated overnight in the refrigerator.

### Spicy Udon and Clam Soup

TOTAL: 30 MIN

4 SERVINGS ● ●

This dish is based on the classic Korean noodle soup *kal gooksu,* or "knife noodles," so named because the handmade dough is cut with a knife.

- ½ pound dried udon noodles
- 2 garlic cloves, very finely chopped
- 2 teaspoons Asian sesame oil
- 1¼ teaspoons Asian chili-garlic sauce, plus more for serving
- 1 teaspoon pure ancho chile powder
- Pinch of sugar
- Salt
- 2 cups clam broth
- 2 cups water
- 24 littleneck clams, scrubbed
- 4 ounces baby spinach (4 cups)
- 2 scallions, thickly sliced

**1.** In a large saucepan of boiling salted water, cook the udon noodles until they are al dente, about 6 minutes. Drain the noodles, shaking off the excess water.

**2.** Meanwhile, in a large saucepan, combine the chopped garlic, sesame oil, 1¼ teaspoons of chili-garlic sauce, chile powder, sugar and a pinch of salt. Add the clam broth and water to the pan and bring to a boil. Add the clams and cook until they are opened, about 5 minutes; transfer the cooked clams to a bowl. Discard any clams that do not open.

**3.** Add the spinach, scallions and udon to the broth and cook until the spinach is wilted, about 1 minute. Ladle the udon soup into 4 bowls and top with the clams. Pass extra chili sauce at the table.
—*Cecilia Hae-Jin Lee*

## F&W taste test

### RAMEN NOODLE SOUPS

Instant ramen are dried noodles packaged with a dried broth mix. Here are F&W's favorites.

**MARUCHAN'S BEEF AND ORIENTAL FLAVORS**
A bargain 25 cents per pack and the best beef-flavored ramen.

**NISSIN TOP RAMEN**
Won for best chicken flavor; a six-pack costs 99 cents.

**SAPPORO ICHIBAN**
Was our top choice for shrimp flavor, and it's just 49 cents a bowl.

● FAST   ● HEALTHY   ● MAKE AHEAD   ● STAFF FAVORITE

**TANGY LEMON-EGG SOUP WITH TINY MEATBALLS**

**FIVE-SPICE SHORT RIBS WITH UDON NOODLES**

### Tangy Lemon-Egg Soup with Tiny Meatballs

**TOTAL: 1 HR**

**4 SERVINGS** ●

With its blend of chicken stock and vitamin-C-rich lemon, this restorative soup (inspired by the classic Greek lemon-egg soup *avgolemono*) is a good way to fight colds or the flu.

- ½ **cup medium-grain white rice**
- 3 **cups water**

**Kosher salt**

- 4 **cups chicken stock**
- 2 **large egg yolks**
- ½ **cup fresh lemon juice**

**Freshly ground pepper**

- ¾ **pound lean ground lamb or turkey**
- ⅓ **cup minced sweet onion**
- 2 **teaspoons finely chopped mint**
- 3 **tablespoons finely chopped dill, plus dill sprigs for garnish**
- 1¼ **teaspoons finely grated lemon zest**

**All-purpose flour, for dusting**

**1.** In a large saucepan, cover the rice with the water, season with salt and bring to a boil. Simmer over moderate heat until the rice is tender and the water is nearly absorbed, about 15 minutes. Transfer ½ cup of the rice to a blender and spread the remaining rice out on a plate.

**2.** Add the chicken stock to the same saucepan and bring it to a simmer. Add 1 cup of the hot stock to the blender, cover it and puree until the rice is smooth. With the machine on, add the egg yolks and the lemon juice and blend until smooth. Season the rice and egg yolk mixture with salt and pepper. Stir the mixture into the stock and keep warm over low heat.

**3.** In a medium bowl, mix the lamb with the onion, mint, 2 tablespoons of the dill, ¼ teaspoon of the lemon zest, 2 teaspoons of salt and ½ teaspoon of pepper. Form the ground lamb mixture into 1-inch balls.

**4.** Lightly dust the meatballs with flour, tapping off any excess and drop them into the warm soup. Increase the heat to moderate and simmer the soup until the meatballs are cooked through, 8 to 10 minutes. Stir in the reserved rice and the remaining 1 tablespoon of dill and 1 teaspoon of lemon zest and season with salt and pepper. Ladle the soup into bowls, garnish with dill sprigs and serve.

—*Grace Parisi*

**MAKE AHEAD** The soup and meatballs can be prepared through Step 3 and refrigerated separately for up to 8 hours. Return the meatballs to room temperature before proceeding with the recipe.

### Five-Spice Short Ribs with Udon Noodles

**ACTIVE: 2 HR; TOTAL: 4 HR**

**4 SERVINGS**

Chewy udon noodles have a mild flavor that is wonderful combined with the delicate spices in this rich beef broth from chef Nobuo Fukuda of Sea Saw in Scottsdale, Arizona. Udon are available at Asian markets and some supermarkets, but if you can't find them, Italian egg noodles are the best alternative.

- 1½ **pounds boneless beef short ribs, cut into 2-inch pieces**
- 1 **tablespoon Chinese five-spice powder**
- ¼ **cup vegetable oil**
- 1 **large onion, chopped**
- 2 **large carrots, thinly sliced**
- 4 **large garlic cloves**
- 1 **small celery rib, thinly sliced**
- One 5-inch piece of peeled fresh **ginger, thinly sliced**
- 6 **thyme sprigs**
- 1 **cup dry red wine, such as Cabernet Sauvignon**
- 4 **cups chicken stock or low-sodium broth**
- 4 **dried shiitake mushrooms**
- 2 **cups water**
- One 4-inch piece of daikon radish, **sliced 1 inch thick**
- One 3-inch piece of *konbu* **(dried kelp; see Note)**
- ⅓ **cup sake**
- ⅓ **cup mirin**
- ⅓ **cup Asian fish sauce**
- ½ **pound dried flat udon noodles or Italian egg noodles, or 1 pound fresh udon noodles (see Note)**

**1.** Dust the boneless short ribs with the five-spice powder and let them stand at room temperature for 20 minutes. In a medium enameled cast-iron casserole, heat 2 tablespoons of the oil. Add the short ribs and cook over moderately high heat until they are browned all over, about 8 minutes. Transfer the short ribs to a plate and pour off the fat.

**2.** Heat the remaining 2 tablespoons of oil in the casserole. Add the onion, carrots, garlic, celery, ginger and thyme sprigs; cook, stirring frequently, until the vegetables are softened, about 10 minutes. Add the wine and cook until it is nearly evaporated, 2 to 3 minutes. Return the short ribs to the casserole. Add the chicken stock and bring to a boil. Cover the casserole with a sheet of parchment paper and simmer over moderately low heat until the meat is very tender, about 3 hours.

**3.** Meanwhile, in a medium saucepan, cover the shiitake mushrooms with the water and bring to a boil. Remove the saucepan from the heat and let the mushrooms soak until they are softened, about 30 minutes. Add the daikon and the *konbu* to the mushroom broth and cook over moderately high heat until the daikon is just tender, about 20 minutes. Drain the mushrooms and daikon and discard the *konbu* and liquid.

**4.** Using tongs, transfer the short ribs to a plate. Strain the broth they were cooked in into a heatproof bowl and discard the solids. Skim as much fat from the surface of the broth as possible. Return the broth to the casserole and keep warm.

**5.** Preheat the broiler and position a rack 8 inches from the heat source. In a medium bowl, combine the sake, mirin and fish sauce. Add the short ribs, shiitake mushrooms and daikon and let marinate for 5 minutes. Transfer the meat and vegetables to a baking sheet and discard the marinade. Broil the meat and vegetables, turning once, until the meat is browned and crisp and the vegetables are golden, about 2 minutes.

**6.** In a large pot of boiling salted water, cook the udon until al dente. Drain and transfer to bowls. Top with the meat and vegetables, spoon in the broth and serve.
—*Nobuo Fukuda*

**NOTE** *Konbu* and udon noodles are available at Asian markets and some well-stocked supermarkets.

**MAKE AHEAD** The five-spice short ribs can be prepared through Step 2 and refrigerated for up to 4 days. Bring the short ribs to room temperature before proceeding with the recipe.

# ingredient
## ASIAN NOODLE PRIMER

### SOBA
Thin, grayish-brown Japanese buckwheat noodles; usually sold dried. In Japan, soba is often eaten chilled with dipping sauce, though it may also be eaten hot in broth.

### UDON
Thick (about ¼ inch wide) white Japanese wheat noodles. Udon are sold round or flat and are used in soups or served cold with dipping sauce.

### CHOW MEIN AND LO MEIN NOODLES
Chinese noodles made from wheat and eggs; lo mein noodles are thicker than chow mein. Available fresh, frozen and dried.

### CELLOPHANE NOODLES
Transparent noodles made from mung bean starch. Cellophane noodles are also called glass noodles, cellophane vermicelli or bean threads.

### SOMEN
Very thin, round, white Japanese wheat noodles. They are frequently tied in small bundles.

### RICE NOODLES
Slightly translucent, dried noodles made from rice flour. Rice vermicelli are thin and wiry, while rice stick noodles are flatter and can vary in width from .05 inch to about ½ inch.

COCONUT-CURRY NOODLE SOUP

## Coconut-Curry Noodle Soup

**TOTAL: 30 MIN**

**4 SERVINGS** ●

 3 ounces baby spinach (3 cups)
¼ pound snow peas,
  halved crosswise
¾ pound dried chow mein noodles
 3 tablespoons vegetable oil
 2 shallots, thinly sliced
 2 garlic cloves, minced
 2 teaspoons Thai red curry paste
1½ teaspoons Madras curry powder
½ teaspoon ground coriander
½ teaspoon ground turmeric
 6 cups chicken stock or
  low-sodium broth
One 13½-ounce can unsweetened
  coconut milk
 2 tablespoons Asian fish sauce
 2 tablespoons sugar
½ pound shredded cooked chicken
¼ cup chopped cilantro leaves
 2 scallions, thinly sliced
Salt
Lime wedges and sliced chiles,
  for serving

1. In a large pot of boiling salted water, cook the spinach and snow peas until the spinach wilts, 30 seconds. Remove the vegetables and add the noodles; cook until al dente, 8 minutes. Drain well. Transfer the spinach, snow peas and noodles to bowls.

2. In a saucepan, heat 1 tablespoon of the oil. Cook the shallots over moderately high heat until lightly browned, 2 minutes; transfer to a plate. Reduce the heat to moderate. Add the remaining 2 tablespoons of oil, the garlic, curry paste, curry powder, coriander and turmeric and stir-fry for 30 seconds. Add the stock, bring to a boil and cook for 3 minutes. Add the coconut milk, fish sauce and sugar, bring to a boil and cook for 5 minutes. Add the chicken, cilantro and scallions and cook just until heated through; season with salt. Ladle the soup over the noodles and serve with the cooked shallots, lime wedges and sliced chiles. —*Mai Pham*

## Jewish Turkey-Wonton Soup

**ACTIVE: 1 HR 20 MIN; TOTAL: 3 HR**

**8 SERVINGS** ● ●

 3 tablespoons vegetable oil
Three 1-pound turkey legs
Kosher salt and freshly ground pepper
 6 cups water
 6 cups chicken stock
 2 garlic cloves
 2 celery ribs, 1 coarsely chopped,
  1 finely diced
 1 large carrot, coarsely chopped
 1 large yellow onion, coarsely chopped
 1 bay leaf
 1 thyme sprig
 1 teaspoon whole black peppercorns
 1 small red onion, finely diced
40 square wonton wrappers
 1 tablespoon plus 1 teaspoon
  chopped fresh dill

1. In a soup pot, heat 2 tablespoons of the oil. Season the turkey legs with salt and pepper, add to the pot and cook over high heat until browned on all sides, 7 minutes. Add the water, stock, garlic, chopped celery, carrot, onion, bay leaf, thyme and peppercorns and bring to a boil. Cover and simmer over moderately low heat until the turkey meat pulls away from the bone, 1 hour.

2. Transfer the turkey legs to a large plate and let cool slightly. Pull the meat off the bones and coarsely chop it; discard the skin. Return the bones to the pot and simmer the turkey stock for 1 hour longer.

3. Meanwhile, in a medium skillet, heat the remaining 1 tablespoon of oil. Add the diced celery and red onion and cook over moderate heat until softened, about 5 minutes; transfer to a food processor. Add the turkey, season with salt and pepper and pulse until the turkey is finely chopped.

4. On a work surface, lay out 10 wonton wrappers. Scoop 1 tablespoon of the turkey filling into the center of each wrapper. Moisten the edges of the wrapper with water and fold it in half on the diagonal, creating a triangle; press the edges to seal. Transfer the wonton to a baking sheet and keep covered with a damp cloth. Repeat with the remaining wrappers and filling.

5. Strain the turkey stock into another pot and skim the fat from the surface. Season with salt and pepper and bring the stock to a simmer. Add the wonton, cover and cook until the wrappers are just tender, about 5 minutes. Ladle the soup into bowls, garnish with the dill and serve. —*David Ansel*

## Hunter's Stew with
## Braised Beef and Wild Rice

**ACTIVE: 45 MIN; TOTAL: 3 HR**

**8 SERVINGS** ●

 3 tablespoons pure olive oil
1½ pounds beef chuck in 1 piece
Kosher salt and freshly ground pepper
10 cups beef stock
¾ cup Madeira
½ pound wild rice (1¼ cups)
 1 medium onion, very finely chopped
 2 carrots, coarsely chopped

1. Preheat the oven to 300°. In a large, heavy ovenproof saucepan, heat 1 tablespoon of the olive oil. Season the meat with salt and pepper. Cook over high heat until browned, 2 minutes per side. Transfer to a plate and wipe out the pan. Add 2 cups of the stock and the Madeira and bring to a simmer. Return the meat to the pan, cover and braise in the oven for 2 to 2½ hours, turning occasionally, until tender.

2. Heat a large enameled cast-iron casserole over high heat. Add the rice and cook, stirring, until it begins to pop, 2 minutes. Add the onion, carrots and the remaining 2 tablespoons of olive oil and cook, stirring, for 2 minutes. Add the remaining 8 cups of stock and bring to a simmer. Reduce the heat to moderate, cover and cook until the rice is tender, 50 minutes.

3. Remove the meat from the liquid and let cool slightly, then shred. Add the meat and liquid to the casserole; season with salt and pepper. Simmer for 5 minutes, ladle into bowls and serve. —*David Ansel*

# soups

## Chicken Pho

**ACTIVE: 45 MIN; TOTAL: 4 HR**

**6 SERVINGS**

This addictive soup, called *pho,* has an intense chicken flavor accented by aromatic roasted onion and ginger. A large pinch of sugar added to the broth balances the pungent fish sauce.

- 2 unpeeled yellow onions, quartered

Three ½-inch-thick slices of
    fresh ginger, smashed
- 4 quarts cold water
- 3 pounds chicken bones
    or wings

One 3½-pound chicken, quartered
- 1 tablespoon salt
- 2 teaspoons sugar
- ¼ cup Asian fish sauce
- 1 pound dried rice noodles
- 1 scallion, white and green
    part, thinly sliced

## health

### THE POWER OF GINGER

Ginger has long been used in Asia to treat everything from the common cold to the plague. Although there's no scientific proof that ginger helps fight colds, recent studies have shown its effectiveness in treating other ailments. Research conducted by the University of Adelaide in Australia and published in *Obstetrics & Gynecology* in 2004 confirms that ginger can help **reduce nausea** in pregnant women. And according to a 2004 article in *Asia Pacific Journal of Clinical Nutrition,* ginger contains high levels of antioxidants, which can help **protect against heart disease, cancer and stroke.** Christine Gerbstadt, a physician and dietitian with the American Dietetic Association, recommends sipping a tea made by steeping slices of ginger in boiling water.

- 1 pound mung bean sprouts
- ½ cup torn basil leaves
- 2 limes, cut into wedges
- 2 jalapeños, thinly sliced

**Asian chili-garlic sauce and hoisin
    sauce, for serving**

**1.** Preheat the oven to 400°. Put the onions and ginger on a baking sheet and roast for 30 minutes, or until they are softened and lightly browned.

**2.** Add the water to a large stockpot and bring to a boil. Add the roasted onions and ginger to the stockpot along with the chicken bones, quartered chicken, salt and sugar and bring to a boil. Lower the heat to moderate and simmer until the chicken is cooked, about 30 minutes.

**3.** Using tongs, transfer the quartered chicken to a plate and let cool slightly. Remove the meat from the bones and refrigerate the meat. Return the chicken skin and bones to the stockpot and simmer for 2 hours longer. Strain the chicken broth into a large soup pot and cook over high heat until the soup is reduced to 12 cups, about 15 minutes. Stir the fish sauce into the chicken broth.

**4.** In a large bowl of warm water, soak the dried rice noodles until they are pliable, about 20 minutes.

**5.** Bring a large saucepan of salted water to a boil. Drain the rice noodles, then add them to the saucepan and boil over high heat until they are tender, about 3 minutes. Drain well. Transfer the rice noodles to 6 large soup bowls and sprinkle them with the thinly sliced scallion. Add the reserved chicken to the broth and simmer until it is heated through. Ladle the broth and chicken over the noodles in the bowls. Serve the soup with the bean sprouts, basil, lime wedges, jalapeños, chili-garlic sauce and hoisin sauce on the side. —*Charles Phan*

**MAKE AHEAD** The Chicken Pho recipe can be prepared through Step 3 and refrigerated for up to 2 days.

## Chicken Soup with Jasmine Rice and Ginger

**ACTIVE: 15 MIN; TOTAL: 1 HR**

**4 SERVINGS** ● ●

This lovely recipe is not only supereasy, it is also quite healthy. Add to that a gingery flavor and aroma, and this is one chicken soup that will undeniably make you feel better when you're under the weather.

- ⅓ cup plus 1 tablespoon
    jasmine rice, rinsed
- 4 cups water

One 3-inch piece of fresh
    ginger, peeled
- 3 cups chicken stock
- 1 tablespoon Asian fish sauce

**Pinch each of salt and sugar**
- ½ cup shredded cooked chicken
- 2 scallions, thinly sliced crosswise
- 2 tablespoons coarsely
    chopped cilantro

**1.** In a medium saucepan, cover the rice with the water. Bring the rice to a boil over high heat. Reduce the heat to low and simmer until the rice is tender and porridge-like, about 25 minutes.

**2.** Meanwhile, cut the piece of peeled ginger into slivers: Thinly slice the ginger crosswise, then stack the slices, removing the bottom rounded slice so the stack is stable and easy to work with. Cut the ginger slices lengthwise into thin slivers.

**3.** Add the chicken stock, fish sauce, salt and sugar to the rice, bring the soup to a simmer and continue cooking over low heat for 10 minutes. Stir in half of the ginger slivers and simmer the soup for 10 minutes longer.

**4.** Ladle the chicken soup into shallow bowls and garnish with the shredded chicken, sliced scallions, chopped cilantro and the remaining slivered ginger. Serve at once. —*Mai Pham*

**MAKE AHEAD** The recipe can be made through Step 3 and refrigerated overnight. When reheating the soup, add extra stock to adjust the consistency.

CHICKEN SOUP WITH
JASMINE RICE AND GINGER

For the June issue, chef Bradford Thompson (pictured here with his fiancée, Kerry-Ann Brown) grilled a terrific lunch with a group of chef friends. On the menu: Farfalle with Salsa Verde and Grilled Ricotta Salata (P. 81).

**pasta**

**PASTA WITH SPICY ALMOND PESTO**

**BAKED FOUR-CHEESE SPAGHETTI**

### Pasta with Spicy Almond Pesto

**ACTIVE: 10 MIN; TOTAL: 25 MIN**

**4 SERVINGS** ●

Until recently, finding a nut butter made from anything but peanuts meant going to the health food store or grinding your own. Today, supermarkets sell a broad range of nut butters, and using one of them makes a great shortcut for this spicy dish.

- ¾ pound fettuccine
- ¾ cup extra-virgin olive oil
- ¼ cup fresh sage leaves
- 1 garlic clove, mashed to a paste
- ¼ cup almond or hazelnut butter
- 1 scallion, minced
- ½ teaspoon finely grated lemon zest

Large pinch of crushed red pepper

- ½ cup freshly grated Parmesan cheese (1½ ounces)

Salt and freshly ground pepper

**1.** In a large pot of boiling salted water, cook the pasta until al dente. Drain, reserving ¾ cup of the cooking water. Meanwhile, in a small skillet, heat ½ cup of the olive oil until shimmering. Fry the sage leaves over moderate heat, turning occasionally, until crisp. Drain the sage leaves on paper towels, then chop half of the leaves.

**2.** In a medium bowl, combine the chopped sage leaves with the garlic, almond butter, the remaining ¼ cup of olive oil, the scallion, lemon zest, crushed red pepper and all but 2 tablespoons of the Parmesan cheese. Toss the drained pasta with the almond pesto; add as much of the reserved pasta water as needed to make a creamy sauce. Season the pasta with salt and pepper. Top with the remaining 2 tablespoons of cheese and the whole sage leaves and serve. —*Grace Parisi*

**WINE** Zippy, fresh Pinot Bianco.

### Baked Four-Cheese Spaghetti

**ACTIVE: 30 MIN; TOTAL: 1 HR 10 MIN**

**8 SERVINGS** ●

Marc Murphy, chef at Landmarc in New York City, grew up eating this intensely cheesy baked spaghetti. "When I was young, we lived in Genoa, where spaghetti is the pasta of choice. This is my mother's version of macaroni and cheese," he says.

- 1½ pounds spaghetti
- ½ pound imported Fontina cheese, coarsely shredded (2 cups)
- ½ pound mozzarella, coarsely shredded (2 cups)
- ½ pound Gruyère cheese, coarsely shredded (2 cups)
- ¼ pound Gorgonzola dolce cheese, crumbled

Salt and freshly ground pepper

1. Preheat the oven to 350°. Lightly butter a 9-by-13-inch baking dish. Cook the spaghetti in a large pot of boiling salted water until al dente. Drain well and spread the spaghetti on a baking sheet; let cool.
2. In a bowl, toss the Fontina, mozzarella and Gruyère. Spread a third of the spaghetti evenly in the prepared baking dish. Sprinkle one-third of the mixed cheeses and half of the Gorgonzola over the spaghetti; season with salt and pepper. Repeat with a layer of spaghetti, mixed cheeses, Gorgonzola and salt and pepper. Top with the remaining spaghetti and cheeses.
3. Bake the spaghetti in the center of the oven until the top is golden brown, about 40 minutes. Let cool slightly before cutting into squares and serving. —*Marc Murphy*
**WINE** Light, crisp white Burgundy.

## Pennette with Spicy Tomato Sauce
**TOTAL: 20 MIN**
4 SERVINGS ● ●
One 28-ounce can whole tomatoes in
   tomato puree, drained
¼ cup extra-virgin olive oil
3 garlic cloves, sliced
1 teaspoon crushed red pepper
Salt
¾ pound whole wheat pennette
2 tablespoons chopped parsley
1. Bring a large pot of water to a boil. In a food processor, puree the tomatoes until smooth. Heat the olive oil in a large, deep skillet; add the garlic and cook over moderately low heat until golden. Add the red pepper and cook for 30 seconds. Add the pureed tomatoes and cook over moderately high heat, stirring occasionally, until thickened, 6 minutes; season with salt.
2. Salt the boiling water. Add the pennette and cook, stirring occasionally, until al dente. Drain the pasta and add to the sauce. Toss well, spoon into bowls, sprinkle with parsley and serve.
—*Mark Strausman*
**WINE** Bright, tart Barbera.

## Farfalle with Salsa Verde and Grilled Ricotta Salata
**TOTAL: 35 MIN**
8 SERVINGS ●
This creative, fresh-tasting pasta salad is nothing like the ones that have given cold pasta a bad name. Chef Shea Gallante of Cru restaurant in New York City forgoes the standard mayonnaise-based dressing in favor of a tangy salsa verde made with tomatillos, garlic, jalapeños, anchovy and herbs. He tosses the salsa verde with warm farfalle, then tops the pasta with grated cheese from a slab of salty grilled ricotta salata.
¾ pound tomatillos—husked,
   rinsed and halved
4 garlic cloves, thinly sliced
2 jalapeños, seeded and sliced
1 anchovy fillet, chopped
¼ cup chopped basil
¼ cup chopped flat-leaf parsley
¼ cup snipped chives
1 cup extra-virgin olive oil, plus
   more for drizzling
1 teaspoon fresh lime juice
Salt and freshly ground pepper
1½ pounds farfalle
One ½-pound piece of ricotta salata
½ cup coarsely chopped
   celery leaves
1. Light a grill. Bring a medium saucepan of water to a boil and cook the tomatillos for 1 minute. Drain the tomatillos and let them cool. In a food processor, pulse the tomatillos with the sliced garlic and jalapeños, the anchovy fillet, basil, parsley and chives until combined. Slowly pour in 1 cup of the olive oil, pulsing until the salsa is blended but still slightly chunky. Stir in the lime juice and season the salsa with salt and pepper.
2. In a large pot of boiling salted water, cook the farfalle until al dente.
3. Drizzle olive oil over the ricotta salata and grill over high heat until lightly charred, about 2 minutes per side.

4. Drain the pasta and return it to the pot. Stir in the salsa and celery leaves. Grate half of the ricotta salata over the pasta and toss well. Season with salt and pepper and transfer to a serving bowl. Grate the remaining ricotta salata over the farfalle and serve. —*Shea Gallante*
**WINE** Fresh, minerally Vermentino.

## Orzo Salad with Feta, Spinach and Mushrooms
**TOTAL: 30 MIN**
8 SERVINGS ● ●
2¼ cups orzo (15 ounces)
3 tablespoons pine nuts
⅓ cup plus 2 tablespoons
   extra-virgin olive oil
6 ounces shiitake mushrooms,
   stemmed, caps cut into
   1-inch pieces
Salt and freshly ground pepper
¼ cup red wine vinegar
2 tablespoons fresh lemon juice
2 cups spinach leaves (1½ ounces),
   cut into thin strips
2 celery ribs, cut into ¼-inch dice
9 ounces feta cheese, crumbled
   (1½ cups)
1. In a large pot of boiling salted water, cook the orzo until al dente. Drain and transfer to a large bowl; let cool.
2. In a medium skillet, toast the pine nuts over moderate heat, shaking the skillet until the nuts are golden, 3 minutes. Transfer to a plate. Add 2 tablespoons of the olive oil to the skillet. Add the shiitake, season with salt and pepper and cook over moderate heat, stirring occasionally, until tender and browned, 5 minutes. Set aside.
3. In a small bowl, whisk together the vinegar, lemon juice and remaining ⅓ cup of olive oil; add to the orzo to loosen it up.
4. Toss the spinach, celery, feta, pine nuts and mushrooms with the orzo and season with salt and pepper. Serve at room temperature or lightly chilled. —*Carrie Dove*
**WINE** Fruity, soft Chenin Blanc.

## Whole Wheat Spaghetti and Turkey Meatballs

**ACTIVE: 45 MIN; TOTAL: 1 HR 30 MIN**

**4 SERVINGS** ● ● ●

- 5 tablespoons extra-virgin olive oil
- ¾ cup finely chopped onion
- 4 garlic cloves, very finely chopped
- 1 small celery rib, very finely chopped
- 1 small carrot, grated
- Two 28-ounce cans whole plum tomatoes with juices, crushed
- ¼ cup finely chopped basil leaves
- Kosher salt and freshly ground pepper
- 2 tablespoons bread crumbs
- 2 tablespoons low-fat milk
- 1 large egg white
- 1 tablespoon chopped fresh oregano
- 1 pound ground turkey
- ½ pound whole wheat spaghetti
- Freshly grated Parmesan cheese, for serving

**1.** In a medium casserole or Dutch oven, heat 2 tablespoons of the olive oil until shimmering. Add ½ cup of the onion and 3 of the very finely chopped garlic cloves along with the celery and carrot and cook over moderately high heat, stirring, until the vegetables are softened but not browned, about 5 minutes. Add the canned tomatoes with their juices and all but 1 teaspoon of the chopped basil; season the sauce with salt and pepper and bring to a simmer. Cook the tomato sauce over moderately low heat for 1 hour, stirring occasionally.

**2.** Meanwhile, in a small skillet, heat 1 teaspoon of the olive oil. Add the remaining ¼ cup of onion and 1 chopped garlic clove and cook over moderately high heat until softened, about 4 minutes. Transfer to a medium bowl and let cool. Stir in the bread crumbs, milk and egg white. Add the oregano, 2 teaspoons of kosher salt, ½ teaspoon of pepper and the remaining 1 teaspoon of basil. Add the ground turkey and knead until combined. With lightly moistened hands, roll the mixture into thirty-six 1-inch meatballs and arrange them on a large baking sheet. Refrigerate the meatballs for 30 minutes.

**3.** In a large nonstick skillet, heat the remaining 2 tablespoons plus 2 teaspoons of olive oil until shimmering. Add half of the meatballs and cook over high heat, turning, until browned and cooked through, about 6 minutes. Using a slotted spoon, transfer the meatballs to a paper towel–lined plate. Repeat with the remaining meatballs. Add the meatballs to the tomato sauce and simmer over low heat for 15 minutes; season with salt and pepper.

**4.** In a large pot of boiling salted water, cook the pasta until al dente. Drain the pasta well and return it to the pot. Add half of the tomato sauce and toss to coat. Transfer the spaghetti to a large serving bowl and pass the remaining sauce, meatballs and Parmesan cheese at the table.
—*Chef Bobo*

**MAKE AHEAD** The meatballs can be refrigerated in their sauce in an airtight container for up to 2 days.

**WINE** Cherry-inflected, earthy Sangiovese.

## Pecorino Ravioli with Walnuts and Marjoram

**TOTAL: 30 MIN**

**4 SERVINGS** ●

In adapting this recipe from chef Shea Gallante at Cru restaurant in New York City, F&W's Marcia Kiesel substituted store-bought wonton wrappers for labor-intensive fresh pasta and was thrilled with the results. Wonton wrappers are milder-tasting than fresh pasta, which makes them a better showcase for the nutty brown butter, delicate young pecorino cheese and fresh marjoram.

- ¾ cup walnuts
- ½ pound young pecorino cheese, such as Rossellino, rind removed, cheese grated (1½ cups)
- ½ cup heavy cream
- Salt and freshly ground pepper
- 48 wonton wrappers
- 6 tablespoons unsalted butter
- 2 tablespoons marjoram leaves

**1.** Preheat the oven to 350°. Put the walnuts in a pie plate and bake them for about 5 minutes, or until they are lightly toasted and fragrant. Let the walnuts cool, then coarsely chop them.

**2.** Bring a large pot of salted water to a gentle simmer. In a medium bowl, stir together the cheese and cream; season lightly with salt and pepper. On a work surface, lay out 4 wonton wrappers and moisten the edges with water. Place 2 teaspoons of the cheese filling in the center of each wrapper. Top the wontons with 4 more wrappers, press to remove any air pockets and then press well around the edges to seal. Transfer the ravioli to a lightly floured baking sheet and cover lightly with plastic wrap. Repeat with the remaining wrappers and cheese filling.

**3.** In a medium skillet, cook the butter over moderate heat until it just begins to brown, about 5 minutes; remove from the heat.

**4.** Add the ravioli to the simmering water and cook until just tender, about 2 minutes. Remove from the heat. With a slotted spoon, carefully transfer the ravioli to a large platter and blot dry with paper towels. Reheat the butter, letting it boil over moderately high heat until richly browned. Add the marjoram leaves and let wilt, about 5 seconds. Pour the browned butter over the ravioli, sprinkle with the toasted walnuts and serve right away.
—*Marcia Kiesel*

**MAKE AHEAD** The assembled ravioli can be covered with plastic wrap and refrigerated for up to 4 hours.

**WINE** Fresh, lively Soave.

PECORINO RAVIOLI WITH
WALNUTS AND MARJORAM

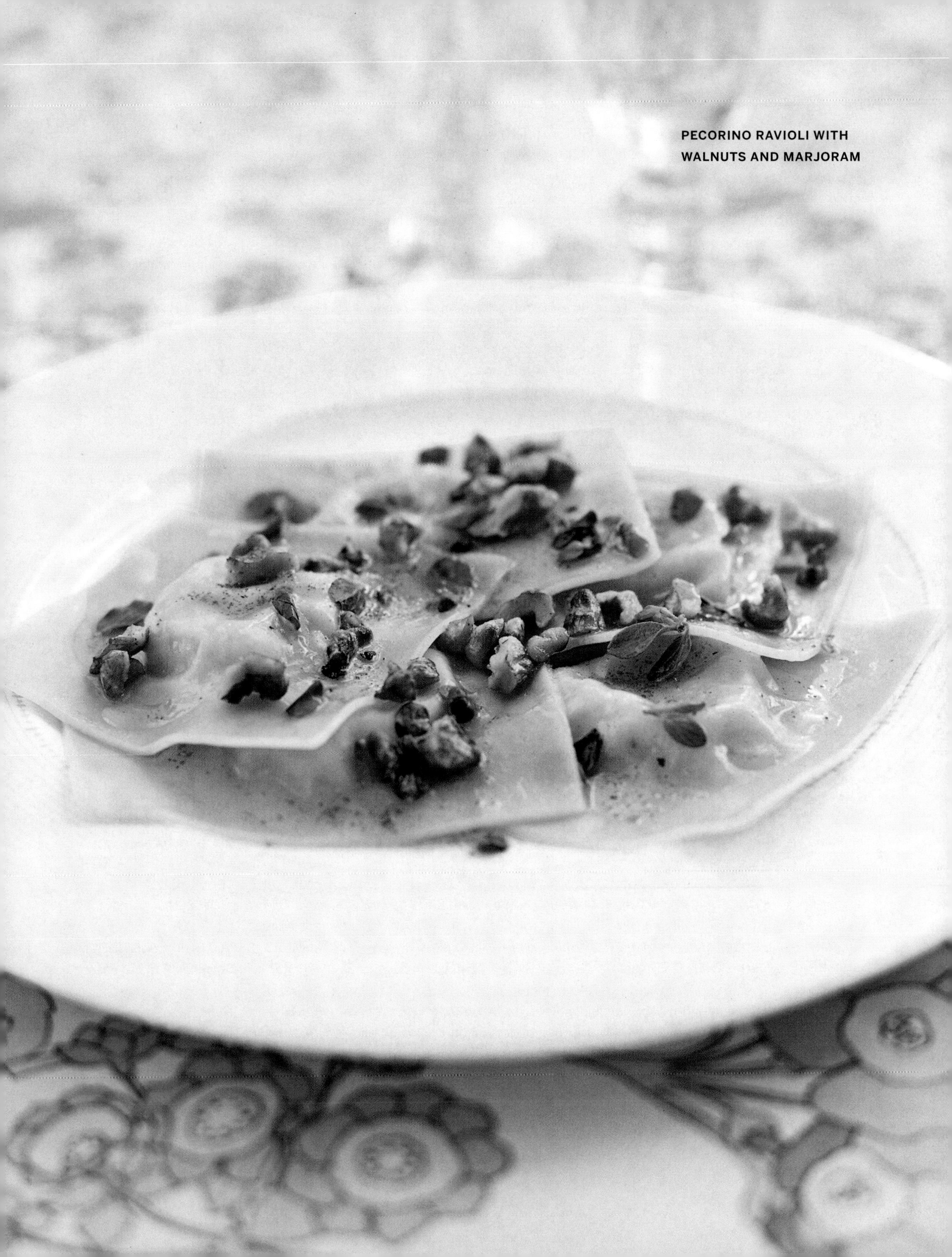

# pasta

## Sweet Potato Gnocchi with Pecans and Brown Butter

**ACTIVE: 1 HR 45 MIN;**

**TOTAL: 2 HR 45 MIN**

10 SERVINGS ●

- 1½ cups plus 2 tablespoons kosher salt
- 3 baking potatoes (1½ pounds)
- 2 medium sweet potatoes (1 pound)
- 2 large egg yolks
- 1½ cups all-purpose flour, plus more for dusting
- 3 tablespoons extra-virgin olive oil
- 6 tablespoons unsalted butter
- 1 cup pecan halves, chopped

**1.** Preheat the oven to 375°. Spread 1½ cups of the salt on a baking sheet. Set all of the potatoes on the salt and bake for 1 hour, or until tender. Let cool.

**2.** Peel the baked potatoes. Work them through a ricer into a large bowl. Mix in the remaining 2 tablespoons of salt, the egg yolks and the 1½ cups of flour. Turn the dough out onto a lightly floured work surface and knead it gently 3 or 4 times; add more flour if necessary to keep the dough from sticking. Cut the dough into 6 pieces and cover with a clean, barely damp kitchen towel.

**3.** Bring a large pot of water to a boil. Prepare a large bowl of ice water. Working with 1 piece at a time, roll the gnocchi dough on a lightly floured work surface into a ¾-inch-thick rope. Cut the rope into ½-inch lengths. Using your thumb, roll each piece along the back of the tines of a fork to make indentations. Transfer the gnocchi to a lightly floured baking sheet.

**4.** Salt the boiling water. Add one-third of the gnocchi and stir gently until they begin to rise to the surface, then cook until the gnocchi are just tender, about 1 minute longer. Using a slotted spoon, transfer the gnocchi to the ice water, then drain well on paper towels. Repeat with the remaining gnocchi. In a large bowl, toss the gnocchi with the olive oil. Spread the gnocchi on 2 baking sheets.

**5.** In a very large skillet, melt 2 tablespoons of the butter. Cook the butter over moderate heat until it begins to brown, about 1 minute. Add one-third of the pecans and cook, stirring, until the nuts are toasted, about 2 minutes. Add one-third of the gnocchi and cook until they are golden brown and warmed through; transfer the gnocchi to a bowl. Repeat with the remaining butter, pecans and gnocchi in 2 more batches. Serve the sweet potato gnocchi immediately. —*Allison Vines-Rushing and Slade Rushing*

**MAKE AHEAD** The gnocchi can be prepared through Step 4, covered tightly with plastic wrap and refrigerated overnight.

**WINE** Complex, aromatic Chenin Blanc.

## Toasted Spaghetti with Clams

**TOTAL: 25 MIN**

4 SERVINGS ● ●

The method used here is very similar to that for cooking risotto, but spaghetti fills in for the arborio rice: Catalan chef Ferran Adrià of El Bulli, in Rosas, Spain, toasts the spaghetti in a pan with a little oil, then adds clam juice until the pasta is fully cooked and loaded with briny flavor.

- 3 tablespoons extra-virgin olive oil
- ¾ pound spaghetti, broken into 2-inch lengths
- 2 garlic cloves, minced

**Crushed red pepper**

- 3 cups bottled clam broth
- 1 cup water
- 3 dozen littleneck clams, rinsed
- ¼ cup minced flat-leaf parsley

In a large, deep skillet, heat the olive oil until shimmering. Add the spaghetti and cook over moderate heat, stirring constantly, until golden, about 3 minutes. Add the garlic and a large pinch of crushed red pepper and cook until fragrant, about 1 minute. Add the clam broth and water and bring to a boil. Cover tightly and cook over moderate heat until the pasta is barely al dente, about 8 minutes. Nestle the clams into the pasta, cover and cook until the pasta is al dente and the clams open, about 7 minutes. Discard any clams that do not open. Add a few tablespoons of water if the pasta is too dry. Stir in the parsley and serve. —*Ferran Adrià*

**WINE** Zesty, fresh Vinho Verde.

## Tonnarelli with Pecorino and Black Pepper

**TOTAL: 15 MIN**

4 SERVINGS ●

For this take on the classic Roman *cacio e pepe* (cheese and pepper), *tonnarelli* (a kind of fresh square spaghetti) is tossed with sheep's-milk cheese and lots of spicy, freshly ground black pepper. Adding vegetable stock to the dish instead of the usual pasta cooking liquid makes the melted cheese even more velvety.

- ¾ pound fresh egg *tonnarelli,* tagliarini or thin fettuccine
- 1 cup freshly grated Pecorino Romano cheese (3 ounces), plus more for serving
- ½ cup freshly grated Parmesan cheese (1½ ounces)
- ½ cup vegetable stock or low-sodium broth, warmed
- 1 teaspoon freshly ground black pepper, plus more for serving

**1.** In a large pot of boiling salted water, cook the *tonnarelli,* stirring, until al dente, about 6 minutes.

**2.** Meanwhile, in a large, warmed pasta bowl, stir the 1 cup of Pecorino Romano with the Parmesan, stock and pepper.

**3.** Drain the *tonnarelli* thoroughly and add it to the bowl. Using 2 forks, toss the pasta until the sauce is creamy. Mound the pasta on plates and serve at once, passing more Pecorino Romano and pepper at the table. —*Marco Gallotta*

**WINE** Fresh, minerally Vermentino.

In an F&W tasting of 65 artisanal extra-virgin olive oils from California, there were six standouts.

**Apollo 2005 Mistral Organic** A soft, round and buttery blend of Provençal varietals. DETAILS $20 for 500 ml; 530-692-2314 or apollooliveoil.com.

**Lila Jaeger** A mix of old-world (Aglandau, Bouteillan) olives; unctuous, smooth and peppery. DETAILS $24 for 375 ml; 800-676-7176 or katzandco.com.

**Olivina Estate Mission** A full-bodied oil with herbal and bitter flavors, made from olives grown on century-old trees. DETAILS $18 for 375 ml; 925-455-8710 or theolivina.com.

**Skipstone Ranch Melina's Harvest** Produced from Manzanillo olives; fruity and spicy with a long, green-olive finish. DETAILS $25 for 375 ml; 707-433-9124 or skipstoneranch.com.

**Stonehouse House Oil** A nicely balanced mix of olives, including Sevillano and Arbequina. DETAILS $11 for 500 ml; 800-865-4836 or stonehouseoliveoil.com.

**Willow Creek Olive Ranch's Pasolivo** A Tuscan-style olive oil with a vibrant green color and a sharp grassy flavor. DETAILS $25 for 500 ml; 805-227-0186 or pasolivo.com.

SEAFOOD PASTA WITH
TUSCAN HOT OIL

## Seafood Pasta with Tuscan Hot Oil

**TOTAL: 25 MIN**
6 SERVINGS ● ●
TUSCAN HOT OIL
½ cup extra-virgin olive oil
¼ cup plus 2 teaspoons
   dried parsley
2 teaspoons crushed red pepper
2 teaspoons sea salt
SEAFOOD PASTA
¼ cup extra-virgin olive oil
1 medium onion, finely chopped
1 garlic clove, minced
½ cup dry white wine
2 cups tomato sauce, preferably
   homemade
½ cup clam broth
1 pound large shrimp, shelled
   and deveined
1 pound mussels, scrubbed
   and debearded
1 pound cockles, scrubbed
   and rinsed
½ pound sea scallops
½ pound red snapper fillets,
   cut into 1½-inch pieces
½ pound small squid, cut into
   ½-inch rings
1 pound bucatini

**1.** MAKE THE TUSCAN HOT OIL: In a small bowl, combine the olive oil with the parsley, crushed red pepper and sea salt.

**2.** MAKE THE SEAFOOD PASTA: In a large, deep skillet, heat the olive oil until shimmering. Add the onion and garlic and cook over moderately high heat until softened, about 5 minutes. Add the wine and cook until reduced by half, about 3 minutes. Add the tomato sauce, clam broth and 1½ tablespoons of the Tuscan hot oil and bring to a boil. Add the shrimp, mussels and cockles and cook, uncovered, until the shells just begin to open and the shrimp start to curl, about 2 minutes. Add the scallops and snapper and cook until the shells are nearly all opened and the fish is nearly cooked through, 2 to 3 minutes.

Add the squid and cook until opaque, about 1 minute. Discard any mussels and cockles that do not open.

**3.** Meanwhile, in a large pot of boiling salted water, cook the bucatini until al dente. Drain the pasta well.

**4.** Transfer the pasta to a large bowl and toss with the seafood and its sauce. Serve the pasta, passing the remaining Tuscan hot oil at the table for drizzling. —*Rolando Beramendi*
**WINE** Light, fresh Pinot Grigio.

## Olive-Mint Pesto Meatballs with Fettuccine

**TOTAL: 30 MIN**
6 SERVINGS ●
If you're pressed for time, good store-bought pesto works here too.
3 slices good-quality packaged
   white bread, crusts removed,
   bread torn
⅓ cup whole milk
Olive-Mint Pesto (recipe follows)
1 scallion, thinly sliced
1 large egg
¾ pound ground turkey
¾ pound ground beef
Kosher salt and freshly ground pepper
2 tablespoons extra-virgin olive oil
¾ pound fettuccine
Freshly grated Parmesan, for serving

**1.** In a large bowl, soak the bread in the milk for 1 minute, mashing it. Using your hand, press out the milk and drain it off. Add ⅓ cup of the pesto, the scallion and the egg to the soaked bread and mash to a paste. Add the turkey and beef and season with 1½ teaspoons of salt and ½ teaspoon of pepper. Mix until well blended.

**2.** Line a baking sheet with plastic wrap. Using lightly moistened hands, roll the meat mixture into twenty-four 1½-inch balls and transfer to the baking sheet.

**3.** In a large skillet, heat the olive oil until shimmering. Add the meatballs in a single layer and cook over moderately high heat,

turning occasionally, until browned and cooked through, about 10 minutes.

**4.** Meanwhile, in a saucepan of boiling salted water, cook the fettuccine until al dente. Drain the pasta, reserving ¼ cup of the cooking water. Transfer the fettuccine to a large bowl. Add the remaining ⅔ cup of pesto and a few tablespoons of the reserved pasta cooking water and toss until the pasta is evenly coated and moistened. Transfer the pasta to a large platter, leaving some of the pesto in the bowl. Add the meatballs to the bowl and toss with any remaining pesto. Scatter the meatballs on the fettuccine, sprinkle with Parmesan and serve. —*Grace Parisi*
**WINE** Minerally Marsanne or Roussanne.

### OLIVE-MINT PESTO

**TOTAL: 10 MIN**
MAKES 1 CUP ● ● ●
F&W's Grace Parisi likes using a mix of brine- and oil-cured olives for a more complex pesto; her favorites are green Sicilian, Calamata, Cerignola and oil-cured Moroccan.
2 tablespoons tightly packed
   mint leaves
2 tablespoons small capers, drained
1 large garlic clove, smashed
½ teaspoon finely grated
   lemon zest
Pinch of crushed red pepper
¼ cup extra-virgin olive oil
1 cup pitted mixed olives, such as
   Calamata and Cerignola
Freshly ground pepper

In a food processor, pulse the mint with the capers, garlic, lemon zest and crushed red pepper. With the machine on, add the olive oil in a thin stream. Add the olives and pulse until coarsely chopped. Season the pesto with pepper. —*G.P.*

**VARIATION** Stir the pesto into mixed ground meats to make meat loaf, serve it on bruschetta with shaved Parmesan cheese, stir it into soups or whisk it into vinaigrettes.

## Sesame Noodles with Prosciutto

**TOTAL: 30 MIN**

4 SERVINGS ● ●

- ¾ pound dried chow mein noodles or thin spaghetti
- 1 tablespoon Asian sesame oil
- 2 tablespoons peanut oil
- 1 large garlic clove, minced
- ¼ cup chunky peanut butter, preferably natural
- 1 tablespoon balsamic vinegar
- 1 tablespoon soy sauce
- 2 teaspoons finely grated fresh ginger
- 2 teaspoons sugar
- ½ teaspoon crushed red pepper
- ¼ cup chicken stock or low-sodium broth

Salt

- 1½ ounces prosciutto, sliced ⅛ inch thick, cut into matchsticks
- 1 scallion, thinly sliced
- 1 kirby cucumber—peeled, seeded and cut into matchsticks

1. In a large pot of boiling salted water, cook the chow mein noodles until al dente, about 8 to 9 minutes. Drain the noodles, reserving ½ cup of the cooking water. Return the chow mein noodles to the pot and toss with the sesame oil.

2. Meanwhile, in a medium skillet, heat the peanut oil until shimmering. Add the garlic and cook over moderate heat, stirring, just until fragrant, 30 seconds. Add the peanut butter, balsamic vinegar, soy sauce, ginger, sugar and crushed red pepper and stir to form a paste. Add the stock and stir until smooth; season with salt.

3. Pour the peanut sauce over the noodles. Add the prosciutto and scallion and toss until the noodles are coated. Add about ¼ cup of the reserved cooking water and toss until the sauce is creamy, adding more water as needed. Transfer the noodles to bowls, garnish with the cucumber and serve. —*Grace Young*

**WINE** Intense, fruity Zinfandel.

## Baked Pasta with Shrimp

**TOTAL: 45 MIN**

4 SERVINGS

This is an easy version of a classic dish from Spain called *fideus,* which requires toasting pasta in a pot on the stove and stirring constantly. In this recipe, the pasta simply gets baked in the oven until it's wonderfully crisp.

- ¼ cup plus 3 tablespoons extra-virgin olive oil, plus more for drizzling
- 1½ pounds large shrimp, shelled and deveined, shells reserved
- 1 quart water
- 2 pounds cockles, scrubbed
- 8 garlic cloves, very finely chopped
- 1 teaspoon Aleppo pepper or ½ teaspoon crushed red pepper
- ¾ pound angel-hair pasta
- ⅛ teaspoon saffron threads
- ¼ cup heavy cream

Salt and freshly ground pepper

- 1 tablespoon plus 1 teaspoon fresh lemon juice
- 2 teaspoons finely chopped mint
- ½ cup salted roasted almonds, coarsely chopped

1. Preheat the oven to 450°. In a medium saucepan, heat 1 tablespoon of the olive oil. Add the reserved shrimp shells and cook over moderately high heat, stirring, until bright pink, about 3 minutes. Add the water, cover and simmer over moderate heat for 5 minutes. Add the cockles, cover and cook until the cockle shells open, about 3 minutes; discard any cockles that do not open. Strain the shellfish broth through a colander set over a bowl. Remove the cockles from their shells and reserve them separately in a small bowl.

2. In a skillet, heat ¼ cup of the olive oil. Add the garlic and Aleppo pepper and cook over low heat until fragrant and the garlic is lightly browned, about 3 minutes. Scrape the chile-garlic oil into a small bowl.

3. In a large pot of boiling salted water, cook the pasta, stirring, until pliable, about 2 minutes. Drain well and transfer to a bowl. Drizzle the pasta with olive oil and toss to coat. As the pasta cools, toss it frequently to loosen the strands.

4. In the pasta pot, combine the strained shellfish broth with the saffron and boil over high heat until the broth is reduced to 3 cups, about 6 minutes. Add the heavy cream and boil for 1 minute. Add the pasta and stir well. Pour the pasta and the broth into a 9-by-13-inch glass or ceramic baking dish. With 2 forks, toss the pasta with the reserved chile-garlic oil and cockles and season it with salt and pepper. Spread the pasta in an even layer and drizzle it with olive oil. Bake the pasta in the upper third of the oven for 15 minutes, or until the top of the pasta is crispy.

5. Meanwhile, in a large skillet, heat the remaining 2 tablespoons of olive oil. Add the shrimp, season with salt and pepper and cook over moderate heat until just opaque throughout, about 4 minutes. Add the lemon juice and toss well. Remove from the heat and stir in the mint.

6. Cut the baked pasta into 4 squares. With a wide spatula, transfer the pasta squares to plates. Top the pasta with the chopped almonds and the shrimp and serve.
—*Marcia Kiesel*

**WINE** Full-bodied, minerally Riesling.

## Cannelloni with Ricotta, Shrimp and Leeks

**TOTAL: 45 MIN**

4 SERVINGS

This unorthodox version of cannelloni pairs a chive-flecked ricotta filling with an intensely flavored topping of leeks and shrimp that are sautéed in olive oil, then flambéed with Armagnac. The sheets of pasta dough are rolled so thin, you can practically see through them.

1 pound fresh ricotta (2 cups)

1 tablespoon minced chives

Salt and freshly ground pepper

2½ tablespoons unsalted
butter, softened

1 tablespoon freshly grated
Parmesan cheese

¼ pound thin sheets of fresh pasta
(see Note)

2 tablespoons extra-virgin olive oil

2 medium leeks, white and tender
green parts only, sliced crosswise
⅓ inch thick

8 large shrimp—shelled, halved
lengthwise and deveined

1 tablespoon Armagnac or
other brandy

1. Preheat the oven to 350°. In a small bowl, blend the ricotta with the chives and season with salt and pepper. Spread 1 tablespoon of the butter in a 9-by-13-inch baking dish. Sprinkle the Parmesan over the bottom of the dish.

2. Bring a medium saucepan of salted water to a boil. Have ready a large bowl of cold water. Cut the pasta sheets into eight 6-inch squares. Add the sheets to the boiling water and cook them until tender, about 2 minutes. Using a slotted spoon or a Chinese wire skimmer, transfer the sheets to the bowl of cold water and let cool. Spread the sheets on paper towels and pat them dry.

3. Transfer the pasta sheets to a work surface. Spread ¼ cup of the ricotta filling at one edge of each pasta sheet and roll up loosely to make flattened cylinders. Transfer the cannelloni to the prepared baking dish and spread ½ tablespoon of the butter over them. Bake the cannelloni for about 12 minutes, or until heated through.

4. Meanwhile, in a medium skillet, heat the olive oil. Add the leeks, season with salt and pepper and cook over moderately low heat, stirring occasionally, until softened, about 8 minutes. Increase the heat to moderate. Add the shrimp, season with

salt and pepper and stir occasionally until the shrimp are cooked, about 3 minutes. Add the Armagnac and carefully light it with a long-handled match. When the flames die down, swirl in the remaining 1 tablespoon of butter. Spoon the leeks and shrimp over the baked cannelloni and serve. —*Marco Gallotta*

**NOTE** If your fresh pasta sheets are not delicately thin (¹⁄₁₆ to ¹⁄₃₂ inch thick), run them through a pasta machine adjusted to the thinnest setting.

**WINE** Fresh, minerally Vermentino.

## Spaetzle with Buttery Japanese Bread Crumbs

**ACTIVE: 30 MIN; TOTAL: 1 HR 30 MIN**

**6 SERVINGS**

Even though the spaetzle look a bit clunky—they're tablespoon-size—they're so deeply satisfying you'll want to roast a chicken or a beef rib eye simply as an excuse to have them as a side dish.

4 cups all-purpose flour

1½ teaspoons salt

8 large eggs

1⅓ cups milk, plus more if needed

6 tablespoons unsalted butter

½ cup *panko* (Japanese
bread crumbs) or plain
dry bread crumbs

1. In a large bowl, mix the flour with the salt and make a well in the center. Add the eggs to the well and lightly beat them. Whisk the flour into the eggs. Gradually whisk in the milk until a very thick batter forms. Cover the bowl with a damp cloth and let stand for 30 minutes.

2. Meanwhile, in a large nonstick skillet, melt 2 tablespoons of the butter. Add the *panko* and cook over moderately high heat, stirring, until golden, about 3 minutes. Transfer the crumbs to a plate and wipe out the skillet.

3. Bring a large pot of salted water to a boil. Working in batches, using a wet spoon, scoop heaping teaspoons of the batter into

the boiling water. When the spaetzle rise to the surface, boil them until cooked through, about 2 minutes. Using a skimmer or slotted spoon, transfer the spaetzle to a platter; repeat with the remaining batter.

4. Melt 2 tablespoons of the butter in the large skillet. Add half of the spaetzle and cook over moderately low heat for 4 minutes, tossing gently. Transfer the spaetzle back to the platter; repeat with the remaining butter and spaetzle. Sprinkle the bread crumbs over the spaetzle and serve. —*Jean-Georges Vongerichten*

**WINE** Peppery, refreshing Grüner Veltliner.

# F&W taste test

## SPAGHETTI

F&W taste-tested 10 brands of dried spaghetti available at supermarkets around the country. These three were our favorites.

**BARILLA**

Barilla's 29 worldwide plants produce 4,000 tons of pasta daily. The company is the world's largest buyer of wheat.

**DELVERDE**

DelVerde's factory is located in Majella National Park in Abruzzo, Italy, also home to a wolf reserve and 116 species of butterflies.

**DE CECCO**

In 1889, Filippo De Cecco created a low-temperature method for drying pasta that simulates old-fashioned sun-drying.

## Dan Dan Noodles with Pickled Mustard Greens

**TOTAL: 25 MIN**

4 SERVINGS ● ●

- 3 tablespoons soy sauce
- 1 tablespoon brandy or whiskey
- 1 teaspoon hoisin sauce
- 1 teaspoon cornstarch
- ¼ pound ground pork
- 1 tablespoon Asian sesame paste
- 1 teaspoon balsamic vinegar
- 1 tablespoon chili oil
- 1 teaspoon Asian sesame oil
- 1 garlic clove, minced
- 1 cup chicken stock or low-sodium broth
- 1 tablespoon vegetable oil
- 4 heads baby bok choy, quartered lengthwise
- ½ pound thin fresh Asian noodles, preferably Shanghainese, or fresh linguine or spaghetti
- 2 tablespoons minced Chinese pickled mustard greens (optional)
- 2 scallions, white parts only, minced

1. Bring a large saucepan of water to a boil. In a small bowl, mix 1 tablespoon of the soy sauce with the brandy, hoisin sauce and cornstarch. Blend the mixture into the ground pork.

2. In a small bowl, whisk the sesame paste with the vinegar and the remaining 2 tablespoons of soy sauce until smooth. In a small saucepan, heat the chili and sesame oils. Add the garlic and cook over high heat for 30 seconds. Add the sesame paste mixture and simmer for 1 minute. Add the stock and simmer over low heat, stirring occasionally, until reduced slightly, about 3 minutes.

3. In a small skillet, heat the vegetable oil. Add the seasoned ground pork and cook over moderately high heat, breaking up the meat with a spatula, until cooked through, about 3 minutes. Cover the skillet and remove from the heat.

4. Add the bok choy to the boiling water and cook until bright green, 10 seconds. Using a slotted spoon, transfer to 4 small bowls. Cook the noodles in the boiling water until al dente, 3 minutes. Drain well and transfer to the bowls. Pour the sauce over the noodles and spoon the pork on top. Garnish with the pickled mustard greens and scallions and serve. —*Susanna Foo*

**WINE** Vivid, lightly sweet Riesling.

## Scallion-Chicken Noodles

**TOTAL: 30 MIN**

4 SERVINGS ● ●

- ½ pound skinless, boneless chicken thighs
- ¾ pound linguine
- ¼ cup peanut oil
- 1 cup finely chopped scallions
- 1 tablespoon finely grated fresh ginger
- 2 tablespoons soy sauce
- 1 teaspoon Asian sesame oil

Pinch of sugar

Salt and freshly ground pepper

- ¼ cup finely chopped cilantro leaves

1. Bring a saucepan of water to a boil. Add the chicken thighs and bring back to a boil. Remove from the heat, cover and let stand until the chicken is cooked through, about 15 minutes. Drain the chicken and cut it into 1-inch pieces.

2. Meanwhile, in a large pot of boiling salted water, cook the linguine until tender, 12 minutes. Drain, shaking out the excess water.

3. Wipe out the pot. Add the oil and heat until shimmering. Add the scallions and ginger and cook over moderately low heat until fragrant, 1 minute. Add the linguine and chicken along with the soy sauce, sesame oil, sugar and a generous pinch each of salt and pepper. Cook over moderately high heat, tossing, until the noodles are coated and heated through, 1 minute. Toss in the cilantro, transfer to bowls and serve. —*Grace Young*

**WINE** Fruity, low-oak Chardonnay.

## Silky Spaghetti with Prosciutto and Egg

**TOTAL: 20 MIN**

4 TO 6 SERVINGS ●

Lusty carbonara is usually made with eggs, cream, Parmesan cheese and bacon. Sydney chef Bill Granger's easy version—he substitutes prosciutto for bacon and omits the cream altogether—is lighter but just as delicious.

- 1 pound spaghetti
- 4 large organic eggs, at room temperature
- ⅓ cup packed freshly grated Parmesan cheese, plus more for serving
- ½ cup thinly sliced scallions

Salt and freshly ground pepper

- ¼ cup extra-virgin olive oil
- 2 large garlic cloves, very thinly sliced
- 2 ounces thinly sliced prosciutto, coarsely chopped
- ¼ cup dry white wine

1. In a large pot of boiling salted water, cook the spaghetti until al dente.

2. Meanwhile, in a large bowl, beat the eggs with the ⅓ cup of Parmesan cheese, the scallions and a generous pinch each of salt and pepper. In a large skillet, heat the olive oil until shimmering. Add the sliced garlic and cook over moderately high heat until it is fragrant, about 10 seconds. Add the chopped prosciutto and cook, stirring occasionally, until the garlic is golden, about 2 minutes longer. Add the white wine to the skillet and cook until it is nearly evaporated, about 1 minute. Scrape the prosciutto mixture into the bowl with the eggs.

3. Drain the spaghetti and add it to the bowl with the sauce. Toss the spaghetti until it is coated with a thick, creamy sauce. Serve the spaghetti right away, passing extra Parmesan cheese on the side. —*Bill Granger*

**WINE** Dry, fruity sparkling wine.

**SILKY SPAGHETTI WITH PROSCIUTTO AND EGG**

**PAD SEE YEW**

## Pad See Yew

**TOTAL: 30 MIN**

4 SERVINGS ● ● ●

Cookbook author Mai Pham gives a twist to this Thai street-food staple by adding bok choy and replacing the usual pork, chicken or beef with shrimp.

- **3** tablespoons Asian
  fish sauce
- **1** tablespoon miso paste or
  fermented yellow beans
- **1** tablespoon oyster sauce
- **4** teaspoons sugar
- **¼** cup low-sodium soy sauce
- **1** pound bok choy, cut into
  2-inch pieces
- **⅔** pound dried rice stick noodles
- **¼** cup plus 3 tablespoons
  vegetable oil
- **¾** pound shelled and deveined
  medium shrimp

Salt

- **4** large garlic cloves, minced
- **3** large eggs, beaten
- **3** Thai bird chiles or serrano chiles,
  thinly sliced
- **2** tablespoons chopped
  roasted, salted peanuts
  (optional)

Lime wedges, for serving

**1.** In a bowl, mix the fish sauce, miso, oyster sauce, sugar and soy sauce.

**2.** In a large pot of boiling, lightly salted water, cook the bok choy until it is crisp-tender, about 2 minutes. With a slotted spoon, transfer the cooked bok choy to a plate. Add the noodles to the boiling water and cook until firm but pliable, 5 minutes. Drain the noodles and rinse them under cold water; shake out any excess water. Transfer the noodles to a bowl and toss with 1 tablespoon of the oil.

**3.** Heat 1 tablespoon of the oil in a large nonstick skillet. Add the shrimp, season with salt and cook over high heat until pink throughout, 2 minutes. Add the shrimp to the bok choy. Add the remaining ¼ cup plus 1 tablespoon of oil to the skillet and heat until shimmering. Add the garlic and cook, stirring, for 30 seconds. Add the eggs and cook over high heat for about 30 seconds, just until lightly scrambled. Add the noodles and toss lightly. Add the fish sauce mixture and toss. Cook, without stirring, just until the liquid is nearly evaporated, about 5 minutes. Stir the noodles once, then cook until browned on the bottom, 2 to 3 minutes longer. Add the shrimp and bok choy; cook just until heated through. Transfer the noodles to a large platter, sprinkle with the chiles and peanuts and serve with lime wedges. —*Mai Pham*
**WINE** Lively, fruity Merlot.

For the November issue, Louisiana chefs Allison Vines-Rushing and her husband, Slade Rushing, created this Slow-Smoked Turkey with Cane Syrup–Coffee Glaze (P. 115).

92

**poultry**

**PERSIAN ROASTED CHICKEN WITH CHERRY-SAFFRON RICE**　　　　**ROTISSERIE CHICKEN WITH DRIED FRUIT AND PINE NUTS**

## Persian Roasted Chicken with Dried Cherry–Saffron Rice

**ACTIVE: 25 MIN; TOTAL: 1 HR PLUS 1 HR MARINATING**

**6 SERVINGS**

Anoosh Shariat, the executive chef at Park Place on Main in Louisville, Kentucky, likes to use supertart dried sour cherries in this buttery, exotically fragrant rice dish. But raisins, dates or pecans are also delicious.

- ¼ cup extra-virgin olive oil
- 1 onion, finely chopped
- 2 tablespoons fresh lemon juice
- 1 teaspoon ground cumin
- ½ teaspoon saffron threads, crushed
- 6 pounds bone-in chicken breasts, thighs and legs, with skin
- Salt and freshly ground pepper
- 2 cups basmati rice
- 1 stick plus 2 tablespoons (5 ounces) unsalted butter
- ½ cup dried sour cherries (4 ounces)
- 2 tablespoons sugar
- ¼ cup slivered almonds

**1.** Preheat the oven to 375°. In a large bowl, combine the olive oil, onion, lemon juice, cumin and half of the saffron. Add the chicken, season with salt and pepper and turn to coat. Let the chicken stand at room temperature for 1 hour.

**2.** Drain the chicken, scraping off the onion and saffron. Transfer to a large metal roasting pan. Add ½ cup of water, cover with foil and bake for 20 minutes. Uncover and bake for 25 minutes, or until cooked through.

**3.** Bring a large saucepan of salted water to a boil. Add the rice and cook until almost tender, about 10 minutes. Drain the rice in a colander and shake out any excess water. In a bowl, dissolve the remaining saffron in 1 tablespoon of water. Return the rice to the pan and stir in the saffron water.

**4.** In a small skillet, melt the butter with the dried sour cherries and sugar. Spoon one-third of the rice into a buttered 2-quart soufflé dish. Top with half of the sour cherries and slivered almonds. Cover with half of the remaining rice and the remaining sour cherries and almonds. Top with a final layer of rice and pour any remaining butter on top. Cover the soufflé dish with foil and bake for about 20 minutes (while the chicken is baking), or until the rice is tender, light and fluffy.

**5.** Preheat the broiler when the rice is done. Broil the chicken, skin side down, for 2 minutes. Turn the chicken and broil until the skin is browned and crisp, about 3 minutes. Transfer the chicken to a platter. Pour the pan juices into a warm gravy boat. Serve the chicken with the rice, passing the pan juices at the table. —*Anoosh Shariat*

**WINE** Fresh, fruity rosé.

## Rotisserie Chicken with Dried Fruit and Pine Nuts

**TOTAL: 15 MIN**

4 SERVINGS ●

Long-simmered stews made with dried fruit and nuts are typically Catalan. This version starts with a store-bought rotisserie chicken—the ones in Spain are supertasty—finished with a quick fruit-and-nut sauce that uses the flavorful poultry drippings.

- 1 tablespoon extra-virgin olive oil
- ½ cup pitted prunes (3 ounces)
- ½ cup dried apricots (3 ounces)
- ¼ cup dried tart cherries
- 2 tablespoons pine nuts
- ½ cup tawny port
- 1 medium cinnamon stick
- ½ cup chicken stock or low-sodium broth
- 1 rotisserie chicken, cut into 8 pieces, drippings reserved

**1.** Heat the olive oil in a large skillet. Add the prunes with the dried apricots and cherries and the pine nuts and cook over moderate heat, stirring, until the pine nuts are golden and the fruit is browned in spots, about 3 minutes. Add the port and cinnamon stick and cook over moderate heat until the sauce is syrupy, about 5 minutes. Add the chicken stock and chicken drippings and bring to a boil.

**2.** Meanwhile, in a large nonstick skillet, brown the chicken pieces over high heat until the skin is golden and crisp, about 2 minutes. Scrape the dried fruit sauce and liquid into the skillet with the chicken and bring to a boil, turning the pieces of chicken until they are nicely coated with sauce, about 1 minute. Transfer the chicken, dried fruit and pine nuts to plates and serve at once. —*Ferran Adrià*

**WINE** Earthy, medium-bodied Tempranillo.

## Roasted Chicken with Tarragon Jus

**ACTIVE: 40 MIN; TOTAL: 1 HR 35 MIN**

4 SERVINGS

At Lever House in New York City, executive chef Dan Silverman serves this dish with poussin, a very small, young chicken. In her simplified version, F&W's Marcia Kiesel replaced the poussin with regular chicken and served it with sauteed wild mushrooms and a rich, tarragon-scented chicken jus.

- One 4-pound chicken—wing tips, neck and gizzard reserved
- 2½ tablespoons unsalted butter, softened
- Salt and freshly ground pepper
- 1 small onion, thickly sliced
- 1 small carrot, thinly sliced
- ½ cup dry white wine
- 1½ cups chicken stock or low-sodium broth
- ½ pound sugar snap peas
- 2½ tablespoons extra-virgin olive oil
- ½ pound white mushrooms, cut into thin wedges
- ½ pound oyster mushrooms, stems discarded, large caps halved
- 1 shallot, thinly sliced
- 2 large tarragon sprigs, plus 2 teaspoons leaves

**1.** Preheat the oven to 400°. Put the chicken in a small roasting pan. Rub 1 tablespoon of the butter over the chicken and season with salt and pepper. Roast for about 1 hour and 20 minutes, rotating the pan once, until the skin is browned and crisp and the chicken is cooked.

**2.** Meanwhile, in a medium saucepan, melt 1 tablespoon of the butter. Add the wing tips, neck, gizzard, onion and carrot, season with salt and pepper and cook over moderate heat until browned all over, about 10 minutes. Add the wine and simmer over moderately high heat until reduced to 2 tablespoons, about 4 minutes. Add the stock and bring to a boil. Simmer over low heat for 20 minutes.

**3.** In a large skillet, bring ½ inch of water to a boil. Add the sugar snaps and cook over high heat until bright green but still crisp, about 2 minutes. Transfer to a plate and set aside.

**4.** Wipe out the skillet and heat 2 tablespoons of the olive oil. Add the white mushrooms, season with salt and pepper and cook over high heat for 1 minute. Stir and cook over moderate heat until any juices evaporate and the mushrooms start to brown, about 7 minutes. Add the remaining ½ tablespoon of olive oil to the skillet. Add the oyster mushrooms, season with salt and pepper and cook over moderately high heat until browned on the bottom, about 4 minutes. Stir and cook until browned all over, about 3 minutes longer. Add the shallot and cook, stirring, until softened, about 2 minutes. Remove the mushroom mixture from the heat.

**5.** When the chicken is done, tilt it to release the juices from the cavity into the pan. Transfer the chicken to a carving board and keep warm. Pour the pan juices into the saucepan with the stock, scraping in any browned bits. Add the tarragon sprigs and simmer the stock over moderate heat for 5 minutes. Strain the jus through a coarse sieve into a small saucepan and skim the fat from the surface. Boil over high heat until the jus is reduced to ¾ cup, about 4 minutes. Stir in half of the tarragon leaves and season the jus with salt and pepper.

**6.** Reheat the mushrooms over moderately high heat. Add the remaining ½ tablespoon of butter and the blanched sugar snap peas and cook, stirring, until the peas are heated through. Season the vegetables with salt and pepper and stir in the remaining tarragon leaves.

**7.** Carve the chicken and arrange on plates. Spoon the mushrooms and sugar snaps alongside and pass the jus at the table. —*Marcia Kiesel*

**WINE** Rich, complex white Burgundy.

## Whole Grilled Chicken with Wilted Arugula

**ACTIVE: 20 MIN; TOTAL: 1 HR**

**4 SERVINGS**

Cooking a whole chicken on the grill can be tricky, but chef Thomas Keller of the French Laundry in Yountville, California, and Per Se in New York City has perfected a method that uses indirect heat. He adds rosemary sprigs to the coals to infuse the smoke and flavor the chicken.

- 1 bunch rosemary sprigs
- One 3½-pound chicken, preferably free-range
- Salt and freshly ground pepper
- 1 tablespoon olive oil
- 1 large bunch arugula, thick stems discarded
- Quick Pickled Pearl Onions (recipe follows)

**1.** Light a grill using 6 pounds of charcoal briquettes or 8 pounds of hardwood charcoal. When the flames have died down and the coals are white on the outside, divide the coals in half and push them to each side of the grill, leaving the center empty. Top each pile of coals with half of the rosemary sprigs.

**2.** Season the chicken inside and out with a good amount of salt and pepper. Fold the wing tips under the back and tie the legs together. Set the chicken in the center of the grill, breast side up. Cover the grill and cook the chicken without turning for about 50 minutes, or until an instant-read thermometer inserted in the thickest part of a thigh registers 160°. Transfer the chicken to a carving board and let rest for 10 minutes.

**3.** Heat the olive oil in a large skillet. Add the arugula; stir over moderately high heat just until wilted, about 1 minute. Season with salt and pepper. Spread the arugula on a platter. Carve the chicken and arrange on the wilted arugula; serve with the Quick Pickled Pearl Onions. —*Thomas Keller*

**WINE** Minerally Marsanne or Roussanne.

## QUICK PICKLED PEARL ONIONS

**ACTIVE: 15 MIN; TOTAL: 1 HR 15 MIN**

**4 SERVINGS** ● ●

As an unconventional accompaniment to his juicy grilled chicken, Keller likes to serve pickled pearl onions, which add a sweet, tart bite. The vinegary mixture is great for pickling other vegetables, like baby carrots and kirby cucumbers.

- 16 white pearl onions (about 1 cup), root ends trimmed and scored with an X
- ½ cup water
- ½ cup red wine vinegar
- ⅓ cup sugar
- 1½ tablespoons mustard seeds
- ½ teaspoon coriander seeds
- ½ teaspoon black peppercorns

**1.** In a medium saucepan of boiling salted water, cook the pearl onions until they are just tender, about 8 minutes. Drain the pearl onions, rinse them under cold water and drain again. Transfer the pearl onions to a glass bowl.

**2.** Meanwhile, in another medium saucepan, bring the water and vinegar to a boil with the sugar, mustard seeds, coriander seeds and peppercorns. Boil until the sugar dissolves, about 2 minutes. Pour the liquid over the onions and refrigerate for at least 1 hour and for up to 2 days. Drain before serving. —*T.K.*

**MAKE AHEAD** The drained pickled onions can be refrigerated for up to 2 weeks.

## Beer Can Chicken

**ACTIVE: 2 HR; TOTAL: 4 HR 30 MIN**

**PLUS 4 HR OR OVERNIGHT MARINATING**

**4 SERVINGS**

Propping a whole chicken on an open can of beer and slow-roasting it on the grill may seem a bit unusual, but the result is incredible. The beer vapors do little to moisten the chicken; rather, the vertical position of the bird allows its juices to flow down over the breast, keeping it succulent.

- 2 tablespoons Garlicky Barbecue Marinade (recipe follows)
- One 4-pound chicken
- 2 tablespoons Seven-Spice Dry Rub (recipe follows)
- One 12-ounce can of beer
- 1 cup hickory or other hardwood chips, soaked in water
- Cider Mop Spray (recipe follows)
- ½ cup Sweet and Sticky Barbecue Sauce (recipe follows) mixed with ½ cup water

**1.** Rub the marinade all over the chicken and refrigerate overnight, or let stand for 4 hours at room temperature.

**2.** Bring the chicken to room temperature and sprinkle the dry rub all over the skin.

**3.** Light a charcoal fire in a covered grill and set it up for indirect grilling: When the temperature reaches 225°, carefully push the hot coals to one side and place a drip pan filled with 1 cup of water on the opposite side. Alternatively, bring a smoker to 225°. Discard (or drink) half of the beer. Stand the chicken upright on the can, with its legs pointing down.

**4.** Transfer the chicken on the beer can to the grill, setting it over the drip pan, and cover the grill; you'll need to cook the chicken for about 3 hours total. To maintain the temperature at 225°, replenish the charcoal with a fresh batch of burning coals every hour. Add more water to the drip pan when half of it is evaporated. After the first 45 minutes, rotate the chicken, then drain ½ cup of the wood chips and scatter them over the coals. After another 45 minutes, drain and scatter the remaining wood chips over the coals. Rotate the chicken again, and spray the chicken with the mop spray. Rotate and spray the bird twice more, at 45-minute intervals. The chicken is done when an instant-read thermometer inserted in an inner thigh registers 165°. Remove and discard the beer can. Transfer the bird to a carving board; let rest for 20 minutes.

**5.** Remove the drip pan from the grill. Stoke the coals and spread them in an even layer. Replenish with fresh coals to make a moderately hot fire. Cut the chicken in half through the backbone and brush it all over with the diluted barbecue sauce. Grill the chicken skin side down until lightly charred. Turn and brush it with more sauce. Continue grilling, brushing and turning until the chicken skin is crisp and glazed, about 15 minutes. Serve at once. —*Adam Perry Lang*

**WINE** Fruity, light-bodied Beaujolais.

### GARLICKY BARBECUE MARINADE

**TOTAL: 10 MIN**

**MAKES ABOUT 1¼ CUPS** ● ●

"Building layer upon layer of flavor is absolutely crucial to great barbecue," says Adam Perry Lang, chef at Daisy May's BBQ USA in New York City. For the first layer, he usually slathers on a marinade or wet rub the night before cooking.

- 10 garlic cloves, coarsely chopped
- ¼ cup Worcestershire sauce
- 2 tablespoons low-sodium soy sauce
- 1 medium onion, chopped
- ¼ cup water

Put all of the ingredients in a blender and pulse until they are throroughly combined. —*A.P.L.*

**MAKE AHEAD** The marinade can be refrigerated for up to 1 week.

### SEVEN-SPICE DRY RUB

**TOTAL: 5 MIN**

**MAKES ABOUT 1¾ CUPS** ● ●

This basic dry rub is delicious on all types of foods, including chicken, although you can add more chili powder and black pepper when using it on heartier meats like beef and lamb. Since the mixture is versatile and keeps well, buy the ground spices in bulk and premix an extra batch to keep on hand.

- ½ cup dark brown sugar
- ½ cup sweet paprika
- ¼ cup kosher salt
- ¼ cup chili powder
- ¼ cup dry mustard
- 1 tablespoon freshly ground black pepper
- 2 teaspoons Old Bay Seasoning
- ½ teaspoon ground ginger

In a small bowl, whisk together the dark brown sugar, sweet paprika, kosher salt, chili powder, dry mustard, black pepper, Old Bay Seasoning and ginger. —*A.P.L.*

**MAKE AHEAD** The dry rub can be refrigerated or frozen for up to 6 months.

### CIDER MOP SPRAY

**TOTAL: 5 MIN**

**MAKES 2¼ CUPS** ● ●

- 1 cup apple juice
- 1 cup water
- ¼ cup cider vinegar

In a large glass measuring cup, combine the apple juice, water and cider vinegar. Pour the Cider Mop Spray into a spray bottle and refrigerate. —*A.P.L.*

**MAKE AHEAD** The mop spray can be refrigerated for up to 1 week.

### SWEET AND STICKY BARBECUE SAUCE

**ACTIVE: 30 MIN; TOTAL: 1 HR**

**MAKES ABOUT 6½ CUPS** ●

- ½ cup vegetable oil
- 5 garlic cloves, chopped
- 1 medium onion, chopped
- 1 green bell pepper, chopped

Salt

- ¼ cup dark rum
- 3 tablespoons chili powder
- 1 tablespoon freshly ground black pepper
- ½ teaspoon ground allspice
- ½ teaspoon ground cloves
- 1 cup dark brown sugar
- 2 cups water
- 2 cups ketchup
- ½ cup molasses
- ½ cup yellow mustard
- ½ cup cider vinegar
- 2 teaspoons hot sauce

**1.** Heat the vegetable oil in a large saucepan. Add the chopped garlic, onion, green pepper and a large pinch of salt and cook over moderate heat, stirring occasionally, until the onion and green pepper are softened, about 10 minutes. Add the rum and simmer for 2 minutes. Add the chili powder, black pepper, ground allspice and cloves and cook, stirring, until fragrant, about 3 minutes. Add the dark brown sugar, the water, ketchup, molasses, yellow mustard, cider vinegar and hot sauce and simmer over moderate heat, stirring often, until the sauce is thickened, about 30 minutes.

**2.** Transfer the barbecue sauce to a large food processor and puree. Season the barbecue sauce with salt. —*A.P.L.*

**MAKE AHEAD** The Sweet and Sticky Barbecue Sauce can be refrigerated for up to 2 weeks.

## tools

### BBQ FIRE STARTERS

**FatWood pitch-pine sticks** are useful to have on hand to help get a charcoal fire started quickly. **DETAILS** $6 for 4 pounds from Ace Hardware; 866-290-5334 or acehardware.com.

## Fried Chicken Cutlets with Salsa

**TOTAL: 30 MIN**

4 SERVINGS ●

- 3 medium tomatoes—halved, seeded and diced
- 1 medium onion, cut into ¼-inch dice
- ¼ cup coarsely chopped basil
- 1 tablespoon fresh lime juice
- 1 tablespoon extra-virgin olive oil

Kosher salt and freshly ground black pepper

Eight 4-ounce chicken breast cutlets

- ½ cup all-purpose flour
- 3 eggs, lightly beaten
- 1 cup plain bread crumbs

Pinch of cayenne pepper

- ½ cup vegetable oil

**1.** In a medium bowl, mix the tomatoes with the onion, basil, lime juice and olive oil. Season the salsa with salt and pepper.

**2.** Season the chicken cutlets with salt and pepper. Put the flour, eggs and bread crumbs in 3 large, shallow bowls. Stir the cayenne into the bread crumbs. Dredge the chicken cutlets in the flour, shaking off any excess. Dip the chicken in the eggs, then dredge in the bread crumbs, pressing to help the crumbs adhere.

**3.** In a very large skillet, heat the vegetable oil. Working in 2 batches, fry the chicken over moderately high heat, turning once, until cooked through, about 6 minutes. Transfer the chicken to a paper towel–lined plate to drain. Serve with the tomato salsa.
—*Daisy Martinez*

**WINE** Fresh, fruity rosé.

## Roasted Chicken with Walnut-Arugula Pesto

**ACTIVE: 20 MIN; TOTAL: 1 HR PLUS OVERNIGHT MARINATING**

4 SERVINGS ●

One 4-pound chicken, cut into 8 pieces

- 3 garlic cloves, thinly sliced
- 3 medium shallots, thinly sliced

Zest and juice of 1 lemon

- 4 thyme sprigs
- 2 tablespoons minced parsley
- ½ cup extra-virgin olive oil
- ½ cup dry white wine

Salt and freshly ground pepper

Walnut-Arugula Pesto (recipe follows)

**1.** In a large bowl, toss the chicken, garlic, shallots, lemon zest and juice, thyme, parsley, olive oil and wine; season with salt and pepper. Cover and refrigerate overnight.

**2.** Preheat the oven to 425°. Set a rack on a rimmed baking sheet. Remove the chicken from the marinade, scraping off the solids. Arrange the chicken on the rack, skin side up. Roast for 35 to 40 minutes, until the skin is golden and crisp and an instant-read thermometer inserted in a thigh registers 165°. Transfer the chicken to a platter and serve with the Walnut-Arugula Pesto.
—*Gail Hobbs-Page*

**WINE** Lush, fragrant Viognier.

### WALNUT-ARUGULA PESTO

**TOTAL: 25 MIN**

MAKES 2 CUPS ● ● ●

This nutty, fresh-tasting pesto is great with roasted chicken, but it's also super tossed with pasta, as a sandwich spread or even served alongside sliced steak.

- ½ cup walnuts
- 2 bunches arugula (½ pound), thick stems discarded
- 4 garlic cloves, smashed
- ¼ pound Manchego cheese, coarsely shredded

Zest and juice of 1 lemon

- ¾ cup extra-virgin olive oil

Salt and freshly ground pepper

**1.** Preheat the oven to 350°. Put the walnuts in a pie plate and toast for about 8 minutes, or until golden and fragrant. Let cool completely.

**2.** In a food processor, pulse the arugula with the walnuts and garlic until finely chopped. Add the Manchego cheese and the lemon zest and juice and pulse until combined. With the machine on, add the olive oil in a steady stream and process to a smooth paste. Season the pesto with salt and pepper, transfer to a bowl and serve.
—*G.H.P.*

**MAKE AHEAD** The pesto can be refrigerated overnight.

## Citrus-and-Ginger-Roasted Chicken

**ACTIVE: 20 MIN; TOTAL: 1 HR 50 MIN**

4 SERVINGS ●

- 3 lemons
- 2 oranges

One 4½-pound chicken

- 3 tablespoons finely grated ginger

Kosher salt and freshly ground pepper

- 5 tablespoons extra-virgin olive oil
- 3 tablespoons honey

**1.** Preheat the oven to 400°. Finely grate the zest of 1 lemon and 1 orange. Quarter the zested lemon and orange. Set the chicken on a rack in a roasting pan. In a small bowl, combine the citrus zests with 1 tablespoon of the ginger. Generously season the cavity of the chicken with salt and pepper and all of the zest mixture. Stuff as many lemon and orange quarters inside the chicken as will fit.

**2.** Juice the remaining 2 lemons and 1 orange. In a small bowl, mix the citrus juice with the remaining 2 tablespoons of ginger, the olive oil and the honey. Brush the chicken with the juice mixture and roast, basting with the juice every 20 minutes, for 1¼ hours, or until an instant-read thermometer inserted in the thickest part of a thigh registers 165°. If the skin browns too quickly, cover the chicken with foil.

**3.** Transfer the chicken to a cutting board and let rest for 15 minutes. Pour the pan juices into a glass measuring cup and skim off the fat. Remove the chicken skin and discard, carve the meat and transfer to plates. Serve with the pan juices.
—*Ann Withey*

**WINE** Full-bodied, rich Pinot Gris.

CITRUS-AND-GINGER-ROASTED
CHICKEN (OPPOSITE)
AND CARROTS WITH LIME
BUTTER (P. 246)

## Chicken with Honey, Lemon and Oregano

**TOTAL: 45 MIN**

**4 SERVINGS**

Chunks of lemon help make this pleasantly sticky honey chicken distinctive. It's lovely served with a salad of chickpeas, feta, cucumber, tomato and parsley.

- 1 tablespoon extra-virgin olive oil
- One 3½-pound chicken, cut into 8 pieces
- Salt and freshly ground pepper
- 1 red onion, thinly sliced
- 1 head garlic, cloves separated and peeled
- 1 lemon, cut into 8 chunks
- ¾ cup chicken stock or low-sodium broth
- ¼ cup honey
- 1 tablespoon very finely chopped oregano

1. Heat the olive oil in a large skillet. Season the chicken pieces with salt and pepper and add them to the skillet. Cook the chicken pieces over high heat, turning them occasionally, until they are browned all over, about 7 minutes. Transfer the chicken to a plate. Add the red onion and the garlic cloves to the skillet and cook them over moderate heat until the onion is barely softened, about 2 minutes. Return the chicken and any accumulated juices to the skillet. Add the lemon chunks, chicken stock and honey and bring the stock to a boil. Cover the skillet and simmer over moderately low heat until the chicken is cooked through, about 17 minutes.

2. Preheat the broiler. Transfer the chicken pieces to a baking sheet, skin side up, and broil them for 1 minute, until they are crisp and browned. Transfer the broiled chicken to a serving platter.

3. In the skillet, boil the sauce until it's thickened and slightly reduced, about 5 minutes; season the sauce with salt and pepper. Pour the sauce over the chicken, sprinkle with the oregano and serve immediately.

—*Bill Granger*

**WINE** Minerally Marsanne or Roussanne.

## Magnolia Chicken Jambalaya

**TOTAL: 40 MIN**

**6 SERVINGS** ● ●

This jambalaya is only mildly spicy, which is true to the Creole tradition of favoring flavor over heat. Feel free to substitute shrimp or crawfish for the chicken.

- 1¼ cups long-grain white rice
- 2 tablespoons vegetable oil
- 1½ pounds skinless, boneless chicken thighs, cut into ¾-inch pieces
- 3 small green bell peppers, seeded and cut into ½-inch pieces
- 1 large Spanish onion, cut into ½-inch pieces
- 1 carrot, finely diced
- 1 celery rib, finely diced
- 1 large garlic clove, very finely chopped
- 1 teaspoon paprika
- 1 bay leaf
- One 14-ounce can diced tomatoes, drained
- 1 cup dry white wine
- 1 cup chicken stock or low-sodium broth
- Kosher salt and freshly ground black pepper
- Cayenne pepper
- 2 tablespoons very finely chopped parsley
- Hot sauce, for serving

1. In a medium saucepan, bring 6 cups of salted water to a boil. Add the long-grain white rice to the saucepan and cook until the rice is just al dente, about 7 minutes. Drain the cooked rice well, shaking out the excess water.

2. In a large enameled cast-iron casserole, heat the vegetable oil until shimmering. Add the chicken thighs and cook over moderately high heat, stirring occasionally, until the thighs are lightly browned, about 7 minutes. Using a slotted spoon, transfer the chicken to a plate. Add the bell peppers, onion, carrot, celery, garlic, paprika and bay leaf to the casserole and cook, stirring occasionally, until the vegetables are softened, about 10 minutes.

3. Add the drained tomatoes and the chicken to the casserole and cook, stirring, until all of the liquid has evaporated, about 3 minutes. Add the white wine and boil over high heat until it is nearly evaporated, about 4 minutes. Stir the rice into the casserole. Add the chicken stock, season the jambalaya with salt, black pepper and cayenne and bring to a boil. Cook the jambalaya, uncovered, until the rice is tender, about 5 minutes. Discard the bay leaf. Stir in the parsley and serve the jambalaya with hot sauce on the side.

—*Howie Velie*

**MAKE AHEAD** The jambalaya can be refrigerated for up to 2 days. Stir in the parsley before serving.

**WINE** Fruity, low-oak Chardonnay.

# equipment
## NONSTICK PANS

The **Urban Trends** line of nonstick pans from the Italian company Bialetti comes in playful, pretty colors; a comfortable grip and solid weight make the pans perfect for serious cooks. **DETAILS** $20 at laprimashops.com.

## Chicken Tagine with Sweet Potatoes

**ACTIVE: 30 MIN; TOTAL: 1 HR 25 MIN**

**4 SERVINGS** ●

Although lamb is the most common meat for tagine, there are numerous versions made with chicken. You can substitute dates or pitted prunes for the sweet potatoes used here.

- ¼ cup plus 1 tablespoon extra-virgin olive oil
- One 4-pound chicken, cut into 8 pieces
- Salt and freshly ground pepper
- 1 large onion, coarsely chopped
- 1 teaspoon ground ginger
- 1 teaspoon ground cinnamon
- ¾ pound white or yellow sweet potatoes, peeled and sliced crosswise ⅛ inch thick
- 2 large tomatoes, finely chopped
- 2 garlic cloves, minced
- 1 tablespoon chopped parsley
- ½ cup water

**1.** In a large enameled cast-iron casserole, heat 2 tablespoons of the olive oil. Season the chicken with salt and pepper and cook over moderately high heat until lightly browned, about 3 minutes per side. Transfer the chicken to a plate.

**2.** Add the remaining 3 tablespoons of olive oil to the casserole along with the onion, ginger, cinnamon and 1 teaspoon of freshly ground pepper. Cook over low heat, stirring occasionally, until the onion is softened, about 7 minutes. Arrange the chicken pieces in the casserole in an even layer. Spread the sweet potato slices over the chicken and season with salt and pepper. Sprinkle evenly with the tomatoes, garlic and parsley. Add the water to the casserole and bring to a simmer. Cover and cook the tagine over low heat until the chicken and sweet potatoes are tender, about 50 minutes.

**3.** Using a spatula, carefully transfer the sweet potatoes to a large bowl. Add the chicken pieces to the bowl and keep warm. Boil the sauce over high heat until slightly thickened, about 5 minutes. Season with salt and pepper. Pour the sauce over the chicken and sweet potatoes and serve. —*Dar Liqama Cooking School*

**MAKE AHEAD** The chicken tagine can be prepared through Step 2 and refrigerated for up to 3 days.

**WINE** Lush, fragrant Viognier.

## Sweet Spiced Chicken Breasts with Anisette

**TOTAL: 20 MIN**

**4 SERVINGS** ● ●

*Aguardiente de anís,* a clear, anise-flavored brandy, is delicious with the cinnamon and other spices in this succulent dish. Use dry *aguardiente* or substitute Pernod.

- ¼ cup dry white wine
- ¼ cup water
- 1 tablespoon anisette or Pernod
- ¼ teaspoon ground cinnamon
- Pinch of ground cloves
- Pinch of freshly grated nutmeg
- Four 6-ounce skinless, boneless chicken breast halves
- Salt and freshly ground pepper
- 2 tablespoons extra-virgin olive oil
- 2 garlic cloves, minced

**1.** In a small bowl, stir together the wine, water and anisette. In another small bowl, mix the cinnamon, cloves and nutmeg.

**2.** Season the chicken with salt and pepper. In a large skillet, heat the olive oil until shimmering. Add the chicken breasts and cook over high heat until browned on the bottom, about 3 minutes. Turn the chicken and scatter the garlic in the skillet.

**3.** Sprinkle the spices over the chicken. Pour the wine mixture into the skillet, cover and simmer over moderate heat until the chicken is cooked through, about 4 minutes; season with salt and pepper. Transfer the chicken to plates, spoon the sauce on top and serve. —*Janet Mendel*

**WINE** Fruity, soft Chenin Blanc.

## Grilled Chicken Breasts with Spicy Pecan Butter

**TOTAL: 30 MIN PLUS 1 HR MARINATING**

**4 SERVINGS** ●

- Four 6-ounce skinless, boneless chicken breast halves, pounded ½ inch thick
- ½ cup Worcestershire sauce
- 2 teaspoons vegetable oil
- ½ cup chopped pecans
- 6 tablespoons unsalted butter
- ¼ cup finely chopped onion
- ⅛ teaspoon cayenne pepper
- Salt

**1.** Put the chicken breast halves in a resealable plastic bag, add the Worcestershire sauce and vegetable oil and seal. Shake the bag to coat the chicken with the marinade, then refrigerate for 1 hour.

**2.** Meanwhile, preheat the oven to 350°. Light a grill. Put the chopped pecans in a pie plate and bake them for 7 minutes, or until they are golden brown; let the pecans cool. In a small skillet, melt the butter. Add the onion and cayenne and cook over moderate heat until the onion has softened, about 4 minutes. Add the pecans to the skillet, season with salt and remove the skillet from the heat. Pour 1 tablespoon of the melted butter into a small bowl.

**3.** Remove the chicken breasts from the marinade and grill them over moderately high heat until they are nicely charred, about 4 minutes. Turn the chicken breasts and brush the cooked side with some of the reserved melted butter. Grill the chicken breasts until charred on the other side and just cooked through, about 4 minutes. Brush the second side of the chicken breasts with more of the reserved melted butter and transfer the chicken to a platter to rest for 5 minutes. Reheat the pecan sauce, spoon it over the chicken breasts and serve immediately. —*Cheryl Alters Jamison and Bill Jamison*

**WINE** Ripe, juicy Pinot Noir.

## Crisp Spiced Chicken

**TOTAL: 30 MIN**
6 SERVINGS ●

- 2 plum tomatoes, diced
- ½ cup crumbled feta cheese (3 ounces)
- 2 tablespoons extra-virgin olive oil
- 1 jalapeño, seeded and minced
- 2 tablespoons chopped flat-leaf parsley
- ½ cup tahini paste
- ½ cup water
- 2 tablespoons fresh lemon juice
- 1 garlic clove, smashed

Salt and freshly ground black pepper
- ½ cup all-purpose flour, for dusting
- 2 large eggs, beaten

One 6-ounce package falafel mix
- 2 pounds thin chicken cutlets

Vegetable oil, for frying

**1.** Preheat the oven to 225°. In a medium bowl, toss the diced plum tomatoes, crumbled feta cheese, olive oil, minced jalapeño and chopped parsley.

**2.** In a mini food processor, puree the tahini with the water, lemon juice and garlic until smooth. Season the sauce with salt and pepper and transfer to a small bowl.

**3.** Put the flour, beaten eggs and falafel mix in 3 shallow bowls. Season the chicken cutlets with salt and pepper on both sides and dust with flour. Dip the chicken in the beaten egg, then coat in the falafel mix.

**4.** In a large nonstick skillet, heat ¼ inch of vegetable oil until shimmering. Working in batches, fry the chicken over moderately high heat, turning once, until crisp, about 6 minutes. Drain on paper towels. Transfer the chicken to an ovenproof platter; keep warm in the oven. Serve the fried chicken with the salad and sauce.
—*Grace Parisi*

**WINE** Fruity, light-bodied Beaujolais.

## Chicken with Mushroom Hash

**TOTAL: 30 MIN**
4 SERVINGS ●

"Making hash is a great way to build a dish from odds and ends," says Marc Meyer of New York City's Cookshop and Five Points restaurants. In fall, when pears and potatoes are abundant, he combines them with shiitake mushrooms for a rustic hash to serve with roasted chicken.

Four 8- to 10-ounce bone-in chicken breast halves
Salt and freshly ground pepper
- 3 tablespoons extra-virgin olive oil
- 1 medium onion, finely chopped
- 2 baking potatoes, peeled and cut into ½-inch cubes
- ¼ pound shiitake mushrooms, stems discarded, caps sliced
- 2 thyme sprigs
- ½ cup water
- 2 Bosc pears, cored and cut into ½-inch pieces

**1.** Preheat the oven to 400°. Season the chicken breasts with salt and pepper. In a large, deep skillet, heat 2 tablespoons of the olive oil until shimmering. Add the chicken, skin side down, and cook over moderately high heat, turning once, until browned, about 6 minutes. Transfer to a baking dish. Roast the chicken for 15 minutes, or until the juices run clear when the breasts are pierced.

**2.** Meanwhile, in the same skillet, heat the remaining 1 tablespoon of oil until shimmering. Add the onion and cook, stirring, until barely softened, 3 minutes. Add the potatoes, shiitake and thyme and cook, stirring, for 2 minutes; season with salt and pepper. Add the water, cover and cook until the potatoes are browned, about 7 minutes. Add the pears, cover and cook over moderately low heat until crisp-tender, about 3 minutes longer. Discard the thyme. Transfer the chicken to plates and serve with the hash. —*Marc Meyer*

**WINE** Ripe, juicy Pinot Noir.

## Grilled Chicken and Watercress Salad with Canadian Bacon

**ACTIVE: 25 MIN; TOTAL: 1 HR**
4 SERVINGS ● ●

- 2 garlic cloves, minced
- 1 teaspoon minced rosemary
- 3 tablespoons plus 1 teaspoon extra-virgin olive oil

Freshly ground pepper
Four 6-ounce skinless, boneless chicken breast halves
- ½ cup whole wheat bread cubes (½-inch cubes)
- 1½ ounces Canadian bacon, cut into ½-inch dice (½ cup)
- ¼ cup golden raisins
- 2 tablespoons sherry vinegar
- 1 tablespoon Dijon mustard
- 1 tablespoon fresh lemon juice

Salt
Two 6-ounce bunches watercress, thick stems discarded
- ¼ cup walnut pieces

**1.** Preheat the oven to 400°. In a dish, mix the garlic, rosemary, 1 tablespoon of the oil, 1 teaspoon of pepper and the chicken; turn to coat. Refrigerate for 30 minutes.

**2.** Light a grill or preheat a grill pan. Bake the bread in a pie plate for 5 minutes. In a nonstick skillet, heat 1 teaspoon of the oil. Add the bacon and raisins and cook over moderately high heat until browned, 1 minute. Transfer to a plate. Add 1 tablespoon of the vinegar, then scrape it onto the plate.

**3.** In a small bowl, mix the mustard with the lemon juice and the remaining 2 tablespoons of olive oil and 1 tablespoon of vinegar; season with salt and pepper.

**4.** Salt the chicken. Grill over high heat until lightly charred and just cooked, 4 minutes per side. Transfer to a carving board.

**5.** In a bowl, toss the watercress, walnuts, croutons, bacon and raisins with the dressing. Cut each breast into 3 crosswise pieces on the bias. Mound the salad and chicken on plates and serve. —*James Boyce*

**WINE** Juicy, spicy Grenache.

CHICKEN AND WATERCRESS SALAD WITH CANADIAN BACON

BAKED CHICKEN WITH POTATOES, FENNEL AND MINT

## Baked Chicken with Potatoes, Fennel and Mint

ACTIVE: 30 MIN; TOTAL: 1 HR 15 MIN

4 SERVINGS ●

- 2 medium fennel bulbs, quartered and cored
- 2 tablespoons extra-virgin olive oil
- Four ¾-pound whole chicken legs—skin discarded and fat trimmed, separated into drumsticks and thighs
- Salt and freshly ground black pepper
- ¾ cup dry white wine
- 1 cup water
- 2 large Yukon Gold potatoes (½ pound each), peeled and sliced ¼ inch thick
- 1 large onion, thinly sliced
- 4 garlic cloves, unpeeled
- 3 bay leaves
- 1 tablespoon chopped rosemary
- 1 tablespoon chopped mint

1. Preheat the oven to 425°. In a saucepan of boiling salted water, cook the quartered fennel bulbs over high heat for 5 minutes. Drain the fennel and pat dry.

2. In a large skillet, heat the olive oil until shimmering. Season the chicken drumsticks and thighs with salt and black pepper and cook the chicken over moderately high heat until browned, about 5 minutes per side. Transfer the chicken to a large roasting pan and arrange the pieces around the edges.

3. Add the white wine to the skillet and simmer over moderate heat for 2 minutes, scraping up any browned bits. Add the water and simmer for 1 minute, then pour the liquid into the roasting pan. Arrange the potatoes in the center of the roasting pan in an even layer. Season the potatoes with salt and pepper. Arrange the onion on top of the potatoes; season with salt and pepper. Scatter the garlic, bay leaves, rosemary and mint over all. Arrange the parboiled fennel quarters over the top of the onions. Cover the roasting pan with foil and bake for about 35 minutes, or until the chicken is cooked and the potatoes and fennel are tender.

4. Transfer the chicken and vegetables to a serving platter. Discard the bay leaves. Set the roasting pan over high heat and boil until the pan juices are reduced to ⅔ cup, about 3 minutes. Season the pan juices with salt and pepper and pour them into a warmed gravy boat. Serve the chicken and vegetables immediately, passing the juices separately at the table.

—Eugenia Giobbi Bone and Edward Giobbi

WINE Fresh, fruity rosé.

## Spicy Lemongrass Chicken

**TOTAL: 25 MIN**

6 SERVINGS ●

1½ pounds skinless, boneless chicken thighs, fat trimmed, meat cut into ¾-inch pieces

¼ cup plus 2 tablespoons canola oil

Kosher salt and freshly ground pepper

2 plump stalks of lemongrass, tender white inner bulbs only, minced

1 medium red onion, quartered lengthwise and thinly sliced crosswise

2 teaspoons minced garlic

¼ cup Chinese cooking wine, sake or water

½ cup Vietnamese Stir-Fry Sauce (p. 240)

1 tablespoon plus 1 teaspoon oyster sauce

1 teaspoon Asian chili paste

4 large scallions, cut into ½-inch lengths

5 small dried red chiles

1 large jalapeño, seeded and thinly sliced

**1.** In a medium bowl, toss the chicken, 2 tablespoons of the oil, 1½ teaspoons of salt and ¾ teaspoon of pepper.

**2.** In a large skillet or a wok, heat 2 tablespoons of the oil until small puffs of smoke begin to appear. Add half of the chicken and stir-fry over high heat until browned in spots, 3 minutes. Transfer to a plate and cook the remaining chicken.

**3.** Heat the remaining 2 tablespoons of oil in the skillet. Add the lemongrass, onion and garlic and cook over high heat, stirring until fragrant, 2 minutes. Add the wine and cook until slightly reduced, about 1 minute. Add the stir-fry sauce, oyster sauce, chili paste, scallions, dried chiles and jalapeño; bring to a boil. Add the chicken to the sauce and simmer until heated through, then serve. —*Charles Phan*

**SERVE WITH** Steamed jasmine rice.

**WINE** Fresh, fruity rosé.

## Creole Fried Chicken

**TOTAL: 1 HR PLUS 1 HR MARINATING**

4 SERVINGS

The late chef Austin Leslie of New Orleans's Chez Helene and Pampy's Creole Kitchen was famous for this fried chicken, which is pleasantly sweetened with condensed milk. And the chicken's crust, fried in lard, is spectacularly crisp.

1 tablespoon salt

1 tablespoon freshly ground pepper

1 tablespoon Creole seasoning

One 3½-pound chicken, cut into 8 pieces, breasts cut in half through the bone

3 pounds all-natural lard (see Note)

One 14-ounce can condensed milk

1 cup water

1 large egg, beaten

1½ cups all-purpose flour

¼ cup finely chopped parsley

2 small garlic cloves, minced

2 dill pickles, thinly sliced crosswise

**1.** In a small bowl, mix the salt, pepper and Creole seasoning. On a platter, sprinkle the chicken with the seasonings. Refrigerate for at least 1 hour or overnight.

**2.** In a large, deep saucepan fitted with a deep-frying thermometer, melt the lard and heat it to 325°. In a bowl, whisk the milk with the water and egg. Pour the flour into a large paper bag. Working with 2 or 3 pieces of chicken at a time, dip them in the milk, add them to the flour and shake to coat. Tap off any excess flour and transfer to a rack while you coat the rest.

**3.** Line another rack with paper towels. Add the chicken to the hot lard and fry until deeply golden and an instant-read thermometer inserted in the meat registers 155° for white meat and 165° for dark meat, about 12 minutes. Reduce the heat if necessary to keep the lard at 325°. Drain the fried chicken on the rack. Transfer to a platter and sprinkle with the parsley, garlic and pickle slices. Serve. —*Austin Leslie*

**NOTE** All-natural lard is available from PrairiePrideMN.com.

**WINE** Lively, fruity Merlot.

## Tomato-Basil Chicken with Spices

**TOTAL: 30 MIN**

4 SERVINGS ● ●

The complex flavor of fresh basil appeals to Jerry Traunfeld, chef at The Herbfarm restaurant near Seattle. He makes a chunky fresh-tomato sauce that enhances basil's natural spiciness with cinnamon, star anise and ginger, creating a simple but exotic topping for moist chicken breasts.

2 tablespoons extra-virgin olive oil

1 small onion, thinly sliced lengthwise

2 large tomatoes, coarsely chopped

2 cinnamon sticks

3 star anise pods

2 teaspoons peeled, minced fresh ginger

Kosher salt and freshly ground pepper

Four 8-ounce skinless, boneless chicken breast halves

1½ cups basil leaves, coarsely chopped

Couscous or orzo, for serving

**1.** In a large skillet, heat the olive oil until shimmering. Add the sliced onion and cook over high heat, stirring, until the onion is softened and lightly browned, about 5 minutes. Add the tomatoes, the cinnamon sticks, star anise and ginger and season the sauce with salt and pepper. Add the chicken breasts to the skillet and season with salt and pepper. Cover and cook over moderate heat, turning the chicken once, until cooked through, about 15 minutes.

**2.** Transfer the chicken to plates. Stir the basil into the sauce. Spoon the sauce over the chicken and serve with couscous. —*Jerry Traunfeld*

**WINE** Savory, spicy Carmenère.

### Thai Chicken Thighs with Garlic and Lime

**TOTAL: 15 MIN PLUS 1 HR MARINATING**

4 SERVINGS ●

Thai recipes often combine sweet, salty, sour and spicy flavors. This dish highlights skinless chicken thighs, which are fattier than breasts but still relatively lean and much more luscious.

- 1½ pounds skinless, boneless chicken thighs, trimmed of all visible fat
- Freshly ground pepper
- 2 large garlic cloves, very finely chopped
- 2½ tablespoons very finely chopped cilantro
- 1½ tablespoons Asian fish sauce
- 1 teaspoon brown sugar
- ½ teaspoon chili powder
- 1½ teaspoons finely chopped basil
- 1½ teaspoons finely chopped mint
- 2 tablespoons vegetable oil
- Lime wedges, for serving

**1.** Season the chicken thighs with pepper. In a bowl, mix the chopped garlic with 2 tablespoons of the chopped cilantro, the fish sauce, brown sugar and chili powder; rub the seasoning mixture all over the chicken and let stand for up to 1 hour.

**2.** In a small bowl, toss the remaining ½ tablespoon of chopped cilantro with the chopped basil and mint. In a large non-stick skillet, heat the vegetable oil until it is shimmering. Add the chicken thighs to the skillet and cook them over high heat, turning once, until the chicken is cooked through, 6 to 7 minutes. Cut each thigh into 3 or 4 pieces. Transfer the chicken thighs to a platter and scatter the herbs all over the chicken. Serve the chicken thighs immediately, with the lime wedges on the side. —*Chef Bobo*

**SERVE WITH** Brown rice.

**WINE** Vivid, lightly sweet Riesling.

### Clay Pot Ginger Chicken

**TOTAL: 45 MIN**

4 SERVINGS ●

- 2 tablespoons plus 2 teaspoons sugar
- ⅓ cup plus ¼ cup hot water
- 2 tablespoons vegetable oil
- 2 Thai red chiles, chopped, or 1 teaspoon crushed red pepper
- 1 garlic clove, minced
- One 4-inch piece of fresh ginger, peeled and cut into slivers
- 1 pound skinless, boneless chicken thighs, cut into 3-by-1-inch pieces
- 1½ tablespoons Asian fish sauce
- ¼ teaspoon salt
- 1 small onion, cut into thin wedges
- 2 scallions, cut into 2-inch lengths
- 6 cilantro sprigs, cut into 1-inch lengths

**1.** In a small, heavy saucepan, cook 2 table-spoons of the sugar over moderate heat until bubbling and beginning to brown around the edge, 4 minutes. Gradually stir in ⅓ cup of the hot water and simmer for 3 minutes to dissolve the caramel. Remove from the heat.

**2.** Heat the oil in a medium Chinese clay pot or a flameproof casserole. Add the chiles, garlic and half of the ginger and stir-fry over moderate heat until fragrant, about 20 seconds. Add the chicken, fish sauce, salt and the remaining 2 teaspoons of sugar and stir until the chicken turns white, 3 to 4 minutes. Add the onion wedges, the remaining ¼ cup of hot water and the caramel sauce and bring to a boil. Cover, reduce the heat to low and simmer until the chicken is cooked through and the sauce is slightly thickened, 8 minutes. Add the scallions and cook for 3 minutes longer. Stir in the remaining ginger and remove the pot from the heat. Garnish with the cilantro and serve. —*Mai Pham*

**WINE** Peppery, refreshing Grüner Veltliner.

### Chicken Legs Marinated in Yogurt and Spices

**TOTAL: 1 HR PLUS 4 HR OR OVERNIGHT MARINATING**

6 SERVINGS ●

This pungent cumin-and-coriander-spiked marinade is reminiscent of restaurant tandoori spicing—without the scary red dye.

- 4 large garlic cloves, minced
- 1½ tablespoons finely grated ginger
- Sea salt
- 2 cups plain low-fat yogurt
- 2 tablespoons extra-virgin olive oil, plus more for brushing
- 1 tablespoon ground cumin
- 1 tablespoon ground coriander
- 1 teaspoon crushed red pepper
- 1 teaspoon sweet paprika
- ½ teaspoon ground turmeric
- ½ teaspoon freshly ground black pepper
- Pinch of cinnamon
- 6 pounds chicken legs, cut into drumsticks and thighs

**1.** In a bowl, using a wooden spoon, mash the garlic and ginger with 1½ teaspoons of salt to a coarse paste. Stir in the yogurt and the 2 tablespoons of oil, then add the cumin, coriander, crushed pepper, paprika, turmeric, black pepper and cinnamon.

**2.** Remove the skin from the chicken thighs and, using a sharp knife, make 3 to 4 deep slashes in the thighs and drumsticks on both sides. Add the chicken to the spiced yogurt marinade, toss to coat and let stand at room temperature for 4 hours, or refrigerate overnight.

**3.** Light a grill. Remove the chicken from the marinade and scrape some of it off. Lightly brush the chicken with olive oil and season with salt. Grill over moderately high heat, turning occasionally, until lightly charred and the juices run clear when the chicken is pierced with a knife, 25 to 30 minutes. Transfer to a platter and serve.
—*Grace Parisi*

**WINE** Bright, tart Barbera.

## Hearty Braised Chicken Legs

**TOTAL: 30 MIN**

**4 SERVINGS** ● ● ○

Pureeing garlic, onion and cilantro, then cooking them with white mushrooms in chicken fat, gives this tomato-based sauce an incredible depth of flavor.

- **3** tablespoons vegetable oil
- **4** whole chicken legs, cut into thighs and drumsticks (2 pounds)

Kosher salt and freshly ground black pepper

- **¾** pound white mushrooms, quartered
- **3** garlic cloves
- **1** medium onion, quartered
- **½** cup cilantro leaves
- **1** cup tomato sauce

**1.** In a very large skillet, heat the vegetable oil. Season the chicken thighs and drumsticks with salt and pepper and add them to the skillet, skin side down. Cook the chicken legs over high heat, turning once, until they are browned, about 8 minutes. Transfer the chicken legs to a plate and pour off all but 3 tablespoons of the fat. Add the quartered mushrooms to the skillet and cook them over moderate heat, undisturbed, until they begin to brown on the bottom, about 2 minutes.

**2.** Meanwhile, in a food processor, puree the garlic cloves with the onion and cilantro leaves. Add the garlic and onion puree to the mushrooms in the skillet and cook over moderate heat until very fragrant, about 1 minute. Stir the tomato sauce into the mushrooms. Return the chicken legs to the skillet and bring to a simmer. Cover the skillet and simmer the sauce until the chicken is cooked through, about 15 minutes. Season the braised chicken legs with salt and pepper, transfer them to plates and serve with the sauce.
—*Daisy Martinez*

**SERVE WITH** White rice.

**WINE** Fresh, minerally Vermentino.

## Chicken Wings with Sweet-and-Spicy Pantry Sauce

**TOTAL: 35 MIN PLUS OVERNIGHT MARINATING**

**4 SERVINGS**

Ray Lampe is a national barbecue champion, a teacher and the owner of a roadside barbecue stand in Lakeland, Florida. His first book, *Dr. BBQ's Big-Time Barbecue Cookbook*, gives advice on how to bump up the flavors in grilled dishes, as in his sweet and sticky chicken wings. His tip: Slash the inside of the joints so they cook through and the seasonings penetrate.

- **16** chicken wings, with the two joints attached, tips removed
- **1** cup ketchup
- **¼** cup Dijon mustard
- **¼** cup hot sauce
- **¼** cup soy sauce
- **1** tablespoon light brown sugar

**1.** Make a slash on the inside of the chicken wing joints, without cutting through the bone, and in a few other places. In a large, shallow baking dish, combine the ketchup with the Dijon mustard, hot sauce, soy sauce and light brown sugar. Add the chicken wings to the marinade and turn to coat. Cover and refrigerate the chicken wings overnight.

**2.** Light a grill. Remove the chicken wings from the marinade (or pantry sauce), leaving some of it on them, and reserve the remaining marinade. Grill the wings over moderately high heat, turning and basting them with the reserved marinade, until they are nicely charred and cooked through, about 30 minutes. Stop basting during the last 5 minutes of grilling and discard any remaining marinade. Serve the chicken wings hot or at room temperature.
—*Ray Lampe*

**NOTE** A "pantry sauce" is one that can be made with ingredients, such as ketchup, mustard and soy sauce, that can be found in the home pantry.

**WINE** Savory, spicy Carmenère.

## Almond-Crusted Chicken Wings

**TOTAL: 30 MIN**

**4 SERVINGS** ○

Andy Nusser, chef and co-owner of Casa Mono in New York City, says these wings, coated with crunchy chopped almonds, are a favorite staff meal at the restaurant. He serves them with a superfast lemon aioli: a mix of store-bought mayonnaise, grated lemon zest and fresh lemon juice.

- **⅓** cup plus ¼ cup extra-virgin olive oil
- **1** tablespoon sweet paprika
- **1** teaspoon ground cumin
- **¾** teaspoon cayenne pepper
- **3** garlic cloves, crushed
- **2½** tablespoons sherry vinegar

Salt and freshly ground black pepper

- **2½** pounds chicken wings
- **¾** cup coarsely chopped natural almonds
- **¼** cup mayonnaise

Zest and juice from 1 lemon

**1.** Preheat the oven to 425°. In a large bowl, combine the ⅓ cup of olive oil with the paprika, cumin, cayenne pepper and crushed garlic. Stir in the sherry vinegar and season with salt and black pepper. Add the chicken wings and almonds and toss. Spread the chicken wings and almonds on a large baking sheet in a single layer and roast for about 25 minutes, until the chicken wings are cooked through.

**2.** Meanwhile, in a mini food processor, combine the mayonnaise with the lemon zest and lemon juice. Add the remaining ¼ cup of olive oil and process until the lemon aioli is smooth, then season it with salt and black pepper.

**3.** Turn on the broiler and broil the chicken wings, turning once, until they are lightly crisp, 2 to 3 minutes. Transfer the chicken wings and almonds to a platter and serve them immediately, with the lemon aioli.
—*Andy Nusser*

**WINE** Full-bodied, rich Pinot Gris.

## Gingery Chicken Satay with Peanut Sauce

**TOTAL: 30 MIN**

6 SERVINGS ●

In this ingenious version of an Indonesian classic, the gingery, lemongrass-scented satay paste is the base for the marinade as well as for the peanut dipping sauce. A few alternatives to the chicken: thinly sliced beef or pork or whole, shelled shrimp.

- 4 large shallots
- 4 large garlic cloves
- 2 stalks of lemongrass—bottom 6 inches only, outer leaves peeled, inner stalk cut into 1-inch pieces
- 2 serrano or jalapeño chiles, stemmed and seeded
- 2 tablespoons minced fresh ginger
- 1 tablespoon soy sauce
- 1 teaspoon ground coriander
- 1 teaspoon freshly ground pepper
- 3 tablespoons light brown sugar
- 2 tablespoon Asian fish sauce
- 2 pounds skinless, boneless chicken breasts, sliced lengthwise 1 inch thick
- 3 tablespoons vegetable oil
- 1 cup unsweetened coconut milk
- ½ cup smooth peanut butter
- 2 tablespoons fresh lime juice
- 2 tablespoons chopped cilantro

**1.** Light a grill. In a mini food processor, combine the shallots, garlic, lemongrass, chiles, ginger, soy sauce, coriander and ground pepper. Add 2 tablespoons of the brown sugar and 1 tablespoon of the fish sauce and process to a fine paste. Transfer half of the seasoning paste to a large bowl. Add the chicken and toss to coat.

**2.** Thread the chicken strips onto skewers. Drizzle with 2 tablespoons of the oil and let stand for 10 minutes.

**3.** Heat the remaining 1 tablespoon of oil in a medium saucepan. Add the remaining seasoning paste and cook over moderate heat, stirring, until fragrant, about 1 minute. Add the coconut milk and bring to a

boil, stirring. Whisk in the peanut butter and the remaining 1 tablespoon each of sugar and fish sauce and bring to a simmer. Transfer to a blender, add the lime juice and puree until smooth. Transfer to a bowl.

**4.** Grill the chicken skewers over high heat until lightly charred and cooked through, about 5 minutes. Transfer the chicken to a platter or bowl and sprinkle with the cilantro. Serve with the peanut sauce. *—Grace Parisi*

**WINE** Vivid, lightly sweet Riesling.

## Chicken Salad with Cumin-Scented Carrot Raita

**TOTAL: 30 MIN**

6 SERVINGS ● ●

A rotisserie bird is wonderful in this Middle Eastern–inspired warm chicken dish. It's a delicious and healthy alternative to a typical mayonnaise-based chicken salad, especially in a sandwich.

- One 3½-pound roasted chicken, meat shredded (4 cups)
- 3 large radishes, thickly sliced
- ¼ small red onion, thinly sliced
- 2 tablespoons coarsely chopped mint leaves
- ¼ teaspoon ground cumin
- Cumin-Scented Carrot Raita (recipe follows)
- Salt
- Cayenne pepper
- Lime wedges and warmed pita

In a bowl, toss the chicken, radishes, onion, mint and cumin. Stir in the raita and season with salt and cayenne. Serve with lime wedges and warmed pita. *—Grace Parisi*

**WINE** Minerally Marsanne or Roussanne.

### CUMIN-SCENTED CARROT RAITA

**TOTAL: 15 MIN**

MAKES ⅔ CUP ● ● ●

This Indian-inspired yogurt sauce is already fast to make, but you can save more time by using ½ cup of thick Greek-style yogurt instead of draining the yogurt.

- ⅔ cup plain whole milk yogurt
- 2 tablespoons extra-virgin olive oil
- 1 garlic clove, minced
- ½ teaspoon cumin seeds
- 2 carrots, coarsely shredded
- 2 scallions, white and tender green parts only, thinly sliced
- 1 tablespoon finely chopped cilantro leaves
- Salt
- Cayenne pepper

**1.** Spoon the yogurt into a coffee filter set in a strainer and let stand until slightly thickened, about 10 minutes. Transfer the yogurt to a medium bowl.

**2.** Meanwhile, heat the olive oil in a small skillet. Add the minced garlic and the cumin seeds and cook over moderate heat, stirring, until the garlic and cumin are fragrant, about 1 minute. Add the carrots and scallions and cook, stirring, until the vegetables are just heated through. Add the carrot mixture and the cilantro to the drained yogurt and season with salt and cayenne. Serve the raita warm, at room temperature or chilled. *—G.P.*

**VARIATIONS** Serve the Cumin-Scented Carrot Raita with grilled and roasted meats and poultry, or stir it into cooked lentils, beans or grains.

**MAKE AHEAD** The raita can be refrigerated overnight.

## Circassian Chicken

**ACTIVE: 30 MIN; TOTAL: 1 HR 30 MIN**

4 SERVINGS ● ●

This cool chicken salad in a creamy walnut sauce supposedly got its name because its color resembles the pale complexions of the Circassian beauties in the sultan's harem during the Ottoman Empire. The mild, slightly nutty chicken is traditionally part of a Turkish meze assortment and can be drizzled with red pepper oil, replaced in this version with ground Turkish red pepper.

One 4-pound chicken, quartered

1 onion, halved

4 allspice berries

4 whole cloves

4 black peppercorns

3 bay leaves

1 teaspoon coriander seeds

Salt

1 pita bread, torn into pieces

½ cup milk or half-and-half

2 cups walnuts (6 ounces)

2 garlic cloves, smashed

Freshly ground black pepper

2 tablespoons finely chopped
cilantro

Turkish red pepper, such as Aleppo
or Urfa (optional)

**1.** Put the chicken in a large soup pot. Add the onion, allspice, cloves, peppercorns, bay leaves and coriander seeds. Add enough water to cover the chicken and bring to a boil. Reduce the heat to low and simmer until the chicken is cooked, about 30 minutes. Transfer the chicken to a plate, and when it is cool enough to handle, discard the skin and pull the meat off the bones in shreds.

**2.** Strain the broth and transfer 3 cups to a small saucepan. Boil until reduced by half, about 10 minutes. Season with salt.

**3.** In a small bowl, mash the pita in the milk until completely soaked. Transfer to a food processor. Add the walnuts and garlic and process to a paste. With the machine on, add about 1 cup of the reduced broth in a thin stream until a thick sauce forms; add more broth if needed. Season the sauce with salt and black pepper; scrape half of it into a bowl. Fold the chicken and cilantro into the walnut sauce. Mound the chicken on a plate, top with a pinch of Turkish red pepper and serve. Pass the extra walnut sauce at the table. —*Eveline Zoutendijk*

**SERVE WITH** Pita or other flat bread.

**MAKE AHEAD** The chicken salad can be refrigerated overnight.

**WINE** Juicy, fresh Dolcetto.

**CHICKEN SALAD WITH CUMIN-SCENTED CARROT RAITA**

**CIRCASSIAN CHICKEN**

## Andean Chicken and Potato Cake

**TOTAL: 1 HR PLUS 1 HR CHILLING**

**6 SERVINGS ●**

This recipe is Peru's version of shepherd's pie. Here the mashed potatoes are flavored with lime juice and chiles, and the filling is shredded chicken seasoned with red onion, celery and mayonnaise. Serve it cold or at room temperature; either way, it's ridiculously good.

1½ **pounds bone-in whole chicken breast**

1½ **pounds Yukon Gold potatoes, peeled and cut into 2-inch chunks**

**Salt**

1 **small yellow bell pepper, quartered**

1 **large jalapeño, seeded and halved lengthwise**

2 **teaspoons fresh lime juice**

¼ **cup extra-virgin olive oil**

**Freshly ground pepper**

½ **cup plus 2 tablespoons mayonnaise**

1 **large celery rib, finely chopped**

½ **small red onion, finely chopped**

1 **Hass avocado—halved lengthwise, pitted and sliced lengthwise ⅛ inch thick**

6 **pitted Calamata olives, sliced crosswise ⅛ inch thick**

3½ **ounces farmer cheese (½ cup), crumbled**

1 **cup alfalfa, radish or broccoli sprouts**

## superfast
### CHICKEN MOLE TACOS

Remove the meat from a store-bought rotisserie chicken and pull it into shreds. Pour a jar of mole sauce into a pan, add the chicken and heat, stirring. Spoon into crisp taco shells. Top with shredded lettuce, chopped cilantro and crumbled goat cheese.

**1.** Put the chicken breast in a medium saucepan of boiling water, reduce the heat to low and simmer until cooked through, about 25 minutes. Transfer to a bowl and let rest for 15 minutes.

**2.** Meanwhile, in a large saucepan, cover the potatoes with water and bring to a boil. Salt the water and simmer over moderately high heat until tender, about 25 minutes.

**3.** In a small saucepan, cover the bell pepper and jalapeño with water; bring to a boil. Simmer over moderately high heat until tender, 8 minutes. Drain and transfer to a blender. Add the lime juice and puree.

**4.** When the potatoes are done, drain in a colander, then return them to the saucepan. Shake the potatoes over high heat for about 15 seconds to dry them out. Using a potato masher, mash the potatoes well, then mash in the olive oil. Stir in the pepper puree and season with salt and pepper.

**5.** Discard the skin and bones from the chicken. Cut the chicken into ¼-inch pieces and transfer to a bowl. Stir in the mayonnaise, celery and red onion and season with salt and pepper.

**6.** Line an 8-inch springform pan with plastic wrap. Spread half of the mashed potatoes in the bottom and partway up the side of the pan. Spread the chicken salad over the potatoes. Spread the remaining potatoes over the chicken and smooth the top. Cover with plastic wrap and refrigerate until lightly chilled, about 1 hour.

**7.** Carefully remove the ring from the pan and peel back the plastic wrap. Using 2 wide spatulas, transfer the cake to a serving plate. Smooth the side if necessary. Garnish the cake with the avocado slices in a fan shape. Sprinkle the olives, cheese and sprouts over the top. Using a sharp knife, cut the cake into wedges and serve. —*Emmanuel Piqueras*

**MAKE AHEAD** The cake can be refrigerated overnight. Decorate the top just before serving cold or at room temperature.

**WINE** Savory, spicy Carmenère.

## Mole Poblano Chicken

**ACTIVE: 20 MIN; TOTAL: 50 MIN**

**4 SERVINGS ●**

Almost every region in Mexico has its own version of mole. The robust, nutty and spicy mole poblano is from the south-central state of Puebla, where, some historians say, an order of nuns developed the recipe for braising turkey in the 17th century to honor an archbishop. Substituting chicken, as here, makes the dish quicker and easier.

**One 3½-pound chicken, cut into 8 pieces**

2 **bay leaves**

1 **medium onion, chopped**

1 **whole head garlic**

1 **teaspoon whole black peppercorns**

**Salt**

3 **cups low-sodium chicken broth**

3 **cups water**

**One 7-ounce jar prepared red mole**

2 **tablespoons sesame seeds, lightly toasted**

**1.** In a medium enameled cast-iron casserole, combine the chicken, bay leaves, onion, garlic, peppercorns and a generous pinch of salt. Add the broth and water and bring to a boil. Simmer over moderate heat for 20 minutes, or until the chicken is almost cooked through. Transfer to a plate and strain the broth into a heatproof bowl. Set aside 4 cups of the broth and refrigerate the remaining broth for another use.

**2.** Wipe out the casserole and add the mole. Whisk in the 4 cups of reserved broth until smooth and bring to a boil. Season with salt. Add the chicken and any accumulated juices and simmer over moderately low heat until cooked through, 10 minutes. Transfer to a platter and skim any fat from the sauce. Spoon 2 cups of mole sauce over the chicken, sprinkle with the sesame seeds and pass the remaining mole sauce at the table. —*Melissa Guerra*

**SERVE WITH** White rice.

**WINE** Rustic, peppery Malbec.

## Chicken Potpie with Cream Biscuit Topping

**ACTIVE: 1 HR 30 MIN; TOTAL: 2 HR 30 MIN**
8 SERVINGS

- ¼ cup extra-virgin olive oil
- 4 pounds skinless, boneless chicken thighs, cut into 1-inch pieces
- Salt and freshly ground pepper
- 2 quarts chicken stock or low-sodium broth
- ½ pound sliced bacon, cut into 1-inch pieces
- ½ cup all-purpose flour
- 3 large carrots, sliced ½ inch thick
- 3 large celery ribs, sliced ½ inch thick
- 1 large white onion, thinly sliced
- 2 large garlic cloves, minced
- ¼ cup brandy
- 2 thyme sprigs
- 1 bay leaf
- Cream Biscuits (p. 269), unbaked

**1.** Heat 2 tablespoons of the olive oil in a large enameled cast-iron casserole or Dutch oven. Season the chicken with salt and pepper and add half of it to the casserole in a single layer. Cook over moderately high heat, turning occasionally, until browned, about 8 minutes. Using a slotted spoon, transfer the chicken to a large platter. Add 1 cup of the chicken stock to the casserole and scrape up the browned bits stuck to the bottom; strain the deglazed drippings into a small heatproof bowl and wipe out the casserole. Repeat with the remaining oil, chicken and 1 cup of stock; add to the reserved juices in the bowl.

**2.** Add the bacon to the casserole; cook over moderate heat until crisp, 6 minutes. Using a slotted spoon, transfer to the platter.

**3.** Pour 4 tablespoons of the bacon fat into a small skillet. Add the flour and cook over moderate heat, stirring, until lightly browned, about 3 minutes. Let cool.

**4.** Add the carrots, celery, onion and garlic to the casserole and cook over moderate heat, stirring occasionally, until softened,

about 8 minutes. Add the brandy and cook until evaporated, 1 to 2 minutes. Add the remaining 6 cups of stock and the thyme and bay leaf and season with salt and pepper. Return the chicken and bacon to the casserole along with the 2 cups of deglazed drippings and bring to a simmer. Cover partially and cook over moderate heat for 30 minutes. Whisk in the bacon fat and flour paste and cook until the sauce has thickened, 5 to 6 minutes.

**5.** Preheat the oven to 375°. Pour the chicken stew into a shallow 3-quart baking dish; discard the thyme sprigs and bay leaf. Arrange the unbaked Cream Biscuits on top of the stew and bake in the upper third of the oven until the biscuits are golden and the stew is bubbling, about 30 minutes. Let cool slightly, then serve. —*Marc Murphy*

**WINE** Cherry-inflected, earthy Sangiovese.

## Free-Form Chicken Potpie

**ACTIVE: 1 HR; TOTAL: 2 HR 30 MIN**
6 SERVINGS

This potless potpie with a Spanish accent (from the Pimentón pepper) doesn't rely on the usual deep dish for serving. The luxurious chicken and vegetable stew simply gets spooned into bowls and garnished with flaky puff pastry rounds.

- One 3½-pound chicken
- ¼ cup extra-virgin olive oil
- Salt and freshly ground pepper
- 1 pound oyster mushrooms, large stems discarded, large caps halved
- 2 tablespoons unsalted butter
- 4 carrots, sliced ¼ inch thick
- 4 celery ribs, cut into ½-inch dice
- 1 large onion, cut into ½-inch dice
- 1 leek, white and tender green parts only, cut into ½-inch dice
- 1 bay leaf
- ⅓ cup all-purpose flour
- 2 cups chicken broth
- 1 cup heavy cream

- ½ cup frozen peas, thawed
- 2 teaspoons chopped thyme
- Pinch of smoked paprika, preferably Pimentón de la Vera
- 14 ounces frozen all-butter puff pastry, thawed but still cold
- 1 large egg beaten with 2 tablespoons heavy cream

**1.** Preheat the oven to 350°. In a roasting pan, rub the chicken with 1 tablespoon of the olive oil; season with salt and pepper. Roast for 1 hour and 30 minutes, or until the juices run clear. Let the chicken rest for 10 minutes. Increase the oven temperature to 450°. Remove all of the meat from the chicken and discard the skin and bones. Cut the chicken into bite-size pieces.

**2.** On a large rimmed baking sheet, toss the oyster mushrooms with 1 tablespoon of the olive oil. Season with salt and pepper. Roast for 8 minutes, or until richly browned. Reduce the oven temperature to 400°.

**3.** In a large, deep skillet, melt the butter in the remaining 2 tablespoons of olive oil. Add the carrots, celery, onion, leek and bay leaf. Cover and cook over low heat, stirring occasionally, until softened, about 10 minutes. Stir in the flour, then gradually whisk in the broth until smooth. Simmer over low heat, stirring often, until no floury taste remains, about 5 minutes. Stir in the cream and simmer until thickened, about 8 minutes. Stir in the peas, thyme, chicken and mushrooms and season with salt, pepper and the smoked paprika. Simmer for 5 minutes. Discard the bay leaf.

**4.** Line a large rimmed baking sheet with parchment paper. On a lightly floured work surface, roll out the puff pastry to a ⅛-inch thickness. Using a 4-inch round cookie cutter, stamp out 6 rounds; transfer to the prepared baking sheet. Brush the rounds with the egg-cream wash and bake for 15 minutes, or until puffed and browned. Ladle the chicken stew into bowls, garnish with the pastry and serve. —*Tom Fundaro*

**WINE** Minerally Marsanne or Roussanne.

**LEMONY CHICKEN FRICASSEE
WITH SHALLOTS AND MORELS**

## Lemony Chicken Fricassee with Shallots and Morels

**TOTAL: 30 MIN**

4 SERVINGS ●

Typically, a fricassee is made with chicken or another kind of white meat stewed in a white sauce with vegetables. In this version, chicken is sizzled in butter until it's crisp, then cooked with shallots and morels and finished with lemon for a hit of tartness.

- 3 tablespoons unsalted butter

One 3- to 4-pound chicken,
    cut into 8 pieces

Salt and freshly ground pepper

- 6 small shallots, peeled and quartered lengthwise
- ¼ pound morels (about 6), quartered lengthwise (see Note)
- 1 cup water
- 1 pound pencil-thin asparagus

Juice and zest of 1 lemon

1. In a large, deep skillet, melt 2 tablespoons of the butter. Season the chicken pieces with salt and pepper, add them to the skillet and cook over high heat, turning occasionally, until browned, about 8 minutes. Add the shallots and morels and cook for 2 minutes. Add the water, cover tightly and simmer over moderately low heat until the chicken is cooked through, about 15 minutes.

2. Meanwhile, in a large saucepan, steam the asparagus over 1 inch of water until crisp-tender, 2 to 3 minutes.

3. Transfer the chicken to a plate. Add the lemon juice and zest to the skillet and cook over high heat for 2 minutes. Swirl the remaining 1 tablespoon of butter into the sauce and season with salt and pepper. Pour the sauce over the chicken and serve with the asparagus. —*Katy Sparks*

**NOTE** If fresh morels are unavailable, you can substitute ½ ounce of dried morels reconstituted in 1 cup of boiling water and then drained.

**WINE** Rich, complex white Burgundy.

## Spicy Chicken Curry

**ACTIVE: 40 MIN; TOTAL: 1 HR 30 MIN**

12 SERVINGS ● ●

Cookbook author Neelam Batra gives Indian food a California-style makeover, making it lighter and brighter. Batra's most recent book is *1,000 Indian Recipes*.

- ½ cup vegetable oil
- 12 pounds skinless chicken drumsticks and thighs

Salt

- 4 jalapeños, coarsely chopped with some seeds
- 2 dried red chiles, broken
- 2 large onions, coarsely chopped
- 8 large garlic cloves, finely chopped

One 3-inch piece of ginger,
    peeled and sliced crosswise
    into paper-thin rounds

- 2 tablespoons ground coriander
- 2 teaspoons ground cumin
- 1½ teaspoons ground fenugreek seeds
- ½ teaspoon ground cinnamon
- ½ teaspoon ground cloves
- ½ teaspoon freshly grated nutmeg
- ½ teaspoon paprika
- 2 pounds tomatoes, chopped
- 1 cup chopped cilantro, plus cilantro leaves for garnish
- ½ cup plain yogurt

Garam masala, for sprinkling

1. Heat 2 very large, deep skillets. Add 2 tablespoons of the oil to each. Season the chicken pieces with salt and add half of them to each skillet. Cook over high heat until golden brown, about 3 minutes per side. Transfer the chicken pieces to a large bowl. Add half of the remaining 4 tablespoons of oil to each of the skillets along with the jalapeños and dried chiles. Cook over moderately high heat until sizzling, about 30 seconds. Divide the onions, garlic and ginger between the skillets and cook, stirring occasionally, until deep brown, about 8 minutes.

2. Spoon the onion mixture into a food processor. Add the coriander, cumin, fenugreek seeds, cinnamon, cloves, nutmeg, paprika and 1 teaspoon of salt and puree. Transfer half of the onion mixture to each of the skillets. Add the tomatoes and chopped cilantro and puree.

3. Return the chicken pieces to the skillets along with any accumulated juices. Cook over moderate heat, stirring, until the onion sauce begins to stick to the skillets, about 8 minutes. Stir half of the yogurt into each skillet, then stir in the tomato and cilantro puree. Simmer the curry over moderately low heat, turning the chicken pieces occasionally, until cooked through, about 50 minutes; add ¼ cup of water to each skillet toward the end of cooking if the sauce gets too thick. Season the curry with salt and transfer the chicken to a platter. Pour the sauce on top, sprinkle with garam masala and cilantro leaves and serve. —*Neelam Batra*

**WINE** Spicy American Gewürztraminer.

## Roasted Turkey with Shallot Butter and Thyme Gravy

**ACTIVE: 45 MIN; TOTAL: 3 HR 30 MIN**

8 TO 10 SERVINGS ●

Shallots and thyme in both the turkey and the gravy provide double the flavor for this simple roasted bird.

- 1 stick (4 ounces) unsalted butter, softened
- 1 tablespoon soy sauce
- ½ cup minced shallots (2 large)
- 3 tablespoons coarsely chopped thyme, plus 8 thyme sprigs

Salt and freshly ground pepper

One 12-pound fresh turkey, rinsed and
    dried, neck and giblets reserved

- ½ cup dry white wine

About 2½ cups chicken stock

- 3 cups water
- ¼ cup Madeira
- 2 teaspoons cornstarch mixed with 1 tablespoon water

1. Preheat the oven to 350°. In a small bowl, blend the butter with the soy sauce, ¼ cup of the shallots, 2 tablespoons of the chopped thyme, ½ teaspoon of salt and ¼ teaspoon of pepper. Separate the skin from the turkey breast and rub two-thirds of the shallot butter over the meat, then smooth out the breast skin. Rub the outside of the turkey with the remaining shallot butter and season liberally inside and out with salt and pepper. Tuck 5 of the thyme sprigs into the cavity.

2. Pour the white wine and ½ cup of the chicken stock into a roasting pan fitted with a V-shaped rack. Set the turkey on the rack and roast for 30 minutes. Baste with the pan juices. Roast the turkey for about 1 hour and 45 minutes longer, basting every 30 minutes and adding chicken stock to the pan as necessary; keep the pan moist throughout roasting so the drippings don't burn. If the turkey starts getting too dark, tent it loosely with foil. The turkey is done when an instant-read thermometer inserted in the inner thigh registers 170°. Transfer the turkey to a carving board and let rest for 20 to 30 minutes.

3. Meanwhile, in a medium saucepan, cover the turkey neck, heart and gizzard with the 3 cups of water. Add the remaining 3 thyme sprigs, season with salt and pepper and simmer for 20 minutes. Strain the turkey broth and reduce it to 2¼ cups.

4. Pour the pan drippings into a fat separator; reserve 2 tablespoons of the fat and all of the drippings. Add 1¼ cups of the turkey broth and the Madeira to the roasting pan; simmer, stirring to dissolve the browned bits; you should have 1¼ cups of jus.

5. In a saucepan, heat the reserved fat. Add the remaining ¼ cup of shallots and cook over moderately high heat, stirring, until softened. Add the remaining 1 tablespoon of chopped thyme and cook for 1 minute longer. Stir in the jus, pan drippings and the remaining 1 cup of broth and bring to a simmer. Stir in the cornstarch slurry and

bring to a boil to thicken very lightly, then season with salt and pepper. Transfer to a gravy boat. Carve the turkey and serve with the gravy. —*Susan Spungen*

**SERVE WITH** Candied Cranberry Sauce (recipe follows).

**WINE** Intense, fruity Zinfandel.

### CANDIED CRANBERRY SAUCE
**TOTAL: 20 MIN**
**MAKES ABOUT 5½ CUPS** ● ● ●

Cooked with a little water in a wide skillet, tart cranberries get candied in sugar syrup and remain almost whole.

- 1½ **pounds cranberries**
- 1 **cup sugar**
- ½ **cup water**

**Zest strips from 1 orange**

- 1 **tablespoon grated fresh ginger**

Combine all of the ingredients in a very large skillet and cook over moderately high heat until the cranberries are candied, about 15 minutes. Let cool and serve. —*S.S.*

**MAKE AHEAD** The sauce can be refrigerated for up to 2 weeks.

### Deep-Fried Turkey Brined in Cayenne and Brown Sugar
**TOTAL: 1 HR PLUS 36 HR BRINING**
**10 SERVINGS, WITH LEFTOVERS** ●

Deep-frying a turkey isn't as hard as it sounds (though it does require caution). And there's a great payoff: an exquisitely moist, crispy bird. You can use different kinds of equipment: a stockpot, an electric fryer, a pot-and-propane setup (you can buy these at hardware stores or online at sites like cajun-outdoor-cooking.com). The best deep fryers come with a thermostat and a metal basket for lowering the turkey into the hot oil and removing it once it's done. Whatever equipment you use, the procedure is the same: Heat the oil—it can take up to an hour— then slowly lower the turkey into it. A 12-pound turkey cooks in just 36 minutes, following the pitch-perfect timing of 3 minutes per pound.

- 3 **cups packed light brown sugar (about 1¼ pounds)**
- 1½ **cups Dijon mustard**
- ¼ **cup plus 2 tablespoons salt**
- 2 **tablespoons cayenne pepper**
- 2 **gallons cold water**
- 1 **bunch thyme**
- 1 **head garlic, separated into cloves and crushed**

**One 12-pound turkey**
2½ **gallons vegetable oil**

1. In a large stockpot, whisk the brown sugar with the mustard, salt and cayenne pepper. Gradually whisk in the water, then add the thyme and the crushed garlic cloves. Add the turkey, cover the pot and brine in the refrigerator for 36 hours.

2. In a turkey fryer or an 18-quart or larger stockpot, bring the vegetable oil to 400°; this can take up to an hour. Remove the turkey from the brine and pat it thoroughly dry inside and out with paper towels. Transfer to a frying basket, breast side up.

3. Lower the turkey in the frying basket into the hot vegetable oil and fry it for 3 minutes per pound, 36 minutes. Lift the basket out of the fryer and drain the turkey on a rack set over a rimmed baking sheet for about 15 minutes. Carve the turkey and serve immediately.

—*Allison Vines-Rushing and Slade Rushing*

**SERVE WITH** Satsuma Orange and Dried-Cranberry Chutney (recipe follows).

**WINE** Ripe, juicy Pinot Noir.

### SATSUMA ORANGE AND DRIED-CRANBERRY CHUTNEY
**ACTIVE: 15 MIN; TOTAL: 1 HR PLUS 1 HR COOLING**
**MAKES 3 CUPS** ● ●

- 2 **pounds satsuma oranges, clementines or juice oranges, with skin, thinly sliced**
- 1 **cup sugar**
- 2 **tablespoons fresh lemon juice**
- ½ **cup dried cranberries**

In a medium saucepan, combine the satsumas, sugar and lemon juice. Simmer over moderately low heat, stirring occasionally, until thick, about 45 minutes. Stir in the cranberries and remove from the heat. Let cool to room temperature, about 1 hour. — A.V.R. and S.R.

### Slow-Smoked Turkey with Cane Syrup–Coffee Glaze

**ACTIVE: 1 HR; TOTAL: 3 HR**

10 SERVINGS, WITH LEFTOVERS ●

If you have a grill with a lid and a bag of hickory chips, you can smoke a turkey. Braising the bird first in a mix of coffee, apple cider vinegar and cane syrup or brown sugar results in marvelously complex flavors—sweet, bitter and herbaceous.

- 2 gallons water
- 1 cup apple cider vinegar
- ½ cup ground coffee, preferably chicory coffee
- 1 large onion, halved
- 12 large thyme sprigs, tied together
- ¼ cup kosher salt
- 1 tablespoon black peppercorns
- 2 cups light brown sugar or 3 cups cane syrup (see Note)

One 11-pound turkey

About 3 cups hickory chips

Vegetable oil, for brushing

**1.** In a large saucepan, bring 1 gallon of the water to a boil; keep warm. In a large stockpot, combine the cider vinegar, coffee, onion, thyme, salt and peppercorns with 1¾ cups of the brown sugar and the remaining gallon of water. Bring to a boil.

**2.** Holding the turkey by the legs, carefully ease the bird into the hot brine, neck end down. Add enough of the hot water to the stockpot to cover the turkey and bring to a simmer. Simmer for 1½ hours.

**3.** Carefully remove the turkey from the stockpot. Strain 2 cups of the braising liquid into a heatproof bowl and stir in the remaining ¼ cup of brown sugar. Discard the remaining braising liquid.

**4.** Meanwhile, light a charcoal grill or preheat a gas grill. A few minutes before the turkey has finished simmering, add 2 cups of the hickory chips to the coals. When the chips start smoking, brush the turkey breast with vegetable oil. Set the turkey breast side down on the grill. Cover and smoke over low heat for 15 minutes. Baste the turkey with the reserved braising liquid; turn it breast side up and baste again. Cover the grill and continue smoking the turkey for about 40 minutes longer, basting occasionally with the braising liquid and adding more coals or hickory chips to the grill as necessary. The turkey is done when an instant-read thermometer inserted in the inner thigh registers 165°. Transfer the turkey to a cutting board and let rest 20 minutes before carving. —Allison Vines-Rushing and Slade Rushing

**NOTE** Cane syrup is available by mail order from Steen's (800-725-1654 or steensyrup.com).

**WINE** Fruity, luscious Shiraz.

### Duck with Cranberry Mostaza

**TOTAL: 30 MIN**

4 SERVINGS ●

Chef Andy Nusser of Casa Mono in New York City has a secret for cooking duck: He slowly sears it over low heat, which crisps the skin while keeping the meat tender. He likes duck best with a sweet-tart sauce like this cranberry *mostaza* (mustard) with a hint of red wine vinegar.

- ¾ cup dry red wine
- ¾ cup sugar
- 1 large bay leaf
- 1 bag cranberries (12 ounces)
- 1½ tablespoons red wine vinegar
- 1½ tablespoons dry mustard

Salt and freshly ground pepper

Two 12-ounce duck breasts

Vegetable oil

- 2 large endives, quartered lengthwise

**1.** In a large saucepan, combine the red wine with the sugar and bay leaf and bring to a boil, stirring to dissolve the sugar. Boil until the wine is syrupy, about 9 minutes. Add the cranberries to the saucepan and cook until they begin to break down, about 5 minutes. In a small bowl, whisk the red wine vinegar with the dry mustard, then whisk the mixture into the cranberries in the saucepan. Season the cranberry *mostaza* with salt and pepper.

**2.** Meanwhile, heat a large, heavy skillet until very hot. Lightly rub the duck skin with vegetable oil and add the duck breasts to the skillet, skin side down. Cook the duck breasts over moderately low heat until the skin is golden and crisp, about 15 minutes. As the fat renders, spoon it into a heatproof bowl. Season the duck breasts with salt and pepper, turn them over and cook over moderately low heat until browned on the bottom, about 8 minutes. Transfer the cooked duck breasts to a plate and keep warm.

**3.** Add 2 tablespoons of the reserved duck fat to the skillet and heat until the fat is shimmering. Add the quartered endives to the skillet, season with salt and pepper and cook over moderately high heat, turning the endives occasionally, until they are softened and golden, about 6 minutes. Slice the duck breasts and transfer to plates. Serve the duck with the quartered endives and the cranberry *mostaza*. —Andy Nusser

**WINE** Earthy, medium-bodied Tempranillo.

# technique
### BRINING

Poultry can easily dry out when roasted. Soaking a bird in salted water (often overnight, as in the deep-fried turkey recipe opposite) is an excellent way to improve the meat's taste and texture. It produces a moist, deeply seasoned result.

## Duck Breasts with Fresh Cherry Sauce and Grilled Apricots

**ACTIVE: 40 MIN; TOTAL: 1 HR 40 MIN**

**4 SERVINGS**

In this delicious recipe, apricots are marinated in garlic and thyme, then served alongside slices of golden duck and a bright cherry sauce.

- 3½ tablespoons extra-virgin olive oil
- 1 tablespoon plus 1 teaspoon chopped thyme
- 1 tablespoon minced garlic
- Salt and freshly ground pepper
- Four 6-ounce apricots, halved and pitted
- 1 cup apple juice or cider
- ½ cup red wine vinegar
- Pinch of sugar
- ½ pound sweet cherries, pitted (2 cups)
- 1 tablespoon minced shallots
- 1 tablespoon fresh lime juice
- 1 large fennel bulb, cored and very thinly sliced
- Four 6-ounce boneless Pekin duck breasts, skin scored in a crosshatch pattern
- ½ cup small arugula leaves
- 2 tablespoons minced chives

**1.** In a shallow dish, combine 2 tablespoons of the olive oil with 1 tablespoon of the thyme and the garlic and season with salt and pepper. Add the apricot halves and toss to coat. Let stand for 1 hour.

**2.** Meanwhile, preheat the oven to 400°. In a medium saucepan, combine the apple juice, vinegar and sugar and boil over moderately high heat until slightly thickened, about 15 minutes. Add the cherries and boil until tender, about 3 minutes. With a slotted spoon, transfer the cherries to a bowl. Add the shallots to the pan and boil over high heat until the liquid has reduced to ½ cup, about 4 minutes. Return the cherries to the saucepan. Stir in the remaining 1 teaspoon of thyme and season with salt and pepper. Keep the sauce warm.

**3.** Light a grill. In a medium bowl, mix the remaining 1½ tablespoons of olive oil with the lime juice and season with salt and pepper. Add the fennel and toss well.

**4.** Grill the apricots over moderately high heat until they are lightly charred and tender, about 3 minutes per side. Transfer to a plate and keep warm.

**5.** Heat a large ovenproof skillet. Season the duck breasts generously with salt and pepper. Add to the skillet, skin side down, and cook over moderately high heat until some of the fat has been rendered, about 3 minutes. Transfer the skillet to the oven and roast the duck breasts for 3 minutes. Turn the breasts and roast for about 3 minutes longer, until medium rare. Transfer the duck breasts to a carving board to rest for 5 minutes.

**6.** Toss the arugula and chives with the fennel salad and arrange on 4 plates. Slice the duck breasts crosswise ¼ inch thick; arrange the slices on the plates and top with the cherry sauce. Garnish with the grilled apricots and serve.

—*Seth Bixby Daugherty*

**MAKE AHEAD** The cherry sauce can be refrigerated overnight. Reheat gently before serving.

**WINE** Earthy, medium-bodied Tempranillo.

## Duck Breasts with Mustard and Candied Kumquats

**ACTIVE: 25 MIN; TOTAL: 1 HR**

**4 SERVINGS** ●

The blend of fiery mustard and jalapeño with sweet candied kumquats make this sauce sensational.

- ½ cup dry white wine
- 1 tablespoon plus 1 teaspoon pure olive oil
- 1½ teaspoons grainy mustard
- 1 teaspoon chopped rosemary
- Four 8-ounce duck breasts, skin and fat removed
- 6 ounces kumquats, sliced crosswise ⅓ inch thick
- ½ cup sugar
- ½ cup water
- Salt and freshly ground pepper
- 2 medium shallots, thinly sliced
- 1 jalapeño, seeded and thinly sliced
- 1 tablespoon Dijon mustard

**1.** In a shallow dish, combine the wine with 1 teaspoon of the olive oil and ½ teaspoon each of the grainy mustard and rosemary. Add the duck breasts and turn to coat. Cover and refrigerate for 30 minutes.

**2.** Bring a saucepan of water to a boil. Add the kumquats and simmer over moderately high heat until tender, about 5 minutes, then drain them. In the same saucepan, combine the sugar and water and bring to a boil, stirring to dissolve the sugar. Add the kumquats and simmer over moderate heat for 8 minutes. Transfer to a heatproof bowl along with the sugar syrup.

**3.** In a large skillet, heat the remaining 1 tablespoon of olive oil. Remove the duck breasts from the marinade; reserve the marinade. Season the duck breasts with salt and pepper and cook over moderately high heat until browned on the bottom, about 3 minutes. Turn the duck breasts, reduce the heat to moderate and cook until browned on the bottom and medium rare, 2 to 3 minutes longer. Transfer the duck breasts to warmed plates.

**4.** Add the shallots, jalapeño and remaining ½ teaspoon of rosemary to the skillet and cook over moderately low heat until softened, about 4 minutes. Add the reserved duck marinade and simmer over moderately high heat until syrupy, about 3 minutes. Add the kumquats and their syrup and bring to a simmer. Blend in the Dijon mustard and remaining 1 teaspoon of grainy mustard and remove from the heat. Season with salt and pepper. Slice the duck, pour the kumquat sauce over the slices and serve. —*Marcia Kiesel*

**MAKE AHEAD** The candied kumquat slices can be refrigerated for up to a week.

**WINE** Full-bodied, rich Pinot Gris.

DUCK BREASTS WITH MUSTARD
AND CANDIED KUMQUATS

GRILLED GAME HENS
WITH FOUR HERBS

## Grilled Game Hens with Four Herbs

ACTIVE: 35 MIN; TOTAL: 1 HR 10 MIN

4 SERVINGS

Before grilling these small hens, Jonathan Benno, executive chef at Per Se in New York City, butterflies them, cutting out the backbones with kitchen scissors or a sturdy knife so they can be flattened. "It's the best way to cook a bird all the way on a grill," he says. "You get those nice grill marks, and by the time the chicken's got good color on both sides, it's cooked all the way through."

- ¼ cup extra-virgin olive oil
- 2 tablespoons fresh lemon juice
- 1 tablespoon finely chopped flat-leaf parsley
- 1 teaspoon finely chopped thyme
- 1 teaspoon finely chopped marjoram
- 1 teaspoon finely chopped rosemary
- 4 Cornish game hens or poussins, backbones removed

Salt and freshly ground pepper

1. Light a charcoal grill. In a small bowl, combine the olive oil, lemon juice, chopped flat-leaf parsley, thyme, marjoram and rosemary. Flatten the game hens and season them all over with salt and pepper. Spread the game hens out on a platter, pour the herb mixture over them and turn to coat well.

2. Grill the game hens over moderately high heat, breast side down, for 10 minutes, or until they are lightly charred. Turn the hens over and grill for about 15 minutes longer, or until an instant-read thermometer inserted in the thickest part of a thigh registers 160°. Transfer the grilled game hens to a cutting board and let rest for 10 minutes, then cut them in half, separating the breasts from the legs. Arrange the hens on a platter and serve at once. —Jonathan Benno

WINE Rustic, peppery Malbec.

## Peking Duck Stir-Fry

TOTAL: 30 MIN

4 SERVINGS ● ●

Ken Hom is an authority on Chinese stir-frying—he's written four books about it. In this recipe, Hom replaces chicken with duck breasts for a stir-fry, an excellent idea: The duck has the flavor to stand up to the chiles, garlic and peanuts here.

- 2 tablespoons soy sauce
- 1 tablespoon Shao-Hsing cooking wine or dry sherry
- 1 tablespoon Asian sesame oil
- 1 tablespoon cornstarch

Salt

Four 6-ounce skinless, boneless Pekin duck breasts, sliced crosswise ½ inch thick

- 3 tablespoons vegetable oil
- 4 large garlic cloves, thinly sliced
- 1 large shallot, thinly sliced
- 1 jalapeño, seeded and thinly sliced
- 1 red chile, seeded and thinly sliced
- 2 teaspoons sugar
- ½ cup chicken stock or water
- ¼ cup salted, roasted peanuts
- 2 tablespoons chopped cilantro

1. In a bowl, stir 1 tablespoon of the soy sauce with the wine, sesame oil, cornstarch and a pinch of salt. Add the duck and turn to coat; let marinate for 10 minutes.

2. In a large skillet or a wok, heat the oil. Add the duck; reserve any excess marinade. Cook over high heat until medium rare, 2 minutes per side. Transfer to a plate.

3. Add the garlic, shallot, jalapeño and chile and cook over moderately high heat, stirring, until golden, about 2 minutes. Add the remaining 1 tablespoon of soy sauce, the reserved marinade, the sugar and stock, then stir-fry, scraping up the browned bits on the bottom of the skillet. Return the duck to the skillet and stir-fry for 30 seconds. Remove from the heat and stir in the peanuts. Transfer to plates, sprinkle with the cilantro and serve. —Ken Hom

WINE Ripe, juicy Pinot Noir.

## Duck Confit Cooked in a Pouch

ACTIVE: 45 MIN; TOTAL: 6 HR PLUS OVERNIGHT SEASONING

MAKES 6 PIECES OF CONFIT ●

Duck confit is a key ingredient in the cassoulet of Toulouse, France. This recipe uses the sous vide technique, cooking the duck legs in a vacuum-sealed pouch. The legs simmer in their own fat so you don't need to cover them with extra duck fat, as in the traditional recipe. If the pouches balloon during cooking, don't worry; they'll contract when chilled.

- 3 tablespoons kosher salt
- 2 teaspoons black peppercorns, lightly crushed
- 1 bay leaf, crumbled
- 1 teaspoon chopped thyme
- 6 large Pekin duck legs, untrimmed

1. In a bowl, mix the salt, peppercorns, bay leaf and thyme. Put the duck legs in a large, shallow container; sprinkle all over with the seasoning. Cover; refrigerate overnight.

2. Rinse the legs and dry them thoroughly with paper towels. Using a vacuum sealer, package and seal the legs in pairs.

3. Set a large enameled cast-iron casserole over a heat diffuser on the stove. Add the pouches and enough hot water to cover generously. Top the pouches with a heat-proof plate to keep them submerged. Cover the pot and bring the water to 180° over moderately low heat. Reduce the heat to low and cook at 180° for 5 hours. The duck legs are ready when they feel very tender and the meat begins to separate from the bone. The joints between the legs and thighs should crack easily when pressed firmly.

4. Prepare an ice water bath. With tongs, transfer the pouches to the water bath. When the legs are cold and the fat solidified, dry the pouches and refrigerate for up to 1 week. If a pouch puffs up, discard it.

5. Open the pouches and scrape the fat off. Roast or pan-fry the confit until warmed through and crisp. —Paula Wolfert

WINE Dry, rich Champagne.

## Roasted Guinea Hens with Cumin-Date Sauce

**ACTIVE: 30 MIN; TOTAL: 2 HR**

4 SERVINGS ●

Two 2¼-pound guinea hens or
    2 small chickens
Salt and freshly ground pepper
  ½ lemon, cut into 8 pieces
   4 tablespoons unsalted
     butter, softened
  ½ cup water
   4 small garlic cloves
   2 plump pitted Medjool dates
  ½ cup Pinot Noir
  ½ teaspoon cumin seeds
   1 tablespoon minced chives
  ½ teaspoon chopped thyme
  ½ cup chicken stock
   2 teaspoons fresh lemon juice

**1.** Preheat the oven to 400°. Fold the guinea hen wing tips under the wings. Season the hen cavities with salt and pepper and tuck 4 pieces of lemon inside each one. Tie the legs together with kitchen string.

## superfast
### USES FOR EXTRA HERBS

Stuff inside a whole fish or chicken before roasting.

Use as a bed for steaming fish, shellfish or vegetables.

Mince and blend with softened butter, then freeze for later use on corn, fish or meat.

Transfer the hens to a medium roasting pan, breasts up. Rub 1 tablespoon of butter all over each guinea hen and season generously with salt and pepper. Pour the water into the roasting pan, add the garlic and dates and roast for 30 minutes.

**2.** Reduce the oven temperature to 350°. Add the Pinot Noir to the roasting pan and roast the hens for about 50 minutes longer, or until the skin is richly browned and crisp and the breasts are just done. Remove the hens from the oven and increase the oven temperature to 400°.

**3.** Meanwhile, in a small dry skillet, toast the cumin seeds over moderately high heat until fragrant, about 30 seconds. Transfer to a mortar and let cool. With a pestle, grind the seeds to a powder. Add the chives, thyme and the remaining 2 tablespoons of butter and stir to blend. Season the cumin butter with salt and pepper.

**4.** Remove the strings from the hens and transfer the hens to a carving board. Using a sharp knife, cut the legs off the hens at the thigh joint. Return the legs to the roasting pan, skin side up, and roast for 10 minutes longer, or until they are cooked through, then transfer to the carving board.

**5.** Set the roasting pan over 2 burners. Add the stock and simmer over moderately high heat, stirring to scrape up any browned bits stuck to the bottom of the pan. Simmer for 1 minute. Strain the juices through a coarse sieve set over a small saucepan. Using a rubber spatula, press the soft garlic and dates through the sieve; scrape the puree from the bottom of the sieve and add to the saucepan. Pour in any accumulated juices from the birds; bring to a simmer, whisking until smooth. Remove from the heat and whisk in the reserved cumin butter and the lemon juice. Season with salt and pepper. Thickly slice the breasts and separate the drumsticks from the thighs. Serve with the sauce.
—*Marcia Kiesel*

**WINE** Complex, elegant Pinot Noir.

## Quail Escabèche

**ACTIVE: 1 HR; TOTAL: 2 HR 40 MIN**

8 FIRST-COURSE SERVINGS ●

Depending on what's available, Bar Pintxo, inside Barcelona's historic La Boqueria market, makes this escabèche with either *codorniz* (quail) or *perdiz* (partridge).

   1 cup plus 2 tablespoons
     extra virgin olive oil
   8 whole quail (not boneless)
Salt and freshly ground pepper
   2 large onions, thinly sliced
     lengthwise
   2 large carrots, thinly sliced
   2 heads garlic, cloves peeled
   1 bay leaf
   1 rosemary sprig
   4 thyme sprigs
   1 teaspoon paprika
One 750-ml bottle dry white wine
   1 cup red wine vinegar

**1.** In a large, deep skillet, heat 2 tablespoons of the oil. Season the quail with salt and pepper, add to the skillet and cook over moderately high heat, turning once, until browned, 10 minutes. Transfer to a platter. Add the onions, carrots, garlic, bay leaf, rosemary, thyme and the remaining 1 cup of oil and cook over moderately high heat, stirring occasionally, until softened, 10 minutes. Add the paprika and cook for 1 minute, stirring. Add the wine and vinegar, season with salt and pepper and bring to a boil.

**2.** Return the quail to the skillet, breast side down. Cover and cook over moderately low heat until the meat is very tender and slightly pulling away from the breast bone, 1 hour. Turn and cook uncovered for 10 minutes. Let cool for 30 minutes.

**3.** Pull off the quail legs, then pull the meat from the breast bone; discard the back- and breastbones. Transfer the meat to bowls. Season the sauce with salt and pepper. Discard the bay leaf, rosemary and thyme. Pour the sauce over the quail. Serve warm or at room temperature. —*Jeff Koehler*

**WINE** Zesty, fresh Albariño.

## Grilled Quail with Mushroom Quinoa Risotto

**TOTAL: 1 HR**

6 SERVINGS

- 1 ancho chile
- 1 cup boiling water
- ½ cup black quinoa, rinsed
- ½ cup white quinoa, rinsed
- 6 medium dried shiitake mushrooms
- ½ cup white wine, heated until hot
- 4 garlic cloves, 3 chopped, 1 minced
- ¼ cup white wine vinegar
- ¼ cup extra-virgin olive oil
- 2 teaspoons sugar
- 1 large red onion, cut into 6 slices
- 6 semiboneless quail

Salt and freshly ground pepper

- 2 tablespoons unsalted butter
- ½ yellow bell pepper, cut into ½-inch dice
- ¼ pound fresh shiitake mushrooms, stems discarded, caps cut into ½-inch dice
- ½ cup heavy cream
- ½ cup water
- ¼ cup freshly grated Parmesan cheese
- 2 tablespoons minced chives
- 2 tablespoons chopped basil

1. In a heatproof bowl, cover the ancho chile with the boiling water and let soak until softened, about 20 minutes.

2. Bring 2 medium saucepans of salted water to a boil. Add the black quinoa to one and the white quinoa to the other. Boil over moderately high heat, stirring occasionally, until al dente, about 10 minutes for the white quinoa and 20 minutes for the black. Drain the quinoa and transfer to a large bowl. Cover with plastic wrap and keep at room temperature.

3. In another heatproof bowl, cover the dried shiitake with the hot wine. Let stand until softened, about 15 minutes. Lift the mushrooms out of the wine; reserve the wine. Discard the shiitake stems and cut the caps into ½-inch dice.

4. Remove the chile from the water; discard the stem and seeds. In a food processor, puree the ancho with ¼ cup of the soaking water, the chopped garlic, vinegar and 2 tablespoons of oil. Transfer 2 tablespoons of the ancho puree to a large, shallow dish, stir in the sugar and add the onion. Turn to coat well; marinate for 15 minutes.

5. In a shallow dish, combine the quail with the remaining puree, turning to coat well. Let marinate for 15 minutes.

6. Light a grill or preheat a grill pan. Oil the grill or grill pan. Season the quail with salt and pepper and grill over high heat until they are lightly charred outside but still pink at the breast, 3 minutes per side. Transfer the quail to a platter and cover loosely with foil. Oil the grill and grill the onion over high heat until charred, 4 minutes per side. Transfer to the platter.

7. In a large saucepan, melt the butter in the remaining 2 tablespoons of oil. Add the bell pepper, the fresh and dried shiitake and the minced garlic. Cook over moderate heat until softened, 8 minutes. Add the reserved wine and cook for 2 minutes. Add the heavy cream and water and bring to a boil. Add the black and white quinoa and stir to heat through. Stir in the cheese, chives and basil. Season with salt and pepper. Transfer the quail and onion slices to plates and serve with the mushroom quinoa risotto. —*Emmanuel Piqueras*

**WINE** Ripe, juicy Pinot Noir.

## Roasted Goose with Crispy Skin

**ACTIVE: 30 MIN; TOTAL: 3 HR 20 MIN PLUS OVERNIGHT DRYING**

6 SERVINGS

One 12-pound goose, neck and giblets reserved, visible fat removed

Salt and freshly ground pepper

- 4¼ cups warm water
- 1½ tablespoons honey
- 1 teaspoon Tabasco
- 1 teaspoon potato starch dissolved in 2 tablespoons red or white wine

1. Beginning at the neck end of the goose, work your fingers under the skin, snipping any fibers and sinews with kitchen scissors; work your fingers as far down over the thighs as possible. Using a sharp knife, cut halfway through the wing and leg joints to help the bird cook evenly. Generously season inside and out with salt and pepper.

2. Set the goose on a rack in a heavy roasting pan, breast side up. Add the neck, gizzard, heart and 4 cups of the water to the pan. Cover the goose with foil and seal the foil all around the edge of the pan. Bring the water to a boil on top of the stove. Reduce the heat to low and steam for 45 minutes. Remove from the heat; let cool. Transfer the rack with the goose to a rimmed baking sheet and strain the pan juices. Refrigerate the juices and the uncovered goose overnight.

3. The next day, bring the goose to room temperature. Preheat the oven to 350°. In a bowl, mix the honey with the Tabasco and the remaining ¼ cup of water. Return the rack to the pan and roast the goose for 1 hour, basting occasionally with the Tabasco mixture. Carefully turn the goose breast side down. Roast for 30 minutes longer, basting occasionally. The goose is done when an instant-read thermometer inserted in the inner thigh registers 170°. Turn off the oven and let the goose cool to 160°. Transfer the goose to a heatproof platter, breast side up. Return the goose to the oven and let rest for 20 minutes.

4. Pour off the fat in the roasting pan. Scrape the solidified fat off the refrigerated pan juices; refrigerate for another use. Add the juices to the pan and bring to a boil, scraping up any browned bits. Pour the juices into a saucepan. Stir in the potato starch slurry and simmer, stirring, until slightly thickened, 1 minute. Season the jus with salt and pepper and strain into a gravy boat. Carve the goose and pass the jus at the table. —*Jacques Pépin*

**WINE** Complex, elegant Pinot Noir.

San Francisco chef Michael Mina's family enjoyed his outstanding Salt-and-Pepper-Crusted Prime Rib with Sage Jus (P. 134) in the December issue.

# beef & lamb

NORI-CRUSTED SIRLOIN WITH SHIITAKE AND WASABI

RIB-EYE TAGLIATA WITH WATERCRESS AND POTATOES

### Nori-Crusted Sirloin with Shiitake and Wasabi

**ACTIVE: 35 MIN; TOTAL: 1 HR**

**4 SERVINGS** ● ●

- 2 bunches scallions, white and tender green parts only
- ½ pound shiitake mushrooms, stems discarded

Kosher salt and coarsely ground black pepper

- 1 pound sirloin steak (1¼ inches thick)

Three 8-inch-square sheets of nori (dried seaweed), torn into small pieces

- 1 tablespoon sesame seeds
- 1 teaspoon crushed red pepper
- 1½ tablespoons extra-virgin olive oil
- 2 tablespoons tamari or soy sauce
- 1 tablespoon mirin (sweet Japanese cooking wine)
- 1½ teaspoons fresh lemon juice
- 2 tablespoons wasabi powder mixed with 2 tablespoons water

**1.** Preheat the oven to 400°. In a small saucepan of boiling water, blanch the scallions for 2 minutes. Drain the scallions and rinse under cold water. Set a rack on a baking sheet and arrange the shiitake caps on the rack, gill side down. Season the shiitake mushroom caps lightly with salt and black pepper.

**2.** Season the sirloin steak with salt. In a food processor, coarsely grind the pieces of nori with the sesame seeds, crushed red pepper and 1 teaspoon of black pepper. Spread the nori mixture on a plate and dredge the sirloin steak in it.

**3.** In a medium skillet, heat 1 tablespoon of the olive oil until shimmering. Add the sirloin steak and cook the steak over moderately high heat until the nori is toasted, about 4 minutes per side. Place the sirloin steak over the mushrooms on the rack and transfer the baking sheet with the mushrooms and steak to the oven to roast for about 15 minutes, or until an instant-read thermometer inserted in the center of the meat registers 130° for medium rare. Transfer the steak to a cutting board and let rest for 10 minutes.

**4.** Meanwhile, halve the scallions lengthwise and quarter the mushroom caps. In a small bowl, whisk the tamari with the mirin, lemon juice and the remaining ½ tablespoon of olive oil.

**5.** Slice the sirloin steak ¼ inch thick and arrange it on plates with the shiitake mushrooms and scallions and a small mound of wasabi. Drizzle the tamari mixture over the steak and serve immediately.
—*Josh DeChellis*

**WINE** Deep, velvety Merlot.

124

## Grilled Rib-Eye Tagliata with Watercress and Potatoes

**ACTIVE: 30 MIN; TOTAL: 1 HR**

**8 SERVINGS**

Feel free to play fast and loose with this recipe: You can use almost any tender cut of beef to make tagliata—thin slices of steak served rare.

½ cup plus 2 tablespoons extra-virgin olive oil
2 tablespoons fresh lemon juice
1½ teaspoons Asian fish sauce
Salt and freshly ground pepper
2 pounds fingerling potatoes
1 large garlic clove, minced
½ teaspoon herbes de Provence
5 pounds rib-eye steaks (½ inch thick)
½ pound watercress or arugula, thick stems discarded
5 ounces Parmesan cheese, shaved with a vegetable peeler (2 cups)
Lemon wedges, for serving

1. Preheat the oven to 350°. Light a grill. In a small bowl, combine 2 tablespoons of the olive oil with the lemon juice, fish sauce and a generous pinch each of salt and pepper. Set the dressing aside.
2. In a medium roasting pan, toss the potatoes with 2 tablespoons of the olive oil and season with salt. Roast for about 30 minutes, or until tender.
3. Meanwhile, in a small bowl, combine the garlic and herbes de Provence with the remaining ¼ cup plus 2 tablespoons of olive oil and a generous pinch each of salt and pepper. Rub the mixture all over the steaks. Grill over high heat until browned but still medium rare, 3 to 4 minutes.
4. In a large bowl, toss the watercress with the dressing and Parmesan shavings and season with salt and pepper. Serve the salad with the steaks and potatoes and pass the lemon wedges at the table. —*Hiro Sone*

**WINE** Rich, ripe Cabernet Sauvignon.

## Smoked Paprika–Rubbed Steaks with Valdeón Butter

**TOTAL: 30 MIN PLUS 1 HR MARINATING**

**4 SERVINGS**

This dish is a brilliant combination of robust flavors. Tender rib eye gets flavored by the smoky garlic marinade as well as by a blue cheese butter that melts down the sides of the steaks. Any creamy blue would be terrific here, but Valdeón, a maple leaf–wrapped cheese from the Picos de Europa region of Spain, adds a special complexity to the dish.

4 large garlic cloves, thinly sliced
½ tablespoon kosher salt
1 tablespoon Pimentón de la Vera (smoked Spanish paprika)
Pinch of cayenne pepper
Pinch of dried oregano
¼ cup extra-virgin olive oil
Four 10-ounce rib-eye steaks (about 1 inch thick)
4 tablespoons unsalted butter, softened
1 tablespoon finely chopped shallot
1 scallion, dark green part only, finely chopped
2 ounces Valdeón or other intense and creamy blue cheese, crumbled (⅓ packed cup), at room temperature

1. On a work surface, using the flat side of a chef's knife, mash the garlic to a paste with the salt. Scrape the garlic into a small bowl. Stir in the paprika, cayenne and oregano. Gradually stir in the olive oil. Spread the mixture on a large platter, add the steaks and turn to coat, rubbing in the marinade. Let stand at room temperature for 1 to 4 hours, or refrigerate overnight.
2. Meanwhile, in a medium bowl, mash the butter with the shallot and scallion. Stir in the Valdeón. Scrape the blue cheese butter onto a sheet of plastic wrap and pat it into a 4-inch log. Wrap and refrigerate until firm, at least 30 minutes.
3. Light a grill or preheat a grill pan. Scrape some of the marinade off the steaks and grill over moderately high heat, turning once, for about 8 minutes for medium rare. Slice the butter 1 inch thick, set a pat on each steak and serve. —*Grace Parisi*

**WINE** Juicy, spicy Grenache.

## Balsamic Steaks

**TOTAL: 25 MIN**

**4 SERVINGS** ●

Donna Hay, the Australian cookbook author, is a terrific representative of Australian cooking. In this recipe, she flavors juicy rib-eye steak with a punchy balsamic glaze and serves it alongside a bright-tasting bean salad. This recipe is also great with boneless chicken breast.

½ pound cherry tomatoes, halved
One 19-ounce can cannellini beans, drained and rinsed
1 tablespoon fresh lemon juice
3 tablespoons extra-virgin olive oil
Salt and freshly ground pepper
Four 8- to 10-ounce rib-eye steaks
¼ cup balsamic vinegar
Pinch of sugar
1 ounce arugula (2 cups)

1. In a bowl, combine the cherry tomatoes and cannellini beans. Add the lemon juice and 1 tablespoon of olive oil and toss; season with salt and pepper.
2. In a skillet, heat the remaining 2 tablespoons of olive oil until shimmering. Season the steaks with salt and pepper and cook over high heat until deeply browned and medium rare, about 3 minutes per side. Transfer the steaks to plates.
3. Pour off the oil in the skillet. Add the balsamic vinegar and sugar and cook over moderate heat, shaking the pan to dissolve the sugar. Pour the vinegar sauce over the steaks. Toss the arugula with the beans and tomatoes and serve with the steaks. —*Donna Hay*

**WINE** Complex, aromatic Nebbiolo.

# beef & lamb

## Grilled Skirt Steak with Fregola and Italian Frying Peppers

**TOTAL: 40 MIN PLUS 1 HR MARINATING**
**8 SERVINGS**

Garlic infuses both the succulent skirt steak and the sweet fried peppers tossed with *fregola*, a small, round Sardinian couscous that is cooked like pasta.

- 1 cup extra-virgin olive oil
- 4 garlic cloves, 2 minced, 2 thinly sliced
- 1 teaspoon chopped thyme

Salt and freshly ground pepper

- 5 pounds skirt steak
- 1 pound Italian frying peppers, cut into 2-inch pieces
- 1½ pounds *fregola* (see Note)

Leaves from 1 bunch flat-leaf parsley

- ½ cup sherry vinegar

**1.** In a small bowl, combine ¼ cup of the olive oil with the minced garlic, the thyme and a generous pinch each of salt and pepper. On a rimmed baking sheet, rub the skirt steak with the flavored oil and let stand at room temperature for 1 hour.

**2.** Meanwhile, heat ¼ cup of the oil in a large skillet. Add the peppers and cook over moderate heat, stirring occasionally, until lightly browned, about 8 minutes. Add the sliced garlic and cook, stirring, until it softens, about 2 minutes. Transfer the peppers to a large bowl.

**3.** Cook the *fregola* in a large pot of boiling salted water, stirring occasionally, until al dente, about 11 minutes. Drain the *fregola* well in a colander and let cool. Add the *fregola* to the peppers along with the parsley, sherry vinegar and the remaining ½ cup of oil. Season generously with salt and pepper and toss well.

**4.** Light a grill. Grill the skirt steak over high heat, turning once, about 8 minutes for medium. Let the steak rest for 5 minutes, then cut it into 5-inch lengths. Thinly slice the steak across the grain and serve with the *fregola* and peppers. —*Marc Murphy*

**NOTE** *Fregola* is available at Italian markets and specialty shops, or online from cybercucina.com.

**MAKE AHEAD** The *fregola* with peppers can stand at room temperature for up to 4 hours. Toss before serving.

**WINE** Firm, complex Cabernet Sauvignon.

## Skirt Steak with Shiso-Shallot Butter

**TOTAL: 45 MIN PLUS 2 HR MARINATING**
**8 SERVINGS**

TV chef Tyler Florence makes a Korean-inspired marinade for skirt steak with hoisin sauce, soy sauce and brown sugar. With what he calls a "king-of-the-grill mentality," he boldly adds even more layers of flavor by topping the steak with a butter he's blended with caramelized shallots and shiso, an aromatic green leaf used frequently in Japanese cooking. In the United States, shiso leaves are available at Asian markets; one tablespoon of chopped fresh tarragon is a fine substitute in this recipe.

**STEAK**

- ½ cup hoisin sauce
- ¼ cup light brown sugar
- ¼ cup soy sauce
- 3 garlic cloves, very finely chopped
- 2 tablespoons finely grated fresh ginger
- 2 tablespoons rice vinegar
- 1 tablespoon sambal oelek or other Asian chili paste
- 4 pounds skirt steaks

**BUTTER**

- 2 tablespoons extra-virgin olive oil
- 5 medium shallots, thinly sliced
- ¼ cup soy sauce
- 14 medium shiso leaves, coarsely chopped (about ⅔ cup), or 1 tablespoon chopped tarragon
- 1 teaspoon crushed black peppercorns

- 1 stick (4 ounces) unsalted butter, softened
- 3 bunches scallions

**1. MARINATE THE STEAK:** In a bowl, mix the hoisin sauce, light brown sugar, soy sauce, garlic, ginger, rice vinegar and sambal oelek. Lay the steaks in a large roasting pan in a single layer. Pour the marinade over the meat and turn to coat. Cover and refrigerate the steaks for 2 hours.

**2. MEANWHILE, MAKE THE BUTTER:** In a medium skillet, heat the olive oil. Add the shallots and cook over moderate heat until softened and lightly browned, 10 minutes. Add the soy sauce and simmer until evaporated, 2 minutes; let cool.

**3.** In a bowl, mix the shallots, shiso leaves and crushed black peppercorns into the butter. Transfer the shiso-shallot butter to the refrigerator.

**4.** Light a grill. Grill the steaks over high heat for 3 to 4 minutes per side for medium-rare meat. Transfer the steaks to a carving board and let them rest for 5 to 10 minutes. Meanwhile, grill the scallions, turning, until lightly charred all over, about 2 minutes. Thinly slice the steaks against the grain and transfer to a platter along with the scallions. Top the skirt steaks with the shiso-shallot butter and serve at once. —*Tyler Florence*

**MAKE AHEAD** The shiso-shallot butter can be refrigerated overnight or frozen for up to 1 month.

**WINE** Round, deep-flavored Syrah.

## Skirt Steak with Onion Marmalade

**TOTAL: 30 MIN**
**4 SERVINGS** ● ●

- 1 cup sugar
- 1 cup dry red wine
- 1 large red onion, thinly sliced
- ¼ cup red wine vinegar
- ¼ cup plus 2 tablespoons extra-virgin olive oil
- 1 large Spanish onion, finely chopped

4 garlic cloves, 2 thinly sliced,
    2 minced

One 8-ounce jar roasted red peppers,
    drained (about 1 cup)

2 tablespoons sherry vinegar

Salt and freshly ground
    black pepper

½ teaspoon cayenne pepper

½ teaspoon ground cumin

1½ pounds skirt steak, cut crosswise
    into 4 pieces

1. In a medium saucepan, combine ½ cup of the sugar with the wine and bring to a boil, stirring to dissolve the sugar. Add the red onion, cover and cook over high heat, stirring occasionally, until softened, about 5 minutes. Drain the onion slices and discard the liquid. Return the onion to the pan. Add the remaining ½ cup of sugar and the red wine vinegar and cook over moderate heat, stirring occasionally, until syrupy, about 6 minutes longer.

2. Meanwhile, in a large skillet, heat 2 tablespoons of the olive oil until shimmering. Add the Spanish onion and cook over moderately high heat, stirring, until softened, about 5 minutes. Add the sliced garlic and roasted red peppers and cook over moderate heat until the garlic is softened, about 5 minutes. Add the sherry vinegar. Scrape the mixture into a food processor and puree until fairly smooth. Season the red pepper sauce with salt and black pepper and transfer to a bowl. Rinse out the skillet and pat dry.

3. Heat the skillet until hot but not smoking. In a small bowl, combine the remaining ¼ cup of olive oil with the minced garlic, the cayenne and the cumin. Rub the mixture over the steaks and season with salt. Add the steaks to the skillet and cook them over high heat, turning once, until they are medium rare, about 5 minutes. Transfer the steaks to plates and serve with the onion marmalade and red pepper sauce.
—*Andy Nusser*

**WINE** Earthy, medium-bodied Tempranillo.

## Pot Roast Smothered in Bacon and Onions

**ACTIVE: 45 MIN; TOTAL: 3 HR 30 MIN**

6 SERVINGS ●

There seems to be a daunting amount of onions in this Portuguese-inspired dish, but with the bacon they cook down to a wonderful, smoky jam.

3 tablespoons unsalted butter

½ pound thick-cut bacon, cut into
    ½-inch pieces

One 2½-pound beef chuck roast, tied
    at 1-inch intervals

Kosher salt and freshly ground pepper

3 pounds onions, very thinly sliced

12 large garlic cloves, chopped

1¼ cups water

20 whole allspice berries

10 black peppercorns

¼ teaspoon crushed red pepper

1 bay leaf

3 cups dry white wine

2 tablespoons minced
    flat-leaf parsley

1. In a large enameled cast-iron casserole, melt 2 tablespoons of the butter. Add the bacon and cook over moderately low heat, stirring occasionally, until most of the fat has been rendered, about 10 minutes. Using a slotted spoon, transfer the bacon to a paper towel–lined plate.

2. Using a sharp knife, carefully cut the roast between the strings into four 1-inch-thick slabs. Season the meat with salt and pepper. Working in 2 batches, brown the meat in the casserole over moderately high heat, turning once, 6 minutes. Transfer to a large plate. Lower the heat to moderate for the second batch if the butter begins to brown too quickly. Remove the strings. Keep the steaks intact, if possible.

3. Preheat the oven to 350°. Add the onions, garlic, ¼ cup of the water and 1 teaspoon of salt to the casserole. Cook over moderately high heat, stirring and scraping up any browned bits stuck to the bottom of the casserole, about 8 minutes.

Transfer half of the onions to a plate. Stir the remaining 1 tablespoon of butter into the onions in the casserole. Nestle the steaks into the onions, overlapping them slightly if necessary. Add the allspice berries, peppercorns, crushed pepper and bay leaf; lay half of the reserved bacon over the steaks. Spread the remaining onions and bacon on top. Add the wine and the remaining 1 cup of water and bring to a simmer, then cover and cook over moderately high heat for 5 minutes.

4. Transfer the casserole to the oven and cook for 30 minutes, then reduce the temperature to 250° and continue braising for 1½ to 2 hours, or until the meat is very tender. Turn the oven off, uncover the casserole and let stand in the oven for 30 minutes. Serve the meat and onions in deep plates; spoon the sauce on top and sprinkle with the parsley. —*Lobel Family*

**SERVE WITH** Steamed rice or crusty country bread.

**MAKE AHEAD** The pot roast can be refrigerated for up to 4 days.

**WINE** Complex, aromatic Nebbiolo.

# F&W taste test
## SOY SAUCE

Beef and soy are natural partners, as in the skirt steak recipe on the opposite page. F&W sampled 30 soy sauces; these are our favorites.

### WAN JA SHAN ORGANIC
Earthy flavor, with a deep, roasted taste. Good as a dipping sauce and for cooking.

### KAGAYA
A rich, full-bodied soy sauce with an almost misolike flavor. Works well as a dipping sauce and for cooking.

### KIKKOMAN
Both the naturally brewed Sushi and Sashimi and Lite Soy sauces are pleasantly tangy and mild.

**GARLICKY HERB-RUBBED HANGER STEAKS**

**CALF'S LIVER WITH GREEN BEANS**

## Garlicky Herb-Rubbed Hanger Steaks

**ACTIVE: 20 MIN; TOTAL: 1 HR PLUS 5 HR MARINATING**

8 SERVINGS

Shea Gallante, chef at Cru restaurant in New York City and an F&W Best New Chef 2005, based this recipe on a classic Florentine dish called *bistecca alla fiorentina*—a thick T-bone grilled rare over hot coals. Here, Gallante substitutes cheaper but equally flavorful hanger steak, which he thinks is an underrated cut, and rubs the meat with dried herbs, garlic and paprika before cooking it.

1½ teaspoons dried thyme
½ teaspoon dried rosemary
½ teaspoon dried marjoram
½ teaspoon dried oregano
1 head garlic, cloves peeled and minced
Three 2-pound hanger steaks
2 tablespoons sweet paprika
Olive oil, for drizzling
Kosher salt and freshly ground pepper

**1.** In a mini food processor or spice grinder, combine the dried thyme with the dried rosemary, marjoram and oregano and blend the herbs until a powder forms. On a work surface, rub the minced garlic cloves all over the hanger steaks and sprinkle them with the sweet paprika. Dust the steaks with the powdered herbs, cover with plastic wrap and refrigerate for at least 4 hours or overnight. Let the steaks stand at room temperature for 1 hour before proceeding with the recipe.

**2.** Light a grill. Drizzle the steaks all over with olive oil and season them generously with salt and pepper. Grill the steaks over moderately high heat until they are charred on the outside and medium rare on the inside, about 12 minutes per side. Transfer the steaks to a carving board to rest for 15 minutes.

3. Working from both sides and using a sharp knife, slice the steaks against the grain until you reach the strip of gristle in the center. Discard the gristle. Arrange the slices on a platter and serve.
—*Shea Gallante*

**WINE** Cherry-inflected, earthy Sangiovese.

## Calf's Liver with Green Beans

**TOTAL: 30 MIN**

**4 SERVINGS** ●

When prepared correctly, calf's liver can be absolutely amazing. This rich and crispy version is served with a tangy salad of wax beans and frisée in a mustardy red wine vinaigrette.

- 1 pound green beans or yellow wax beans, trimmed
- 1 shallot, minced
- 1½ tablespoons red wine vinegar
- 1½ teaspoons Dijon mustard
- ¼ cup extra-virgin olive oil

Salt and freshly ground pepper

- 1 pound thinly sliced calf's liver
- ½ cup all-purpose flour
- ½ cup pure olive oil
- 6 ounces frisée, leaves torn

1. Bring a saucepan of lightly salted water to a boil. Add the green beans and boil until tender, about 5 minutes. Drain the beans and pat dry.

2. Meanwhile, in a medium bowl, whisk together the shallot, vinegar and mustard. Whisk in the extra-virgin olive oil and season with salt and pepper. Add the beans and toss well.

3. Season the calf's liver with salt and pepper and dust all over with the flour, tapping off any excess. In a very large skillet, heat the pure olive oil until shimmering. Add the calf's liver and cook over moderately high heat, turning the slices once, until they're golden, 3 to 4 minutes.

4. Add the frisée to the beans and toss to coat. Serve the liver with the beans and frisée. —*Marc Meyer*

**WINE** Firm, complex Cabernet Sauvignon.

## Soy-Ginger Flank Steak with Grilled Eggplant

**TOTAL: 30 MIN**

**4 SERVINGS** ●

The secret to this dish is the marinade, a simple mix of soy sauce, lime juice and ginger. Scoring the flank steak helps the marinade penetrate quickly.

One 2-pound flank steak

- ½ cup soy sauce
- ¼ cup plus 2 tablespoons fresh lime juice
- 2 tablespoons finely grated fresh ginger
- ¼ cup extra-virgin olive oil
- 1 medium eggplant (about 1½ pounds), cut lengthwise into 8 spears

Salt and freshly ground pepper

1. Using a small, sharp knife, score the flank steak on both sides in a shallow crosshatch pattern and transfer to a shallow baking dish. In a small bowl, combine the soy sauce, lime juice and ginger. Pour ⅔ cup of the soy marinade over the flank steak and turn to coat. Let the flank steak stand for 10 minutes. Reserve the remaining marinade.

2. Meanwhile, light a grill or preheat a grill pan. Brush 2 tablespoons of the olive oil over the cut sides of the eggplant and season with salt and pepper.

3. Remove the steak from the marinade and pat dry. Brush the steak with the remaining 2 tablespoons of olive oil and season with pepper. Grill the steak over moderately high heat, turning occasionally, for about 11 minutes for medium to medium-rare meat. Simultaneously grill the eggplant until tender and browned, 11 minutes. Transfer the steak to a cutting board and let rest for 5 minutes. Thinly slice the meat against the grain. Transfer the meat and eggplant to plates, drizzle with the reserved marinade and serve.
—*Katy Sparks*

**WINE** Rustic, peppery Malbec.

## Peruvian Beef and Noodle Stew

**TOTAL: 30 MIN**

**4 SERVINGS** ●

Daisy Martinez was working off-camera as a prep-kitchen chef for Lidia Bastianich's *Italian-American Kitchen* when she was "discovered" by the producer and given her own PBS series, *Daisy Cooks!* Here, Martinez shares one of her great fast Latin recipes, the kind of dish she might make at home for her own kids.

- 4 tablespoons vegetable oil
- 1½ pounds beef sirloin, cut into 1-inch cubes
- 1 large onion, cut into ½-inch dice
- ½ red bell pepper, cut into ½-inch dice
- 2 garlic cloves, minced
- 5 cups beef stock or low-sodium broth
- 1 large baking potato, peeled and cut into ½-inch dice
- 1 teaspoon ground cumin
- 1 bay leaf
- 4 ounces dried fideos or spaghettini, crushed

Kosher salt and freshly ground pepper

1. In a soup pot, heat 2 tablespoons of the vegetable oil. Add the sirloin cubes and cook over high heat until they are browned all over, 6 to 8 minutes. Transfer the meat to a plate.

2. Heat the remaining 2 tablespoons of vegetable oil in the pot. Add the onion, bell pepper and garlic and cook over moderately high heat until softened, about 4 minutes. Add the stock, potato, cumin and bay leaf. Bring to a simmer and cook for 10 minutes.

3. Add the noodles and simmer until al dente, about 5 minutes. Return the meat and any accumulated juices to the pot and cook until warmed through, about 1 minute. Discard the bay leaf. Season the stew with salt and pepper, ladle into bowls and serve. —*Daisy Martinez*

**WINE** Savory, spicy Carmenère.

# beef & lamb

## Fiery Grilled Beef Salad with Oranges and Crispy Shallots

**TOTAL: 45 MIN PLUS 2 HR MARINATING**

6 SERVINGS ●

You can use any leafy green in this spicy main-course salad, although watercress adds another subtle, peppery layer of heat to the dish. It's fine to partially cook the shallots ahead of time (even the night before) until they are golden, then let them cool; when you refry them before serving, they'll become extra crispy.

- 1 tablespoon black peppercorns
- 1 tablespoon coriander seeds
- 2 tablespoons minced garlic
- ¼ cup plus 1½ tablespoons low-sodium soy sauce
- ¼ cup plus 1 tablespoon sugar
- 1½ pounds New York strip steaks (1 inch thick)
- 2 cups canola oil
- 4 large shallots, thinly sliced

Salt
- 2 navel oranges
- ¼ cup fresh orange juice
- 1 tablespoon fresh lime juice
- 2 teaspoons unseasoned rice vinegar
- 1 serrano chile, minced

Freshly ground pepper

One 6-ounce bunch watercress, thick stems discarded

One 6-ounce head frisée, torn into pieces

1. In a small dry skillet, toast the peppercorns and coriander seeds over moderately high heat, shaking the pan frequently, until fragrant, about 1 minute. Transfer the toasted peppercorns and coriander seeds to a work surface and let cool. Using the back of a heavy knife, coarsely crack the peppercorns and coriander. Transfer to a large, sturdy, resealable plastic bag. Add the minced garlic and ¼ cup each of the soy sauce and sugar, then add the steaks and seal the bag, carefully pressing out as much air as possible. Refrigerate the steaks in their marinade for 2 hours.

2. Meanwhile, in a medium saucepan, heat the oil until shimmering. Add the shallots and cook over moderate heat, stirring frequently, until golden and crisp, about 10 minutes. Using a slotted spoon, transfer to a paper towel–lined plate. Sprinkle with salt and let cool. Reserve the oil; let cool.

3. Using a very sharp knife, peel the oranges, carefully removing all of the bitter white pith. Working over a bowl, cut in between the membranes, releasing the orange sections into the bowl.

4. Light a grill. Remove the steaks from the marinade and scrape off some of the solids. Grill the steaks over moderately high heat, turning occasionally, about 10 minutes for medium rare. Transfer to a cutting board and let rest for 15 minutes.

5. In a large bowl, combine the orange juice, lime juice, vinegar, serrano chile and the remaining 1½ tablespoons of soy sauce and 1 tablespoon of sugar. Slowly whisk in ½ cup of the reserved oil (reserve the remaining oil for another use) and season the dressing with salt and pepper. Add the orange segments, watercress and frisée. Season the salad with salt and pepper and toss well. Transfer to large plates. Slice the steak across the grain and arrange on the salads. Sprinkle with crispy shallots and serve immediately. —*Charles Phan*

**MAKE AHEAD** The orange sections can be refrigerated overnight. The shallots can be stored in an airtight container. Briefly refry to recrisp.

**WINE** Vivid, lightly sweet Riesling.

## Beef Sukiyaki Noodles

**TOTAL: 30 MIN**

4 SERVINGS ● ●

In ancient Japan, farmers often used a plow (*suki*) for grilling (*yaki*) meat. Thus, sukiyaki was born. In her riff on that dish, Japanese cookbook author Hiroko Shimbo sears thinly sliced beef in a wok until it's tender, then mixes it with onions, mushrooms, tofu, watercress and fettuccine.

- ½ pound dried fettuccine
- ¼ cup plus 2 tablespoons soy sauce
- ¼ cup plus 2 tablespoons sake
- ¼ cup plus 2 tablespoons water
- 2 tablespoons sugar
- 2 tablespoons vegetable oil
- ¾ pound beef sirloin, thinly sliced across the grain and cut into 2-inch lengths

Salt
- 1 medium sweet onion, cut into ½-inch wedges
- 8 large shiitake mushrooms, stems discarded, caps quartered
- 3 scallions, cut into matchsticks
- 1 bunch watercress, thick stems discarded
- ½ pound (about ½ block) firm tofu, cut into 1-inch cubes

1. In a large saucepan of boiling salted water, cook the pasta until al dente, about 12 minutes. Drain and rinse the pasta under hot water. Transfer to 4 bowls and keep the pasta warm.

2. Meanwhile, in a medium bowl, combine the soy sauce, sake, water and sugar and stir until the sugar is dissolved.

3. In a large skillet, heat 1 tablespoon of the oil until shimmering. Season the beef with salt, add to the skillet and cook over high heat, stirring occasionally, until half-cooked, 2 minutes. Transfer to a plate.

4. Add the remaining 1 tablespoon of oil to the skillet. Add the onion and cook over moderate heat until lightly browned, 5 minutes. Add the shiitake and cook until softened, 5 minutes. Add the scallions and watercress and cook, stirring gently, until the watercress is just wilted, 1 minute. Return the meat and any accumulated juices to the skillet, along with the tofu. Add half of the soy-sake sauce. Bring to a boil and simmer just until the meat is cooked through, 1 minute. Spoon the sukiyaki over the noodles and drizzle with the remaining soy-sake sauce. Serve. —*Hiroko Shimbo*

**WINE** Fruity, luscious Shiraz.

## BEEF SUKIYAKI NOODLES

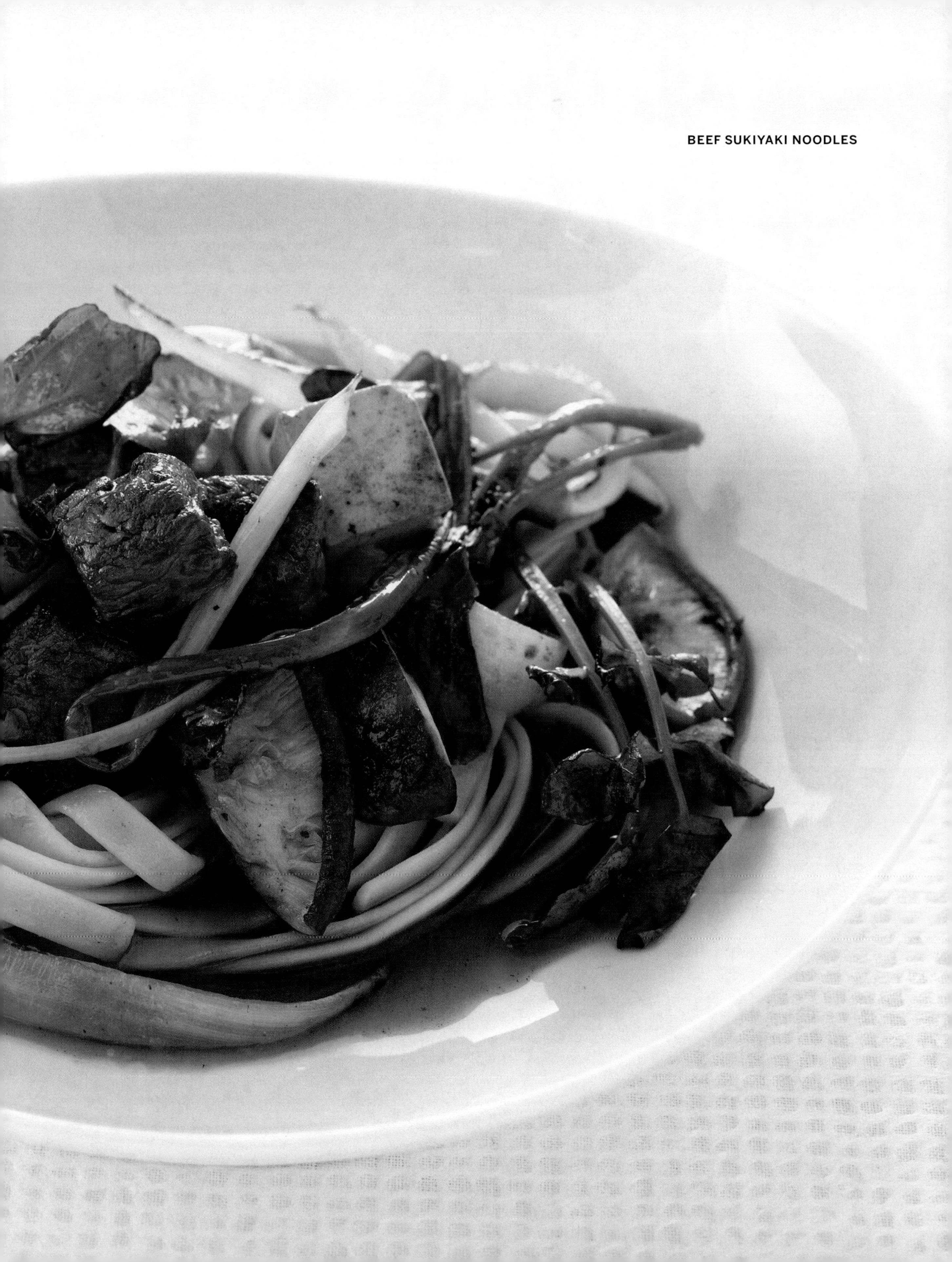

# beef & lamb

## Steak Salad with Creamy Italian Dressing

**TOTAL: 30 MIN**

6 SERVINGS ●

A perfectly grilled steak is delicious with good vegetables, like this salad of bitter greens, peppery radishes and crunchy croutons in an herb-packed dressing.

- 1 **large garlic clove, thickly sliced**

Kosher salt

- 3 **tablespoons heavy cream or crème fraîche**
- 3 **tablespoons mayonnaise**
- 2 **tablespoons white wine vinegar**
- 1 **teaspoon Dijon mustard**
- ¼ **cup plus 2 tablespoons extra-virgin olive oil, plus more for brushing**
- 1 **tablespoon finely chopped flat-leaf parsley**
- 1 **teaspoon chopped oregano**

Freshly ground pepper

- 2 **pounds boneless sirloin, rib-eye or strip steak (1 inch thick)**

Six 1-inch-thick baguette slices

- 1 **large head escarole, tender inner leaves only, torn**
- 3 **endives, sliced crosswise 1 inch thick**
- 6 **large radishes, thinly sliced**
- 1 **Hass avocado, thinly sliced lengthwise**

**1.** Light a grill. Using the flat side of a chef's knife, mash the garlic with a large pinch of salt. Transfer the garlic paste to a bowl and whisk in the heavy cream, mayonnaise, white wine vinegar and mustard. Whisk in the ¼ cup plus 2 tablespoons of olive oil in a thin stream until emulsified. Add the parsley and oregano and season the dressing with salt and pepper.

**2.** Brush the sirloin steak with olive oil and season it generously with salt and pepper. Grill the steak over moderately high heat, turning occasionally, about 10 minutes for

medium-rare meat. Transfer the steak to a cutting board and let it rest for 10 minutes, then slice thinly.

**3.** Meanwhile, brush the baguette slices with olive oil and grill the bread until it is toasted, 2 to 3 minutes. Cut the toasted baguette slices into cubes.

**4.** In a large bowl, combine the escarole with the endives, radishes, avocado and bread cubes. Add the dressing and toss to coat. Transfer the salad to a large platter or plates, top with the steak and serve.
—*Grace Parisi*

**WINE** Fresh, fruity rosé.

## Beef Stew with Port and Porcini

**ACTIVE: 1 HR; TOTAL: 3 HR PLUS OVERNIGHT MARINATING**

6 SERVINGS ● ●

Gail Hobbs-Page, former chef at musician Dave Matthews's Virginia farm, Best of What's Around, developed this beef stew recipe with chuck in mind. She marinates the meat overnight to tenderize it, simmers it slowly, then adds port, red wine and porcini mushrooms to create a rich, deeply flavored sauce.

- 3 **pounds beef chuck roast, fat trimmed, meat cut into 1-inch pieces**
- 2 **large onions, coarsely chopped**
- 4 **large garlic cloves, thinly sliced**
- 4 **thyme sprigs, plus 2 teaspoons finely chopped thyme leaves**
- 2 **bay leaves**
- 1 **cup pure olive oil**

One 750-ml bottle dry red wine

Salt and freshly ground pepper

- ½ **ounce dried porcini mushrooms (½ cup)**
- 1 **cup ruby port**
- 2 **tablespoons tomato paste**
- ¼ **cup extra-virgin olive oil**
- 3 **slices of thick-cut bacon, cut into 1-inch pieces**
- 2 **celery ribs, finely chopped**
- ½ **cup all-purpose flour**

- 2 **large carrots, cut into 1-inch pieces**
- 4 **large shiitake mushrooms, stems discarded, caps thinly sliced**
- 2 **cups chicken stock or low-sodium broth**
- 2 **tablespoons minced flat-leaf parsley**

**1.** In a large bowl, toss the beef chuck with the onions, garlic, thyme sprigs, bay leaves, pure olive oil and 1 cup of the red wine; season with salt and pepper. Cover with plastic wrap and refrigerate overnight.

**2.** Drain the meat. Transfer the meat to a paper towel–lined plate and pat dry; reserve the onion mixture separately.

**3.** In a medium heatproof bowl, cover the dried porcini with the port. Microwave at high power for 1 minute, until the porcini are softened; let cool. Using a slotted spoon, transfer the porcini to a food processor. Add the tomato paste and half of the porcini soaking liquid and process until smooth. Reserve the remaining porcini soaking liquid.

**4.** In a large, heavy casserole, heat 2 tablespoons of the extra-virgin olive oil. Add the bacon and cook over moderately high heat until crisp, about 5 minutes. Add the reserved onion mixture and the celery and cook over moderately high heat, stirring occasionally, until softened, about 8 minutes. Using a slotted spoon, transfer the onion-bacon mixture to a bowl.

**5.** Heat the remaining 2 tablespoons of extra-virgin olive oil in the casserole. Dust the meat with the flour, shaking off any excess. Add half of the meat to the casserole and cook over moderately high heat until browned all over, about 10 minutes. Transfer the meat to the bowl with the onion-bacon mixture. Lower the heat to moderate and brown the remaining meat.

**6.** Return all of the meat and the onion mixture to the casserole and stir until sizzling. Add the porcini paste and stir for

1 minute. Stir in the carrots and sliced shiitake caps. Add the stock, the remaining red wine and the remaining porcini soaking liquid and bring to a boil. Season the stew with salt and pepper. Cover and simmer the stew over low heat until the meat is tender, about 2 hours. Discard the thyme sprigs and bay leaves.

**7.** Uncover the stew and cook over moderate heat until the sauce is slightly thickened, about 10 minutes. Add the parsley and chopped thyme, season with salt and pepper and serve. —*Gail Hobbs-Page*

**MAKE AHEAD** The stew can be refrigerated for up to 3 days.

**WINE** Rustic, peppery Malbec.

## Braised Short Ribs with Celery-Root Pancakes

**ACTIVE: 45 MIN; TOTAL: 2 HR 45 MIN**
**4 SERVINGS**

These short ribs are braised until the meat is fork-tender, then paired with celery-root pancakes and soft, buttery cipollini onions.

- 2 tablespoons vegetable oil
- 5½ pounds beef short ribs (8 ribs), trimmed of excess fat
- Salt and freshly ground pepper
- 8 large garlic cloves, coarsely chopped
- 1 medium carrot, thinly sliced
- 1 medium onion, coarsely chopped
- 1 medium celery rib, thinly sliced crosswise
- 2 tablespoons tomato paste
- 1 cup dry red wine
- 2 cloves
- 1 cinnamon stick, broken in half
- 1 bay leaf
- 5 cups water
- ¾ pound cipollini onions (about 20), peeled
- 2 tablespoons unsalted butter
- Celery-Root Pancakes (recipe follows)

**1.** Preheat the oven to 325°. In a medium roasting pan, heat the vegetable oil. Season the ribs with salt and pepper and cook over moderately high heat until browned on both sides, about 10 minutes. Transfer the ribs to a large bowl. Add the garlic, carrot, onion and celery to the roasting pan and cook over moderate heat, stirring occasionally, until softened, about 8 minutes. Add the tomato paste and cook, stirring, until glossy, about 1 minute. Add the red wine and boil over high heat until reduced by half, scraping up the browned bits from the bottom of the pan, about 4 minutes. Add the cloves, cinnamon stick, bay leaf and water and bring to a boil. Return the ribs to the pan and simmer for 1 minute. Remove from the heat.

**2.** Cover the ribs with a sheet of parchment paper, then cover with foil. Bake until the short ribs are very tender, about 2 hours. Let the ribs cool slightly.

**3.** Skim the fat from the surface of the ribs, then transfer the ribs to a large bowl. Strain the pan sauce into a medium saucepan and skim off the fat. Boil the pan sauce over high heat until reduced to 1½ cups, about 12 minutes; season with salt and pepper. Return the ribs to the roasting pan, pour the sauce on top and keep hot over low heat.

**4.** Meanwhile, in a medium saucepan of boiling salted water, cook the cipollini until just tender, about 10 minutes; drain well.

**5.** In a medium skillet, melt the butter. Add the cipollini, season with salt and pepper and cook over moderate heat until nicely browned, about 8 minutes.

**6.** Transfer the short ribs to plates and spoon the cipollini alongside. Spoon the sauce over the ribs and serve, passing the Celery-Root Pancakes at the table.
—*Marcia Kiesel*

**MAKE AHEAD** The ribs can be prepared through Step 1 and refrigerated overnight. Skim off the fat before reheating.

**WINE** Juicy, spicy Grenache.

## CELERY-ROOT PANCAKES

**TOTAL: 35 MIN**
**4 SERVINGS** ● ●

- 1 pound celery root, peeled
- 1 large russet potato (½ pound), peeled
- 2 tablespoons coarsely grated onions
- 1 teaspoon kosher salt
- 3 tablespoons vegetable oil
- Freshly ground pepper

**1.** Preheat the oven to 400°. Working over a large bowl, coarsely shred the celery root and potato on the large holes of a box grater. Using 2 forks, toss the celery root and potato with the onion and salt.

**2.** In a large nonstick skillet, heat 1½ tablespoons of the oil. Scoop four ½-cup mounds of the vegetable mixture into the skillet and flatten them into cakes. Cook the pancakes over moderately high heat until browned and crisp, about 4 minutes per side. Transfer to a large baking sheet and season with pepper; keep warm in the oven. Repeat with the remaining oil and vegetable mixture. Serve hot. —*M.K.*

**MAKE AHEAD** The fried pancakes can be refrigerated overnight. Bring to room temperature before reheating in a 375° oven.

# ingredient
## BEEF CUTS FOR BRAISING

Tough cuts of meat are often less expensive than premium cuts, and they make the most flavorful meals. The catch? They require hours of slow, moist cooking, a method called braising. The best beef cuts for braising include the **chuck** and the **brisket.** The chuck comes from the shoulder of the cow and includes the meatiest short ribs. The brisket comes from the underside of the cow, below the chuck. These cuts are available in supermarkets, often cut into chunks for stewing.

# beef & lamb

## Salt-and-Pepper-Crusted Prime Rib with Sage Jus
**ACTIVE: 45 MIN; TOTAL: 4 HR**

10 SERVINGS ●

One 14-pound bone-in prime rib
    roast, tied
Kosher salt and freshly
    ground pepper
20  large sage sprigs
20  large thyme sprigs
  8  bay leaves
  8  shallots, peeled and halved
  1  head garlic, cloves crushed, plus
    4 cloves thinly sliced
  2  cups water
  1  onion, thinly sliced
  3  tablespoons freshly cracked
    black peppercorns
  1  cup dry red wine
  5  cups beef stock or
    low-sodium broth
  2  tablespoons all-purpose flour

**1.** Preheat the oven to 400°. Set the meat in a large roasting pan, fat side up. Season the meat generously with salt and pepper. Around the roast, scatter 10 sprigs each of sage and thyme, 6 of the bay leaves, the shallots and the crushed garlic cloves. Pour in 1 cup of the water and roast for 45 minutes. Reduce the temperature to 275°. Roast the meat for about 2 hours and 15 minutes longer, adding the remaining 1 cup of water to the pan as the juices evaporate. The roast is done when an instant-read thermometer inserted in the thickest part registers 135°.

**2.** Transfer the roast to a large carving board. Pour the fat in the roasting pan into a large heatproof bowl, stopping when you reach the syrupy pan juices at the bottom. Pour the pan juices into a small bowl and discard the vegetables and herbs.

**3.** Set the pan over 2 burners and add 2 tablespoons of the reserved fat. Add the onion, peppercorns, sliced garlic, remaining 2 bay leaves and 10 sprigs each of sage and thyme. Cook over moderate heat until the onion is softened, 8 minutes. Add the wine and cook, scraping up any bits stuck to the bottom and sides of the pan. Pour the mixture into a medium saucepan and bring to a boil over high heat. Add the stock and pan juices and cook over moderate heat until slightly reduced, 15 minutes.

**4.** In a small bowl, whisk the flour with 2 tablespoons of the reserved fat. Whisk the paste into the saucepan and simmer the gravy until thickened, about 5 minutes. Strain the gravy through a fine sieve and keep warm until ready to serve.

**5.** Cut the bones off the roast and slice the meat ½ inch thick. Cut in between the bones and serve them on the side. Pass the gravy at the table. —*Michael Mina*
**WINE** Firm, complex Cabernet Sauvignon.

## Smoky Barbecued Brisket
**ACTIVE: 4 HR; TOTAL: 9 HR 30 MIN**
**PLUS OVERNIGHT MARINATING**

6 TO 8 SERVINGS ●

A barbecued brisket has a slightly denser texture than one that has been braised, but it can be just as tender if you buy the right cut. Ask the butcher for the packers cut or whole brisket: It will have a thick layer of fat that adds about 3 or 4 pounds to the typical 5- or 6-pound brisket. You can trim away some of the fat, but leave enough to keep the meat moist while it cooks.

¼  cup Garlicky Barbecue Marinade
    (p. 97)
One 10-pound beef brisket with a nice
    layer of fat
¼  cup plus 2 tablespoons Seven-
    Spice Dry Rub (p. 97)
  4  cups hickory or other hardwood
    chips, soaked in water for
    at least 30 minutes
Cider Mop Spray (p. 97)
  2  cups Sweet and Sticky Barbecue
    Sauce (p. 97) mixed with
    2 cups water
Hamburger buns and hot sauce,
    for serving

**1.** Rub the Garlicky Barbecue Marinade all over the beef brisket and refrigerate the brisket overnight.

**2.** Bring the brisket to room temperature and sprinkle the Seven-Spice Dry Rub all over the meat.

**3.** Light a charcoal fire in a covered grill and set it up for indirect grilling: When the temperature reaches 225°, carefully push the hot coals to one side and place a drip pan filled with 1 cup of water on the opposite side. Alternatively, bring a smoker to 225°. Place the brisket over the drip pan, fat side up, and cover the grill; you'll need to cook the brisket for a total of about 8 hours, rotating the meat (but not turning it over) every 2 hours. Maintain the temperature at 225° by replenishing the charcoal with a fresh batch of burning coals every hour. Every hour, drain ½ cup of the wood chips and scatter them over the hot coals. Add more water to the drip pan when half of it is evaporated.

**4.** After the first 6 hours, spray the brisket generously with the Cider Mop Spray. Continue cooking the brisket, spraying it with the Mop Spray every 30 minutes, until an instant-read thermometer registers 190° when inserted in the thickest part of the meat. Transfer the brisket to a carving board and let rest for 30 minutes.

**5.** Pour the diluted Sweet and Sticky Barbecue Sauce into a roasting pan and bring the sauce to a simmer on the stovetop. Slice the brisket ¼ inch thick against the grain and transfer the sliced brisket to the roasting pan. Simmer the meat over low heat, basting it with the sauce until it is heated through, about 5 minutes. Serve the barbecued brisket immediately, with the hamburger buns and the hot sauce. —*Adam Perry Lang*

**MAKE AHEAD** The barbecued brisket can be refrigerated overnight. Bring the meat to room temperature before carving and reheating.

**WINE** Round, deep-flavored Syrah.

## Spicy Beef with Fermented Black Beans and Scallions

**TOTAL: 25 MIN**

**4 SERVINGS** ●

At South Beauty in Beijing, cooks simmer beef tableside in pots of boiling oil lavishly seasoned with red chiles and Sichuan peppercorns. The beef becomes exquisitely tender, fragrant and spicy. Susanna Foo, a Philadelphia chef who specializes in Chinese cuisine, makes this lovely version of the dish with just a fraction of the oil.

½ cup vegetable oil

1½ tablespoons Sichuan peppercorns

10 dried red chiles

6 garlic cloves, thinly sliced

One 3-inch piece of fresh ginger, peeled and thinly sliced

1½ tablespoons fermented black beans, rinsed and chopped

¾ cup chicken stock

Salt

1½ pounds trimmed beef tenderloin, halved lengthwise and sliced ½ inch thick

4 scallions, cut into 2-inch lengths

¼ cup cilantro leaves

1. Heat the oil in a saucepan. Add the peppercorns; cook over moderate heat until darkened, 4 minutes. Strain into a bowl.

2. Return 2 tablespoons of the strained oil to the pan and heat. Add the chiles, garlic and ginger and cook over moderate heat, stirring, until darkened, 3 minutes. Add the beans and cook for 30 seconds. Add the stock; boil over high heat until reduced by half, 3 minutes. Season lightly with salt.

3. In a skillet, heat the remaining strained oil until shimmering. Season the meat with salt. Add half of the meat in a single layer and cook over high heat until browned and medium rare, 1 minute per side. Transfer to a serving platter and repeat. Reheat the sauce and add the scallions to the pan. Pour the sauce over the meat, scatter on the cilantro and serve. —*Susanna Foo*

**WINE** Juicy, spicy Grenache.

## BLT Burgers with Garlicky Mayonnaise

**TOTAL: 30 MIN**

**4 SERVINGS** ●

This burger has all the components of a BLT—they're just not configured in the usual way. Crumbled bacon and intense sun-dried tomatoes are mixed into a garlicky mayonnaise, which gets slathered on a juicy burger. The lettuce part, arugula, adds a crunchy, peppery hit.

8 strips of bacon

8 oil-packed, sun-dried tomatoes, drained (¼ cup)

1 garlic clove

1 chipotle in adobo sauce, seeded, or 1 teaspoon hot sauce

1 teaspoon cider vinegar

½ cup mayonnaise

Salt and freshly ground pepper

2 pounds ground beef chuck

Extra-virgin olive oil, for brushing

4 kaiser rolls, split

1 bunch arugula, thick stems discarded (6 ounces)

1. Light a grill. In a large skillet, cook the bacon over moderate heat until crisp, about 7 minutes. Drain on paper towels, then chop finely.

2. In a mini food processor, pulse the sun-dried tomatoes with the garlic, chipotle and vinegar until finely chopped. Add the mayonnaise and puree until smooth. Add the bacon, season with salt and pepper and pulse just until combined.

3. Form the meat into 4 large patties about 1 inch thick and brush lightly with olive oil. Season with salt and pepper and grill over moderately high heat for 9 minutes for medium meat. Brush the cut sides of the rolls with olive oil and grill until lightly browned, about 2 minutes.

4. Spread the mayonnaise on the cut sides of the rolls and set the burgers on the bottom halves. Top with the arugula, close the sandwiches and serve. —*Grace Parisi*

**WINE** Deep, velvety Merlot.

# ingredient
**STAR SALTS**

**1 Kosher** This inexpensive, widely available coarse-grained salt has a clean taste.

**2 Maldon** These flat crystals, which look like snowflakes, have a mild and subtle flavor.

**3 Sel Gris** Colored by the clay from which it's harvested, this salt is moist and large grained.

**4 Hawaii Pink** Volcanic minerals turn this salt pink and give it a singular mellow flavor.

# beef & lamb

# ingredient
## CHILES

Chiles don't just heat up recipes—they add flavor and complexity and make other ingredients taste better. Farmers' markets and supermarkets are selling more chile varieties, so experiment with them.

**HABANERO CHILE**

**GREEN JALAPEÑO**

**ANAHEIM CHILE**

**RED JALAPEÑO**

**BANANA CHILE**

**BIRD CHILE**

**SCOTCH BONNET CHILE**

**RED HOLLAND CHILE**

## Chile-Stuffed Cheeseburgers
**TOTAL: 30 MIN**
**4 SERVINGS** ●

The gooey filling for these juicy, spicy burgers was inspired by *chile con queso*, a Mexican dip made with melted cheese and roasted chiles.

- 2 Anaheim chiles and 2 jalapeños
- Extra-virgin olive oil, for brushing
- 1 large garlic clove, unpeeled
- 4 ounces shredded Monterey Jack cheese
- Salt and freshly ground pepper
- 1½ pounds ground beef
- 4 kaiser rolls, split
- Lettuce leaves, sliced onion and tomato, mayonnaise and ketchup, for serving

**1.** Light a grill. Rub the Anaheim and jalapeños chile peppers with olive oil. Thread the jalapeños and garlic onto a skewer and grill until charred all over. Using tongs, repeat with the Anaheims. Peel the chiles and discard the stems and seeds. Peel the garlic. Chop the chiles and garlic and transfer to a bowl. Fold in the cheese and season with salt and pepper.

**2.** Cut eight 6-inch squares of wax paper; divide the beef among them. Pat each portion into a 5-inch round, a little thicker in the center. Using a ¼ cup measure, mound one-fourth of the cheese mixture in the centers of 4 patties. Top with the remaining patties; press the edges to seal. Flatten the centers so that the burgers are even. Brush with oil and season with salt and pepper. Brush the cut sides of the rolls with oil.

**3.** Lightly oil the grate. Grill the burgers over high heat, turning once, about 7 minutes for medium to medium-rare meat. Toast the kaiser rolls. Place the burgers on the rolls and top with lettuce, onion and tomato. Serve with mayonnaise and ketchup. —*Grace Parisi*

**SERVE WITH** Garlicky Chile Pickles (recipe follows).

**WINE** Fruity, luscious Shiraz.

## GARLICKY CHILE PICKLES
**TOTAL: 20 MIN PLUS OVERNIGHT PICKLING**
**MAKES 1 QUART** ● ● ●

The longer these pickles sit, the spicier they get.

- 4 kirby cucumbers, cut lengthwise into eighths
- 2 Holland red and 2 yellow chiles, thinly sliced on the diagonal
- 2 jalapeños, thinly sliced crosswise
- 3 garlic cloves, thinly sliced
- 1½ cups water
- ¾ cup white wine vinegar
- 1 tablespoon kosher salt
- 2 teaspoons pickling spice

Pack the cucumbers, upright, into a 1-quart mason jar. Tuck the chiles and garlic in all around. In a saucepan, bring the water, vinegar, salt and pickling spice to a boil. Slowly pour the hot liquid into the jar. Close the lid and refrigerate overnight. —*G.P.*

**MAKE AHEAD** The pickles can be refrigerated in the tightly closed jar for 2 weeks.

## Greek Island Lamb Burgers with Grilled Feta
**TOTAL: 35 MIN**
**6 SERVINGS**

- 2½ pounds ground lamb
- 2 garlic cloves, minced
- ½ teaspoon dried oregano, plus more for sprinkling
- 1 teaspoon minced mint leaves
- ⅛ teaspoon cinnamon
- 1 teaspoon kosher salt
- ½ teaspoon freshly ground black pepper
- 2 cups pitted oil-cured black Greek olives
- ¼ cup extra-virgin olive oil, plus more for brushing
- 1 tablespoon chopped parsley
- One 10-ounce piece of firm feta cheese, cut into 6 slices
- 6 kaiser rolls, split and toasted
- 1 large tomato, cut into 6 slices

CHILE-STUFFED CHEESEBURGER

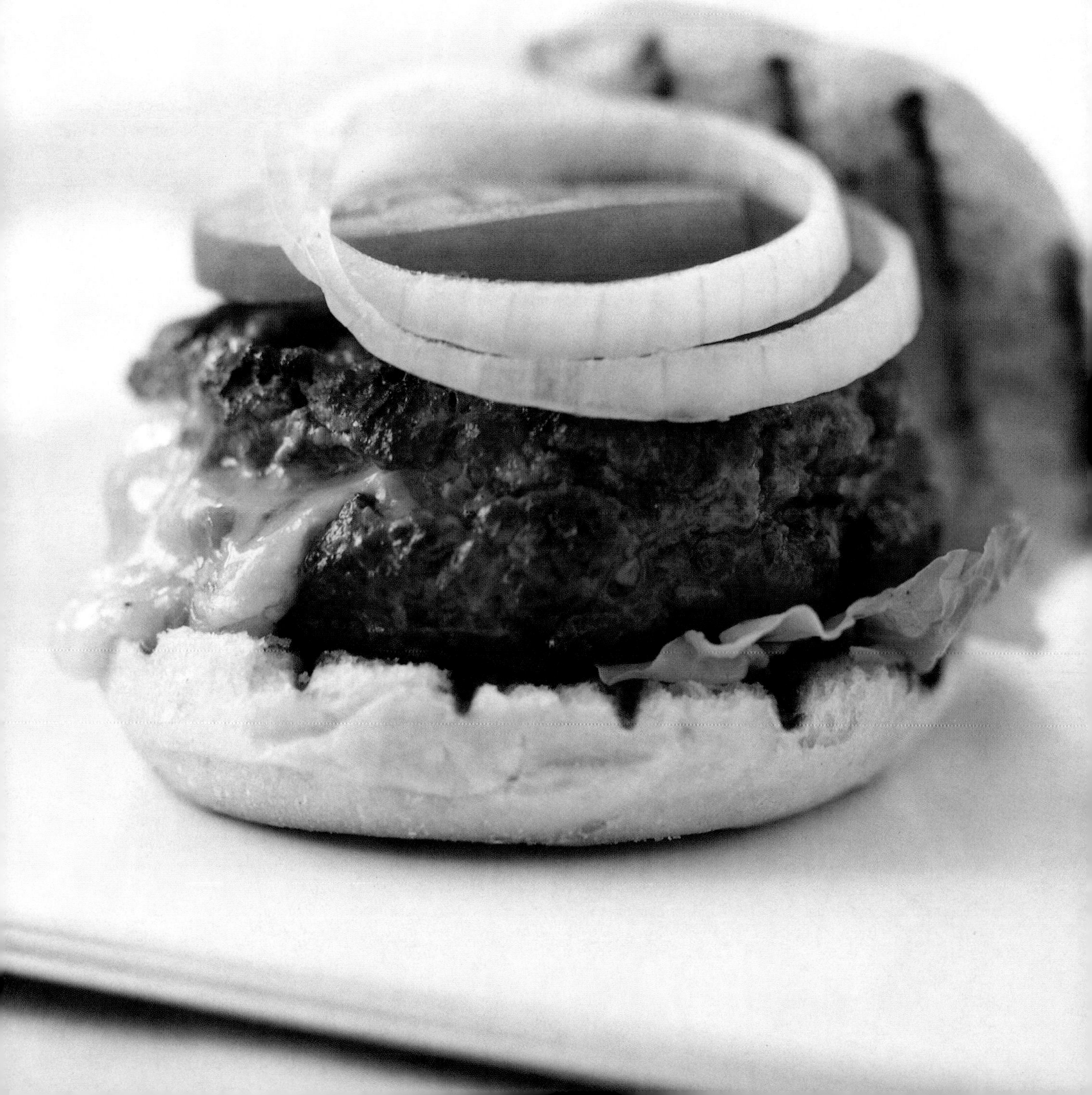

# beef & lamb

1. Light a grill. In a large bowl, combine the ground lamb with half of the minced garlic, the ½ teaspoon of oregano and the mint, cinnamon, salt and pepper. Mix gently and pat into 6 burgers. Let the burgers stand for 15 minutes.

2. In a food processor, combine the pitted black olives with the remaining minced garlic and process until coarsely chopped. Add the ¼ cup of olive oil and process to a paste. Scrape the tapenade into a bowl and stir in the parsley.

3. Brush the lamb burgers with olive oil and grill them over high heat until they are medium rare, 4 minutes per side. Carefully put the feta slices on the grill and grill them just until they are hot, about 10 seconds per side. Sprinkle the feta with oregano and set each slice on a burger.

4. Spread the tapenade on the rolls. Top with the lamb burgers and tomato slices, close the rolls and serve immediately.
—*Christopher Bakken*

**WINE** Intense, spicy Syrah.

## Rolled Lamb Cutlets Stuffed with Pancetta and Pecorino
**ACTIVE: 1 HR; TOTAL: 2 HR 30 MIN**
6 SERVINGS ● ●
If you don't own a meat mallet, use the flat side of a small, heavy skillet to pound the lamb for these hearty rolls.

- 2 tablespoons extra-virgin olive oil
- ¼ pound thinly sliced pancetta
- 4 hard-cooked eggs, finely chopped
- 1 cup freshly grated Pecorino Romano cheese (4 ounces)
- ½ cup plain dry bread crumbs
- ½ cup very finely chopped flat-leaf parsley
- 5 large garlic cloves, minced
- Kosher salt and freshly ground pepper
- 4 pounds boneless leg of lamb, trimmed of excess fat, meat cut into 12 pieces
- 1 large onion, finely chopped
- 2 tablespoons tomato paste
- 1 cup dry white wine
- 1 cup water
- One 28-ounce can peeled Italian tomatoes, drained and chopped
- ½ teaspoon crushed red pepper

1. In a deep 12-inch skillet, heat the oil until shimmering. Add the pancetta slices and cook over moderate heat, turning occasionally, until browned and crisp, about 6 minutes. Transfer to a work surface and finely chop. Reserve the skillet and fat.

2. In a large bowl, mix the pancetta, eggs, cheese, bread crumbs, 6 tablespoons of the parsley and half of the garlic. Season with ½ teaspoon each of salt and pepper.

3. Working with 1 piece of lamb at a time, place the meat on a work surface between 2 sheets of plastic wrap and pound it into a roughly 4-by-6-inch rectangle ¼ inch thick. Spoon the filling onto the lamb, leaving a 1-inch border on one of the shorter sides. Starting on the shorter end, press the filling to compact it slightly and roll into a tight cylinder. Tuck in any loose flaps of lamb; tie up the rolls with kitchen string.

4. Set the skillet over moderately high heat until the fat shimmers. Add the lamb rolls in a single layer and cook, turning occasionally, until browned all over, 10 to 12 minutes. Transfer the rolls to a large plate. Add the onion to the skillet and cook over moderate heat, stirring, until softened, about 8 minutes. Add the remaining garlic and cook until fragrant. Add the tomato paste and cook, stirring, for 1 minute. Pour in the wine and simmer until slightly reduced, scraping up any browned bits stuck to the bottom of the skillet, about 3 minutes. Add the water, chopped tomatoes, crushed red pepper and a pinch of salt.

5. Return the lamb rolls and any accumulated juices to the skillet and bring to a boil. Cover tightly and simmer over moderately low heat until the lamb is tender, about 1½ hours. Transfer the lamb to a deep platter, cover with foil and keep warm.

6. Boil the sauce over high heat, stirring, until slightly thickened, about 5 minutes. Pour over the lamb rolls, sprinkle with the remaining parsley and serve.
—*Lobel Family*

**MAKE AHEAD** The lamb rolls can be refrigerated in their sauce for up to 3 days.

**WINE** Juicy, fresh Dolcetto.

## Lamb Meatballs with Mint
**TOTAL: 50 MIN**
MAKES ABOUT 32 MEATBALLS ●
This recipe is an adaptation of the outstanding meatballs made with lamb and mint that are served at the bar of Seville's Enrique Becerra restaurant.

- 1 pound lean ground lamb
- 1 egg, lightly beaten
- ¼ cup dry bread crumbs
- 2 tablespoons finely chopped mint
- Salt and freshly ground pepper
- ½ cup extra-virgin olive oil
- 1 medium onion, finely chopped
- 1 garlic clove, finely chopped
- ½ cup dry white wine
- ½ cup beef broth
- 1 cup tomato puree

1. In a bowl, mix the lamb, egg, crumbs and 1 tablespoon of the mint. Season with salt and pepper. Form into 1-inch balls.

2. Heat the olive oil in a very large skillet. Add the meatballs and fry over moderately high heat until browned all over, about 4 minutes. Transfer to a plate.

3. Add the onion and garlic to the skillet and cook over moderate heat until softened, 8 minutes. Add the wine and cook, stirring, until reduced by half, 5 minutes. Transfer to a food processor. Add the remaining 1 tablespoon of mint and puree.

4. Return the onion puree to the skillet. Add the broth, tomato puree and meatballs and simmer over low heat until the meatballs are cooked through, about 10 minutes. Season with salt and pepper and serve. —*Jeff Koehler*

**WINE** Rustic, peppery Malbec.

GRILLED LEG OF LAMB
WITH GARLIC AND
ROSEMARY (P. 146)

JICAMA, KIRBY AND CARROT SALAD WITH CHARRED LAMB

ROASTED SADDLE OF LAMB WITH ANCHOVY-HERB STUFFIN

### Jicama, Kirby and Carrot Salad with Charred Lamb

**TOTAL: 1 HR**

**4 SERVINGS** ● ○

Because chef and restaurateur Jean-Georges Vongerichten is constantly opening new restaurants, it's easy to forget his breakout place: Vong, in New York City. This smoky lamb salad dates to Vong's 1992 opening. With crunchy carrots, cucumbers and bean sprouts and a spiced vinegar dressing, it is one of the dishes that launched the Asian-fusion trend in America.

- ¼ cup distilled white vinegar
- 2 teaspoons sugar
- 2 garlic cloves, minced
- 2 red or green Thai chiles, minced
- 1 tablespoon Asian fish sauce
- 1 tablespoon vegetable oil, plus more for rubbing

Salt and freshly ground pepper
- 2 pounds well-trimmed boneless leg of lamb, cut into 3 equal pieces
- 3 medium carrots, finely julienned
- 2 kirby cucumbers (¼ pound each), very thinly sliced on a mandoline
- 10 ounces peeled jicama, cut into ⅓-inch dice (2 cups)
- 1 cup mung bean sprouts
- ¼ cup small mint leaves
- ¼ cup chopped cilantro
- 2 stalks of fresh lemongrass, tender inner bulbs only, thinly sliced crosswise (2 tablespoons)

**1.** Light a grill. In a small saucepan, combine the white vinegar with the sugar, minced garlic and chiles. Bring to a boil. Transfer the vinegar mixture to a small bowl and let cool. Stir in the fish sauce and the 1 tablespoon of oil and season the dressing with salt and pepper.

**2.** Rub the lamb all over with oil and season with salt and pepper. Grill the lamb over moderately high heat, turning, for 25 to 30 minutes, or until it is nicely charred and an instant-read thermometer inserted into the thickest part registers 135° for medium-rare meat. Transfer the leg of lamb to a carving board and let it rest for 10 minutes before carving.

**3.** In a large bowl, toss the carrots with the cucumbers, jicama, bean sprouts, mint, cilantro and lemongrass. Add the dressing and toss to coat. Transfer the salad to a platter. Thinly slice the lamb. Arrange overlapping slices on the salad and serve.
—*Jean-Georges Vongerichten*

**WINE** Intense, spicy Syrah.

## Roasted Saddle of Lamb with Anchovy-Herb Stuffing

**ACTIVE: 35 MIN; TOTAL: 2 HR**

8 SERVINGS

- 4 medium garlic cloves, minced
- 4 anchovy fillets, minced
- 1 teaspoon minced rosemary
- 1 teaspoon minced thyme
- 3 tablespoons plus 2 teaspoons extra-virgin olive oil

One 5½- to 6-pound boneless saddle of lamb, with side flaps of meat intact

Sea salt and freshly ground pepper

- ¼ cup water
- 2 teaspoons aged balsamic vinegar

**1.** Preheat the oven to 350°. In a mortar or mini processor, pound or pulse the garlic to a paste. Add the anchovies and pound or pulse until smooth. Stir in the rosemary and thyme and 2 tablespoons of the oil.

**2.** Spread the saddle of lamb on a work surface, fat side up. Using a sharp knife, lightly score the fat in a crosshatch pattern. Turn the saddle over and trim any excess fat from the loin, tenderloin and flap pieces. Season the lamb with salt and pepper. Rub the anchovy-herb filling over the inside of the lamb. Roll up the roast, wrapping the flaps around the outside to form a neat cylinder, then tie at 1-inch intervals with kitchen string. Season the outside of the roast with salt and pepper.

**3.** In a very large ovenproof skillet, heat 1 tablespoon of the oil. Add the roast and cook over moderately high heat until nicely browned all over, about 10 minutes. Transfer the skillet to the oven and roast the lamb for about 1 hour, or until an instant-read thermometer inserted into the center of the roast registers 120°. Transfer to a carving board and let rest for 15 minutes.

**4.** Pour the skillet juices into a small saucepan and skim off the fat. Add any juices that have collected around the roast. Add the water and bring to a simmer. Stir in the remaining 2 teaspoons of olive oil and the balsamic vinegar and season with salt and pepper. Strain the jus through a fine sieve into a warmed gravy boat.

**5.** Cut and discard the strings from the roast. Thickly slice the roast crosswise and serve with the jus. —*Michael Cimarusti*

**SERVE WITH** Tangy Salt-Roasted Fennel (p. 229).

**WINE** Firm, complex Cabernet Sauvignon.

## Lamb Chops with Garlic Custards

**ACTIVE: 45 MIN; TOTAL: 1 HR 20 MIN**

4 SERVINGS

CUSTARDS

- 6 large garlic cloves, halved
- 2 teaspoons extra-virgin olive oil
- ½ teaspoon chopped thyme
- 3 large egg yolks
- 2 large eggs
- 1½ cups milk
- ½ teaspoon salt
- ⅛ teaspoon freshly ground pepper

SALAD

- 2 tablespoons extra-virgin olive oil
- ½ ounce pancetta or lean bacon, finely chopped
- 1 medium shallot, thinly sliced
- 10 ounces frozen peas (2 cups), thawed
- 1 tablespoon plus 1 teaspoon red wine vinegar

Salt and freshly ground pepper

- 1 tablespoon chopped mint
- 2 ounces arugula (4 cups)

LAMB CHOPS

- 1 tablespoon extra-virgin olive oil
- 8 lamb loin chops, trimmed of excess fat

Salt and freshly ground pepper

- ¼ cup Riesling wine

**1. MAKE THE CUSTARDS:** Preheat the oven to 325°. Lightly butter four ⅔-cup ramekins and place in a small baking dish.

**2.** Bring a small saucepan of water to a simmer. Add the garlic and cook over moderate heat until very tender, about 10 minutes. Drain and transfer to a medium bowl.

Smash the garlic to a puree. Stir in the olive oil and thyme. Whisk in the egg yolks and whole eggs, then whisk in the milk, salt and pepper. Pour the custard into the ramekins and add enough very hot tap water to the baking dish to reach halfway up the sides of the ramekins. Bake for about 25 minutes, until the custards are just set and slightly jiggly in the center. Remove the ramekins from the water bath and set aside.

**3. MAKE THE SALAD:** In a medium skillet, heat 1 tablespoon of the olive oil. Add the pancetta and cook over moderate heat until lightly browned, about 3 minutes. Add the shallot and cook until softened, about 3 minutes. Add the peas and cook until heated through, about 2 minutes. Add 1 teaspoon of the vinegar and season with salt and pepper.

**4.** In a bowl, combine the remaining 1 tablespoon each of olive oil and vinegar and season with salt and pepper. Add the mint and arugula and toss the salad well.

**5. MAKE THE LAMB CHOPS:** Increase the oven temperature to 425°. In a very large ovenproof skillet, heat the olive oil. Season the lamb chops with salt and pepper, add to the skillet and cook over high heat until browned, about 3 minutes per side. Transfer the skillet to the oven and bake the chops for about 6 minutes, until medium rare. Meanwhile, reheat the garlic custards in the oven for 2 minutes.

**6.** Transfer the lamb to warm plates. Set the skillet over moderately high heat, add the wine and cook for 1 minute, scraping up any browned bits; season with salt and pepper. Drizzle the sauce over the chops.

**7.** Run a thin knife around the inside of the ramekins and invert the custards onto the plates. Toss the pea mixture with the salad and serve at the table. —*Marcia Kiesel*

**MAKE AHEAD** The custards can be refrigerated overnight. Bring them to room temperature and reheat them in a microwave oven for 15 seconds.

**WINE** Firm, complex Cabernet Sauvignon.

# beef & lamb

## Lamb Rib Chops with Vegetable Hash

ACTIVE: 50 MIN; TOTAL: 1 HR 15 MIN

8 SERVINGS

*Samfaina* is a quick Catalan hash of diced eggplant, bell pepper and zucchini.

- ¼ cup plus 2 tablespoons extra-virgin olive oil
- 1 large Spanish onion, cut into ½-inch dice
- 4 garlic cloves, minced
- ¼ pound smoked ham or prosciutto, sliced ¼ inch thick
- 2 pounds tomatoes, cut into ½-inch dice
- ½ cup dry white wine
- ½ cup brandy
- 2 pounds zucchini, cut into ½-inch dice
- One 1½-pound eggplant, cut into ½-inch dice
- 1 medium red bell pepper, cut into ½-inch dice
- 16 oil-cured black olives, pitted and chopped
- 2 tablespoons chopped oregano
- 2 teaspoons chopped thyme
- 2 teaspoons chopped rosemary
- 1 bay leaf
- Salt and freshly ground pepper
- 16 lamb rib chops (3¼ pounds)

1. In an enameled cast-iron casserole, heat ¼ cup of the oil. Add the onion, garlic and ham. Cook over moderate heat, stirring occasionally, for 8 minutes. Add the tomatoes. Cook over high heat for 3 minutes. Add the wine; cook for 3 minutes. Add the brandy; simmer for 3 minutes. Stir in the zucchini, eggplant, bell pepper, olives, oregano, thyme, rosemary and bay leaf. Cover and simmer over moderately low heat, stirring occasionally, until tender, 35 minutes. Discard the bay leaf; reserve the ham for another use. Season with salt and pepper.

2. In each of 2 very large skillets, heat 1 tablespoon of the remaining olive oil. Season the lamb chops with salt and pepper.

Add the chops to the skillets and cook over high heat for 1 minute. Reduce the heat to moderately high and cook until browned on the bottom, 2 minutes. Turn and cook until browned on the second side and medium rare, 2 minutes. Place 2 lamb chops on each plate, spoon the *samfaina* alongside and serve. —*Sergi Millet*

**WINE** Firm, complex Cabernet Sauvignon.

## Lamb Chops Sizzled with Garlic

TOTAL: 20 MIN

4 SERVINGS ●

Las Pedroñeras, a village in the Castilla–La Mancha region, is considered the garlic capital of Spain. These juicy, meaty lamb chops sizzled in extra-virgin olive oil with plenty of garlic cloves are cookbook author Janet Mendel's homage to the village.

- Eight ½-inch-thick lamb loin chops (about 2 pounds), fatty tips trimmed
- Salt and freshly ground pepper
- Pinch of dried thyme
- 3 tablespoons extra-virgin olive oil
- 10 small garlic cloves, halved
- 3 tablespoons water
- 2 tablespoons fresh lemon juice
- 2 tablespoons minced parsley
- Pinch of crushed red pepper

1. Season the lamb with salt and pepper and sprinkle lightly with thyme. In a very large skillet, heat the oil until shimmering. Add the lamb and garlic and cook over moderately high heat until the chops are browned on the bottom, 3 minutes. Turn the chops and garlic; cook until the chops are browned, about 2 minutes longer for medium meat. Transfer the chops to plates, leaving the garlic in the skillet.

2. Add the water, lemon juice, parsley and crushed pepper to the pan and cook, scraping up any browned bits, until sizzling, about 1 minute. Pour the garlic and pan sauce over the lamb chops and serve immediately. —*Janet Mendel*

**WINE** Savory, spicy Carmenère.

## Lamb Chops with Parsnips

TOTAL: 30 MIN

4 SERVINGS ●

When parsnips are sautéed until soft on the inside and brown on the outside, their unique sweetness emerges. Mixed with apple juice, lemon and horseradish, they make a terrific side dish for chops.

- 2½ tablespoons extra-virgin olive oil
- 4 medium parsnips (about 1 pound), peeled and sliced ⅓ inch thick
- ¾ cup frozen apple juice concentrate (6 ounces), thawed
- Zest and juice from 1 lemon
- 2 tablespoons drained prepared horseradish
- Salt and freshly ground pepper
- Eight 1-inch-thick lamb loin chops (2½ pounds)

1. In a large skillet, heat 2 tablespoons of the olive oil until shimmering. Add the parsnips and cook over moderately high heat, turning once, until they are golden and tender, 6 to 7 minutes. Transfer the parsnips to a plate.

2. Add the apple concentrate to the skillet and boil until syrupy and reduced to ¼ cup, about 8 minutes. Add the lemon zest and juice, the parsnips and 1 tablespoon of the horseradish. Season the parsnips with salt and pepper and keep warm.

3. Meanwhile, in another large skillet, heat the remaining ½ tablespoon of olive oil until shimmering. Season the lamb loin chops with salt and pepper, add them to the skillet and cook the chops over high heat, turning once, until the meat is cooked but still pink throughout, about 7 minutes.

4. Transfer the lamb and parsnips to plates. Spoon the sauce over the lamb, top with the remaining 1 tablespoon of horseradish and serve. —*Andy Nusser*

**WINE** Round, deep-flavored Syrah.

## Oven-Braised Lamb with Gremolata

**ACTIVE: 30 MIN; TOTAL: 3 HR 45 MIN**

**6 SERVINGS**

Cal Peternell, a chef at Chez Panisse Café in Berkeley, California, makes a simple cooking method—braising—even easier. By baking the lamb uncovered and turning it twice, the parts of the roast that are not submerged brown nicely.

- 2½ tablespoons extra-virgin olive oil
- One 5½-pound boneless lamb shoulder roast, tied at 2-inch intervals
- Salt and freshly ground pepper
- 2 large onions, thickly sliced
- 2 medium carrots, sliced ¼ inch thick
- 2 medium celery ribs, sliced ¼ inch thick
- 1 leek, white and tender green parts only, thickly sliced crosswise
- 6 thyme sprigs
- ¼ cup coarsely chopped flat-leaf parsley, plus 6 parsley sprigs
- 1 head garlic, halved crosswise, plus 1 small garlic clove minced
- 1 bay leaf
- 1½ quarts water
- 2 cups dry white wine
- 2 teaspoons finely grated lemon zest

**1.** Preheat the oven to 400°. Rub ½ tablespoon of the olive oil all over the lamb and season with salt and pepper. In a medium roasting pan, heat the remaining 2 tablespoons of olive oil until shimmering. Add the onions, carrots, celery, leek, thyme, parsley sprigs, head of garlic and bay leaf. Cook over moderate heat, stirring occasionally, until softened, about 10 minutes. Add the water and wine; bring to a boil.

**2.** Set the lamb on the vegetables, fat side up, and put the roasting pan in the oven. Reduce the oven temperature to 325° and roast the lamb for about 3 hours, turning it twice to brown the exposed sides. The lamb should be very tender.

**3.** Transfer the lamb to a carving board, cover loosely with foil and let rest for 10 minutes. Strain the pan juices into a medium saucepan, pressing on the solids to extract as much liquid as possible. Skim the fat from the surface and boil the juices over high heat until reduced by half, about 8 minutes. Season with salt and pepper.

**4.** Finely chop the lemon zest, chopped parsley and minced garlic, then transfer this gremolata to a bowl. Thickly slice the lamb and transfer to a platter. Sprinkle the gremolata over the lamb and serve with the pan juices. —*Cal Peternell*

**WINE** Cherry-inflected, earthy Sangiovese.

## Lamb Tagine with Prunes

**ACTIVE: 30 MIN; TOTAL: 2 HR 20 MIN**

**6 SERVINGS** ●

- 1 teaspoon sesame seeds
- 3 tablespoons vegetable oil
- 3 pounds trimmed boneless lamb shoulder, cut into 2½-inch pieces
- 1 medium onion, halved
- 1 bunch cilantro, tied with kitchen string
- 1 cinnamon stick, broken in half
- ½ teaspoon ground ginger
- Pinch of saffron threads
- Salt and freshly ground pepper
- 4½ cups water
- 3 cups pitted prunes, halved
- 1 tablespoon honey
- 1 teaspoon orange-flower water (optional)

**1.** In a small dry skillet, toast the sesame seeds over moderate heat until golden, 45 seconds. Transfer to a plate.

**2.** In a large enameled cast-iron casserole, add the oil, lamb, onion, cilantro, cinnamon, ginger, saffron, a pinch of salt and ½ teaspoon of pepper. Add the water and bring to a boil. Reduce the heat to moderately low; cook, skimming the stew a few times, until the lamb is tender, 1½ hours.

**3.** With a slotted spoon, remove the onion, cilantro and cinnamon stick and discard.

Add the prunes to the casserole and simmer for 15 minutes. With a slotted spoon, transfer the lamb and prunes to a bowl. Boil the cooking liquid over high heat until slightly reduced, 5 minutes. Add the honey and boil for 5 minutes. Return the lamb and prunes to the casserole and stir in the orange-flower water. Season with salt. Transfer to a bowl, sprinkle with the sesame seeds and serve. —*Anissa Helou*

**SERVE WITH** Couscous or crusty bread.

**WINE** Round, deep-flavored Syrah.

# equipment
## CHEFS' FAVORITE PANS

**ALL-CLAD BRAND**
These pans distribute heat evenly. "They're as good for sautéing as for braising," says chef Todd Gray of Equinox in Washington, D.C.

**CAST IRON**
Black cast-iron pans (above) "hold their heat well and pick up the seasonings you cook with," says chef Trey Foshee of George's at the Cove in La Jolla, California.

**BLUE STEEL**
Many chefs favor these inexpensive pans, which sell for about $40. Heat-treating the steel strengthens the metal and turns it blue.

# beef & lamb

## Rack of Lamb with Mustard Crumbs

**ACTIVE: 25 MIN; TOTAL: 1 HR**

4 SERVINGS ●

    3 thick slices of sourdough bread
      with crust (6 ounces)
    ¼ cup plus 2 tablespoons
      extra-virgin olive oil
    ¼ cup chopped flat-leaf parsley
  1½ teaspoons grated lemon zest
    5 garlic cloves, 1 minced, 4 unpeeled
Salt and freshly ground pepper
Two racks of lamb, frenched
    2 tablespoons Dijon mustard
  1½ pounds cherry tomatoes on the vine

**1.** Preheat the oven to 350°. Put the bread on a cookie sheet and toast for 10 minutes, until golden brown. Let cool, then crumble into pieces. Leave the oven on.

**2.** Put the toast pieces in a food processor and process into crumbs. Transfer the crumbs to a bowl and stir in ¼ cup of the olive oil, the parsley, lemon zest and minced garlic. Season with salt and pepper.

**3.** In a large skillet, heat 1 tablespoon of the olive oil until shimmering. Season the lamb with salt and pepper and cook, meaty side down, over high heat until browned, about 2 minutes per side. Transfer to a rimmed sheet pan, meaty side up, and let cool.

**4.** Spread the mustard over the meaty sides of the racks. Press on the bread crumbs. Put the tomatoes and 4 unpeeled garlic cloves on another rimmed baking sheet and rub with the remaining 1 tablespoon of olive oil. Season with salt and pepper. Put the tomatoes and garlic on the lower rack of the oven; bake for about 25 minutes, until soft. Meanwhile, put the lamb racks in the center of the oven. Roast the lamb until an instant-read thermometer registers 125° when inserted in the thickest part, 25 minutes for medium rare. Transfer to a carving board and let rest for 10 minutes. Carve the lamb into chops and serve with the tomatoes and garlic. —*Bill Granger*

**WINE** Firm, complex Cabernet Sauvignon.

## Lamb Stew with Swiss Chard and Garlic-Parsley Toasts

**ACTIVE: 1 HR 35 MIN;**

**TOTAL: 2 HR 45 MIN**

4 SERVINGS ● ● ●

This robust, satisfying stew is made with lamb shanks, a relatively lean cut with marvelous flavor.

    ¼ cup dried porcini mushrooms
    4 thyme sprigs
One 3-inch strip of orange zest
One 3-inch piece of ancho chile
    1 bay leaf
    1 celery rib, quartered crosswise
    ¼ cup extra-virgin olive oil
Four 1-pound lamb shanks, fat trimmed
Salt and freshly ground pepper
    1 medium red onion, finely chopped
    8 garlic cloves, minced
    1 large tomato—peeled, seeded
      and chopped
    ½ cup dry red wine
    1 quart water
    2 medium carrots, cut into
      1-by-⅓-inch pieces
    ½ pound small turnips, peeled
      and cut into wedges
    ½ pound Swiss chard, stemmed
Eight ½-inch-thick slices of crusty
      whole wheat baguette
    ¼ cup chopped flat-leaf parsley

**1.** Preheat the oven to 275°. In the center of a double-ply 5-inch piece of dampened cheesecloth, combine the porcini, thyme, orange zest, ancho chile, bay leaf and celery. Tie into a neat package with kitchen string. Trim any excess cheesecloth and string from the bouquet garni.

**2.** In a 12-inch enameled cast-iron casserole, heat 2 tablespoons of the olive oil until shimmering. Season the lamb with salt and pepper and cook 2 shanks over moderate heat until browned, 7 minutes per side. Transfer the lamb to a bowl and repeat with the remaining lamb shanks.

**3.** Add 2 teaspoons of olive oil, the onion and three-quarters of the minced garlic to the casserole. Cook over moderately low heat, stirring occasionally, until softened, 7 minutes. Add the tomato and cook over moderately high heat for 3 minutes. Stir in the wine and simmer until reduced by half. Return the lamb shanks to the casserole, nestling them in an even layer. Add the water and bouquet garni and bring to a gentle simmer. Cover the shanks with a sheet of parchment paper and the lid and bake for 1 hour. Turn the shanks, cover again with the parchment and the lid and bake for 1 hour longer, or until the meat is very tender.

**4.** Meanwhile, in a medium saucepan of boiling salted water, cook the carrots until tender, about 5 minutes. Using a slotted spoon, transfer the carrots to a bowl. Add the turnips to the saucepan and boil until tender, about 4 minutes. Transfer to the bowl. Add the Swiss chard to the saucepan and blanch for 1 minute. Drain, chop coarsely and transfer to the bowl.

**5.** Transfer the shanks to a bowl and let cool slightly. Increase the oven temperature to 400°. Simmer the braising liquid over moderate heat, skimming the surface occasionally, until slightly reduced, about 5 minutes. Squeeze the bouquet garni into the liquid, then discard it.

**6.** Remove the meat from the shanks. Cut or tear it into bite-size pieces and return it to the casserole. Add the carrots, turnips and Swiss chard and season the stew with salt and pepper; keep warm.

**7.** Arrange the baguette slices on a baking sheet and brush with 1 tablespoon of olive oil. In a bowl, combine the remaining olive oil and garlic with the parsley. Spread the garlic-parsley mixture on the slices and bake for 7 minutes, or until toasted. Halve the toasts crosswise and serve with the stew. —*Marcia Kiesel*

**MAKE AHEAD** The recipe can be prepared through Step 6 and refrigerated overnight.

**WINE** Intense, spicy Syrah.

LAMB STEW WITH SWISS CHARD
AND GARLIC-PARSLEY TOASTS

# beef & lamb

### Grilled Leg of Lamb with Garlic and Rosemary

**TOTAL: 45 MIN PLUS 4 HR MARINATING**
6 TO 8 SERVINGS

Instead of butterflying a boned leg of lamb and cooking it whole, carefully cut along the four natural muscle separations (they're easily visible) and pull the four pieces apart with your fingers. Grilling the lamb this way is quicker, makes it easier to determine doneness and also simplifies carving.

One 4- to 5-pound boneless leg of lamb, not butterflied
¼ cup extra-virgin olive oil
8 large garlic cloves, smashed and coarsely chopped
2 tablespoons minced rosemary
Salt and freshly ground black pepper

1. Spread the lamb on a work surface. With a boning or paring knife, cut between the muscles and separate them with your fingers. Trim any excess fat and gristle.
2. In a large, shallow dish, combine the olive oil, garlic and rosemary. Add the lamb and turn to coat. Let the meat marinate at room temperature for 4 hours, turning a few times.
3. Light a grill. Season the lamb with salt and pepper; do not scrape off the garlic or rosemary. Grill over high heat, turning often, until an instant-read thermometer inserted in each piece registers 125° to 130° for medium rare. The times will vary according to size and shape, anywhere from 8 minutes for a 6-ounce piece to 20 minutes for a 1½-pound piece. Transfer to a carving board as each one is done, cover loosely with foil and let rest for 15 minutes. Thinly slice and serve. —*Cal Peternell*
**SERVE WITH** Grilled asparagus and white bean salad.
**MAKE AHEAD** The lamb can marinate in the refrigerator overnight. Bring to room temperature before grilling.
**WINE** Intense, spicy Syrah.

### Lamb Kebabs with Cool Cucumber Salad

**TOTAL: 30 MIN**
4 SERVINGS ●

These lamb kebabs are coated with a garlicky, salty cumin rub. Leg of lamb is ideal here because it stays juicy and tender during grilling without shredding or falling apart. If you are really short on time, you can skip cutting and skewering the leg of lamb steaks and just grill the whole steaks for 2 minutes longer.

2 tablespoons ground cumin
3 large garlic cloves, very finely chopped
3 tablespoons extra-virgin olive oil
Salt and freshly ground pepper
1¼ pounds boneless leg of lamb steaks (1 inch thick), cut into 1-inch cubes
1 European cucumber, peeled and cut into 3-inch lengths
1 cup plain whole milk yogurt

1. Light a grill or preheat a grill pan. In a large bowl, combine the cumin, minced garlic and olive oil. Season the marinade generously with salt and pepper, then add the lamb and turn to coat. Thread the lamb onto 8 skewers. Let the kebabs stand for 10 minutes.
2. Meanwhile, working over a medium bowl, grate the cucumber on the large holes of a box grater, stopping when you get to the seedy center. Stir the yogurt into the grated cucumber. Transfer the yogurt mixture to a strainer lined with a coffee filter or paper towel and let drain for about 10 minutes. Transfer the cucumber salad to a serving bowl.
3. Grill the lamb kebabs over moderately high heat until the meat is charred and medium rare, about 7 minutes. Let the lamb kebabs rest for 5 minutes, then serve them immediately, with the cucumber salad alongside. —*Katy Sparks*
**WINE** Fresh, fruity rosé.

### Braised Lamb Shanks with Trahana Pasta and Ricotta Salata

**ACTIVE: 45 MIN; TOTAL: 3 HR 30 MIN**
6 SERVINGS

*Trahana,* a Greek pasta made from bulgur wheat, can be sweet or sour. The sour variety is mixed with thick goat's-milk yogurt before it is dried, giving the pasta a distinctive tangy flavor that is great with this oven-braised lamb. If you can't find sour *trahana* pasta at a Middle Eastern market, substitute couscous and add an extra squirt of lemon.

Six 1-pound lamb shanks
Salt and freshly ground black pepper
¾ cup extra-virgin olive oil
3 tablespoons unsalted butter
1 very large white onion, chopped
8 large garlic cloves, thinly sliced
12 thyme sprigs
1½ quarts chicken stock or low-sodium broth
3 large shallots, finely chopped
Two 28-ounce cans Italian pureed tomatoes
1 cinnamon stick
3 cups sour *trahana* pasta or couscous
¼ cup plus 2 tablespoons minced dill
¼ cup plus 2 tablespoons minced flat-leaf parsley
¼ cup plus 2 tablespoons snipped chives
¼ cup fresh lemon juice
¾ pound ricotta salata, shredded

1. Season the lamb shanks with salt and pepper. In a very large skillet, heat 2 tablespoons of the olive oil. Add the lamb shanks and cook them over moderately high heat until they are browned, about 10 minutes. Transfer the lamb shanks to a medium roasting pan.

**LAMB KEBABS WITH COOL CUCUMBER SALAD**

**BRAISED LAMB SHANK WITH TRAHANA PASTA**

**2.** Meanwhile, preheat the oven to 325°. Melt the butter in the same very large skillet that was used to brown the lamb shanks. Add the chopped sliced garlic and 8 of the thyme sprigs to the skillet and cook over moderate heat, stirring occasionally, until the onion and garlic are softened, about 7 minutes. Scrape the onion and garlic into the roasting pan with the lamb shanks and add the chicken stock to the roasting pan. Cover the roasting pan with foil and braise the lamb shanks in the oven for 2½ hours, or until the lamb shanks are very tender.

**3.** Transfer the cooked lamb shanks to a large ovenproof platter. Strain the lamb braising liquid into a bowl through a fine sieve and skim off the fat from the top of the braising liquid. You should have 7½ cups of braising liquid; if necessary, add water to the braising liquid to make up the

difference. Cover the cooked lamb shanks with foil and keep them warm in the oven while you prepare the sauce.

**4.** In a medium saucepan, heat ¼ cup of the olive oil. Add the chopped shallots and the remaining 4 thyme sprigs to the saucepan and cook the shallots over moderate heat, stirring occasionally, until they are softened, about 7 minutes. Add the tomato puree and cinnamon stick to the saucepan and cook over moderate heat until the tomato sauce is very thick and has reduced to 3 cups, about 30 minutes. Season the tomato sauce with salt and pepper. Remove the cinnamon stick and the thyme sprigs from the tomato sauce and discard them.

**5.** In a large saucepan, bring the reserved braising liquid to a boil. Add the sour trahana pasta and bring it to a boil, stirring constantly. Reduce the heat to low, cover

and cook the pasta for 10 minutes, or until all of the liquid has been absorbed; stir the pasta occasionally. Transfer the *trahana* to a large bowl and stir in the tomato sauce, the minced dill and parsley, the snipped chives and the lemon juice. Fold in half of the shredded ricotta salata cheese and the remaining ¼ cup plus 2 tablespoons of olive oil and season the pasta with salt and pepper. Mound the *trahana* on a large platter. Sprinkle the remaining shredded ricotta salata cheese on top of the pasta. Arrange the lamb shanks on top of the *trahana* and serve immediately.
—*Pano Karatassos*

**MAKE AHEAD** The lamb shanks can be refrigerated in their braising liquid for up to 3 days. Let the lamb shanks stand at room temperature for 1 hour, then reheat them in a 325° oven before serving.

**WINE** Intense, spicy Syrah.

PISTACHIO-CRUSTED RACK
OF LAMB WITH PANCETTA

## Pistachio-Crusted Rack of Lamb with Pancetta

**ACTIVE: 20 MIN; TOTAL: 1 HR 10 MIN**

**4 SERVINGS**

Something as conventional as rack of lamb would never find its way into Catalan chef Ferran Adrià's ultra-experimental kitchen at El Bulli in Rosas, Spain. But in his book *Cocinar en Casa* (Cooking at Home), he converts it into an unexpected, wonderful dish that anyone can make. Who else would think to coat a rack of lamb with a pistachio pesto, then wrap it in pancetta to keep it nicely moist and make it even richer as it roasts?

⅓ **cup unsalted pistachios**
1 **tablespoon chopped thyme**
1½ **teaspoons chopped rosemary**
⅓ **cup extra-virgin olive oil**
**Salt and freshly ground pepper**
**One 1½-pound rack of lamb, frenched**
6 **ounces thinly sliced pancetta**
8 **scallions, white and tender green parts only**

1. Preheat the oven to 400°. In a mini processor, finely chop the pistachios with the chopped thyme and rosemary. Add half of the olive oil to the mini processor and process to a paste; season the pistachio paste with salt and pepper and reserve half of it. Scrape the other half into a small bowl and stir in the remaining olive oil to make a pistachio pesto.

2. Coat the rack of lamb with half of the reserved pistachio paste. Wrap the pancetta slices around the lamb between the bones, leaving the bones exposed. Spread the remaining half of the reserved pistachio paste over the pancetta and set the rack of lamb in a small roasting pan. Roast the rack of lamb for about 40 minutes, or until an instant-read thermometer inserted in the center of the meat registers 130° for medium rare. Transfer the rack of lamb to a cutting board and let rest for 5 minutes. Reserve the pan drippings.

3. Meanwhile, spoon 1 teaspoon of the rendered pancetta fat from the roasting pan into a medium skillet and heat the fat until shimmering. Add the scallions and cook over high heat until softened and browned in spots, about 4 minutes. Carve the lamb rack into four 2-chop servings and transfer them to plates along with the scallions. Drizzle the pistachio pesto all around and serve the rack of lamb right away.
—*Ferran Adrià*

**MAKE AHEAD** The pistachio pesto can be refrigerated overnight.

**WINE** Earthy, medium-bodied Tempranillo.

## Grilled Leg of Lamb with Feta and Herb Salsa

**ACTIVE: 45 MIN; TOTAL: 1 HR 45 MIN**
**PLUS OVERNIGHT MARINATING**

**8 SERVINGS**

In this spin on the classic pairing of lamb and mint, the butterflied leg of lamb is rubbed with a garlicky, spicy mint pesto, which is also used to flavor a feta-herb salsa. The feta-herb salsa makes a fantastic sandwich spread for any leftovers.

1½ **cups mint leaves**
1½ **cups flat-leaf parsley leaves**
6 **garlic cloves, thickly sliced**
¾ **teaspoon crushed red pepper**
¾ **cup plus 2 tablespoons extra-virgin olive oil, plus more for brushing**
¼ **cup plus 2 tablespoons freshly grated Parmesan cheese**
½ **teaspoon grated lemon zest**
**Salt and freshly ground pepper**
**One 5½- to 6-pound butterflied leg of lamb**
1 **pound feta cheese, preferably French, crumbled (4 cups)**

1. In a food processor, pulse the mint leaves with the parsley leaves, sliced garlic and the crushed red pepper until finely chopped. Add ¼ cup plus 2 tablespoons of the olive oil and process to a coarse paste. Add the Parmesan cheese and the lemon zest and pulse to combine. Season the mint pesto with salt and pepper.

2. Spread the lamb on a cutting board and, using a paring knife, poke the meat all over. Using your fingers, work ⅓ cup of the mint pesto into the slashes and crevices. Season the lamb generously with salt and pepper and transfer to a roasting pan. Cover and refrigerate overnight.

3. Meanwhile, transfer the remaining mint pesto to a bowl and stir in the feta and the remaining ½ cup of olive oil. Season with salt and pepper and refrigerate.

4. Light a grill. Bring the marinated lamb to room temperature, about 1 hour, then brush it all over with olive oil. Season generously with salt and pepper and grill the lamb over moderately high heat, turning occasionally, for about 20 minutes, or until an instant-read thermometer inserted into the thickest part registers 125° (150° in the thinnest part). Transfer the lamb to a cutting board and let it rest for 10 minutes. Thinly slice the lamb and serve with the feta salsa. —*Grace Parisi*

**MAKE AHEAD** The feta salsa can be refrigerated overnight.

**WINE** Intense, spicy Syrah.

# technique
## FRENCHING A RACK OF LAMB

Frenching a rack of lamb refers to trimming the meat on the rib ends of the bones to expose them. Most butchers sell lamb that has been frenched or will french a rack of lamb by request. **To french at home: Make a long, horizontal cut** across the bones, just above the meatiest part of the rack. **Cut away the fat and meat** from between the bones. **Scrape both sides of the bones with** the back of a knife until clean.

# beef & lamb

## Roasted Rack of Lamb with Walnut Sauce

**TOTAL: 1 HR**

4 SERVINGS

Familiar Mediterranean flavors are made into something new here. Lamb is paired with a luscious, silky Northern Italian–inspired sauce made with walnuts that are simmered in milk, then pureed and enriched with butter.

- 1 cup shelled walnuts (3 ounces)
- 1½ cups milk
- 1 medium Yukon Gold potato (6 ounces), peeled and cut into 1-inch cubes
- ¼ cup extra-virgin olive oil
- 1 large shallot, finely chopped
- 1 green bell pepper, cut into 1-inch pieces
- 1 pound eggplant, peeled and cut into 1-inch cubes
- 2 medium zucchini, cut into 1-inch cubes
- ¾ cup vegetable stock or low-sodium broth
- 2 tablespoons coarsely chopped basil
- Salt and freshly ground pepper
- Two 1¼-pound frenched racks of lamb
- 1 tablespoon unsalted butter

**1.** Preheat the oven to 450°. In a small saucepan, combine the walnuts with the milk and simmer over low heat until the milk has reduced slightly, so it just covers the walnuts, about 20 minutes. Cover the saucepan and keep warm.

**2.** Meanwhile, in another small saucepan, cover the potato with water and bring to a boil. Cook over moderately high heat until just tender, about 6 minutes. Drain well.

**3.** In a large skillet, heat 2 tablespoons of the olive oil. Add the shallot and cook over moderate heat until softened, about 3 minutes. Add the bell pepper and cook,

stirring, for 4 minutes. Add the eggplant and 1 tablespoon of the olive oil, cover and cook, stirring a few times, until the eggplant is just tender, about 4 minutes. Add the zucchini and stock, cover and cook for 3 minutes longer, stirring once. Gently stir in the potato and basil, season with salt and pepper and stir again. Cover the skillet and remove it from the heat.

**4.** In a large ovenproof skillet, heat the remaining 1 tablespoon of olive oil until shimmering. Cut each lamb rack in half and season with salt and pepper. Add the lamb racks to the skillet, meaty side down, and cook them over high heat until richly browned on the bottom, about 4 minutes. Turn and cook on the bony side for 2 minutes. Transfer the skillet to the oven and cook the lamb for about 15 minutes, or until an instant-read thermometer inserted in the center of the meat registers 135° for medium rare. Transfer the lamb racks to a carving board and let them rest for about 10 minutes.

**5.** Transfer the walnuts and milk to a blender and puree. Return the walnut sauce to the saucepan and rewarm over moderate heat. Stir in the butter and season with salt and pepper. Reheat the vegetables, if necessary. Carve the lamb into chops and serve with the walnut sauce and vegetables. —*Marco Gallotta*

**NOTE** The creamy walnut sauce would also be wonderful with veal or chicken.

**MAKE AHEAD** The recipe can be prepared through Step 3 up to 4 hours ahead.

**WINE** Firm, complex Cabernet Sauvignon.

## Crusty Roasted Leg of Lamb with British Mint Sauce

**ACTIVE: 30 MIN; TOTAL: 5 HR PLUS OVERNIGHT MARINATING**

8 SERVINGS

- 20 garlic cloves, peeled
- ½ cup red wine vinegar
- 2 tablespoons thyme
- 1½ cups water

- One 9- to 10-pound whole leg of lamb
- 1 medium onion, coarsely chopped
- 2 cups dry white wine
- 2 tablespoons extra-virgin olive oil
- 4 bay leaves
- Salt and freshly ground pepper
- ½ cup white wine vinegar
- ½ cup finely chopped mint
- 1 tablespoon unsalted butter

**1.** In a blender, puree 10 of the garlic cloves with the red wine vinegar, thyme and ½ cup of the water. Put the lamb in a roasting pan and pour the marinade over it. Cover and refrigerate overnight.

**2.** Preheat the oven to 325°. Spread the onion and the remaining 10 garlic cloves under the leg of lamb. Add the wine to the pan and rub the lamb with the olive oil. Top with the bay leaves and season with salt and pepper. Roast the lamb for about 4½ hours, or until an instant-read thermometer inserted in the thickest part of the meat registers 160°. If the pan begins to look dry during cooking, add ½ cup of water.

**3.** Transfer the lamb to a carving board. In a small saucepan, combine the remaining ½ cup of water with the white wine vinegar, mint, butter and a pinch of salt and bring to a boil. Simmer over moderate heat until the broth resembles mint tea, about 3 minutes. Carve the lamb and serve with the mint broth. —*Victoria Amory*

**VARIATION** Make a pan sauce: Once the lamb is cooked, strain the contents of the roasting pan into a bowl, pressing hard on the solids. Skim off the fat. Set the roasting pan over 2 burners. Add 2 cups of water and boil over moderately high heat, stirring and scraping up the browned bits, until the liquid is reduced to 1 cup, about 5 minutes. Stir in the pan juices. Strain the pan sauce and season with salt.

**SERVE WITH** Roasted new potatoes.

**WINE** Earthy, medium-bodied Tempranillo.

CRUSTY ROASTED LEG OF LAMB WITH BRITISH MINT SAUCE (OPPOSITE)

TOMATO SALAD WITH MINT DRESSING (P. 46)

TENDER ARTICHOKE HEART STEW WITH PEAS (P. 228)

In the October issue, the Lobel family—legendary New York City butchers—shared their recipe for Sautéed German Sausages with Bacon and Apple Sauerkraut (P. 174). Here, Mark Lobel shows off his wurst.

# pork & veal

**PORK STEW WITH COCKLES AND SPICY RED PEPPER SAUCE**

**TWO-DAY SPICE-RUBBED PORK CHOPS**

## Pork Stew with Cockles and Spicy Red Pepper Sauce

ACTIVE: 1 HR 20 MIN; TOTAL: 3 HR

6 SERVINGS

This combination of briny cockles and smoky pork is traditional in southern Portugal's Alentejo region, but the red chiles in the sauce add a distinctive twist (for a less spicy version, use red bell peppers).

½ cup extra-virgin olive oil

3 pounds boneless pork blade chops (1 inch thick), cut into 1-inch cubes

Kosher salt

1 large onion, minced

5 large garlic cloves, 4 minced

1½ cups dry white wine

1 tablespoon tomato paste

1½ cups water

Finely grated zest of 1 lemon

3 large bay leaves

3 large thyme sprigs

1½ teaspoons sweet paprika

1 baguette, sliced ½ inch thick

1½ pounds kale, inner ribs and stems discarded, leaves coarsely chopped

Spicy Red Pepper Sauce (recipe follows)

Freshly ground pepper

3 pounds cockles, rinsed

3 tablespoons chopped cilantro

1. In a large enameled cast-iron casserole, heat ¼ cup of olive oil until shimmering. Sear the pork in 3 batches over moderately high heat until browned all over, 7 minutes per batch; you shouldn't need to add more oil. Using a slotted spoon, transfer the pork to a platter and season with salt.

2. Preheat the oven to 325°. Add half each of the minced onion and garlic to the pan. Cook over moderate heat, stirring occasionally, until softened, 8 minutes. Add the wine and cook over moderately high heat until reduced by a third, scraping up browned bits from the bottom of the pan. Whisk in the tomato paste, water, lemon zest, bay leaves, thyme, paprika and a generous pinch of salt. Return the meat and any accumulated juices to the pan; bring to a boil. Cover and cook over moderately low heat, stirring occasionally, until the meat is tender, 1½ hours. Skim the fat.

3. Meanwhile, brush the baguette slices with 2 tablespoons of the olive oil and arrange on a baking sheet; bake until lightly toasted. Rub the toasts with the whole garlic clove while they're still warm.

4. Add the kale to the stew a handful at a time; let it wilt slightly and add more. Stir in ⅓ cup of the Spicy Red Pepper Sauce and season with pepper. Cover and keep warm over very low heat.

**5.** In a large saucepan, heat the remaining 2 tablespoons of olive oil. Add the remaining minced onion and garlic and cook over moderate heat until softened, 8 minutes. Add the cockles and the remaining Spicy Red Pepper Sauce, cover and cook until most of the shells have opened, 4 minutes. Pour the cockles and their juices into the stew and gently stir. Cook for 1 minute, or until heated through. Discard any cockles that do not open. Ladle the stew into shallow bowls, top with the cilantro and serve with the garlic toasts. —*Lobel Family*
**WINE** Earthy, medium-bodied Tempranillo.

### SPICY RED PEPPER SAUCE
**TOTAL: 15 MIN**
**MAKES ABOUT ½ CUP** ● ● ●

- ¼ pound fresh red chiles, halved lengthwise and seeded
- 1 small garlic clove, thinly sliced
- ½ teaspoon kosher salt
- 2 tablespoons extra-virgin olive oil

In a mini food processor, pulse the chiles with the garlic and salt until finely chopped. With the machine on, slowly add the olive oil and process until a fairly smooth paste forms. —*Lobel Family*

### Two-Day Spice-Rubbed Pork Chops
**ACTIVE: 45 MIN; TOTAL: 3 HR PLUS 2 DAYS CURING**
**4 SERVINGS**

Sam Hayward of Fore Street restaurant in Portland, Maine, prefers cooking with pork from small farmers who raise heritage breeds, such as Berkshire, Gloucestershire or Old Spot. This pork is deeply colored and often as marbled as high-quality beef, and Hayward treats it with the special care it deserves. His two-day curing process is worth the time because it allows the spices to penetrate these juicy chops.

- Two 1¼-pound double-cut, bone-in pork rib chops
- 3 garlic cloves, 2 minced, 1 crushed
- 2 teaspoons chopped thyme leaves, plus 2 thyme sprigs
- Kosher salt
- 1½ tablespoons turbinado sugar
- 1 tablespoon juniper berries
- 1 tablespoon coriander seeds
- 2 teaspoons crushed black peppercorns, plus 6 whole peppercorns
- ½ teaspoon fennel seeds
- 1 star anise pod, crushed
- 3 tablespoons vegetable oil
- ½ pound pork shoulder, cut into 1-inch pieces
- 1 medium carrot, thinly sliced
- 2 medium shallots, thinly sliced
- 1 rosemary sprig
- 1 flat-leaf parsley sprig
- 1½ cups dry white wine
- 2 tablespoons honey
- 1 quart chicken stock

**1.** Put the pork chops in a glass baking dish and rub them all over with the minced garlic, chopped thyme and 1 tablespoon of salt. Cover and refrigerate overnight.
**2.** In a spice grinder or a clean coffee mill, combine the turbinado sugar with the juniper berries, coriander seeds, crushed peppercorns, fennel seeds and star anise and grind to a sandy powder. Sprinkle the spice rub all over the chops. Cover and refrigerate again overnight.
**3.** In a medium saucepan, heat 1 tablespoon of the oil. Add the pork shoulder and cook over moderately high heat, stirring once, until browned, about 4 minutes. Add the carrot, shallots, rosemary, parsley, crushed garlic, whole peppercorns and thyme sprigs; cook until the shallots begin to brown, about 3 minutes. Add the wine and honey and boil over high heat until reduced by half, about 5 minutes. Add the stock and bring to a boil. Simmer over low heat until the pork stock has reduced to ¾ cup, about 1½ hours. Strain the jus into a small saucepan and skim off the fat.

**4.** Preheat the oven to 375°. In a large ovenproof skillet, heat the remaining 2 tablespoons of oil. Add the pork chops and cook over moderately high heat until browned on the bottom, about 3 minutes. Turn and cook for 1 minute. Transfer the skillet to the oven and roast the pork chops for 35 to 40 minutes, until an instant-read thermometer inserted in the thickest part registers 150°. Remove from the oven and let the chops rest in the skillet for 8 minutes.
**5.** Reheat the pork jus and season with salt. Cut the pork between the rib bones into 4 chops; transfer to plates, browned side up. Serve with the jus. Alternatively, cut the meat off the bones and carve the chops as you would a roast. —*Sam Hayward*
**WINE** Rustic, peppery Malbec.

### Crisp Green Beans with Pork Belly
**TOTAL: 20 MIN**
**6 SERVINGS** ●

- 1 pound green beans, cut into 2-inch lengths
- 1 tablespoon canola oil
- ½ pound skinless pork belly or pancetta, sliced ¼ inch thick and cut crosswise into 2-inch pieces
- ¼ cup Chinese cooking wine, sake or water
- ½ cup Vietnamese Stir-Fry Sauce (p. 240)

**1.** In a saucepan of boiling water, cook the green beans until crisp-tender, 5 minutes. Drain and rinse under cold water; pat dry.
**2.** In a skillet or wok, heat the oil until small puffs of smoke appear. Add the pork belly in a single layer; cook over high heat, turning once, until golden, 3 minutes. Add the wine and cook for 1 minute. Pour in the Vietnamese Stir-Fry Sauce and cook over moderate heat until the pork is tender, 3 minutes. Add the beans and cook over moderate heat until tender, 1 to 2 minutes. Transfer to a platter and serve. —*Charles Phan*
**SERVE WITH** Steamed jasmine rice.
**WINE** Peppery, refreshing Grüner Veltliner.

**PAN-FRIED PORK CHOPS WITH QUINOA PILAF**

**SPICE-CRUSTED PORK-BLADE STEAKS**

## Pan-Fried Pork Chops with Quinoa Pilaf and Dried Fruit
**TOTAL: 35 MIN**

4 SERVINGS ●

2¼ cups chicken stock

1 small shallot, minced

1 garlic clove, minced

⅔ cup quinoa

2 tablespoons wheat berries

1 thyme sprig

1 bay leaf

2 tablespoons extra-virgin olive oil

Four 5-ounce boneless pork loin
 chops, trimmed of fat

Salt and freshly ground pepper

2 dried pear halves, diced

4 dried apricot halves, sliced

¼ cup dried sour cherries (1 ounce)

2 tablespoons ruby port

**1.** Preheat the oven to 350°. In a skillet, combine ¼ cup of the stock, the shallot and garlic and cook over moderate heat for 2 minutes. Add the quinoa, wheat berries, thyme and bay leaf. Add 1 cup of the stock and bring to a simmer. Scrape the mixture into a 9-inch square baking dish, cover with foil and bake for 15 minutes, until the quinoa and wheat berries are tender. Remove from the oven; keep covered.

**2.** Heat the olive oil in a large skillet. Season the pork chops with salt and pepper and brown them in the skillet over moderately high heat, 4 minutes per side. Transfer to a plate. Add the dried pears, apricots and cherries to the skillet and cook for 1 minute. Add the port and cook for 1 minute. Add the remaining 1 cup of stock and simmer over moderately high heat until reduced to ⅓ cup, 5 minutes. Add the pork and any accumulated juices and cook over moderate heat, turning a few times, until hot and just cooked, 2 minutes.

**3.** Fluff the pilaf with a fork, season with salt and pepper and mound it on plates. Set the pork chops on the pilaf, top with the sauce and serve. —*James Boyce*
**WINE** Intense, fruity Zinfandel.

### Spice-Crusted Pork-Blade Steaks

**TOTAL: 25 MIN**
4 SERVINGS ●

- 1 tablespoon cumin seeds
- 2 tablespoons chili powder
- 1 teaspoon ground chipotle
- 1 teaspoon dried oregano
- 1 teaspoon dried parsley
- Four 10-ounce pork shoulder blade steaks (about 1 inch thick)
- Salt
- 2 tablespoons Dijon mustard
- Extra-virgin olive oil, for drizzling

**1.** Light a grill. In a skillet, toast the cumin seeds over moderately high heat until fragrant, about 20 seconds. Let cool.

**2.** In a small bowl, combine the chili powder with the chipotle, oregano and parsley. Season the pork on both sides with salt. Spread with the mustard. Sprinkle with the cumin, then the chili mixture.

**3.** Drizzle the pork with oil and grill over moderately high heat until nicely charred and cooked through, 8 minutes per side. Transfer to a platter and let rest for 5 minutes before serving. —*Ron Shewchuk*
**WINE** Rich, ripe Cabernet Sauvignon.

### Pork Chops with Sautéed Apples

**TOTAL: 30 MIN**
4 SERVINGS ●

- ¼ cup extra-virgin olive oil
- 4 boneless pork chops, about 1 inch thick (about 2 pounds)
- Salt and freshly ground pepper
- 2 large Granny Smith apples, cored and cut into ½-inch-thick rounds
- 1½ tablespoons honey
- 1½ tablespoons sherry vinegar
- ½ cup pomegranate seeds (from ½ small pomegranate)

**1.** In a medium skillet, heat 1 tablespoon of the olive oil until shimmering. Season the chops with salt and pepper, add to the skillet and cook over high heat, turning once, until golden, about 7 minutes. Transfer to a plate, cover loosely and keep warm.

**2.** Add the apples to the skillet and cook over high heat, turning once, until softened and golden, about 6 minutes.

**3.** In a small bowl, whisk the honey and vinegar with the remaining 3 tablespoons of olive oil; season with salt and pepper. Stir in the pomegranate seeds. Transfer the pork and apples to plates, scatter the pomegranate seeds and vinaigrette on top and serve. —*Andy Nusser*
**WINE** Juicy, spicy Grenache.

### Stuffed Pork Chops with Onion and Shiitake

**TOTAL: 45 MIN**
4 SERVINGS ●

- ¼ cup extra-virgin olive oil
- ¼ cup finely chopped sweet onion
- 2 scallions, thinly sliced
- 1 small garlic clove, minced
- ¼ pound shiitake mushrooms, stems discarded, caps thinly sliced
- Salt and freshly ground pepper
- 1 tablespoon finely chopped parsley
- 1 teaspoon thyme leaves
- ¼ teaspoon minced rosemary
- Four 5-ounce boneless pork chops (1 inch thick), butterflied
- 8 large sage leaves
- ½ cup chicken stock

**1.** Preheat the oven to 350°. In a large ovenproof skillet, heat 2 tablespoons of the olive oil until shimmering. Add the onion, scallions and garlic and cook over moderately high heat until just softened, about 3 minutes. Add the mushrooms, season with salt and pepper and cook until tender and golden, about 7 minutes. Transfer to a bowl and add the parsley, thyme and rosemary; let cool slightly.

**2.** On a work surface, open the butterflied pork chops and season the inside with salt and pepper. Place a sage leaf on each side of each chop. Stuff with the mushroom mixture and close. Using four 8-inch lengths of kitchen string, tie up each pork chop across the middle.

**3.** Wipe out the skillet. Heat the remaining 2 tablespoons of oil until shimmering. Season the chops with salt and pepper and cook over high heat, turning once, until browned. Add the stock and bring to a simmer. Cover the skillet and bake the chops until cooked through, 6 minutes. Transfer to a plate and cover loosely with foil.

**4.** Return the skillet to high heat and cook until the liquid is reduced, 3 minutes. Untie the chops and transfer to plates. Spoon on the sauce and serve. —*Chef Bobo*
**WINE** Complex, elegant Pinot Noir.

### Grilled Pork with Curried Apricots and Napa Cabbage

**TOTAL: 30 MIN**
4 SERVINGS ● ●

- 1 cup dried apricots
- 1 cup water
- 1 pound pork tenderloin, cut into 4 pieces
- Extra-virgin olive oil
- Salt and freshly ground pepper
- 2 tablespoons unsalted butter
- 2 teaspoons mild curry powder
- 1 head napa cabbage (2 pounds), shredded
- 1½ teaspoons minced rosemary

**1.** Light a grill. In a saucepan, cover the apricots with the water. Bring to a boil. Remove from the heat and let stand for 3 minutes, then drain.

**2.** Rub the pork with olive oil; season with salt and pepper. Grill over moderately high heat, turning occasionally, until cooked through, 10 minutes. Let rest for 5 minutes, then cut each piece into 3 slices.

**3.** In a skillet, melt the butter and add the curry powder. Cook over moderate heat, stirring, until fragrant, 2 minutes. Add the cabbage, apricots and rosemary, season with salt and pepper and cook over high heat, stirring, until the cabbage wilts. Transfer the cabbage and apricots to plates, top with the pork and serve. —*Katy Sparks*
**WINE** Fruity, soft Chenin Blanc.

# pork & veal

### Pork with Strawberry-Herb Sauce

**TOTAL: 25 MIN**

4 SERVINGS ●

Luscious herb-scented pork gets a subtle sweetness from strawberry jam. Slicing the meat into medallions and pounding it makes it cook especially fast.

- 1 tablespoon extra-virgin olive oil
- Two ¾-pound pork tenderloins, each cut crosswise into 4 pieces and pounded 1 inch thick
- Salt and freshly ground pepper
- 2 tablespoons unsalted butter
- 1 shallot, very finely chopped
- ¾ cup chicken stock or low-sodium broth
- 2 tablespoons strawberry jam or preserves
- Scant 1 teaspoon chopped thyme
- 1 teaspoon Dijon mustard

**1.** In a large skillet, heat the olive oil until shimmering. Season the pork tenderloins with salt and pepper and cook the meat over high heat, turning once, until the tenderloins are browned and just cooked through, about 8 minutes. Transfer the pork to a plate and cover loosely with foil.

**2.** Melt 1 tablespoon of the butter in the skillet. Add the chopped shallot and cook over moderate heat, stirring, until the shallot is softened. Add the chicken stock, strawberry jam and chopped thyme and cook over high heat, stirring, until the sauce is thickened, about 3 minutes. Whisk the mustard into the sauce, reduce the heat to low and then whisk the remaining 1 tablespoon of butter into the sauce. Season the sauce with salt and pepper. Return the pork tenderloins and any juices on the plate to the skillet, turn the meat to coat with the sauce and serve immediately.
—*Grace Parisi*

**WINE** Intense, fruity Zinfandel.

### Pork with Parsley and Olives

**TOTAL: 25 MIN**

4 SERVINGS ● ●

Jerry Traunfeld, chef at The Herbfarm restaurant near Seattle, likes to treat parsley more like a green vegetable than like an herb. Here he mixes it with black olives and aromatic oregano to create a vibrant side dish that's great with succulent pork tenderloin or grilled steak.

- Two ¾-pound pork tenderloins
- Kosher salt and freshly ground pepper
- 2 tablespoons olive oil, plus more for drizzling
- ½ cup water
- 3 cups flat-leaf parsley leaves, coarsely chopped (from 2 bunches)
- 2 tablespoons coarsely chopped oregano
- ¼ cup pitted black olives, such as Calamata, chopped

**1.** Preheat the oven to 400°. Season the pork tenderloins with salt and pepper. In a large ovenproof skillet, heat the 2 tablespoons of olive oil until shimmering. Add the tenderloins and cook them over moderately high heat, turning occasionally, until browned all over, about 5 minutes. Transfer the skillet to the oven and roast the pork tenderloins for about 10 minutes, or until an instant-read thermometer inserted in the thickest part registers 140° for medium. Transfer the pork tenderloins to a cutting board and keep warm.

**2.** Return the skillet to the stovetop and set it over moderate heat. Add the water and bring it to a simmer, scraping up any browned bits stuck to the pan. Add the parsley, oregano and olives to the pan sauce and season with salt and pepper.

**3.** Slice the tenderloins crosswise and arrange the slices on a platter. Spoon the parsley all around the pork, drizzle with olive oil and serve. —*Jerry Traunfeld*

**WINE** Cherry-inflected, earthy Sangiovese.

### Pork Chops with Nectarine Relish

**TOTAL: 30 MIN**

4 SERVINGS ●

In the summertime, TV chef Bobby Flay loves eating relishes made with either fresh or grilled fruit. For this dish, he mixes smoky-sweet grilled nectarines with honey, balsamic vinegar and crunchy pine nuts to make a fantastic accompaniment for pork chops. This fast recipe is one of Flay's favorites; it was inspired by the journeys he made across America for his TV shows as well as by the regional ingredients he highlights at his new restaurant in New York City, Bar Americain.

- ¼ cup pine nuts
- Four 6-ounce center-cut boneless pork chops (about 1 inch thick)
- Olive oil, for brushing
- Salt and freshly ground pepper
- 4 firm nectarines, halved and pitted
- 2 tablespoons balsamic vinegar
- 1 tablespoon honey
- ½ small red onion, thinly sliced
- 1 tablespoon shredded basil

**1.** Light a grill. In a skillet, toast the pine nuts over high heat, stirring, until golden, 4 minutes. Transfer to a small bowl.

**2.** Brush the pork chops with olive oil and season with salt and pepper. Grill the chops over high heat, turning once, until they are cooked through, 10 to 11 minutes. Transfer the pork chops to a plate and let them rest for 5 minutes.

**3.** Meanwhile, brush the nectarines with olive oil and grill, cut side down, until browned, about 3 minutes. Turn the nectarines and grill until they are charred and softened, about 2 minutes longer. Cut the nectarine halves into ½-inch dice. Put them in a medium bowl and stir in the balsamic vinegar and honey. Add the onion, basil and pine nuts to the nectarines and season the relish with salt and pepper. Serve the pork chops topped with the nectarine relish.
—*Bobby Flay*

**WINE** Fruity, luscious Shiraz.

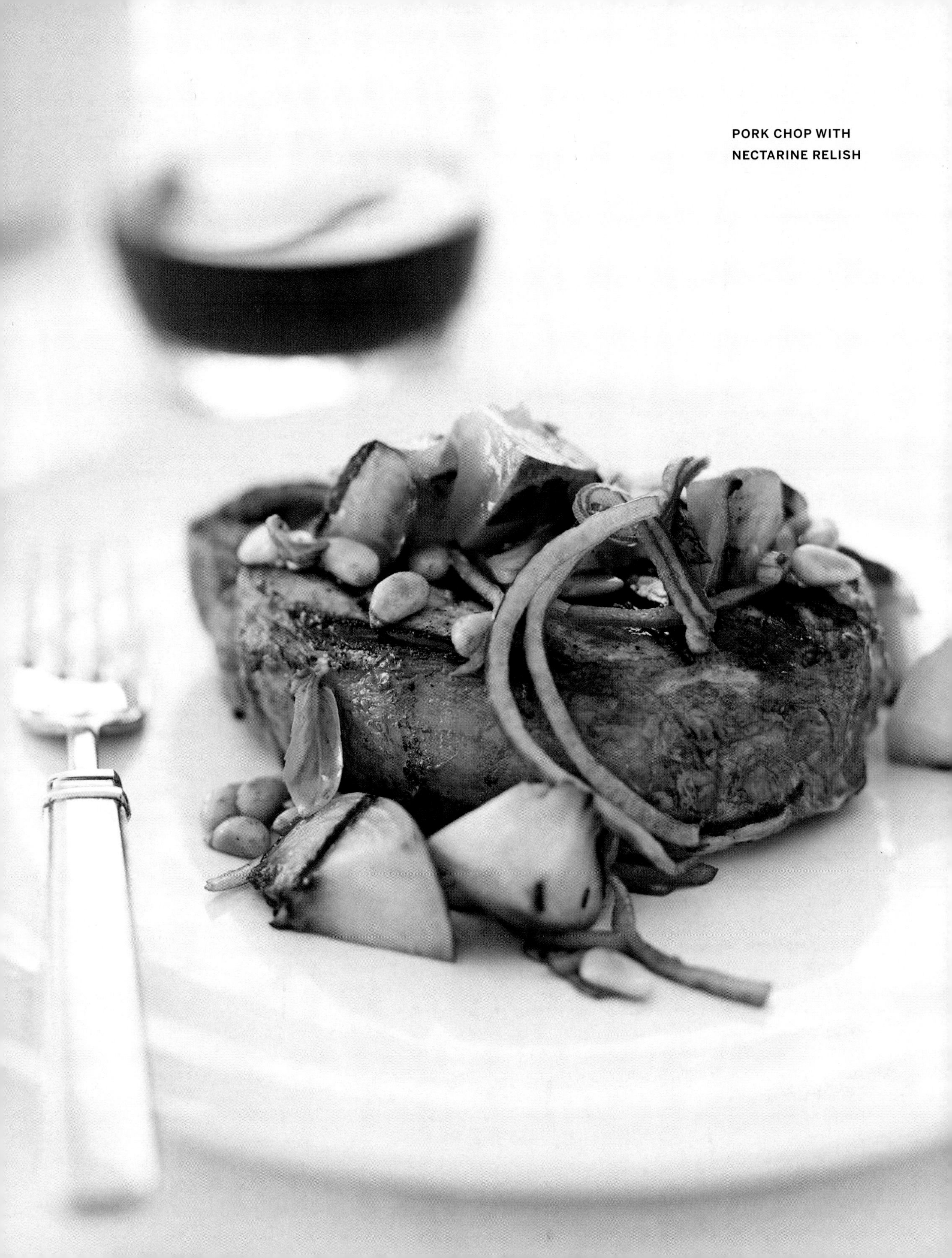

PORK CHOP WITH
NECTARINE RELISH

### Baked Pork Tamale

**ACTIVE: 30 MIN; TOTAL: 2 HR 30 MIN**
**8 SERVINGS** ●

This hearty casserole of succulent mole-braised pork, sandwiched between layers of tender, cakey masa dough, is like a supersized tamale.

- **3 pounds trimmed boneless pork shoulder, cut into 1½-inch pieces**
- **2 quarts water**
- **4 garlic cloves**
- **2 bay leaves**
- **1 medium onion, halved**
- **1 teaspoon freshly ground pepper**
- **2 tablespoons kosher salt**
- **4 cups instant masa harina (see Note)**
- **¾ cup solid vegetable shortening**
- **2 teaspoons baking powder**
- **1 cup prepared black or red mole**

Sour cream, chopped cilantro, lime wedges and sliced scallions, for serving

**1.** Preheat the oven to 350°. In a 6-quart pot, cover the pork with the water. Add the garlic, bay leaves, onion, pepper and 1 tablespoon of the salt; bring to a boil over high heat, skimming the surface once or twice. Cover and simmer over low heat until the pork is cooked through, about 30 minutes. Using a slotted spoon, transfer the pork to a bowl and let cool, then finely chop. Reserve the broth; you should have about 7½ cups.

**2.** In a large bowl, combine the masa harina with the vegetable shortening, baking powder and the remaining 1 tablespoon of salt. Add 4 cups of the reserved broth and knead the masa with your hands until a soft, sticky dough forms.

**3.** In a very large skillet, bring 3 cups of the reserved broth to a simmer over moderately low heat. Whisk in the mole until smooth; whisk in the remaining ½ cup of broth if the sauce seems too thick. Add the pork and simmer over moderately low heat for 10 minutes, stirring occasionally.

**4.** With wet hands, spread a little less than half of the masa dough on the bottom of a 9-by-13-inch glass or ceramic baking dish. Spoon the mole on top. Cover with the remaining dough, spreading it to completely enclose the filling. Tightly cover the dish with foil and bake for 1 hour, or until the crust is puffed and set and the filling is bubbling. Remove the foil and bake for 15 minutes, until golden. Let stand for 10 minutes. Serve with sour cream, cilantro, lime wedges and scallions. —*Melissa Guerra*

**NOTE** Masa harina is flour made from finely milled hominy (dried corn kernels that have been soaked in lime) and is used for making tortillas and tamales. It is available at Latin markets and many supermarkets.

**MAKE AHEAD** The tamale can be made earlier in the day and kept at room temperature. Reheat gently to serve.

**WINE** Savory, spicy Carmenère.

### Meat Tacos with Mole Sauce

**TOTAL: 20 MIN**
**4 SERVINGS** ●

If you're short on time, you can braise the meat in the mole sauce for just 10 minutes—it will be great. But refrigerating the braised meat for two to three days will allow the dish's complex flavors to meld.

- **⅓ cup prepared red or black mole**
- **2 cups low-sodium chicken broth**
- **3 cups shredded roast pork or chicken (about 1 pound)**

Twelve 8-inch corn tortillas
- **1 cup shredded Monterey Jack (4 ounces)**

Chopped cilantro, sliced scallions and lime wedges, for serving (optional)

**1.** In a medium saucepan, whisk the mole into the broth and bring to a boil. Add the pork and simmer over moderately low heat for 10 minutes. Keep warm.

**2.** Wrap the corn tortillas in a clean kitchen towel, then warm them in a microwave at high power for 2 minutes, or until they are hot and pliable.

**3.** Lay 4 tortillas on a work surface; keep the rest covered with the towel. Fill each tortilla with a few tablespoons of the meat. Roll up the tortillas into tight cylinders and transfer to a platter. Repeat with the remaining tortillas and meat. Spoon about ¾ cup of the mole sauce on top. Garnish with the cheese, cilantro, scallions and lime wedges, then serve with the remaining mole sauce. —*Melissa Guerra*

**WINE** Ripe, juicy Pinot Noir.

### Glazed Pork Tenderloin with Cumin-Spiked Corn Sauce

**ACTIVE: 1 HR; TOTAL: 1 HR 30 MIN**
**PLUS OVERNIGHT MARINATING**
**6 SERVINGS** ●

- **3 large tomatillos or ½ pound cape gooseberries, husked and chopped**
- **3 jalapeños, seeded and chopped**
- **2 scallions, chopped**
- **½ teaspoon chopped rosemary**
- **4 garlic cloves, minced**
- **7 tablespoons extra-virgin olive oil**
- **1 tablespoon plus 1 teaspoon honey**

Two 1-pound pork tenderloins
- **3 cups fresh corn kernels (from 6 ears of corn)**
- **½ yellow bell pepper, chopped**
- **1 medium red onion, cut into ⅓-inch dice**
- **¼ pound smoked ham, cut into ⅓-inch dice**
- **¼ cup plus 2 tablespoons pisco or other brandy**
- **2½ cups vegetable stock**
- **2 tablespoons chopped parsley**
- **¼ teaspoon ground cumin**

Salt and freshly ground pepper

**1.** In a food processor, puree the tomatillos with the jalapeños, scallions, rosemary, one-fourth of the garlic, 2 tablespoons of the olive oil and 1 tablespoon of the honey. Pour the puree into a sturdy, resealable plastic bag. Add the pork tenderloins, coat well and refrigerate overnight.

**2.** In a medium saucepan of boiling water, cook the corn until just tender, about 3 minutes; drain. In a food processor, coarsely puree the corn with the yellow pepper.

**3.** In a medium skillet, heat 2 tablespoons of the olive oil. Add the diced red onion, diced ham and the remaining three-fourths of the garlic and cook over moderate heat until the onion is softened, about 7 minutes. Add 2 tablespoons of the pisco and light carefully with a long match. When the flames die down, add the corn and pepper puree and 1 cup of the vegetable stock and simmer over low heat for 15 minutes, stirring occasionally. Add the chopped parsley and the cumin and season with salt and pepper. Cover the corn puree and set aside.

**4.** Remove the pork tenderloins from the marinade; reserve the marinade. In a large skillet, heat the remaining 3 tablespoons of olive oil. Season the tenderloins with salt and pepper, add them to the skillet and cook over moderate heat until they are browned on all sides, about 1 minute per side. Add the remaining ¼ cup of pisco and light carefully with a long match. When the flames die down, add the reserved marinade and the remaining 1½ cups of vegetable stock to the skillet and bring to a boil. Cover the skillet and simmer over moderately low heat, turning occasionally, until the pork tenderloins are pink in the center, about 20 minutes.

**5.** Transfer the pork tenderloins to a carving board and cover loosely with foil. Boil the pan sauce over moderately high heat for 3 minutes. Set a fine sieve over a small saucepan and strain the sauce, pressing on the solids. Add the remaining 1 teaspoon of honey and season the sauce with salt and pepper. Gently reheat the corn puree. Thickly slice the pork and transfer to plates. Pour the sauce over the pork, spoon the corn puree alongside and serve at once. —*Emmanuel Piqueras*
**WINE** Rustic, peppery Malbec.

**MEAT TACOS WITH MOLE SAUCE**

**GLAZED PORK TENDERLOIN WITH CUMIN-SPIKED CORN SAUCE**

# pork & veal

## Pork in Adobo Sauce

**ACTIVE: 1 HR 15 MIN; TOTAL: 2 HR**
**8 FIRST-COURSE SERVINGS** ●

This recipe was inspired by Bar Juanito in Jerez de la Frontera, Spain, which is famed for its *costillas de cerdo en adobo.* Jerez is a center of sherry production, so it's no surprise that the pork gets its tanginess from sherry vinegar.

- 1 head garlic, cloves peeled
- ⅓ cup sweet paprika
- ¼ cup ground cumin
- 2 tablespoons dried oregano
- 1⅓ cups sherry vinegar
- 1 cup extra-virgin olive oil
- 2¼ pounds boneless pork shoulder, trimmed and cut into 2-by-1-inch strips

Salt and freshly ground pepper
- 4 pounds baby back ribs, cut into individual ribs

About 6 cups water

1. In a food processor, puree the garlic, paprika, cumin, oregano and ⅓ cup of the vinegar until smooth. Add the remaining 1 cup of vinegar; process until blended.
2. Heat ⅓ cup of the olive oil in a large enameled cast-iron casserole. Season the pork shoulder with salt and pepper and cook over moderately high heat, turning occasionally, until browned, about 13 minutes. Transfer the pork to a platter.
3. Add the remaining ⅔ cup of olive oil to the casserole and heat until shimmering. Season the ribs with salt and pepper and add half of them to the pan in a single layer. Cook over moderately high heat, turning occasionally, until browned, about 10 minutes. Add them to the pork and brown the remaining ribs. Do not pour off the oil.
4. Return the meat to the casserole; season with salt and pepper. Add the vinegar mixture and enough water to cover and bring to a boil. Simmer over moderate heat until very tender, 45 to 50 minutes. Transfer to a plate and serve. —*Jeff Koehler*
**WINE** Rich, ripe Cabernet Sauvignon.

## Oven-Fried Pork Carnitas with Guacamole and Orange Salsa

**ACTIVE: 1 HR 30 MIN;**
**TOTAL: 3 HR 30 MIN**
**6 SERVINGS** ●

Chef Richard Sandoval of Isla in Las Vegas first tasted the moist, creamy, slightly sweet Spanish Requeson cheese used here during childhood trips to the market in Mexico City with his grandmother. In the United States, Requeson is sold at Latin markets. If you can't find it, substitute fresh whole-milk ricotta.

- ½ cup tamarind concentrate (see Note)
- 2 tablespoons honey
- 2 tablespoons sherry vinegar
- 2½ cups vegetable oil, plus more for brushing
- 2½ pounds boneless pork shoulder, cut into 1½-inch pieces

Salt and freshly ground pepper
- 1 medium white onion, finely chopped
- 2 garlic cloves, unpeeled
- 1 Hass avocado, pitted and peeled
- 3 tablespoons fresh lime juice
- 2 navel oranges
- 1 small red onion, thinly sliced
- ¼ cup coarsely chopped cilantro
- ½ habanero chile, seeded and finely chopped
- 1 cup fresh Requeson or ricotta cheese
- 1 small plum tomato, chopped
- 1 jalapeño or serrano chile, seeded and finely chopped
- 12 flour tortillas

1. In a large bowl, mix the tamarind concentrate with the honey, sherry vinegar and ¼ cup of the vegetable oil. Add the pork shoulder, season with salt and pepper and stir to coat. Let the pork marinate at room temperature for 1 hour. Drain the pork and pat dry.

2. Preheat the oven to 375°. In a large enameled cast-iron casserole, heat 2 tablespoons of the oil. Add half of the marinated pork and cook over moderately high heat, turning occasionally, until the meat is browned all over, about 6 minutes. Transfer the pork to an 8-by-11-inch baking dish. Repeat with 2 more tablespoons of oil and the remaining meat. Add two-thirds of the chopped white onion and 2 cups of oil to the baking dish. Cover with foil and bake for about 2 hours, or until the meat is very tender.
3. Meanwhile, wrap the garlic cloves in foil and bake for 1 hour, or until softened. Let cool slightly, then peel the cloves. In a small bowl, mash the avocado with the garlic. Stir in 1 tablespoon of the lime juice and season with salt and pepper.
4. Using a sharp knife, peel the oranges, removing all the bitter white pith. Working over a bowl, cut in between the membranes to release the segments. Squeeze the orange membranes to extract the juice. Stir in the red onion, cilantro and habanero chile and the 2 remaining tablespoons of fresh lime juice.
5. In a medium bowl, combine the Requeson cheese with the tomato, jalapeño and the remaining one-third of the chopped white onion. Season the Requeson with salt and pepper.
6. Brush the tortillas lightly with oil, then stack and wrap them in foil. Heat the tortillas in the oven until warm. Drain the pork on paper towels. Serve the carnitas by filling the tortillas with the Requeson, meat and guacamole. Serve the orange salsa on the side. —*Richard Sandoval*
**NOTE** Tamarind concentrate is used in Latin and South Asian dishes to add a slightly sweet and sour flavor. It is available at most Latin and Indian markets.
**MAKE AHEAD** The recipe can be prepared through Step 3 and refrigerated overnight. Reheat the carnitas in a 325° oven.
**WINE** Intense, fruity Zinfandel.

### Barbecued Baby Back Ribs

**ACTIVE: 2 HR; TOTAL: 5 HR 30 MIN**
**PLUS OVERNIGHT MARINATING**
**6 SERVINGS** ●

Baby back ribs (also known as loin back ribs because they are next to the pork loin) are more tender than spareribs. When buying them, avoid racks with protruding bones, which means the butchers have sacrificed more meat to the loin cut. If you do substitute spareribs here, be sure to allow an additional 2 hours of cooking time.

**Four 1¼-pound racks baby back ribs**
- ½ cup Garlicky Barbecue Marinade (p. 97)
- ¼ cup Seven-Spice Dry Rub (p. 97)
- 2 cups hickory or other hardwood chips, soaked in water

**Cider Mop Spray (p. 97)**
- ½ cup Sweet and Sticky Barbecue Sauce (p. 97) mixed with ½ cup water

1. Rub each rack of ribs all over with 2 tablespoons of the Garlicky Barbecue Marinade and refrigerate overnight.
2. Bring the ribs to room temperature and sprinkle each rack with 1 tablespoon of the Seven-Spice Dry Rub.
3. Light a charcoal fire in a covered grill and set it up for indirect grilling: When the temperature reaches 225°, carefully push the hot coals to one side and place a drip pan filled with 1 cup of water on the opposite side. Alternatively, bring a smoker to 225°. Put the ribs on the grill over the drip pan, overlapping them slightly, and cover the grill; you'll need to cook the ribs for about 4 hours total, or until the meat pulls away from the bones and is very tender. Maintain the temperature at 225° by replenishing the charcoal with a fresh batch of burning coals every hour. Every hour, drain ½ cup of the chips and scatter over the hot coals. Add water to the drip pan when half of it is evaporated. After 1½ hours, spray the ribs with the Cider Mop Spray and rotate on the grill; repeat spraying every 45 minutes.

4. Remove the drip pan. Spread the coals in an even layer. Replenish with fresh coals to make a moderately hot fire. Brush the ribs with the diluted Sweet and Sticky Barbecue Sauce and cook for 30 minutes, turning often. Repeat 4 or 5 times to build a sticky glaze. Transfer the ribs to a carving board; let rest for 10 minutes. Cut between each rib and serve. —*Adam Perry Lang*
**MAKE AHEAD** The glazed ribs can be refrigerated overnight. Serve cold or reheat in a 325° oven.
**WINE** Intense, fruity Zinfandel.

### Mahogany Glazed Spareribs

**TOTAL: 40 MIN**
**6 SERVINGS**

Brushing spareribs with a glaze of ginger, soy sauce and chili sauce turns them deep mahogany as they're grilled. The meat cooks surprisingly quickly because it's cut into individual ribs.

- ¼ cup rice vinegar
- ¼ cup water
- 2 large garlic cloves, crushed
- 5 pounds spareribs, cut into individual ribs
- ½ cup hoisin sauce
- 1½ tablespoons minced fresh ginger
- 1½ tablespoons soy sauce
- 1 teaspoon Chinese chili-garlic sauce

1. Light a grill. In a small bowl, combine the vinegar and water with the garlic. Grill the spareribs over moderately low heat until golden brown, brushing frequently with the garlic mixture and turning occasionally, about 25 minutes.
2. Meanwhile, in a small bowl, combine the hoisin sauce with the ginger, soy sauce and chili-garlic sauce. Brush the hoisin glaze on the spareribs and grill, turning occasionally, until they're deep mahogany, 9 to 10 minutes longer. Transfer the spareribs to a platter and serve at once, with lots of napkins. —*Grace Parisi*
**WINE** Round, deep-flavored Syrah.

### Chipotle-Cherry Barbecue Glaze

**TOTAL: 20 MIN**
**MAKES 1¼ CUPS** ● ● ●

- 2 tablespoons unsalted butter
- 1 medium onion, finely chopped
- 8 ounces cherry preserves (¾ cup)
- ¼ cup seeded, minced chipotle chile in adobo sauce
- ¼ cup ketchup
- ¼ cup cider vinegar

In a small saucepan, melt the butter. Add the onion and cook over moderate heat, stirring occasionally, until softened, 5 to 6 minutes. Add the remaining ingredients and cook over moderate heat, stirring, until bubbling, about 5 minutes longer. Transfer the mixture to a food processor and process until fairly smooth. Transfer to a bowl and let cool before using. —*Grace Parisi*
**SERVE WITH** Grilled meat or poultry.

## tools
### GRILLING GEAR

BBQ expert Steven Raichlen has tested a lot of grilling tools in his life. Now he's introduced his own line of tools, Best of Barbecue. Some of the products he's proudest of: strong, **extra long tongs**—the longest on the market, Raichlen says—that keep hands far from the flames ($17); elbow-length **heavy-duty suede gloves** that provide extra protection when you're raking embers ($20 a pair); and the **divided grill basket,** with four lids, that lets you remove each type of food when it's cooked ($25). **DETAILS** From barbecue-store.com; 888-789-0650.

**PORK RIB ROAST WITH SWEET ONION PUREE AND SAGE TEMPURA**

**PORK RIBS WITH ORANGE AND TOMATO GLAZE**

## Pork Rib Roast with Sweet Onion Puree and Crisp Sage Tempura

**ACTIVE: 50 MIN; TOTAL: 3 HR**
**PLUS 24 HR MARINATING**
**8 SERVINGS**

Govind Armstrong (at left), chef at Table 8 in Los Angeles, adores the variety of heady spices in his aromatic brine, which includes cloves, juniper and mustard seeds. He often uses them to flavor a whole rack of pork, which he finds easier to cook than individual chops. He also likes to finish the rack on a grill to add smoky flavor.

- ¼ cup juniper berries
- ¼ cup fennel seeds
- 2 tablespoons coriander seeds
- 1 tablespoon whole cloves
- ¼ cup coarsely chopped dried red chiles, such as árbol chiles
- ¼ cup black mustard seeds
- 6 bay leaves
- ½ cup dried thyme
- 5 quarts cold water
- 1 cup sugar

Kosher salt
One 5½-pound pork rib roast
Freshly ground black pepper
Sweet Onion Puree (recipe follows)
Crisp Sage Tempura (recipe follows)

**1.** In a large saucepan, combine the juniper berries, fennel, coriander and cloves; cook over moderately high heat, shaking the pot, until the spices are toasted and fragrant, 3 minutes. Add the chiles, mustard seeds and bay leaves; toast for 30 seconds longer. Stir in the thyme, add 1 quart of the water and bring to a boil. Remove from the heat and whisk in the sugar and ¾ cup of salt until dissolved. Transfer the mixture to a stockpot and let cool to room temperature. Stir in the remaining 4 quarts of cold water, then add the pork roast. Cover and refrigerate for 24 hours.

**2.** Preheat the oven to 375°. Remove the pork from the brine; discard the brine. Rinse the roast and pat dry with paper towels. Season well with salt and pepper.

3. Heat a very large ovenproof skillet over moderately high heat. Add the pork fat side down and brown all over, about 5 minutes per side. Transfer the skillet to the oven and cook for about 1 hour and 15 minutes, or until the roast is well browned and an instant-read thermometer inserted in the center registers 145°. Transfer the roast to a cutting board and let rest for 15 minutes. Carve the pork roast into 8 chops. Serve with Sweet Onion Puree and Crisp Sage Tempura. —*Govind Armstrong*

**WINE** Deep, velvety Merlot.

### SWEET ONION PUREE
**ACTIVE: 20 MIN; TOTAL: 3 HR**
8 SERVINGS ●

Creamy long-cooked onions, a simplified version of classic French onion *soubise,* are an ideal accompaniment to the savory rack of pork, but they're also great with duck or any other poultry.

- 2 thyme sprigs
- 1 bay leaf
- 1½ teaspoons whole black peppercorns

Pinch of crushed red pepper

- 4 tablespoons unsalted butter
- 4 medium onions, coarsely chopped
- 4 garlic cloves, peeled
- 1 small baking potato, peeled and cut into large dice
- 2 tablespoons dry white wine
- 1½ teaspoons sherry vinegar

Salt and freshly ground black pepper

1. Wrap the thyme, bay leaf, peppercorns and crushed pepper in a piece of cheesecloth and secure with kitchen string. In a medium saucepan, melt the butter. Add the onions, garlic, potato, wine and the herb bundle and bring to a simmer over moderately high heat. Reduce the heat to low, cover and cook until the onions are very soft, about 2½ hours.

2. Drain the vegetables, reserving the cooking liquid; discard the herb bundle. Transfer the vegetables to a food processor and puree with 2 tablespoons of the cooking liquid and the vinegar. Pass the puree through a sieve, then transfer to a bowl, season with salt and black pepper and serve warm. —*G.A.*

**MAKE AHEAD** The Sweet Onion Puree can be refrigerated for up to 2 days. Rewarm the puree over low heat.

### CRISP SAGE TEMPURA
**TOTAL: 50 MIN**
8 SERVINGS ●

Poppy-seed-studded batter makes a light and pleasantly crunchy coating for pungent, addictive sage leaves.

- ½ cup rice flour (see Note)
- 1½ teaspoons poppy seeds

Salt

- ⅛ teaspoon freshly ground pepper
- ½ cup cold club soda
- 1 tablespoon cold water

Vegetable oil, for frying

- 1 bunch sage (about 24 leaves), stems trimmed to ¼ inch

1. In a medium bowl, mix the rice flour with the poppy seeds, ½ teaspoon of salt and the pepper. Whisk in the club soda and cold water. Let the tempura batter rest for 20 minutes.

2. Heat ½ inch of vegetable oil in a small skillet just until shimmering. Holding each sage leaf by the stem, dip it into the batter to coat both sides. Add the battered sage leaves to the oil and fry them over moderately high heat until they are lightly golden, about 30 seconds. Drain the fried sage leaves on paper towels and sprinkle them lightly with salt. Serve the sage tempura warm or at room temperature. —*G.A.*

**NOTE** Rice flour is available at Asian markets and health food stores.

**MAKE AHEAD** The fried sage leaves can be stored in an airtight container overnight.

### Pork Ribs with Orange and Tomato Glaze
**ACTIVE: 20 MIN; TOTAL: 2 HR 30 MIN**
**PLUS 6 HR MARINATING**
10 SERVINGS

- 2 shallots
- 5 garlic cloves

One 2-ounce can oil-packed flat anchovies, drained

- 8 oil-packed sun-dried tomatoes, drained
- 3 tablespoons tomato paste
- 2 bay leaves
- ⅓ cup orange marmalade
- 1½ cups dry white wine
- 1½ cups fresh orange juice
- ¼ cup red wine vinegar
- 2 tablespoons minced rosemary
- 2 teaspoons finely grated orange zest
- 2 tablespoons kosher salt
- 1 tablespoon crushed red pepper
- 1 teaspoon freshly ground black pepper
- 4½ pounds baby back ribs, cut into individual ribs

1. In a food processor, process the shallots, garlic, anchovies, tomatoes, tomato paste, bay leaves and marmalade to a smooth paste. Transfer to a bowl and add the wine, juice, vinegar, rosemary, zest, salt, crushed pepper and black pepper. Add the ribs and toss to coat. Cover and refrigerate, turning occasionally, for 6 hours or overnight.

2. Preheat the oven to 375°. Remove the ribs from the marinade and arrange in a single layer on 2 large rimmed baking sheets. Cover with foil and bake for 1 hour. Pour the marinade into a medium saucepan and bring to a boil; let cool.

3. Drain any fat and liquid from the ribs. Continue baking, uncovered, for about 1 hour, turning and basting occasionally with the reserved marinade, until the meat is very tender. Transfer the ribs to a platter and serve right away. —*Seen Lippert*

**WINE** Lively, fruity Merlot.

# pork & veal

## Roasted Veal Chops with Young Garlic Vinaigrette

**ACTIVE: 45 MIN; TOTAL: 1 HR 30 MIN**

4 SERVINGS

So immature that they haven't yet formed a papery skin, young garlic bulbs are pearly white and still have their green stems attached. The garlic is mild, with a delicate flavor that makes for a fantastic vinaigrette that F&W Best New Chef 2005 Colby Garrelts of Bluestem restaurant in Kansas City, Missouri, drizzles over plump roasted veal chops. Look for young garlic at farmers' markets and specialty food shops in the late spring.

- 1 whole head young garlic, trimmed, cloves separated, plus 2 extra cloves peeled and thinly sliced (see Note)
- 10 medium shallots (14 ounces), 2 peeled and thinly sliced
- ¼ cup plus 2 tablespoons extra-virgin olive oil, plus more for drizzling
- Salt and freshly ground pepper
- 3 ears of corn, shucked
- 2 tablespoons chopped marjoram
- 1 tablespoon white wine vinegar
- ½ pound fava beans, shelled
- 2 tablespoons vegetable oil
- Four 14-ounce veal rib chops (1½ inches thick)
- 1 cup orzo
- 1 tablespoon unsalted butter
- ½ cup freshly grated Parmesan cheese (2 ounces)

1. Preheat the oven to 350°. Put the whole garlic cloves and whole, unpeeled shallots on a rimmed baking sheet. Drizzle lightly with olive oil and season with salt and pepper. Bake the garlic cloves for 15 minutes, or until softened; transfer to a plate. Bake the shallots for 30 minutes, until softened. Let the garlic and shallots cool, then peel the shallots. Turn the oven temperature up to 425°.

2. Preheat a grill pan and lightly oil it. Put the corn on the grill, cover loosely with foil and cook over moderately high heat, turning occasionally, until lightly charred and crisp-tender, about 20 minutes. Let the corn cool slightly, then cut the kernels from the cobs.

3. In a saucepan, heat 1 tablespoon of the olive oil. Add the sliced garlic and sliced shallots and cook over moderate heat until softened, 4 minutes. Scrape the shallots and garlic into a blender, add the marjoram and vinegar and puree. With the machine on, add ¼ cup of the olive oil. Season the vinaigrette with salt and pepper.

4. In a small saucepan of boiling water, cook the fava beans until just tender, about 2 minutes. Drain and peel. In a large skillet, heat 1 tablespoon of the vegetable oil until shimmering. Season the veal chops with salt and pepper. Add 2 of the chops to the skillet and cook over moderately high heat until browned, about 3 minutes per side. Transfer the chops to a rimmed baking sheet and repeat with the remaining 2 chops and 1 tablespoon of vegetable oil. Bake the chops for about 15 minutes, until just pink in the center.

5. Meanwhile, in a medium saucepan of boiling salted water, cook the orzo until al dente. Drain, reserving ¼ cup of the cooking water. Return the saucepan to the stove. Add the butter and the charred corn and cook over moderately high heat until heated through. Stir in the orzo and the reserved cooking water, then stir in the Parmesan. Season with salt and pepper.

6. In a small skillet, heat the remaining 1 tablespoon of olive oil. Add the baked shallots and garlic cloves, then add the fava beans and season with salt and pepper. Cook over moderately high heat until warmed through, about 1 minute.

7. Spoon the orzo onto plates and top with the veal chops. Spoon the shallots, garlic and favas alongside. Spoon the vinaigrette around the veal and serve.

—*Colby Garrelts*

**NOTE** If you can't find young garlic, regular garlic is a fine substitute; bake for 30 minutes in Step 1.

**MAKE AHEAD** The vinaigrette can be refrigerated overnight.

**WINE** Fresh, fruity rosé.

## Catalan-Style Braised Veal Ribs with Green Olives

**ACTIVE: 1 HR; TOTAL: 4 HR PLUS OVERNIGHT MARINATING**

6 TO 8 SERVINGS ●

Finding veal ribs isn't always easy, but they're so tender, they're worth the search. Because they're milder than beef ribs, the rich braising liquid here adds even more complexity, while the nutty *picada* spooned in at the end imparts a sweet, earthy depth.

## equipment
### BBQ THERMOMETER

This thermometer by Tel Tru allows BBQ buffs to check the temperature of their grill or smoker constantly. The **glow-in-the-dark dial** clearly shows if the temperature inside is in the right zone for smoking, barbecuing or grilling, so you know when the fire needs stoking. This handy piece of equipment ensures perfect results whether you're grilling hamburgers for 10 minutes or smoking pork butt for a whole day. **DETAILS** $49 from Tel Tru; 800-232-5335 or teltru.com.

7 pounds veal ribs, trimmed, ribs
   cut between the bones
1¼ cups extra-virgin olive oil
40 thyme sprigs
25 large garlic cloves, smashed
 2 large onions, finely chopped
 2 large celery ribs, finely chopped
 1 large carrot, finely chopped
 1 red bell pepper, finely chopped
One 28-ounce can peeled Italian
   tomatoes, drained and chopped
Salt and freshly ground black pepper
All-purpose flour, for dusting
 3 cups dry white wine
 3 cups beef stock
 3 bay leaves
 2 teaspoons sweet paprika
 ½ teaspoon cayenne pepper
 1 cup water
1½ cups pitted Spanish green olives
Catalan Picada (recipe follows)

1. In a large roasting pan, toss the ribs with ½ cup of the oil, the thyme and the garlic. Refrigerate for at least 8 hours, or overnight. Return the ribs to room temperature. Reserve the garlic; discard the thyme.

2. Preheat the oven to 275°. In a very large, deep skillet, heat ¼ cup of the oil until shimmering. Add the onions and cook over moderate heat, stirring occasionally, until softened, 5 minutes. Add the celery, carrot and bell pepper and cook until softened, 5 minutes. Add the reserved garlic and cook for 1 minute. Add the tomatoes, season with salt and pepper and cook over moderately high heat, stirring occasionally, until thickened, 15 minutes. Transfer to a bowl and rinse and dry the skillet.

3. Add ¼ cup of the oil to the skillet; heat until shimmering. Season half of the ribs with salt and pepper, then dust with flour, tapping off any excess. Add the floured ribs to the skillet and cook over moderately high heat, turning occasionally, until browned all over. Using tongs, transfer to the roasting pan. Wipe out the skillet. Repeat with the remaining oil and ribs.

4. Pour off all but 2 tablespoons of the fat in the skillet, add the wine and cook over moderate heat until reduced to 2 cups, 7 minutes. Add the tomato sauce, stock, bay leaves, paprika and cayenne. Bring to a boil and pour over the ribs. Season generously with black pepper. Add the water. Cover the roasting pan tightly with foil and bring the ribs to a simmer over 2 burners. Carefully transfer the pan to the lower third of the oven and bake for 2½ hours, or until the meat is falling-off-the-bone tender.

5. Preheat the broiler. Using a slotted spoon, arrange the ribs on a large baking sheet. Broil the ribs 8 inches from the heat, turning occasionally, until lightly browned. Transfer the ribs to a platter and cover loosely with foil.

6. Stir the olives and the Catalan Picada into the braising sauce. Set the roasting pan over 2 burners and boil the sauce over moderately high heat until the sauce is slightly reduced, about 10 minutes. Discard the bay leaves. Pour the sauce over the ribs and serve. —Lobel Family

WINE Juicy, spicy Grenache.

### CATALAN PICADA
**TOTAL: 15 MIN**
MAKES ABOUT ¼ CUP ● ● ●

 3 tablespoons extra-virgin olive oil
Two ½-inch-thick baguette slices
 6 roasted, blanched almonds
 6 roasted hazelnuts
 1 large garlic clove
 1 tablespoon water
 2 tablespoons minced parsley

1. In a small skillet, heat 2 tablespoons of the olive oil until shimmering. Add the bread and cook over high heat, turning, until toasted; cut into small cubes.

2. Transfer the cubes to a mini food processor. Add the almonds, hazelnuts and garlic and pulse until finely chopped. Add the remaining 1 tablespoon of olive oil and the water and process to a paste. Add the parsley and pulse to combine. —Lobel Family

### Veal Milanese with Eggplant and Onions
**TOTAL: 30 MIN**
4 SERVINGS ●

 4 small eggplants (about
   7 ounces each),
   quartered lengthwise
 1 large onion, cut into 8 wedges
   through the root end
1¼ cups pure olive oil
 3 tablespoons balsamic vinegar
Salt and freshly ground pepper
 2 cups dry bread crumbs
 1 cup freshly grated
   Parmesan cheese (4 ounces)
 2 tablespoons finely
   chopped sage
 1 cup all-purpose flour
 3 large eggs, beaten
1¼ pounds thin veal cutlets

1. Preheat the oven to 375°. In a large bowl, toss the eggplant and onion wedges with ¼ cup of the olive oil and the vinegar; season with salt and pepper. Spread the vegetables on a rimmed baking sheet and roast for about 20 minutes, turning occasionally, until tender and browned.

2. Meanwhile, in a large pie plate, toss the bread crumbs with the Parmesan and sage. Put the flour and eggs in 2 separate pie plates. Season the veal cutlets with salt and pepper, then dredge lightly in flour and dip in the eggs, letting any excess drip back into the plate. Dredge the cutlets in the bread crumbs, pressing lightly to help the crumbs adhere.

3. In a very large skillet, heat ½ cup of the olive oil until shimmering. Add half of the cutlets and cook over moderately high heat, turning once, until cooked through and crisp, about 4 minutes. Transfer to a platter and keep warm. Add the remaining ½ cup of olive oil to the skillet and fry the remaining cutlets. Serve the veal cutlets with the eggplant and onions.
—Marc Meyer

WINE Fruity, light-bodied Beaujolais.

ROASTED VEAL LOIN WITH CHESTNUT
STUFFING AND PICKLED RAISINS

## Roasted Veal Loin with Chestnut Stuffing and Pickled Raisins

ACTIVE: 30 MIN; TOTAL: 1 HR 30 MIN
PLUS 2 HR MARINATING

12 SERVINGS

- 2 tablespoons rosemary leaves, plus 3 sprigs broken into 3-inch pieces
- 2 tablespoons thyme leaves, plus 8 sprigs
- ¼ cup extra-virgin olive oil

One 5-pound boneless veal loin

Kosher salt and freshly ground pepper

- 6 tablespoons unsalted butter, cut into 6 pieces
- 24 garlic cloves, smashed and peeled

Chestnut Stuffing with Fennel (recipe follows), for serving

Pickled Golden Raisins (recipe follows), for serving

1. In a small bowl, combine the rosemary leaves, thyme leaves and 2 tablespoons of the olive oil. Set the veal in a baking dish and rub with the herb oil. Cover and refrigerate for at least 2 hours or overnight. One hour before roasting, remove the veal from the refrigerator.

2. Preheat the oven to 350°. Season the veal well with salt and pepper. In a large ovenproof skillet, heat the remaining 2 tablespoons of olive oil until almost smoking. Add the veal and sear over high heat until well browned all over, about 8 minutes. Remove from the heat. Arrange the rosemary and thyme sprigs on the roast and top with the butter. Scatter the garlic around the meat. Roast for about 1 hour, basting with the butter, until an instant-read thermometer inserted in the center registers 140°. Remove the veal from the oven and let rest for at least 10 minutes.

3. Slice the veal ¼ inch thick and arrange on a platter. Pile the roasted garlic alongside. Spoon the pan juices over the veal and serve with the Chestnut Stuffing with Fennel and the Pickled Golden Raisins.
—*Suzanne Goin*

**WINE** Dry, rich Champagne.

## CHESTNUT STUFFING WITH FENNEL

ACTIVE: 1 HR; TOTAL: 1 HR 50 MIN

12 SERVINGS ● ●

When Suzanne Goin, chef at Lucques in Los Angeles, was a child, making stuffing for the holidays was one of her first forays into cooking. "My mom always used store-bought crumbs, and it became my job to doctor them up," says Goin. "I'd just raid the spice cabinet and the first batches were a little crazy. But I figured out what I liked best." This chestnut-laced stuffing with pancetta and fennel is adapted from *Sunday Suppers at Lucques*. The bread cubes on top are especially delectable.

- 1½ pounds country bread, crusts removed, bread torn into 1-inch pieces
- ½ cup plus 2 tablespoons extra-virgin olive oil
- 1½ tablespoons fennel seeds
- 4 ounces pancetta, sliced ⅛ inch thick and the slices cut into dice
- 1 small rosemary sprig
- 1 dried árbol chile or other dried red chile, stemmed and broken in half
- 1 small onion, finely chopped
- 1 small fennel bulb, halved lengthwise and finely diced
- 1½ teaspoons thyme leaves

Kosher salt and freshly ground pepper

- 1 tablespoon finely grated lemon zest
- ¾ cup dry white wine, such as Chardonnay
- 2¼ cups chicken stock or low-sodium broth
- 6 tablespoons unsalted butter

One 10-ounce vacuum-packed jar chestnuts, very coarsely crumbled

- 2 large eggs, lightly beaten
- 3 tablespoons chopped flat-leaf parsley

1. Preheat the oven to 400°. On a baking sheet, toss the bread with ½ cup of the olive oil. Spread the bread in a single layer and toast in the oven for 15 minutes, stirring once, until golden brown. Let the croutons cool, then transfer to a large bowl. Leave the oven on.

2. In a small skillet, toast the fennel seeds over moderate heat until fragrant and lightly golden, about 2 minutes. Transfer to a mortar or spice grinder; coarsely grind.

3. In a large skillet, heat the remaining 2 tablespoons of olive oil. Add the pancetta and cook over high heat, stirring, until crisp, about 3 minutes. Lower the heat to moderate, add the rosemary and chile and cook for 1 minute. Add the onion, fennel, fennel seeds and thyme and season with salt and pepper. Cook, stirring, until the vegetables are lightly caramelized, about 8 minutes; discard the rosemary and chile. Stir in the lemon zest and add to the croutons.

4. Set the skillet over high heat. Add the wine and bring to a boil, scraping up the browned bits. Boil until reduced to ⅓ cup, about 4 minutes. Add the chicken stock and bring to a boil. Pour the hot stock mixture over the croutons and toss well.

5. Wipe out the skillet. Add 3 tablespoons of the butter and the chestnuts and cook over moderately high heat, stirring, until lightly browned, about 5 minutes. Add the chestnuts to the stuffing, season with salt and pepper and let cool completely. Add the eggs and parsley and toss well.

6. Transfer the stuffing to a 9-by-13-inch baking dish. Cover with foil and bake for 30 minutes. Remove the foil and dot the stuffing with the remaining 3 tablespoons of butter. Bake for about 20 minutes, or until crisp on top. Serve hot. —*S.G.*

**MAKE AHEAD** Bake the chestnut stuffing, covered with foil, for 30 minutes, then refrigerate it overnight. Heat the stuffing, covered, until cooked through, about 20 minutes, then uncover and bake for 20 minutes longer.

## PICKLED GOLDEN RAISINS

**TOTAL: 15 MIN**

**MAKES 1½ CUPS** ● ● ●

Suzanne Goin borrowed this recipe from Brian Wolff, her sous-chef at Lucques and a compulsive pickler. The piquant raisins are a great accompaniment to roasted poultry or pork as well as veal.

- 2 teaspoons yellow mustard seeds
- ½ cup sugar
- 1 cup water
- 3 tablespoons Champagne vinegar
- 1 dried árbol chile or other dried red chile, stemmed and crumbled
- 1 bay leaf
- 1⅓ cups golden raisins (½ pound)
- 3 thyme sprigs
- 1 small rosemary sprig
- 1 teaspoon kosher salt

**1.** In a small saucepan, toast the mustard seeds over moderate heat, shaking the pan, until the seeds just start to pop, about 2 minutes.

**2.** Add the remaining ingredients and bring to a boil. Reduce the heat to low and simmer gently until the liquid has reduced by half, about 8 minutes. Let the raisins cool completely and drain them before serving. —S.G.

**MAKE AHEAD** The raisins can be refrigerated in the pickling liquid for 3 days.

## Seared Tuscan-Style Meat Loaf

**ACTIVE: 1 HR; TOTAL: 2 HR 45 MIN**

**6 SERVINGS** ● ●

The Lobel family of Lobel's Prime Meats in New York City uses the traditional Tuscan method of searing the meat loaf in a roasting pan before baking it to produce an amazing crust.

- 2 cups crustless country bread cubes (1-inch cubes)
- ¼ cup milk
- ¾ pound ground pork
- ¾ pound ground veal
- ¾ pound ground beef
- ¼ pound thinly sliced mortadella, finely chopped
- ½ cup freshly grated Parmesan cheese (2 ounces)
- ¼ teaspoon freshly grated nutmeg

Kosher salt

- 4 large eggs
- ½ cup extra-virgin olive oil
- 1 very large onion, finely chopped
- 1 medium carrot, finely chopped
- 1 large celery rib, finely chopped
- 3 large garlic cloves, very finely chopped
- 3 tablespoons very finely chopped flat-leaf parsley
- 1½ teaspoons very finely chopped sage
- 1¼ cups dry white wine
- ½ cup water

**1.** Lightly oil a baking sheet. In a large bowl, mash the bread cubes with the milk until a paste forms. Add the ground pork, veal and beef, then the mortadella, Parmesan cheese and nutmeg. Season the meat loaf with 1 tablespoon of kosher salt.

**2.** In a small bowl, lightly beat 3 of the eggs and pour over the meat. Using your hands, gently work the beaten eggs into the meat loaf. Pat the meat into a large ball. Lift the meat from the bowl and gently toss it back and forth to compact it slightly. Transfer the meat to the prepared baking sheet and pat it into a 10-by-5-inch loaf. Cover the meat loaf with plastic wrap and refrigerate for 1 hour.

**3.** Meanwhile, in a large skillet, heat ¼ cup of the olive oil until shimmering. Add the chopped onion, carrot, celery, garlic, parsley and sage and cook the vegetables over moderate heat, stirring, until they are softened and just beginning to brown, about 8 minutes.

**4.** Preheat the oven to 325°. Heat the remaining ¼ cup of olive oil in a medium roasting pan set over a burner. Season the meat loaf with salt and carefully slide it into the roasting pan. Cook the meat loaf over moderately high heat, undisturbed, until it is browned on the bottom, about 7 minutes. Remove the pan from the heat and, using a spatula, loosen the meat loaf from the roasting pan. Using 2 spatulas, carefully transfer the meat loaf to the baking sheet, browned side up, then slide it back into the roasting pan.

**5.** Return the roasting pan to the burner, add the wine and cook over moderate heat until slightly reduced, about 5 minutes. Add the cooked vegetables, spreading some of them over the meat; spoon some of the liquid on top. Place a sheet of parchment paper directly on the meat loaf, pressing it all around. Cover the roasting pan tightly with foil and bake the meat loaf for 35 minutes, or until an instant-read thermometer inserted in the center registers 155°. Remove the parchment paper and let the meat loaf rest in the roasting pan for 15 minutes.

**6.** Transfer the meat loaf to a cutting board and cover it loosely with foil. Set the roasting pan over low heat and add the water. Using a spatula, scrape up any browned bits stuck to the bottom and sides of the pan and bring the pan juices to a simmer. In a small bowl, lightly whisk the remaining egg. Measure out 1 cup of the hot pan juices and whisk them into the egg. Gradually whisk the egg mixture back into the roasting pan and whisk until the gravy is slightly thickened and creamy, about 2 minutes. Pour the gravy into a warm gravy boat and cover. Cut the meat loaf into ½-inch slices and serve at once with the gravy. —*Lobel Family*

**MAKE AHEAD** The cooked meat loaf can be refrigerated for up to 5 days. It can be served hot or at room temperature.

**WINE** Fresh, minerally Vermentino.

## Sizzled Veal with Fresh-Herb Salad

**TOTAL: 30 MIN**

4 TO 6 SERVINGS ●

2½ tablespoons fresh lemon juice

¼ cup plus 2 tablespoons
   extra-virgin olive oil

2 cups arugula

1 cup flat-leaf parsley leaves

½ cup small or torn basil leaves

¼ cup snipped chives
   (½-inch lengths)

¼ cup mint leaves

1½ pounds veal scallopine
   (⅛ inch thick)

Salt and freshly ground pepper

All-purpose flour, for dusting

1 stick (4 ounces) unsalted butter

1½ lemons, very thinly sliced
   crosswise and seeded

1. In a small bowl, combine ½ tablespoon of the lemon juice and 1 tablespoon of the olive oil. In a large bowl, toss the arugula with the parsley, basil, chives and mint.

2. Put the veal on 2 large baking sheets. Season both sides with salt and pepper. Dust with flour and shake off the excess.

3. In each of 2 large skillets, heat 2 tablespoons of oil until shimmering. Add the scallopine to the skillets in a single layer, without crowding, and cook over high heat until browned, about 2 minutes per side. Transfer to a platter and keep warm. Add the remaining 1 tablespoon of oil to one of the skillets and cook the remaining veal.

4. Pour off the oil and add the butter to the skillet. Cook over moderately high heat until the butter starts to brown, about 3 minutes. Add the lemon slices and the remaining 2 tablespoons of lemon juice to the skillet and cook until the slices sizzle, about 1 minute. Season the sauce with salt and pepper. Transfer the veal to plates and pour the sauce on top. Toss the herb salad with the vinaigrette, mound alongside the veal and serve right away.

—*Suzanne Goin*

**WINE** Bright, tart Barbera.

## Veal Chops with Chorizo Stuffing

**TOTAL: 50 MIN**

4 SERVINGS ●

One 3-ounce dry-cured chorizo

¼ cup plus 3 tablespoons
   extra-virgin olive oil

5 large white mushrooms, ends
   trimmed, very thinly sliced

Salt and freshly ground pepper

2 medium leeks, white and
   tender green parts only, very
   thinly sliced crosswise

1½ cups packed baby spinach

¼ cup coarsely shredded young
   pecorino cheese, such as
   Pecorino Toscano

Four 1-pound veal rib chops
   (1½ inches thick)

½ cup fruity Pinot Noir

¼ cup dry Marsala

½ cup chicken stock

2 tablespoons unsalted butter

Fried Polenta with Fresh Corn (p. 262),
   for serving

1. Preheat the oven to 425°. Bring a small saucepan of water to a boil. Add the chorizo and simmer over low heat until softened, about 5 minutes. Transfer the chorizo to a plate and let cool. Thinly slice the chorizo crosswise, then coarsely chop it.

2. In a medium skillet, heat 3 tablespoons of the olive oil. Add the mushrooms in a single layer, season with salt and pepper and cook over high heat until browned on the bottom, about 4 minutes. Add the leeks, cover and cook over moderate heat, stirring occasionally, until softened, about 5 minutes. Add the chorizo and cook, stirring, for 1 minute. Add the spinach and stir just until wilted. Transfer the stuffing to a bowl and let cool slightly. Stir in the cheese and season with salt and pepper.

3. Using a thin, sharp knife, cut a pocket in each veal chop: Insert the blade 2 inches into the center of the chop, cutting horizontally from one side to the other without cutting completely through. Generously fill the chops with the stuffing and secure the openings by threading them closed with bamboo skewers. Break off the ends of the skewers that protrude from the meat.

4. Heat 2 tablespoons of the olive oil in each of 2 large skillets. Season the veal chops with salt and pepper. Cook 2 chops in each skillet over moderately high heat, turning once, until nicely browned, about 9 minutes. Transfer the skillets to the top and bottom racks of the oven and roast the chops for 5 minutes. Turn the veal chops, switch the pans between racks and roast for 5 minutes longer, or until just pink. Transfer the chops to a warmed platter.

5. Pour off the fat from each skillet and set the skillets over moderate heat. Add half of the Pinot Noir to each skillet and scrape up any browned bits stuck to the bottom. Pour the wine from one skillet into the other and simmer for 1 minute. Add the Marsala and stock and simmer until slightly reduced, about 3 minutes. Off the heat, whisk in the butter and season the sauce with salt and pepper.

6. Remove the skewers from the meat and spoon the pan sauce over the veal chops. Serve with Fried Polenta with Fresh Corn.

—*Marcia Kiesel*

**MAKE AHEAD** The filling can be refrigerated overnight. Bring to room temperature before stuffing the chops.

**WINE** Complex, elegant Pinot Noir.

## superfast
### VEAL SCALLOPINE

Cut veal scallopine into one-by-two-inch strips and season with salt and pepper. **Pan-fry** the strips in a tablespoon each of extra-virgin olive oil and canola oil over moderately high heat for about one minute, turning once. Add the strips to **cooked pasta** tossed with pesto, or serve them over a plate of mixed greens dressed in a vinaigrette.

# pork & veal

## Veal Meatballs with Fried Sage Leaves

**TOTAL: 35 MIN**

4 SERVINGS ●

- 1 cup crustless day-old bread cubes (1-inch cubes)
- ¾ cup milk
- 1 pound ground veal (see Note)
- 2 scallions, minced
- 1 garlic clove, minced
- 1 teaspoon salt
- ¼ teaspoon freshly ground pepper
- 4 tablespoons unsalted butter
- 12 sage leaves

All-purpose flour, for dusting

- ¾ cup dry white wine
- 6 tablespoons vegetable stock

**1.** In a small bowl, soak the bread in the milk until softened, about 10 minutes.

**2.** In a bowl, mix the veal, scallions, garlic, salt and pepper. Squeeze the bread dry and add to the veal. Using your hands, mix the ingredients thoroughly and shape into 30 meatballs. Transfer to a baking sheet.

**3.** In a large skillet, melt the butter. Add the sage leaves, laying them flat, and cook over moderately high heat until crisp, about 2 minutes; transfer to a plate.

**4.** Dust the meatballs lightly with flour and shake off the excess. Add the meatballs to the skillet and cook them over moderate heat until browned all over and cooked through, about 12 minutes. Transfer the meatballs to a platter and keep warm.

**5.** Add the wine to the skillet and simmer over moderately high heat, scraping up the browned bits on the bottom of the skillet, until almost evaporated, 5 minutes. Add the stock and simmer until slightly reduced, about 2 minutes. Transfer the meatballs to a platter and pour the pan sauce over them. Garnish with the fried sage leaves and serve. —*Marco Gallotta*

**NOTE** These meatballs are also delicious when made with ground pork or a mixture of ground pork and veal.

**WINE** Cherry-inflected, earthy Sangiovese.

## Poor Man's Paella

**TOTAL: 30 MIN**

4 SERVINGS ● ●

- ⅓ cup extra-virgin olive oil
- 2 tablespoons annatto seeds (achiote)
- ½ small onion
- 2 garlic cloves
- ¼ red bell pepper
- 1 small tomato, coarsely chopped
- ½ cup cilantro leaves
- ½ pound ham steak, cut into ½-inch dice
- 3 cups chicken stock or low-sodium broth
- 2 cups long-grain rice
- ½ teaspoon ground cumin

Salt and freshly ground pepper

- 1 cup frozen peas

**1.** In a small skillet, warm the olive oil with the annatto seeds over moderate heat until bright orange, about 3 minutes. Strain the annatto oil into a large saucepan.

**2.** In a food processor, puree the onion, garlic, bell pepper, tomato and cilantro. Reheat the annatto oil. Add the onion mixture and ham and cook over moderately high heat until fragrant. Stir in the stock, rice and cumin; season with salt and pepper. Bring to a boil; stir in the peas. Reduce the heat to moderately low, cover and simmer for 15 minutes. Remove from the heat and let stand, covered, for 3 minutes, then transfer to bowls and serve. —*Daisy Martinez*

**WINE** Earthy, medium-bodied Tempranillo.

## Sausages with Grilled-Onion Chowchow

**TOTAL: 35 MIN**

6 SERVINGS

Chowchow is a sweet-and-sour relish. The version here is studded with pieces of charred and crunchy onions, which have a smoky flavor that's delicious with grilled sausage. The chowchow is perfect with all types of grilled meat or poultry or as a hot dog relish.

- 2 sweet onions, sliced ½ inch thick
- 2 jalapeños

Extra-virgin olive oil, for brushing

- ½ cup cider vinegar
- ¼ cup plus 2 tablespoons light brown sugar
- ¼ cup grainy mustard
- ¼ cup Dijon mustard
- ¼ teaspoon caraway seeds
- ¼ teaspoon turmeric
- 1 teaspoon cornstarch dissolved in 2 teaspoons water

Salt and freshly ground pepper

- 3 pounds mixed sausages (see Note)

**1.** Light a grill. Skewer each onion slice with a toothpick. Thread the jalapeños on a skewer. Brush the onions and jalapeños with olive oil and grill over high heat until charred but still slightly crisp, about 10 minutes. Remove the toothpicks and the skewer. Coarsely chop the onions. Peel and chop the jalapeños.

**2.** In a medium saucepan, combine the cider vinegar with the light brown sugar, grainy and Dijon mustards, caraway seeds and turmeric and bring to a simmer. Add the onions and jalapeños and cook over moderate heat, stirring frequently, until the liquid is slightly reduced, about 12 minutes. Stir the cornstarch mixture, add it to the onions and cook, stirring occasionally, until slightly thickened, about 2 minutes. Season with salt and pepper.

**3.** Grill the sausages over moderately high heat until golden and cooked through, 10 to 12 minutes. Serve the sausages with the grilled-onion chowchow.
—*Grace Parisi*

**NOTE** The sausages can include Italian fennel, merguez, turkey and chicken sausages, which will cook in about 12 minutes, and andouille and kielbasa sausages, which will cook in about 10 minutes.

**MAKE AHEAD** The chowchow can be refrigerated for up to 1 week.

**WINE** Intense, fruity Zinfandel.

## Sautéed German Sausages with Bacon and Apple Sauerkraut

**ACTIVE: 30 MIN; TOTAL: 1 HR 30 MIN**

6 SERVINGS

- ¼ cup vegetable oil
- 5 ounces thick-cut bacon, cut into ½-inch pieces
- 1 very large onion, coarsely chopped
- 2 tablespoons off-dry white wine, such as Riesling
- 1 large sweet apple, such as Gala or Fuji—peeled, cored and cut into ½-inch pieces
- 12 juniper berries
- 4 bay leaves
- ½ teaspoon sugar

Kosher salt and freshly ground pepper

- 1 cup water
- 2½ pounds sauerkraut—drained, rinsed and squeezed dry (4 packed cups)
- 12 German-style sausages, such as weisswurst or bratwurst

Grainy mustard, for serving

**1.** In a large enameled cast-iron casserole, heat 2 tablespoons of the oil until shimmering. Add the bacon and cook over moderately high heat until the fat is rendered and the bacon is crisp, about 5 minutes. Using a slotted spoon, transfer the bacon to a paper towel–lined plate.

**2.** Add the onion to the casserole, cover partially and cook over moderately low heat, stirring occasionally, until very soft, 20 minutes. Increase the heat to moderately high. Add the wine, apple, juniper berries, bay leaves, sugar, 1 teaspoon of salt and ½ teaspoon of pepper and boil for 3 minutes. Add the water and sauerkraut. Reduce the heat to low, cover and cook until the apple is very tender, 45 minutes.

**3.** In a skillet, heat the remaining 2 tablespoons of oil until shimmering. Prick the sausages several times with a fork and cook over moderate heat, turning several times, until golden, 8 minutes.

**4.** Spoon the sauerkraut onto a platter and arrange the sausages on top. Sprinkle the reserved bacon over the sausages and serve with mustard. —*Lobel Family*

**MAKE AHEAD** The sauerkraut can be prepared through Step 2 and refrigerated for up to 2 days.

**WINE** Vivid, lightly sweet Riesling.

## Curly Corn Dogs

**TOTAL: 45 MIN**

8 SERVINGS

These hot dogs are quartered lengthwise, dipped in batter, then skillet-fried in a shallow pool of oil. The hot dogs curl as they cook and become wonderfully crunchy.

- 1⅓ cups fine cornmeal
- ⅔ cup all-purpose flour
- 2½ teaspoons baking powder
- 1 teaspoon salt
- ½ teaspoon freshly ground pepper
- ½ teaspoon onion powder
- 2 large eggs
- 1½ cups milk
- ¼ cup honey

Vegetable oil, for frying

- 8 hot dogs, quartered lengthwise

Mustard, for serving

**1.** Preheat the oven to 300°. In a large bowl, whisk together the cornmeal, flour, baking powder, salt, pepper and onion powder. In another bowl, whisk the eggs, then whisk in the milk and honey. Using a rubber spatula, fold the dry ingredients into the wet until just blended. Let stand for 15 minutes.

**2.** In a large, deep skillet, heat ½ inch of vegetable oil to 350°. Set a large rack over a large rimmed baking sheet. Dip 4 hot dog strips in the batter to coat, then slip them into the hot oil. Fry over moderate heat until browned and crisp, about 2 minutes. Transfer to the rack to drain; keep the corn dogs warm in the oven while you finish frying. Repeat, frying up to 6 strips at a time. Serve hot, with mustard.
—*Jeremy Jackson*

**WINE** Juicy, fresh Dolcetto.

## Hot Dog Melts

**TOTAL: 30 MIN**

6 SERVINGS

- ½ cup plus 2 tablespoons mayonnaise
- ¼ cup sour cream
- ¼ cup drained prepared horseradish
- ¼ cup Dijon mustard
- 1 tablespoon honey
- 1 tablespoon minced shallots
- 1 tablespoon minced chives
- 1 tablespoon fresh lemon juice

Salt and freshly ground pepper

- 6 slices of Gruyère cheese
- 6 hot dogs, slit lengthwise
- 6 thin slices of lean bacon
- 6 hot dog buns

**1.** Preheat the oven to 425°. In a small bowl, combine the mayonnaise, sour cream, horseradish, mustard, honey, shallots, chives and lemon juice and season with salt and pepper.

**2.** Place a slice of cheese in the center of each splayed hot dog, breaking the slice if necessary to fit it in. Wrap a slice of bacon around each hot dog and secure it with toothpicks.

**3.** Arrange the hot dogs on a rimmed baking sheet and bake in the upper third of the oven until the bacon is crisp, about 12 minutes. Place each hot dog in a bun and serve, passing the horseradish sauce on the side. —*Wolfgang Puck*

**WINE** Lively, fruity Merlot.

## Toulouse-Style Cassoulet

**ACTIVE: 2 HR 30 MIN; TOTAL: 7 HR**
**PLUS 2 DAYS SOAKING AND RESTING**

10 TO 12 SERVINGS

- 2 fresh ham hocks
- 1 pound boneless pork shoulder, cut into 1½-inch cubes
- 6 ounces fresh pork skin with ¼ inch of fat attached

Salt and freshly ground pepper

- 2 ounces salt pork, skin removed
- ⅓ cup duck fat (see Note)

3 small carrots, thinly sliced

2 medium onions, diced

One 5-ounce piece of pancetta

One 5-ounce piece of prosciutto

1 head garlic, unpeeled, plus
4 small garlic cloves, peeled

1 large plum tomato, chopped

2 quarts plus 2 cups chicken broth

Bouquet garni: 4 parsley sprigs,
3 small celery ribs, 2 thyme sprigs
and 1 bay leaf, tied with string

2 pounds dried Tarbais (see Note)
or cannellini beans—picked over,
rinsed and soaked overnight

6 duck confit legs (see Note for
availability, or recipe on p. 119)

1 tablespoon vegetable oil

1 pound French-style fresh pork
sausages, such as *saucisses
de Toulouse,* pricked with a fork

¼ cup fresh bread crumbs

1. Put the ham hocks, pork shoulder cubes and pork skin in a dish; season with salt and pepper. Cover and refrigerate overnight.

2. The next day, in a saucepan, cover the salt pork and seasoned skin with water. Bring to a boil, then simmer over moderate heat until the skin is supple, 30 minutes. Drain and cool. Refrigerate the salt pork. Cut the pork skin into 5 long pieces and roll each piece into a bundle; tie with string.

3. Dry the ham hocks and pork shoulder cubes with a paper towel. In a very large enameled cast-iron casserole, heat the duck fat. Add half of the pork cubes and cook over moderately high heat until lightly browned all over; transfer to a plate. Repeat with the remaining pork cubes. Add the ham hocks to the casserole and brown them lightly. Add the carrots and onions and cook over moderate heat, stirring occasionally, until the onions are golden, about 7 minutes. Add the pancetta and brown it lightly. Add the prosciutto, the head of garlic and the tomato and cook, stirring, for 1 minute. Add 2 quarts of the broth, the bouquet garni, pork skin bundles

and the browned pork and its juices and bring to a boil. Cover the casserole and gently simmer the ragout over low heat for 1½ hours, stirring occasionally.

4. Drain the beans. In a large saucepan, cover the beans with water and bring to a boil over moderate heat. Simmer the beans for 3 minutes, then drain. Add the beans to the ragout and simmer until the beans are just tender, about 2 hours. Let the ragout cool, then refrigerate overnight.

5. Remove as much of the solidified fat as you can from the surface of the ragout; reserve ¼ cup of the fat. Let the ragout return to room temperature. Pick out the ham hocks, pancetta and prosciutto. Cut the meats into bite-size pieces; discard the bones, skin and gristle. Pick out the pork skin bundles and the head of garlic and reserve. Discard the bouquet garni.

6. Preheat the oven to 400°. Bring the ragout to a simmer. Cut the blanched salt pork into small pieces. Squeeze the cooked garlic cloves into a food processor. Add the salt pork and the raw garlic cloves and process to a smooth paste. Stir the paste into the ragout and simmer over low heat for 15 minutes, stirring occasionally. Stir in all of the cooked and cured meats.

7. Meanwhile, arrange the duck confit legs in a baking dish and roast just until heated through, about 15 minutes. Remove the meat from the bones in large pieces. Cut the skin into strips. Discard the bones.

8. Turn the oven down to 325°. Untie and unroll the pork skin. Line the bottom of a 5- to 6-quart earthenware casserole with the pork skin, fat side down, and, using a large slotted spoon, transfer half of the ragout to the casserole. Top with the duck confit in an even layer, then cover with the rest of the ragout. Add the remaining 2 cups of broth to the cast-iron casserole and season lightly with salt and pepper. Pour the liquid over the ragout and drizzle with 2 tablespoons of the reserved skimmed fat. Bake for 1½ hours.

9. Heat the oil in a medium skillet. Add the sausages and cook over moderately high heat until browned all over. Let cool, then cut the sausages into 3-inch pieces.

10. Reduce the oven temperature to 275°. Gently stir in the skin that has formed on the cassoulet. Nestle in the sausages and drizzle with the remaining 2 tablespoons of reserved fat. Sprinkle with the bread crumbs. Bake for 1 hour longer, until richly browned on the surface. Transfer to a cloth-lined rack and let rest for at least 20 minutes before serving. —*Paula Wolfert*

**NOTE** Duck fat and confit legs can be ordered from dartagnan.com; Tarbais beans and Toulouse-style sausages from frenchselections.com.

**MAKE AHEAD** The cassoulet can be prepared through Step 6 up to 3 days ahead. Let cool, then refrigerate. Bring to room temperature before proceeding.

**WINE** Intense, spicy Syrah.

# ingredient
## ARTISANAL CHARCUTERIE

**Armandino Batali** (father of superstar chef Mario) of Seattle's Salumi sells delicious dry-cured meats, including mole-flavored salami and hot soppressata. Try the three-salami pack. **DETAILS** $34; salumicuredmeats.com.

The May issue featured a story on a sailboat cruise along the Turkish coast, with delicious food like these Swordfish Kebabs with Lemon and Bay Leaves (P. 185).

**fish**

**SALMON WITH LEMON GLAZE AND ROSEMARY CRUMBS**

**SALMON RICE BOWL WITH GINGER-LIME SAUCE**

## Salmon with Lemon Glaze and Rosemary Crumbs

**TOTAL: 30 MIN**

4 SERVINGS ● ●

These plump center-cut salmon fillets are lacquered with mint-and-lemon-infused honey, then topped with crisp rosemary-scented bread crumbs.

¼ cup extra-virgin olive oil, plus more for brushing

1 garlic clove, smashed

One 4-inch rosemary sprig

¾ cup *panko* (Japanese bread crumbs)

½ teaspoon grated lemon zest

Salt and freshly ground pepper

¼ cup honey

1½ tablespoons fresh lemon juice

2 mint sprigs

Four 8-ounce skinless salmon fillets

**1.** Light a grill. In a skillet, warm the ¼ cup of olive oil with the garlic and rosemary over moderate heat until fragrant, about 1 minute. Add the *panko* and cook, stirring constantly, until golden and crisp, about 5 minutes. Remove the skillet from the heat, add the zest and season with salt and pepper. Discard the rosemary and garlic.

**2.** In a small saucepan, combine the honey, lemon juice and mint and cook over high heat, stirring frequently, for 1 minute.

**3.** Brush the salmon with olive oil. Season well with salt and pepper. Grill the fish over moderately high heat, turning once, until lightly charred and pink in the center, 10 minutes. Brush the honey and lemon glaze all over the fish. Grill until lightly lacquered, turning and brushing both sides, 2 minutes. Transfer to plates, sprinkle with the crumbs and serve. —*Grace Parisi*

**WINE** Complex, elegant Pinot Noir.

## Salmon Rice Bowl with Ginger-Lime Sauce

**TOTAL: 30 MIN**

4 SERVINGS ● ● ●

1¾ cups water

1¼ cups long-grain rice, rinsed

2 tablespoons peeled, minced fresh ginger

3½ tablespoons sugar

1 Thai red chile, chopped

10 small garlic cloves, 2 chopped

2 tablespoons fresh lime juice

2 tablespoons Asian fish sauce

2 kirby cucumbers (10 ounces), cut into thin strips

2 tablespoons vegetable oil

Four 6-ounce skinless salmon fillets

Salt and freshly ground pepper

1. In a medium saucepan, bring 1½ cups of the water and the rice to a boil. Cover the saucepan, reduce the heat to low and cook the rice for 12 minutes. Remove the cooked rice from the heat and let stand for about 5 minutes.

2. Meanwhile, in a mortar, pound the minced fresh ginger with the sugar, the Thai red chile and the chopped garlic to a coarse paste. Transfer the ginger paste to a bowl and stir in the remaining ¼ cup of water, the lime juice and the fish sauce. Add the cucumber strips.

3. Heat the vegetable oil in a large nonstick skillet. Season the salmon fillets with salt and pepper. Add the salmon fillets to the skillet and cook over moderately high heat until they are lightly browned, about 3 minutes. Add the whole garlic cloves. Turn the salmon over and cook the other side over moderate heat until opaque throughout, about 4 minutes.

4. Mound the rice in bowls. Top with the salmon, garlic cloves and ginger-lime sauce with cucumber strips and serve. Pass any extra ginger-lime sauce at the table.
—*Mai Pham*

**WINE** Ripe, juicy Pinot Noir.

## Pan-Roasted Salmon with Soy-Ginger Glaze
**TOTAL: 15 MIN**
4 SERVINGS ● ●
Salmon is especially delicious when brushed with honey, soy, ginger and mustard and roasted until sticky and glazed.

¼ cup soy sauce
1 teaspoon finely grated fresh ginger
1 teaspoon honey
1 teaspoon Dijon mustard
2 teaspoons extra-virgin olive oil
Four 6-ounce skinless salmon fillets
Freshly ground pepper
Cilantro leaves, for garnish

1. Preheat the oven to 350°. In a small saucepan, combine the soy sauce and ginger and bring to a simmer. Remove the pan from the heat and stir in the honey and the mustard.

2. Heat the olive oil in a large nonstick ovenproof skillet. Season the salmon fillets with pepper and add them to the skillet, skinned side up. Cook the salmon over high heat until golden and crusty, 2 to 3 minutes. Turn the salmon and spoon the soy-ginger glaze on top. Transfer the skillet to the oven and bake the salmon for 5 minutes, or until cooked through. Using a slotted spatula, transfer the salmon fillets to plates, garnish with the cilantro and serve immediately. —*Chef Bobo*

**WINE** Ripe, juicy Pinot Noir.

## Roast Salmon with Couscous Crust
**TOTAL: 45 MIN**
4 SERVINGS
F&W's Marcia Kiesel used to make a crust for salmon with bread crumbs, but she created this clever alternative as a way to use up leftover cooked couscous. She now prefers the couscous crust because it holds its shape better than the bread-crumb one and delivers a much more satisfying crunch.

1 cup boiling water
1 cup instant couscous
2 tablespoons extra-virgin olive oil
2 slices of lean bacon, cut into ¼-inch dice
1 garlic clove, minced
6 oil-packed black olives, pitted and chopped
1 tablespoon chopped flat-leaf parsley
Salt and freshly ground pepper
Four 6-ounce skinless center-cut salmon fillets
1 large leek, white and tender green parts only, halved lengthwise and sliced crosswise ¼ inch thick
½ cup fruity Pinot Noir
2 tablespoons red wine vinegar
1 medium shallot, thinly sliced
1 stick (4 ounces) unsalted butter, well chilled and sliced into tablespoons

1. Preheat the oven to 500°. In a small heatproof bowl, pour the boiling water over the instant couscous. Cover the bowl with a plate and let the couscous stand until the water has been completely absorbed, about 20 minutes.

2. In a small skillet, heat 1 tablespoon of the olive oil. Add the diced bacon and cook over moderate heat until lightly crisp, about 4 minutes. Add the garlic and cook until fragrant. Remove the skillet from the heat and stir in the olives, parsley and couscous. Season the couscous lightly with salt and pepper.

3. Put the salmon fillets skinned side down on a lightly oiled baking sheet and season with salt and pepper. Carefully mound the couscous on the fillets, pressing lightly to help it adhere. Bake the salmon in the upper third of the oven for about 10 minutes, or until the couscous topping is crisp and the salmon is just cooked through.

4. Meanwhile, in a medium saucepan, heat the remaining 1 tablespoon of olive oil. Add the sliced leek, cover and cook over moderately low heat until softened, about 6 minutes. Scrape the leek onto a plate. Add the Pinot Noir, vinegar and sliced shallot to the saucepan and boil over moderately high heat until the liquid has reduced to 2½ tablespoons, about 4 minutes. Remove the saucepan from the heat and whisk in the butter, 1 tablespoon at a time; return the saucepan to the heat only as necessary to keep the sauce warm. Do not let the sauce boil. Stir the leek into the sauce and cook just until heated through. Season the sauce with salt and pepper. Serve the sauce at once with the salmon.
—*Marcia Kiesel*

**WINE** Complex, elegant Pinot Noir.

## Salmon Fillets with Leek Fondue

**TOTAL: 25 MIN**

**4 SERVINGS** ●

The creamy, piquant leek fondue in this recipe is marvelous with salmon but would be equally good with cod or halibut, or even chicken.

- 4 tablespoons unsalted butter
- 2 tablespoons white wine vinegar
- 2 medium leeks (about 1 pound), white and light green parts only, halved lengthwise and thinly sliced crosswise
- 1 medium onion, cut into ½-inch dice
- 4 garlic cloves, smashed

Kosher salt and freshly ground pepper

- 2 tablespoons all-purpose flour
- 1¼ cups chicken stock or low-sodium broth
- ⅓ cup heavy cream
- 2 tablespoons extra-virgin olive oil

Four 6- to 7-ounce skinless salmon fillets

- 1 tablespoon minced flat-leaf parsley

**1.** In a medium skillet, melt the butter with the vinegar. Add the leeks, onion and garlic and season with salt and pepper. Cook over moderate heat until the leeks and onion have softened, about 5 minutes. Stir in the flour, then stir in the stock and simmer until slightly thickened, about 2 minutes. Transfer the leek mixture to a blender and puree until smooth. Return the puree to the skillet and stir in the cream. Simmer over low heat until the sauce thickens, about 5 minutes. Season with salt and pepper.

**2.** In a large nonstick skillet, heat the olive oil. Season the salmon with salt and pepper and cook over moderately high heat until light pink throughout, about 4 minutes per side. Transfer the salmon to plates and top with the leek fondue. Garnish with the parsley and serve immediately.

—Daisy Martinez

**WINE** Ripe, luxurious Chardonnay.

## Crispy-Skin Salmon with Vegetable-Noodle Salad

**TOTAL: 30 MIN**

**4 SERVINGS** ● ●

- ½ pound dried Chinese egg noodles or 14 ounces fresh noodles
- 2 tablespoons low-sodium soy sauce
- 1 tablespoon fresh lime juice
- 1 teaspoon sugar
- 1 teaspoon balsamic vinegar
- ½ teaspoon Asian sesame oil
- ½ European cucumber—peeled, seeded and finely julienned
- 1 cup julienned daikon
- 2 scallions, thinly sliced
- 1 small hot red chile, thinly sliced
- 2 tablespoons cilantro leaves
- 1 tablespoon extra-virgin olive oil

Four 8-ounce center-cut salmon fillets with skin

Salt and freshly ground pepper

Lime wedges, for serving

**1.** In a large pot of boiling salted water, cook the dried noodles until al dente, about 5 minutes. Drain and cool under running water, then shake dry.

**2.** In a medium bowl, combine the soy sauce, lime juice, sugar, vinegar and sesame oil and stir until the sugar dissolves. Add the noodles, cucumber, daikon, scallions, chile and cilantro and toss. Transfer the noodle salad to plates.

**3.** In a large skillet, heat the olive oil until almost smoking. Season the salmon with salt and pepper and cook over moderately high heat, skin side down, until browned and crispy, about 3 minutes. Turn and cook until browned and crusty and slightly rare in the center, about 3 minutes longer. Place the salmon skin side up on the noodle salad and serve with lime wedges.

—Bill Granger

**WINE** Fruity, low-oak Chardonnay.

## Spicy Thai Pomelo Salad with Smoked Salmon

**TOTAL: 25 MIN**

**4 SERVINGS** ● ●

Two 1¾-pound pomelos, peeled

- 2 tablespoons vegetable oil
- 1 large shallot, thinly sliced, slices separated into rings
- 3 Thai chiles, thinly sliced
- 1 tablespoon Asian fish sauce
- 1 teaspoon sugar
- 6 ounces thinly sliced smoked salmon, cut crosswise into ½-inch-wide strips
- ¼ cup chopped basil
- ¼ cup chopped cilantro
- ¼ cup roasted, unsalted peanuts, chopped

**1.** On a work surface, separate the pomelos into sections, then peel each section. Using a fork or knife, gently break up the sections until the flesh separates into juicy, translucent pieces (these are called pearls) and transfer them to a bowl.

**2.** Heat the oil in a small saucepan. Add the shallot rings and cook over moderate heat, stirring occasionally, until browned, about 5 minutes. Using a slotted spoon, transfer to paper towels to drain.

**3.** In a small bowl, stir the chiles with the fish sauce and sugar. In a large bowl, combine the pomelo pearls with the salmon, basil, cilantro, peanuts, shallots and chile dressing and toss to coat. Mound the salad on plates and serve. —Marcia Kiesel

**WINE** Tart, citrusy Riesling.

## Miso-Cured Salmon with Endive and Ginger-Pickled Shallot Salad

**TOTAL: 30 MIN PLUS 4 HR 30 MIN FOR MARINATING**

**4 SERVINGS** ●

- 1 cup water
- ½ cup plus 1½ tablespoons red miso
- ¼ cup plus 1 teaspoon soy sauce

Four 6-ounce salmon fillets with skin

One 2-inch piece of peeled
     fresh ginger
 1 tablespoon plus 1 teaspoon
     unseasoned rice vinegar
 2 medium shallots, thinly sliced
1½ teaspoons honey
 ¼ teaspoon Asian sesame oil
 1 teaspoon vegetable oil
 2 Belgian endives, sliced
     crosswise ½ inch thick
 ½ cup shiso leaves or sweet basil,
     cut into thin ribbons

1. In a bowl, whisk the water with ½ cup of the miso and ¼ cup of the soy sauce. Put the salmon in a sturdy, resealable 1-gallon plastic bag. Add the miso, seal the bag and turn to coat the salmon. Refrigerate for at least 4 hours and up to 8 hours.

2. Meanwhile, finely grate the ginger into a fine strainer set over a small bowl. Press to extract as much ginger juice as possible. Add 1 tablespoon of the rice vinegar and the shallots, toss well and let stand at room temperature for 1 hour.

3. Preheat the oven to 350°. In a small bowl, whisk the remaining 1½ tablespoons of miso with the honey, sesame oil and the remaining 1 teaspoon each of soy sauce and rice vinegar.

4. Set a large cast-iron skillet over high heat for 3 minutes. Remove the salmon fillets from the marinade and pat dry. Add the vegetable oil to the skillet and heat until shimmering. Add the salmon fillets, skin side down, and cook over high heat until the skin is well-browned and crisp, about 3 minutes; turn and cook for 1 minute longer. Transfer the fillets to a rimmed baking sheet, skin side up, and bake for 6 minutes, or until medium.

5. In a bowl, toss the endives and shiso. Using a fork, lightly drain the shallots and add them to the salad. Spread the miso-honey sauce on plates, top with the salmon fillets and serve the salad alongside. —Josh DeChellis

**WINE** Creamy, supple Pinot Blanc.

## Salmon Burgers with Horseradish-Dill Sauce
TOTAL: 35 MIN
4 SERVINGS ●
This supermoist, flavorful and healthy fish burger is the runner-up recipe from the 2004 F&W Readers' Burger Contest.
 ½ cup plain whole-milk yogurt
 2 tablespoons drained prepared horseradish
 2 tablespoons chopped capers
Finely grated zest of 1 lemon
 ¼ cup plus 1 tablespoon extra-virgin olive oil
 2 celery ribs, finely chopped
 1 small onion, finely chopped
 1 pound skinless center-cut salmon fillet, cut into ¼-inch dice
 ½ cup fresh bread crumbs
 3 tablespoons chopped dill
 1 large egg, lightly beaten
 ¾ teaspoon kosher salt
 ¼ teaspoon freshly ground black pepper
 4 kaiser rolls, split and lightly toasted

1. In a small bowl, mix the yogurt with the horseradish, capers and half of the zest.
2. In a medium skillet, heat 2 tablespoons of the olive oil. Add the chopped celery and onion and cook over moderately low heat until the vegetables are translucent, about 7 minutes. Transfer to a bowl and let cool. Add the diced salmon, crumbs, dill, egg, salt, pepper and the remaining zest; mix gently and pat into 4 burgers.
3. In a skillet, heat the remaining 3 tablespoons of olive oil until shimmering. Add the burgers and cook over moderately high heat until browned outside and medium in the center, about 4 minutes per side.
4. Spread the sauce on both sides of the rolls. Add the burgers, close the sandwiches and serve. —Terese Fantasia

**MAKE AHEAD** The horseradish sauce and the uncooked burgers can be refrigerated separately overnight.

**WINE** Ripe, luxurious Chardonnay.

## Plank Barbecued Salmon
TOTAL: 50 MIN PLUS 1 HR 30 MIN
MARINATING AND SOAKING
4 SERVINGS ●
 ½ cup dry white wine
 ½ cup apple juice
 1 tablespoon sea salt
 3 bay leaves, crumbled
 2 tablespoons pink peppercorns, crushed
 1 tablespoon juniper berries, crushed
One 1¾- to 2-pound center-cut salmon fillet with skin
Olive oil, for brushing
 ½ cup prepared barbecue sauce

1. Soak a 16-by-8-inch cedar plank in water for 1 hour. In a large, shallow baking dish, combine the wine with the apple juice, salt, bay leaves, peppercorns and juniper berries. Add the salmon, turn to coat and refrigerate for 30 minutes.
2. Light a grill. If using charcoal, push the coals to the sides when covered with light gray ash. Set a disposable drip pan in the center. If using a gas grill, turn off the center burner. Remove the fish from the marinade, brush off the seasonings and lay it skin side down on the plank. Brush the fish with oil and set in the center of the cooking grate for indirect grilling. Cover and grill until just cooked, 30 minutes; brush with sauce during the last 10 minutes. Serve directly from the plank. —Elizabeth Karmel

**WINE** Juicy, fresh Dolcetto.

## superfast
### QUICK SALMON RECIPES

Bake salmon fillets at 350° until almost cooked. Cover them with honey and place under the broiler until they are nicely caramelized.

Drizzle a mixture of soy sauce, lemon juice, salt, pepper and peanut oil over salmon fillets wrapped individually in foil, then steam.

### Seared Tuna with Potatoes and Anchovy Vinaigrette

**TOTAL: 40 MIN**

8 SERVINGS ● ●

1¾ pounds medium Yukon Gold
   potatoes, scrubbed but not peeled
  4 anchovy fillets, finely chopped
  4 garlic cloves, 1 minced, 3 chopped
  2 tablespoons finely chopped parsley
Pinch of crushed red pepper
  ¼ cup plus 2 tablespoons
   sherry vinegar
  ¾ cup extra-virgin olive oil
Salt and freshly ground pepper
  1 large red onion, halved lengthwise
   and sliced into ¼-inch wedges
  1 pint cherry or grape
   tomatoes, halved
  4 pounds tuna steaks
   (¾ inch to 1 inch thick)

**1.** Preheat the oven to 225°. Put the potatoes in a large pot of water and bring to a boil. Cook over moderate heat until tender when pierced, about 30 minutes. Drain and let cool slightly; cut into ½-inch wedges.
**2.** In a bowl, mix the anchovies, minced garlic, parsley, crushed pepper and 2 tablespoons of vinegar. Whisk in ¼ cup of the olive oil. Season with salt and pepper.
**3.** Heat ¼ cup of the olive oil in a very large nonstick skillet. Add the chopped garlic and cook until softened. Add the potatoes, onion and tomatoes; cook over moderately high heat until warmed through, 4 minutes. Add the remaining ¼ cup of vinegar, season with salt and pepper and cook, stirring, for 1 minute. Transfer to a large heatproof platter and keep warm in the oven.
**4.** Wipe out the skillet. Add 2 tablespoons of the olive oil and heat until shimmering. Season the tuna with salt and pepper and add half of the steaks to the skillet. Cook the tuna over high heat, turning once, until lightly browned outside but still pink inside, about 5 minutes. Transfer the tuna steaks to the platter. Repeat with the remaining 2 tablespoons of olive oil and tuna steaks.

Drizzle the dressing over the tuna and serve hot, warm or at room temperature.
—Marc Murphy
**WINE** Rich Alsace Gewürztraminer.

### Peppery Tuna with Dilled Potato Salad

**TOTAL: 35 MIN**

4 SERVINGS ●

  1 pound small red potatoes
  ½ teaspoon coriander seeds
  ½ teaspoon fennel seeds
  ½ teaspoon crushed red pepper
Kosher salt and freshly ground pepper
Four 6-ounce tuna steaks
  2 tablespoons extra-virgin olive oil
  2 tablespoons balsamic vinegar
  1 tablespoon grainy mustard
  2 tablespoons chopped dill
  2 cups packed baby greens

**1.** In a medium saucepan, cover the potatoes with water and bring to a boil. Cook over moderately high heat until tender, about 20 minutes. Drain and let cool.
**2.** In a spice grinder, grind the coriander seeds and fennel seeds to a powder. Transfer to a small bowl and stir in the crushed red pepper and 1 teaspoon each of salt and pepper. Sprinkle the tuna steaks on both sides with the spice mixture and let stand for 15 minutes.
**3.** In a small bowl, combine 1 tablespoon of the olive oil with the vinegar, mustard and dill and season with salt and pepper. Slice the potatoes ½ inch thick and toss with 2 tablespoons of the dressing. Mound the potato salad on plates.
**4.** In a large skillet, heat the remaining 1 tablespoon of olive oil until shimmering. Add the tuna steaks and cook over high heat until browned on the outside and rare within, about 1 minute per side. Set the tuna steaks over the potato salad and scatter the greens on top. Drizzle with the remaining dressing and serve.
—James Boyce
**WINE** Fruity, light-bodied Beaujolais.

### Tuna Tacos with Onions

**TOTAL: 30 MIN**

4 SERVINGS ● ●

To accompany his tuna tacos, chef Aarón Sanchez of New York City's Paladar and Centrico makes a supercrunchy red-onion pickle. It's lovely with the soft tortillas.

  3 tablespoons olive oil, plus
   more for the grill
  2 medium red onions, thinly sliced
Salt
  1 teaspoon chipotle powder
   or hot paprika
  1 teaspoon dried oregano
  1 tablespoon red wine vinegar
  1 ripe mango—peeled, pitted and
   cut into ¼-inch dice
  1 medium cucumber—peeled,
   seeded and cut into ¼-inch dice
  1 serrano or jalapeño chile,
   seeded and very finely chopped
  2 tablespoons fresh lime juice
  1 tablespoon chopped cilantro
One 1-pound tuna steak (1 inch thick)
Eight 6-inch corn tortillas

**1.** Light a grill or preheat a grill pan. In a large skillet, heat 2 tablespoons of the olive oil. Add the onions, season with salt and cook over moderately high heat until softened and browned, about 8 minutes. Add the chipotle powder and cook for 30 seconds. Add the oregano and vinegar and cook for 1 minute. Transfer to a plate.
**2.** In a bowl, combine the mango, cucumber, serrano, lime juice, cilantro and salt.
**3.** Oil the grill. Rub the tuna with the remaining olive oil and season with salt. Grill over high heat until lightly charred and pink within, about 3 minutes per side. Transfer to a plate. Grill the tortillas until hot and soft, about 10 seconds. Stack the tortillas and wrap in foil to keep warm.
**4.** Thinly slice the tuna and transfer to a platter. Serve with the onions, salsa and tortillas. Let everyone make their own tacos.
—Aarón Sanchez
**WINE** Spicy American Gewürztraminer.

TUNA TACOS WITH ONIONS

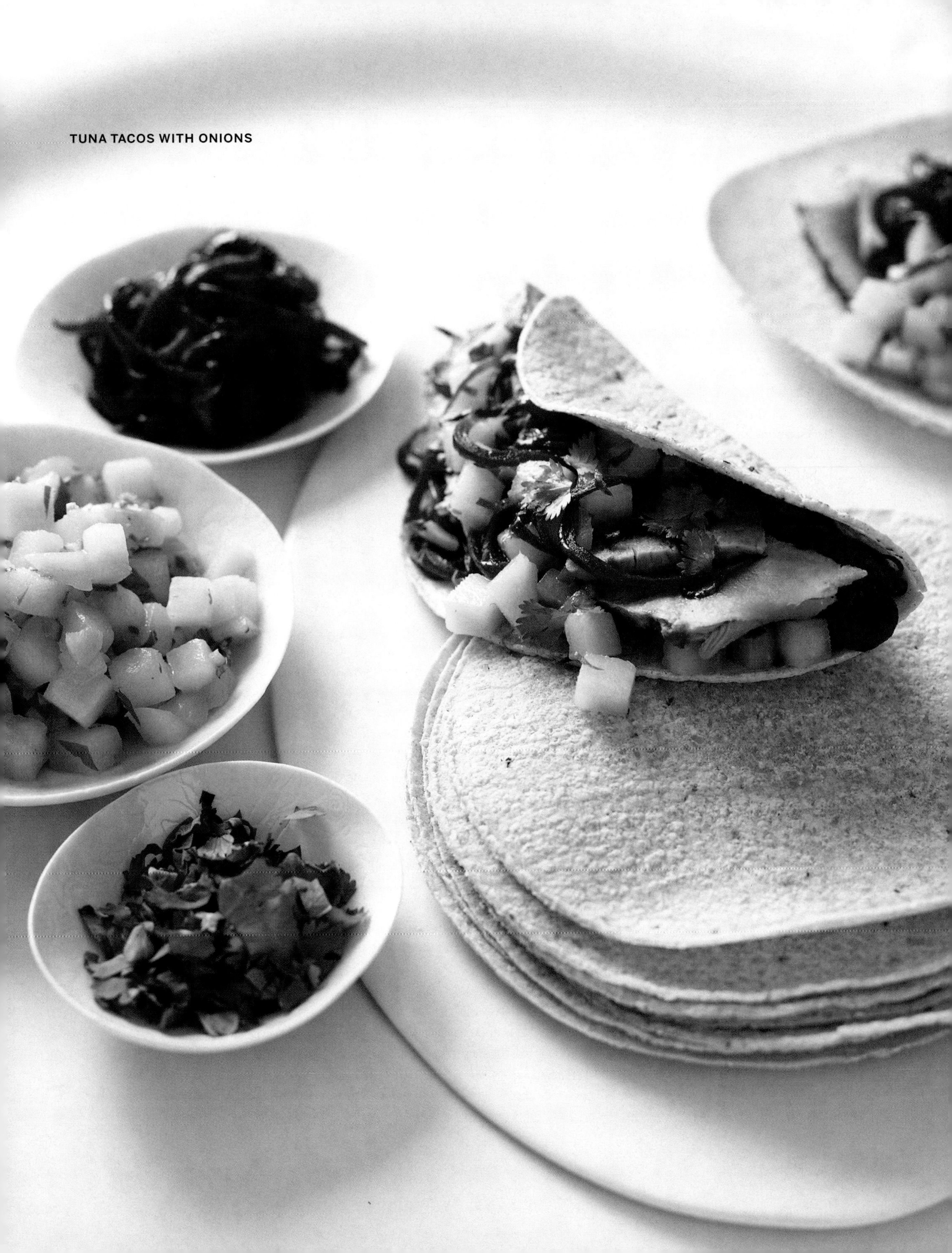

## Tuna Steaks with Currant and Fresh-Herb Salsa

**ACTIVE: 45 MIN; TOTAL: 1 HR 30 MIN**

10 SERVINGS ● ●

Ten 5-ounce tuna steaks
(about 1 inch thick)

½ cup plus 3 tablespoons
extra-virgin olive oil

Kosher salt and freshly
ground pepper

½ small baguette, crusts
trimmed, bread cut
into 1-inch cubes (1½ cups)

3 shallots, minced

3 tablespoons red
wine vinegar

½ cup dried currants

¼ cup finely chopped mint

¼ cup finely chopped
flat-leaf parsley

2 tablespoons finely
chopped tarragon

2 tablespoons small capers,
drained and chopped

1 tablespoon balsamic vinegar,
preferably aged

**1.** Light a grill and preheat the oven to 350°. Brush the tuna steaks with 2 tablespoons of the olive oil and season with salt and pepper. Grill the tuna over moderately high heat until lightly browned outside but still pink in the center, about 3 minutes per side. Transfer the tuna to a large platter and let cool.

**2.** In a food processor, pulse the bread cubes until coarsely chopped. Transfer the crumbs to a baking sheet, toss with 1 tablespoon of the olive oil and spread evenly. Toast for about 15 minutes, or until lightly golden and dry; let cool.

**3.** In a small bowl, mix the shallots with the red wine vinegar and ½ teaspoon of salt and let stand for 15 minutes. Drain the shallots and transfer them to a large bowl. Add the currants, mint, parsley, tarragon, capers, balsamic vinegar and the remaining ½ cup of olive oil. Season with salt and

pepper. Add the toasted bread crumbs and toss well. Spoon the salsa over the grilled tuna steaks and serve right away.
*—Seen Lippert*

**MAKE AHEAD** The grilled tuna and fresh-herb salsa can be prepared up to 6 hours ahead. Refrigerate the tuna steaks, then let them return to room temperature before serving.

**WINE** Ripe, juicy Pinot Noir.

## Bacon-Wrapped Tuna Steaks with Frisée and Avocado Salad

**TOTAL: 30 MIN**

4 SERVINGS ●

4 slices of smoked bacon

One 1-pound tuna steak (1 inch thick),
cut into 4 pieces

Salt and freshly ground pepper

3 tablespoons extra-virgin
olive oil

2 tablespoons balsamic vinegar

1 head frisée, torn into bite-size
pieces (about 4 cups)

2 Hass avocados, thinly sliced

**1.** Lay the bacon strips on a cutting board and place a piece of tuna in the center of each; season with salt and pepper. Fold the bacon around the tuna and secure with toothpicks.

**2.** In a large nonstick skillet, heat 1 tablespoon of the olive oil until shimmering. Add the tuna and cook over moderately high heat, turning once, until the bacon is crisp and the tuna is still pink inside, about 6 minutes.

**3.** Meanwhile, in a medium bowl, whisk the remaining 2 tablespoons of olive oil with the vinegar; season with salt and pepper. Toss in the frisée and avocados and transfer to plates.

**4.** Remove the toothpicks from the tuna and cut each piece in half. Arrange the tuna over the frisée and serve right away, drizzling any remaining dressing left in the bowl over the fish. *—Katy Sparks*

**WINE** Fruity, light-bodied Beaujolais.

## Grilled Tuna with Tomato and Cucumber Salad

**TOTAL: 25 MIN**

4 SERVINGS ● ●

¼ cup extra-virgin olive oil, plus
more for brushing

2 tablespoons red wine vinegar

Salt and freshly ground pepper

2½ pounds tomatoes, cut into
½-inch dice

2 scallions, thinly sliced

1 large cucumber—peeled,
seeded and sliced
crosswise ¼ inch thick

1 small red onion,
thinly sliced

1 cup torn basil leaves

1½ tablespoons Dijon mustard

1½ tablespoons balsamic vinegar

1 tablespoon hot water

Four 6-ounce tuna steaks

2 teaspoons dried oregano

**1.** Light a grill. In a large bowl, whisk the ¼ cup of olive oil with the red wine vinegar and season with salt and pepper. Add the tomatoes, scallions, cucumber, red onion and basil and toss to coat. Refrigerate the tomato and cucumber salad.

**2.** In a small bowl, whisk the mustard with the balsamic vinegar and blend in the hot water. Season with salt and pepper. Set the balsamic dressing aside.

**3.** Brush the tuna steaks with olive oil and season with salt, pepper and the oregano. Grill the tuna over high heat until the steaks are lightly charred on the outside and rare inside, about 2 minutes per side. Transfer the tuna steaks to a carving board.

**4.** Mound the tomato and cucumber salad on serving plates. Thickly slice the tuna steaks and transfer the tuna to the plates. Drizzle the grilled tuna with the balsamic dressing and serve.
*—Mark Strausman*

**MAKE AHEAD** The salad can be refrigerated for up to 2 hours.

**WINE** Ripe, juicy Pinot Noir.

## Soba Salad with Tuna Tartare

**TOTAL: 30 MIN**

4 SERVINGS ●●

- 10 ounces dried soba (3 bundles)
- 2 eggs
- 1 teaspoon sugar

Salt

- ½ tablespoon vegetable oil
- 1 carrot, shredded
- 1 European cucumber, seeded and shredded
- 2 large radishes, shredded
- ¼ cup mirin
- ¼ cup plus 2 teaspoons soy sauce
- ½ pound sushi-grade tuna or smoked salmon, finely diced
- 3 scallions, thinly sliced
- 1 teaspoon Sriracha (Thai hot chili sauce)
- 1 teaspoon Asian sesame oil
- 2 tablespoons sesame seeds

Wasabi paste, for serving

**1.** In a large pot of boiling water, cook the soba until al dente, 6 minutes. Drain, cool under running water and shake out the excess water; transfer to a large bowl.

**2.** Meanwhile, in a small bowl, beat the eggs with the sugar and a pinch of salt. In a medium nonstick skillet, heat the vegetable oil. Add the eggs and cook over moderate heat, tilting the pan to form a very thin omelet. Cook on one side only, just until golden on the bottom and barely set on top, about 3 minutes. Cover, remove from the heat and let stand until the top is just set, about 5 minutes. Slide the omelet onto a cutting board and slice it into very thin strips.

**3.** Add the omelet strips, carrot, cucumber, radishes, mirin and ¼ cup of the soy sauce to the soba and toss; transfer to bowls.

**4.** Chop the tuna with the scallions; transfer to a bowl. Stir in the Sriracha, sesame oil and the remaining 2 teaspoons of soy sauce. Mound the tuna on the soba, sprinkle with the sesame seeds, top each serving with a dab of wasabi and serve. —*Hiroko Shimbo*
**WINE** Fruity, soft Chenin Blanc.

## Moroccan Swordfish Kebabs

**ACTIVE: 15 MIN; TOTAL: 1 HR 15 MIN**

6 SERVINGS ●

Fish kebabs are a favorite of home cooks and street vendors throughout Casablanca and other coastal towns in Morocco—probably because they're so easy to make and because smoky, juicy pieces of swordfish (or monkfish, if you prefer) pair so effortlessly with almost any of the wonderful vegetable salads common in Morocco.

- 3 tablespoons extra-virgin olive oil
- 2 garlic cloves, minced
- 2 teaspoons ground cumin
- 2 teaspoons sweet paprika
- ¼ cup chopped flat-leaf parsley
- ½ teaspoon crushed red pepper
- 2 pounds swordfish steaks, cut into 1½-inch cubes

Salt

Lemon wedges and *harissa* (see Note), for serving

**1.** In a large, shallow dish, combine the olive oil, garlic, cumin, paprika, parsley and crushed red pepper. Add the swordfish and stir to coat. Refrigerate for 1 hour.

**2.** Light a grill. Thread the salmon onto 6-inch skewers. Season with salt. Grill the kebabs over high heat, turning once, until lightly charred and cooked through, about 8 minutes. Serve hot, with lemon wedges and *harissa*. —*Anissa Helou*
**SERVE WITH** Tangy Roasted Beet Salad (p. 51).
**NOTE** *Harissa*, a North African chile paste, is available at Middle Eastern markets and specialty food stores.
**WINE** Fresh, lively Soave.

## Swordfish Kebabs with Lemon and Bay Leaves

**TOTAL: 20 MIN**

4 SERVINGS ●●

- 24 bay leaves, preferably Turkish
- 1¼ pounds skinless swordfish steaks (1 inch thick), cut into 1-inch cubes

- 2 lemons, each cut into 8 wedges

Extra-virgin olive oil, for drizzling
Salt and freshly ground pepper

Light a grill. Soak the bay leaves in hot water for 10 minutes, then drain. Alternately thread the swordfish cubes, soaked bay leaves and lemon wedges onto skewers. Drizzle the kebabs with olive oil and season them with salt and pepper. Grill the kebabs over high heat, turning occasionally, until the swordfish is cooked through and the lemon wedges are charred in spots, about 5 minutes. Serve right away. —*Eveline Zoutendijk*
**WINE** Light, crisp white Burgundy.

## Swordfish with Orzo, Pistachios and Olives

**TOTAL: 25 MIN**

4 SERVINGS ●●

- ¾ cup orzo
- ½ cup pitted mixed olives (2 ounces), coarsely chopped
- 2 tablespoons fresh lemon juice
- 2 tablespoons unsalted butter
- 3 tablespoons extra-virgin olive oil

Salt and freshly ground pepper
Four 5-ounce skinless swordfish steaks (1 inch thick)

- ½ cup roasted, shelled pistachios, coarsely chopped

**1.** In a saucepan of boiling water, cook the orzo until al dente. Drain and return it to the saucepan. Stir in the olives, lemon juice, butter and 2 tablespoons of the olive oil; season with salt and pepper.

**2.** Meanwhile, light a grill or heat a grill pan until very hot. Brush the swordfish with the remaining 1 tablespoon of olive oil and season with salt and pepper. Grill over moderately high heat, turning once, until browned and just cooked through, about 7 minutes. Stir the pistachios into the orzo and serve with the swordfish. —*Katy Sparks*
**WINE** Fruity, low-oak Chardonnay.

**COD WITH BASQUE WINE SAUCE**　　　　　**SUMAC-CRUSTED BLACK COD SALAD**

### Cod with Basque Wine Sauce

**TOTAL: 30 MIN**

**4 SERVINGS** ● ●

This fast and festive seafood recipe from Janet Mendel, author of *Food of La Mancha,* calls for cod with a generous topping of shrimp, cockles and bright green peas.

- 3 tablespoons extra-virgin olive oil
- Four 5-ounce skinless cod fillets, halved crosswise
- Salt and freshly ground pepper
- 2 tablespoons all-purpose flour
- 3 large garlic cloves, thinly sliced
- ¾ cup frozen peas
- ⅓ cup finely chopped flat-leaf parsley
- ½ cup dry white wine
- 1 pound cockles, rinsed
- 6 ounces shelled and deveined medium shrimp

In a large nonstick skillet, heat the olive oil until shimmering. Season the cod fillets with salt and pepper and dust them all over with 1 tablespoon of the flour. Add the cod and garlic to the skillet and cook over moderately high heat until barely golden, about 2 minutes. Sprinkle the remaining 1 tablespoon of flour over the cod. Turn the fillets and add the peas, half of the parsley, the wine and the cockles. Cook, shaking the pan occasionally, until the cod is almost cooked, about 4 minutes. Add the shrimp to the skillet, tucking them into the liquid. Cover the skillet and cook for 2 to 3 minutes, until the shrimp are pink and curled and the cockles have opened. Discard any cockles that do not open. Sprinkle the fish with the remaining parsley and serve at once in shallow bowls.

—*Janet Mendel*

**WINE** Zesty, fresh Albariño.

### Sumac-Crusted Black Cod Salad

**ACTIVE: 30 MIN; TOTAL: 2 HR 45 MIN**

**4 SERVINGS** ● ●

F&W Best New Chef 2005 Maria Hines of Earth & Ocean in Seattle coats buttery-rich cod with ground sumac, a tart berry that grows wild in the Middle East and Italy.

- 8 red or yellow tomatoes—4 cored, halved crosswise and seeded
- 6½ tablespoons extra-virgin olive oil
- ¼ cup plus 1 tablespoon chopped flat-leaf parsley, plus ¼ cup parsley leaves for garnish
- 1 tablespoon red wine vinegar
- Salt and freshly ground pepper
- 4 ounces baby spinach
- ¼ cup dried ground sumac (1 ounce; see Note)
- Four 6-ounce skinless black cod fillets

1. Preheat the oven to 275°. Put the halved tomatoes on a rimmed baking sheet and toss them with 2 tablespoons of the olive oil, 1 tablespoon of the chopped parsley and 2 teaspoons of the vinegar; season the tomatoes with salt and pepper. Turn the tomatoes cut side up and bake for 1 hour. Turn the tomatoes over and bake them for 1 hour longer.

2. Increase the oven temperature to 300°. Peel the warm tomatoes and reserve the skins. Cut the tomato halves in half again and transfer them to a plate along with any accumulated juices. Put the tomato skins on a pie plate and bake them for about 15 minutes, turning once, until the skins are crisp.

3. In a small bowl, combine 2 tablespoons of the olive oil with the remaining ¼ cup of chopped parsley and 1 teaspoon of vinegar. Season the parsley vinaigrette with salt and pepper.

4. In a small saucepan of boiling water, cook the spinach for 30 seconds. Drain the spinach and lightly squeeze out the excess water.

5. Put the sumac in a shallow bowl. Season the cod fillets with salt and pepper and dredge them in the sumac to coat completely. In a large nonstick skillet, heat 2 tablespoons of the olive oil until shimmering. Add the cod fillets and cook over moderately high heat until they are browned and crisp and barely cooked through, about 4 minutes per side. If the fish is browning too quickly, reduce the heat to moderate toward the end of cooking.

6. Meanwhile, in a medium saucepan, heat the remaining ½ tablespoon of olive oil. Add the baby spinach and the tomato quarters and any accumulated juices and cook the spinach and tomatoes over moderately high heat, stirring, until hot. Season with salt and pepper; keep warm.

7. Slice the remaining 4 whole tomatoes into wedges and arrange the tomatoes on 4 plates. Drizzle the tomatoes with the parsley vinaigrette. Arrange the spinach and quartered tomatoes on the plates and top with the black cod fillets. Break the tomato skins into large pieces and scatter over the fish. Garnish the cod salad with the parsley leaves and serve at once.
—Maria Hines

**NOTE** Sumac is available at Middle Eastern markets and some supermarkets.

**WINE** Full-bodied, rich Pinot Gris.

## Green Bell Peppers Stuffed with Salt Cod
**ACTIVE: 40 MIN; TOTAL: 1 HR 10 MIN**
**4 SERVINGS** ●

- ¼ cup plus 2 tablespoons kosher salt
- 1 tablespoon sugar
- 1 pound center-cut cod fillet (¾ inch to 1 inch thick), skinned and cut into 3 pieces
- 4 green bell peppers, stemmed and seeded
- ¾ cup extra-virgin olive oil
- 4 garlic cloves, thinly sliced
- 1 small dried red chile, stemmed

Table salt

- 1½ teaspoons sherry vinegar

Freshly ground pepper

- 1 tablespoon chopped flat-leaf parsley

1. Preheat the oven to 425°. In a small bowl, mix the kosher salt with the sugar. Spread half of the salt mixture in the bottom of a shallow bowl that is just big enough to hold the 3 pieces of cod fillet. Lay the cod on the salt and sprinkle the remaining salt on top. Cover the cod fillet pieces with a plate and weight the pieces down with a large, heavy can. Let the cod stand at room temperature for 30 minutes or refrigerate the cod for up to 4 hours. When you are ready to cook the fish, rinse the pieces and pat dry.

2. Meanwhile, stand the green bell peppers, rounded side up, on a rimmed baking sheet. Bake the bell peppers for about 25 minutes, or until the skins are blistered. When the bell peppers are cool enough to handle, peel them and gently tear each one in half lengthwise.

3. In a medium saucepan, simmer the olive oil with the garlic and chile over moderate heat until the garlic is golden, about 3 minutes. Add the cod fillet pieces and simmer over low heat until just cooked, 3 to 4 minutes per side. Transfer the cod to a bowl. Strain the oil through a coarse sieve into a glass measuring cup; reserve the garlic and chile.

4. Break up the cod into small flakes and season lightly with table salt if needed. Cut four 8-inch squares of plastic wrap. Lightly oil a baking sheet and lay 2 bell pepper halves on it, shiny side down, overlapping slightly. Shape one-fourth of the cod into a tight ball and set it in the center of the pepper. Wrap the cod in the pepper, twisting the plastic wrap around the pepper to give it a neat round shape. Transfer the stuffed bell pepper to a plate, twisted side down. Repeat with the remaining peppers and flaked cod.

5. In a blender, puree the sherry vinegar with the reserved garlic and chile. With the machine on, slowly pour in the reserved garlic oil until emulsified. Season the sauce with salt and pepper.

6. Put the cod packages in a microwave oven and cook at high power for 1 minute, or until the cod stuffing is just hot in the center. Carefully unwrap each package and transfer the stuffed bell peppers to serving plates. Spoon the sauce over the bell peppers, sprinkle with parsley and serve.
—Alex Raij

**MAKE AHEAD** The recipe can be prepared through Step 5 and refrigerated overnight. Let the sauce return to room temperature before serving.

**WINE** Zesty, fresh Albariño.

## Seared Cod with Chile Sauce

**TOTAL: 25 MIN**

4 SERVINGS ● ●

- 4 dried *guajillo* or ancho chiles, stemmed and seeded
- 2 small plum tomatoes, halved
- ½ medium onion
- 1 garlic clove
- 1 cup chicken stock or low-sodium broth
- 2½ tablespoons vegetable oil
- 1 tablespoon all-purpose flour
- Salt and freshly ground pepper
- Four 6- to 7-ounce skinless cod fillets

1. In a medium cast-iron skillet, toast the *guajillo* chiles over moderately high heat until the chiles are fragrant, about 1 minute. Fill a small bowl with very hot water and submerge the toasted chiles in it to soak until they are softened, about 5 minutes. Drain the soaked chiles and discard the soaking liquid.

2. Meanwhile, in the same skillet, cook the plum tomatoes and the onion, cut side down, over high heat until the tomatoes and the onion begin to blacken, about 3 minutes. Transfer the tomatoes and onion to a blender and add the softened *guajillos,* the garlic and the chicken stock; puree the chile sauce until smooth.

3. In a medium saucepan, heat 1½ tablespoons of the vegetable oil. Add the flour to the pan and whisk over moderate heat until the mixture is smooth. Slowly whisk in the chile sauce and season with salt and pepper. Simmer the sauce, stirring occasionally, until it has thickened slightly, about 8 minutes.

4. Season the cod with salt and pepper. In a large nonstick skillet, heat the remaining 1 tablespoon of vegetable oil. Add the fish fillets and cook them over moderately high heat until white throughout, about 4 minutes per side. Transfer the cod fillets to plates, spoon the *guajillo* chile sauce on top and serve. —*Daisy Martinez*

**WINE** Ripe, juicy Pinot Noir.

## Halibut with Fresh Fennel and New Potatoes

**TOTAL: 30 MIN**

4 SERVINGS ● ●

Use unblemished small fennel bulbs; they're usually more tender than big ones.

- 2 pounds small new potatoes, halved
- 2 tablespoons unsalted butter
- 1 tablespoon extra virgin olive oil
- 1 fennel bulb, sliced lengthwise ½ inch thick
- ½ cup fresh orange juice
- 1 teaspoon finely grated orange zest
- Four 6-ounce skinless halibut fillets
- Salt and freshly ground pepper
- 1 tablespoon finely chopped tarragon

1. In a large pot of warm salted water, bring the potatoes to a boil. Cook over moderate heat until tender, about 15 minutes; drain.

2. In a large, deep skillet, melt the butter in the oil. Add the fennel and cook over moderately high heat, stirring, until browned, about 8 minutes. Add the orange juice and zest. Set the fish on the fennel; season with salt and pepper. Cover and simmer until just cooked through, about 8 minutes.

3. Transfer the halibut to plates. Toss the potatoes with the fennel, sprinkle with the tarragon and serve with the fish. —*Katy Sparks*

**WINE** Light, fresh Pinot Grigio.

## Halibut with Walnut-Olive Relish

**TOTAL: 30 MIN**

4 SERVINGS ● ●

- 1¼ pounds small fingerling potatoes, scrubbed
- 3 tablespoons extra-virgin olive oil
- Salt and freshly ground pepper
- Four 6-ounce skinless halibut fillets
- 12 walnut halves
- ¼ cup pitted green olives, chopped
- 2 tablespoons brined capers, rinsed and chopped
- ½ teaspoon finely grated lemon zest
- 1 tablespoon fresh lemon juice

1. Preheat the oven to 300°. In a saucepan, cover the potatoes with hot tap water and bring to a boil. Cook over moderately high heat until tender, 15 minutes. Drain, then return to the pot and toss with 1 tablespoon of oil. Season with salt and pepper.

2. Meanwhile, set the fish in a lightly oiled baking dish and season with salt and pepper. Bake for about 15 minutes, until the flesh just begins to flake. Put the walnuts on a pie plate and toast for 8 minutes, until fragrant. Coarsely chop the nuts.

3. In a bowl, mix the walnuts, olives, capers, lemon zest, lemon juice and the remaining 2 tablespoons of olive oil; season with salt and pepper. Transfer the fish and potatoes to plates, spoon the walnut-olive relish on top and serve. —*Marc Meyer*

**WINE** Minerally Marsanne or Roussanne.

## Roasted Halibut with Vegetables en Papillote

**TOTAL: 40 MIN**

8 SERVINGS ●

Cooking halibut and vegetables *en papillote* (in paper) preserves the flavor of the delicate fish, crisp asparagus, sugar snaps and carrots, with only a little fat.

- 2 medium carrots, cut into straws
- ¾ pound thin asparagus, cut into 3-inch lengths
- ½ pound sugar snap peas
- 2 tablespoons extra-virgin olive oil, plus more for brushing
- 1 medium onion, thinly sliced
- ½ pound white mushrooms, sliced
- Salt and freshly ground pepper
- 2½ pounds skinless halibut fillet (about 1½ inches thick), cut into 8 pieces
- ½ cup chicken stock
- ¼ cup dry sherry

1. Preheat the oven to 375°. In a saucepan of boiling water, cook the carrots for 1 minute. Add the asparagus and sugar snaps and cook until crisp-tender, 2 minutes. Drain and spread on a plate to cool.

**ROASTED HALIBUT WITH VEGETABLES EN PAPILLOTE**

**RIO GRANDE TROUT WITH RIESLING**

**2.** In a nonstick skillet, heat the 2 tablespoons of olive oil until shimmering. Add the onion and mushrooms, season with salt and pepper and cook over moderately high heat, stirring, until softened, 7 minutes. Transfer to the plate; let cool slightly.

**3.** Heat 2 large, sturdy baking sheets in the oven. Lay out 8 long (14-inch) parchment paper sheets; brush with oil. Mound one-eighth of the vegetables on half a sheet. Set a fillet on top; season with salt and pepper. Fold in half, then fold in the sides, leaving the top open. In a bowl, mix the stock and sherry; spoon 1½ tablespoons into the packet. Fold in the top, sealing tightly. Repeat.

**4.** Transfer the packets to the heated baking sheets. Bake for 9 minutes, until the fish is cooked through. Open the packets at once and transfer the fish, vegetables and broth to plates. Serve. —*André Soltner*
**WINE** Full-bodied, rich Pinot Gris.

## Rio Grande Trout with Riesling
**TOTAL: 30 MIN**
**4 SERVINGS** ●●
Chef Kevin Graham of El Monte Sagrado in Taos, New Mexico, rolls up trout fillets and poaches them in a delicate white wine broth flavored with juniper berries.

- 1 **cup dry Riesling**
- 1 **large carrot, finely julienned**
- 1 **large celery rib, finely julienned**
- ½ **small sweet onion, thinly sliced**
- 4 **whole black peppercorns**
- 3 **juniper berries, crushed**
- 1 **garlic clove, crushed**
- 1 **bay leaf**
- 1 **thyme sprig**
- 1 **oregano sprig**
- 1 **tablespoon canola oil**

**Four 7-ounce skinless trout fillets**
**Salt and freshly ground pepper**
- 1 **tablespoon unsalted butter**

**1.** Preheat the oven to 375°. In a saucepan, combine the wine, carrot, celery, onion, peppercorns, juniper berries, garlic, bay leaf, thyme and oregano; bring to a boil.

**2.** Meanwhile, coat the bottom of a large ovenproof skillet with the oil. Season the fish with salt and pepper. Skinned side up and starting from the tail end, roll up each fillet and secure with 2 toothpicks. Transfer the trout rolls to the skillet.

**3.** Pour the Riesling mixture over the trout rolls and bake for 15 minutes, or until the fish flakes. Let rest for 5 minutes, then carefully remove the toothpicks. Transfer the rolls to shallow bowls and spoon the vegetables on top. Remove the bay leaf, herb sprigs and peppercorns from the broth. Whisk the butter into the broth, season with salt and pepper and spoon over the trout; serve. —*Kevin Graham*
**WINE** Vivid, lightly sweet Riesling.

## Spanish Mackerel with Three Sauces

**TOTAL: 1 HR**

**4 SERVINGS**

F&W Best New Chef 2005 Christophe Emé, of Ortolan Restaurant in Los Angeles, pan-fries mackerel until the skin is beautifully crisp, then serves it alongside a trio of deeply flavored sauces.

**CONFIT**

**Zest of 1 lemon, cut into ⅛-inch dice, plus 3 tablespoons fresh lemon juice**

**3 tablespoons sugar**

**2 tablespoons water**

**½ mango—peeled, pitted and cut into ⅛-inch dice**

**½ teaspoon chopped lemon thyme**

**PESTO**

**1½ cups basil leaves**

**3 tablespoons extra-virgin olive oil**

**1 tablespoon freshly grated Parmesan cheese**

**1 small garlic clove, chopped**

**½ tablespoon pine nuts**

**Salt**

**OLIVE CREAM**

**½ cup heavy cream**

**3 tablespoons black olive tapenade**

**Salt**

**FISH**

**2 tablespoons extra-virgin olive oil**

**Four 6-ounce Spanish mackerel fillets with skin**

**Cayenne pepper**

**Salt and freshly ground black pepper**

**1. MAKE THE CONFIT:** In a small saucepan of boiling water, cook the lemon zest for 1 minute; drain. Repeat 2 more times. In the saucepan, combine the blanched lemon zest with the lemon juice, sugar and water and simmer over moderate heat until syrupy, about 8 minutes. Add the mango and simmer for 1 minute. Stir in the lemon thyme.

**2. MAKE THE PESTO:** In a mini food processor, pulse the basil leaves with the olive oil, Parmesan, garlic and pine nuts until a sauce forms. Season the pesto with salt.

**3. MAKE THE OLIVE CREAM:** In a saucepan, simmer the cream over moderately low heat until reduced by one-fourth, about 4 minutes. Add the tapenade and simmer for 1 minute. Season lightly with salt.

**4. COOK THE FISH:** In a large skillet, heat the olive oil until shimmering. Season the mackerel with cayenne, salt and black pepper. Add the fillets to the skillet, skin side down, and cook over high heat until browned and crisp, about 4 minutes. Turn and cook just until done, about 2 minutes longer.

**5.** Spoon the olive cream onto 4 plates and top with the mackerel. Dollop the lemon-mango confit on each plate and spoon the pesto alongside. Serve at once. —*Christophe Emé*

**MAKE AHEAD** The lemon-mango confit can be covered and refrigerated for up to 2 days. The pesto and olive cream can be refrigerated overnight.

**WINE** Complex, aromatic Chenin Blanc.

## Mackerel Escabèche with Asparagus and Artichoke Hearts

**TOTAL: 30 MIN**

**8 SERVINGS** ● ●

A traditional escabèche is made by soaking fried fish overnight in a pungent blend of vinegar and garlic. In his riff on this recipe, Catalan chef Ferran Adrià of El Bulli, near Barcelona, skips the marinating, which not only speeds things up but keeps the tastes fresh. The fish is delicious with these piquant, potent flavors.

**½ cup extra-virgin olive oil**

**Four 8-ounce Spanish mackerel fillets with skin, each halved crosswise**

**Salt and freshly ground pepper**

**8 thick asparagus spears**

**One 6.5-ounce jar marinated artichoke hearts, drained**

**4 large garlic cloves, unpeeled**

**2 bay leaves**

**¼ teaspoon Pimentón de la Vera (smoked Spanish paprika)**

**½ cup sherry vinegar**

**1.** In a large nonstick skillet, heat 2 tablespoons of the olive oil until shimmering. Season the fish fillets with salt and pepper, add them to the skillet and cook over moderately high heat, turning once, until browned, about 10 minutes. Transfer the fillets to a deep platter or shallow baking dish and discard the oil in the skillet.

**2.** Add the remaining ¼ cup plus 2 tablespoons of olive oil to the skillet and heat until shimmering. Add the asparagus, artichoke hearts, garlic, bay leaves and *pimentón* and cook over moderate heat until the vegetables are lightly browned and the asparagus is just tender, about 6 minutes. Remove from the heat, add the vinegar and pour over the fish. Let cool slightly, then serve. —*Ferran Adrià*

**WINE** Lively, tart Sauvignon Blanc.

## Grilled Trout with Ginger and Vinegar

**TOTAL: 15 MIN**

**4 SERVINGS** ● ●

**4 butterflied trout**

**Olive oil, for brushing**

**Salt and freshly ground pepper**

**¼ cup balsamic vinegar**

**1 tablespoon finely grated ginger**

**1 tablespoon minced parsley**

**1.** Light a grill. Brush the trout with olive oil and season with salt and pepper. Grill the butterflied trout over high heat, skin side down, for 3 minutes. Turn and grill until the fish is just cooked through, about 3 minutes longer. Transfer the trout to plates, skin side down.

**2.** In a small skillet, warm the balsamic vinegar with the ginger and parsley. Spoon the vinegar over the fish and serve. —*Eveline Zoutendijk*

**WINE** Fruity, low-oak Chardonnay.

SPANISH MACKEREL
WITH THREE SAUCES

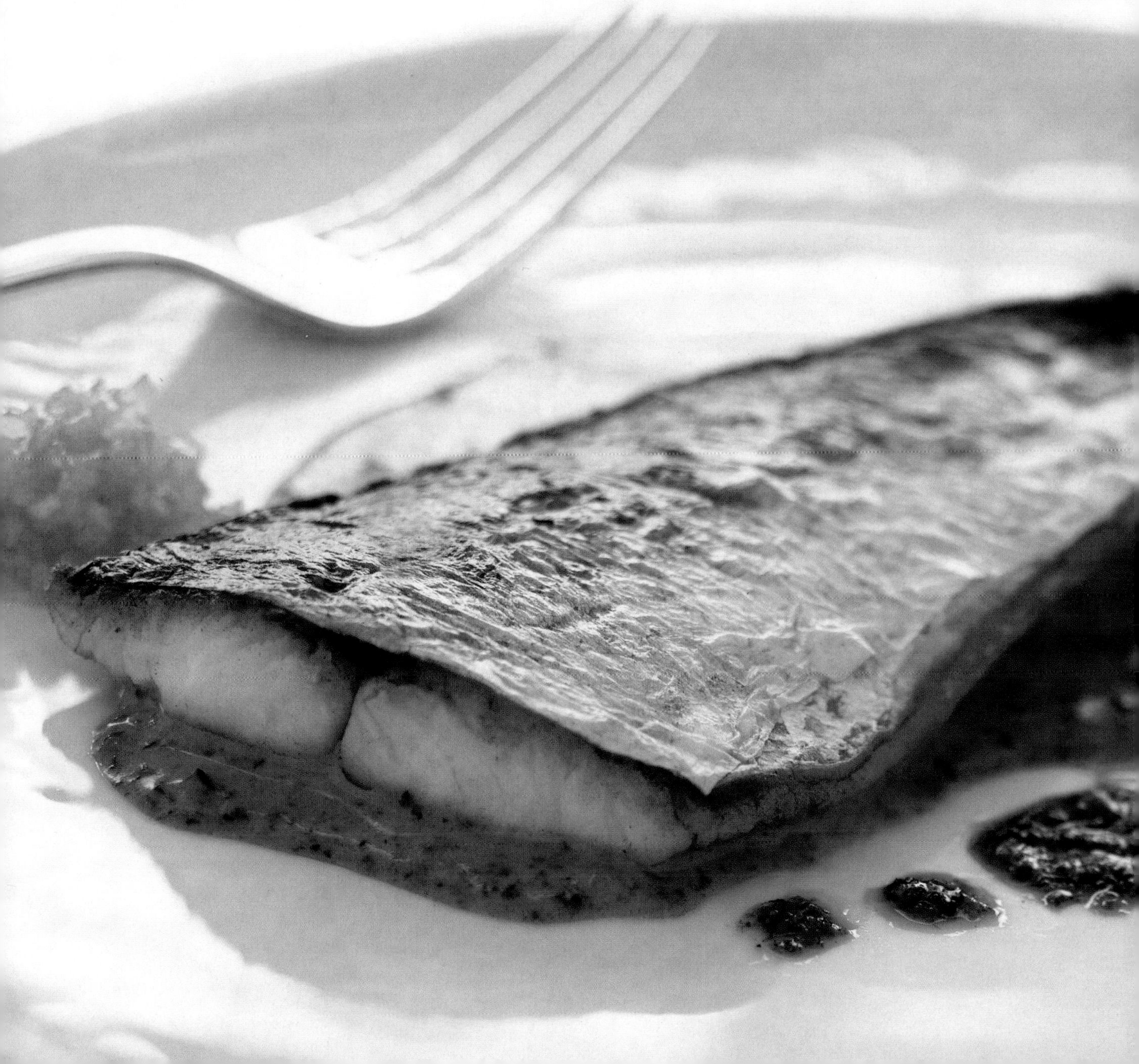

## Stuffed Trout with Purple-Potato Gratin

**TOTAL: 1 HR**

6 SERVINGS

- ½ pound smoked ham, sliced ¼ inch thick and cut into ¼-inch dice
- 1 tablespoon coarsely chopped mint
- 1 tablespoon coarsely chopped parsley
- Six 8- to 10-ounce boneless, butterflied trout, heads removed
- 3 tablespoons extra-virgin olive oil, plus more for rubbing and drizzling
- Salt and freshly ground pepper
- 3 medium purple potatoes (1 pound), scrubbed
- ½ pound fresh fava beans, shelled (½ cup)
- 3 garlic cloves, minced
- 1 small red onion, cut into ½-inch dice
- 1 small red bell pepper, thinly sliced
- 1 cup hominy, drained (from a 15-ounce can)
- 3 ounces skinless, boneless, smoked trout, flaked
- ½ pound fresh mozzarella, sliced crosswise into 6 rounds
- 3 tablespoons freshly grated Parmesan cheese
- ¼ cup plus 2 tablespoons vegetable oil

**1.** Preheat the oven to 450°. In a small bowl, toss the ham with the mint and parsley. Open the trout on a work surface, skin side down. Rub the flesh with olive oil and season with salt and pepper. Spread the ham mixture on one side of each trout. Close the trout and press to flatten evenly. Secure the trout with 8-inch bamboo skewers. Lightly rub the trout with olive oil and refrigerate them.

**2.** In a saucepan, cover the potatoes with water and bring to a boil; boil until tender, about 20 minutes. Drain and let cool, then peel and cut into ½-inch dice.

**3.** Meanwhile, put the fava beans in a strainer. Lower them into the saucepan of boiling potato water and cook until just tender, about 2 minutes. Transfer the favas to a plate and peel them.

**4.** In a medium skillet, heat the 3 tablespoons of olive oil. Add the garlic, onion and red pepper and cook over moderate heat until softened, about 7 minutes. Add the hominy, smoked trout, favas and potatoes and cook, stirring, until heated through, about 2 minutes. Season with salt and pepper. Transfer the mixture to a 10-inch gratin dish and arrange the mozzarella on top. Sprinkle with the Parmesan. Lightly drizzle with oil and bake in the upper third of the oven for about 10 minutes, or until the gratin is sizzling and the mozzarella has melted. Leave the oven on.

**5.** Meanwhile, heat 3 tablespoons of the vegetable oil in a large skillet. Season the butterflied trout with salt and pepper. Add 3 of the trout to the skillet and cook over high heat until they are browned and crisp, about 4 minutes per side. Transfer the trout to a baking sheet. Discard the oil. Repeat with the remaining 3 tablespoons of vegetable oil and 3 trout. Bake the trout in the oven for about 4 minutes, or until they are cooked through.

**6.** Preheat the broiler. Broil the gratin for about 1 minute, or until richly browned on top. Remove the skewers and transfer the trout to plates. Serve the gratin alongside. —*Emmanuel Piqueras*

**MAKE AHEAD** The stuffed trout and the assembled gratin can be refrigerated overnight. Bring to room temperature and add both cheeses and the drizzle of olive oil just before baking.

**WINE** Ripe, luxurious Chardonnay.

## Warm Seafood and Spinach Salad

**TOTAL: 40 MIN**

4 FIRST-COURSE SERVINGS

- ¼ cup dry white wine
- ¼ cup water
- 12 littleneck clams, scrubbed
- 1 tablespoon extra-virgin olive oil, plus more for drizzling
- 5 ounces spinach, thick stems discarded
- 1 slice of center-cut bacon, chopped
- 1 tablespoon minced shallot
- 1 medium garlic clove, finely chopped
- 1 tablespoon minced roasted red pepper (from a jar)
- 1 tablespoon toasted nori powder (see Note)
- Pinch of cayenne pepper
- 1 pound cleaned squid bodies, sliced lengthwise ½ inch thick
- Salt and freshly ground black pepper
- ½ teaspoon finely grated lemon zest

## ingredient
### SMELTS

Smelts are a small local Maine fish that come from the same family as salmon. They are often served bones, head and all, and have a wonderfully delicate, clean flavor that is often compared to violets or cucumbers. Mid- to late winter is the best season for smelts. That's when fishermen set up smelt shacks on frozen lakes and streams and dangle their lines through holes in the ice.

1. In a medium saucepan, bring the white wine and water to a boil. Add the clams, cover and cook over high heat until they open, about 4 minutes. Discard any clams that do not open. Transfer the clams to a small bowl and discard the shells. Pour the cooking liquid over the clams, stopping before you reach the grit at the bottom of the saucepan.

2. Heat the 1 tablespoon of olive oil in a large skillet. Add the spinach and stir-fry over moderately high heat until wilted. Transfer the spinach to a bowl and let cool slightly, then coarsely chop it.

3. Set the skillet over low heat. Add the bacon and cook until slightly crisp, about 4 minutes. Increase the heat to moderate, add the shallot and garlic and cook until fragrant, about 1 minute. Stir in the roasted red pepper, nori powder and cayenne. Add the clams and their cooking liquid and the chopped spinach and stir until heated through, about 1 minute. Remove from the heat.

4. In a large saucepan fitted with a steamer basket, bring ½ inch of water to a boil. Scatter the squid in the basket and season with salt and black pepper. Cover the steamer and steam the squid over high heat until they are white, about 2 minutes. Add the squid to the cooked spinach and clams along with the lemon zest and toss well. Season the salad with salt. Transfer to plates, drizzle with olive oil and serve. —*Josh DeChellis*

**NOTE** To make the toasted nori powder, use tongs to hold half a nori sheet 4 inches from the heat, either over a gas flame or under the broiler, turning constantly, until the nori begins to curl, about 10 seconds. Let the nori cool slightly, then tear it into small pieces and grind them in a spice grinder. Half a sheet makes 1 tablespoon of nori powder.

**MAKE AHEAD** The clams and the spinach can be refrigerated separately overnight. **WINE** Fresh, lively Soave.

## Oven-Roasted Smelts with Cornichon Mayonnaise
**TOTAL: 35 MIN**
**4 FIRST-COURSE SERVINGS** ●

- ¾ cup mayonnaise
- 6 sour cornichons, diced, plus 2 tablespoons brine from the jar
- 2 teaspoons fresh lemon juice
- Pinch of cayenne pepper
- Kosher salt and freshly ground black pepper
- 5 tablespoons vegetable oil
- 1 tablespoon finely chopped celery
- 1 tablespoon finely chopped Granny Smith apple
- 2 teaspoons finely chopped shallot
- 4 ounces sourdough bread, crust removed, bread torn into ½-inch pieces (about 2 cups)
- 1 tablespoon chopped chives
- ½ teaspoon chopped rosemary
- 1¼ pounds medium smelts, gutted

1. Preheat the oven to 400°. In a small bowl, combine the mayonnaise with the cornichons, lemon juice and cayenne. Season with salt and black pepper and stir until blended, then refrigerate.

2. In a medium skillet, heat 3 tablespoons of the oil. Add the celery, apple and shallot and cook over moderate heat until softened. Add the bread and cook, stirring, until golden, 5 minutes. Stir in the chives and rosemary; season with salt and black pepper. Remove from the heat.

3. Brush a 9-by-13-inch glass baking dish with 1 tablespoon of the oil. Arrange the smelts in the dish in a single layer and season lightly with salt and black pepper. Top with the croutons and drizzle with the remaining 1 tablespoon of oil. Roast the smelts for 12 minutes, or until they are firm and the croutons are crisp. Transfer to a platter, drizzle with the brine and serve with the mayonnaise. —*Sam Hayward*

**WINE** Fresh, lively Soave.

## Grilled Fish with Citrus Pearl Sauce
**TOTAL: 30 MIN**
**4 SERVINGS** ● ● ●

When you peel citrus fruit and remove the membranes, then break up the sections, you end up with juicy, translucent "pearls." This sweet and tart sauce gets a flavor boost by using both the pearls and the juice.

- 2 navel oranges
- 1 large grapefruit
- 1 lime
- Four 6-ounce pompano, Spanish mackerel or halibut fillets, skin removed
- 1 tablespoon extra-virgin olive oil, plus more for brushing
- Salt and freshly ground pepper
- 1 tablespoon cold unsalted butter

1. Using a sharp knife, peel 1 of the navel oranges, removing all of the bitter white pith, then cut in between the membranes to release the sections into a bowl. Using a fork, gently break up the sections into pearls; you will need 2 tablespoons. Repeat with 2 sections of the grapefruit to yield 2 tablespoons of grapefruit pearls, and with the lime to yield 1 tablespoon of pearls. Juice the remaining orange and grapefruit to yield ½ cup each of juice.

2. In a small skillet, simmer the orange and grapefruit juices over moderately high heat until they are reduced by half, about 10 minutes.

3. Light a grill. Brush the fish with olive oil and season with salt and pepper. Grill over high heat until just cooked through, 3 minutes per side for pompano or mackerel, 5 minutes for halibut. Transfer to plates.

4. Bring the reduced juice to a boil and add the citrus pearls. Remove from the heat and whisk in the 1 tablespoon of olive oil, then the butter. Season with salt. Spoon over the fish and serve. —*Marcia Kiesel*

**WINE** Dry, light Champagne.

## Sea Bass with Caper Berries, Green Olives and Meyer Lemon

**TOTAL: 20 MIN**

**4 SERVINGS** ● ●

Fragrant Meyer lemons are sweeter and more fragrant than the regular variety. They are excellent in this bold, Mediterranean-accented recipe.

- 2 large Meyer or regular lemons

Four 6-ounce sea bass fillets
    with skin

Salt and freshly ground pepper

- ¼ cup extra-virgin olive oil
- 12 green olives, pitted and coarsely chopped (¼ cup)
- 8 caper berries, sliced (2 tablespoons)
- 1 large garlic clove, finely chopped
- 2 tablespoons chicken stock or low-sodium broth
- 2 tablespoons finely chopped flat-leaf parsley

**1.** Using a sharp knife, peel the lemons, removing all of the bitter white pith. Working over a bowl, cut in between the membranes, releasing the sections. Cut each section in half.

**2.** Season the sea bass fillets with salt and pepper. In a large nonstick skillet, heat 2 tablespoons of the olive oil. Add the sea bass, skin side down, and cook over high heat until the fillets are golden on the bottom, about 5 minutes. Flip the fish and cook until golden on the second side and cooked through, about 4 minutes longer. Transfer the sea bass fillets to plates, cover and keep warm.

**3.** Discard the olive oil from the skillet. Add the remaining 2 tablespoons of olive oil to the skillet along with the olives, caper berries and garlic. Cook over moderate heat until fragrant, about 1 minute. Add the lemon sections, stock and parsley and cook just until heated through, about 10 seconds. Spoon half of the sauce over the fish and pass the rest at the table.
—*Grace Parisi*

**WINE** Fresh, minerally Vermentino.

## Sautéed Calamari with Chorizo

**TOTAL: 25 MIN**

**4 SERVINGS** ● ●

Sautéing delicate squid with spicy, fat-flecked chorizo is a clever way to baste it, keeping it moist and flavorful.

- 1 dry-cured chorizo sausage, cut into thin half-moons
- 1 pound cleaned squid, bodies cut into ¼-inch-thick rings, tentacles halved

Salt

- 2 tablespoons extra-virgin olive oil, plus more for drizzling
- ½ cup water
- 2 garlic cloves, thinly sliced
- 1 small tomato—peeled, seeded and coarsely chopped

One 15-ounce can chickpeas, drained

- 1 tablespoon red wine vinegar
- 2 tablespoons minced parsley

Pinch of crushed red pepper

- 1 large bunch arugula, thick stems discarded

**1.** In a bowl, toss the chorizo and squid and season with salt. In a large skillet, heat ½ tablespoon of the olive oil. Add half of the squid mixture. Cook over high heat, stirring, until the squid is firm, 1 minute. Transfer to a plate. Add ¼ cup of the water to the skillet and scrape up any browned bits in the pan. Pour the juices into a bowl. Repeat with the remaining squid and chorizo, using another ½ tablespoon of olive oil and the remaining ¼ cup of water.

**2.** Heat the remaining 1 tablespoon of olive oil in the skillet. Add the garlic and cook over moderately high heat until soft. Add the tomato, chickpeas, vinegar and reserved pan juices and cook over moderate heat for 2 minutes. Return the squid mixture to the skillet; toss with the parsley and crushed red pepper and season with salt. Mound the arugula on plates, drizzle with olive oil and top with the squid and chorizo mixture. —*Rick Stein*

**WINE** Fresh, fruity rosé.

## Crispy Salt-and-Pepper Squid

**TOTAL: 30 MIN**

**6 FIRST-COURSE SERVINGS** ● ●

Ice-cold seltzer is used to lighten the tempura batter for this squid recipe. The result is an outrageously crispy, golden crust that doesn't get soggy. The squid spends no more than a couple of minutes in the hot oil, making this a perfect quick dish.

- ⅓ cup all-purpose flour
- ⅓ cup cornstarch
- 1 teaspoon each of sea salt and crushed black peppercorns
- 1 teaspoon crushed Sichuan peppercorns (optional)

Pinch of Chinese five-spice powder

- 6 ounces ice-cold seltzer
- 1 quart vegetable oil
- 1 pound cleaned squid, bodies cut into ½-inch-thick rings, tentacles halved

Soy sauce, cilantro leaves and sliced hot chiles, for serving

**1.** In a large bowl, whisk the flour with the cornstarch, sea salt, peppercorns and five-spice powder. Lightly whisk in the seltzer to make a batter. The batter should be a little lumpy.

**2.** In a large saucepan, heat the vegetable oil to 375°. Meanwhile, set a wire rack over a baking sheet. Working in 5 batches, add the squid rings and tentacles to the batter: Lift each piece from the batter, drag it against the side of the bowl to remove any excess batter and drop it gently into the hot oil. Use a frying screen to prevent the hot oil from splattering. Continue adding the squid to different parts of the saucepan until the whole batch has been added to the oil. Fry the squid over high heat until it is deep golden, about 2 minutes. Using a slotted spoon, transfer the fried squid to the wire rack. Repeat with the remaining 4 batches of squid. Serve the fried squid at once, with the soy sauce, cilantro and chiles. —*Rick Stein*

**WINE** Full-bodied, minerally Riesling.

### Monkfish in Tomato-Garlic Sauce

**TOTAL: 40 MIN**

8 SERVINGS ●

This Catalan-style dish of silky monkfish is cooked in a tomato sauce, then sprinkled with paprika and topped with a scattering of nutty chips of crisp sautéed garlic.

- ¼ cup plus 3 tablespoons extra-virgin olive oil
- 2 heads garlic plus 4 large cloves, peeled and very thinly sliced
- 1 tablespoon sweet paprika
- 1 cup canned crushed tomatoes
- 2 cups water

**Salt and freshly ground pepper**

**Eight 6-ounce cleaned monkfish fillets (about 2 inches thick)**

**1.** Preheat the oven to 400°. In a large skillet, warm the ¼ cup of olive oil. Add the sliced garlic to the skillet and cook slowly over very low heat, shaking the skillet, until the garlic is deep golden, about 15 minutes. Remove about ¼ cup of the garlic slices to a plate and reserve. Add the paprika to the garlic in the skillet and cook for 1 minute. Add the crushed tomatoes to the skillet and cook them over moderately high heat for 1 minute. Add the water to the skillet and simmer until the sauce has reduced to 1½ cups, about 10 minutes. Season the sauce with salt and pepper.

**2.** In a very large skillet, heat the remaining 3 tablespoons of olive oil. Season the monkfish fillets with salt and pepper. Cook the monkfish over high heat until browned on the bottom, about 2 minutes. Turn the monkfish fillets, transfer them to the oven and roast until they are just cooked through, about 15 minutes.

**3.** Transfer the monkfish fillets to a large warmed platter. Pour any juices from the skillet into the sauce and simmer for 2 minutes. Spoon the sauce onto plates and set the monkfish on top. Scatter the fried garlic over the fish and serve right away.
—*Sergi Millet*

**WINE** Minerally, complex Sauvignon Blanc.

**CRISPY SALT-AND-PEPPER SQUID**

**MONKFISH IN TOMATO-GARLIC SAUCE**

## Snapper with Spicy Crab-and-Andouille Sauce

**TOTAL: 30 MIN**

**6 SERVINGS** ●

A buttery crab-and-andouille sausage sauce tops succulent sautéed red snapper fillets in this French-Cajun dish from John Folse, a restaurateur turned owner of a New Orleans–based specialty food company. This recipe gets its kick from Louisiana Gold Pepper Sauce, Folse's favorite hot sauce. It has a pure chile flavor that is not masked by the taste of vinegar, which Folse thinks interferes with the subtle flavor of foods.

## equipment
### CHEFS' TOP KNIVES

**1 Wüsthof** Strong blades; good for all kinds of chopping and prep. **DETAILS** $90 for a chef's knife; wusthof.com.

**2 Misono** Sharp, superthin blades; great for precision slicing and fine dicing. **DETAILS** $143 for a chef's knife; Korin Japanese Trading Corp., korin.com.

**3 R. H. Forschner** Durable, budget-priced knives; easy to sharpen. **DETAILS** About $40 for a chef's knife; swissarmy.com.

---

2 ounces lump crabmeat, picked over (¼ cup)
2 ounces andouille sausage, thinly sliced (¼ cup)
½ cup dry white wine
3 tablespoons Louisiana Gold Pepper Sauce or any hot sauce
1 tablespoon fresh lemon juice
1 scallion, thinly sliced
1 garlic clove, minced
1½ sticks (6 ounces) unsalted butter, cut into tablespoons
Salt and freshly ground pepper
2 cups white rice flour or all-purpose flour, for dredging
1 large egg, lightly beaten
½ cup milk
½ cup water
Six 7-ounce red snapper fillets
½ cup vegetable oil

**1.** In a medium skillet, combine the crabmeat, sausage, wine, pepper sauce, lemon juice, scallion and garlic and simmer over moderate heat until the liquid has reduced by half, about 4 minutes. Reduce the heat to moderately low and add 3 or 4 tablespoons of the butter, shaking and swirling the pan until it is melted. Continue adding the butter a few tablespoons at a time, shaking and swirling the pan until all of the butter is incorporated and the sauce is thick and creamy; do not let the sauce boil. Season with salt and pepper and keep warm over very low heat.

**2.** Put the rice flour in a shallow bowl and season it with salt and pepper. In another shallow bowl, whisk the egg with the milk and water. Dip the snapper fillets in the egg wash, then dredge them in the rice flour, pressing to help it adhere.

**3.** In each of 2 very large skillets, heat ¼ cup of oil until shimmering. Add the snapper fillets to the skillets and fry over high heat, turning once, until golden and crisp, about 6 minutes. Spoon the sauce over the fillets and serve. —*John Folse*

**WINE** Lush, fragrant Viognier.

---

## Flounder Rolls with Pesto

**TOTAL: 30 MIN**

**4 SERVINGS** ●

Chef Gennaro Contaldo of Passione restaurant in London combines fish and vegetables in a Parmesan-rich pesto sauce. He uses delicate sole here, but flounder, which is also light and flaky, is a fine and less expensive substitute.

3½ ounces basil leaves (5 packed cups)
2 garlic cloves, chopped
¼ cup freshly grated Parmesan cheese
⅔ cup extra-virgin olive oil, plus more for drizzling
Salt and freshly ground pepper
Four 6- to 7-ounce sole or flounder fillets
1 small zucchini, cut into matchsticks
1 red bell pepper, seeded and julienned

**1.** In a food processor, combine the basil leaves, garlic, grated Parmesan cheese and ⅔ cup of olive oil and process to a puree. Scrape the pesto into a bowl and season with salt and pepper.

**2.** Lay the flounder fillets, boned side down, on a work surface. Season the flounder fillets with salt and pepper and place an equal amount of the zucchini and red pepper strips across the narrow end of each fillet. Tightly roll up the flounder fillets and secure the rolls with toothpicks. Season the flounder rolls with salt and pepper and lightly drizzle them all over with olive oil.

**3.** Lightly oil a large steamer basket and place it in a large saucepan over ½ inch of boiling water. Put the flounder rolls in the basket, cover and steam over moderately high heat until they are just cooked through, about 10 minutes. Transfer the rolls to plates, spoon some of the pesto alongside and serve at once. —*Gennaro Contaldo*

**WINE** Light, fresh Pinot Grigio.

SNAPPER WITH SPICY
CRAB-AND-ANDOUILLE SAUCE

Cookbook author Linda Greenlaw went clamming in Maine in the August issue, using her catch for Amazing Stuffed Clams (P. 210).

# shellfish

**SHRIMP WITH BACON AND CHILES**

**CRISPY VIETNAMESE CRÊPES WITH SHRIMP AND PORK**

### Shrimp with Bacon and Chiles

**TOTAL: 25 MIN**

**4 SERVINGS** ● ●

For this singular stir-fry, Jerry Traunfeld, chef at The Herbfarm restaurant near Seattle and the author of *The Herbal Kitchen: Cooking with Fragrance and Flavor*, combines sweet shrimp with salty bacon, then adds hot chiles, vermouth and a healthy dose of fresh mint.

- **2 teaspoons vegetable oil**
- **¼ pound thickly sliced bacon, cut crosswise ¼ inch thick**
- **3 garlic cloves, very finely chopped**
- **8 Thai bird chiles or 4 serrano chiles**
- **1½ pounds shelled and deveined large shrimp**
- **Salt and freshly ground black pepper**
- **¼ cup vermouth or dry white wine**
- **¼ cup plus 2 tablespoons coarsely chopped mint**

In a large skillet, heat the vegetable oil. Add the bacon and cook it over moderate heat, stirring occasionally, until most of the fat has been rendered. Spoon off all but 1 tablespoon of the bacon fat from the skillet. Stir in the chopped garlic and whole chiles and cook until the garlic and chiles are fragrant, about 1 minute. Add the shrimp, season with salt and pepper and cook over moderately high heat, stirring occasionally, until the shrimp are pink and curled, about 3 minutes longer. Add the vermouth and cook until it is nearly evaporated, about 1 minute. Stir in the mint, then transfer the shrimp, bacon and chiles to plates and serve immediately.
—*Jerry Traunfeld*

**WINE** Vivid, lightly sweet Riesling.

### Crispy Vietnamese Crêpes with Shrimp, Pork and Bean Sprouts

**TOTAL: 1 HR 30 MIN**

**MAKES 12 CRÊPES**

When Charles Phan, the chef and owner of San Francisco's Slanted Door, samples *banh xeo* ("happy pancakes") at other Vietnamese restaurants, he often finds that they aren't crisp enough. Phan thinks the perfect crêpe should be lacy thin and crackly. After years of obsessive experimentation, he recommends refrigerating the batter overnight, so the starches have time to relax, then cooking the crêpes in a nonstick pan.

- **½ cup dried mung beans**
- **1 cup unsweetened coconut milk, stirred before using**
- **2 cups white rice flour**
- **1 cup cornstarch**
- **4 cups water**

2 scallions, thinly sliced

1½ teaspoons turmeric

Salt

Vegetable oil

¾ pound boneless pork loin, cut into ¼-inch-thick slices

¾ pound medium shrimp—shelled, deveined and halved lengthwise

1 medium white onion, halved lengthwise and thinly sliced

3 cups bean sprouts

Red leaf lettuce and mint leaves, for serving

Sweet and Spicy Vietnamese Dipping Sauce (recipe follows), for serving

**1.** In a small bowl, soak the mung beans in warm water until softened, about 30 minutes. Drain the beans and transfer to a blender. Add the coconut milk and puree until very smooth. Transfer the bean puree to a large bowl and whisk in the rice flour, cornstarch, water, scallions and turmeric; season the batter lightly with salt. Let the batter rest for at least 20 minutes or refrigerate overnight.

**2.** Heat 1 teaspoon of oil in a 10-inch nonstick skillet. Add a few slices of the pork, a couple of the shrimp and a few slices of the onion and cook for 30 seconds. Stir the batter and pour ⅔ cup of it into the pan; tilt and swirl the pan to coat the bottom with a very thin layer of batter, letting it come up the side of the pan. Scatter ¼ cup of the bean sprouts over the crêpe and drizzle 2 teaspoons of oil around the edge. Cover the skillet and cook over moderately high heat until the bottom of the crêpe is golden and crisp, about 2 minutes. Slide the crêpe onto a plate and serve with lettuce leaves, mint and Sweet and Spicy Vietnamese Dipping Sauce. Repeat with the remaining ingredients, serving the crêpes as soon as they are cooked. —*Charles Phan*

**MAKE AHEAD** The batter can be refrigerated overnight. Let return to room temperature and stir before making the crêpes.

**WINE** Vivid, lightly sweet Riesling.

## SWEET AND SPICY VIETNAMESE DIPPING SAUCE

**TOTAL: 5 MIN**

MAKES ABOUT 1½ CUPS ● ●

2 large garlic cloves, coarsely chopped

1 Thai chile, thinly sliced

¼ cup plus 2 tablespoons sugar

¼ cup unseasoned rice vinegar

½ cup Asian fish sauce

1½ cups water

In a large mortar, pound the chopped garlic with the chile. Add the sugar and mash the ingredients to a paste, adding a few drops of the rice vinegar as needed to moisten the mixture. Pound until the sugar is completely dissolved. Stir in the remaining rice vinegar along with the fish sauce and water and transfer the dipping sauce to a bowl. —*C.P.*

**MAKE AHEAD** The dipping sauce can be refrigerated overnight.

## Stir-Fried Sichuan Shrimp with Dried Red Chiles

**TOTAL: 25 MIN**

4 SERVINGS ●

⅓ cup vodka

3 tablespoons soy sauce

2 tablespoons ketchup

2 teaspoons rice wine vinegar or white wine vinegar

¼ cup vegetable oil

10 dried red chiles

One 2-inch piece of fresh ginger, peeled and very thinly sliced

1 teaspoon Sichuan peppercorns

3 large garlic cloves, thinly sliced

1¾ pounds medium shrimp, shelled and deveined

Salt

3 scallions, white parts only, coarsely chopped

**1.** In a small bowl, stir the vodka with the soy sauce, ketchup and vinegar. In a large skillet, heat the oil. Add the chiles, ginger and Sichuan peppercorns and stir-fry over high heat until the chiles and peppercorns darken and the ginger starts to brown, about 2 minutes. Add the garlic and stir-fry until golden, about 10 seconds. Add the shrimp, season lightly with salt and stir-fry until just cooked, about 3 minutes.

**2.** Remove the skillet from the heat and slowly add the vodka sauce. Using a long match, carefully light the sauce. Return the skillet to the heat and bring the sauce to a simmer, stirring. Add the scallions and serve at once. —*Susanna Foo*

**WINE** Fresh, lively Soave.

## Grilled Shrimp with Habanero-Garlic Vinaigrette

**TOTAL: 25 MIN**

4 SERVINGS ● ●

6 garlic cloves

½ cup pure olive oil, plus more for brushing

½ habanero chile, seeded and chopped

5 tablespoons chopped cilantro

¼ cup fresh lime juice

1 tablespoon honey

Salt and freshly ground pepper

16 jumbo shrimp, deveined

**1.** Light a grill. In a small saucepan, combine the garlic and the ½ cup of olive oil and simmer over low heat until the garlic is golden brown, about 8 minutes. Transfer the garlic to a blender and pour the oil into a glass measuring cup. Let the oil cool slightly. Add the habanero chile to the blender with ¼ cup of the cilantro, the lime juice and honey and puree. With the blender on, slowly add the garlic olive oil. Season with salt and pepper.

**2.** Brush the shrimp with olive oil and season with salt and pepper. Grill over high heat until lightly charred, about 4 minutes per side. Shell the shrimp and transfer to plates. Drizzle with the vinaigrette, sprinkle with the remaining cilantro and serve. —*Bobby Flay*

**WINE** Lush, fragrant Viognier.

# shellfish

## Shrimp Boil with Three-Bean Salad

**ACTIVE: 25 MIN; TOTAL: 1 HR 40 MIN**

**4 SERVINGS** ●

- ¼ cup extra-virgin olive oil, plus more for drizzling
- 10 large garlic cloves, unpeeled, plus 3 garlic cloves thinly sliced
- 2 quarts water
- ¾ pound yellow wax beans
- 2 bay leaves
- 1½ teaspoons thyme leaves
- Finely grated zest and juice of 1 lemon
- ½ teaspoon cayenne pepper
- Salt and freshly ground black pepper
- 1 pound large shrimp, shelled
- 2 tablespoons Creole mustard
- 2 tablespoons rice vinegar
- 1½ teaspoons honey
- ¾ cup shelled thawed edamame
- 1 cup canned chickpeas, drained

**1.** Preheat the oven to 400°. On a sheet of foil, drizzle some olive oil on the unpeeled garlic cloves, then wrap them up and bake for about 40 minutes.

**2.** In a medium saucepan, bring the water to a boil, add the wax beans and cook until they are just tender, about 4 minutes. Using a slotted spoon, transfer the wax beans to a large bowl. Add the sliced garlic, bay leaves, thyme, lemon zest and juice, cayenne and 1½ teaspoons each of salt and black pepper to the saucepan. Bring to a boil and cook for 5 minutes. Add the shrimp and simmer for 3 minutes. Transfer the shrimp to a baking sheet. Let the shrimp boil cool to room temperature, then return the shrimp to it.

**3.** Peel the roasted garlic. In a mini food processor, puree the roasted garlic with the mustard, vinegar and honey. Slowly blend in the ¼ cup of olive oil. Season the dressing with salt and black pepper.

**4.** Toss the wax beans with the edamame, chickpeas and dressing. Using a slotted spoon, mound the salad on plates, top with the shrimp and serve. —*Corbin Evans*

**WINE** Tart, citrusy Riesling.

## Shrimp with Tangy Tomato Sauce

**TOTAL: 30 MIN**

**4 SERVINGS** ● ●

Tamarind concentrate (sold at Asian and Latin markets) adds a tangy edge to this dish. Lemon juice is a fine substitute.

- 2 tablespoons vegetable oil
- 1 medium red onion, chopped
- 4 garlic cloves, minced
- 2 serrano chiles, minced
- 1 teaspoon ground cumin
- ¾ teaspoon ground coriander
- ¾ teaspoon garam masala
- ½ teaspoon turmeric
- 2 medium tomatoes, chopped
- 2 tablespoons plus ½ teaspoon fresh lemon juice, or 1 tablespoon tamarind concentrate dissolved in 2 tablespoons warm water
- 1 teaspoon dark brown sugar
- 1 cup coarsely chopped cilantro
- 1½ teaspoons kosher salt
- ½ cup water
- 1½ pounds shelled and deveined large shrimp

Heat the vegetable oil in a large skillet. Add the chopped onion and cook over moderately high heat, stirring frequently, until the onion is golden, about 5 minutes. Add the minced garlic and chiles and cook until softened, about 2 minutes. Stir in the cumin, coriander, garam masala and turmeric. Cook the ground spices for 1 minute, stirring constantly. Reduce the heat to moderate, add the chopped tomatoes and cook, stirring occasionally, until the sauce is thickened slightly, about 5 minutes. Stir in the lemon juice, brown sugar, cilantro, salt and water. Bring to a boil. Add the shrimp and cook, stirring frequently, until they're pink and curled, about 5 minutes. Transfer the shrimp and sauce to a shallow bowl and serve at once.
—*Heather Carlucci-Rodriguez*

**SERVE WITH** Steamed basmati rice.

**WINE** Vivid, lightly sweet Riesling.

## Shrimp, Asparagus and Eggs in Spicy Tomato Sauce

**TOTAL: 35 MIN**

**4 SERVINGS** ●

- ½ pound asparagus
- 2 tablespoons extra-virgin olive oil
- ½ pound large shrimp, shelled and deveined
- Salt and freshly ground pepper
- 1 small onion, thinly sliced
- ¼ cup torn basil leaves
- 3 garlic cloves, minced
- Pinch of crushed red pepper
- 1 cup tomato sauce
- 1 cup water
- 4 large eggs
- 1 ounce ricotta salata (3 tablespoons), grated

**1.** In a large skillet of boiling salted water, cook the asparagus for 3 minutes. Drain, pat dry and cut into 1½-inch lengths.

**2.** Heat the olive oil in the same skillet. Add the shrimp, season them with salt and pepper and cook over moderate heat, stirring, until they are pink, about 3 minutes. Transfer the shrimp to a plate. Add the onion slices to the skillet and cook until they are softened. Add the basil, garlic and crushed red pepper and cook until the garlic is golden. Add the tomato sauce and water and simmer until the sauce is slightly thickened, about 3 minutes. Season the tomato sauce with salt and pepper.

**3.** Break each egg into a ramekin, then gently pour the eggs, one at a time, into the simmering tomato sauce. Cover the skillet and cook over low heat until the whites are just firm and the yolks are still runny, about 3 minutes. Using a large spoon, transfer the eggs to serving plates. Add the asparagus and shrimp to the tomato sauce and heat through, then spoon the asparagus and shrimp around the eggs. Sprinkle with the ricotta salata and serve.
—*Corbin Evans*

**WINE** Fresh, fruity rosé.

## Shrimp and Coconut Curry

**TOTAL: 30 MIN**

**4 TO 6 SERVINGS** ●

Cookbook author Maya Kaimal has a deft hand with Indian sauces. (She even sells an eponymous line of them at specialty food stores.) The light and fragrant sauce here is based on a Keralan shrimp curry.

- 2 tablespoons vegetable oil
- 1 medium onion, thinly sliced
- 4 whole cloves
- 2 cardamom pods, crushed

One 3-inch cinnamon stick, broken

- 2 cups unsweetened coconut milk
- 1 cup water
- 12 thin slices of fresh ginger
- 3 jalapeños—stemmed, quartered and seeded

Salt

- 1¼ pounds shelled and deveined medium shrimp
- 1 teaspoon fresh lime juice

Steamed rice and lime wedges, for serving

**1.** In a large skillet, heat the vegetable oil. Add the onion slices to the skillet and cook over moderately high heat, stirring occasionally, until they are browned, about 5 minutes. Add the cloves, cardamom and cinnamon stick to the skillet and cook, stirring, for 2 minutes. Add 1½ cups of the coconut milk, the water, ginger, jalapeños and ½ teaspoon of salt and simmer the coconut-curry sauce over moderate heat for about 10 minutes.

**2.** Add the shrimp to the sauce and simmer, stirring a few times, until they are just cooked, about 4 minutes. Add the remaining ½ cup of coconut milk and bring the sauce back to a simmer. Remove the skillet from the heat and add the lime juice. Season the curry with salt and transfer to plates. Serve with steamed rice and lime wedges. —*Maya Kaimal*

**WINE** Rich Alsace Gewürztraminer.

## Quick Curried Shrimp Salad

**TOTAL: 30 MIN**

**4 SERVINGS** ● ● ●

- ¾ cup plain nonfat yogurt
- 2 tablespoons extra-virgin olive oil
- 4 scallions, thinly sliced
- 1 small garlic clove, finely chopped
- 1 teaspoon curry powder
- 1 pound cleaned, cooked shrimp, cut into 1 inch pieces
- 1 cucumber—peeled, halved, seeded and thinly sliced

Salt and freshly ground pepper

- ¼ cup roasted, salted shelled sunflower seeds

**1.** Scoop the yogurt into a paper towel–lined colander set over a bowl. Let stand at room temperature for 30 minutes. You should end up with ½ cup of yogurt.

**2.** Heat the olive oil in a small skillet. Add the scallions and garlic and cook over high heat, stirring, until softened, 1 to 2 minutes. Add the curry powder and cook, stirring, for 1 minute. Scrape into a medium bowl and let cool slightly. Stir in the shrimp, cucumber and drained yogurt; season with salt and pepper. Sprinkle the sunflower seeds over the salad and serve. —*Grace Parisi*

**SERVE WITH** Whole wheat pita.

**MAKE AHEAD** The shrimp salad can be refrigerated in an airtight container for up to 6 hours. Sprinkle the sunflower seeds over the salad just before serving.

**WINE** Zesty, fresh Albariño.

## Fried Parsley-Flecked Shrimp Cakes

**TOTAL: 45 MIN**

**MAKES ABOUT 30 CAKES** ●

These golden, bite-size, can't-stop-eating-them pancakes are called *tortitas de camarones*. They were invented in the fishing village of Zahara de los Atunes, in the Andalusian province of Cadiz. Their fame spread, and soon they became a trendy tapas at dinner parties all through southern Spain.

- 2 large eggs
- 2 cups all-purpose flour
- 1 cup water
- 1 teaspoon salt
- 1 pound medium shrimp— shelled, deveined and finely chopped
- 1 large onion, coarsely grated
- 2 tablespoons chopped parsley
- ¼ cup plus 2 tablespoons extra-virgin olive oil

**1.** Preheat the oven to 300°. In a large bowl, whisk the eggs. Whisk in the flour, water and salt until just blended; some lumps are fine. Using a rubber spatula, fold the chopped shrimp, onion and parsley into the batter.

**2.** In a large nonstick skillet, heat ¼ cup of the olive oil until shimmering. Drop 6 rounded tablespoons of the batter into the skillet and spread each mound into a 2½-inch round. Fry the cakes over moderately high heat until browned, about 3 minutes per side. Drain on paper towels, then transfer to a large rimmed baking sheet. Repeat with the remaining batter, adjusting the heat if the cakes brown too quickly and adding the remaining 2 tablespoons of olive oil to the skillet as needed. Rewarm the shrimp cakes in the oven and serve. —*Victoria Amory*

**WINE** Minerally, complex Sauvignon Blanc.

# health

### GOOD NEWS ABOUT SHRIMP

Shrimp are loaded with lean **protein:** One serving (about three ounces) supplies a third of the recommended daily intake and, miraculously, only 84 **calories,** with less than one-third the saturated fat of chicken breast. But watch how much you eat: One serving contains more than half the amount of **cholesterol** you should have in a day.

# shellfish

## Flat Breads with Shrimp and Romesco Sauce

**ACTIVE: 50 MIN; TOTAL: 2 HR**

MAKES 2 DOZEN HORS D'OEUVRES ●

**FLAT BREADS**

- 2 tablespoons extra-virgin olive oil
- ½ cup minced onion
- ¼ cup warm water
- 1½ teaspoons sugar
- 1 envelope (¼ ounce) active dry yeast
- 1½ cups all-purpose flour, plus more for dusting
- ½ teaspoon salt
- ¼ cup dry white wine

**ROMESCO SAUCE**

- 1 medium red bell pepper
- 1 cup roasted, salted almonds (4 ounces), chopped
- ¼ cup red wine vinegar
- 2 tablespoons chopped parsley
- 1 large garlic clove, chopped
- ½ cup extra-virgin olive oil

Salt

**SHRIMP**

- 2 tablespoons extra-virgin olive oil
- 24 medium shrimp (about ¾ pound), shelled and deveined

Salt and freshly ground pepper

**1. MAKE THE FLAT BREADS:** In a small skillet, heat the olive oil. Add the onion and cook over moderate heat until softened, about 5 minutes. Let the onion cool to room temperature.

**2.** In a small bowl, mix the water with the sugar and yeast. Let stand until foamy, about 5 minutes. In a food processor fitted with the plastic dough blade, blend the 1½ cups of flour and the salt. Add the cooked onion, the wine and the yeast mixture and process until a ball forms. On a lightly floured work surface, knead the dough briefly until smooth. Transfer it to a lightly oiled bowl, cover with a sheet of plastic wrap and let stand in a warm place until doubled in bulk, about 1 hour.

**3.** Preheat the oven to 375°. Punch down the flat bread dough. On a lightly floured work surface, roll out the dough to a 12-inch round about ⅛ inch thick. Cover the dough with plastic wrap and let rest for 15 minutes. Using a 2-inch round biscuit cutter, stamp out 24 rounds and transfer them to a large baking sheet. Bake the flat breads for about 15 minutes, or until they are just cooked through and pale.

**4. MEANWHILE, MAKE THE ROMESCO SAUCE:** Roast the bell pepper directly over a gas flame or under a preheated broiler until blackened all over. Transfer the red bell pepper to a plate and let cool. Peel, discard the stem and seeds and coarsely chop the pepper.

**5.** In a food processor, process the roasted red bell pepper with the almonds, vinegar, parsley and garlic to a paste. With the machine on, slowly blend in the olive oil. Transfer the *romesco* sauce to a bowl and season with salt.

**6. COOK THE SHRIMP:** In a large skillet, heat the olive oil. Add the shrimp, season with salt and pepper and cook over moderately high heat until white throughout, about 2 minutes per side.

**7.** Spread a teaspoon of *romesco* sauce on each flat bread, top with a shrimp and serve immediately. —*Sergi Millet*

**WINE** Spicy American Gewürztraminer.

## Grilled Shrimp Rolls with Sorrel

**TOTAL: 40 MIN PLUS 2 TO 4 HR MARINATING**

8 SERVINGS ● ● ●

- ¼ cup extra-virgin olive oil, plus more for brushing
- 1 tablespoon rosemary leaves

Finely grated zest of 1 lemon

- 3 garlic cloves, very finely chopped
- 40 large shrimp (about 1½ pounds), shelled and deveined
- ½ cup mayonnaise
- 2 scallions, finely chopped
- 3 cornichons, finely chopped
- 1 shallot, finely chopped
- 1 large celery rib, finely chopped
- 2 teaspoons very finely chopped tarragon
- 1 teaspoon sherry vinegar
- ½ teaspoon sweet paprika
- ¼ teaspoon celery seeds

Salt and freshly ground pepper

- 1 tablespoon gin
- 1 tablespoon dry sherry
- 8 hot dog rolls (preferably potato rolls), split in half lengthwise
- 8 large sorrel or arugula leaves

**1.** In a large, shallow dish, combine the ¼ cup of olive oil with the rosemary leaves, lemon zest and two-thirds of the chopped garlic. Stir in the shrimp and refrigerate for 2 to 4 hours.

**2.** In a bowl, stir the mayonnaise with the chopped scallions, cornichons, shallot and celery and the minced tarragon, sherry vinegar, paprika, celery seeds and the remaining chopped garlic. Season the dressing with salt and pepper.

**3.** Light a grill. Toss the shrimp with the gin and the dry sherry. Thread the shrimp onto 8 skewers. Season the shrimp with salt and pepper. Grill the shrimp over high heat until they are lightly charred and cooked through, about 3 minutes per side; let cool slightly. Stir the grilled shrimp into the mayonnaise dressing.

**4.** Brush the cut sides of the hot dog rolls with olive oil and grill until toasted. Place a sorrel leaf in each roll, then spoon the shrimp salad into the rolls and serve at once. —*Shea Gallante*

**MAKE AHEAD** The shrimp salad can be refrigerated overnight. Let the shrimp salad stand at room temperature for 30 minutes before serving.

**WINE** Light, crisp white Burgundy.

GRILLED SHRIMP
ROLLS WITH SORREL

## Grilled Spot Prawns with Crispy Shaved Vegetables

**ACTIVE: 30 MIN; TOTAL: 1 HR 30 MIN**

8 SERVINGS ●

Pacific Coast spot prawns are named for the distinctive white spots on their reddish-brown shells. They have an unbelievably sweet flavor and firm, meaty texture. Since they can be hard to find, you can substitute almost any kind of jumbo head-on shrimp. You can even use big, fresh sardines (Japanese iwashi are the best); just debone them and grill them quickly over high heat.

12 large spot prawns or jumbo shrimp

12 asparagus tips (2 inches long)

16 baby orange and yellow carrots with ½ inch of the green stems attached, peeled

4 baby turnips with ½ inch of the green stems attached, peeled

4 small red radishes with ½ inch of the green stems attached, peeled

1 small red onion

1 kirby or Japanese cucumber, halved and seeded

½ cup celery leaves

½ cup flat-leaf parsley leaves

8 tarragon leaves

½ cup extra-virgin olive oil, plus more for brushing

¼ cup fresh lemon juice

1 teaspoon finely grated lemon zest

Salt and freshly ground pepper

**1.** Using a pair of kitchen scissors, cut down the middle of the backs of the prawn shells. Leave the prawn shells on and pull out the central vein.

**2.** Fill a large bowl with ice water. Using a mandoline-style slicer and holding the vegetables lengthwise, very thinly slice the asparagus tips, carrots, turnips, radishes, red onion and cucumber directly into the ice water bath. Add the celery, parsley and tarragon leaves and refrigerate until the vegetables are crisp, at least 30 minutes or up to 1 hour.

**3.** Light a grill. In a small bowl, mix the ½ cup of olive oil with the lemon juice and zest. Season the dressing with salt and pepper. Drain the vegetables and herbs and dry thoroughly in a salad spinner. Wrap the vegetables and herbs in paper towels and keep in the refrigerator.

**4.** Brush the prawns with olive oil and season with salt and pepper. Grill over moderately high heat until just cooked through, about 3 minutes per side. Transfer to a platter and let rest for 5 minutes.

**5.** In a bowl, toss the vegetables and herbs with half of the dressing, then arrange them on 8 plates. Halve each prawn lengthwise through the shell. Top each salad with 3 prawn halves, drizzle with the remaining dressing and serve. —*Michael Cimarusti*
**WINE** Peppery, refreshing Grüner Veltliner.

## Garlicky Shrimp with Olive Oil

**TOTAL: 20 MIN**

8 FIRST-COURSE SERVINGS ● ● ●

These *gambas al ajillo* (shrimp with garlic) from La Casa del Abuelo, a tiny *taberna* in Madrid, are traditionally cooked in individual earthenware *cazuelitas* and served with plenty of bread to dip into the garlicky oil once the shrimp have been eaten. This dish can also be prepared in a skillet.

1 cup extra-virgin olive oil

4 garlic cloves, minced

6 whole dried red chiles

¼ cup minced flat-leaf parsley

2 pounds shelled and deveined medium shrimp

Salt

**Crusty bread, for serving**

In a very large, deep skillet, heat the olive oil until shimmering. Add the garlic, chiles and parsley and cook over moderately high heat for 10 seconds, stirring. Add the shrimp and cook over high heat, stirring once, until pink and curled, 3 to 4 minutes. Season with salt and transfer to bowls. Serve with crusty bread. —*Jeff Koehler*
**WINE** Dry, earthy sparkling wine.

## Smoky Shrimp and Cheesy Grits

**TOTAL: 25 MIN**

4 SERVINGS ●

The steaming hot grits here are mixed with plenty of white cheddar cheese, then topped with shrimp cooked with garlic and smoky slab bacon.

3 cups chicken stock or low-sodium broth

¾ cup quick grits

4 ounces white cheddar cheese, shredded (1 cup)

3 tablespoons unsalted butter

Salt and freshly ground pepper

2 tablespoons extra-virgin olive oil

¾ pound slab bacon, cut into ¼-inch matchsticks

4 garlic cloves, minced

1 pound shelled and deveined large shrimp

2 tablespoons chopped parsley

**1.** In a saucepan, bring the chicken stock to a boil. Whisk in the grits and cook over moderately high heat, stirring constantly, until the consistency is thick and the grains are tender, about 5 minutes. Add the shredded cheese and butter, season with salt and pepper and whisk just until the cheese is melted. Cover and remove from the heat.

**2.** In a large, deep skillet, heat the olive oil until shimmering. Add the bacon and cook over moderately high heat, stirring occasionally, until the fat is rendered and the bacon is golden, about 8 minutes. Using a slotted spoon, transfer the bacon to a paper towel–lined plate to drain.

**3.** Pour off all but 4 tablespoons of the fat in the skillet. Add the garlic and cook over moderately high heat just until fragrant. Add the shrimp and cook until curled and pink, about 3 minutes. Stir in the parsley and bacon; season with salt and pepper.

**4.** Spoon the warm, cheesy grits into shallow bowls and top with the shrimp and bacon. Serve right away. —*Bobby Flay*
**WINE** Ripe, luxurious Chardonnay.

## Spicy Shrimp and Chorizo Kebabs

**TOTAL: 45 MIN**

6 SERVINGS

The superfast, supertasty marinade for the shrimp, flavored with caraway seeds and ancho powder, would also be delicious with chicken, pork tenderloin or steak.

- 2 large garlic cloves, thickly sliced
- 2 teaspoons sea salt
- 2 teaspoons caraway seeds
- 2 tablespoons pure chile powder, such as ancho
- ¼ cup extra-virgin olive oil
- 2 pounds large shrimp, shelled and deveined
- 8 small chorizo (about ½ pound total), sliced ½ inch thick

**1.** On a cutting board, using the flat side of a chef's knife, mash the garlic and salt to a coarse paste. Add the caraway seeds and finely chop them. Transfer to a large bowl and stir in the chile powder and olive oil. Add the shrimp and toss to coat.

**2.** Meanwhile, bring a small saucepan of water to a boil. Add the chorizo and cook over high heat for 5 minutes. Drain and pat dry. Let cool slightly.

**3.** Light a grill. Tuck a chorizo slice in the crook of a shrimp and thread onto a skewer; the shrimp should be attached at both ends. Push it to the end of the skewer and repeat with 2 more shrimp and chorizo slices. Using more skewers, repeat with the remaining shrimp and chorizo.

**4.** Grill the kebabs over high heat, turning once or twice, until the chorizo is charred and the shrimp are cooked through, 5 minutes. Serve immediately. —*Grace Parisi*
**WINE** Fruity, light-bodied Beaujolais.

## Roasted Shrimp with Lentils and Sun-Dried Tomatoes

**TOTAL: 40 MIN**

4 SERVINGS ●

- ¼ cup extra-virgin olive oil
- 2 garlic cloves, minced
- 1 small onion, minced
- 1 small carrot, finely diced
- 1 small celery rib, finely diced
- 1 quart water
- 1 cup French green lentils, rinsed
- 1 bay leaf
- 6 sun-dried tomato halves (not oil-packed)
- ¼ cup chopped mint
- 1½ teaspoons balsamic vinegar
- 1 teaspoon honey
- Salt and freshly ground pepper
- 1 pound large shrimp, shelled and deveined

**1.** Preheat the oven to 425°. In a medium saucepan, heat 1 tablespoon of the olive oil. Add the garlic, onion, carrot and celery and cook over moderately high heat, stirring occasionally, until the vegetables are starting to brown, about 5 minutes. Add the water, lentils and bay leaf and bring to a boil. Simmer over low heat, stirring a few times, until the lentils are tender, about 25 minutes. Set a colander over a large bowl and drain the lentils; transfer the cooking liquid to a cup. Discard the bay leaf.

**2.** Meanwhile, in a small saucepan, cover the sun-dried tomatoes with water and bring to a boil. Simmer the tomatoes over low heat until they are softened, about 5 minutes. Drain and cool, then cut the tomatoes into ¼-inch dice.

**3.** In the large bowl, mix the mint, vinegar, honey and 2 tablespoons of the olive oil. Stir in the lentils and tomatoes. Season with salt and pepper and stir in 2 tablespoons of the reserved cooking liquid; add more of the liquid if the lentils seem dry.

**4.** In a 9-inch square baking dish, toss the shrimp with the remaining 1 tablespoon of olive oil and season with salt and pepper. Spread the shrimp in the baking dish and roast for about 6 minutes, or until just cooked. Mound the lentil salad on plates, top with the shrimp and drizzle the roasting juices over them. —*Corbin Evans*
**WINE** Creamy, supple Pinot Blanc.

## Sizzled Shrimp Provençal

**TOTAL: 15 MIN**

4 SERVINGS ● ●

- ¼ cup extra-virgin olive oil
- 1½ pounds jumbo shrimp, peeled and deveined
- Salt and freshly ground pepper
- 2 large garlic cloves, minced
- 2 tablespoons small capers, drained
- ¼ cup fresh lemon juice
- 2 tablespoons finely chopped flat-leaf parsley

**1.** In a very large skillet, heat 2 tablespoons of the olive oil until shimmering. Season the shrimp generously with salt and pepper, add them to the skillet and cook over high heat until lightly browned and barely opaque, about 2 minutes.

**2.** Add the remaining 2 tablespoons of olive oil to the skillet along with the garlic and capers and cook for 30 seconds. Turn the shrimp and add the lemon juice and 1 tablespoon of the chopped parsley. Cover and cook over low heat until the shrimp are cooked through and the sauce is slightly reduced, 4 to 5 minutes. Transfer the shrimp to plates and spoon the Provençal sauce on top. Sprinkle the shrimp with the remaining 1 tablespoon of parsley and serve. —*Chef Bobo*
**SERVE WITH** Crusty whole wheat bread.
**WINE** Fresh, fruity rosé.

# ingredient
## WILD SHRIMP

Most shrimp sold in the U.S. come from farms overseas, but you can buy fresh, wild American shrimp at **farmers' markets** along the Gulf Coast from April through January. These shrimp tend to be especially firm and tasty, and unlike farmed varieties, they're antibiotic-free. You can also buy frozen wild shrimp at **supermarkets.** Look for the Wild American Shrimp certification label.

## Shrimp with Creamy Grits

**TOTAL: 30 MIN**

**4 SERVINGS** ●

This dish has all of the luscious appeal of traditional Southern shrimp and grits—warm, cheesy cornmeal topped with tender, sweet seafood. But what makes this version even better is the brilliant addition of a spicy, garlicky sauce.

- **2** quarts water
- Salt
- **2** cups stone-ground white grits
- **4** ounces white cheddar cheese, shredded (1 cup)
- **4** tablespoons unsalted butter
- **2** jalapeño chile peppers
- **2** poblano chiles
- **6** large garlic cloves, thickly sliced
- **½** cup pure olive oil
- **¼** cup orange juice
- Freshly ground pepper
- **1¼** pounds shelled and deveined large shrimp

**1.** In a large saucepan, bring the water to a boil. Season with a pinch of salt. Whisk the grits into the water and cook them over moderate heat, stirring often, until their consistency is very thick and the grains are tender, about 15 minutes. Stir the cheddar cheese and butter into the grits and keep them warm.

**2.** Meanwhile, thread the jalapeño chile peppers onto skewers. Roast the jalapeño skewers along with the poblano chiles over a gas flame or under a broiler as close to the heat as possible until the chile peppers are blackened, about 3 minutes. Transfer all of the chile peppers to a bowl and let them cool for 10 minutes, then rub off the skins under running water. Stem and seed the chile peppers.

**3.** In a small saucepan, cook the garlic in the olive oil over moderate heat, stirring, until the garlic is softened and very lightly browned, about 5 minutes. Using a slotted spoon, transfer the garlic to a blender. Add the chiles and the orange juice and puree until smooth. Add all but 2 tablespoons of the garlic oil and puree the sauce until creamy. Season the garlic-chile sauce with salt and pepper.

**4.** Toss the shrimp with the remaining 2 tablespoons of garlic oil. Heat a very large skillet until very hot, about 2 minutes. Add the shrimp in a single layer and cook until they are browned and just cooked through, about 1 minute per side.

**5.** Spoon the grits into a serving bowl and top with the shrimp. Spoon the chile-garlic sauce all around and serve at once.
—*Marc Meyer*

**WINE** Ripe, luxurious Chardonnay.

## Maine Shrimp and Scallop Stew

**ACTIVE: 20 MIN; TOTAL: 2 HR 20 MIN**

**4 TO 6 SERVINGS** ● ●

- **4** tablespoons unsalted butter
- **¼** teaspoon sweet paprika
- Freshly ground pepper
- **1** pound sea scallops, halved horizontally
- **1** pound medium shrimp, shelled and deveined
- **1** quart light cream
- Salt

**1.** Melt the butter in a large saucepan. Add the paprika and a pinch of pepper. Add the scallops and cook over moderate heat for 2 minutes, stirring a few times. Add the shrimp and cook, stirring, for 1 minute. Add the heavy cream and heat until it is steaming. Do not let the cream boil. Remove the pan from the heat and let the stew stand for 2 hours.

**2.** Reheat the stew over low heat; do not let it boil. Season the shrimp and scallop stew with salt and pepper and serve in bowls.
—*Diana Santospago*

**MAKE AHEAD** The stew can be refrigerated overnight and gently reheated.

**WINE** Minerally Marsanne or Roussanne.

## Steamed Tofu with Shrimp and Black Bean Sauce

**TOTAL: 30 MIN**

**4 SERVINGS** ● ●

Corinne Trang, author of *Essentials of Asian Cuisine*, offers this pungent, garlicky take on the Chinese dish of tofu stuffed with shrimp in black bean sauce. The shrimp here are stir-fried just until they curl, then served alongside firm tofu.

- **½** cup whole fermented black beans
- **1½** pounds firm tofu (two 1½-inch-thick squares), each cut into 8 triangles
- **3** tablespoons vegetable oil
- **24** medium shrimp (10 ounces), shelled and deveined
- Salt and freshly ground pepper
- **¼** cup peeled and finely julienned fresh ginger
- **2** garlic cloves, minced
- **½** cup Chinese cooking wine
- **½** cup vegetable stock
- **1** teaspoon sugar
- **12** cilantro sprigs

**1.** In a bowl, cover the black beans with water and let soak for 10 minutes. Drain.

**2.** In a wok, bring 2 inches of water to a boil. Set a bamboo steamer in the wok. Spread the tofu pieces on a heatproof plate and set it in the steamer. Cover and steam the tofu over moderately high heat for 5 minutes.

**3.** In a skillet, heat 1 tablespoon of the oil. Add the shrimp, season with salt and pepper and cook over high heat until pink and curled, about 1 minute per side. Transfer to a bowl. Add the remaining 2 tablespoons of oil to the skillet and heat until shimmering. Add the ginger and garlic and cook over moderate heat until fragrant, about 2 minutes. Add the black beans and stir-fry for 1 minute. Add the cooking wine, stock and sugar and simmer until slightly reduced, 2 to 3 minutes. Transfer the tofu and shrimp to plates, top with the sauce and cilantro and serve. —*Corinne Trang*

**WINE** Lively, tart Sauvignon Blanc.

### Citrus-Marinated Shrimp with Grilled-Onion and Orange Salad

**TOTAL: 25 MIN**

**6 SERVINGS** ● ●

This recipe gets its bold flavors from chipotles, grilled onions and citrus juice.

- ½ cup fresh orange juice
- 1 large garlic clove, minced
- 2 canned chipotle chiles in adobo—stems discarded, chiles seeded and thinly sliced—plus 1 teaspoon of the adobo sauce from the can
- 2 tablespoons fresh lime juice
- 1½ pounds shelled and deveined large shrimp
- Salt and freshly ground pepper
- 1 large sweet onion, cut crosswise into 3 thick slabs
- 1 tablespoon extra-virgin olive oil
- 3 large navel oranges—peeled, halved lengthwise and thinly sliced crosswise
- 2 tablespoons chopped cilantro

**1.** In a medium bowl, combine the orange juice, garlic, adobo sauce and 1 tablespoon of the lime juice. Add the shrimp and season with salt and pepper; let stand at room temperature for 10 minutes.

**2.** Preheat a grill pan. Thread the onion slices on skewers to hold them together. Brush the onions with some of the olive oil and season with salt and pepper. Grill the slices over high heat, turning once, until softened and charred, about 3 minutes per side. Let cool slightly, then coarsely chop the onions and transfer them to a medium bowl. Add the orange slices, chipotles, cilantro and the remaining 1 tablespoon lime juice. Season with salt and pepper.

**3.** Drain the marinated shrimp and thread them onto 6 skewers. Brush the shrimp lightly with the remaining olive oil and grill over moderately high heat, turning occasionally, until charred in spots, about 5 minutes. Serve the shrimp with the onion and orange salad. —*Grace Parisi*

**WINE** Minerally, complex Sauvignon Blanc.

**TOFU WITH SHRIMP AND BLACK BEAN SAUCE**

**CITRUS-MARINATED SHRIMP WITH ONION-ORANGE SALAD**

# shellfish

## Saucy Clams and Shrimp with Wild Mushrooms

**TOTAL: 20 MIN**

**8 FIRST-COURSE SERVINGS** ● ●

One of the specialties of Seville's Modesto restaurant is this wonderful saucy clam dish cooked in Marqués de Lillalúa, a wine from the neighboring province of Huelva. Any dry, fruity white can be substituted.

- ½ cup extra-virgin olive oil
- ½ pound shiitake mushrooms, stems discarded, caps thickly sliced
- Salt and freshly ground pepper
- 1 bunch scallions, white and light green parts only
- 1 large hot red chile, seeded and thinly sliced
- 2 dozen littleneck clams, scrubbed
- 1¼ cups dry, fruity white wine
- 1 pound shelled and deveined medium shrimp
- Crusty bread, for serving

1. In a large, deep skillet, heat the olive oil until shimmering. Add the shiitake mushrooms and cook over high heat, stirring occasionally, until lightly browned, about 5 minutes. Season with salt and pepper. Add the scallions and chile and cook for 2 minutes, until just softened.

# ingredient
## MUSSELS

Buy mussels with unbroken, tightly closed shells. To prepare, **clean** them under cold running water and rub them with a stiff brush if they seem gritty. Just before cooking, **remove the fibrous beard** from between the two shells, grasping it with a kitchen towel and pulling firmly. **Tap** all open shells, and if they do not close, discard them, because the mussel is dead. After cooking, the shells should open; **discard** mussels that remain closed.

2. Add the clams and wine and cook uncovered, stirring, until half of the clams are open, 4 minutes. Add the shrimp and cook, stirring, until all of the clams are open and the shrimp are pink and cooked through, 4 minutes. Discard any clams that do not open. Serve in bowls with crusty bread to sop up the sauce. —*Jeff Koehler*

**WINE** Zesty, fresh Albariño.

## Mussels Roasted in Almond-Garlic Butter

**TOTAL: 35 MIN**

**4 SERVINGS**

The savory combination of garlic, chiles and toasted almonds reflects a Spanish influence.

- ½ cup roasted, salted almonds, chopped
- 1 stick unsalted butter, softened
- 2 garlic cloves, minced
- 1 medium shallot, minced
- 2 tablespoons chopped parsley
- 1 tablespoon fresh lemon juice
- 1 teaspoon finely grated lemon zest
- 1 teaspoon minced jalapeño
- 1 teaspoon freshly ground pepper
- Salt
- 4 pounds mussels, scrubbed and debearded
- ½ cup dry white wine

1. Preheat the oven to 450°. In a processor, coarsely grind the almonds. Add the butter, garlic, shallot, parsley, lemon juice, lemon zest, jalapeño and pepper; process until blended and season with salt.

2. Put the mussels in a large roasting pan; add the wine. Spoon the butter over the mussels and roast for 12 minutes, stirring the mussels and shaking the pan a few times, until all of the mussels have opened; discard any that do not open.

3. With a slotted spoon, transfer the mussels to bowls. Spoon the butter on top and serve. —*Sam Hayward*

**SERVE WITH** Hot crusty bread.

**WINE** Light, crisp white Burgundy.

## Amazing Stuffed Clams

**ACTIVE: 35 MIN; TOTAL: 1 HR 10 MIN**

**MAKES 30 STUFFED CLAMS** ●

- One 6-inch pepperoni, chopped
- One 2-ounce chorizo sausage, chopped
- 15 quahogs or chowder clams, scrubbed
- 1 pound sweet Italian sausage, casings removed
- 1 stick (4 ounces) unsalted butter
- ½ cup minced onion
- ½ cup minced celery
- ½ cup minced green bell pepper
- 6 cups dry finely diced bread

1. Preheat the oven to 350°. Put the pepperoni and chorizo in a food processor and pulse until crumbly. Transfer to a bowl.

2. In a pot, boil 2 inches of water. Add the clams, cover and steam over high heat until open, 5 minutes. Transfer to a bowl. Pour the broth into a glass measuring cup, stopping when you reach the grit. Remove the clams from their shells; separate the shells and reserve. Discard the round muscles on both sides of each clam; quarter the clams; coarsely chop in a food processor.

3. In a large nonstick skillet, cook the sausage over moderate heat, breaking up the clumps; stir until no pink remains, about 5 minutes. Scrape into a large bowl.

4. Melt the butter in the skillet. Add the onion, celery and bell pepper and cook over moderately high heat, stirring occasionally, until softened and browned, 5 minutes. Add the reserved pepperoni and chorizo and cook, stirring, until heated through, 2 minutes. Scrape into the large bowl. Add the bread and clams and stir in 2 cups of the reserved clam broth. Lightly pack the stuffing into the shells.

5. Arrange the clams on 2 large baking sheets and cover with foil. Bake for 30 minutes. Uncover and bake 5 minutes longer, or until lightly browned and crisp on top. —*Linda and Martha Greenlaw*

**WINE** Fresh, fruity rosé.

### Sizzled Scallops

**TOTAL: 30 MIN**

4 SERVINGS ● ●

Chef Daniel Boulud of Daniel in New York City is famous for elaborate four-star dinners, but surprisingly, he's also a genius at creating fast one-dish meals with a French accent. Here he prepares a complete meal in a single skillet: crusty sea scallops, fresh green snow peas and golden potatoes.

1½ pounds large sea scallops
Salt and freshly ground pepper
3 tablespoons vegetable oil
2 large Yukon Gold potatoes (¾ pound), peeled and cut into 1-inch cubes
6 large scallions, cut into 1-inch lengths
1 teaspoon chopped rosemary
6 ounces snow peas, trimmed (2 cups)
2 tablespoons water

**1.** Season the scallops with salt and pepper. In a very large skillet, heat the oil until shimmering. Add the scallops to the skillet, evenly spaced apart. Add the potatoes in an even layer around the scallops and cook over high heat until the scallops are browned, about 3 minutes per side. Transfer the scallops to a plate.

**2.** Season the potatoes with salt and pepper and turn them over. Add the scallions and rosemary and cook over moderate heat, undisturbed, for 5 minutes. Add the snow peas to the skillet and cook, stirring a few times, until they are tender, about 3 minutes. Transfer the potatoes and snow peas to plates.

**3.** Add the water to the skillet along with the scallops and any accumulated juices and cook, stirring, until they are heated through, about 30 seconds. Spoon the scallops over the potatoes and snow peas, drizzle with pan juices and serve.
—*Daniel Boulud*

**WINE** Full-bodied, rich Pinot Gris.

### Steamed Mussels with Pesto and Tomatoes

**TOTAL: 30 MIN**

8 SERVINGS ● ●

2 cups basil leaves (from one 2-ounce bunch)
¼ cup coarsely chopped walnuts
5 garlic cloves, 4 thinly sliced
¼ cup freshly grated Parmesan cheese
¼ cup plus 2 tablespoons extra-virgin olive oil
4 tablespoons unsalted butter, softened
1 cup cherry or grape tomatoes, halved
Salt and freshly ground pepper
3 large shallots, thinly sliced
1 cup dry white wine
5 pounds mussels, scrubbed and debearded
Crusty bread, for serving

**1.** In a mini food processor, combine the basil, walnuts and whole garlic clove and pulse until fine. Add the Parmesan and 2 tablespoons of the olive oil; process until smooth. Transfer the pesto to a medium bowl and add the butter. Stir in the tomatoes and season with salt and pepper.

**2.** In a very large, deep skillet or large soup pot, heat the remaining ¼ cup of olive oil until shimmering. Add the shallots and sliced garlic and cook over high heat, stirring, until they are lightly golden, about 4 minutes. Add the white wine and a generous pinch each of salt and pepper and bring to a boil. Add the mussels and stir for 1 minute. Cover and cook, stirring occasionally, until all of the mussels are open, about 6 minutes. Discard any mussels that do not open. Add the pesto and tomatoes and stir until the butter is thoroughly melted and the mussels are evenly coated. Transfer the mussels and broth to bowls and serve with crusty bread.
—*Marc Murphy*

**WINE** Lively, tart Sauvignon Blanc.

### Steamed Mussels with Coconut Milk and Thai Chiles

**TOTAL: 40 MIN**

8 SERVINGS

This one-pot dish is perfect for parties because it requires so little cleanup. You simply steam plump mussels in lager, then toss them in a creamy, spicy, slightly tart sauce made with ginger, chiles, coconut milk and fresh lime juice. The result is a Thai-inflected version of the French classic.

4 garlic cloves, coarsely chopped
2 Thai chiles, thickly sliced
One 1½-inch piece of fresh ginger, peeled and coarsely chopped
1 cup cilantro leaves
Finely grated zest of 1 lime
¼ cup extra-virgin olive oil
Two 13½-ounce cans unsweetened coconut milk
Juice of 2 limes
Salt
One 11- to 12-ounce bottle lager
5 pounds mussels, scrubbed

**1.** In a food processor, combine the garlic, chiles, ginger, cilantro, lime zest and olive oil and process to a paste; transfer to a large bowl. Whisk in the coconut milk and lime juice and season with salt.

**2.** In a large soup pot, bring the lager to a boil over high heat. Boil until reduced to ½ cup, about 7 minutes. Add the mussels, cover and cook, shaking the pot a few times, until the mussels just begin to open, about 4 minutes.

**3.** Uncover the mussels and stir in the coconut milk mixture. Cover and cook, shaking the pot a few times, until all of the mussels have opened, about 8 minutes. Discard any that do not open. Spoon the mussels and broth into bowls and serve.
—*Tyler Florence*

**MAKE AHEAD** The recipe can be prepared through Step 1 and refrigerated overnight.

**WINE** Fruity, low-oak Chardonnay.

## Dungeness Crab Cioppino

**TOTAL: 1 HR 30 MIN**

**10 SERVINGS** ●

- ¾ cup extra-virgin olive oil
- 8 large garlic cloves, 6 finely chopped
- 3 jalapeños, seeded and minced
- 2 red bell peppers, finely chopped
- 1 large onion, finely chopped
- 1 large bay leaf
- 2 tablespoons tomato paste
- ½ cup dry red wine

One 28-ounce can peeled tomatoes, finely chopped, juices reserved

Four 8-ounce bottles clam broth

1½ cups water

Salt and freshly ground pepper

- ½ cup packed basil leaves
- ½ teaspoon crushed red pepper
- 4 steamed Dungeness crabs, about 2 pounds each (see Note)
- 24 littleneck clams, scrubbed
- 2 pounds firm, white-fleshed fish fillets such as halibut, skinned and cut into 1½-inch chunks
- 2 pounds large shrimp, shelled and deveined
- 2 pounds mussels, scrubbed
- 1 pound sea scallops, halved vertically if large

Crusty bread, for serving

**1.** In a very large soup pot, heat ¼ cup of the olive oil until shimmering. Add the chopped garlic, jalapeños, bell peppers, onion and bay leaf and cook over moderately high heat, stirring occasionally, until the vegetables soften and begin to brown, about 10 minutes. Add the tomato paste and cook, stirring, for 1 minute. Add the wine and cook until nearly evaporated, 1 minute. Add the tomatoes and their juices and cook over moderately high heat until slightly thickened, about 5 minutes. Add the clam broth and water, season lightly with salt and generously with pepper and bring to a boil. Simmer over moderate heat until reduced to 8 cups, about 20 minutes.

**2.** Meanwhile, in a mini food processor, combine the basil leaves with the whole garlic cloves and process until the garlic is finely chopped. Add the remaining ½ cup of olive oil and the crushed red pepper and process until smooth. Season the basil puree with salt and pepper.

**3.** Working over the sink, pull off the flap on the undersides of the crabs. Remove the top shells and discard. Pry out the brownish insides and pull off the feathery lungs and discard. Rinse the crab bodies in cold water and quarter them so that each piece has body and leg.

**4.** Add the crabs and clams to the pot. Cover and cook over high heat, stirring occasionally, until the clams begin to open, 5 minutes. Using tongs, transfer the crabs to a platter. Add the fish, shrimp, mussels and scallops to the pot, pushing them into the broth. Return the crabs to the pot, cover and cook, stirring occasionally, until the clams and mussels are open and the fish, shrimp and scallops are cooked through, 8 minutes. Discard the bay leaf and any clams and mussels that do not open.

**5.** Ladle the cioppino into deep bowls and drizzle each with some basil puree. Serve with crusty bread and pass the remaining basil puree. —*Michael Mina*

**NOTE** Have the fishmonger steam the crabs for you.

**MAKE AHEAD** The cioppino can be prepared through Step 1 and refrigerated for up to 3 days.

**WINE** Bright, tart Barbera.

## San Francisco Seafood Stew

**TOTAL: 30 MIN**

**4 SERVINGS** ● ●

Fisherman's Wharf in San Francisco can be touristy, but TV chef Bobby Flay goes there to eat "literally boatloads" of its famous seafood stews. Flay's version uses generous portions of fresh shrimp, littleneck clams and snapper quickly cooked in a tasty tomato broth spiked with wine.

- 2 tablespoons extra-virgin olive oil
- 1 large shallot, thinly sliced
- 2 large garlic cloves, minced
- ½ cup dry white wine
- 1½ cups chicken stock or low-sodium broth
- 1 cup bottled clam juice
- 1 cup drained, diced tomatoes (from one 15-ounce can)
- 2 thyme sprigs
- 1 bay leaf
- ½ teaspoon hot sauce, plus more for serving

Salt and freshly ground pepper

- 2 dozen littleneck clams, scrubbed
- ¾ pound snapper fillets, cut into 2-inch pieces
- ½ pound shelled and deveined medium shrimp
- 2 tablespoons unsalted butter
- 2 tablespoons coarsely chopped flat-leaf parsley

Sourdough toast, for serving

**1.** In a large soup pot, heat the olive oil. Add the shallot and garlic and cook over high heat, stirring, until they are softened, about 3 minutes. Add the wine and boil until it is reduced by half, about 3 minutes. Add the stock, clam juice, tomatoes, thyme, bay leaf and hot sauce and season with salt and pepper. Bring to a boil over high heat and cook until slightly reduced, about 10 minutes.

**2.** Add the clams, cover and cook just until most of them open, about 5 minutes. Add the snapper and shrimp, cover and simmer until they are cooked through and the remaining clams have opened, 2 to 3 minutes. Discard any clams that do not open. Discard the bay leaf. Using a slotted spoon, transfer the seafood to 4 bowls. Add the butter and parsley to the soup pot and cook over moderate heat for 1 minute, swirling the pot. Spoon the broth over the seafood and serve with sourdough toast. —*Bobby Flay*

**WINE** Fresh, minerally Vermentino.

SAN FRANCISCO
SEAFOOD STEW

## Salt-and-Pepper Crab

**TOTAL: 45 MIN**

**4 FIRST-COURSE SERVINGS** ●

- 1 Dungeness or Jonah crab (2½ to 3 pounds)
- 2 tablespoons vegetable oil
- 2 garlic cloves, minced

One 3-inch piece of fresh ginger, peeled and cut into slivers

- 1 shallot, minced
- 2 teaspoons kosher salt
- 1 teaspoon sugar
- 1 teaspoon soy sauce
- ½ teaspoon freshly ground black pepper
- ⅓ teaspoon crushed red pepper
- 3 tablespoons water
- 2 scallions, cut into 2-inch lengths
- 4 cilantro sprigs, coarsely chopped

**1.** In a large pot of boiling water, cook the crab until it turns pink, 8 to 10 minutes; drain. Remove and reserve the tomalley (the greenish liver). Using a large knife, crack the crab legs at the joints and quarter the body.

**2.** Heat the oil in a large skillet. Add the garlic, ginger and shallot and stir-fry until fragrant, about 15 seconds. Add the reserved tomalley and stir to break it up. Add the salt, sugar, soy sauce, black pepper, crushed red pepper and crab and stir-fry until the crab is evenly coated with the seasonings. Add the water and scallions and cook for 3 minutes. Transfer the crab to a bowl, garnish with the cilantro and serve with lots of napkins. *—Mai Pham*
**WINE** Zippy, fresh Pinot Bianco.

## Seafood Paella with Spinach and Arugula

**TOTAL: 30 MIN**

**4 TO 6 SERVINGS** ● ●

Quick-cooking Bomba rice (a short-grain white rice popular in Spain) has a distinctive chewiness that's perfect in recipes like this outrageously crusty and very fast seafood paella.

- ¼ cup extra-virgin olive oil
- 1 bunch scallions, thinly sliced
- 6 ounces baby spinach and arugula (4 packed cups)
- 2 cups Bomba rice (15 ounces) or other short-grain rice
- 7 cups low-sodium chicken broth
- 1 medium tomato, seeded and diced
- ½ teaspoon smoked paprika
- ¼ teaspoon saffron threads, crushed and mixed with 1 tablespoon water

Kosher salt and freshly ground pepper

- 1 pound peeled and deveined medium shrimp
- 1 pound mussels, scrubbed

**1.** Heat the olive oil in a deep 12-inch skillet. Add the scallions and cook over high heat for 1 minute, until barely softened. Add the spinach and arugula and cook, stirring, just until wilted, about 2 minutes. Add the rice and cook, stirring, until it's coated with the olive oil and the grains begin to turn a milky-white color, about 3 minutes.

**2.** Stir 3½ cups of the broth into the rice. Add the tomato, paprika, the saffron and its soaking water, 1 tablespoon of salt and ½ teaspoon of pepper; bring to a boil. Cook over moderately high heat, stirring occasionally, until some of the chicken broth has been absorbed, about 5 minutes. Add the remaining 3½ cups of broth and cook over moderately high heat, without stirring at all, until the level of liquid is just under the surface of the rice, about 8 minutes.

**3.** Working quickly, arrange the shrimp and mussels on top of the rice, tucking them slightly under the surface. Continue cooking over moderate heat until the shrimp curl and turn pink, the mussel shells open and the rice is tender and starting to sizzle and form a crust on the bottom of the skillet, about 10 minutes longer. Discard any mussels that do not open. Serve the paella at once. *—Amaryll Schwertner*
**WINE** Fresh, fruity rosé.

## Crab, Avocado and Sorrel Salad

**TOTAL: 30 MIN**

**4 SERVINGS** ● ●

Sorrel is a leafy green that resembles baby spinach and has a lively, mildly sour taste. It's a great complement to the delicate crab morsels and creamy avocado in this recipe. If you can't find sorrel, substitute the same amount of basil or ¼ cup of chopped fresh dill.

- ½ cup fresh carrot juice
- 1 small shallot, minced
- 1 tablespoon Champagne vinegar
- ¼ cup plus 2 tablespoons extra-virgin olive oil

Kosher salt and freshly ground pepper

- 1 tablespoon fresh lemon juice
- 2 tablespoons finely chopped red onion
- ¾ pound lump crabmeat, picked over
- 2 ounces coarsely shredded sorrel leaves (½ cup)
- 2 ripe Hass avocados, peeled and cut into ½-inch dice

**1.** In a small saucepan, combine the carrot juice and minced shallot and boil over moderate heat until the carrot juice is reduced to 2 tablespoons, about 6 minutes. Transfer the reduced carrot juice to a blender. Add the Champagne vinegar to the blender and let cool slightly, then puree until the dressing is smooth. With the machine on, slowly blend in 2 tablespoons of the olive oil. Season the vinaigrette with salt and pepper.

**2.** In a medium bowl, whisk the lemon juice with the remaining ¼ cup of olive oil. Add the onion, crab and sorrel and toss gently. Add the avocado, season with salt and pepper and gently fold together. Mound the salad on plates, drizzle the carrot vinaigrette around the salad and serve. *—Jerry Traunfeld*
**WINE** Zesty, fresh Albariño.

## Point Lookout Lobster Salad

**TOTAL: 30 MIN**

4 FIRST-COURSE OR 2 MAIN-COURSE SERVINGS ● ● ●

The best thing about this lemony, crunchy, celery-studded salad is that there's no mayonnaise to mask the lobster's natural sweetness. Instead, the lobster is dressed with olive oil and fresh lemon juice.

**Salt**

**Two 1½-pound lobsters**

½ cup peas

¼ cup extra-virgin olive oil

2½ tablespoons fresh lemon juice

½ cup thinly sliced celery

1 tablespoon coarsely chopped basil

1 teaspoon finely grated lemon zest

**Freshly ground white pepper**

**1.** Bring a large pot of water to a boil. Salt the water. Carefully add the live lobsters, cover and cook over high heat until they're bright red, 6 to 8 minutes. Using tongs, transfer the lobsters to a large bowl and let them cool slightly. Remove the rubber bands from the lobster claws, then crack the claws and knuckles and remove the meat. Using scissors, slit the tail shells and remove the meat. Remove the dark intestinal veins from the tails. Cut the lobster meat into ½-inch pieces.

**2.** In a small saucepan of boiling water, cook the peas until they are tender, about 2 minutes. Drain the peas well.

**3.** In a bowl, mix the olive oil, lemon juice, celery, basil and lemon zest. Add the lobster meat and the peas to the vinaigrette, then season the salad with salt and white pepper and toss. Mound the lobster salad on plates and serve at once.

*—Linda and Martha Greenlaw*

**MAKE AHEAD** The cooked lobster meat can be chilled before dressing, if you prefer. Serve the salad slightly chilled or at room temperature.

**WINE** Ripe, luxurious Chardonnay.

## Lobster and Pea Shoots with Butter-Fried Garlic and Ginger

**TOTAL: 35 MIN**

4 SERVINGS

**Two 1½-pound lobsters**

4 tablespoons unsalted butter

2 large garlic cloves, thinly sliced

3 tablespoons finely julienned fresh ginger

2 red Thai chiles, thinly sliced

**Salt**

3½ ounces pea shoots, or one 4-ounce bunch watercress, rinsed but not dried, thick stems discarded

½ cup finely shredded basil leaves

**Lemon wedges, for serving**

**1.** Bring a large pot of water to a boil. Carefully add the lobsters head first and cook until bright red, about 5 minutes. Using tongs, transfer to a bowl. Pour out all but ½ inch of the cooking water; set a steamer basket in the pot and cover with a lid.

**2.** When the lobsters are cool enough to handle, twist off the claws, then twist off and discard the heads. Using a large knife, cut the tails in half lengthwise and discard the intestinal veins. Loosen the meat in the tail shells, leaving it in the shell. Crack the claws so the meat can be removed easily. Remove the meat from the knuckles.

**3.** In a small saucepan, melt the butter over low heat. Skim off the foam. Add the garlic and cook until golden, about 4 minutes. Add the ginger and chiles and cook over moderate heat until fragrant, about 3 minutes. Season the butter with salt.

**4.** Bring the water in the pot to a simmer. Add the lobster pieces, cover and steam until heated through, about 1 minute.

**5.** Set a medium skillet over high heat. Add the pea shoots and toss until barely wilted, about 1 minute; transfer to a platter. Top with the lobster, garlic butter and basil and serve with lemon wedges.

*—Jean-Georges Vongerichten*

**WINE** Rich, complex white Burgundy.

## Seafood Newburg

**TOTAL: 25 MIN**

6 SERVINGS ●

This recipe is a variation on the classic lobster Newburg, with its sherry-spiked cream sauce. Here, scallops, haddock and shrimp have been added to the shellfish.

1 stick (4 ounces) unsalted butter

3 tablespoons all-purpose flour

2 cups light cream

½ cup dry sherry, such as fino or amontillado

½ teaspoon sweet paprika

**Pinch of freshly grated nutmeg**

½ pound sea scallops, halved horizontally

½ pound haddock or hake fillet, skinned and cut into 1½-inch pieces

½ pound medium shrimp, shelled and deveined

½ pound cooked lobster meat, cut into bite-size pieces

**Salt and freshly ground pepper**

**1.** Melt 4 tablespoons of the butter in a medium saucepan. Whisk in the flour and cook over low heat for 1 minute. Whisk in the cream and sherry and bring to a simmer over moderately high heat. Whisk the paprika and nutmeg into the cream sauce over low heat. Cook the sauce, whisking often, until no floury taste remains, about 5 minutes.

**2.** Meanwhile, in a large saucepan, melt the remaining 4 tablespoons of butter. Add the scallops and haddock and cook them over moderate heat, stirring gently, until the haddock starts to turn white, about 3 minutes. Add the shrimp and lobster and cook, stirring, for 2 minutes. Add the cream sauce and simmer over low heat until the seafood is cooked, about 3 minutes longer. Season the seafood with salt and pepper and serve. *—Diana Santospago*

**WINE** Rich, complex white Burgundy.

# shellfish

## Creamy Crab Stew

**TOTAL: 30 MIN**

**4 SERVINGS** ●

This outrageously creamy seafood stew can be made with various kinds of crab. Use Jonah crab, often marketed as peeky-toe, if it's available where you live. Cooks living south of New York City can substitute blue crab, and those living in the West can use Dungeness.

6 **tablespoons unsalted butter**
¼ **pound medium shrimp in their shells, coarsely chopped**
¼ **cup dry sherry**
2 **cups bottled clam juice**
1 **cup water**
1 **small onion, minced**
1 **garlic clove, minced**
2 **tablespoons sweet paprika**
¾ **teaspoon chipotle chile powder**
2 **tablespoons all-purpose flour**
½ **cup heavy cream**
**Salt and freshly ground pepper**
1 **pound lump crabmeat, picked over**
2 **cups steamed rice, for serving**
1 **tablespoon chopped flat-leaf parsley**

1. In a medium saucepan, melt 1 tablespoon of butter. Add the shrimp and cook over moderately high heat until they start to brown. Add the sherry and cook for 2 minutes. Add the clam juice and water; bring to a boil. Simmer over moderately low heat for 10 minutes. Strain the broth; you should have 2½ cups.

2. In a medium saucepan, melt 2 tablespoons of butter. Add the onion and garlic; cook over moderate heat until softened. Add the paprika and chile powder and cook, stirring, for 3 minutes. Stir in the flour.

3. Whisk the broth into the saucepan; cook until smooth, then bring to a boil. Simmer over low heat, whisking until just thickened, about 5 minutes. Stir in the cream and simmer for 5 minutes. Season the shellfish sauce with salt and pepper.

4. In a large skillet, melt the remaining 3 tablespoons of butter. Gently stir in the crab and cook over moderate heat, tossing a few times, until warmed through, about 4 minutes. Season with salt and pepper.

5. Spoon the steamed rice into shallow bowls. Ladle the shellfish sauce over the rice and top with the crab. Sprinkle with parsley and serve. —*Sam Hayward*

**WINE** Fruity, low-oak Chardonnay.

## Italian Seafood Salad with String Beans

**ACTIVE: 50 MIN; TOTAL: 1 HR 30 MIN**

**6 SERVINGS** ●

In this recipe, chef Michael Romano of New York City's Union Square Cafe sautés the seafood in several batches, deglazing the browned bits from the bottom of the skillet after each batch. He then combines the pan juices to create a luscious broth in which to marinate the cooked seafood before serving.

½ **cup extra-virgin olive oil**
¾ **pound shelled and deveined large shrimp**
**Salt and freshly ground black pepper**
1½ **teaspoons finely chopped garlic**
1 **cup water**
½ **pound cleaned squid, bodies cut crosswise into ½-inch-thick rings, tentacles halved lengthwise**
½ **pound bay scallops or quartered sea scallops**
1 **pound mussels, scrubbed and debearded**
1½ **pounds cockles, scrubbed**
3 **tablespoons fresh lemon juice**
1 **pound mixed yellow wax and green beans, ends trimmed, beans cut into 2-inch lengths**
2 **tablespoons shredded basil leaves**
1 **tablespoon minced flat-leaf parsley**
**Cayenne pepper**
**Lemon wedges, for serving**

1. In a large skillet, heat 1 tablespoon of the olive oil until shimmering. Add the shrimp, season with salt and black pepper and cook over high heat, stirring occasionally, for 1 minute. Add ½ teaspoon of the garlic and cook, stirring, until the shrimp are opaque, about 1 minute. Transfer the shrimp to a platter. Add the water to the skillet and cook over high heat, scraping up any browned bits stuck to the bottom of the pan. Pour the pan juices into a bowl and wipe out the skillet.

2. Heat 1 tablespoon of the olive oil in the skillet. Add the squid and scallops. Season with salt and black pepper and cook, stirring, for 1 minute. Add ½ teaspoon of the garlic and cook just until fragrant, about 1 minute longer. Transfer to the platter.

3. Pour the reserved pan juices into the skillet and cook over high heat, scraping up any browned bits from the bottom. Add the mussels, cockles and the remaining ½ teaspoon of garlic and bring to a boil. Cover and cook over high heat until the shells open, about 5 minutes. Using a slotted spoon, transfer the mussels and cockles to a large bowl; discard any that do not open. When cool enough to handle, remove the meat and add it to the platter.

4. Pour any accumulated shellfish juices into the skillet and bring the liquid to a boil. Simmer over moderate heat until reduced to ¼ cup. Pour the liquid into a large bowl. Add the lemon juice and the remaining olive oil and let cool. Stir in all of the seafood and let marinate in the refrigerator for 30 minutes.

5. Meanwhile, in a medium saucepan of boiling salted water, cook the beans until crisp-tender, about 5 minutes. Drain and cool under running water; pat dry. Add the beans, basil and parsley to the seafood salad. Season with salt and cayenne and serve with lemon wedges. —*Michael Romano*

**SERVE WITH** Salad greens.

**WINE** Fresh, lively Soave.

ITALIAN SEAFOOD SALAD
WITH STRING BEANS

Chef Thomas Keller of New York City's Per Se (here with protégé Jonathan Benno, at right) invented a quick recipe for Heirloom Tomatoes Stuffed with Summer Succotash (P. 224), featured in the August issue.

# vegetables

**EGGPLANT CAPONATA**

**SARDINIAN STUFFED EGGPLANT**

## Eggplant Caponata

ACTIVE: 20 MIN; TOTAL: 1 HR

4 SERVINGS ● ●

Sicily's caponata is a tangy eggplant salad that is served as a side dish or appetizer. This version departs from tradition by adding bits of velvety avocado.

- 2 **tablespoons brined capers, drained**
- ¼ **cup extra-virgin olive oil**
- One 1-pound eggplant, peeled and **cut into ⅓-inch dice**
- 1 **medium onion, finely chopped**
- 1 **celery rib, finely chopped**
- 1 **medium tomato, finely chopped**
- 2 **tablespoons red wine vinegar**
- 2 **teaspoons sugar**
- 1 **teaspoon pine nuts**
- **Salt and freshly ground pepper**
- 1 **Hass avocado, diced**

1. In a small bowl, cover the capers with water and let soak for 15 minutes; drain.
2. Meanwhile, in a large skillet, heat 3 tablespoons of the olive oil. Add the eggplant and cook over moderately high heat until the bottom browns, 5 minutes. Stir and cook until browned all over, 10 minutes longer. Transfer the eggplant to a bowl.
3. Add the remaining 1 tablespoon of olive oil, the onion and celery to the skillet. Cover and cook over low heat, stirring occasionally, for 10 minutes. Add the tomato, cover and cook until soft, about 5 minutes.
4. In a saucepan, simmer the vinegar and sugar to dissolve the sugar. Add the pine nuts and capers and cook for 1 minute.
5. Return the eggplant to the pan. Stir in the vinegar and cook over low heat for 3 minutes. Season with salt and pepper; transfer to a bowl. Let cool, then fold in the avocado.
—*Eugenia Giobbi Bone and Edward Giobbi*

## Sardinian Stuffed Eggplant

ACTIVE: 1 HR; TOTAL: 2 HR

6 SERVINGS ● ●

Efisio Farris, the executive chef at Arcodoro in Houston, says that his mother used only eggplants from the first pick of the season (*le primizie*) for this dish because of their supple texture and earthy-sweet flavor without a hint of bitterness. But if you don't have the *primizie* option, you should seek out firm, heavy eggplants with smooth, evenly colored skin. Check for ripeness by pressing them lightly; if this leaves an imprint, the eggplant is ready to use.

- **Five 1-pound Italian eggplants, 3 halved lengthwise**
- **Kosher salt**
- 4 **tablespoons extra-virgin olive oil**
- 1 **medium white onion, finely chopped**

2 small bay leaves, crushed
  to a powder
½ cup dry white wine
½ pound ground veal
1 cup freshly grated fresh
  pecorino cheese, preferably
  Fiore Sardo (4 ounces)
2 large eggs, lightly beaten
½ cup plain dry bread crumbs
Pinch of freshly grated nutmeg
1 tablespoon chopped basil
1 tablespoon chopped mint
Freshly ground pepper
3 garlic cloves, thickly sliced
One 35-ounce can Italian
  peeled tomatoes, drained
  and coarsely chopped

1. Peel the 2 whole eggplants; coarsely chop the flesh and transfer to a large colander. Using a spoon, scoop out the flesh from the 6 eggplant halves, leaving a ¼-inch-thick shell to hold the eggplant stuffing. Chop the scooped-out flesh and add it to the colander with the other eggplant. Toss all of the chopped eggplant with 2 tablespoons of kosher salt and let it drain for 30 minutes, then rinse it well. Working with handfuls of the chopped eggplant, squeeze out as much of the water as possible. You should have about 4 cups of chopped eggplant.

2. Meanwhile, bring a large pot of salted water to a boil. Set a wire rack on a baking sheet. Add the 6 eggplant shells to the pot and cook, gently poking them under to keep them submerged, until just tender, about 3 minutes. Using a slotted spoon, transfer the eggplant shells to the wire rack to drain and cool. Lightly oil a 9-by-13-inch baking dish and arrange the eggplant shells in it, cut side up.

3. In a large, deep skillet, heat 3 tablespoons of the olive oil until shimmering. Add the onion and bay leaves and cook over moderate heat until the onion is softened, about 5 minutes. Add the chopped eggplant and wine to the skillet and cook over moderate heat, stirring occasionally, until the eggplant is tender and just beginning to brown, 15 minutes. Add the veal and cook over moderately high heat, stirring and breaking up the meat, until it is cooked through and lightly browned, about 5 minutes longer. Transfer the eggplant filling to a bowl and stir in ½ cup of the pecorino, the eggs, bread crumbs, nutmeg, basil and mint. Season the filling with salt and pepper. Spoon the filling into the eggplant shells in the baking dish.

4. Preheat the oven to 350°. In a medium saucepan, heat the remaining 1 tablespoon of olive oil. Add the garlic and cook over moderate heat until golden, about 1 minute. Add the chopped tomatoes and cook over moderate heat, stirring, until thickened, about 10 minutes. Season the tomatoes with salt and pepper. Spoon half of the sauce over the eggplant and sprinkle with the remaining ½ cup of grated pecorino. Bake the stuffed eggplant until browned and bubbling, about 35 minutes. Let cool slightly, then serve. Pass the remaining tomato sauce on the side. —Efisio Farris

**MAKE AHEAD** The baked stuffed eggplant can be refrigerated overnight. Let the eggplant return to room temperature, then reheat in a 325° oven.

### Garlicky Eggplant Salad with Tomato Sauce
**ACTIVE: 35 MIN; TOTAL: 1 HR**
**6 SERVINGS** ● ●
Like many Moroccan salads, this supersmooth and intensely flavored version of ratatouille is made from spiced or sweetened cooked vegetables that are mashed rather than cut into pieces. Like Italian antipasti, Moroccan salads are often served as an appetizer.

2 pounds small eggplants—
  peeled, quartered lengthwise,
  then halved crosswise
6 medium garlic cloves, halved
2 tablespoons extra-virgin
  olive oil
One 28-ounce can peeled Italian
  plum tomatoes, coarsely
  chopped, juices reserved
½ cup coarsely chopped
  cilantro
1 teaspoon ground cumin
1 teaspoon sweet paprika
⅛ teaspoon crushed red pepper
2 tablespoons fresh lemon juice
Kosher salt and freshly
  ground pepper

1. In a large saucepan fitted with a large steamer basket, bring ½ inch of water to a simmer. Add the eggplant and garlic to the steamer. Cover the saucepan and steam the eggplant over moderate heat until tender, about 20 minutes.

2. Meanwhile, in a large, deep skillet, heat the olive oil. Add the chopped tomatoes and their juices along with the chopped cilantro, ground cumin, ground paprika and crushed red pepper. Cook the tomatoes over moderately high heat, stirring occasionally, until they are thickened, about 15 minutes.

3. Drain the steamed eggplant and garlic in a colander, pressing gently to extract any excess water. Transfer the eggplant and garlic to a bowl. Finely mash the garlic with a fork and coarsely mash the eggplant with a fork, then scrape them both into the tomato sauce. Add the fresh lemon juice and simmer over moderate heat for 5 minutes, stirring a few times. Season the eggplant with salt and pepper and transfer to a serving bowl. Serve the eggplant salad at room temperature or slightly chilled. —Anissa Helou

**SERVE WITH** Warm pita bread or sliced Moroccan Olive Bread (p. 270).

**MAKE AHEAD** The eggplant salad can be prepared early in the day and stored in an airtight container at room temperature. If you prefer to serve the salad chilled, it can also be refrigerated.

## Creamy Eggplant with Green Peas

**ACTIVE: 40 MIN; TOTAL: 1 HR 5 MIN**

**12 SERVINGS** ● ●

Cookbook author Neelam Batra's American friends so love her eggplant dish, flavored with turmeric, fenugreek seeds and chiles, that now she can't imagine preparing it the classic Indian way, seasoned simply with salt and pepper.

Six 1¼-pound eggplants
¼ cup vegetable oil
2 teaspoons cumin seeds
1 large Spanish onion, minced
3 jalapeños, minced with some seeds
3 large garlic cloves, minced
2½ tablespoons peeled, minced fresh ginger
2 dried red chiles, broken
6 medium tomatoes, finely chopped
1½ teaspoons ground fenugreek seeds
1 teaspoon paprika
¾ teaspoon turmeric
One 15-ounce package frozen peas, thawed (2½ cups)
2 cups chopped cilantro
¾ cup plain yogurt
Salt
½ teaspoon garam masala

1. Preheat the oven to 500°. Put the eggplants on 2 rimmed baking sheets and pierce them all over with the tip of a small knife. Bake for about 1 hour, or until the skin is blackened and the flesh is very soft. Let cool slightly. Peel off the skin and scrape the flesh into a large bowl, then mash coarsely.
2. Meanwhile, heat the oil in a large, deep skillet. Add the cumin seeds and cook over high heat until they sizzle, about 10 seconds. Add the onion and cook, stirring occasionally, until softened and starting to brown, about 10 minutes. Add the jalapeños, garlic, ginger and chiles and cook, stirring, until fragrant, about 3 minutes. Add the tomatoes and boil until all the liquid has evaporated, about 8 minutes. Add the fenugreek, paprika and turmeric and cook, stirring, until fragrant, about 3 minutes. Stir in the eggplant and cook over low heat for 10 minutes to blend the flavors. Add the peas and cook for 5 minutes longer. Stir in the cilantro and yogurt and season with salt. Transfer the eggplant to a bowl and sprinkle with the garam masala. Serve hot. *—Neelam Batra*

**MAKE AHEAD** The recipe can be refrigerated overnight.

## Quick-Braised Eggplant with Coconut Milk and Scallions

**TOTAL: 25 MIN**

**6 SERVINGS** ● ●

Adding unsweetened coconut milk to the eggplant after it's been stir-fried keeps the texture silky.

¼ cup canola oil
1 medium onion, quartered lengthwise and thinly sliced crosswise
2 teaspoons minced garlic
1¼ pounds Asian or Italian eggplants (about 4), cut into 3-by-½-inch pieces
¼ cup Chinese cooking wine, sake or water
½ cup Vietnamese Stir-Fry Sauce (p. 240)
½ cup plus 2 tablespoons water
¼ cup unsweetened coconut milk, stirred just before using
2 teaspoons Asian chili paste
4 large scallions, white and tender green parts only, cut into ¾-inch lengths

Heat the oil in a large skillet or a wok until small puffs of smoke begin to appear. Add the onion and garlic and stir-fry over high heat until the onion is crisp-tender, about 1 minute. Add the eggplant and stir-fry until browned in spots and just tender, about 5 minutes. Add the cooking wine and cook until nearly evaporated, about 1 minute. Add the Vietnamese Stir-Fry Sauce, water, coconut milk and chili paste. Cook over high heat, stirring occasionally, until the eggplant is very tender and the sauce is slightly reduced, about 5 minutes. Add the scallions and cook for 30 seconds. Serve hot. *—Charles Phan*

**SERVE WITH** Steamed jasmine rice.

**MAKE AHEAD** The eggplant can be refrigerated overnight. Reheat gently on the stovetop before serving.

## Fried Green Tomatoes

**TOTAL: 25 MIN**

**6 SERVINGS** ●

When firm, tart green tomatoes are coated in bread crumbs and Parmesan cheese, then pan-fried, they become amazingly crispy on the outside and warm and juicy on the inside. If green tomatoes are difficult to find, fresh tomatillos make an excellent substitute.

¼ cup all-purpose flour
Salt and freshly ground pepper
2 large eggs, beaten
⅔ cup plain dry bread crumbs
⅓ cup freshly grated Parmesan cheese
1 pound green tomatoes or large tomatillos, sliced ½ inch thick
½ cup extra-virgin olive oil
Old Bay Seasoning, for serving
Hot sauce, for serving

1. In a medium bowl, season the flour with salt and pepper. Put the eggs in another medium bowl and toss the bread crumbs and grated Parmesan in a third bowl. Dredge the tomato slices in the flour, then coat them with the egg, letting any excess drip back into the bowl. Coat with the bread crumbs, pressing to help them adhere.
2. In a large nonstick skillet, heat the olive oil until shimmering. Add the breaded tomatoes in a single layer and cook them over moderately high heat, turning once, until deeply golden and crisp, 5 to 6 minutes. Transfer the tomato slices to paper towel–lined plates. Sprinkle with salt and Old Bay and serve immediately, with hot sauce. *—Laurent Tourondel*

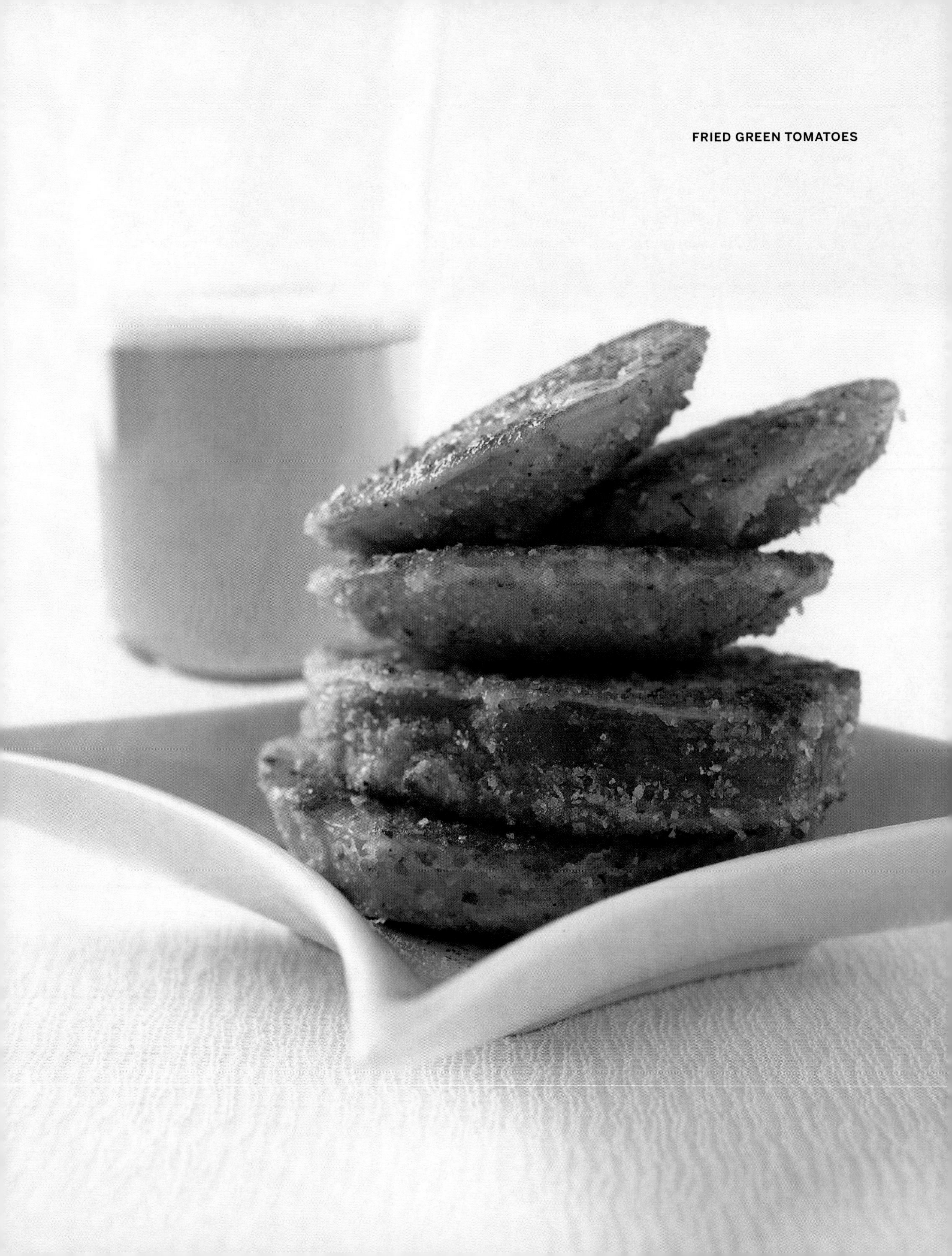
FRIED GREEN TOMATOES

### Heirloom Tomatoes Stuffed with Summer Succotash

**TOTAL: 35 MIN**

4 SERVINGS ● ●

- ¾ cup shelled lima beans (4 ounces)
- 1 large ear of corn, kernels cut off the cob (about ¾ cup)
- 8 firm, ripe heirloom tomatoes (about 5 ounces each)
- 1 tablespoon extra-virgin olive oil, plus more for brushing

Salt and freshly ground pepper

- 1 tablespoon unsalted butter
- 1 medium red or yellow bell pepper, finely diced
- 1½ tablespoons snipped chives

1. Preheat the oven to 425°. Bring a large saucepan of salted water to a boil. Add the lima beans and corn and boil until tender, about 3 minutes. Drain the beans and corn, transfer to a bowl and let cool.

2. Slice off the bottom of each tomato so it sits flat. Using a knife, cut around the center of each tomato to form a cone that can easily be removed once the tomato is baked. Brush the tomatoes with olive oil and set them in a large pie plate, cut side up. Season the tomatoes with salt and pepper and roast just until tender, about 5 minutes. Let cool slightly, then spoon out and discard the centers.

3. Meanwhile, in a large skillet, melt 1½ teaspoons of the butter in the 1 table-spoon of olive oil. Add the bell pepper and cook over moderately high heat, stirring occasionally, until crisp-tender, about 3 minutes. Add the limas and corn and cook, stirring, for 2 minutes. Remove from the heat. Stir in the remaining 1½ teaspoons of butter and the chives and season with salt and pepper. Spoon the succotash into the tomatoes and serve warm or at room temperature.
—*Thomas Keller*

**MAKE AHEAD** The stuffed tomatoes can be prepared early in the day; let stand at room temperature.

### Warm Mushroom and Bacon Salad

**TOTAL: 50 MIN**

8 SERVINGS

- ¼ cup plus 2 tablespoons vegetable oil
- 2 shallots, thinly sliced
- ¼ cup sherry vinegar
- 1½ teaspoons Dijon mustard

Salt and freshly ground pepper

- ½ pound bacon, sliced ¼ inch thick and cut into 1-inch matchsticks
- ¼ cup extra-virgin olive oil
- 1 pound oyster mushrooms, thickly sliced
- 1 garlic clove, thinly sliced
- 1 pound cremini mushrooms, thickly sliced
- 1 pound frisée, torn into bite-size pieces

1. In a small skillet, heat 1 tablespoon of the vegetable oil. Add half of the shallots and cook over moderately low heat, stirring frequently, until softened and golden, about 10 minutes. Add the vinegar and cook over moderately high heat until reduced by half, about 5 minutes. Transfer the contents of the skillet to a blender and let cool. Add the mustard and blend until smooth. With the machine on, add the remaining ¼ cup plus 1 tablespoon of vegetable oil in a thin stream and blend until emulsified. Season the dressing with salt and pepper.

2. In a large skillet, fry the bacon over moderately high heat until crisp, about 7 minutes. Drain the bacon on paper towels. Pour off the fat from the skillet. Add 2 tablespoons of the olive oil to the pan and heat until shimmering. Add the oyster mushrooms and garlic and cook over moderate heat, stirring occasionally, until the mushrooms are tender and browned, about 8 minutes. Scrape the mushrooms into a large bowl.

3. Heat the remaining 2 tablespoons of olive oil in the skillet. Add the cremini mushrooms and the remaining shallots and cook over moderate heat until golden and tender, about 10 minutes. Add the cremini mushrooms and shallots to the bowl and season with salt and pepper. Add the frisée, the cooked bacon and the vinaigrette, season with salt and pepper and toss. Transfer the salad to plates and serve right away. —*Marc Murphy*

### Garlicky Wild Mushroom Sauté

**TOTAL: 30 MIN**

8 SERVINGS ● ● ●

- 6 tablespoons extra-virgin olive oil
- 1 pound oyster mushrooms, tough stems trimmed, large mushrooms halved
- ¾ pound shiitake mushrooms, stems discarded, caps quartered
- ½ pound chanterelle mushrooms, halved
- ½ pound enoki mushrooms

Salt and freshly ground pepper

- 1 large garlic clove, thinly sliced
- 1 teaspoon crushed red pepper
- 3 tablespoons dry sherry

1. Heat 2 large skillets over high heat. Add 2 tablespoons of olive oil to each skillet and heat until shimmering. Add half of the oyster, shiitake, chanterelle and enoki mushrooms to each skillet. Season with salt and pepper and cook without stirring until browned on the bottom, about 4 minutes. Stir and cook until browned all over, about 3 minutes. Reduce the heat to moderate and cook until all of the mushrooms are tender, about 3 minutes longer. Transfer to a platter.

2. Add the remaining 2 tablespoons of olive oil to one of the skillets and heat until shimmering. Add the garlic and crushed red pepper and cook over low heat until the garlic is golden, about 1 minute. Add the sherry and bring to a simmer; pour over the mushrooms, season with salt and pepper and toss. Serve the mushrooms warm or at room temperature.
—*Victoria Amory*

**SERVE WITH** Toasted baguette slices.

## White Asparagus and Ham Gratin

**ACTIVE: 30 MIN; TOTAL: 1 HR**

6 SERVINGS

Like a frugal Alsatian housewife, Jean-Georges Vongerichten, chef and owner of restaurants in New York City, London, Paris and elsewhere, uses the asparagus peels to make a fragrant broth.

- 2 pounds fat white or green asparagus, peeled and tied into 6 bundles, peels reserved

Salt

- 3 tablespoons unsalted butter
- 3 tablespoons all-purpose flour

Freshly ground pepper

- 1 teaspoon fresh lemon juice

Pinch of freshly grated nutmeg

- 6 thin slices of smoked ham, such as Virginia ham or Black Forest
- 1 cup shredded Comté or Gruyère cheese (¼ pound)

**1.** Preheat the oven to 350° and lightly butter a 9-by-13-inch shallow baking dish. Bring 8 cups of water to a boil in a very large, deep skillet. Add the asparagus peels and salt the water. Add the asparagus bundles to the skillet and cook over high heat until tender, about 12 minutes. Transfer the asparagus to a platter and pat dry. Strain the asparagus broth into a large glass measuring cup.

**2.** Melt the butter in a medium saucepan. Whisk in the flour and cook over moderately high heat for 1 minute. Add 1½ cups of the asparagus broth and cook over moderate heat, whisking constantly, until the sauce thickens, about 5 minutes. Season the sauce with salt, pepper, lemon juice and nutmeg.

**3.** Remove the strings from the asparagus and loosely roll a slice of ham around each bundle. Transfer the bundles to the baking dish and pour the sauce on top. Sprinkle with the cheese and bake in the upper third of the oven for about 25 minutes, or until the cheese is melted and the sauce is bubbling. —*Jean-Georges Vongerichten*

## Two-Cheese Moussaka with Sautéed Mushrooms and Zucchini

**ACTIVE: 1 HR; TOTAL: 2 HR 45 MIN**

12 SERVINGS ●

Rock musician Dave Matthews loves making this casserole, with layers of roasted zucchini, mushrooms, tomato sauce, feta and provolone. It's his version of the Croatian moussaka in *Moosewood Cookbook*.

- ½ cup extra-virgin olive oil
- 2 large onions, coarsely chopped
- 1 large garlic clove, minced

One 28-ounce can whole tomatoes, chopped, juices reserved

- 2 tablespoons tomato paste
- 2 cups water
- 2 tablespoons finely chopped basil

Salt and freshly ground pepper

- 2 pounds cremini mushrooms, thinly sliced
- ½ cup dry white wine
- 2 tablespoons tamari soy sauce
- 2 tablespoons finely chopped dill
- 2 pounds zucchini, sliced crosswise ½ inch thick
- ⅔ pound dried lasagna noodles (about 15 noodles)
- 6 large eggs, beaten
- 1 pound feta cheese, crumbled
- ¼ pound provolone cheese, shredded

**1.** Preheat the oven to 450°. In a large saucepan, heat 2 tablespoons of the olive oil until shimmering. Add one-fourth of the onions and the garlic and cook over moderately high heat, stirring occasionally, until softened. Add the tomatoes and their juices, the tomato paste and water and bring to a boil. Simmer the sauce over moderate heat until reduced to 4 cups, about 20 minutes. Stir in the basil; season with salt and pepper.

**2.** In a large, deep skillet, heat ¼ cup of the olive oil. Add the mushrooms, season with salt and pepper and cook over high heat until the mushrooms begin to brown, about 8 minutes. Add the remaining chopped onions and cook, stirring occasionally, until softened, about 5 minutes longer. Add the wine and tamari and boil until the liquid has reduced, about 5 minutes. Add the dill.

**3.** Toss the zucchini with the remaining 2 tablespoons of olive oil and season with salt and pepper. Spread the zucchini on a baking sheet and roast for about 10 minutes, until golden on the bottom and softened. Lower the oven to 350°.

**4.** Spread ½ cup of the tomato sauce in a 10½-by-14-inch baking dish. Arrange one-third of the uncooked noodles on the sauce, overlapping them slightly. Top with another ½ cup of sauce, one-third of the mushrooms and half of the zucchini; season with salt and pepper. Repeat with another ½ cup of sauce, another layer of noodles, ½ cup of sauce, one-third of the mushrooms and the remaining zucchini; season again. Top with ½ cup of sauce and the remaining noodles, then cover with the remaining sauce and mushrooms. Press the moussaka down slightly.

**5.** In a bowl, whisk the eggs with the feta; pour over the mushrooms. Season with pepper and sprinkle with the provolone. Bake the moussaka for about 45 minutes, until the top is golden. Cover with foil and bake for 25 minutes longer, or until piping hot in the center. Uncover and let rest for 20 minutes before serving. —*Dave Matthews*

**MAKE AHEAD** The moussaka can be refrigerated overnight.

# technique
## MUSHROOM PREP

Just before using, clean mushrooms by **wiping them** gently with a damp cloth or paper towel, or rinse them briefly under cold running water and dry them immediately. **Do not soak them** in water because they quickly absorb liquid. For hard-to-reach dirt, clean mushrooms with a soft brush (a small paintbrush works well).

**LEEKS ROMESCO WITH CRUMBLED GARROTXA CHEESE**

**CAULIFLOWER GRATIN WITH MANCHEGO AND ALMOND SAUCE**

## Leeks Romesco with Crumbled Garrotxa Cheese

**ACTIVE: 35 MIN; TOTAL: 1 HR**

**4 TO 6 SERVINGS** ●

Inspired by a traditional Catalan dish that pairs tart *romesco* sauce with a sweet Spanish green onion, this salad highlights the mildly earthy flavor of Garrotxa, a semi-soft Catalan goat's-milk cheese.

- 1 small red bell pepper
- ½ cup plus 2 tablespoons extra-virgin olive oil, plus more for brushing
- ¼ cup blanched whole unsalted almonds
- ½ cup firm-textured white-bread cubes (¼ inch), without crusts
- 2 garlic cloves, smashed
- 2 plum tomatoes—peeled, seeded and coarsely chopped
- 3 tablespoons sherry vinegar

Salt and cayenne pepper

- 6 medium leeks, white and tender green parts only, halved lengthwise
- ¼ cup chicken stock or low-sodium broth
- 4 ounces crumbled Garrotxa or other tangy semi-aged goat's-milk cheese (1 cup)

Crusty sourdough bread, for serving

**1.** Lightly brush the bell pepper with olive oil and roast it directly over a gas flame or under the broiler, turning frequently, until charred all over. Transfer to a bowl, cover with plastic wrap and let stand for 15 minutes. Peel, core and seed the pepper and cut it into thick strips.

**2.** Meanwhile, in a medium skillet, heat 1 tablespoon of the olive oil until shimmering. Add the almonds and cook over moderate heat, stirring constantly, until they are golden, about 5 minutes. Transfer the almonds to a cutting board and let cool slightly, then coarsely chop.

# vegetables

3. Heat 1 tablespoon of the olive oil in the skillet. Add the bread cubes and cook over moderate heat, stirring frequently, until golden and crisp, about 5 minutes. Transfer to a plate. Heat another tablespoon of the olive oil in the skillet. Add the bell pepper strips and garlic and cook, stirring occasionally, until the garlic is lightly golden and softened, about 5 minutes. Add the tomatoes and cook for 1 minute longer. Transfer to a large mortar or food processor and let cool.

4. Add the fried almonds to the bell pepper mixture and, using a pestle, pound the mixture to a coarse paste, or pulse it in the food processor. Add the toasted bread cubes and 1 tablespoon of the olive oil, then pound and stir, or pulse, until the sauce is emulsified. Gradually add ¼ cup of olive oil, stirring and pounding, or pulsing, until the sauce is emulsified. Stir in 2 tablespoons of the sherry vinegar and season with salt and cayenne.

5. In a large, deep skillet, heat the remaining 2 tablespoons of olive oil until shimmering. Add the leeks and cook over moderate heat, turning occasionally, until they are lightly browned and barely softened, about 10 minutes. Add the chicken stock and the remaining 1 tablespoon of sherry vinegar to the leeks, season with salt and cayenne and bring to a boil. Cover the leeks and cook over moderate heat until tender, 10 to 12 minutes longer. Let the leeks cool, then drain them.

6. Arrange the braised leeks on a large platter. Spoon half of the *romesco* sauce over the leeks. Sprinkle the crumbled Garrotxa cheese on top and serve with crusty bread and the remaining *romesco* sauce on the side. —*Grace Parisi*

**MAKE AHEAD** The *romesco* sauce can be refrigerated for up to 4 days and the cooked leeks can be refrigerated overnight. Let the sauce and leeks return to room temperature before assembling the dish and serving.

## Cauliflower Gratin with Manchego and Almond Sauce
**ACTIVE: 30 MIN; TOTAL: 1 HR**
6 SERVINGS ●
- ¾ cup half-and-half
- ½ cup plus 2 tablespoons whole roasted almonds with skin (3 ounces), 2 tablespoons coarsely chopped
- 4 tablespoons unsalted butter
- 2 tablespoons all-purpose flour
- 1 cup whole milk
- ¾ cup plus 2 tablespoons finely shredded Manchego or other mildly nutty semi-aged sheep's- or cow's-milk cheese (3½ ounces), such as Gouda

Pinch of freshly grated nutmeg
Salt and freshly ground pepper
One 2-pound head cauliflower, cut into 1½-inch florets
- 1 medium onion, finely chopped
- ¼ teaspoon Pimentón de la Vera (smoked Spanish paprika)

1. Preheat the oven to 400°. In a saucepan, heat the half-and-half until steaming, then transfer it to a food processor or blender. Add the ½ cup of whole almonds and process until finely ground. Let stand for 10 minutes. Strain the half-and-half through a fine sieve set over a bowl, pressing on the almonds to extract as much liquid as possible. Discard the ground almonds.

2. In a medium saucepan, melt 2 tablespoons of the butter. Add the flour and whisk over moderately high heat for 1 minute. Add the milk and the half-and-half and cook, whisking constantly, until thickened, 5 minutes. Remove from the heat. Add ¾ cup of the Manchego and whisk until melted. Whisk in the nutmeg; season with salt and pepper. Keep warm.

3. In a large skillet, bring ½ inch of salted water to a boil. Add the cauliflower, cover and cook over high heat until crisp-tender, about 4 minutes. Drain the cauliflower in a colander. Wipe out the skillet.

4. Melt the remaining butter in the skillet. Add the onion and cook over moderately high heat, stirring, until lightly browned, 5 minutes. Add the cauliflower and cook, stirring, until lightly golden, 2 minutes. Season lightly with salt and pepper. Transfer to a 7-by-10-inch glass or ceramic baking dish; spread the sauce on top.

5. Sprinkle the gratin with the remaining cheese, the 2 tablespoons of chopped almonds and the paprika and bake in the center of the oven for 20 minutes, or until bubbling and browned on top. Let stand for 10 minutes before serving. —*Grace Parisi*

**MAKE AHEAD** This dish can be prepared through Step 4 and refrigerated overnight. Bring to room temperature before baking.

## Cauliflower in a Caper Vinaigrette
**TOTAL: 20 MIN**
4 SERVINGS ● ●
Andy Nusser, executive chef and co-owner of Casa Mono in New York City, loves the tangy flavor of marinated vegetables. But when he's pressed for time, he tosses cooked vegetables (like the cauliflower here) with a vinaigrette, then serves them at room temperature.
- 1 head cauliflower (about 1¾ pounds), cut into 1-inch florets
- 2 tablespoons drained capers, chopped
- 1 large garlic clove, minced
- 1 shallot, minced
- 2 tablespoons red wine vinegar
- ¼ cup extra-virgin olive oil

Salt
Cayenne pepper

1. In a large saucepan of boiling salted water, cook the cauliflower florets until they are crisp-tender, 5 to 6 minutes. Drain the cauliflower well and pat dry.

2. In a medium bowl, mix the capers, garlic, shallot and vinegar. Whisk in the olive oil and season with salt and cayenne. Add the cauliflower and toss to coat. Serve warm or at room temperature. —*Andy Nusser*

### Tender Artichoke Heart Stew with Peas

**ACTIVE: 30 MIN; TOTAL: 1 HR**

8 SERVINGS ●

- 1 lemon, halved
- 6 large artichokes
- 1 bay leaf

Salt

- ¼ cup extra-virgin olive oil
- 4 garlic cloves, thinly sliced
- 1 small onion, thinly sliced
- 1½ teaspoons all-purpose flour
- 1 cup dry white wine
- ½ cup finely julienned serrano ham
- 1 cup frozen peas

Freshly ground pepper

**1.** Fill a large bowl with water and squeeze the juice from a lemon half into it. Working with 1 artichoke at a time, snap off the tough outer leaves. Using a sharp knife, cut off the top two-thirds of the leaves and trim the base and stem. Using a melon baller or teaspoon, scrape out the hairy choke. Rub the remaining lemon half all over the artichoke, then add the artichoke to the lemon water. Repeat with the remaining artichokes.

**2.** Bring a medium saucepan of water to a boil. Add the bay leaf, a large pinch of salt and the drained artichoke hearts. Simmer over moderate heat until tender, about 15 minutes. Drain and cut each artichoke heart into 8 wedges.

**3.** In a skillet, heat the olive oil. Add the garlic and onion and cook over moderate heat until softened, 4 minutes. Stir in the flour, then stir in the wine until smooth. Add the serrano ham and artichoke wedges and simmer over low heat, stirring occasionally to blend the flavors, 5 minutes. Add the peas and simmer until heated through, 5 minutes. Season with salt and pepper and serve. —*Victoria Amory*

**MAKE AHEAD** The artichokes can be prepared through Step 2 and refrigerated overnight. Bring to room temperature before proceeding.

### Braised Artichoke Hearts with Vegetables

**ACTIVE: 25 MIN; TOTAL: 1 HR 25 MIN**

4 SERVINGS ● ●

- ½ lemon, plus 1½ tablespoons fresh lemon juice
- 4 large artichokes
- 1 carrot, cut into ¼-inch dice
- 1 medium Yukon Gold potato, peeled and cut into ¼-inch dice
- ¾ cup frozen baby peas
- ½ small onion, peeled
- ¼ cup extra-virgin olive oil
- 1 teaspoon all-purpose flour

Pinch of sugar

- ¼ cup water

Salt and freshly ground pepper

- 2 tablespoons finely chopped dill

**1.** Fill a medium bowl with water and squeeze the lemon half into it. Working with 1 artichoke at a time, snap off the tough outer leaves until you reach the tender yellow leaves. Using a sharp knife, cut off the top two-thirds of the leaves, leaving 1½ inches at the base. Cut off the stem and peel the artichoke bottom, then scoop out the hairy choke with a melon baller or teaspoon. Add the artichoke to the lemon water. Repeat with the remaining artichokes.

**2.** Scatter the diced carrot in a large saucepan and arrange the drained artichoke bottoms on top. Scatter the potato and peas around the artichokes and nestle the onion in the center.

**3.** In a small bowl, whisk the olive oil with the flour, sugar and 1 tablespoon of the lemon juice. Stir in the ¼ cup of water and season with salt and pepper. Pour the mixture over the artichokes. Cover with a moistened piece of parchment paper and bring to a boil. Reduce the heat to moderately low and cook the vegetables until they are tender, about 1 hour. Check occasionally and add a few tablespoons of water as necessary if the vegetables begin to look dry.

**4.** Transfer the artichokes to a small platter. Stir the dill and the remaining ½ tablespoon of lemon juice into the vegetables in the pan, then spoon them over the artichokes. Serve warm or at room temperature. —*Eveline Zoutendijk*

**MAKE AHEAD** The artichokes can be refrigerated for up to 2 days.

### Artichoke, Cauliflower and Mushroom Barigoule

**ACTIVE: 45 MIN; TOTAL: 1 HR 30 MIN**

8 SERVINGS ● ●

*Barigoule* is a traditional Provençal dish of braised artichokes in a warm and slightly tangy white wine broth. With the addition of cauliflower and carrots, it's a fabulous vegetable alternative to a salad.

- 1 lemon, halved, plus 3 tablespoons fresh lemon juice
- 8 large artichokes
- ¼ cup extra-virgin olive oil
- 1 large white onion, thinly sliced
- 3 small carrots, thinly sliced
- 5 small garlic cloves, halved
- 2 bay leaves
- 2 thyme sprigs
- ½ teaspoon coriander seeds
- 1½ cups dry white wine
- 1½ cups water
- ¾ pound cauliflower, cut into 1-inch florets (4 cups)
- ¾ pound white mushrooms, quartered if large

Salt and freshly ground pepper

**1.** Fill a large bowl with water and squeeze the lemon halves into it. Using a sharp knife, halve the artichokes crosswise. Discard the tops. Working with 1 artichoke at a time, pull off the tough outer leaves until you reach the tender yellow leaves. Scrape out the hairy choke with a melon baller or teaspoon. Trim and peel the base and stem, then quarter the heart and add the artichoke quarters to the lemon water. Repeat with the remaining artichokes.

**2.** In a large, deep skillet, heat the olive oil. Add the onion and carrots and cook over moderate heat, stirring, until softened but not browned, about 7 minutes. Add the garlic, bay leaves, thyme and coriander seeds and cook for 1 minute. Add the wine, water and the 3 tablespoons of lemon juice and bring to a boil over high heat. Cook until the carrots are barely tender, about 3 minutes.

**3.** Drain the artichokes and add them to the skillet along with the cauliflower and mushrooms. Season with salt and pepper and bring to a boil over high heat. Cover and cook over low heat until tender, about 20 minutes. Uncover and let cool to room temperature, about 30 minutes. Transfer the vegetables and broth to shallow bowls and serve. —*André Soltner*

**MAKE AHEAD** The *barigoule* can be refrigerated overnight. Bring to room temperature before serving.

### Balsamic-Glazed Onion Wedges with Fennel

**ACTIVE: 10 MIN; TOTAL: 1 HR**

**8 SERVINGS** ● ●

When Los Angeles chef and restaurateur Nancy Silverton makes these richly flavored onions at her house in Umbria, Italy, she roasts them with the wild fennel that grows on her property. To replicate the complex flavor of wild fennel in Los Angeles, Silverton uses a combination of fennel stalks, fronds and pollen.

>  2  **tablespoons extra-virgin olive oil**
>  4  **teaspoons balsamic vinegar**
> **Sea salt**
> **Fronds and stalks from 1 fennel bulb, the bulb reserved for another use**
>  1  **very large red onion, cut into 8 wedges through the root end**
>  8  **bay leaves**
>  1  **teaspoon fennel pollen or finely ground fennel seeds**

**1.** Preheat the oven to 400°. In a 10-inch ovenproof skillet, mix 4 teaspoons of the olive oil with 2 teaspoons of the balsamic vinegar and a pinch of sea salt. Spread the fennel fronds and stalks over the oil and vinegar in the skillet and top the fennel with the onion wedges. Drizzle the remaining 2 teaspoons each of olive oil and balsamic vinegar over the onion wedges and top each wedge with a bay leaf. Sprinkle the onion wedges with the fennel pollen and a pinch of salt.

**2.** Cut out a round of parchment paper slightly larger than the skillet. Crumple the round under running water, then open it up and place it directly over the onion wedges. Cover the skillet with foil and bake the onion wedges in the center of the oven for 40 minutes, or until they are tender. Remove the foil and parchment paper from the skillet.

**3.** Turn the onion wedges over and cook them over high heat on the stove until most of the liquid in the skillet has evaporated, about 1 minute. Transfer the onion wedges and fennel to a serving platter, discarding the bay leaves, and serve immediately. —*Nancy Silverton*

**MAKE AHEAD** The onion wedges can be refrigerated overnight. Let return to room temperature before serving.

### Tangy Salt-Roasted Fennel

**ACTIVE: 25 MIN; TOTAL: 1 HR 25 MIN**

**8 SERVINGS** ● ●

>  2  **medium lemons**
>  8  **medium fennel bulbs, halved lengthwise and cored**
> **Salt and freshly ground black pepper**
>  8  **small thyme sprigs**
>  2  **garlic cloves, thickly sliced**
>  8  **Gaeta or Calamata olives, pitted and coarsely chopped**
> **Extra-virgin olive oil, for drizzling**
>  1¼  **pounds kosher salt**

**1.** Preheat the oven to 400°. Peel the lemons, removing all of the bitter white pith. Cut each lemon crosswise into 4 slices.

**2.** Cut eight 12-inch squares of aluminum foil. Set a lemon slice in the center of each square. Top the lemon with 2 fennel halves, overlapping them slightly. Season with salt and pepper. Scatter the thyme, garlic and olives over the fennel, drizzle with olive oil and fold each square into a package.

**3.** Spread the kosher salt on a large rimmed baking sheet. Nestle the foil packets into the salt, seam side up. Bake the fennel for about 1 hour, or until very tender. Carefully open the packets over a bowl to catch the roasting juices. Transfer the fennel to a deep platter, pour the juices on top and serve. —*Michael Cimarusti*

## equipment
### DOUBLE-DUTY BOWL AND LID

The cleverly designed **"Spurgo"** glass bowl has a walnut lid that is flat on one side and concave on the other, so it can be flipped over and used as an extra serving dish. Use the lid to seal the bowl when you put leftovers in the refrigerator. The Pucci-esque pot holder adds a touch of '70s-inspired design to the kitchen. **DETAILS** Bowl by Maxjenny Forslund for Scandinaviaform, $38 from Space Downtown; 212-352-9968. Pot holder $15 from Milli Home; millihome.com.

## Maple-Roasted Brussels Sprouts

**TOTAL: 30 MIN**

10 SERVINGS ● ●

This unbelievably simple side dish counters the slight bitterness of brussels sprouts with a sweet maple-syrup pan sauce.

- ¼ cup canola oil
- 2¼ pounds baby brussels sprouts or regular brussels sprouts that are halved lengthwise
- Salt and freshly ground black pepper
- 1 stick (4 ounces) unsalted butter, cut into tablespoons and softened
- 2 tablespoons light brown sugar
- ¼ cup Grade A pure maple syrup
- 1½ tablespoons cider vinegar
- 1 cup vacuum-packed roasted chestnuts (6 ounces), coarsely chopped
- 1 tablespoon walnut oil

1. Heat the canola oil in a very large skillet until shimmering. Add the baby brussels sprouts to the skillet and season them with salt and pepper. Cook the brussels sprouts over high heat without stirring until they are browned, about 2 minutes. Add the butter and brown sugar and continue cooking over moderately high heat, stirring occasionally, until the brown sugar is melted. Add the maple syrup to the skillet and cook, stirring occasionally, until the brussels sprouts are just crisp-tender, about 7 minutes. Stir the cider vinegar into the brussels sprouts. Add the chopped chestnuts and walnut oil to the skillet and cook until the chestnuts are heated through, about 3 minutes.

2. Using a slotted spoon, transfer the brussels sprouts and chestnuts to a serving bowl. Boil the cooking liquid over high heat until it has thickened slightly, about 2 minutes. Pour the maple sauce over the brussels sprouts and chestnuts and serve them immediately.

—*Julie Taras and Tasha Garcia*

## Tofu, Green Bean and Shiitake Salad

**TOTAL: 30 MIN**

4 SERVINGS ● ●

Nancie McDermott, author of the cookbook *Real Thai*, explains that this style of fiery, tangy chopped Thai salad is called *yum*. The Thai generally eat this type of salad on lettuce leaves in a café or restaurant while deciding what to order for dinner.

- ½ pound firm tofu, halved crosswise
- 2 tablespoons fresh lime juice
- 1 tablespoon Asian fish sauce
- 3 tablespoons soy sauce
- 2 teaspoons sugar
- ¾ teaspoon crushed red pepper
- 1 tablespoon vegetable oil
- 3 garlic cloves, very finely chopped
- ¼ pound shiitake mushrooms, stems discarded, caps sliced ½ inch thick
- ¼ pound green beans, sliced on the diagonal into ⅓-inch lengths
- 3 scallions, very finely chopped
- 1 medium shallot, very finely chopped
- ¼ cup coarsely chopped cilantro
- ¼ cup coarsely chopped mint
- 4 whole Boston lettuce leaves, washed and dried

1. Arrange the tofu halves in a single layer on a rimmed baking sheet, then place another baking sheet on top of the tofu. Set 2 large, heavy cans on top and press the tofu for 30 minutes. Drain the tofu and cut it into ½-inch dice.

2. In a small bowl, stir the lime juice with the fish sauce, 1 tablespoon of the soy sauce, the sugar and the crushed red pepper. Set aside.

3. In a medium skillet, heat the vegetable oil. Add the chopped garlic and cook over moderately high heat until the garlic

is fragrant, about 30 seconds. Add the shiitake mushrooms and cook, stirring, until they are softened, about 1 minute. Add the remaining 2 tablespoons of soy sauce and cook over moderate heat until the shiitake are tender, about 4 minutes longer. Transfer the mushrooms to a large bowl. Add the diced tofu, the green beans, scallions, shallot, cilantro, mint and dressing and toss. Spread the Boston lettuce leaves on a platter. Spoon the tofu salad onto the leaves and serve.

—*Nancie McDermott*

## Smoky Brussels Sprouts

**TOTAL: 30 MIN**

4 SERVINGS ●

Marc Meyer, chef and owner of New York City's Cookshop and Five Points, is a fan of much-maligned brussels sprouts. He sautés them with smoky bacon, then adds sour cream to the dish for richness.

- 1¼ pounds brussels sprouts, halved lengthwise
- ¼ pound thick-cut bacon, cut into ¼-inch strips
- ¼ cup plus 2 tablespoons sour cream
- Salt and freshly ground pepper

1. Bring a medium saucepan of salted water to a boil. Add the halved brussels sprouts to the pan and cook them over high heat until tender but still bright green, about 3 minutes. Drain the brussels sprouts well, reserving about 2 tablespoons of the cooking liquid.

2. In a large skillet, cook the bacon over moderate heat, stirring occasionally, until browned, 7 minutes. Add the brussels sprouts and cook over moderately high heat for 2 minutes, stirring occasionally. Add the sour cream and the reserved cooking liquid and simmer over moderate heat until the brussels sprouts are coated with the sauce. Season the brussels sprouts with salt and pepper, transfer them to a bowl and serve at once. —*Marc Meyer*

### Green Bean and Tomato Salad with Green Apple and Cider Dressing

**TOTAL: 30 MIN**

6 SERVINGS ● ●

Diced raw onions make this refreshing salad extra crisp and pungent.

- 2 tablespoons cider vinegar
- 1 small shallot, coarsely chopped
- ½ teaspoon Dijon mustard
- ½ teaspoon kosher salt
- ¼ cup plus 2 tablespoons extra-virgin olive oil
- 1½ tablespoons boiling water
- 1 pound green beans, trimmed
- 2 pints grape tomatoes, halved
- 1 large Granny Smith apple— peeled, cored and cut into ¼-inch matchsticks
- ½ small red onion, thinly sliced
- 2 tablespoons chopped flat-leaf parsley
- 2 tablespoons very finely chopped chives

1. In a blender, combine the cider vinegar with the chopped shallot, mustard and salt and puree. With the machine on, gradually add the olive oil until blended, then mix the boiling water into the dressing.

2. In a large saucepan of boiling salted water, cook the green beans until barely tender, about 4 minutes. Drain the green beans and spread them out on a paper towel–lined baking sheet. Set the green beans aside and let cool.

3. In a large bowl, toss the cooled green beans with the tomatoes, apple, onion, parsley and chives. Add the dressing to the green bean and tomato salad, toss well and serve at once. —*Adam Perry Lang*

**MAKE AHEAD** The cider dressing and the blanched green beans can be refrigerated separately in airtight containers overnight. Let the green beans return to room temperature before making the salad.

### Stir-Fried Green Beans in Tortilla Wraps

**TOTAL: 30 MIN**

8 SERVINGS ● ●

Wrapping these crispy, sesame-spiked green beans in flour tortillas turns them into finger food. This recipe works well as a first course.

- ¾ cup water
- 3 tablespoons sugar
- 2 tablespoons sake
- 1½ tablespoons miso
- 1 tablespoon soy sauce
- 1 tablespoon rice vinegar
- 1 tablespoon cornstarch
- 1½ teaspoons chile-garlic sauce
- 3 tablespoons vegetable oil
- 1½ pounds green beans, cut into 2-inch lengths
- 3 scallions, thickly sliced
- 1 teaspoon toasted-sesame oil
- 1 teaspoon toasted white sesame seeds (see Note)

Four 8-inch flour tortillas, warmed and cut into 4 wedges each

1. In a medium bowl, combine the water with the sugar, sake, miso, soy sauce, rice vinegar, cornstarch and the chile-garlic sauce. Set the sauce aside.

2. Heat a large, deep skillet for 2 minutes. Add the vegetable oil and heat until smoking. Add the green beans and the scallions and cook over high heat, stirring occasionally, until the beans are just tender and browned in spots, about 6 minutes. Stir the sauce mixture, add it to the beans and bring to a boil. Cook until the sauce is glossy and slightly thickened, about 1 minute. Stir in the sesame oil. Transfer the green beans to a serving platter and garnish with the toasted sesame seeds. Serve the green beans with the tortilla wedges alongside for wrapping. —*Hiro Sone*

**NOTE** In a small skillet, toast the sesame seeds over moderate heat, stirring occasionally, until they are lightly browned, about 2 minutes.

### Anise-Scented Corn with Fresh Cheese and Jalapeño Sauce

**TOTAL: 35 MIN**

6 SERVINGS

This is the kind of simple appetizer or side dish you'd eat in a Peruvian home. Many Peruvians make the soft, sliceable cheese themselves by adding lime juice to milk, then draining, salting and pressing the curds, ending up with something similar to American farmer cheese. Eating corn on the cob rolled in this garlicky, cumin-flecked cheese is an unbelievable treat.

- 5 large jalapeños, 4 halved lengthwise and seeded, 1 minced
- 2 medium tomatillos (¼ pound), cored and halved lengthwise
- ½ cup chopped red onion
- ¼ cup chopped roasted, salted peanuts
- 2 tablespoons chopped basil

Salt and freshly ground pepper

- 1 pound farmer cheese, at room temperature
- 2 tablespoons extra-virgin olive oil
- 2 tablespoons fresh lime juice
- 2 tablespoons chopped parsley
- 1 teaspoon ground cumin
- 1 garlic clove, minced
- 2 teaspoons sugar
- 2 teaspoons anise seeds
- 6 ears of corn, shucked

1. In a saucepan of boiling salted water, cook the halved jalapeños and tomatillos over moderately high heat until tender, 8 minutes. Drain and transfer to a blender. Add the onion, peanuts and basil and puree. Scrape into a bowl; season with salt and pepper.

2. In a bowl, mash the cheese, olive oil, lime juice, parsley, cumin, garlic and minced jalapeño; season with salt and pepper.

3. Boil a pot of water with the sugar, anise seeds and 2 teaspoons of salt. Add the corn and boil for 5 minutes. Turn off the heat. Leave the corn in the hot water. Serve the corn piping hot. Pass the sauce and cheese at the table. —*Emmanuel Piqueras*

## Spicy Corn Pudding with Roasted Red Pepper

**ACTIVE: 30 MIN; TOTAL: 1 HR 40 MIN**

**6 SERVINGS**

Inspired by a recipe from the 1993 cookbook *Lee Bailey's Corn,* chef Michael Romano of New York City's Union Square Cafe uses pureed corn to give this kernel-studded pudding a fresh flavor and creamy texture.

- 1 small red bell pepper
- 1 tablespoon unsalted butter
- 3 cups fresh corn kernels (from about 8 ears)

Kosher salt and freshly ground black pepper

- 1½ cups half-and-half
- 1½ tablespoons cornstarch
- 2 large eggs, lightly beaten
- 1 tablespoon minced flat-leaf parsley
- 1 tablespoon minced cilantro

Pinch each of sugar and ground allspice

- ⅛ teaspoon cayenne pepper

1. Preheat the oven to 325°. Roast the bell pepper over a gas flame or under the broiler until charred all over. Transfer to a small bowl, cover with plastic wrap and let cool slightly. Peel and seed the pepper and cut it into ¾-inch dice.

2. Generously butter a 6-cup soufflé dish. In a medium skillet, melt the 1 tablespoon of butter. Add half of the corn and cook over moderately high heat, stirring, until crisp-tender, about 2 minutes. Stir in the roasted bell pepper and season with salt and black pepper; let cool.

3. In a blender, combine the remaining corn with the half-and-half and the cornstarch and puree until smooth. Strain the mixture through a fine sieve set over a bowl, pressing hard on the solids. Discard the solids. Add the eggs, parsley, cilantro, sugar, allspice, cayenne, 1½ teaspoons of kosher salt and ¼ teaspoon of black pepper to the bowl. Stir in the corn and red pepper mixture and pour into the prepared soufflé dish.

4. Set the dish in a roasting pan and pour enough hot water into the pan to reach halfway up the side of the dish. Bake the pudding in the center of the oven until golden and just set, about 1 hour. Carefully remove the soufflé dish from the roasting pan and let stand for 15 minutes before serving. —*Michael Romano*

## Crunchy Coleslaw with Cayenne and Toasted Caraway Seeds

**ACTIVE: 25 MIN; TOTAL: 2 HR 25 MIN**

**8 TO 10 SERVINGS ●**

The cabbage for this spicy coleslaw is lightly salted first to draw out some of the liquid, so it doesn't dilute the dressing.

One 3-pound head green cabbage, cored and finely shredded

One 2-pound head red cabbage, cored and finely shredded

Kosher salt

- 1 teaspoon caraway seeds
- 1 teaspoon celery seeds
- ½ cup water
- 1 cup mayonnaise
- ½ cup heavy cream
- ¼ cup sugar
- ½ small onion, minced
- 2 garlic cloves, minced
- 3 tablespoons cider vinegar
- 1 tablespoon fresh lemon juice
- ½ teaspoon cayenne pepper
- ½ teaspoon freshly ground black pepper
- 1 large carrot, coarsely shredded
- 1 large Granny Smith apple, peeled and cut into ¼-inch matchsticks
- ½ cup coarsely chopped flat-leaf parsley

1. Put the green and red cabbage in 2 colanders and toss each with 1 teaspoon of salt. Let drain in the sink for 2 hours. Pat the cabbage dry.

2. In a small dry skillet, toast the caraway and celery seeds over moderately high heat until fragrant, about 20 seconds. Add the water and let cool.

3. In a blender, combine the mayonnaise, cream, sugar, onion, garlic, vinegar, lemon juice, cayenne and black pepper. Pour in the caraway and celery seeds and their liquid; blend until the dressing is smooth.

4. In a large bowl, combine the green and red cabbages, carrot, apple and parsley; toss with the dressing. Season with salt and serve. —*Adam Perry Lang*

**MAKE AHEAD** The coleslaw can be refrigerated overnight.

## Tangy Cabbage Slaw with Golden Raisins

**TOTAL: 30 MIN**

**6 SERVINGS ● ● ●**

This coleslaw is nothing like the white drippy slaw that's standard at summer barbecues. Instead of mayonnaise, the slaw is mixed with a tangy dressing of vinegar, mustard and olive oil. Plump golden raisins add a little sweetness to the slaw.

- ¾ cup golden raisins
- ¼ cup red wine vinegar
- 3 tablespoons whole-grain mustard
- 1 tablespoon sugar
- ¼ cup grapeseed oil
- 2 tablespoons walnut oil

Salt and freshly ground pepper

- ½ medium head green cabbage, cored and shredded (8 cups)
- 1 large carrot, shredded
- ½ small red onion, thinly sliced crosswise
- ¼ cup snipped chives

1. In a small bowl, soak the raisins in hot water for 10 minutes. Drain the raisins, pressing out any liquid.

2. In a large bowl, whisk the vinegar, mustard and sugar. Whisk in the grapeseed and walnut oils. Season with salt and pepper. Add the cabbage, carrot, onion, chives and raisins and toss well. Season with salt and pepper and toss again. Refrigerate until chilled, about 10 minutes. Transfer to a bowl and serve. —*Laurent Tourondel*

### Spicy Red Cabbage with Raisins

**TOTAL: 20 MIN**

4 SERVINGS ● ● ●

- 2 tablespoons extra-virgin olive oil
- 1 teaspoon coriander seeds, finely crushed
- 2 medium shallots, thinly sliced
- 1 teaspoon ground cumin
- 1 teaspoon crushed red pepper
- 3 cups finely shredded red cabbage (¾ pound)

One 14-ounce can diced tomatoes with their juices

- ⅓ cup golden raisins
- 2 tablespoons fresh lemon juice
- ½ cup coarsely chopped cilantro leaves

Salt

In a large skillet, heat the olive oil. Add the coriander seeds and cook over moderate heat for 1 minute. Add the shallots, cumin and crushed red pepper and cook over moderately high heat, stirring, for 2 minutes. Add the cabbage, the tomatoes and their juices and the raisins and bring to a boil. Cover and cook over moderate heat, stirring occasionally, until the cabbage is tender, 8 minutes. Stir in the lemon juice and cilantro, season with salt and serve. —*Peter Berley*

**MAKE AHEAD** The cabbage can be refrigerated overnight.

### Broccoli Rabe with Garlic, Chile and Mustard Bread Crumbs

**TOTAL: 50 MIN**

12 SERVINGS ● ●

Chef Suzanne Goin of Lucques in Los Angeles reports that her snack of choice is broccoli or broccoli rabe. She reserves the crunchy, mustard-spiked bread crumb topping for special occasions.

- 2 tablespoons unsalted butter
- 1 tablespoon Dijon mustard
- 1 teaspoon chopped flat-leaf parsley
- 1 tablespoon thyme leaves
- 1 cup fresh bread crumbs

Kosher salt

- 3 pounds broccoli rabe, thick stems discarded
- ⅔ cup extra-virgin olive oil
- 6 garlic cloves, thinly sliced
- 4 shallots, thinly sliced
- 2 dried árbol chiles or other dried red chiles, stemmed and thinly sliced on the diagonal

Freshly ground pepper

**1.** Preheat the oven to 375°. In a medium saucepan, melt the butter. Whisk in the mustard, parsley and 1 teaspoon of the thyme and remove from the heat; let cool for 3 minutes. Add the bread crumbs, season with salt and toss to coat. Spread the bread crumbs on a baking sheet and toast for 10 minutes, until crisp and golden.

**2.** Meanwhile, bring a large pot of salted water to a boil. Add the broccoli rabe and boil until just tender, 3 minutes. Drain and rinse under cold water to cool. Drain the broccoli rabe and pat thoroughly dry.

**3.** Heat a very large skillet over high heat for 2 minutes, or heat 2 large skillets. Add ⅓ cup of the olive oil to the skillet along with the garlic, shallots, chiles and the remaining 2 teaspoons of thyme. Cook until the shallots are softened, about 2 minutes. Add the broccoli rabe and season with salt. Stir well to coat the broccoli rabe with the oil. Drizzle the remaining ⅓ cup of oil over the broccoli rabe and cook for 2 minutes, tossing often. Season with salt and pepper. Mound the broccoli rabe on a platter, scatter the mustard bread crumbs on top and serve hot or warm. —*Suzanne Goin*

### Broccoli with Herbed Hollandaise Sauce and Toasted Bread Crumbs

**TOTAL: 40 MIN**

4 SERVINGS

The long, thick broccoli florets are perfect for mopping up the creamy, herbed hollandaise sauce.

- 1 stick plus 2 tablespoons (5 ounces) unsalted butter, cut into pieces
- 1 slice of sourdough bread (about 2 ounces), crust removed, bread torn into pieces
- 2 tablespoons plus 1 teaspoon extra-virgin olive oil

Salt and freshly ground pepper

- 1½ pounds broccoli, peeled and cut lengthwise into long, thick florets
- 2 large egg yolks
- 1 tablespoon boiling water
- 1 tablespoon fresh lemon juice

Tabasco

- 1 tablespoon plus 1 teaspoon chopped mint
- ½ teaspoon chopped thyme

**1.** Preheat the oven to 450°. In a small saucepan, melt the butter over low heat. Skim the foam from the surface of the butter. Remove from the heat.

**2.** In a food processor, pulse the bread to coarse crumbs. Transfer to a small cookie sheet, toss with 1 teaspoon of the olive oil and season lightly with salt and pepper. Bake for 2 minutes, until golden brown.

**3.** On a large rimmed baking sheet, toss the broccoli with the remaining 2 tablespoons of olive oil; season with salt and pepper. Arrange the broccoli in an even layer and roast for about 15 minutes, until just tender and starting to brown.

**4.** Meanwhile, in a medium saucepan, bring 1 inch of water to a simmer. In a stainless steel bowl, mix the egg yolks with the boiling water. Set the bowl over the saucepan and whisk the yolks constantly until thickened slightly and bright yellow, about 1 minute. Remove from the heat.

**5.** Gently reheat the butter. Gradually whisk the butter into the yolks until a slightly thick sauce forms. Whisk in the lemon juice and a dash of Tabasco and season lightly with salt and pepper. Whisk in the mint and thyme.

**6.** Transfer the broccoli to a platter, pour the hollandaise over it, sprinkle with the bread crumbs and serve. —*Marcia Kiesel*

BROCCOLI WITH HERBED
HOLLANDAISE AND
TOASTED BREAD CRUMBS

## Roasted Broccoli with Brazil-Nut Pesto

**TOTAL: 30 MIN**

6 SERVINGS ● ● ●

- ½ cup coarsely chopped flat-leaf parsley
- ¼ cup Brazil nuts, coarsely chopped
- 2 tablespoons water
- 1 tablespoon chopped tarragon
- 1 large garlic clove, chopped
- ½ teaspoon finely grated lemon zest
- 5 tablespoons extra-virgin olive oil
- 3 tablespoons freshly grated Parmesan cheese

Salt and freshly ground pepper

- 2½ pounds broccoli, large stems discarded, cut into 4-inch-long florets

1. Preheat the oven to 500°. In a mini food processor, combine the parsley with the Brazil nuts, water, tarragon, garlic and lemon zest and pulse to a coarse paste. Add 3 tablespoons of the olive oil and the Parmesan and process to a slightly smooth paste. Season with salt and pepper.

2. On 2 large rimmed baking sheets, toss the broccoli florets with the remaining 2 tablespoons of olive oil and spread the florets in an even layer. Season the broccoli florets with salt and pepper. Roast the broccoli in the center of the oven for 8 minutes. Switch the baking sheets and continue to roast for about 8 minutes longer, or until the broccoli is browned and crisp-tender. Transfer the broccoli to a platter, drizzle the pesto on top and serve. —*Melissa Clark*

**MAKE AHEAD** The Brazil-nut pesto can be refrigerated overnight. Bring to room temperature before using.

## Charred Broccolini with Anchovies and Garlic Confit

**TOTAL: 45 MIN**

8 SERVINGS ● ●

Rather than roasting garlic in aluminum foil, you can make a supereasy garlic confit by slow-cooking the peeled cloves in olive oil. The garlic's marvelous pungent flavor infuses the oil, which gets tossed with the smoky vegetables. The garlic oil is also delicious in a vinaigrette or brushed on slices of toasted bread.

- ¾ cup extra-virgin olive oil
- 2 heads garlic, cloves peeled

One 2-inch strip of lemon zest, plus ½ teaspoon finely grated lemon zest

- 2 small dried hot chiles
- 1 bay leaf
- 12 flat anchovy fillets, drained
- ¼ teaspoon crushed red pepper
- 2 pounds Broccolini, bottom 2 inches of stalks discarded

Salt

1. In a small saucepan, combine the olive oil, garlic cloves, lemon zest strip, dried chiles and bay leaf and bring to a simmer. Reduce the heat to moderately low and cook, stirring occasionally, until the garlic is very soft, about 35 minutes. Strain the oil into a measuring cup and let cool. Discard the lemon zest, chiles and bay leaf and reserve the garlic.

2. Spoon 1 tablespoon of the garlic oil onto a plate. Add the anchovies, crushed red pepper and grated lemon zest and toss.

3. In a large bowl, toss the Broccolini with ½ cup of the garlic oil. Season with salt. Heat a large, deep skillet. Add half of the Broccolini and cook over high heat, without stirring, until browned in spots, about 2 minutes. Turn and cook for 2 to 3 minutes, or until the Broccolini is just tender. Transfer to a platter and repeat with the remaining Broccolini.

4. Scatter the garlic confit and the anchovies over the Broccolini and serve. —*Nancy Silverton*

**MAKE AHEAD** The Broccolini can be kept at room temperature for up to 2 hours. Top with the garlic confit and anchovies just before serving.

## Crispy Baked Kale with Gruyère Cheese

**ACTIVE: 25 MIN; TOTAL: 1 HR**

4 SERVINGS ●

Chef Sam Hayward of Fore Street restaurant in Portland, Maine, usually tops these lush onion-sweetened greens with an excellent aged raw-milk cheese from Vermont called Tarentaise. Gruyère or any other Alpine-style cheese is a great substitute, but if you want to try Tarentaise, you can order it from thistlehillfarm.com.

One 4-ounce piece of sourdough bread, crusts removed, bread torn into ½-inch pieces (2 cups)

- ¼ cup plus 1 tablespoon extra-virgin olive oil
- 1 medium shallot, minced
- 1 small onion, thinly sliced
- 1 garlic clove, thinly sliced
- 1½ pounds kale, thick stems discarded, leaves chopped
- 1 teaspoon chopped thyme leaves

Salt and freshly ground pepper

- 1¼ cups shredded Tarentaise or Gruyère cheese (3½ ounces)

## health

### BROCCOLI BOON

Broccoli is full of vitamins A and, especially, C (one cup provides more than the recommended daily amount). A study published last year in *Nutrition and Cancer* found that eating four or more three-ounce servings of broccoli a month may **reduce the risk of prostate cancer** by as much as 30 percent. Eating seven or more servings may **reduce the risk of breast cancer** by up to 40 percent.

**1.** Preheat the oven to 350°. Spread the bread pieces on a baking sheet and toss with 1 tablespoon of the olive oil. Bake the bread for 8 minutes, or until it is lightly toasted. Let the croutons cool on the baking sheet.

**2.** In a large, deep skillet, heat the remaining ¼ cup of olive oil. Add the shallot, onion and garlic and cook over moderate heat, stirring occasionally, until softened, 7 minutes. Add the kale, cover and cook over moderately low heat, stirring occasionally, until tender, about 15 minutes. Stir in the thyme and season with salt and pepper.

**3.** Transfer the kale to an 8-by-10-inch glass baking dish. Scatter the cheese over the kale and top with the croutons. Bake for about 20 minutes, or until the cheese is bubbling and the croutons are golden. Let stand for 5 minutes, then serve. —*Sam Hayward*

**MAKE AHEAD** The recipe can be made a day ahead through Step 2. Store the croutons in an airtight container and the kale in the refrigerator overnight.

## Tian of Creamed Greens
**ACTIVE: 30 MIN; TOTAL: 1 HR 30 MIN**
6 SERVINGS

A *tian* (TEE-yan) is a Provençal earthenware dish used for gratins. The gratins themselves are also called *tians*.

- 5 **tablespoons unsalted butter**
- 2 **large onions, coarsely chopped**
- 1 **pound spinach, stemmed and coarsely chopped**

One 6-ounce bunch watercress, thick stems discarded, leaves coarsely chopped

- 1 **cup salad burnet**
- 1 **tablespoon minced garlic**

**Salt and freshly ground pepper**

1½ **tablespoons all-purpose flour**

- 1 **cup hot milk**

**Pinch of freshly grated nutmeg**

- ½ **cup coarse fresh bread crumbs**
- 2 **teaspoons extra-virgin olive oil**

**1.** Preheat the oven to 375°. In a very large skillet, melt 2½ tablespoons of the butter. Add the onions, cover and cook over moderate heat until softened, about 10 minutes. Add the spinach, watercress, salad burnet and garlic and season with salt and pepper, Cook over low heat, stirring occasionally, until the greens are very tender, about 10 minutes. Pour off any liquid from the greens and reserve.

**2.** Meanwhile, in a small saucepan, melt the remaining 2½ tablespoons of butter. Stir in the flour and cook over moderate heat for 1 minute. Gradually whisk in the milk, nutmeg and any reserved liquid from the greens. Bring to a boil, whisking until the sauce is creamy. Reduce the heat and simmer, whisking, until thickened, about 3 minutes. Stir the sauce into the greens and season with salt and pepper.

**3.** Transfer the mixture to a 10-inch round earthenware baking dish. Sprinkle with the bread crumbs and drizzle with the olive oil. Bake in the upper third of the oven until the *tian* is bubbling and the crumbs are golden brown, 25 minutes. Let cool for 15 minutes before serving. —*Paula Wolfert*

## Creamy Spinach with Smoked Gouda Gratin
**TOTAL: 30 MIN**
6 SERVINGS ●

To make sure this gratin is luscious, take care to squeeze all the excess liquid from the wilted spinach before adding the creamy béchamel sauce.

1½ **pounds baby spinach**
- 1 **tablespoon extra-virgin olive oil**
- 1 **small onion, finely chopped**

**Smoked Gouda Béchamel (recipe follows)**

**Salt and freshly ground pepper**
- 3 **tablespoons fine dry bread crumbs**
- 2 **tablespoons coarsely shredded smoked Gouda cheese**

**1.** Preheat the broiler and position a rack 10 inches from the heat. In a large soup pot, bring ¼ inch of water to a boil. Add the spinach and cook over high heat, tossing with long tongs, until completely wilted, about 3 minutes. Transfer the spinach to a colander and drain, pressing out as much liquid as possible.

**2.** In a medium ovenproof skillet, heat the olive oil. Add the onion and cook over high heat, stirring, until softened, about 3 minutes. Add the wilted spinach and cook, stirring, for 1 minute. Add the Smoked Gouda Béchamel and cook over moderate heat, stirring, until bubbling, about 1 minute. Season with salt and pepper. Sprinkle with the bread crumbs and shredded Gouda and broil for 2 minutes, until golden and bubbling. Serve hot. —*Grace Parisi*

## SMOKED GOUDA BÉCHAMEL
**TOTAL: 10 MIN**
MAKES 1½ CUPS ● ●

Béchamel is a classic white sauce made by stirring milk into a cooked mixture of flour and butter. Adding smoked Gouda makes it thick, creamy, cheesy and irresistible.

- 2 **tablespoons unsalted butter**
- 2 **tablespoons all-purpose flour**
1½ **cups whole milk**
- ¼ **cup heavy cream**
- ¼ **pound smoked Gouda cheese, coarsely shredded**
- ½ **teaspoon smoked paprika (optional)**

**Pinch of freshly grated nutmeg**
**Salt and freshly ground pepper**

In a medium saucepan, melt the butter. Add the flour and whisk over moderately high heat for 30 seconds. Add the milk and bring to a boil, whisking constantly. Cook over moderate heat, whisking constantly, until thickened, 4 to 5 minutes. Add the cream, Gouda, paprika and nutmeg and whisk just until the cheese is melted, about 2 minutes. Season with salt and pepper. Use right away or cover directly with plastic wrap and refrigerate. —*G.P.*

CREAMED COLLARD GREENS

CHICKPEA AND SPINACH STEW

### Creamed Collard Greens

TOTAL: 1 HR

10 SERVINGS ●

It's important to shred the collard greens finely before you simmer them in the cream or they'll never get tender.

- 8 **pounds collard greens (8 bunches), tough stems and ribs removed**
- 1 **stick (4 ounces) unsalted butter**
- 6 **large shallots, very finely chopped**
- 4 **large garlic cloves, very finely chopped**
- 1 **quart heavy cream**

**Pinch of freshly grated nutmeg**

**Kosher salt and freshly ground pepper**

1. Bring a very large stockpot of water to a boil. Prepare a large bowl of ice water. Add half of the collard greens to the boiling water, a little at a time, and push them down into the water. Let the water return to a boil, then cook until tender, about 10 minutes. Using tongs, transfer the greens to the ice water. Repeat with the remaining greens. Drain the greens very well and squeeze them dry in a clean kitchen towel, then finely shred.

2. In a very large skillet, melt the butter. Add the shallots and garlic and cook over moderate heat until softened, about 6 minutes. Stir in the cream and simmer, stirring occasionally, until reduced by half, about 25 minutes. Add the greens to the cream and toss until warmed through, about 3 minutes. Season the collard greens generously with nutmeg, salt and pepper and serve them at once.

*—Allison Vines-Rushing and Slade Rushing*

**MAKE AHEAD** The creamed greens can be refrigerated overnight.

### Chickpea and Spinach Stew

TOTAL: 30 MIN

4 SERVINGS ● ● ● ●

In Seville, chickpeas and spinach (*garbanzos con espinacas*) is a popular dish served in both fine restaurants and tapas bars.

- 10 **ounces baby spinach**
- 2 **large garlic cloves, crushed**

**Kosher salt**

**Pinch of saffron threads**

- 2 **teaspoons sweet paprika**
- ¼ **teaspoon ground cumin**

**Pinch of ground cloves**

**Pinch of freshly ground pepper**

**Two 15-ounce cans chickpeas with their liquid**

- ¼ **cup extra-virgin olive oil**
- 1 **small onion, finely chopped**
- 1 **large tomato—peeled, seeded and coarsely chopped**
- ¼ **cup golden raisins**

1. In a large, deep skillet, bring 1 cup of water to a boil. Add the spinach and cook over high heat, tossing frequently, until wilted, about 2 minutes. Drain in a colander, pressing hard on the leaves to extract the liquid. Coarsely chop the spinach.

2. Using the flat side of a large knife, mash the garlic to a paste with ½ teaspoon of salt and the saffron. Transfer the paste to a small bowl. Add the paprika, cumin, cloves and black pepper; mash until combined. Stir in ¼ cup of the chickpea liquid.

3. Wipe out the skillet. Add 2 tablespoons of the olive oil and heat until shimmering. Add the onion and tomato and cook over moderately high heat, stirring occasionally, until softened, about 3 minutes. Add the sauce and cook for 1 minute.

4. Add the chickpeas and the remaining liquid to the skillet. Add the raisins and bring to a boil over moderately high heat. Add the spinach, reduce the heat to moderate and simmer for 15 minutes. Transfer the chickpea stew to deep bowls, drizzle with the remaining 2 tablespoons of olive oil and serve. —*Janet Mendel*
**SERVE WITH** Crusty bread.

## Smoky Chard Sauté
**TOTAL: 25 MIN**
4 SERVINGS ● ● ●
This lovely dish, full of hearty chard greens, is an appealing combination of smoky and tangy. It is perfect for serving alongside poached eggs or pork chops.

- 1¾ pounds Swiss chard, stems trimmed and finely diced, leaves coarsely chopped
- 2 tablespoons extra-virgin olive oil
- 2 garlic cloves, minced
- ½ cup drained canned diced tomatoes
- ½ teaspoon Pimentón de la Vera (smoked Spanish paprika)
- Pinch of fennel seeds
- 2 tablespoons water
- 2 teaspoons white wine vinegar
- Salt and freshly ground pepper

1. In a large, deep skillet, bring 2 cups of water to a boil. Add the chard stems and leaves and cook over high heat until just tender, about 8 minutes. Drain, pressing on the leaves to extract excess liquid.

2. Wipe out the skillet. Add the oil and heat until shimmering. Add the garlic and cook over moderately high heat, stirring, until lightly browned. Add the tomatoes and paprika and cook for 2 minutes. Add the chard, fennel seeds and water and cook over moderate heat for 3 minutes. Stir in the vinegar; season with salt and pepper. Transfer to plates and serve. —*Janet Mendel*

## Bitter Greens with Quince Vinaigrette and Blue Cheese
**TOTAL: 30 MIN**
8 SERVINGS ● ●
The array of bitter greens, lightly wilted by hot garlic oil, is delicious with the flavors of balsamic vinegar and sweet quince paste in the dressing. Govind Armstrong, chef at Table 8 in Los Angeles, recommends using a soft blue like Gorgonzola for making a creamy dish. The firm blue cheese here creates a more crumbly topping.

- 3 ounces quince paste, cut into small pieces
- 2 tablespoons water
- 1 tablespoon plus 1 teaspoon balsamic vinegar
- ¼ cup plus 2 tablespoons extra-virgin olive oil
- Salt and freshly ground pepper
- 4 garlic cloves, smashed
- 2 Belgian endives (¾ pound), cored and sliced crosswise 1 inch thick
- 1 head escarole (10 ounces), tough outer leaves discarded, inner leaves torn into bite-size pieces
- 2 small heads frisée (10 ounces total), torn into bite-size pieces
- 1 small head radicchio (6 ounces), torn into bite-size pieces
- 4 ounces firm blue cheese, such as Maytag Blue, crumbled

1. In a mini food processor, puree the quince paste with the water and the balsamic vinegar. Add ¼ cup of the extra-virgin olive oil to the processor and process the quince vinaigrette until it is emulsified. Pour the quince vinaigrette into a small bowl and season the dressing to taste with salt and pepper.

2. In a small saucepan, cook the smashed garlic in the remaining 2 tablespoons of olive oil over moderate heat until it is golden brown, about 4 minutes. Discard the garlic and reserve the flavored olive oil.

3. Put the endives, escarole, frisée and radicchio in a large bowl. Pour the hot garlic oil on top and toss the salad. Add the quince vinaigrette and the blue cheese to the salad, toss again and serve.
—*Govind Armstrong*

## Peas and Carrots with Two Onions
**TOTAL: 35 MIN**
6 SERVINGS ● ●
- 2 tablespoons unsalted butter
- 1 small onion, finely chopped
- 3 large scallions, minced
- 1 tablespoon all-purpose flour
- 1¼ cups water
- ½ pound carrots, diced
- ¾ teaspoon salt
- ½ teaspoon freshly ground pepper
- ½ teaspoon thyme leaves
- 1 pound frozen petite peas

In a large saucepan, melt the butter over moderately high heat. Add the chopped onion and the minced scallions and cook, stirring, until the onion and scallions are softened. Stir in the flour. Add the water, diced carrots, salt, pepper and thyme and bring to a boil. Cover, reduce the heat to moderate and cook until the carrots are just tender, about 8 minutes. Add the peas. Cover and simmer until the carrots and peas are tender, about 5 minutes longer. Serve the hot peas and carrots immediately. —*Jacques Pépin*

## Smashed Mixed Root Vegetables

**ACTIVE: 30 MIN; TOTAL: 1 HR 15 MIN**

**8 SERVINGS** ● ●

This quintessential fall dish can be made with almost any root vegetable; parsnips and earthy sweet potatoes are especially good with the butter and maple syrup that are mixed in just before serving.

- ½ bunch thyme sprigs
- 3 bay leaves
- 1 teaspoon whole black peppercorns
- 1 teaspoon whole cloves
- 5 pounds mixed root vegetables— such as carrots, parsnips, Yukon Gold potatoes, sweet potatoes and rutabagas—peeled and cut into 2-inch chunks
- 1 large Spanish onion, coarsely chopped
- 8 garlic cloves, smashed
- 1 cup dry white wine
- 3 tablespoons unsalted butter
- 1 tablespoon maple syrup

Salt and freshly ground pepper

1. Wrap the thyme sprigs, bay leaves, peppercorns and cloves in a piece of cheesecloth and tie together with kitchen string. Put the bundle in a large saucepan and add the root vegetables, onion, garlic and white wine. Add enough water to cover the vegetables by 1 inch and bring to a boil over high heat. Reduce the heat to moderately low and simmer until the vegetables are tender, about 45 minutes. Drain the vegetables and discard the herb bundle.

2. Return the vegetables to the pan and cook over high heat, stirring, until the vegetables are dry, about 3 minutes. Remove from the heat and smash the vegetables with a potato masher. Stir the butter and maple syrup into the vegetables and season with salt and pepper. Serve hot. —*Govind Armstrong*

**MAKE AHEAD** The smashed vegetables can be refrigerated for up to 2 days. Rewarm in a double boiler.

## Vegetable-Noodle Tangle

**TOTAL: 30 MIN**

**4 SERVINGS** ● ●

There are many traditional Korean ingredients here: sesame oil, chopped scallions, toasted sesame seeds. *Somen,* a thin Japanese wheat noodle, is commonly used in Korean cooking too. It is perfect for slurping up along with the zucchini, cucumbers and carrots. If you want an extra dose of authentic flavor, add some spicy Korean chili paste before serving.

- 1 pound dried *somen*
- ⅓ cup soy sauce
- 2 tablespoons Asian sesame oil
- 1½ tablespoons sugar
- 2 tablespoons vegetable oil
- 3 small zucchini, thinly sliced crosswise

Salt

- 3 carrots, coarsely shredded
- 3 scallions, coarsely chopped
- 2 kirby cucumbers, seeded and coarsely shredded

Toasted sesame seeds, for serving

1. In a large saucepan of boiling salted water, cook the *somen* until al dente, about 4 minutes. Drain and rinse under lukewarm water. Shake well and transfer the *somen* to 4 soup bowls.

2. In a small bowl, combine the soy sauce with the sesame oil and sugar and stir until the sugar is dissolved.

3. In a large skillet, heat 1 tablespoon of the vegetable oil until shimmering. Add the zucchini, season with salt and cook over high heat until softened and just beginning to brown, 5 minutes. Transfer to a bowl. Add the remaining 1 tablespoon of oil to the skillet. Add the carrots and cook over high heat, stirring occasionally, until softened, 5 minutes. Transfer to the bowl with the zucchini. Add the scallions and toss. Mound the vegetables on the noodles and drizzle the soy mixture on top. Garnish with the cucumbers and sesame seeds and serve. —*Cecilia Hae-Jin Lee*

## Stir-Fried Baby Bok Choy with Shiitake Mushrooms

**TOTAL: 15 MIN**

**6 SERVINGS** ●

- ¼ cup plus 2 tablespoons canola oil
- 2 large garlic cloves, minced
- 6 ounces shiitake mushrooms, stems discarded, caps cut into 1-inch pieces
- 1½ pounds baby bok choy, leaves separated from the stems
- ¼ cup plus 2 tablespoons Chinese cooking wine
- ¾ cup Vietnamese Stir-Fry Sauce (recipe follows)

In a large skillet or a wok, heat the oil until small puffs of smoke begin to appear. Add the garlic and stir-fry over high heat for 10 seconds. Add the shiitake and stir-fry for 1 minute. Add the bok choy and stir-fry until crisp-tender, about 3 minutes. Add the wine and cook until slightly reduced, about 1 minute. Add the Vietnamese Stir-Fry Sauce and cook until the bok choy is tender but still bright green and the sauce is slightly reduced, about 4 minutes longer. Serve hot. —*Charles Phan*

**SERVE WITH** Steamed jasmine rice.

### VIETNAMESE STIR-FRY SAUCE

**TOTAL: 10 MIN**

**MAKES ABOUT 1¾ CUPS** ● ●

The key ingredient here is a fish sauce that lends a faintly nutty, pungent and quintessentially Vietnamese character to this versatile sauce.

- 1½ cups chicken stock, preferably homemade
- ¼ cup plus 1 tablespoon Asian fish sauce
- 1 tablespoon sugar

In a small saucepan, bring the stock to a boil. Remove from the heat and add the fish sauce and sugar; stir until the sugar is dissolved. Let cool. —*C.P.*

**MAKE AHEAD** The sauce can be refrigerated for up to 2 days.

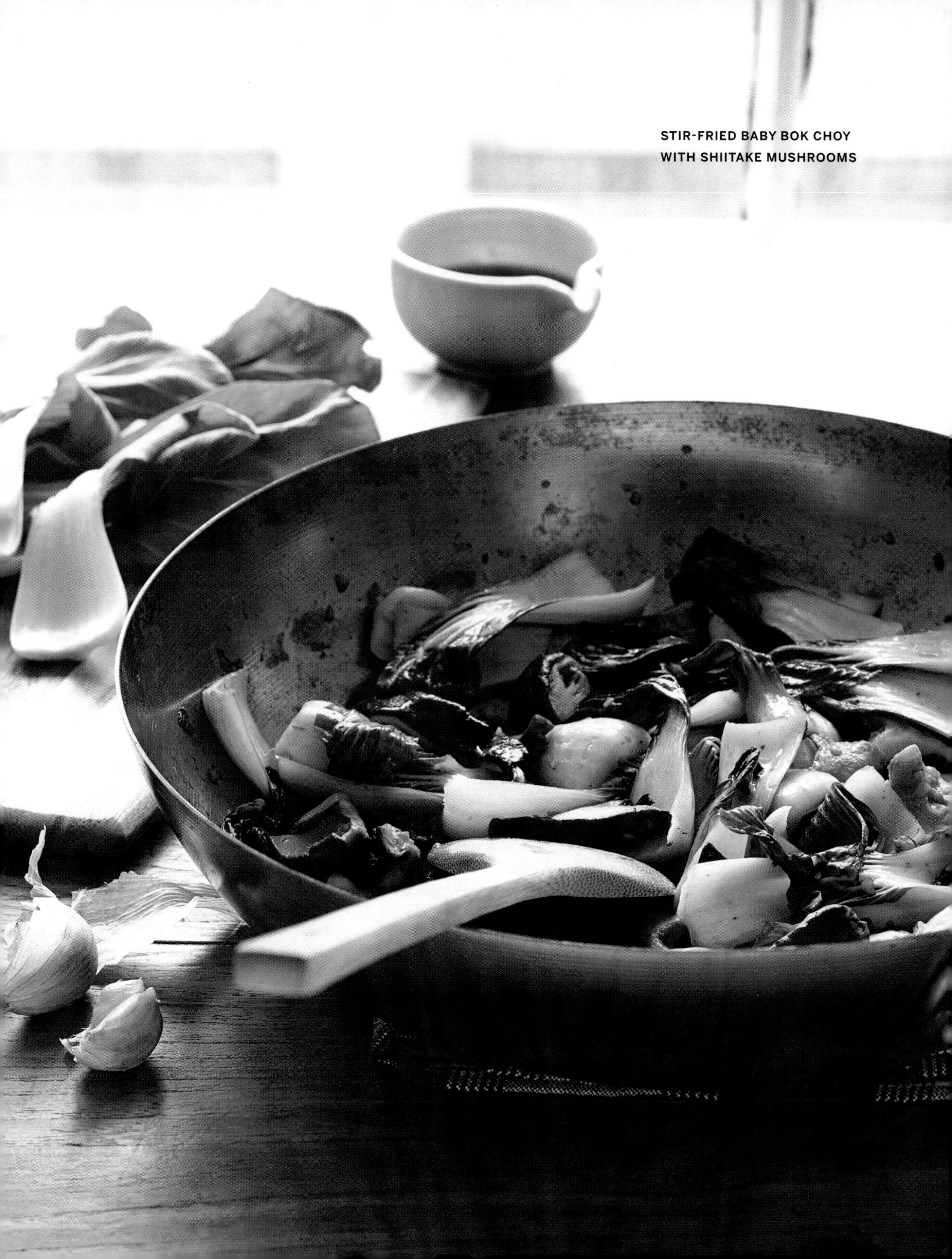

STIR-FRIED BABY BOK CHOY
WITH SHIITAKE MUSHROOMS

## Spicy Carrots with Parsley and Cilantro

ACTIVE: 20 MIN; TOTAL: 40 MIN

6 SERVINGS ● ●

This recipe is great for entertaining because you can serve it warm, at room temperature or even slightly chilled. And it goes with almost any main course.

- 1½ pounds large carrots, quartered lengthwise, then halved crosswise
- 4 garlic cloves, halved
- ¼ cup plus 1 tablespoon extra-virgin olive oil
- 2 tablespoons fresh lemon juice
- ¼ cup coarsely chopped flat-leaf parsley
- ¼ cup chopped cilantro
- 1½ teaspoons sweet paprika
- ½ teaspoon crushed red pepper

Salt

- 2 tablespoons sliced blanched almonds

1. In a large, deep skillet, cover the carrots and garlic with water and bring to a boil. Cook over moderately high heat until the carrots are tender, 10 minutes. Drain and let cool; discard the garlic.

2. In a bowl, combine the olive oil, lemon juice, parsley, cilantro, paprika and crushed pepper. Season with salt. Add the carrots, toss to coat and sprinkle the almonds on top. Serve warm, at room temperature or slightly chilled. —Anissa Helou

MAKE AHEAD The carrots can be prepared early in the day and kept at room temperature or refrigerated.

## Dreamy Creamed Carrots, Onions and Mushrooms

ACTIVE: 1 HR; TOTAL: 4 HR

10 SERVINGS ● ●

These vegetables served in a cream sauce may seem familiar, but pay attention: The carrots are spiked with ginger, the onions are made slightly pungent with the addition of horseradish and the mushrooms are slyly seasoned with garlic and thyme.

- 3 tablespoons canola oil
- 6 large shallots, sliced (1½ cups)
- 1½ cups dry white wine
- 1½ quarts heavy cream

Kosher salt and freshly ground pepper

- 2 pounds carrots—peeled, halved lengthwise and sliced crosswise ½ inch thick on the diagonal
- 6 tablespoons unsalted butter
- 2 tablespoons finely grated fresh ginger
- 2 pounds pearl onions
- 2 tablespoons drained prepared horseradish
- 4 large garlic cloves, finely chopped
- 3 pounds mixed mushrooms— such as shiitake, cremini and oyster—stems trimmed, caps thickly sliced
- 1 tablespoon finely chopped thyme

1. In a large saucepan, heat the oil until shimmering. Add the shallots and cook over moderate heat, stirring occasionally, until softened, about 8 minutes. Add the wine and cook until reduced to ¼ cup, about 25 minutes. Add the cream and bring to a boil. Simmer over moderately low heat until thickened and reduced to 4½ cups, about 1½ hours. Strain the cream sauce through a fine sieve into a medium bowl, then season with salt and pepper.

2. Bring a large saucepan of salted water to a boil. Add the carrots and cook over high heat until crisp-tender, about 5 minutes. Drain and pat dry. Melt 2 tablespoons of the butter in the same saucepan. Add the ginger and cook over moderate heat until fragrant, about 2 minutes. Add the carrots and cook, tossing, until coated. Add 1½ cups of the cream sauce and simmer over moderately low heat until the carrots are tender and the sauce is slightly reduced, about 4 minutes. Transfer to a bowl, cover and keep warm. Clean the saucepan.

3. Fill the same saucepan with water and bring to a boil. Add the onions and cook over high heat until crisp-tender, about 5 minutes. Drain the onions and rinse in cold water. Trim the root ends and pull off the skins. Return the peeled onions to the saucepan. Add 1½ cups of the cream sauce and the horseradish. Simmer over moderate heat until the sauce is slightly reduced and the onions are tender, about 2 minutes longer. Transfer the onions to a bowl, cover and keep warm.

4. Melt the remaining 4 tablespoons of butter in a very large, deep skillet. Add the garlic and cook over moderately high heat until lightly browned. Add the mushrooms and thyme and cook, stirring occasionally, until the liquid is evaporated and the mushrooms are golden, about 15 minutes. Stir in the remaining 1½ cups of cream sauce, season with salt and pepper and cook until the sauce is slightly reduced and the mushrooms are very tender. Transfer to a bowl. Serve all of the vegetables. —Michael Mina

MAKE AHEAD The creamed vegetables can be refrigerated overnight.

## Tricolor Roasted Carrots and Parsnips

ACTIVE: 25 MIN; TOTAL: 1 HR

8 TO 10 SERVINGS ● ●

- 3½ pounds parsnips and multicolored carrots, peeled and quartered lengthwise if large
- 2 tablespoons unsalted butter, melted
- 2 tablespoons extra-virgin olive oil

Pinch of sugar

Salt and freshly ground pepper

Preheat the oven to 425°. On a large rimmed baking sheet, toss the carrots and parsnips with the butter, oil and sugar. Spread the vegetables in a single layer and season with salt and pepper. Roast for about 35 minutes, or until tender. Serve hot or warm. —Susan Spungen

## Roasted Root Vegetable Salad with Persimmons

**ACTIVE: 40 MIN; TOTAL: 2 HR**

**6 SERVINGS** ● ●

Tom Fundaro, chef at Villa Creek in Paso Robles, California, looks forward to fall just so he can eat Fuyu persimmons that are as sweet as sugar. Fundaro features them in this satisfying and nicely bitter fall salad.

1½  pounds rutabagas, peeled and cut into 1-inch dice

1½  pounds parsnips, peeled and cut into 1-inch dice

1½  pounds turnips, peeled and cut into 1-inch dice

3  large carrots, peeled and cut into 1-inch dice

½  cup plus 1 tablespoon extra-virgin olive oil

Salt and freshly ground pepper

2  medium shallots, thinly sliced

5  tablespoons sweet white wine

3  tablespoons white wine vinegar

1½  teaspoons chopped thyme

3  Fuyu persimmons, cut into 1-inch dice

One 3-ounce head frisée, torn

2  Belgian endives, cored and sliced crosswise ½ inch thick

½  cup pomegranate seeds

**1.** Preheat the oven to 375°. On a large rimmed baking sheet, toss the rutabagas, parsnips, turnips and carrots with 3 tablespoons of the olive oil. Spread in an even layer and season with salt and pepper. Bake for about 1 hour, stirring occasionally, or until just tender. Let cool.

**2.** In a small skillet, heat the remaining 6 tablespoons of olive oil. Add the shallots and cook over moderate heat until starting to brown, 6 minutes. Transfer to a large bowl and let cool. Stir in the wine, vinegar and thyme. Season with salt and pepper.

**3.** Add the vegetables, persimmons, frisée and endives to the bowl; toss well. Transfer to a platter, sprinkle with the pomegranate seeds and serve. —*Tom Fundaro*

**TRICOLOR ROASTED CARROTS AND PARSNIPS**

**ROASTED ROOT VEGETABLE SALAD WITH PERSIMMONS**

### Fried Okra with Sweet Chile Sauce

**TOTAL: 1 HR**

6 SERVINGS

Howie Velie, chef and owner of Magnolia in Scottsville, Virginia, dips tender, young okra in a cornmeal batter, then fries it until it's puffy, golden and crusty. Make sure to serve the okra right away, since it can get soggy if it sits.

Vegetable oil, for frying

1 cup white cornmeal

1 cup all-purpose flour

1 teaspoon baking powder

Kosher salt

Freshly ground white pepper

1 cup plus 2 tablespoons milk

2 large eggs

1 pound large okra,
   halved lengthwise

Sweet Chile Sauce (recipe follows)

**1.** Fill a large saucepan with 2 inches of oil and heat to 350°. In a medium bowl, mix the cornmeal, flour, baking powder, 1 teaspoon of kosher salt and ½ teaspoon of white pepper. Add the milk and eggs and whisk until the batter is smooth. Add the okra and turn to coat.

**2.** Line a baking sheet with paper towels. Add 10 or 12 pieces of okra at a time to the hot oil and fry over moderately high heat for 2 to 3 minutes, until crisp. Drain on paper towels and sprinkle with salt. Serve right away, with the Sweet Chile Sauce. *—Howie Velie*

### SWEET CHILE SAUCE

**TOTAL: 25 MIN**

MAKES 2 CUPS ● ● ●

1 red bell pepper—cored, seeded and finely chopped

1 red jalapeño or other small red chile, seeded and minced

1 shallot, minced

1 garlic clove, minced

1 cup water

½ cup honey

2 tablespoons soy sauce

Combine all of the ingredients in a saucepan; bring to a boil. Simmer over moderate heat, stirring occasionally, until thickened slightly and syrupy, about 20 minutes. Serve at room temperature. *—H.V.*

**MAKE AHEAD** The sauce can be refrigerated for up to 1 week.

### Cheesy Zucchini Casserole

**ACTIVE: 15 MIN; TOTAL: 40 MIN**

8 SERVINGS ●

4 tablespoons unsalted
   butter, melted

1 tablespoon vegetable oil

3 medium zucchini (about
   2 pounds), cut into 1-inch dice

1 medium onion, very
   finely chopped

Salt and freshly round pepper

1½ cups finely crushed
   saltine crackers

7½ ounces farmer cheese (1 cup)

2 large eggs, beaten

**1.** Preheat the oven to 350°. In a 12-inch ovenproof skillet, stir 2 tablespoons of the melted butter into the vegetable oil. Add the zucchini and onion, season with salt and pepper and cook over moderate heat, stirring occasionally, until the vegetables are softened, about 10 minutes. Remove the zucchini and onion from the heat and let cool slightly.

**2.** In a medium bowl, stir the cracker crumbs with the farmer cheese. Stir half of the mixture into the zucchini and season generously with salt and pepper. Stir in the beaten eggs. Spread the remaining cracker crumb and farmer cheese mixture on top of the zucchini. Drizzle the casserole with the remaining 2 tablespoons of melted butter and bake for 25 minutes, or until lightly browned and crisp on top. Let stand for 5 minutes, then serve warm. *—Jeremy Jackson*

**MAKE AHEAD** The casserole can be prepared earlier in the day and reheated in a 350° oven.

### Roasted Squash with Chestnuts and Pomegranate

**ACTIVE: 30 MIN; TOTAL: 1 HR 30 MIN**

8 SERVINGS ● ● ●

A drizzle of tangy pomegranate molasses gives this oven-roasted squash a more exotic taste.

2 small organic red kuri or kabocha squash (3 pounds total)—washed, halved lengthwise and seeded

5 tablespoons unsalted butter, 3 tablespoons melted

3 tablespoons dark brown sugar

Salt and freshly ground pepper

6 ounces vacuum-packed whole roasted peeled chestnuts (about 1 cup)

12 thyme sprigs

½ cup red currants or seeds from 1 pomegranate

1½ tablespoons pomegranate molasses (see Note)

**1.** Preheat the oven to 350°. Set the squash cut side up on a large rimmed baking sheet; brush with the melted butter. Sprinkle the sugar in the cavities; season with salt and pepper. Turn the squash over on the sheet and roast for about 1 hour, until tender and browned at the edges.

**2.** Meanwhile, heat the remaining 2 tablespoons of butter in a medium skillet. Add the chestnuts and thyme sprigs and cook over moderate heat, stirring occasionally, until the chestnuts are lightly browned and glazed with the butter, 8 to 10 minutes. Discard the thyme sprigs.

**3.** Cut each squash half into 4 wedges and arrange on a large platter. Scatter the chestnuts and currants over the squash. Drizzle with the pomegranate molasses and serve. *—Govind Armstrong*

**NOTE** Sweet-tart pomegranate molasses is available at specialty food shops and Middle Eastern markets.

**MAKE AHEAD** The baked squash can be refrigerated overnight; rewarm in the oven before drizzling with the molasses.

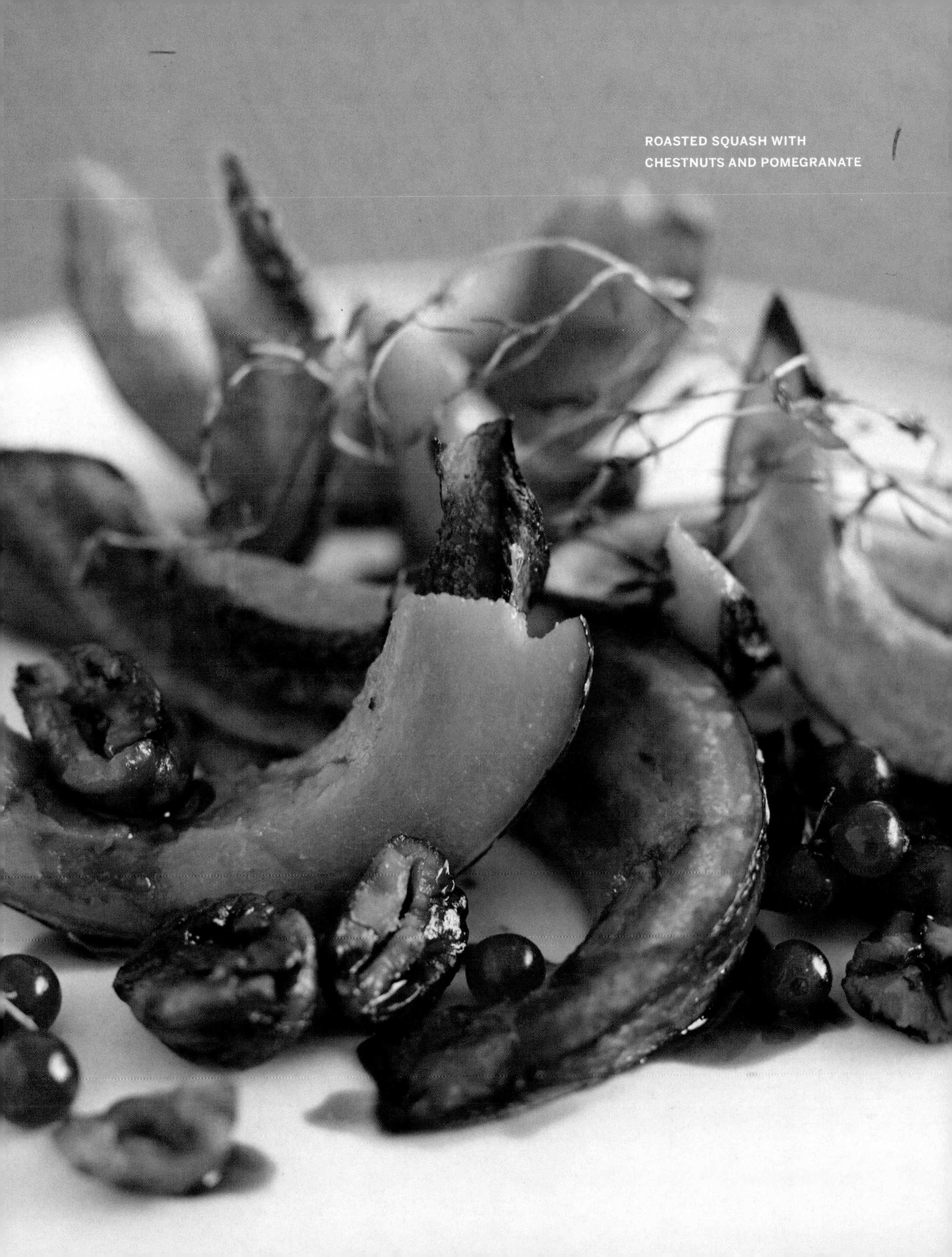
ROASTED SQUASH WITH
CHESTNUTS AND POMEGRANATE

## Carrots with Lime Butter

**TOTAL: 25 MIN**

**4 SERVINGS** ● ●

2 tablespoons unsalted butter

1½ pounds carrots, sliced ½ inch thick on the diagonal

2 scallions, thinly sliced

2 tablespoons fresh lime juice

1 teaspoon grated lime zest

Kosher salt and freshly ground pepper

2 tablespoons chopped pecans

1 tablespoon chopped parsley

Melt the butter in a large skillet. Add the sliced carrots and scallions and cook over moderate heat, stirring occasionally, until the scallions are softened, about 3 minutes. Add the lime juice and lime zest and season the carrots with salt and pepper. Cover the skillet and cook the carrots until they are crisp-tender, about 15 minutes. Stir in the chopped pecans and parsley and serve at once. —*Ann Withey*

## Thai-Style Tofu and Vegetables

**TOTAL: 30 MIN**

**4 SERVINGS** ● ●

1 tablespoon vegetable oil

1 onion, thinly sliced lengthwise

1 tablespoon grated fresh ginger

1 garlic clove, thinly sliced

1 large jalapeño, thinly sliced crosswise with seeds

1 teaspoon turmeric

# ingredient
**LEMONGRASS**

Lemongrass is an herb often used in Thai and Vietnamese cooking. Citral, an oil also found in lemon peel, gives lemongrass its delicate lemony flavor and aroma. **Wrap** fresh lemongrass in plastic and store for up to two weeks in the refrigerator. **When cooking,** use only the softer inner core, as the outer leaves are tough and woody.

4 large shiitake mushrooms, stems discarded, caps thickly sliced

2 cups small broccoli florets

1 medium carrot, thinly sliced crosswise

3 canned plum tomatoes, chopped

1¼ cups light unsweetened coconut milk

1 pound firm tofu, cut into 1-inch cubes

½ cup water

2 tablespoons soy sauce

½ cup coarsely chopped basil

Lime wedges, for serving

**1.** In a large skillet or wok, heat the vegetable oil. Add the onion, ginger, garlic and jalapeño and stir-fry over moderately high heat for 2 minutes. Add the turmeric, shiitake caps, broccoli and carrot and stir-fry for 3 minutes.

**2.** Add the tomatoes, coconut milk, tofu, water and soy sauce to the skillet and simmer over moderately high heat, stirring a few times, until al dente, about 4 minutes. Stir the basil into the vegetables, transfer to plates and serve with the lime wedges on the side. —*Peter Berley*

## Aromatic Yellow Curry Sauce

**TOTAL: 40 MIN**

**MAKES 2½ CUPS** ● ●

3 tablespoons Asian fish sauce

2 stalks of fresh lemongrass—tender inner cores only, thinly sliced crosswise—4 inches of the tops reserved

2 medium shallots, thinly sliced

2 garlic cloves, smashed

1 tablespoon sugar

1 tablespoon curry powder

2 tablespoons vegetable oil

1 medium onion, thinly sliced

One 13½-ounce can unsweetened coconut milk

4 canned plum tomatoes, drained and chopped

1¼ teaspoons turmeric

Seasoning sachet made with 20 cilantro stems, 1 lime leaf, 1 red Thai chile and the reserved lemongrass tops, tied with string

⅓ cup salted roasted peanuts

Salt

**1.** In a food processor, pulse the fish sauce, lemongrass slices, shallots, garlic, sugar and curry to a fine paste.

**2.** In a medium saucepan, heat the oil. Add the onion and cook over moderately low heat until softened, about 7 minutes. Stir in the coconut milk, tomatoes, turmeric and the spice paste and bring to a boil. Add the seasoning sachet and simmer over low heat, stirring occasionally, until the sauce coats the back of a spoon, about 15 minutes. Let cool slightly, then discard the sachet. Transfer the contents of the saucepan to a blender. Add the peanuts and blend to a puree. Season with salt. —*Jean-Georges Vongerichten*

**SERVE WITH** Steamed vegetables.

**MAKE AHEAD** The sauce can be refrigerated for up to 2 days.

## Fresh Green Curry Sauce

**TOTAL: 40 MIN**

**MAKES 2½ CUPS** ●

2 cups packed chopped cilantro leaves and stems

3 green Thai chiles, thinly sliced

1 ounce fresh ginger, peeled and thinly sliced (3 tablespoons)

2 stalks of fresh lemongrass, tender inner cores only, thinly sliced crosswise

1 garlic clove, smashed

1 teaspoon ground coriander

½ teaspoon ground cumin

½ cup water

One 13½-ounce can unsweetened coconut milk

½ cup chicken stock or low-sodium broth

Salt

1. In a food processor, combine the cilantro, chiles, ginger, lemongrass, garlic, coriander, cumin and water and process the spices to a fine paste.

2. In a medium saucepan, combine the coconut milk, chicken stock and the spice paste and bring to a boil. Simmer over moderate heat, stirring occasionally, until the sauce coats the back of a spoon, about 15 minutes. Season with salt.

—*Jean-Georges Vongerichten*

**SERVE WITH** Raw or steamed vegetables, chicken or fish.

**MAKE AHEAD** The sauce can be refrigerated for up to 2 days.

## Seven-Vegetable Couscous
**ACTIVE: 1 HR; TOTAL: 2 HR 15 MIN**
6 SERVINGS

- 1 stick (4 ounces) unsalted butter
- 4 medium tomatoes, coarsely chopped
- 2 pounds well-trimmed boneless lamb shoulder, cut into 1-inch cubes
- 1 large onion, finely chopped
- 1 teaspoon ground cumin

Kosher salt and freshly ground pepper
- 1 tablespoon *harissa* (see Note), plus more for serving

10¾ cups water
- 3 cups couscous
- 2 tablespoons vegetable oil
- 3 large carrots, peeled and quartered lengthwise, quarters halved crosswise
- 2 medium white turnips, peeled and cut into ½-inch wedges
- ½ head Savoy cabbage, cut into 6 wedges

One ½-pound eggplant—peeled, halved crosswise and cut into 1-inch-thick sticks
- ½ medium butternut squash, peeled and cut into 1-inch-wide sticks
- 3 medium zucchini, quartered lengthwise

1. In a large enameled cast-iron casserole, melt the butter. Add the chopped tomatoes, cubed lamb and chopped onion, then season the stew with the cumin and 1 teaspoon each of salt and pepper. Cook the stew over moderate heat, stirring occasionally, until the onion is softened, about 10 minutes. Stir in the 1 tablespoon of *harissa* and 4 cups of the water and bring to a simmer. Cover and gently simmer over low heat until the lamb is almost tender, about 45 minutes.

2. Meanwhile, in a large bowl, toss the couscous with the vegetable oil. Stir in 6 cups of the water. Drain the couscous in a fine sieve and return it to the bowl, fluffing it with your hands to remove any lumps. Cover the couscous with plastic wrap.

3. Add the carrots, turnips and Savoy cabbage to the casserole. Line a large bamboo steamer with cheesecloth and set it over the casserole, then bring the stew to a brisk simmer over moderate heat. Spread ½ cup of the couscous in the steamer and steam for 5 minutes. Gradually sprinkle the remaining couscous on top, mounding it slightly. Steam the couscous over the stew for 20 minutes.

4. Scrape the couscous into a large, shallow bowl and sprinkle the remaining ¾ cup of water and 1 teaspoon of salt over it. Fluff the couscous with a wooden spoon and let it cool for 10 minutes, stirring occasionally with your hands to remove any lumps.

5. Add the eggplant, squash and zucchini to the casserole; bring the stew to a simmer over moderate heat. Set the steamer over the stew once again and gradually sprinkle the couscous back into the steamer, mounding it slightly. Let the couscous steam for 15 minutes longer.

6. Transfer the steamed couscous to a large serving bowl; form a well in the center. Season the cooked lamb with salt and pepper, spoon it into the well in the center of the couscous and arrange the vegetables around it. Pour the sauce around the couscous and serve at once, with *harissa* on the side.
—*Dar Liqama Cooking School*

**NOTE** *Harissa,* a North African chile paste, is available at Middle Eastern markets and specialty food stores.

## Sautéed Asparagus with Wild Mushroom Sauce
**TOTAL: 30 MIN**
6 SERVINGS ●

- 2 pounds thick asparagus, peeled
- 2 tablespoons extra-virgin olive oil
- 1 pound chanterelle or oyster mushrooms, thickly sliced
- 3 medium shallots, minced
- 1 garlic clove, minced

Salt and freshly ground pepper
- ½ cup dry white wine
- 1 cup chicken stock
- 1 cup heavy cream
- 1 tablespoon minced parsley
- 1 tablespoon unsalted butter

1. Bring a large pot of salted water to a boil. Add the asparagus and cook until crisp-tender, about 5 minutes. Drain, rinse under cold water and pat dry.

2. In a large, deep skillet, heat the olive oil until shimmering. Add the chanterelles and cook over high heat, stirring occasionally, until golden and dry, 6 minutes. Add the shallots and garlic, season with salt and pepper and cook until softened, about 2 minutes. Add the wine and cook until nearly evaporated, scraping up any bits stuck to the bottom of the pan. Add the stock and cook until reduced by half, about 3 minutes. Add the cream and cook until reduced by half, about 5 minutes. Season the sauce with salt and pepper and stir in the parsley; keep warm.

3. Melt the butter in a large skillet. Add the asparagus and cook over high heat, shaking the pan until the asparagas are heated through, about 2 minutes. Transfer to plates and spoon the sauce on top.
—*Dominique Filoni*

BBQ obsessive Adam Perry Lang of New York City's Daisy May's BBQ USA concocted this incredible Baked Three-Bean Casserole with Crispy Bacon (P. 258) for the April issue.

# potatoes, grains & beans

**VANILLA BEAN–WHIPPED SWEET POTATOES**

**MAPLE-BAKED SWEET POTATOES**

## Vanilla Bean–Whipped
## Sweet Potatoes

**ACTIVE: 15 MIN; TOTAL: 45 MIN**

10 SERVINGS ●

- 4 pounds medium sweet potatoes
- 1 cup heavy cream
- 4 tablespoons unsalted butter
- ½ vanilla bean, slit lengthwise, seeds scraped

**Kosher salt and freshly ground pepper**

**1.** Preheat the oven to 400°. Poke the sweet potatoes several times with a fork and bake for about 35 minutes, or until tender. Let cool slightly, then peel and transfer them to a food processor. Puree until fairly smooth.

**2.** In a small saucepan, combine the cream with the butter and the vanilla bean and seeds. Bring to a simmer. Remove the vanilla bean. With the processor on, carefully pour the vanilla cream into the sweet potatoes and process until smooth. Season the sweet potato puree with salt and pepper, transfer to a bowl and serve. —*Gerry Hayden*

**MAKE AHEAD** The sweet potatoes can be refrigerated overnight.

## Maple-Baked Sweet Potatoes

**ACTIVE: 20 MIN; TOTAL: 1 HR**

6 SERVINGS ● ●

Parboiling the sweet potatoes first helps keep them supermoist.

- 3 pounds medium sweet potatoes, peeled and cut into 1½-inch pieces
- ½ teaspoon salt
- ¾ teaspoon freshly ground pepper
- 3 tablespoons unsalted butter, cut into ½-inch pieces
- ⅓ cup pure maple syrup
- ⅓ cup water

**1.** Preheat the oven to 400°. In a large saucepan, cover the sweet potatoes with water and bring to a boil. Reduce the heat to moderate and cook the sweet potatoes until they are just tender, about 5 minutes. Drain the potatoes well.

**2.** Arrange the sweet potatoes in a large gratin dish. Season them with the salt and pepper, then dot with the butter pieces. Drizzle the maple syrup over the potatoes. Sprinkle the sweet potatoes with the water and bake them for 15 minutes. Turn the potatoes over and bake them for about 25 minutes longer, or until they are tender and lightly browned. If necessary, broil the sweet potatoes for 1 or 2 minutes before serving to caramelize the maple syrup a bit more. —*Jacques Pépin*

**MAKE AHEAD** The potatoes can be parboiled earlier in the day and kept at room temperature.

## Crispy Scallion Potato Pancakes

**TOTAL: 40 MIN**

**8 TO 10 SERVINGS** ●

- 4½ pounds baking potatoes, peeled and shredded on the large holes of a box grater
- 1 bunch scallions, white and green parts, finely chopped
- 1 large egg white
- 1 tablespoon kosher salt
- ½ teaspoon freshly ground pepper
- ¾ cup vegetable oil

**1.** Squeeze the shredded potatoes dry. In a large bowl, using 2 forks, mix the shredded potatoes with the scallions, egg white, salt and pepper.

**2.** Set two 10-inch nonstick skillets over high heat. Add 3 tablespoons of oil to each skillet. Add half of the potato mixture to each skillet and press into firm cakes. Set a heatproof plate or glass pie plate over each cake just to cover it. Weight each plate with a large, heavy can and reduce the heat to moderate. Cook for 5 minutes. Uncover carefully and slide the potato cakes onto plates. Add 3 tablespoons of the remaining oil to each skillet. Carefully invert the potato cakes and return them to the skillets. Press the cakes firmly and cook until they are browned and crisp on the bottom, about 12 minutes longer. Slide the potato cakes onto a work surface, cut into wedges and serve. —*Tyler Florence*

**MAKE AHEAD** The potato cakes can be cooked up to 4 hours ahead. Just before serving, cut them into wedges and cook in a nonstick skillet over moderate heat for about 4 minutes per side.

## Creamy Fennel-Mashed Potatoes

**ACTIVE: 30 MIN; TOTAL: 1 HR**

**6 TO 8 SERVINGS** ●

Instead of relying on heavy cream and butter, this recipe uses lighter ingredients like olive oil and half-and-half for creaminess. The fennel puree adds an aromatic twist to the familiar potato flavor.

- 2 pounds baking potatoes, peeled and quartered
- 2 pounds Yukon Gold potatoes, peeled and quartered
- Salt
- 3 medium fennel bulbs—halved lengthwise, cored and sliced ¼ inch thick
- 1 cup half-and-half, warmed until hot
- ½ cup extra-virgin olive oil
- Freshly ground pepper

**1.** In a large pot, cover the potatoes with water, add salt and bring to a boil. Cook the potatoes over moderately high heat until fork-tender, about 25 minutes.

**2.** Set a steamer basket in a large saucepan with ½ inch of boiling water. Add the fennel, cover and steam over moderate heat until tender, about 12 minutes. Transfer the fennel to a blender or food processor, add the half-and-half and olive oil and puree.

**3.** Drain the potatoes and return them to the pot. Shake the potatoes over high heat until thoroughly dry. Working over a large bowl, mash the potatoes through a ricer. Stir in the fennel puree, season with salt and pepper and serve. —*Cal Peternell*

**MAKE AHEAD** The potatoes can be prepared 1 hour ahead. Keep warm in a covered pot, then reheat gently, stirring often.

## Three-Mustard Potato Salad

**ACTIVE: 15 MIN; TOTAL: 1 HR PLUS OVERNIGHT CHILLING**

**8 SERVINGS** ● ●

This potato salad is made with three different mustards—yellow, Dijon and whole-grain—to get a complex layering of heat and flavor. Flecks of red pepper, red onion and parsley enliven the salad as well.

- 2 pounds medium red potatoes
- ½ cup plus 2 tablespoons mayonnaise
- 2 tablespoons Dijon mustard
- 1 tablespoon whole-grain mustard
- 1 tablespoon yellow mustard
- 2 tablespoons red wine vinegar
- 2 tablespoons extra-virgin olive oil
- 1 small red onion, finely chopped
- ½ cup finely chopped roasted red peppers
- 2 tablespoons finely chopped flat-leaf parsley
- Salt and freshly ground pepper

**1.** Put the potatoes in a pot of water and bring to a boil. Cook over moderate heat until tender, 25 minutes. Drain and let cool completely, then cut into 1-inch pieces.

**2.** In a large bowl, combine the mayonnaise with the mustards, vinegar and olive oil and whisk until smooth. Add the onion, roasted red peppers and parsley. Gently fold in the potatoes and season with salt and pepper. Cover and refrigerate overnight. —*Todd English*

**MAKE AHEAD** The potato salad can be refrigerated for up to 3 days. Let stand for 30 minutes before serving.

## Rustic Mashed Potatoes and Cabbage

**ACTIVE: 20 MIN; TOTAL: 40 MIN**

**8 SERVINGS** ●

- 2 pounds baking potatoes, peeled and cut into 2-inch chunks
- ¼ pound Savoy cabbage, diced
- Salt
- 1 tablespoon unsalted butter
- 1 tablespoon extra-virgin olive oil
- ¼ cup whole milk
- Freshly ground pepper

Put the potatoes and cabbage in a large saucepan, cover with water and bring to a boil. Add salt and simmer over moderately high heat until the potatoes are tender, about 20 minutes. Drain in a colander and return to the pan. Shake the pan over moderately high heat to dry out the potatoes. Remove from the heat. Using a potato masher, mash the potatoes with the cabbage. Mash in the butter and olive oil. Stir in the milk, season with salt and pepper and serve. —*Sergi Millet*

# potatoes, grains & beans

## Coriander-Spiced New Potatoes in Spinach Sauce

**ACTIVE: 45 MIN; TOTAL: 1 HR 10 MIN**

**12 SERVINGS ● ●**

This recipe is cookbook author Neelam Batra's riff on the ubiquitous restaurant dish *saag paneer* (spinach with Indian cheese), with tender chunks of potato coated in a silky spinach puree.

- **2½ pounds small red potatoes (about 1½ inches in diameter), scrubbed**
- **¼ cup water**
- **2 pounds baby spinach**
- **3 tablespoons vegetable oil**
- **1 large onion, finely chopped**
- **3 large garlic cloves, minced**
- **2 tablespoons peeled, minced fresh ginger**
- **2 jalapeños, minced with some seeds**
- **3 large tomatoes, finely chopped**
- **1 cup coarsely chopped cilantro, plus cilantro leaves for garnish**
- **2 tablespoons ground coriander**
- **2 teaspoons ground cumin**
- **1 teaspoon paprika**
- **1 teaspoon garam masala**
- **¾ cup plain yogurt**
- **Salt**
- **Cherry tomatoes, quartered, for garnish**

1. Put the potatoes in a large pot of salted water and bring to a boil. Boil over moderate heat until tender when pierced with a knife, about 25 minutes. Drain and let cool, then halve the potatoes.

2. Meanwhile, in a large, deep skillet, bring the water to a boil. Working in batches, add the baby spinach by the handful and cook it over moderately high heat until it is wilted. Using tongs, transfer the baby spinach to a colander set in the sink to drain and repeat with the remaining spinach. Squeeze the spinach dry, then transfer it to a food processor and puree. Wipe out the skillet before proceeding.

3. Heat the oil in the same skillet. Add the chopped onion and cook over moderately high heat, stirring occasionally, until the onion is beginning to brown, about 8 minutes. Add the garlic, ginger and jalapeños and cook, stirring, until fragrant, about 3 minutes. Add the tomatoes and cilantro and cook over moderate heat until most of the liquid has evaporated, 10 minutes. Add the coriander, cumin, paprika and garam masala and cook, stirring, for 2 minutes.

4. Slowly stir in the yogurt. Add the potatoes and a large pinch of salt, cover and cook over moderately low heat for 5 minutes, stirring occasionally. Add the pureed spinach and stir well. Cover and simmer for 10 minutes to blend the flavors. Season with salt. Transfer the potatoes and spinach to a platter or bowl, garnish with the cilantro leaves and cherry tomatoes and serve. —*Neelam Batra*

**MAKE AHEAD** The recipe can be prepared up to 4 hours ahead; reheat gently.

## Twice-Baked Potatoes with Tetilla and Roasted Fennel

**ACTIVE: 25 MIN; TOTAL: 1 HR 15 MIN**

**4 SERVINGS**

Melting the cheese a bit before mashing it into the potatoes and mixing in caramelized fennel gives these twice-baked potatoes a light, fluffy filling. Monterey Jack or Fontina cheese are good substitutes for the Tetilla here.

- **4 large Yukon Gold potatoes, scrubbed**
- **1 medium fennel bulb—halved lengthwise, cored and cut into ½-inch wedges—plus 1 tablespoon chopped fronds**
- **3 tablespoons dry white wine**
- **2 tablespoons extra-virgin olive oil**
- **Salt and freshly ground pepper**
- **½ pound Tetilla or other young cow's-milk cheese, such as Monterey Jack or Fontina**
- **⅔ cup whole milk**
- **1 tablespoon unsalted butter, softened**
- **1 small garlic clove, very finely chopped**

1. Preheat the oven to 425°. Bake the potatoes directly on the upper rack of the oven for 40 minutes, or until tender.

2. Meanwhile, spread the fennel wedges in a shallow glass baking dish and drizzle with the wine and olive oil. Season with salt and pepper. Cover the dish with foil and bake in the bottom third of the oven for 40 minutes, or until the fennel is tender and golden brown on the bottom. Let cool slightly, then chop enough of the roasted fennel to measure ¾ cup.

3. Cut one-quarter of the cheese into 8 slices. Cut the remaining cheese into small dice and transfer to a medium glass bowl. Add the milk and cook in a microwave at high power for 1 minute, or until the milk is very hot and the cheese is softened.

4. Halve the warm baked potatoes lengthwise. With a spoon and working over a bowl, scoop out the potatoes to within ¼ inch of the skins. Using a masher or a large fork, coarsely mash the potatoes with the butter. Pour in the hot milk, stopping before you reach the cheese at the bottom of the bowl. Add the garlic and mash the potatoes until smooth and fluffy. Stir in the softened cheese, then the chopped roasted fennel. Season with salt and pepper. Spoon the stuffing into the potato skins and transfer to a baking sheet. Top each potato half with a slice of the remaining cheese.

5. Bake the potatoes in the upper third of the oven for 12 minutes, or until they are hot throughout and the cheese is melted. Sprinkle the chopped fennel fronds over the potatoes and serve with the roasted fennel wedges. —*Marcia Kiesel*

**MAKE AHEAD** The potatoes can be prepared through Step 4 and refrigerated earlier in the day. Let the potatoes return to room temperature before baking.

## Potatoes with Goat Cheese Fondue

**TOTAL: 25 MIN**

**4 SERVINGS** ●

This light fondue is made with sabayon, a frothy custard that gets whisked in a bowl set over the pot of simmering water that was used to cook the potatoes. The fondue is silky, slightly tangy and sublime with the warm new potatoes—or even with chunks of bread.

- **1 pound tiny new potatoes (1 inch in diameter), scrubbed**
- **Kosher salt**
- **2 large egg yolks**
- **3 tablespoons half-and-half**
- **3 tablespoons dry white wine, such as Chardonnay**
- **1 tablespoon coarsely chopped marjoram**
- **5 ounces crumbled fresh goat cheese (1 cup)**
- **Freshly ground pepper**

**1.** Put the new potatoes in a medium saucepan and cover them with water. Add 2 tablespoons of salt and bring to a boil. Cook the potatoes over moderate heat until tender, about 15 minutes. Using a slotted spoon, transfer the cooked potatoes to a plate. Return the saucepan of water that was used to cook the potatoes to the stove and keep the water at a low simmer.

**2.** Meanwhile, in a medium stainless steel bowl, whisk the egg yolks with the half-and-half, white wine and chopped marjoram. Set the bowl of whisked egg yolks over the saucepan of simmering water and cook, whisking constantly, until the egg yolk mixture is frothy, tripled in volume and thickened, about 3 minutes. Add the crumbled goat cheese to the egg yolks and whisk until the fondue is smooth and creamy. Season the fondue with salt and pepper and transfer to 4 ramekins. Serve immediately, with the new potatoes. —*Jerry Traunfeld*

## Salt-Baked Yukon Golds with Three Seasoned Butters

**ACTIVE: 45 MIN; TOTAL: 1 HR 30 MIN**

**10 SERVINGS**

Baking creamy Yukon Golds in a bed of salt results in evenly cooked, moist and tender potatoes. Try serving them with three flavored butters—scallion, mustard and horseradish—as an upscale take on a basic, homey side dish.

- **About 4½ pounds kosher salt**
- **10 large Yukon Gold potatoes (about 4½ pounds), scrubbed**
- **6 scallions, white and light green parts thinly sliced, dark green parts cut into 1-inch lengths**
- **3 sticks (¾ pound) unsalted butter, softened**
- **Table salt and freshly ground pepper**
- **2 tablespoons grainy mustard**
- **1½ teaspoons Dijon mustard**
- **1½ tablespoons drained prepared horseradish**
- **1 tablespoon fresh lemon juice**

**1.** Preheat the oven to 400°. Spread a layer of kosher salt ½ inch thick in a large, deep roasting pan. Nestle the potatoes in the salt and cover with the remaining kosher salt. Bake in the center of the oven for about 1¼ hours, or until tender.

**2.** Meanwhile, in a small saucepan of boiling water, cook the dark scallion greens until softened and bright green, about 20 seconds. Drain and rinse the scallion greens in cold water, transfer to a mini food processor and finely chop. Add 1 stick of the butter and pulse until combined. Add the white and light green scallion slices and a pinch each of table salt and pepper and pulse until incorporated. Scrape the butter into a ramekin and refrigerate until firm, or keep at room temperature.

**3.** Wipe out the food processor. Add a stick of butter, the grainy and Dijon mustards and a pinch each of salt and pepper. Pulse just until blended. Scrape the butter into a ramekin and refrigerate until firm, or keep at room temperature. Repeat with the remaining butter, the horseradish, lemon juice and a pinch each of salt and pepper.

**4.** When the potatoes are done, carefully brush off the salt and transfer them to a platter. Serve the potatoes with the flavored butters. —*Michael Mina*

# equipment
### NEW EUROPEAN RANGES

**AGA**

The cult British cast-iron-stove company has introduced all-electric versions of its cooker (above). The enamel finish is available in 15 colors. **DETAILS** From $9,975; 866-4AGA-4USA or aga-ranges.com.

**DELAUBRAC**

These antique-style French ranges have stainless steel bodies and cast-iron cooktops. Designed with chefs in mind, they have professional features like oven doors that can be kicked shut. **DETAILS** From $12,000; 714-669-8461 or delaubrac.com.

**LA CORNUE**

At half the price of the original La Cornue stoves, the CornuFé line offers limited customizability but plenty of style and functionality. **DETAILS** From $8,000; 800-892-4040 or la-cornue.com.

# potatoes, grains & beans

## Brown Rice Pilaf with Mushrooms

**ACTIVE: 20 MIN; TOTAL: 1 HR 20 MIN**

4 SERVINGS ●

2½ tablespoons extra-virgin olive oil
½ pound small white
   mushrooms, quartered
5 scallions, thinly sliced
Salt and freshly ground pepper
4 large garlic cloves,
   coarsely chopped
1 tablespoon soy sauce
1 cup long-grain brown rice
1 cup chicken stock
   or low-sodium broth
1 cup water
¼ lime

**1.** Preheat the oven to 350°. In a medium skillet, heat 2 tablespoons of the olive oil. Add the mushrooms and all but 2 tablespoons of the scallions; season with salt and pepper. Cook over moderate heat, stirring occasionally, until any liquid has evaporated and the mushrooms are browned, 8 minutes. Add the garlic and the remaining olive oil and cook over moderately high heat, stirring, until the garlic is golden, 2 minutes. Stir in the soy sauce and rice. Add the stock and water and bring to a boil. Add a large pinch each of salt and pepper.

**2.** Scrape the rice into a 9-inch square glass or ceramic baking dish. Cover the rice with foil and bake for 45 minutes, or until the liquid has been absorbed and the rice is tender. Let the pilaf stand, covered, for 10 minutes.

**3.** Squeeze the lime quarter over the pilaf and fluff with a spoon. Season with salt, sprinkle with the remaining sliced scallions and serve. —*Marcia Kiesel*

## Citrus Risotto with Seared Garlic-Chile Shrimp

**TOTAL: 45 MIN**

4 SERVINGS

This recipe calls for red Thai chiles, which are very spicy. Use a less fiery chile, such as jalapeño or serrano, for a milder dish.

2 garlic cloves, chopped
2 small red Thai chiles, chopped
6 cups chicken stock
3 tablespoons unsalted butter
3 tablespoons extra-virgin olive oil
1 small onion, minced
1½ cups arborio rice
1 tablespoon fresh lemon juice
1½ teaspoons grated lemon zest
Salt and freshly ground pepper
½ pound medium shrimp, shelled
   and deveined
¼ cup chopped flat-leaf parsley
Lemon wedges, for serving

**1.** In a mortar, pound the garlic and chiles to make a paste. Cover and set aside.

**2.** In a saucepan, bring the stock to a boil. Cover and keep hot. In a saucepan, melt 1 tablespoon of the butter in 1 tablespoon of the olive oil. Add the onion and cook over moderate heat until softened, 4 minutes. Add the rice and cook, stirring, for 1 minute. Gradually add the stock, 1 cup at a time, stirring constantly, until the stock has been absorbed before adding more, 25 minutes total. The risotto is done when the grains are just tender and the sauce is creamy. Remove from the heat and stir in the lemon juice and zest and the remaining butter. Season with salt and pepper and cover.

**3.** In a skillet, heat the remaining olive oil. Add the shrimp, season with salt and pepper and cook over high heat until the shrimp are almost pink throughout, 2 minutes. Add the chile-garlic paste and cook, stirring, for 1 minute. Stir in the parsley.

**4.** Stir the risotto, spoon into bowls and top with the shrimp. Serve with lemon wedges. —*Bill Granger*

## Chimayó-Chile Risotto with Shiitake Mushrooms

**ACTIVE: 45 MIN; TOTAL: 1 HR 30 MIN**

4 SERVINGS ●

This risotto is infused with moderately hot Chimayó chile powder from the town of the same name in northern New Mexico.

4 quarts water
1 cup dry white wine
1 large onion, halved
1 large tomato, halved
1 large carrot, quartered
1 zucchini, halved lengthwise
1 yellow squash, halved lengthwise
1 leek, halved lengthwise
3 large white mushrooms, sliced
2 thyme sprigs
2 rosemary sprigs
2 garlic cloves, crushed
1 bay leaf
1 teaspoon celery seeds
6 whole black peppercorns
Salt
2 tablespoons canola oil
2 small shallots, minced
¾ cup arborio rice
1 teaspoon pure chile powder,
   such as Chimayó or ancho
1 bay leaf
4 large shiitake mushrooms,
   stemmed, caps thinly sliced
1 tablespoon heavy cream
1 tablespoon unsalted butter
¼ cup grated Parmesan cheese
Freshly ground pepper

**1.** In a pot, bring the water to a boil with the wine, onion, tomato, carrot, zucchini, squash, leek, white mushrooms, thyme, rosemary, garlic, bay leaf, celery seeds, peppercorns and 1 teaspoon of salt. Reduce the heat to moderately low and simmer for 40 minutes. Strain the stock into a large heatproof bowl. Transfer 4 cups to a saucepan. Freeze the rest for another use. Bring the reserved stock to a simmer; keep hot.

**2.** In a heavy, medium saucepan, heat 1 tablespoon of the oil. Add the shallots and cook over moderately high heat, stirring constantly, for 1 to 2 minutes. Add the rice, chile powder and bay leaf and cook, stirring, for 2 minutes. Add 1 cup of the hot stock and cook, stirring frequently, until it is nearly absorbed. Continue adding stock, ½ cup at a time, and stirring constantly until it is nearly absorbed before adding more. The risotto is done when the rice is tender and the liquid is creamy.

**3.** In a nonstick skillet, heat the remaining 1 tablespoon of oil. Add the shiitake and brown over moderately high heat, 5 to 6 minutes. Stir the shiitake, cream, butter and cheese into the risotto. Season with salt and pepper and serve. —*Kevin Graham*

## Bulgur Pilaf with Mixed Greens and Garlic

**ACTIVE: 20 MIN; TOTAL: 1 HR**

**4 SERVINGS** ● ● ◐

- 1 small head garlic, cloves peeled and coarsely chopped

Salt

- 1 pound yellow onions, finely chopped
- 1 pound mixed sweet and earthy greens, such as Tuscan kale, Swiss chard and beet greens, stemmed and finely shredded
- 1 cup coarse bulgur (3½ ounces)
- ¼ cup extra-virgin olive oil
- 2½ teaspoons Turkish red pepper paste (see Note)
- ½ teaspoon freshly ground black pepper
- ¼ teaspoon Turkish red pepper flakes
- ½ cup water

Scallions and lemon slices, for serving

**1.** On a work surface, mash the chopped garlic with 1 teaspoon of salt. In a large, deep saucepan, combine the mashed garlic with the onions, mixed greens, bulgur, olive oil, red pepper paste, black pepper and red pepper flakes. Season with salt.

**2.** Using your hands, work the water into the bulgur mixture until absorbed, then cover with a paper towel. Set the pan over low heat, cover and steam the greens and bulgur until very tender, about 30 minutes. Serve hot or cold, garnished with the scallions and lemon slices. —*Paula Wolfert*

**NOTE** Turkish red pepper paste is available at Middle Eastern markets.

**CHIMAYÓ-CHILE RISOTTO WITH SHIITAKE MUSHROOMS**

**BULGUR PILAF WITH MIXED GREENS AND GARLIC**

SUMMER BULGUR AND
GREEN BEAN SALAD

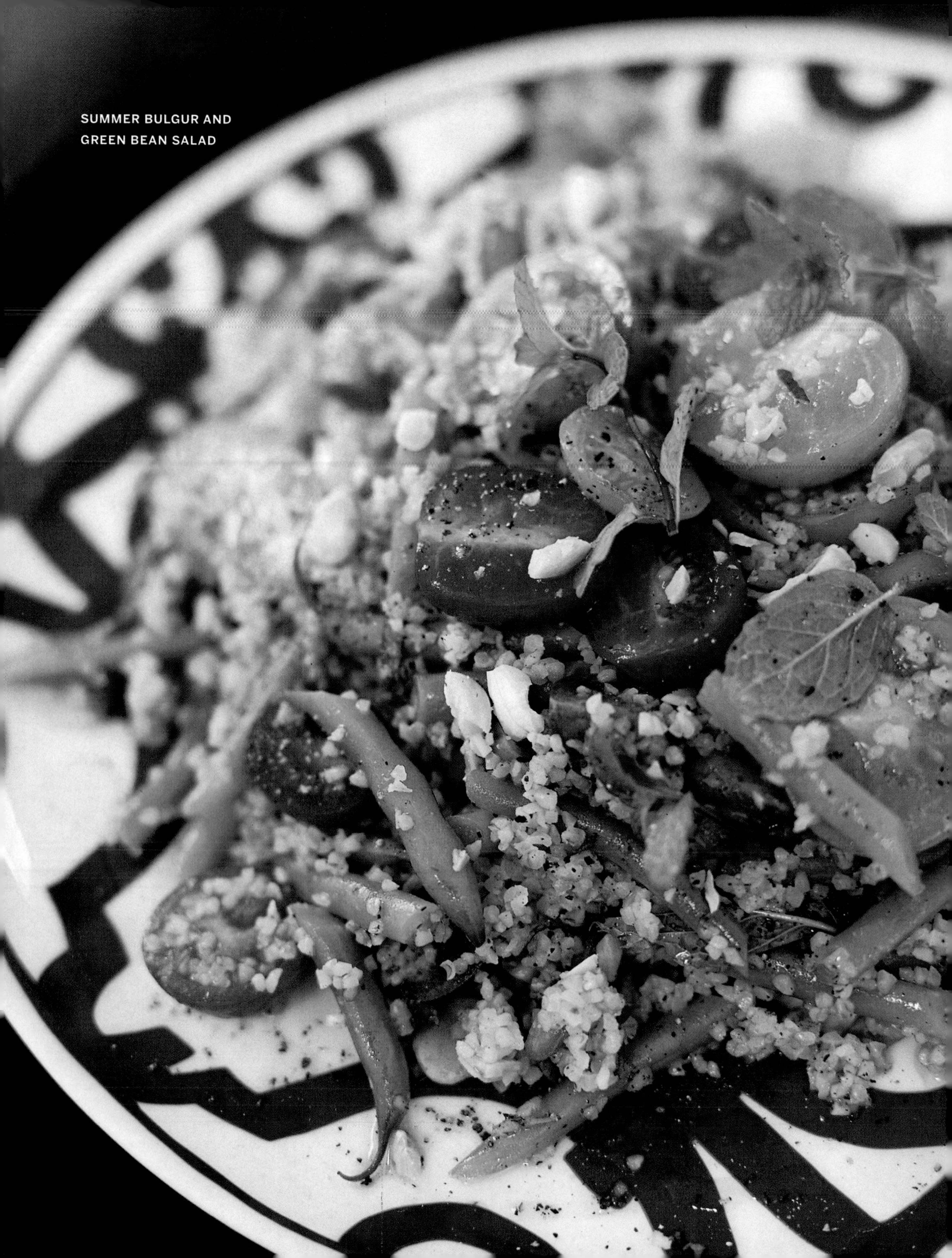

## Summer Bulgur and Green Bean Salad

**TOTAL: 30 MIN**

8 SERVINGS ● ●

- 2 cups boiling water
- 2 cups medium-grind bulgur (11 ounces)
- 1 pound thin green beans

Juice of 2 lemons

- ¼ cup extra-virgin olive oil
- 1 cup red and yellow cherry tomatoes, halved
- ½ cup roasted, salted almonds, coarsely crushed
- ¼ cup coarsely shredded mint leaves

Salt and freshly ground pepper

**1.** In a large heatproof bowl, pour the boiling water over the bulgur. Cover with plastic wrap and let stand until the water is absorbed, about 20 minutes.

**2.** Bring a large pot of salted water to a boil. Add the beans and boil over high heat until just tender, about 4 minutes. Drain and refresh under cold running water, then pat dry. Cut the green beans crosswise.

**3.** In a small bowl, stir together the lemon juice and olive oil. Fluff the bulgur with 2 forks. Add the green beans, cherry tomatoes, almonds, mint and lemon dressing. Season with salt and pepper and mix well. Transfer the bulgur salad to a large serving bowl and serve lightly chilled or at room temperature. —*Tyler Florence*

## Bulgur Salad with Tomatoes, Scallions and Herbs

**ACTIVE: 15 MIN; TOTAL: 1 HR**

4 SERVINGS ● ●

Similar to a tabbouleh, this refreshing grain dish from southeastern Turkey is flavored with lots of scallions and mint.

- ½ cup medium-grind bulgur
- 2 large tomatoes, finely chopped
- 4 scallions, thinly sliced
- 4 garlic cloves, minced
- 1 jalapeño, seeded and finely chopped
- 2 tablespoons tomato paste
- 2 tablespoons extra-virgin olive oil
- ⅓ cup chopped mint
- ⅓ cup chopped flat-leaf parsley
- ½ teaspoon crushed red pepper

Salt and freshly ground pepper

Balsamic vinegar (see Note)

**1.** In a large bowl of hot water, soak the bulgur until softened, about 1 hour. Drain the bulgur well and press out as much water as possible.

**2.** Transfer the bulgur to a large bowl. Add the tomatoes, scallions, garlic, jalapeño, tomato paste, olive oil, mint, parsley and crushed red pepper; mix well. Season with salt, pepper and balsamic vinegar. Serve at room temperature. —*Eveline Zoutendijk*

**NOTE** The pomegranate vinegar that is typically used in this dish isn't widely available in this country, so we used balsamic vinegar in its place.

**MAKE AHEAD** The bulgur salad can be refrigerated overnight.

## Kasha Varnishkes with Mushroom Gravy

**TOTAL: 30 MIN**

4 SERVINGS ● ●

Kasha varnishkes is a classic Jewish dish from Russia and Eastern Europe made with bow-tie pasta and buckwheat groats, which have a marvelous earthy flavor.

- 3½ cups water
- ½ cup coarse kasha (buckwheat groats)

Salt

- 1½ cups bow-tie pasta
- 2 tablespoons extra-virgin olive oil
- 1 medium onion, finely chopped
- 1 garlic clove, minced
- ½ pound cremini mushrooms, thinly sliced
- 2 teaspoons chopped thyme
- 3 tablespoons all-purpose flour
- 2 tablespoons soy sauce

Freshly ground pepper

**1.** In a small saucepan, bring 1 cup of the water to a boil. Add the kasha and ½ teaspoon of salt, cover and cook over low heat until the water has been absorbed, about 10 minutes. Stir well, cover and set aside.

**2.** In a saucepan of boiling salted water, cook the bow-tie pasta until al dente. Drain, reserving ½ cup of the cooking water. Return the bow-ties to the saucepan.

**3.** In a skillet, heat the oil. Add the onion, garlic, creminis and thyme. Cook over high heat, stirring occasionally, until the onion is softened and caramelized, 5 minutes. Stir in the flour, the remaining water and the soy sauce. Stir constantly until a smooth sauce forms. Simmer over moderate heat, stirring a few times, until thickened, 3 minutes; season with salt and pepper.

**4.** Reheat the kasha, stirring in some of the reserved cooking water to loosen it. Stir the kasha into the bow-ties and spoon into bowls. Top with the mushroom gravy and serve. —*Peter Berley*

# tool

## MODERN MEZZALUNA

This mezzaluna is the perfect tool for tackling woody herbs like rosemary. It includes a **round chopper** that rocks against the **cutting board,** which is concave on both sides. Created by Danish designer Jesper Ranum for MoMA Design Store. **DETAILS** $120 at momastore.org.

# potatoes, grains & beans

### Quinoa, Artichoke and Hearts of Palm Salad

**TOTAL: 35 MIN**

6 SERVINGS ●

1½ cups black quinoa (9 ounces), rinsed (see Note)

½ lemon

3 medium artichokes

½ cup avocado oil or extra-virgin olive oil

¼ cup white wine vinegar

Salt and freshly ground pepper

4 canned hearts of palm (5 ounces), sliced crosswise ¼ inch thick

1 small red bell pepper, cut into ¼-inch dice

1 small yellow bell pepper, cut into ¼-inch dice

6 small Boston lettuce leaves

**1.** In a saucepan of boiling salted water, cook the quinoa over moderately high heat, stirring occasionally, until al dente, 20 minutes. Drain in a fine sieve; spread on a baking sheet. Cool to room temperature.

**2.** Squeeze some of the juice from the lemon half into a small bowl of water; reserve the lemon half. Working with 1 artichoke at a time, snap off the outer leaves. Using a sharp knife, cut off the leaves, leaving the artichoke bottom. Cut off the stem and peel the artichoke bottom. Using a spoon, scrape out the furry choke. Rub the artichoke bottom all over with the lemon half and drop it into the lemon water. Repeat with the remaining 2 artichokes.

**3.** In a saucepan of boiling salted water, cook the artichokes over moderately high heat until tender, about 10 minutes. Drain and let cool, then cut into ½-inch dice.

**4.** In a bowl, mix the oil and vinegar; season with salt and pepper. Add the quinoa, artichokes, hearts of palm and peppers and toss. Mound on lettuce leaves and serve.

—*Emmanuel Piqueras*

**NOTE** Black quinoa is available from kalustyans.com.

### Baked Three-Bean Casserole with Crispy Bacon

**ACTIVE: 25 MIN; TOTAL: 3 HR**

6 SERVINGS ● ●

By doctoring three different types and sizes of canned beans with barbecue sauce and bacon, Adam Perry Lang, chef and owner of Daisy May's BBQ USA in New York City, creates an outrageously good version of baked beans. He often cooks his beans over a fire in a cast-iron casserole, but they're terrific baked in an indoor oven too.

3 tablespoons vegetable oil

5 garlic cloves, minced

1 green bell pepper, chopped

1 medium onion, coarsely chopped

1 tablespoon minced fresh ginger

Kosher salt

2 cups Sweet and Sticky Barbecue Sauce (p. 97) mixed with ½ cup water

Two 15½-ounce cans baked beans

One 19-ounce can red kidney beans, drained and rinsed

One 19-ounce can pinto beans, drained and rinsed

6 slices of lean bacon

**1.** Preheat the oven to 375°. Heat the oil in a large saucepan. Add the garlic, green pepper, onion, ginger and 1 teaspoon of salt and cook over moderate heat, stirring occasionally, until the vegetables are softened, about 8 minutes. Add the diluted Sweet and Sticky Barbecue Sauce and all of the beans and simmer over low heat for 30 minutes, stirring occasionally.

**2.** Transfer the beans to a 9-by-13-inch baking dish and arrange the bacon strips on top. Bake for 45 minutes, or until the beans are bubbling and the bacon is crisp. Let cool for 15 minutes before serving.

—*Adam Perry Lang*

**MAKE AHEAD** The beans can be made through Step 1 and refrigerated. Bring to room temperature before baking.

### Barley Chupe with Queso Fresco

**TOTAL: 30 MIN**

4 SERVINGS ● ● ●

In many South American countries, thick soups or stews are called *chupes*. This comforting *chupe* is made with barley, potatoes and lima beans in a savory chicken broth.

5 cups chicken stock or low-sodium broth

1 cup pearl barley, rinsed

4 small red potatoes, each cut into 8 wedges

2 bay leaves

½ teaspoon ground cumin

1 tablespoon extra-virgin olive oil

1 small onion, cut into ½-inch dice

3 garlic cloves, minced

½ cup frozen baby lima beans

2 plum tomatoes—halved, seeded and diced

Kosher salt and freshly ground pepper

1 cup crumbled *queso fresco* or farmer cheese (6½ ounces)

1 tablespoon chopped flat-leaf parsley

**1.** In a large saucepan, combine the stock with the barley, potatoes, bay leaves and cumin and bring to a boil. Simmer over moderate heat until the barley begins to soften, about 15 minutes.

**2.** In a skillet, heat the olive oil. Add the onion and garlic to the saucepan and cook over moderately high heat until they begin to brown, about 7 minutes.

**3.** Add the lima beans and the onion and garlic to the barley and simmer until the barley and potatoes are tender, about 10 minutes. Add the tomatoes, season with salt and pepper and simmer until the *chupe* is piping hot, about 2 minutes. Discard the bay leaves. Ladle the soup into bowls, top with the cheese and parsley and serve.

—*Daisy Martinez*

**MAKE AHEAD** The barley *chupe* can be refrigerated overnight. Add the parsley just before serving.

BARLEY CHUPE WITH QUESO FRESCO

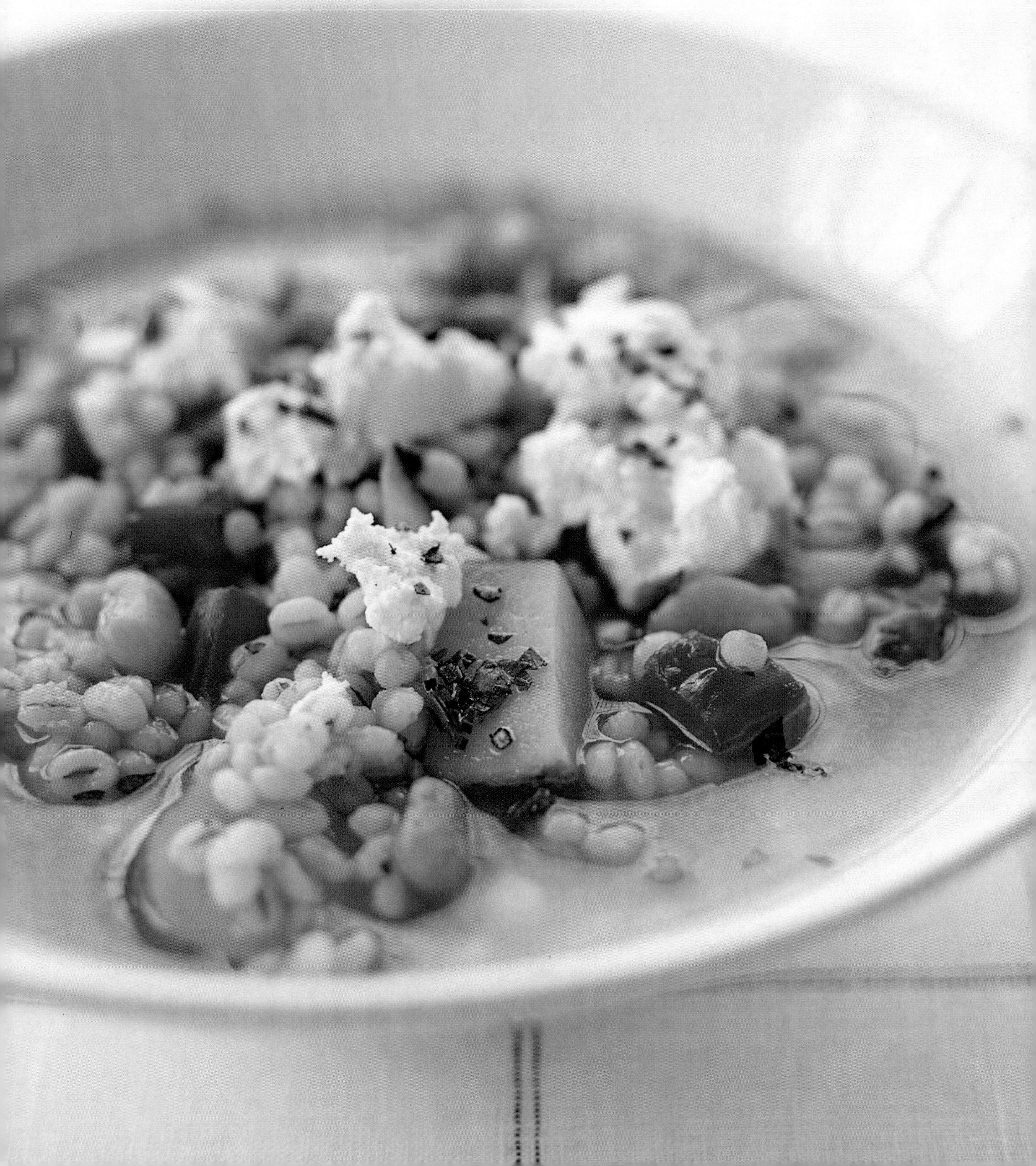

# potatoes, grains & beans

## Black Bean Chili with Mushrooms

**TOTAL: 25 MIN**

**4 SERVINGS** ● ● ●

Since it includes no meat, this quick vegetarian recipe gets its flavor from smoky ancho and chipotle chiles as well as from meaty portobello mushrooms and sweet sun-dried tomatoes. Serve the soup with a bowl of sour cream and some chopped cilantro on the side.

- 2 **dried ancho chiles, stemmed and seeded**
- ½ **cup sun-dried tomatoes**
- 1½ **cups water**
- 2 **tablespoons extra-virgin olive oil**
- 2 **portobello mushrooms, stems and black gills removed, caps cut into ¼-inch dice**
- 2 **garlic cloves, thinly sliced**
- 1 **medium sweet onion, coarsely chopped**
- 1 **red bell pepper, finely chopped**
- 1 **tablespoon ground cumin**
- 1 **canned chipotle chile, stemmed and seeded**

Two 19-ounce cans black beans, drained
- 1 **tablespoon soy sauce**

Salt and freshly ground black pepper

Chopped cilantro and low-fat sour cream, for serving

**1.** In a small saucepan, cover the anchos and sun-dried tomatoes with 1 cup of the water; bring to a boil. Simmer over moderate heat for 2 minutes. Set aside.

**2.** In a large skillet, heat the olive oil. Add the diced portobello mushrooms, sliced garlic, chopped onion and chopped red bell pepper and cook over high heat, stirring until the vegetables are softened, about 5 minutes. Add the cumin and cook, stirring, for about 1 minute. Stir in the remaining ½ cup of water, then reduce the heat to low.

**3.** In a food processor, puree the chipotle with the anchos and sun-dried tomatoes and their soaking water. Stir the puree into the portobello mixture in the skillet. Add the black beans and soy sauce and simmer over moderate heat for 6 minutes, stirring occasionally. Season with salt and pepper. Ladle the chili into bowls and serve with the cilantro and sour cream.   *Peter Berley*

**MAKE AHEAD** The chili can be refrigerated for up to 2 days.

## Cumin-Spiced Red Lentil Burgers

**TOTAL: 1 HR**

**4 SERVINGS** ●

The red lentils in these spicy, Indian-inspired vegetarian burgers don't need to be soaked before cooking.

- 1½ **cups red lentils (see Note)**
- ¼ **cup plus 2 tablespoons extra-virgin olive oil**
- 1 **small onion, finely chopped**
- 3 **medium carrots, finely chopped**
- 3 **garlic cloves, minced**
- 1½ **teaspoons ground cumin**
- ¼ **teaspoon cayenne pepper**
- ¾ **cup plain dry bread crumbs**
- ¼ **cup coarsely chopped flat-leaf parsley**
- 2 **large eggs, lightly beaten**
- 1 **tablespoon kosher salt**
- ½ **teaspoon freshly ground pepper**
- 1 **cup plain low-fat yogurt**
- 1 **teaspoon fresh lemon juice**

**1.** In a large saucepan, cover the lentils with cold water by 2 inches and bring to a boil over high heat. Reduce the heat to moderate and simmer the lentils until they are very tender, about 10 minutes. Drain the lentils well.

**2.** Preheat the broiler. In a medium skillet, heat 2 tablespoons of the olive oil. Add the onion and cook over moderately high heat, stirring frequently, until golden, about 6 minutes. Add the carrots and two-thirds of the garlic and cook until the carrots begin to soften, about 4 minutes. Stir in the cumin and cayenne and remove from the heat. Mix in the bread crumbs, 3 tablespoons of the parsley, the eggs, salt and pepper. Form the mixture into sixteen ¼-cup burgers.

**3.** Line a baking sheet with foil. Brush the foil and both sides of the burgers with the remaining ¼ cup of olive oil. Broil until golden, about 3 minutes per side.

**4.** Meanwhile, in a small bowl, mix the yogurt with the lemon juice and the remaining garlic and 1 tablespoon of chopped parsley. Serve the lentil burgers hot, with the yogurt sauce on the side. —*Ann Withey*

**NOTE** Red lentils are available at health food stores and Middle Eastern markets.

**MAKE AHEAD** The red lentil burgers can be prepared through Step 2 and refrigerated overnight.

## Cranberry Bean and Mixed-Herb Salad

**ACTIVE: 30 MIN; TOTAL: 1 HR 15 MIN**

**10 SERVINGS** ● ●

- 7 **pounds fresh cranberry beans, shelled (about 7 cups), or 1½ pounds dried beans (4 cups)**
- 1 **small onion**
- 2 **garlic cloves**
- 1 **bay leaf**
- 3 **thyme sprigs, plus 1 teaspoon finely chopped thyme**

Salt
- ¼ **cup plus 2 tablespoons extra-virgin olive oil**
- 3 **tablespoons red wine vinegar**
- ¼ **cup finely chopped flat-leaf parsley**
- 1 **tablespoon finely chopped fresh sage**
- 1 **bunch scallions, thinly sliced**

Freshly ground pepper

**CRANBERRY BEAN AND MIXED-HERB SALAD**

**WHITE BEAN AND CHORIZO SALAD WITH OLIVES**

**1.** If using dried cranberry beans rather than the fresh, cover them with water and let soak overnight; drain. In a pot, cover the fresh or soaked dried beans with 2 inches of cold water and bring to a boil. Skim the beans and add the onion, garlic, bay leaf and thyme sprigs, then simmer over moderate heat until the beans are just tender, about 40 minutes for fresh and 1 hour for dried.

**2.** Add 2 tablespoons of salt to the cranberry beans and cook them for 5 minutes longer. Drain the beans and discard the onion, garlic, thyme sprigs and bay leaf. Stir in the olive oil, vinegar, parsley, sage, chopped thyme and sliced scallions. Season the beans with salt and pepper and serve. —*Seen Lippert*

**MAKE AHEAD** The bean salad can be refrigerated overnight. Let return to room temperature before serving.

### White Bean and Chorizo Salad with Olives

**TOTAL: 25 MIN**

**4 SERVINGS** ● ●

- 2 large eggs
- One 15-ounce can small white beans, drained
- 1 ready-to-eat chorizo link (3 ounces), finely diced
- ½ small onion, very finely chopped
- ¼ cup very finely chopped red bell pepper
- ¼ cup very finely chopped flat-leaf parsley
- ¼ teaspoon dried oregano
- ⅛ teaspoon cumin seeds
- ¼ cup extra-virgin olive oil
- 2 tablespoons sherry vinegar
- Salt and freshly ground black pepper
- 4 Boston lettuce leaves
- ¼ cup pitted Calamata olives
- 1 radish, very thinly sliced

**1.** Put the eggs in a small saucepan, cover with water and bring to a boil. Remove the eggs from the heat, cover and let stand for 12 minutes. Drain and run under cold water, gently shaking the pan. Peel the eggs and pat them dry.

**2.** Meanwhile, in a medium bowl, toss the beans with the chorizo, onion, bell pepper, parsley, oregano and cumin seeds. Add the olive oil and vinegar, season with salt and pepper and toss well. Let stand for 10 minutes.

**3.** Arrange the lettuce leaves in bowls and mound the bean salad on top. Scatter the olives and radish slices all around. Quarter the eggs, arrange them around the salads and serve. —*Janet Mendel*

**SERVE WITH** Crusty bread.

● **FAST** ● **HEALTHY** ● **MAKE AHEAD** ● **STAFF FAVORITE**

# potatoes, grains & beans

## Fried Polenta with Fresh Corn

**TOTAL: 1 HR PLUS OVERNIGHT CHILLING**

**4 SERVINGS** ●●

F&W's Marcia Kiesel says the secret to this recipe is stirring the cornmeal vigorously and often while cooking it on the stovetop, then refrigerating it overnight until firm; this helps prevent the polenta from sticking to the pan while you are frying it.

- **7 cups water**
- **Kosher salt**
- **1 cup fine stone-ground yellow cornmeal**
- **1 cup coarse stone-ground yellow cornmeal**
- **1 cup fresh corn kernels**

## F&W taste test

### INSTANT POLENTA

Polenta is ground cornmeal that's slowly cooked with water or stock for about half an hour, until thick and creamy. The good news is that you can get great results from instant polenta, which cooks in about five minutes. F&W tried a wide variety of supermarket brands and found these three were the best.

**La Gallinella** $4 for 26 ounces.

**La Grande Ruota** $3 for 18 ounces.

**Il Riso Beretta** $3 for 16 ounces.

- **6 tablespoons (3 ounces) unsalted butter**
- **1 cup freshly grated Parmesan cheese (3 ounces)**
- **Freshly ground pepper**
- **4 tablespoons extra-virgin olive oil**

**1.** Lightly oil a 9-by-5-inch glass loaf pan. In a large saucepan, bring the 7 cups of water to a boil. Add a large pinch of salt, then slowly add the fine and coarse cornmeals by handfuls, whisking constantly. Cook the polenta over low heat, whisking vigorously and often, until the polenta is thickened and no longer gritty, about 45 minutes.

**2.** Meanwhile, in a small saucepan of boiling salted water, cook the corn kernels until they are tender, about 3 minutes. Drain the corn kernels.

**3.** Stir the corn into the polenta, followed by 2 tablespoons of the butter and all of the Parmesan. Season the polenta with salt and pepper, then scrape it into the prepared loaf pan and smooth the surface. Cover the polenta with plastic wrap and let it cool to room temperature. Refrigerate the cooled polenta overnight.

**4.** Cut the chilled polenta into 8 thick slices. In each of 2 large nonstick skillets, melt 2 tablespoons of the remaining butter in 2 tablespoons of the olive oil. Add 4 polenta slices to each skillet and cook over moderate heat until the polenta slices are browned on the bottom, about 5 minutes. Using a spatula, scrape the slices from the bottom of the skillets and flip them over. Cook the polenta until it is browned on the second side, about 5 minutes longer. Serve the fried polenta at once.
—*Marcia Kiesel*

**MAKE AHEAD** The boiled polenta can be refrigerated in the loaf pan for up to 2 days before being fried. The polenta slices can be fried earlier in the day and then reheated in a 375° oven for 10 minutes before serving.

## Polenta with Pinto Beans and Roasted Vegetables

**TOTAL: 30 MIN**

**4 SERVINGS** ●●

- **Large pinch of saffron threads**
- **1½ quarts plus 1 tablespoon hot water**
- **2 medium red onions, each cut into 6 wedges**
- **5 tablespoons extra-virgin olive oil**
- **1½ pounds cauliflower (from 1 small head), cut into 1-inch florets**
- **1 medium sweet potato, peeled and cut into 1-inch cubes**
- **Salt and freshly ground pepper**
- **2 garlic cloves, very thinly sliced**
- **One 15-ounce can pinto beans, drained**
- **One 14-ounce can diced tomatoes with their juices**
- **½ cup dry white wine**
- **1 teaspoon ground cumin**
- **¼ teaspoon crushed red pepper**
- **1½ cups instant polenta**
- **½ cup freshly grated Parmesan**

**1.** Preheat the oven to 450°. In a bowl, cover the saffron with 1 tablespoon of the water.

**2.** On a rimmed baking sheet, toss the onions with 1 tablespoon of the oil. In a roasting pan, toss the cauliflower and sweet potato with 2 tablespoons of the oil. Season with salt and pepper; roast for 10 minutes; add the garlic to the onions in the last 3 minutes. Remove from the oven.

**3.** Add the beans, tomatoes and their juices, wine, cumin, crushed red pepper and saffron water to the cauliflower and sweet potatoes; roast for 10 minutes longer.

**4.** In a saucepan, bring the remaining 1½ quarts of water to a boil. Whisk in the polenta; cook over moderate heat, whisking constantly, until thickened, 5 minutes. Stir in the remaining olive oil and ¼ cup of the Parmesan; season with salt and pepper.

**5.** Spoon the polenta into bowls. Stir the onions and garlic into the vegetables, season with salt and pepper and ladle the vegetables over the polenta. Serve with the remaining Parmesan. —*Peter Berley*

POLENTA WITH PINTO BEANS
AND ROASTED VEGETABLES

# potatoes, grains & beans

## Tender Chickpea Pancakes

**TOTAL: 50 MIN**

**MAKES EIGHT 10-INCH PANCAKES** ● ● ●

These light, earthy chickpea-flour pancakes, called *socca,* are a popular street food from the south of France. As with crêpes, griddling the perfect *socca* takes some experimentation, but the key is to be sure they are completely set before flipping them. If you like denser, thicker pancakes, use more batter and finish them in a 400-degree oven to cook them completely through.

- 2¼ cups water
- 2 cups chickpea flour (see Note)
- 2 tablespoons extra-virgin olive oil, plus more for frying
- 1 teaspoon salt
- ¼ teaspoon freshly ground pepper

**1.** In a large bowl, whisk the water into the chickpea flour until smooth. Whisk in the 2 tablespoons of olive oil and the salt and pepper. Let the batter rest for 15 minutes.

**2.** Preheat the oven to 350°. Preheat a 10-inch cast-iron skillet over moderate heat. Using a paper towel, coat the bottom of the skillet with a thin film of olive oil. When the skillet is hot but not smoking, add a rounded ¼ cup of batter and tilt the skillet to distribute it evenly. Cook the pancake until it is browned around the edge and set on top, about 3 minutes. Turn the pancake over with a spatula and cook it for 1 minute longer. Fold the pancake into quarters and transfer it to a baking sheet. Repeat with the remaining pancake batter; add a light coating of oil to the skillet for each new pancake. Reduce the heat to moderately low if the pancakes begin to stick.

**3.** When all of the pancakes have been cooked, cover them loosely with foil and reheat in the oven before serving.
—*Michael Cimarusti*

**NOTE** Chickpea flour, also known as *besan,* is available at health food stores as well as at Indian and Mediterranean markets and some supermarkets.

**MAKE AHEAD** The chickpea pancakes can be prepared up to 2 hours ahead. Cover the cooked pancakes with foil and reheat in a 350° oven.

## Marinated Chickpea Salad with Radishes and Cucumber

**TOTAL: 30 MIN**

**6 SERVINGS** ● ● ●

This refreshing salad mixes crunchy cucumber and radishes with red onion slivers and chewy chickpeas in a tart cumin-spiked lemon dressing.

- ¼ cup extra-virgin olive oil
- 2 tablespoons fresh lemon juice
- 1 garlic clove, very finely chopped
- ½ teaspoon finely grated lemon zest
- ¼ teaspoon ground cumin
- Salt and freshly ground pepper
- One 19-ounce can chickpeas, drained and rinsed
- 1 pound seedless European or kirby cucumbers, thinly sliced crosswise
- 6 large red radishes, thinly sliced
- ½ medium red onion, thinly sliced
- ¼ cup finely chopped flat-leaf parsley

In a large bowl, combine the olive oil, lemon juice, chopped garlic, lemon zest and cumin and season the dressing with salt and pepper. Add the chickpeas and let them marinate for at least 25 minutes, stirring occasionally. Just before serving, stir in the cucumbers, radishes, onion and parsley and season the salad with salt and pepper. —*Marcia Kiesel*

**MAKE AHEAD** The chickpeas can be refrigerated overnight in the dressing; add the vegetables just before serving.

## Lemony Chickpea Salad

**ACTIVE: 20 MIN; TOTAL: 2 HR 20 MIN**

**PLUS OVERNIGHT SOAKING**

**8 SERVINGS** ● ●

Serve this fresh-tasting chickpea salad with warm, soft pita bread to soak up the olive oil dressing.

- 2 tablespoons pure olive oil
- 1 yellow onion, quartered
- 2 carrots, halved
- 1 celery rib, halved crosswise, plus 4 small celery ribs finely diced
- 1 pound dried chickpeas, soaked overnight and drained
- 4 rosemary sprigs and 4 thyme sprigs, tied together with string
- Kosher salt and freshly ground pepper
- 1 medium red onion, finely chopped
- ½ cup red wine vinegar
- Finely shredded zest and juice of 1 lemon
- 2 garlic cloves, minced
- 1 teaspoon minced rosemary
- ½ teaspoon dried oregano
- 1½ teaspoons finely chopped peperoncini
- 1 cup extra-virgin olive oil
- ¾ cup finely chopped flat-leaf parsley

**1.** In a soup pot, heat the pure olive oil. Add the yellow onion, the carrots and the halved celery rib and cook over moderate heat, stirring occasionally, until golden, about 10 minutes. Add the chickpeas, the herb sprig bundle and enough water to cover by 2 inches and bring to a boil. Reduce the heat and simmer over moderately low heat until the chickpeas are tender, about 1½ hours. Add a large pinch of salt and pepper and cook the chickpeas for 10 minutes longer. Remove from the heat and cool for 15 minutes, then drain the chickpeas. Discard the herb sprigs, onion, carrots and celery.

**2.** Meanwhile, in a large bowl, soak the red onion in the vinegar for 15 minutes. Drain, discarding the vinegar. Return the onion to

**LEMONY CHICKPEA SALAD**

**CHICKPEA STEW WITH SPINACH AND CHORIZO**

the bowl and add the diced celery, lemon zest, lemon juice, garlic, rosemary, oregano and peperoncini. Add the chickpeas and extra virgin olive oil; season with salt and pepper. Fold in the parsley and serve.
—*Tom Colicchio*

**MAKE AHEAD** The chickpea salad can be refrigerated overnight. Add the parsley just before serving.

## Chickpea Stew with Spinach and Chorizo

**ACTIVE: 30 MIN; TOTAL: 2 HR 30 MIN**
**PLUS OVERNIGHT SOAKING**
**8 SERVINGS** ●

This stew, like many in Catalonia, starts with a *sofrito,* a thick sauce made with onions and tomatoes. Once you get the ingredients in the pot, there's not much to do besides enjoy the aroma wafting from this hearty stew as it slowly cooks.

2 **cups dried chickpeas, soaked overnight and drained**
¼ **cup plus 2 tablespoons extra-virgin olive oil**
4 **garlic cloves, minced**
1 **large onion, finely diced**
1½ **teaspoons minced rosemary**
1 **bay leaf**
One 28-ounce can Italian tomatoes, **chopped, 1 cup juices reserved**
½ **pound soft cooked chorizo, sliced ¼ inch thick**
1 **pound spinach, thick stems discarded**
**Salt and freshly ground pepper**

**1.** In a medium saucepan, cover the chickpeas with 2 inches of water and bring to a boil. Reduce the heat to low and simmer until tender, about 2 hours; add more water as necessary to maintain the level. Drain; reserve 1 cup of the cooking water.

**2.** In a medium enameled cast-iron casserole, heat the olive oil. Add the garlic, onion, rosemary and bay leaf and cook over moderate heat until the onion is softened, about 7 minutes. Add the chopped tomatoes and cook over moderately high heat until sizzling, about 4 minutes. Add the sliced chorizo, the cooked chickpeas and their reserved cup of cooking water and the cup of reserved tomato juices and bring the chickpea stew to a simmer. Stir in half of the spinach and cook until it is wilted, then stir in the remaining half of the spinach. Simmer the chickpea stew over moderately low heat for 10 minutes, stirring occasionally. Season the stew with salt and pepper to taste and serve immediately. —*Sergi Millet*

**MAKE AHEAD** The chickpea stew can be refrigerated for up to 3 days. Reheat the stew gently before serving.

● FAST ● HEALTHY ● MAKE AHEAD ● STAFF FAVORITE

Crispy, chewy bread in two distinctive forms: Pizza with Tomatoes, Mozzarella and Basil (P. 271) from the May issue and decadent Grilled Ham-and-Cheese Sandwiches with Tapenade from February (P. 272).

266

# breads, pizzas & sandwiches

CRÈME FRAÎCHE BISCUITS

CRANBERRY-PECAN BREAD

## Crème Fraîche Biscuits

**ACTIVE: 20 MIN; TOTAL: 1 HR 10 MIN**

**MAKES ABOUT 22 BISCUITS** ● ●

Crème fraîche takes the place of butter-milk in these extremely fluffy biscuits.

- 4 cups all-purpose flour, plus more for dusting
- 2 tablespoons baking powder
- 2 teaspoons kosher salt
- 1 teaspoon sugar
- 2 sticks (½ pound) cold unsalted butter, cut into tablespoons
- 1¼ cups heavy cream
- ½ cup crème fraîche
- 1 large egg

**1.** Preheat the oven to 400°. In a large bowl, whisk the 4 cups of flour with the baking powder, salt and sugar. Cut the butter into the flour until the particles are the size of peas. Make a well in the center of the flour-and-butter mixture.

**2.** In a small bowl, whisk the heavy cream with the crème fraîche and the egg and pour the liquid into the dry ingredient well. Stir the ingredients with a fork until the dough mixture is evenly moistened, then turn the crème fraîche biscuit dough out onto a lightly floured work surface and gently knead it 2 or 3 times, until the biscuit dough holds together.

**3.** Roll out the dough 1 inch thick. Using a 2¼-inch round cookie cutter, stamp out the biscuits as close together as possible. Gently press the scraps together and stamp out more biscuits. Transfer to baking sheets and refrigerate until the biscuits are firm, about 30 minutes.

**4.** Bake the biscuits for 18 minutes, or until they are golden on top. Serve the Crème Fraîche Biscuits warm from the oven or at room temperature.

—*Allison Vines-Rushing and Slade Rushing*

## Cranberry-Pecan Bread

**ACTIVE: 1 HR; TOTAL: 6 HR PLUS OVERNIGHT RISING**

**MAKES TWO 2-POUND LOAVES** ● ●

- 3⅓ cups all-purpose flour, plus more for dusting
- 3⅓ cups white whole wheat flour, preferably King Arthur brand
- 1 tablespoon instant dry yeast

About 3½ cups warm water

- 4 teaspoons fine table salt
- 1½ cups dried cranberries (7 ounces)
- 2 cups pecan halves (7 ounces)

Vegetable oil

**1.** In a bowl, combine both flours with the yeast. Add 3¼ cups of warm water and stir until a soft dough forms. If the dough is too stiff, add 2 more tablespoons of warm water. Let the dough rest for 15 minutes.

**2.** Scrape the dough onto a lightly floured surface. Knead and work the dough until smooth but still very sticky, about 5 minutes. Flatten the dough and sprinkle it with the salt; knead until the salt is evenly incorporated, about 5 minutes. The dough will tighten slightly. Flatten the dough and scatter the cranberries and pecans on top. Fold the dough over the fruit and nuts and knead them in. Lightly oil the bowl, add the dough and turn to coat. Cover and let stand until doubled in volume, about 2 hours.

**3.** Line 2 large baking sheets with parchment paper; brush the sheets with vegetable oil. Punch down the dough, then cut it into 2 equal pieces. Flatten each piece into a 10-inch oval. Fold in the short ends and pinch the ends. Pat the piece of dough into a 9-inch oval loaf; transfer to one of the baking sheets, seam side down. Repeat to form the second loaf. Lightly brush 2 pieces of plastic wrap with vegetable oil and loosely cover the loaves. Refrigerate overnight.

**4.** Uncover the loaves; let the bread stand at room temperature for 2 hours, or until the loaves are slightly risen. Using a knife, make a ½-inch-deep slash down the length of each loaf.

**5.** Preheat the oven to 400°. Bake the loaves for about 40 minutes, shifting the baking sheets halfway through. The loaves are done when they're browned and an instant-read thermometer inserted in the center registers 170°. Transfer the loaves to a rack and let cool before slicing. —*Maggie Glezer*

## Herb-Topped Sweet Potato Biscuits

**ACTIVE: 40 MIN; TOTAL: 2 HR**
**MAKES ABOUT 2½ DOZEN BISCUITS** ●

These biscuits get a nice kick from cayenne pepper. Mashing the sweet potatoes with a fork means that the biscuits will be flecked throughout with orange.

- 1 **pound sweet potatoes, scrubbed**
- 2½ **cups all-purpose flour, plus more for dusting**
- 3 **tablespoons light brown sugar**
- 1 **tablespoon baking powder**
- 1 **teaspoon salt**
- ¼ **teaspoon cayenne pepper**
- 1 **stick cold unsalted butter, diced**
- ⅓ **cup whole milk**
- 1 **egg yolk mixed with 1 tablespoon heavy cream**
- 30 **small, sturdy herb sprigs, such as sage, thyme and rosemary**

**1.** Preheat the oven to 400°. Pierce the sweet potatoes all over with a fork. Set the potatoes on a cookie sheet and bake for 1 hour, or until tender. Let cool slightly. Using a spoon, scoop the potato flesh from the skins into a bowl and mash with a fork; you should have 1½ cups of mashed sweet potatoes. Refrigerate until chilled.

**2.** In a large bowl, mix the 2½ cups of flour with the brown sugar, baking powder, salt and cayenne. Cut in the butter with a pastry blender. In a small bowl, mix the sweet potatoes with the milk. Add to the dry ingredients and stir with a wooden spoon until all of the flour is incorporated; the dough will be quite sticky. Refrigerate the dough for at least 15 minutes.

**3.** Preheat the oven to 425°. On a well-floured work surface, pat out the dough until it is ½ inch thick. Using a floured 2-inch round or fluted cutter, stamp out as many biscuits as you can and transfer them to a parchment paper–lined baking sheet. Pat out the scraps and stamp out more biscuits. Brush the tops with the egg wash and press a small herb sprig into each one. Bake the biscuits for about 20 minutes, or until golden. Serve warm or at room temperature. —*Susan Spungen*

**MAKE AHEAD** Once cooled, the biscuits can be frozen in a resealable plastic bag for up to 2 weeks. Bake the frozen biscuits in a 350° oven for 10 to 12 minutes, or until heated through.

## Cream Biscuits

**TOTAL: 30 MIN**
**MAKES 18 BISCUITS** ● ●

- 4 **cups all-purpose flour, plus more for dusting**
- 2 **tablespoons baking powder**
- 2 **teaspoons salt**
- 1 **teaspoon freshly ground pepper**
- 2¼ **cups heavy cream**

**1.** Preheat the oven to 375°. In a bowl, mix the 4 cups of flour, baking powder, salt and pepper. Add 2 cups plus 2 tablespoons of the cream and stir with a wooden spoon until a stiff, shaggy dough forms. Turn the dough out onto a lightly floured work surface; knead until evenly moistened.

**2.** Roll out half of the dough ½ inch thick. Using a 2½-inch round cookie cutter, stamp out 8 biscuits; arrange the biscuits on a sturdy baking sheet. Repeat with the remaining dough. Gather the scraps, pat out and stamp out 2 more biscuits. Brush the tops of the biscuits with the remaining 2 tablespoons of heavy cream. Bake the biscuits until well-risen and browned, about 20 minutes. —*Marc Murphy*

## Grilled Garlic-Herb Bread

**TOTAL: 15 MIN**
**4 SERVINGS** ●

Chef Thomas Keller of The French Laundry in Yountville, California, grills bread to make it crisp and smoky before topping it with garlic-and-parsley-spiked oil.

- 1 **medium ciabatta or baguette, split lengthwise**
- ½ **cup extra-virgin olive oil**
- 3 **garlic cloves, minced**
- ½ **cup chopped flat-leaf parsley**

**Coarse sea salt**

Light a grill. Grill the bread over moderate heat for 5 minutes, turning occasionally, until toasted. In a bowl, combine the oil, garlic and parsley and spoon onto the cut sides of the bread, spreading it right to the edges. Sprinkle with salt, cut into large pieces and serve. —*Thomas Keller*

# breads, pizzas & sandwiches

## Moroccan Olive Bread

**ACTIVE: 15 MIN; TOTAL: 3 HR**

**MAKES 1 LOAF** ●

Thickly slicing olives before placing them on the unbaked bread allows their briny oil to seep into the dough.

1½ teaspoons active dry yeast
1 cup tepid water
2½ cups all-purpose flour,
plus more for dusting
½ teaspoon salt
½ teaspoon anise seeds
6 pitted green or black olives,
sliced crosswise

1. In a small bowl, mix the yeast and ¼ cup of the water; let stand for 5 minutes. Sift the 2½ cups of flour into a medium bowl. Stir in the salt and anise. With a wooden spoon, stir in the yeast and remaining ¾ cup of water until a raggy dough forms.
2. Transfer the dough to a lightly floured surface and knead until smooth and elastic, 5 minutes. With lightly floured hands, shape the dough into a ball, then flatten it into a 7-inch disk. Press the olives into the top of the loaf. Set the bread on a lightly floured baking sheet and let rise in a warm place for 1½ hours, or until doubled.
3. Preheat the oven to 400°. Bake the bread for 45 minutes, or until it sounds hollow when tapped on the bottom. Transfer to a rack; let cool slightly. —*Anissa Helou*

## ingredient
### CHEESE SOURCES

**NEW YORK CITY**
**Murray's Cheese Shop**
254 Bleecker St.; murrayscheese.com

**ANN ARBOR, MICHIGAN**
**Zingerman's**
3723 Plaza Dr.; zingermans.com

**SAN FRANCISCO**
**Cowgirl Creamery**
1 Ferry Building, #17;
cowgirlcreamery.com

## Flat Bread with Spinach and Feta

**ACTIVE: 40 MIN; TOTAL: 1 HR**

**4 SERVINGS**

The dough for this tasty Anatolian street snack has been baked in a pan since nomadic times. Spinach is the most popular of many fillings.

**DOUGH**
1 cup all-purpose flour
½ teaspoon salt
4½ tablespoons water
1 tablespoon extra-virgin olive oil,
plus more for brushing

**FILLING**
2 tablespoons unsalted butter
1 medium onion, finely chopped
3 garlic cloves, minced
7 ounces baby spinach (7 cups)
½ teaspoon crushed red pepper
Pinch of freshly grated nutmeg
1 tablespoon all-purpose flour
¼ cup plus 2 tablespoons milk
¼ cup crumbled feta cheese
Salt and freshly ground pepper

1. **MAKE THE DOUGH:** In a bowl, mix the flour and salt. Add the water and 1 tablespoon of olive oil; stir with a wooden spoon until a dry, shaggy dough forms. Turn the dough out onto a work surface and knead until smooth, 5 minutes. Quarter the dough and roll each piece into a ball. Cover the balls with a damp paper towel and plastic wrap and let stand for 30 minutes.
2. **MEANWHILE, MAKE THE FILLING:** In a skillet, melt the butter over moderate heat. Add the onion and garlic, increase the heat to moderately high and cook until softened. Add the spinach, crushed pepper and nutmeg and cook, stirring, until the spinach wilts, 2 to 3 minutes. Add the flour and cook for 1 minute, then stir in the milk and cook until thickened. Remove from the heat. Fold the feta into the spinach mixture and season with salt and pepper.
3. On a work surface, roll out each ball of dough to a 7-inch round. Heat a large griddle. Brush one side of a dough round

with oil and transfer to the griddle, oiled side down. Brush the top with oil and cook over moderately high heat for 2 minutes, or until browned on the bottom. Turn the flat bread over and spread one-fourth of the spinach mixture all over it.
4. Cook the bread until browned on the second side, 2 minutes longer. Transfer the flat bread to a work surface, roll it into a cone and serve right away. Repeat with the remaining dough to make 3 more spinach flat breads. —*Eveline Zoutendijk*

## Bikini Pizza with Sun-Dried Tomatoes

**TOTAL: 20 MIN**

**4 SERVINGS** ●

*Bikini*, the Catalan term for grilled cheese sandwiches with ham, are a favorite snack in Barcelona. Catalan chef Ferran Adrià loves these sandwiches, which is rather astonishing for an experimental Spanish chef to admit. He calls his hamless version—made with mozzarella, sun-dried tomatoes, mushrooms and basil—pizza.

8 slices of sourdough bread
½ pound buffalo mozzarella, drained
well and thinly sliced
½ cup oil-packed sun-dried tomatoes,
drained, plus 4 teaspoons oil
reserved from the jar
4 small white mushrooms,
thinly sliced
4 large basil leaves
2 tablespoons extra-virgin olive oil

1. Arrange 4 slices of the bread on a work surface; top with mozzarella. Cover with the sun-dried tomatoes and mushrooms. Drizzle 1 teaspoon of the tomato oil over each sandwich and top with a basil leaf. Close the sandwiches.
2. Heat a griddle. Brush the sandwiches with the olive oil, transfer to the griddle and weight down with a heavy pan. Cook over moderate heat, turning once, until golden and the cheese melted, 9 minutes. Cut into pieces and serve. —*Ferran Adrià*

## Tomato-Basil Pizza

ACTIVE: 20 MIN; TOTAL: 1 HR

8 SERVINGS ●

- 1 tablespoon extra-virgin olive oil
- 1 large garlic clove, minced

Large pinch of crushed red pepper

One 14-ounce can plum tomatoes, crushed, juices reserved

Kosher salt and freshly ground black pepper

All-purpose flour and cornmeal, for dusting

- 2 pounds fresh or frozen pizza dough, thawed if frozen
- ½ pound fresh or smoked mozzarella, cut into ½-inch dice
- 6 large basil leaves, torn into pieces

1. Set a pizza stone or large inverted baking sheet on the bottom of the oven and preheat to 500°.

2. Heat the olive oil in a medium saucepan. Add the garlic and cook over moderate heat, stirring frequently, until lightly golden, about 2 minutes. Add the red pepper and cook, stirring, for 30 seconds. Add the tomatoes and their juices. Increase the heat to high and bring to a boil, then simmer the tomato sauce over moderate heat until slightly thickened, 20 minutes. Season with salt and pepper.

3. On a lightly floured work surface, using a rolling pin or your hands, roll or stretch 1 pound of the dough into a rough 14-inch round. Generously dust a pizza peel or another inverted baking sheet with cornmeal and transfer the dough to it. Make sure the dough doesn't stick to the sheet.

4. Spread half of the tomato sauce onto the pizza, leaving a ½-inch border. Top with half of the diced mozzarella. Slide the pizza onto the hot stone and bake for 11 minutes, or until the crust is deep golden and the cheese is bubbling. Remove from the oven. Sprinkle with half of the basil and serve immediately. Repeat with the remaining dough, tomato sauce, mozzarella and basil. —Melissa Rubel

## Pizza with Tomatoes, Mozzarella and Basil

ACTIVE: 30 MIN; TOTAL: 1 HR 10 MIN

4 SERVINGS

- 1 tablespoon extra-virgin olive oil, plus more for drizzling

One 28-ounce can whole tomatoes, drained and chopped

Salt

- 1 pound room-temperature pizza dough
- 10 ounces buffalo mozzarella, thinly sliced
- 16 basil leaves, torn into pieces

1. Put a pizza stone on the oven floor and preheat the oven to 500°, allowing at least 45 minutes to heat the stone.

2. Meanwhile, in a medium skillet, heat the 1 tablespoon of olive oil. Add the tomatoes and cook over high heat, stirring a few times, until slightly thickened, about 4 minutes. Season with salt.

3. Cut the pizza dough into 4 pieces and pat each one into a disk. Transfer the disks to a floured baking sheet, cover with plastic wrap and let rest for 20 minutes.

4. On a lightly floured work surface, roll 1 disk of dough into a 9-inch round. Transfer it to a floured pizza peel or flat cookie sheet. Spoon about ¼ cup of the tomatoes over the dough. Top with one-fourth of the mozzarella and drizzle with olive oil. Slide the pizza onto the hot stone and bake for about 4 minutes, or until browned around the edge and bubbling. Transfer to a work surface and sprinkle with one-fourth of the basil. Cut the pizza into wedges and serve immediately. Repeat with the remaining pizza dough, tomatoes, cheese, olive oil and basil. —Marco Gallotta

## Squash and Potato Pizzas

ACTIVE: 45 MIN; TOTAL: 1 HR 30 MIN

4 SERVINGS

- 1 pound medium red or Yukon Gold potatoes, scrubbed well but not peeled

- 3 tablespoons extra-virgin olive oil, plus more for drizzling
- 1 pound medium yellow squash, sliced lengthwise ⅛ inch thick

Salt and freshly ground pepper

All-purpose flour, for dusting

- 1½ pounds thawed frozen pizza dough, cut into 4 pieces
- 24 cherry tomatoes, coarsely chopped (1 cup)
- 2½ cups Manchego cheese (7½ ounces), shredded
- 2 ounces frisée, torn into large pieces (optional)

1. Set a pizza stone on the bottom of the oven and preheat the oven to 500° for 30 minutes. In a medium saucepan, cover the potatoes with water and bring to a boil. Simmer over moderate heat until the potatoes are just tender, 20 minutes. Drain and let cool, then slice ⅛ inch thick.

2. In a large skillet, heat 1 tablespoon of the olive oil. Add one-third of the squash in a single layer, season with salt and pepper and cook over moderately high heat, turning once, until golden brown, about 2 minutes. Transfer to a plate. Repeat with the remaining 2 tablespoons of olive oil and squash in 2 batches.

3. Generously flour a pizza peel or a large rimless baking sheet. On a lightly floured work surface, roll out 1 piece of pizza dough into a 12-inch round ⅛ inch thick. Transfer the round to the pizza peel and top with one-fourth of the potato slices. Drizzle lightly with olive oil and season with salt and pepper. Arrange one-fourth of the squash over the potato, then scatter one-quarter of the tomatoes followed by one-quarter of the Manchego on top.

4. Transfer the pizza to the hot stone and bake for 7 minutes, or until the crust is golden and the cheese bubbling. Transfer to a work surface and cut into wedges. Top the wedges with some of the torn frisée and serve. Repeat with the remaining dough and toppings. —Marcia Kiesel

# breads, pizzas & sandwiches

## Oyster–Corn Bread Dressing

**ACTIVE: 30 MIN; TOTAL: 2 HR**

10 SERVINGS ● ●

When you're making this dressing, it's essential to buy fresh oysters and shuck them the same day. Be sure to cut the oysters in large pieces.

CORN BREAD

- 2 cups all-purpose flour
- 2 cups yellow cornmeal
- ¼ cup sugar
- 1½ teaspoons salt
- 2 cups milk
- 2 large eggs
- 1 stick (4 ounces) unsalted butter, melted
- 5 shallots, minced

DRESSING

- 1 stick (4 ounces) unsalted butter
- 4 celery ribs, cut into ¼-inch dice
- 3 garlic cloves, minced
- 1 large onion, cut into ¼-inch dice
- 1 thyme sprig
- 24 oysters, shucked and coarsely chopped, liquor reserved
- 2½ cups chicken broth
- Finely grated zest and juice of 1 lemon
- ¾ cup chopped parsley
- Kosher salt and freshly ground pepper
- 3 large eggs, lightly beaten

1. MAKE THE CORN BREAD: Preheat the oven to 450°. Line a 12-by-16-inch rimmed baking sheet with parchment paper and lightly grease the paper. In a large bowl, whisk the flour with the cornmeal, sugar and salt. In another bowl, whisk the milk with the eggs, melted butter and shallots. Stir the milk mixture into the dry ingredients until blended. Spread the batter on the prepared baking sheet and bake for 12 minutes, or until the corn bread is firm in the center. Transfer to a rack and let cool in the pan, about 30 minutes. Reduce the oven temperature to 350°.

2. MAKE THE DRESSING: Butter a deep 9-by-13-inch casserole. In a large skillet, melt the butter. Add the celery, garlic,

onion and thyme and cook over moderate heat, stirring frequently, until the celery is softened, 8 minutes. Discard the thyme sprig. In a large bowl, break the corn bread into 1-inch pieces. Stir in the celery mixture, the oysters and their liquor, the broth, lemon zest, lemon juice and parsley. Season with salt and pepper; mix in the eggs. Spread the dressing in the casserole. Cover with foil and bake for 40 minutes; uncover and bake for 25 minutes longer, or until the top is lightly browned. —*Allison Vines-Rushing and Slade Rushing*

**MAKE AHEAD** Once assembled, the dressing can be refrigerated for 4 hours. Bring to room temperature before baking. The baked corn bread can be wrapped and frozen for up to 2 weeks. Thaw before using.

## Hot Cheddar-Garlic Rolls

**TOTAL: 15 MIN**

6 SERVINGS ●

At BLT Fish restaurant in New York City, chef Laurent Tourondel serves customers this decadent garlic bread, which is made with puffy round rolls instead of a long loaf and topped with plenty of melted cheddar cheese.

- ¾ cup flat-leaf parsley
- 2 small garlic cloves
- 4 tablespoons unsalted butter, softened
- Salt and freshly ground pepper
- Six 6-inch ciabatta rolls, split
- ½ pound sharp cheddar cheese, shredded (2 cups)

Preheat the oven to 375°. Put the parsley and garlic in a mini food processor and pulse until finely chopped. Add the butter and pulse until blended. Season the butter with salt and pepper. Spread the butter on the cut sides of the rolls and top with the cheese. Arrange the rolls on a large baking sheet and bake for about 6 minutes, or until the bread is toasted and the cheese is melted. Serve the cheddar-garlic rolls immediately. —*Laurent Tourondel*

## Grilled Ham-and-Cheese Sandwiches with Tapenade

**TOTAL: 25 MIN**

4 SERVINGS ●

To make a gooey grilled cheese sandwich, you need a good melting cheese like Mahón; be sure to choose a young semisoft variety rather than a hard aged one. Meaty lomo, a newly imported ham made from dry-cured pork loin accented with garlic and paprika, is definitely worth seeking out, though serrano ham is a very acceptable substitute.

- 2 ounces Spanish green olives, pitted and coarsely chopped (¼ cup)
- 1 small garlic clove, minced
- 1 tablespoon minced flat-leaf parsley
- 1 teaspoon fresh lemon juice
- Pinch of crushed red pepper
- 1½ teaspoons extra-virgin olive oil, plus more olive oil for brushing
- Eight ½-inch-thick slices of peasant bread from a 1-pound loaf
- 6 ounces sliced young Mahón or other young, mildly tangy cow's-milk cheese, such as Edam or Gouda
- 3 ounces thinly sliced lomo ham or thinly sliced serrano ham, trimmed of all fat

1. In a bowl, combine the olives with the garlic, parsley, lemon juice, crushed red pepper and 1½ teaspoons of olive oil.

2. Preheat a grill pan or panini press. Arrange the bread on a work surface and brush one side with olive oil. Turn the oiled sides face down. Spread the olive tapenade on 4 slices of the bread. Top with the sliced Mahón cheese and lomo ham. Close the sandwiches with the remaining bread and grill over moderate heat, turning once, until the bread is lightly toasted and the cheese is melted, 5 to 6 minutes. Transfer the sandwiches to a cutting board, halve and serve. —*Grace Parisi*

GARROTXA

RONCAL

LA SERENA

MAJORERO

AGED MAHÓN

MANCHEGO

IDIAZÁBAL

VALDEÓN

TETILLA

**Idiazábal D.O.** (eedeeah-TZAH-bal) Made from raw sheep's milk. Compact and tender, with a nutty flavor.

**Majorero D.O.** (mahoe-RARE-roe) Made from raw or pasteurized goat's-milk cheese. Piquant and fruity.

**La Serena D.O.** Soft, creamy, ripe, aromatic, runny cheese made from raw sheep's milk.

**Garrotxa** (gar-RO-cha) Made from pasteurized goat's milk. Firm, with a mild, earthy, slightly acidic flavor.

**Roncal** A raw, cured sheep's-milk cheese with a slightly salty, buttery flavor.

**Manchego D.O.** A sheep's-milk cheese that can be semihard to very hard, depending on how long it

has been aged. Piquant, salty and slightly nutty.

**Tetilla D.O.** (teh-TEA-ya) A semisoft cheese made from cow's milk. Sweet, mild and slightly salty.

**Mahón D.O.** (ma-HONE) This cow's-milk cheese is tender and slightly acidic when young; it becomes crumbly and rich as it ages.

**Valdeón** A soft and creamy blue cow's-milk cheese with a sharp, piquant flavor.

**The initials D.O.** stand for *denominación de origen*. This means the cheese has been recognized by the European and U.S. governments as being from a clearly defined geographic area.

# breads, pizzas & sandwiches

## Roasted Pork Sandwiches with Sauerkraut Relish

**ACTIVE: 45 MIN;**

**TOTAL: 1 HR 30 MIN**

**8 SERVINGS** ●

For this sandwich, San Francisco Bay Area caterer Carrie Dove lays slices of roasted pork tenderloin on a baguette, then piles on smoky sauerkraut-bacon relish and a sweet-tart chutney of pears, ginger, vinegar and mustard seeds.

- 3 tablespoons extra-virgin olive oil
- 2 ripe but firm Bartlett pears— peeled, halved, cored and thinly sliced
- ½ cup light brown sugar
- ⅓ cup apple cider vinegar
- ¾ teaspoon mustard seeds
- ¾ teaspoon very finely chopped fresh ginger
- 3 slices of thick-cut bacon
- 1 medium onion, finely chopped
- 1½ cups drained sauerkraut (about 1 pound)
- ¾ cup pear puree (see Note) or applesauce
- 1 teaspoon caraway seeds
- 3 pork tenderloins (about 2½ pounds)

Salt and freshly ground pepper

- 2 baguettes, slit lengthwise but still attached
- 1½ ounces baby spinach (2 cups)

## superfast
### SANDWICHES

Spread halved baguettes with apricot chutney, then fill with grilled split chicken sausages and arugula.

Shred leftover roasted chicken and mix with curry powder, mayonnaise and your favorite chutney. Serve this chicken salad on whole-grain bread.

**1.** Preheat the oven to 350°. In a medium saucepan, heat 1 tablespoon of the olive oil. Add the pear slices and cook them over high heat, stirring occasionally, until they are golden, about 4 minutes. Add the brown sugar, cider vinegar, mustard seeds and ginger and simmer the chutney over moderately low heat until it is slightly reduced and jamlike, about 30 minutes. Let the chutney cool.

**2.** Meanwhile, in a large skillet, heat 1 table-spoon of the olive oil. Add the bacon and cook over moderate heat until it is crisp, about 5 minutes. Transfer the bacon to a work surface and coarsely chop. Add the chopped onion to the skillet and cook over moderate heat until it is softened, about 6 minutes. Add the sauerkraut and cook, stirring, until it is slightly dry, about 3 minutes. Add the pear puree, caraway seeds and chopped bacon and cook for 1 minute longer. Transfer the relish to a bowl and set aside to cool.

**3.** Wipe out the skillet and heat the remaining 1 tablespoon of olive oil until shimmering. Season the pork with salt and pepper, add it to the skillet and cook over moderately high heat, turning occasionally, until browned all over, about 6 minutes. Transfer the pork to a roasting pan and roast until an instant-read thermometer inserted in the thickest part registers 140°, about 10 minutes. Transfer the pork to a cutting board and let cool, then cut into ¼-inch-thick slices.

**4.** Spread the relish on the bottom halves of the baguettes and cover with the pork; season with salt and pepper. Top with the chutney and spinach; close the baguettes. Cut into 8 sandwiches and serve.

—*Carrie Dove*

**NOTE** To make your own pear puree, drain one 15-ounce can of pears, then puree the pears in a food processor until smooth.

**MAKE AHEAD** The Roasted Pork Sandwiches with Sauerkraut Relish can be wrapped in plastic and refrigerated overnight.

## Prosciutto and Mozzarella Heros with Olive Relish

**TOTAL: 30 MIN**

**6 SERVINGS** ●

F&W's Marcia Kiesel layers her hero with prosciutto, mozzarella, tomato, pickled peppers and arugula. An olive relish with slices of crunchy celery gives the sandwich an invigorating bite.

- 3 large celery ribs, halved lengthwise and thinly sliced crosswise
- 4½ ounces pitted mixed black and green olives (¾ cup), chopped
- 3 tablespoons chopped flat-leaf parsley
- 1½ tablespoons coarsely chopped capers
- ¼ cup plus ½ tablespoon extra-virgin olive oil

Six 6-inch-long hero rolls, split

- 12 large arugula leaves
- ¾ pound thinly sliced prosciutto
- ¾ pound fresh, lightly salted mozzarella, cut into 12 slices
- 3 large tomatoes, each cut into 6 slices
- ¾ cup thinly sliced pickled peppers, preferably spicy

**1.** Preheat the oven to 425°. In a medium bowl, toss the celery, olives, parsley and capers, then stir in the olive oil.

**2.** Spread the hero rolls open on a cookie sheet and bake for about 3 minutes, or until they are lightly crisp. Arrange 2 arugula leaves on the bottom half of each roll and top with 2 ounces of prosciutto, 2 mozzarella slices and 3 tomato slices. Top each sandwich with a layer of pickled peppers and about ¼ cup of the olive relish. Close the hero sandwiches and serve at once.

—*Marcia Kiesel*

**MAKE AHEAD** The relish can be refrigerated for up to 3 days.

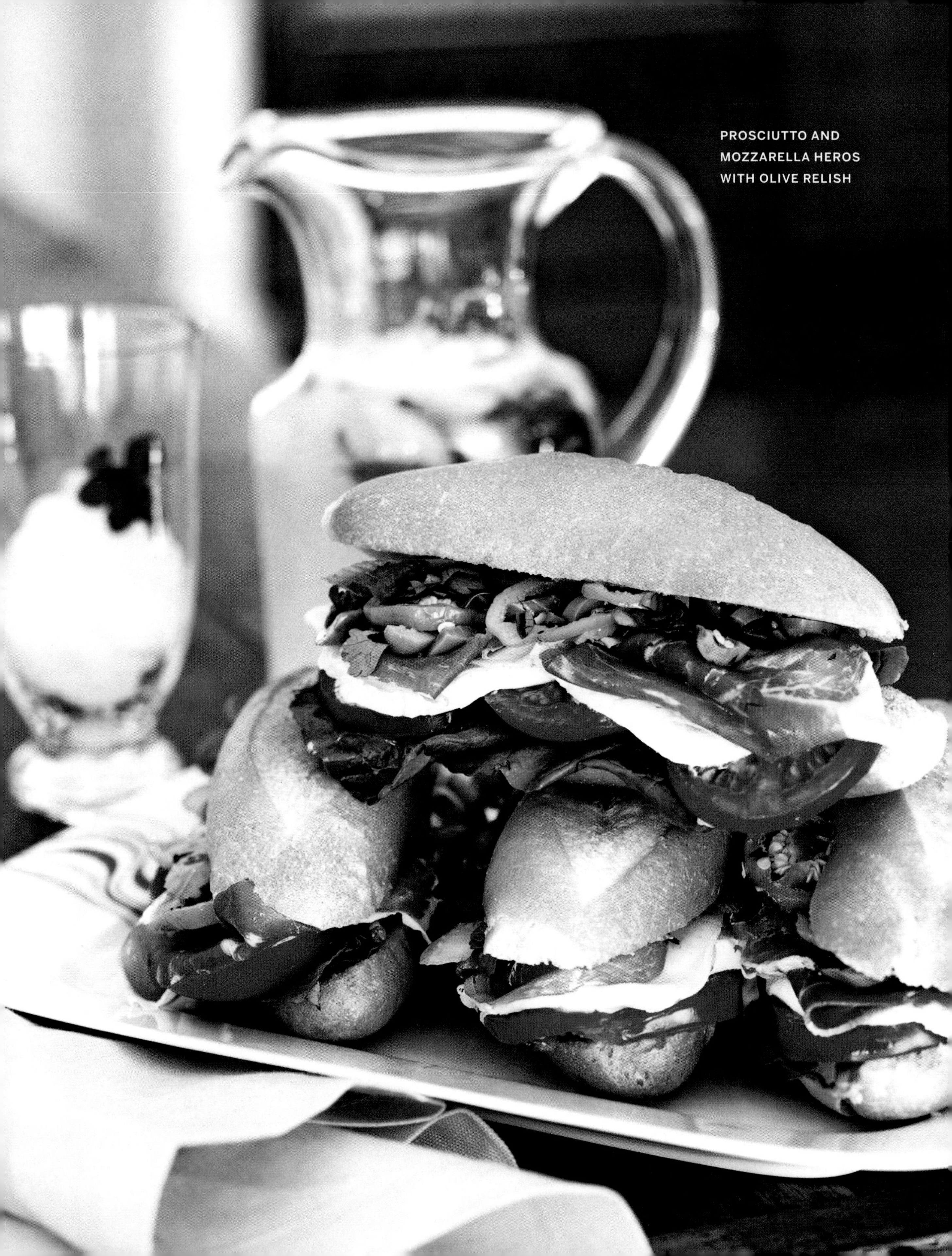

PROSCIUTTO AND MOZZARELLA HEROS WITH OLIVE RELISH

**HAM AND CHILE-CHEDDAR CALZONE**

**STRIP STEAK SANDWICH**

## Ham and Chile-Cheddar Calzones

**TOTAL: 30 MIN**

**4 SERVINGS** ●●

A fast, easy homemade pimiento spread adds a little kick to the cheddar filling in this clever version of grilled ham-and-cheese sandwiches.

**All-purpose flour, for dusting**

2 **pounds thawed frozen pizza dough, formed into 4 balls**

2 **poblano chiles—roasted, peeled, seeded and chopped**

2 **packed cups farmstead cheddar cheese, shredded**

2 **tablespoons chopped jarred pimientos**

**Salt and freshly ground pepper**

½ **pound smoked ham, sliced ¼ inch thick**

**Two 4-ounce bunches arugula, thick stems discarded**

**1.** Preheat a large baking sheet in a 500° oven for 10 minutes and carefully spray it with oil. Meanwhile, on a lightly floured work surface, roll or stretch each ball of dough into a 9-inch round.

**2.** In a medium bowl, combine the chiles, 1¾ cups of the cheddar, the pimientos, a pinch of salt and ¼ teaspoon of pepper; mash to a coarse paste with a fork.

**3.** Arrange the ham on the bottom half of each dough round. Top with the arugula and season lightly with salt and pepper. Spread the cheddar mixture over the arugula to within ½ inch of the edge, pressing slightly to compact. Fold the top half of the dough over the filling, pressing to release any trapped air; pinch the edges to seal.

**4.** Transfer the calzones to the baking sheet. Sprinkle the remaining ¼ cup of cheddar on top and bake for 8 minutes, or until golden and crisp. —*Grace Parisi*

## Strip Steak Sandwiches

**TOTAL: 20 MIN**

**4 SERVINGS** ●

½ **cup plus 2 tablespoons olive oil, plus more for brushing**

1 **tablespoon finely grated lemon zest**

2 **teaspoons minced rosemary**

½ **teaspoon crushed red pepper**

**Sea salt and freshly ground black pepper**

1¾ **pounds New York strip steaks (1 inch thick)**

6 **ounces pitted green olives (1 cup), finely chopped**

3 **tablespoons minced parsley**

2 **teaspoons chopped oregano**

1 **tablespoon chopped mint**

2 **teaspoons chopped capers**

1 **tablespoon fresh lemon juice**

4 **crusty rolls, split**

2 **medium tomatoes, thinly sliced**

**1.** Preheat a grill. In a small bowl, combine 2 tablespoons of the olive oil with the lemon zest, rosemary, crushed red pepper, 1 tablespoon of sea salt and ½ teaspoon of black pepper. Rub the mixture all over the steaks and let stand for 10 minutes.

**2.** Meanwhile, in a small bowl, mix the olives with the parsley, oregano, mint, capers, lemon juice, ½ teaspoon of pepper and the remaining ½ cup of olive oil.

**3.** Scrape the marinade off the steaks and season them with salt and pepper. Grill the steaks over moderately high heat, turning them occasionally, about 10 minutes for medium-rare meat. Let the steaks rest on a cutting board for 10 minutes, then thinly slice them crosswise.

**4.** Meanwhile, brush the cut sides of the rolls with olive oil and grill until toasted, about 1 minute. Spoon half of the olive relish on the rolls and top with the sliced steak and tomatoes. Sprinkle lightly with salt and spoon the remaining relish on top. Close the sandwiches and serve.

*—Suzanne Goin*

## Emeril's Muffuletta

**ACTIVE: 20 MIN; TOTAL: 1 HR 45 MIN**

**8 SERVINGS** ●●

The muffuletta is the quintessential New Orleans sandwich of cured meats, cheese and tangy olive salad piled onto a sturdy Italian loaf. TV chef Emeril Lagasse's delicious muffuletta is packed with briny olives and pickled vegetables.

- **5 ounces pimiento-stuffed olives (1 cup), sliced, plus 2 tablespoons liquid from the jar**
- **6 ounces chopped giardiniera (pickled Italian vegetables; 1 cup), plus 1 tablespoon liquid from the jar**
- **2 tablespoons drained capers, plus 2 teaspoons liquid from the jar**
- **3 ounces pitted Calamata olives (½ cup), sliced**

- **2½ teaspoons minced garlic**
- **1 tablespoon minced shallot**
- **1 teaspoon dried oregano**
- **1 teaspoon dried parsley**

**Pinch of dried thyme**

**Pinch of crushed red pepper**

- **½ cup extra-virgin olive oil**
- **1 large loaf seeded Italian bread (about 1¼ pounds), split**
- **¼ pound sliced fresh mozzarella**
- **6 ounces sliced capocollo or prosciutto**
- **¼ pound sliced Genoa salami**
- **¼ pound sliced mortadella**
- **¼ pound sliced mild provolone cheese**

**Peperoncini, for serving**

**1.** In a bowl, stir the pimiento-stuffed olives with the giardiniera, the capers and their liquids. Add the Calamata olives, garlic, shallot, oregano, parsley, thyme and red pepper. Stir in the olive oil and let the mixture stand for 1 hour.

**2.** Open the Italian bread on a work surface. Spoon the olive salad on both sides of the bread and spread evenly. Arrange the mozzarella slices on the bottom half of the bread, then top with the capocollo, Genoa salami and mortadella. Arrange the provolone cheese on the top half of the bread, covering the olive salad completely. Carefully close the sandwich. Wrap the sandwich tightly in plastic and let stand for 30 minutes or up to 2 hours. Cut the muffuletta sandwich into 8 pieces and serve peperoncini on the side.

*—Emeril Lagasse*

## Pork Tenderloin Sandwiches with Creamy Blue Cheese Dressing

**TOTAL: 30 MIN**

**8 SERVINGS** ●●

This rendition of Iowa's famous pork tenderloin sandwiches showcases another state classic, Maytag blue cheese, in a creamy, tangy dressing. The sandwich is even better with a dash of hot sauce.

- **¾ cup mayonnaise**
- **½ cup plain yogurt**
- **½ cup extra-virgin olive oil**
- **6 ounces blue cheese, preferably Maytag Blue, crumbled**
- **1 tablespoon red wine vinegar**

**Salt and freshly ground pepper**

**All-purpose flour, for dredging**

- **3 large eggs, lightly beaten**
- **2 cups fine dry bread crumbs**

**Two 1¼-pound pork tenderloins, each sliced on the bias into 4 pieces and pounded ¼ inch thick**

**Vegetable oil, for frying**

- **8 kaiser rolls, split**
- **4 cups shredded iceberg lettuce**
- **2 large tomatoes, each cut crosswise into 4 slices**

**Hot sauce, for serving**

**1.** Preheat the oven to 400°. In a bowl, whisk the mayonnaise and yogurt, then whisk in the olive oil until smooth. Stir in the cheese and vinegar; season with salt and pepper.

**2.** Put the flour, eggs and bread crumbs into 3 shallow bowls. Season the cutlets with salt and pepper. Dredge the cutlets in the flour, shaking off the excess, then dip in the beaten eggs and bread crumbs.

**3.** In a large nonstick skillet, heat ¼ inch of vegetable oil until shimmering. Fry 3 pork cutlets over moderately high heat until browned, 2 minutes per side. Drain on paper towels, then transfer the cutlets to a rimmed baking sheet. Repeat with the remaining cutlets, adding more oil to the skillet as needed. Reduce the heat to moderate if they start browning too quickly.

**4.** Transfer the cutlets to the oven; bake for 3 to 4 minutes, until just cooked through. Put the rolls in the oven, cut side up, and bake for 1 minute, until lightly toasted.

**5.** Spread 2 tablespoons of the cheese dressing on each side of the rolls. Mound ½ cup of lettuce on the bottom half of each roll. Top with a tomato slice and a cutlet and close. Cut the sandwiches in half and serve with hot sauce. *—Jeremy Jackson*

# breads, pizzas & sandwiches

## Garlic-Brined Pork Banh Mi

**ACTIVE: 45 MIN; TOTAL: 3 HR PLUS OVERNIGHT BRINING**

**MAKES 6 SANDWICHES PLUS EXTRA ROASTED PORK**

Chef Charles Phan of San Francisco's the Slanted Door thinks these French-Vietnamese sandwiches, *banh mi,* "are fusion food at its best." This particular recipe is inspired by a tiny sandwich shop Phan happened upon in Hoi An, Vietnam, that stays open until 4 A.M. Not only does the owner of the shop make his own pâté, but he also soaks his pork overnight in a garlicky brine before roasting it, as Phan does here.

- 1 tablespoon each of whole white and black peppercorns
- ¾ cup plus 2 tablespoons kosher salt
- ½ cup light brown sugar
- 2 serrano chiles, crushed
- 2 tablespoons minced garlic
- 3 jalapeños, thinly sliced
- 2 cups warm water

One 3-pound boneless pork shoulder

About 6 cups cold water

- ½ cup distilled white vinegar
- ½ cup granulated sugar
- ½ teaspoon table salt
- 1½ cups coarsely shredded carrots (about 6 carrots)
- 6 ciabatta rolls or 2 long baguettes, split lengthwise, roll centers slightly hollowed out

Mayonnaise

- ½ pound fine-textured pork pâté, thinly sliced (optional)
- 1 European seedless cucumber—halved crosswise and thinly sliced lengthwise
- 1 cup cilantro leaves
- 2 tablespoons soy sauce

Hot sauce, for serving

**1.** In a small skillet, toast the white and black peppercorns over moderately high heat until they are fragrant, about 1 minute. Transfer the peppercorns to a work surface and, using the side of a heavy knife, coarsely crack them. Transfer the peppercorns to a large, deep bowl. Add the kosher salt and brown sugar, then add the serrano chiles, garlic and one-third of the jalapeños. Add the warm water and stir until the sugar and salt are dissolved. Add the pork shoulder and enough cold water to submerge the roast. Cover the bowl and refrigerate overnight.

**2.** Preheat the oven to 400°. Drain the pork shoulder and pat it dry, then transfer to a roasting pan. Let the pork return to room temperature. Roast the pork for about 1 hour and 15 minutes, turning once; the pork is done when an instant-read thermometer inserted in the thickest part registers 165°. Let the pork rest for 30 minutes before slicing thinly.

**3.** Meanwhile, in a medium bowl, combine the vinegar, granulated sugar and table salt and stir until dissolved. Add the shredded carrots and let stand until softened, about 30 minutes. Drain the carrots well.

**4.** Spread the cut sides of the ciabatta rolls with mayonnaise and layer the sliced pâté on the bottom halves. Top the pâté with the roasted pork, sliced cucumber, cilantro leaves, pickled carrots and the remaining sliced jalapeños. Sprinkle the sandwich filling lightly with the soy sauce and close the sandwiches. Cut the ciabatta rolls in half or the baguettes in thirds and serve with hot sauce. —*Charles Phan*

## Glazed Tofu Sandwiches with Jicama Slaw

**ACTIVE: 25 MIN; TOTAL: 1 HR 25 MIN**

**4 SERVINGS ● ●**

Tofu doesn't sound like a reasonable substitute for steak, but when it's pressed until firm, then glazed with a sweet, spicy sauce and topped with a crisp slaw of jicama and carrots, you won't miss the meat.

- 2 large blocks extra-firm tofu (14 ounces each), drained and halved horizontally
- 2 tablespoons jalapeño jelly
- 1 tablespoon ketchup
- 2 teaspoons soy sauce
- ½ teaspoon Asian sesame oil
- 2 tablespoons fresh lime juice
- 1 tablespoon sugar
- 1 garlic clove, crushed
- 1 teaspoon minced jalapeño or serrano chile
- 1 tablespoon Asian fish sauce
- 1 small jicama (1 pound), peeled and julienned
- 2 large carrots, julienned
- ¼ cup chopped cilantro
- 2 tablespoons chopped mint
- 4 kaiser rolls, split

Vegetable oil, for brushing

Mayonnaise

**1.** Set the tofu on a cutting board and top it with a cookie sheet and 2 or 3 heavy cans. Let stand for 1 hour, or until the tofu is very firm and the liquid has been pressed out. Pat the tofu dry.

**2.** Meanwhile, in a small bowl, whisk the jalapeño jelly with the ketchup, soy sauce, sesame oil and 1 tablespoon of the lime juice. In a large bowl, mix the sugar with the garlic and minced jalapeño. Using the side of a spoon, mash the mixture until it becomes a paste. Add the fish sauce and the remaining 1 tablespoon of lime juice. Stir in the julienned jicama and the carrots, cilantro and mint.

**3.** Light a grill. Brush the pressed tofu and the cut sides of the rolls with the vegetable oil. Lightly grill the rolls, about 2 minutes. Grill the tofu over a hot fire until it is lightly charred, 8 to 10 minutes. Brush the jalapeño jelly glaze on the tofu and grill, turning and brushing until the tofu is nicely glazed, 2 to 3 minutes longer.

**4.** Spread a thin layer of mayonnaise on both halves of each roll. Mound the jicama slaw on the toasted rolls and top with the glazed tofu steaks. Close the sandwiches, cut them in half and serve. —*Grace Parisi*

## Barbecue Tempeh Sandwiches

**TOTAL: 30 MIN**

**4 SERVINGS** ● ● ●

Tempeh is a fermented soybean cake with a mild, nutty flavor and a texture similar to that of soft tofu. It's a great meat substitute and a very good source of fiber. Look for tempeh in the refrigerator case in the health food section of large supermarkets or in health food stores.

- ⅓ cup cider vinegar
- ⅓ cup soy sauce
- ⅓ cup pure maple syrup
- 2 teaspoons ground cumin
- 2 teaspoons ground chipotle chile powder or 1 canned chipotle—drained, seeded and finely chopped
- 1 teaspoon sweet paprika
- 1⅓ cups water
- ¼ cup extra-virgin olive oil
- 1 pound tempeh (2 pieces), each halved horizontally, then lengthwise to make eight 4-inch squares
- 1 cup sun-dried tomatoes (not oil-packed)
- ¼ cup very finely chopped onion

Salt and freshly ground black pepper

- 4 kaiser rolls, split
- 4 romaine lettuce leaves
- 2 cups alfalfa sprouts

**1.** In a large skillet, whisk the cider vinegar with the soy sauce, maple syrup, cumin, chipotle and paprika until combined. Add ⅓ cup of the water and 3 tablespoons of the olive oil and bring to a boil. Add the tempeh pieces and cook them over low heat, turning a few times, until the tempeh pieces are heated through and the barbecue sauce is slightly reduced, about 10 minutes.

**2.** Meanwhile, in a small saucepan, cover the sun-dried tomatoes with the remaining 1 cup of water and bring to a boil over moderately high heat. Cover the saucepan, remove from the heat and let the sun-dried tomatoes stand until they are softened, about 3 minutes. Drain and coarsely chop the sun-dried tomatoes.

**3.** Add the onion and the remaining tablespoon of olive oil to the saucepan and cook over moderate heat, stirring occasionally, until softened, about 5 minutes. Stir the sun-dried tomatoes and onion into the tempeh sauce and simmer over high heat until the sauce is thickened, about 3 minutes; season with salt and black pepper.

**4.** Open the kaiser rolls and place a lettuce leaf on each bottom half; top with ½ cup of sprouts. Place 2 pieces of tempeh on each kaiser roll and top with some of the chunky barbecue tomato sauce. Close the sandwiches, cut them in half and serve immediately. —*Peter Berley*

## Crispy Chicken Picnic Subs

**ACTIVE: 45 MIN; TOTAL: 1 HR 45 MIN**

**8 SERVINGS**

This chicken sandwich is deliciously over the top. The chicken is marinated in mustard and vinegar, fried until it's crispy, then topped with a tangy tomato-onion salad, crumbled blue cheese and salty bits of bacon.

- 1 teaspoon Dijon mustard
- 1 tablespoon red wine vinegar
- ¼ cup plus 2 tablespoons extra-virgin olive oil

Salt and freshly ground black pepper

Cayenne pepper

- 1½ pounds skinless, boneless chicken breasts, sliced on the bias ¾ inch thick
- 1½ pounds skinless, boneless chicken thighs, trimmed of excess fat and sliced on the bias ¾ inch thick
- 2 tablespoons balsamic vinegar
- 2 tablespoons chopped basil
- 1 teaspoon chopped thyme
- 2 medium tomatoes, thinly sliced
- 1 small red onion, thinly sliced
- 8 slices of bacon
- ½ cup buttermilk
- 2 cups plain coarse bread crumbs

Vegetable oil, for frying

Eight 7- to 8-inch-long rolls, split

- 3 ounces blue cheese, crumbled
- 1 large bunch arugula, stemmed

**1.** In a large bowl, whisk the mustard with the red wine vinegar, ¼ cup of the olive oil and a pinch each of salt, black pepper and cayenne pepper. Add the chicken and let stand at room temperature for 1 hour.

**2.** Meanwhile, in a medium bowl, combine the remaining 2 tablespoons of olive oil with the balsamic vinegar, basil and thyme and season with salt and pepper. Add the tomato and onions; let stand for 1 hour.

**3.** In a large skillet, cook the bacon over moderately high heat until browned, about 6 minutes. Drain and coarsely chop.

**4.** Remove the chicken from the marinade and pat dry; discard the marinade. Return the chicken to the bowl, add the buttermilk and toss. Put the bread crumbs in a large plastic bag and season with salt and cayenne. Add the chicken a few pieces at a time, seal the bag and shake to coat. Transfer the coated chicken to a large plate and press the crumbs to help them adhere.

## equipment
### INDOOR GRILL

**Breville's** countertop grill has nearly 370 square inches of nonstick working space and does double duty as a perfect panini press.

**DETAILS** $180 from Williams-Sonoma; williams-sonoma.com.

**5.** In a large nonstick skillet, heat ¼ inch of vegetable oil. Working in batches, fry the chicken over moderately high heat, turning once, until golden and crisp, 5 minutes. Transfer to a rack to cool.

**6.** Spoon the tomatoes and onions onto the bottom halves of the rolls and drizzle with any leftover dressing. Top with the chicken, blue cheese, bacon and arugula. Close the sandwiches and serve.
—*Bradley Ogden*

## Juicy Pulled-Pork Sandwiches
**ACTIVE: 4 HR; TOTAL: 9 HR 30 MIN**
**PLUS OVERNIGHT MARINATING**
6 TO 8 SERVINGS ●

Pork shoulder is a natural cut for barbecue because it becomes amazingly tender and juicy when slow-roasted over low heat. A whole pork shoulder (which takes about 18 hours to cook) consists of two main parts: the pork butt and the picnic shoulder. Chef Adam Perry Lang of Daisy May's BBQ USA in New York City often uses just the pork butt end of the shoulder because it takes less time (about 8 to 10 hours) and there is less fat to trim after the meat is cooked.

- ¼ cup Garlicky Barbecue Marinade (p. 97)
- One 8-pound pork butt, skin removed
- ¼ cup plus 2 tablespoons Seven-Spice Dry Rub (p. 97)
- 4 cups hickory or other hardwood chips, soaked in water
- Cider Mop Spray (p. 97)
- ½ cup pan drippings or water
- 2 cups Sweet and Sticky Barbecue Sauce (p. 97)
- Hamburger buns, raw onion slices and hot sauce, for serving
- Crunchy Coleslaw with Cayenne and Toasted Caraway Seeds (p. 233), for serving

**1.** Rub the Garlicky Barbecue Marinade all over the pork butt and refrigerate the meat overnight.

**2.** About 10 hours before serving the pulled-pork sandwiches, bring the chilled pork butt to room temperature and sprinkle the meat all over with the Seven-Spice Dry Rub.

**3.** Light a charcoal fire in a covered grill. Set up the grill for indirect grilling: When the temperature reaches 225°, carefully push the hot coals to one side and place a drip pan filled with 1 cup of water on the opposite side of the grill. Alternatively, bring a smoker to 225°. Put the pork butt over the drip pan and cover the grill; you'll need to cook the pork butt for about 8 hours. Maintain the temperature at 225° by replenishing the charcoal with a fresh batch of burning coals every hour. Also, every hour drain ½ cup of the soaked wood chips and scatter them over the hot coals. Add more water to the drip pan when half of it is evaporated.

**4.** After the first 6 hours of cooking, spray the pork butt with the Cider Mop Spray every 30 minutes and continue to cook it for about 2 hours longer, or until an instant-read thermometer inserted into the thickest part of the pork registers 195°. Transfer the pork butt to a roasting pan and let the meat rest for about 30 minutes.

**5.** Skim most of the fat from the liquid in the drip pan. Measure out ½ cup of the liquid and transfer it to a small saucepan. Add the Sweet and Sticky Barbecue Sauce to the saucepan and bring the sauce to a simmer. Scrape any excess fat from the pork butt. With 2 forks, remove the meat from the pork butt and pull it into long, thick shreds. Discard the fat and bones. Add the diluted Sweet and Sticky Barbecue Sauce to the roasting pan and simmer it gently, without stirring too much, until heated through. Serve the pork with the buns, raw onion slices and hot sauce. Serve the Crunchy Coleslaw with Cayenne and Toasted Caraway Seeds on the side.
—*Adam Perry Lang*

**MAKE AHEAD** The barbecued pork butt can be refrigerated overnight in the roasting pan with a little water. Cover the pan with foil and bake the pork butt at 325° until it is heated through, about 1½ hours, before proceeding with Step 5 of the recipe.

## Bouillabaisse Sandwiches
**TOTAL: 30 MIN**
4 SERVINGS ● ●

In his interpretation of bouillabaisse, the classic Provençal seafood stew, chef Aaron Whitcomb of Table 6 in Denver piles seared fish, tomato and fennel on bread slathered with saffron mayonnaise.

- ⅛ teaspoon saffron threads in 2 teaspoons hot water
- ⅓ cup mayonnaise
- Salt and freshly ground pepper
- 2 cups watercress sprigs
- 1 small fennel bulb—halved, cored and very thinly sliced
- 1 medium shallot, thinly sliced
- 2 tablespoons fresh lemon juice
- 1 tablespoon unsalted butter
- 2 tablespoons vegetable oil
- Four 4-ounce skinless halibut or mahimahi fillets
- 8 slices of country bread, toasted and rubbed with garlic
- Hot paprika, for sprinkling
- 4 piquillo peppers, or 2 roasted bell peppers, halved
- 1 large plum tomato, thinly sliced

**1.** In a bowl, stir the saffron into the mayonnaise; season with salt and pepper.

**2.** In a medium bowl, toss the watercress with the fennel, shallot and lemon juice; season the salad with salt and pepper.

**3.** In a large skillet, melt the butter in the oil. Season the fillets with salt and pepper, then cook them over high heat for 3 minutes per side. Spread the bread with the saffron mayonnaise; sprinkle with paprika. Fill the sandwiches with the fish, peppers, tomato and watercress salad and serve.
—*Aaron Whitcomb*

For the March issue, Australian chef Bill Granger and his daughter, Edie, prepared their favorite Coconut Pancakes with Bananas and Passion Fruit Syrup (P. 296).

282

# breakfast & brunch

**HERBED EGG CRÊPES WITH SMOKED SALMON**

**SAUTÉED CAULIFLOWER FRITTATA WITH THYME**

### Herbed Egg Crêpes with Smoked Salmon

**TOTAL: 50 MIN**

10 TO 12 SERVINGS ●

These egg crêpes are filled with smoked salmon and crème fraîche, but they're also wonderful with a mix of softened goat cheese and olive tapenade.

- 10 **large eggs, at room temperature**
- ½ **cup heavy cream**
- ⅓ **cup coarsely chopped tarragon**
- ⅓ **cup coarsely chopped chervil or flat-leaf parsley**
- ⅓ **cup snipped chives, plus more for garnish**

**Kosher salt and freshly ground pepper**

**Olive oil, for brushing**

- 1 **cup crème fraîche**
- 1 **pound thinly sliced smoked salmon**

**1.** In a large bowl, whisk the eggs and heavy cream until blended. Add the tarragon, chervil and ⅓ cup of chives; season with 1 teaspoon of salt and ½ teaspoon of pepper. Let the batter rest for 15 minutes.
**2.** Lightly brush an 8-inch nonstick skillet with olive oil and set over moderate heat. When the pan is hot, add 3 tablespoons of batter, swirling to coat the bottom, and cook until golden around the edge, 30 seconds. Carefully turn the crêpe and cook just until set, 15 seconds longer. Transfer to a large plate lined with wax paper. Continue making crêpes with the remaining batter, brushing the pan with oil as necessary and layering the crêpes with wax paper.
**3.** Arrange the crêpes on a work surface; spread lightly with crème fraîche and top with salmon. Fold the crêpes in half, then in half again to form triangles. Transfer to plates and sprinkle with chives. —*Seen Lippert*

### Sautéed Cauliflower Frittata with Thyme

**TOTAL: 25 MIN**

8 SERVINGS ● ●

Chef and restaurateur Nancy Silverton often prepares a tender frittata for the antipasti table at La Terza in Los Angeles. This version includes sautéed cauliflower topped with homemade bread crumbs for a lovely bit of crunch. Silverton's trick for making small amounts of bread crumbs is to toast a slice of sourdough bread, rub it with a garlic clove and then grind it in a mortar.

- 3 **tablespoons unsalted butter**
- 1 **tablespoon extra-virgin olive oil**
- ½ **medium head cauliflower, cut into 1-inch florets (2 cups)**

**Sea salt**

- 1 **large onion, halved and thinly sliced**

3 small garlic cloves, thinly sliced

10 large eggs, at room temperature, lightly beaten

2 tablespoons dry bread crumbs from 1 piece of toast

2 teaspoons thyme leaves

Freshly grated Parmesan cheese

Truffle salt (see Note) or fleur de sel and aged balsamic vinegar, for serving

**1.** Preheat the oven to 400°. In a 10-inch nonstick ovenproof skillet, melt 1 tablespoon of butter in the olive oil. Add the cauliflower, season with sea salt and cook over high heat, without stirring, until golden brown on the bottom, 2 minutes. Toss the cauliflower and cook until golden brown all over and just tender, 3 minutes longer. Add the onion and 1 tablespoon of butter and cook, stirring occasionally, until softened, 3 minutes. Reduce the heat to moderate, add the garlic and cook until softened, 1 minute. Add the remaining 1 tablespoon of butter and swirl the pan to melt it.

**2.** In a large bowl, whisk the eggs with ¾ teaspoon of sea salt. Pour the eggs over the cauliflower and cook, without stirring, until the bottom of the frittata is just set, about 2 minutes. Lift the edge of the frittata and tilt the pan to allow the uncooked eggs to seep underneath. Cook the frittata until the bottom is golden and the top is just slightly runny, about 3 minutes.

**3.** Sprinkle the crumbs and thyme over the frittata and bake until just set, 3 minutes longer. Sprinkle the frittata with Parmesan and slide it onto a work surface or platter. Cut into wedges and serve warm or at room temperature with truffle salt and balsamic vinegar. —Nancy Silverton

**NOTE** Truffle salt tastes much better than cloying white truffle oil; it contains real black truffles—it's not just an infusion ($21 for 3.5 ounces from the Cheese Store of Beverly Hills; 800-547-1515).

**MAKE AHEAD** The frittata can be kept at room temperature for up to 2 hours.

## Chanterelle and Fontina Frittata

**TOTAL: 30 MIN**

4 SERVINGS ● ●

8 large eggs, beaten

1 tablespoon chopped tarragon

¼ cup extra-virgin olive oil

½ pound chanterelle mushrooms, sliced if large (see Note)

Salt and freshly ground pepper

2 ounces Fontina or Gruyère cheese, shredded (½ cup)

**1.** Preheat the oven to 350°. In a medium bowl, beat the eggs with the tarragon. In a large nonstick ovenproof skillet, heat 2 tablespoons of the olive oil until shimmering. Add the chanterelle mushrooms, season them with salt and pepper and cook them over moderately high heat, stirring occasionally, until they are browned, about 8 minutes.

**2.** Add the remaining 2 tablespoons of olive oil to the skillet. Add the beaten eggs and cook until they begin to set at the edge, about 30 seconds. Using a spatula, lift the edge of the frittata and tilt the pan, allowing the uncooked eggs to seep underneath. Cook the frittata until the bottom is set, about 3 minutes. Sprinkle the cheese on top and bake the frittata for about 8 minutes, or until fluffy and set. Slide the mushroom and cheese frittata onto a platter, cut into wedges and serve at once. —Marc Meyer

**NOTE** Cremini or oyster mushrooms can be substituted

**MAKE AHEAD** The baked mushroom and cheese frittata can be kept at room temperature for up to 2 hours.

## Classic Potato Tortilla

**TOTAL: 25 MIN**

6 TO 8 SERVINGS ● ●

2 pounds all-purpose potatoes, peeled

2 cups extra-virgin olive oil

10 large eggs, beaten

Salt

**1.** Quarter the potatoes lengthwise and thinly slice them crosswise. In a large skillet, heat all but 2 tablespoons of the olive oil until shimmering. Carefully add the potatoes and cook over high heat, stirring once or twice, until softened and just beginning to brown, about 15 minutes. Using a slotted spoon, transfer the potatoes to a colander to drain. Pour off the oil in the skillet.

**2.** Return the skillet to high heat and add the remaining 2 tablespoons of olive oil. In a large bowl, combine the potatoes with the beaten eggs and season with salt. Add the mixture to the skillet and cook, lifting the edge of the tortilla and tilting the pan to allow the uncooked eggs to seep underneath; cook until the bottom is golden and set, about 5 minutes. Slide the tortilla onto a large plate and pour off any oil. Cover the tortilla with the inverted skillet; using 2 oven mitts, grasp the skillet and the plate and quickly invert the tortilla back into the pan. Cook the tortilla over high heat until the bottom is set and lightly browned, about 2 minutes longer. Slide the tortilla onto a plate, cut into wedges and serve. —Jeff Koehler

# ingredient
## SPECIALTY EGGS

### ORGANIC EGGS
Come from hens whose feed is organic (free of pesticides and herbicides). Hens receive no antibiotics and are free to roam outside. Certified by the USDA.

### FREE-RANGE EGGS
Come from hens that have access to the outdoors and are free to lay their legs where they choose.

### CAGE-FREE EGGS
Come from hens that are not raised in cages but may not have access to the outdoors.

● FAST   ● HEALTHY   ● MAKE AHEAD   ● STAFF FAVORITE

## Tomato and Feta Cheese Strata

**TOTAL: 30 MIN**

**4 SERVINGS** ● ●

- 4 large eggs
- ½ cup low-fat yogurt
- 3 tablespoons chopped parsley
- 1 tablespoon extra-virgin olive oil
- 1 medium onion, thinly sliced
- 1 large garlic clove, thinly sliced
- 2 tablespoons finely chopped sage
- ½ teaspoon crushed red pepper

One 16-ounce can diced tomatoes with their juices

Salt and freshly ground pepper

- 5 ounces whole wheat peasant bread, cut into 1-inch cubes (4 cups)
- 2 ounces feta cheese, crumbled

**1.** Preheat the oven to 450°. In a medium bowl, whisk the eggs, then whisk in the yogurt and parsley.

**2.** In a 10-inch ovenproof skillet, heat the oil. Add the onion, garlic, sage and crushed pepper. Cook over moderately high heat, stirring, until the onion is softened and lightly browned, 3 minutes. Add the tomatoes and their juices, season with salt and pepper and bring to a simmer. Stir in the bread and sprinkle with feta. Pour on the eggs and bake for 20 minutes, until golden. Let cool slightly; serve. —*Peter Berley*

## Egg and Bacon Sandwiches with Tomato Relish

**TOTAL: 20 MIN**

**4 SERVINGS** ● ●

- 4 slices of bacon
- 2 large tomatoes—halved, seeded and thinly sliced
- 1 large shallot, very thinly sliced
- ¼ cup flat-leaf parsley leaves
- 2 tablespoons extra-virgin olive oil
- 1 teaspoon fresh lemon juice

Salt and freshly ground pepper

- 4 soft hero rolls, split
- 4 large eggs

**1.** In a large nonstick skillet, cook the bacon over moderately high heat, turning once, until crisp, about 6 minutes. Drain on paper towels. Wipe out the skillet.

**2.** In a bowl, toss the tomatoes, shallot and parsley with 1 tablespoon of the olive oil and the lemon juice; season with salt and pepper. Put the bacon on the bottom half of each roll and top with the tomatoes.

**3.** Heat the remaining 1 tablespoon of olive oil in the skillet until shimmering. Crack an egg into the skillet and cook over moderately high heat until the white is just set, about 2 minutes. Flip the egg and cook for 1 minute longer. Repeat with the remaining eggs. Carefully transfer each egg to a roll and season with salt and pepper. Close the sandwiches and serve. —*Bill Granger*

## Souffléed Asparagus Omelet

**TOTAL: 15 MIN**

**2 SERVINGS** ● ●

- 1 tablespoon plus 1 teaspoon extra-virgin olive oil
- ½ pound pencil-thin asparagus, tips reserved, stems thinly sliced on the diagonal
- 2 large egg whites, at room temperature

Salt

- 2 large eggs, at room temperature
- 1 tablespoon minced parsley

Freshly ground white pepper

- 1 tablespoon snipped chives
- 2 tablespoons finely grated Parmesan cheese

**1.** In a nonstick skillet, heat 1 teaspoon of the olive oil. Add the asparagus stems and cook over moderate heat, stirring, until crisp-tender, 4 minutes. Transfer to a mini food processor and finely chop. Add the asparagus tips to the pan and cook over moderate heat for about 4 minutes. Transfer to a plate.

**2.** In a medium bowl, using a handheld mixer, beat the 2 egg whites with a pinch of salt at medium-high speed until soft peaks form. In another bowl, beat the whole eggs with the asparagus puree and parsley; season with salt and white pepper. Fold the whites into the asparagus mixture.

**3.** Heat the remaining 1 tablespoon of oil in the skillet. Add the egg mixture, smooth the top and cover. Cook over moderately low heat for 3 minutes. Sprinkle the chives, Parmesan and asparagus tips over half of the omelet; fold the other half of the omelet over the filling and hold it for 30 seconds before serving. —*Constance Snow*

## Scrambled Eggs and Cockles

**TOTAL: 25 MIN**

**4 SERVINGS** ● ●

In this recipe, which chef Andy Nusser of Casa Mono in New York City adapted from a dish at Barcelona tapas spot Bar Pinotxo, eggs are scrambled with clams and serrano ham. Sparkling wine lightens the texture.

- ¼ cup extra-virgin olive oil
- 4 ounces serrano ham, cut into ¼-inch dice (1 cup)
- 2 garlic cloves, thinly sliced
- 1 cup cava or dry sparkling white wine
- 1 pound cockles, scrubbed and rinsed

Pinch of crushed red pepper

- 8 large eggs, beaten
- 4 scallions, thinly sliced

Toasted country or sourdough bread, for serving

**1.** In a 10-inch nonstick skillet, heat the olive oil. Add the ham and garlic and cook over moderately high heat, stirring, until the garlic is lightly golden, 5 minutes. Add the wine, cockles and crushed pepper, cover and cook until the cockles open, 3 minutes. Transfer the cockles to a plate. Discard any that do not open.

**2.** Boil the liquid in the skillet until it is reduced to ¼ cup. Add the eggs and scallions and cook, stirring, until soft curds form. Transfer the scrambled eggs to plates, top them with the cockles and serve with toast. —*Andy Nusser*

## Layered Eggplant, Zucchini and Spinach Tortilla

**TOTAL: 50 MIN**

**8 SERVINGS**

Every Spanish housewife has her recipe for this *tortilla* cake (a kind of omelet) served with a creamy tomato béchamel sauce. Usually one of the layers is tuna, spaghetti or macaroni—to make the kids happy. This recipe strays from the classic by calling for only vegetable fillings.

- 2 tablespoons unsalted butter
- 2 tablespoons all-purpose flour
- 1½ cups milk
- 2 tablespoons tomato paste

Salt and freshly ground pepper

- ¼ cup plus ½ tablespoon extra-virgin olive oil
- 10 ounces spinach, thick stems discarded
- 2 medium zucchini (6 ounces each), cut into ½-inch dice
- 2 medium Asian eggplants (6 ounces each), peeled and cut into ½-inch dice
- 12 large eggs

**1.** Preheat the oven to 300°. In a small saucepan, melt the butter over moderately high heat. Whisk in the flour until blended. Slowly pour in the milk, whisking constantly until smooth, and bring to a simmer. Cook the sauce over low heat, whisking often, until no floury taste remains, about 10 minutes. Whisk the tomato paste into the sauce until smooth, then season with salt and pepper. Remove the pan from the heat, cover and keep the sauce warm.

**2.** In a large skillet, heat 1 tablespoon of the olive oil until shimmering. Add the spinach, season with salt and cook over high heat, stirring, until it has wilted and any moisture has evaporated, about 3 minutes. Transfer the spinach to a work surface and coarsely chop it. Add 1 tablespoon of the olive oil to the skillet and heat until shimmering. Add the zucchini, season with salt and cook over high

heat, stirring, until just tender, about 4 minutes. Transfer to a plate to cool. Heat another tablespoon of the olive oil in the skillet until shimmering. Add the eggplant, season with salt and cook over moderate heat until browned on the bottom, about 3 minutes. Stir and cook until tender, about 2 minutes longer. Transfer to a plate.

**3.** In a medium bowl, beat 4 of the eggs with a pinch of salt. In an 8-inch nonstick ovenproof skillet, heat ½ tablespoon of the olive oil. Add the spinach and cook over moderate heat until sizzling. Pour in the eggs and stir to combine with the spinach. Cover and cook over moderate heat until partially set, 5 minutes. Using 2 spatulas, carefully flip the *tortilla* and cook over moderately high heat until completely set, 1 minute. Transfer to a large baking sheet. Repeat with ½ tablespoon of oil and 4 eggs at a time to make 2 more *tortillas,* one with the zucchini and one with the eggplant. Rewarm the *tortillas* in the oven.

**4.** Reheat the tomato sauce over low heat. Transfer the spinach *tortilla* to a large cake plate and spread a thin layer of tomato sauce on top. Top with the zucchini *tortilla* and a thin layer of sauce, then cover with the eggplant *tortilla.* Pour some of the sauce over the layered *tortilla,* letting it drip down the sides. Cut the *tortilla* into wedges and serve with the remaining sauce. —*Victoria Amory*

**MAKE AHEAD** The recipe can be prepared through Step 2 one day ahead. Refrigerate the creamy tomato sauce and each vegetable separately.

## Egg and Potato Chip Tortilla

**TOTAL: 10 MIN**

**2 SERVINGS** ●

*Tortillas de patata,* potato omelets cooked on both sides, are among Spain's signature dishes. Catalan chef Ferran Adrià is particularly proud of his inspired use of potato chips as a fast, easy alternative to fried potatoes. Spanish cooks might use fresh

chips from a *churreria* (a shop specializing in fried crullers), but thin supermarket chips like Lay's are a good substitute.

- 4 large eggs

Two 1-ounce bags potato chips, coarsely crushed (2 cups)

- 2 tablespoons finely chopped serrano ham
- 2 tablespoons finely chopped piquillo peppers

Freshly ground pepper

- 1 teaspoon extra-virgin olive oil

**1.** Preheat the broiler and position a rack 8 inches from the heat. Beat the eggs in a medium bowl. Transfer half of the eggs to another medium bowl, stir in the crushed potato chips and let stand until the chips are slightly softened, about 5 minutes. Add the remaining beaten eggs to the potato chips along with the serrano ham and piquillo peppers and season the mixture with pepper.

**2.** In a small nonstick ovenproof skillet, heat the olive oil. Add the egg mixture and cook over moderately high heat until the bottom is set and golden, about 3 minutes. Transfer the skillet to the broiler and broil for 2 minutes, or until the top of the *tortilla* is golden and the center is slightly jiggly. Slide onto a plate, cut the *tortilla* into quarters and serve. —*Ferran Adrià*

# health

### ARE EGGS BAD FOR YOU?

Are eggs good or bad for you? Good, it turns out—in moderation. One large egg provides more than 12 percent of the recommended daily intake of protein, with only 1.5 grams of saturated fat and **74 calories.** Yolks supply lots of vitamins A and B-12, as well as iron and folate. But keep in mind that one egg also has **212 mg of cholesterol,** and that the American Heart Association suggests consuming no more than a daily average of 300 mg.

## Torta di Napoli

**ACTIVE: 45 MIN; TOTAL: 2 HR**

**10 TO 12 SERVINGS** ●

This savory Italian pie has three kinds of cured meat and three types of cheese stuffed into an extremely flaky crust. Because the *torta* is served at room temperature, it's great for picnics.

- **1 ounces prosciutto, sliced ½ inch thick and cut into ½-inch dice**
- **4 ounces Genoa salami, sliced ½ inch thick and cut into ½-inch dice**
- **4 ounces mortadella, sliced ½ inch thick and cut into ½-inch dice**
- **2 ounces provolone, shredded**
- **1 cup fresh ricotta cheese**
- **⅓ cup freshly grated Parmesan cheese**
- **1 large egg, lightly beaten**
- **¼ teaspoon freshly ground pepper**
- **Flaky Double-Crust Pastry (recipe follows)**
- **1 large egg yolk mixed with 1 tablespoon milk**

1. Preheat the oven to 375° and position a shelf in the lower third. In a food processor, pulse the prosciutto, salami and mortadella just until they are finely chopped. Transfer the chopped meat mixture to a large bowl and stir in the provolone, ricotta and Parmesan cheeses, then the lightly beaten egg and the pepper.

2. On a lightly floured work surface, roll out one of the disks of the Flaky Double-Crust Pastry to a 13-inch round. Loosely wrap the pastry around a rolling pin and transfer it to a 9-inch glass pie plate; press the pastry gently into the pie plate. Roll out the remaining pastry disk to a 13-inch round and reserve.

3. Spread the meat and cheese filling in the pastry shell in an even layer. Brush the pastry rim with water and cover the pie with the second pastry round. Press the pastry edges together to seal, then trim the overhang to ½ inch. Fold the overhang under and crimp the edge of the pastry decoratively. Brush the top crust with the egg wash and bake the meat and cheese pie for 45 minutes, or until the crust is golden on the top and bottom. Transfer the Torta di Napoli to a wire rack to cool, cut into wedges and serve.
—*Seen Lippert*

**MAKE AHEAD** The baked *torta* can be refrigerated for up to 2 days. Bring to room temperature before cutting into wedges.

### FLAKY DOUBLE-CRUST PASTRY

**ACTIVE: 10 MIN; TOTAL: 40 MIN**

**MAKES TWO 9-INCH CRUSTS** ●

This recipe can be used for almost any double-crusted 9- or 10-inch pie, sweet or savory. If you're making the pastry for a pie that has a single crust, wrap the dough you don't need and freeze it for another use.

- **2 cups all-purpose flour**
- **½ teaspoon kosher salt**
- **½ cup solid vegetable shortening**
- **1 stick (4 ounces) cold unsalted butter, cut into ½-inch pieces**
- **¼ cup plus 3 tablespoons ice water**

1. In a food processor, combine the flour and salt. Add the shortening and pulse until the mixture resembles coarse meal. Add the butter and pulse several times more, until the butter is the size of small peas. Sprinkle the ice water evenly over the flour and butter mixture and pulse just until the dough comes together.

2. Transfer the pastry dough to a lightly floured work surface and knead it lightly once or twice. Divide the dough in half, then pat each half into a 6-inch disk. Wrap the pastry disks in plastic wrap and refrigerate them until they are firm, at least 30 minutes or overnight. —*S.L.*

**MAKE AHEAD** The unbaked pastry can be frozen for up to 1 month.

## Deviled Eggs with Crab on Mixed Baby Greens

**TOTAL: 45 MIN**

**4 SERVINGS** ●

- **6 large eggs**
- **5 tablespoons extra-virgin olive oil**
- **1 teaspoon fresh lemon juice**
- **Cayenne pepper**
- **1 tablespoon finely chopped flat-leaf parsley**
- **1 tablespoon minced scallion**
- **1 tablespoon small capers, rinsed, plus more for garnish**
- **½ pound jumbo lump crabmeat, picked over (1 cup)**
- **Salt and freshly ground black pepper**
- **1 tablespoon sherry vinegar**
- **½ teaspoon Dijon mustard**
- **5 ounces mixed greens, such as mâche, frisée, baby spinach and amaranth (5 cups)**

1. In a medium saucepan, cover the eggs with 1½ inches of cold water. Bring the water to a rolling boil. Remove the pan from the heat, cover and let the eggs stand for 12 minutes. Prepare a medium bowl of ice water. Drain the eggs and add to the water for 5 minutes. Peel the eggs and halve them lengthwise.

2. Scoop the egg yolks into a bowl. Using a fork, mash the yolks with 2 tablespoons of the olive oil, the lemon juice and a generous pinch of cayenne. Stir in the parsley, scallion and the 1 tablespoon of capers, then gently fold in the crabmeat. Season the deviled egg filling with salt and black pepper. Generously mound the filling in the egg white halves.

3. In a large bowl, whisk the vinegar with the mustard and the remaining 3 tablespoons of olive oil and season the dressing with salt and black pepper. Add the greens and toss to coat. Mound the greens on plates and arrange the deviled eggs on top. Garnish the deviled eggs with capers.
—*Constance Snow*

DEVILED EGGS WITH CRAB
ON MIXED BABY GREENS

SPRING ONION AND GOAT
CHEESE BREAD PUDDING

### Spring Onion and Goat Cheese Bread Pudding

**ACTIVE: 20 MIN; TOTAL: 1 HR 30 MIN**

**8 SERVINGS** ● ●

When Hiro Sone, chef and co-owner of Terra restaurant in Napa, California, first attempted to make stuffing, he used only bread, onion, celery and stock. That recipe evolved into his first for bread pudding. Since then, Sone has expanded his bread pudding repertoire, and this rich, tangy version, packed with goat cheese and scallions, is a highlight.

- 1 pound sourdough bread, crust removed, bread cut into ¾-inch cubes
- 5 tablespoons unsalted butter
- 3 bunches scallions, cut into ½-inch lengths
- 1 large garlic clove, finely chopped

Kosher salt and freshly ground pepper

- 4 large eggs
- 1½ cups heavy cream
- ¾ cup sour cream
- 1 tablespoon chopped basil

One 10½-ounce log fresh goat cheese, crumbled

**1.** Preheat the oven to 400°. Spread the sourdough bread cubes on a baking sheet and toast in the oven for 10 minutes, or until they are golden.

**2.** In a large skillet, melt the butter over moderately high heat. Add the scallions and garlic and cook, stirring, until the scallions are crisp-tender, about 3 minutes. Season the scallions and garlic with salt and pepper.

**3.** In a large bowl, whisk the eggs with the heavy cream and sour cream to combine them. Gently fold in the sourdough bread cubes, the scallions, basil and half of the goat cheese. Season the mixture with salt and pepper. Let the bread pudding stand until all of the liquid has been absorbed, about 30 minutes.

**4.** Transfer the bread pudding to a 12-by-8-by-2-inch baking dish or a favorite casserole. Scatter the remaining goat cheese on top. Set the baking dish in a roasting pan and add enough hot water to the pan to reach halfway up the side of the baking dish. Bake the bread pudding for 40 minutes, or until the custard is set and the top of the pudding is golden brown. Serve hot or warm. —*Hiro Sone*

**MAKE AHEAD** The unbaked bread pudding can be refrigerated overnight. Bring to room temperature before baking.

### Cheddar-Olive Mini Muffins

**TOTAL: 25 MIN**

**MAKES 3 DOZEN MINI MUFFINS** ● ● ●

These supremely cheesy and crusty little muffins have shredded cheddar folded into the batter and sprinkled on top. If miniature food is not your thing, you can also use this recipe to make 12 standard-size muffins. You'll need to bake them for about 20 to 22 minutes.

- 1 cup buttermilk
- 1 large egg, lightly beaten
- 1¼ cups all-purpose flour
- ½ cup yellow cornmeal
- 1 teaspoon baking powder
- ½ teaspoon baking soda
- ½ teaspoon sugar
- ¼ teaspoon salt
- 2 tablespoons chopped chives
- 2 tablespoons Spanish green olives, pitted and chopped
- 1¼ cups packed farmstead cheddar cheese, shredded
- 6 tablespoons unsalted butter, melted

**1.** Preheat the oven to 400°. Line three 12-cup mini-muffin tins with paper or foil liners. Alternatively, lightly butter and flour the cups, tapping out any excess flour.

**2.** In a small bowl, whisk the buttermilk with the egg. In a medium bowl, whisk the flour with the cornmeal, baking powder, baking soda, sugar and salt. Whisk in the chives and olives and ¾ cup of the shredded cheddar. Add the buttermilk mixture and the melted butter; stir just until moistened. Spoon the batter into the prepared tins and sprinkle with the remaining ½ cup of cheese. Bake the muffins for about 16 minutes, or until golden. Let cool in the tins for 10 minutes before serving. —*Grace Parisi*

### Jam and Bread Pudding

**TOTAL: 30 MIN**

**6 TO 8 SERVINGS** ● ●

This breakfast treat is terrific drizzled with maple syrup. It also makes a homey and comforting dessert.

One 1-pound loaf challah bread, sliced ½ inch thick

- ¾ cup plus 3 tablespoons strawberry jam or preserves
- 4 large eggs
- ½ cup granulated sugar
- 2½ cups plus 1 tablespoon whole milk
- 1 teaspoon pure vanilla extract
- 6 tablespoons unsalted butter, melted
- ¾ cup confectioners' sugar

**1.** Preheat the oven to 375°. Butter a 9-by-13-inch glass baking dish. Arrange half of the challah in the dish; tear the slices to fit. Spread ¾ cup of the strawberry jam on top; cover with the remaining challah.

**2.** Whisk the eggs with the granulated sugar, 2½ cups of the milk and the vanilla and pour over the challah, pressing to soak. Brush the bread pudding with 4 tablespoons of the butter. Cover with foil and bake for 24 minutes, or until set. Remove the foil halfway through.

**3.** Preheat the broiler. Blend the remaining 1 tablespoon of milk with the confectioners' sugar. Add the remaining butter and strawberry jam and stir until the glaze is smooth. Spread all but ¼ cup of the glaze over the bread pudding and broil until golden. Drizzle the bread pudding with the remaining glaze and serve. —*Grace Parisi*

## Mama's Blueberry Buckle

**ACTIVE: 15 MIN; TOTAL: 1 HR**
**6 SERVINGS ●**

1⅓ cups all-purpose flour
1 cup sugar
1 teaspoon cinnamon
4 tablespoons unsalted butter, cut into small pieces
1½ teaspoons baking powder
½ teaspoon salt
¼ cup solid vegetable shortening, at room temperature
1 large egg
⅓ cup milk
2 cups blueberries
Whipped cream, for serving

**1.** Preheat the oven to 350°. Butter an 8-inch square glass baking dish. In a medium bowl, combine ⅓ cup of the flour with ½ cup of the sugar and the cinnamon. Using your fingers, rub in the butter until the mixture is crumbly.

**2.** In a small bowl, whisk the remaining 1 cup of flour with the baking powder and salt. In a large bowl, using a handheld mixer, beat the remaining ½ cup of sugar with the shortening. Beat in the egg. Beat in the flour mixture in 2 batches, alternating with the milk. Spread the batter in the prepared baking dish. Scatter the blueberries over the batter. Sprinkle with the cinnamon topping and bake for 40 minutes. Let cool slightly. Serve warm or at room temperature with whipped cream. —*Martha Greenlaw*

## Parmesan Cookies

**ACTIVE: 15 MIN; TOTAL: 1 HR**
**MAKES 4 DOZEN COOKIES ●**

These tender, crumbly, buttery Parmesan coins are a clever twist on sweet slice-and-bake shortbread cookies.

2 sticks (½ pound) unsalted butter, softened
½ pound Parmesan cheese, freshly grated (2 cups)
1¾ cups all-purpose flour

**1.** Preheat the oven to 350° and position racks in the upper and lower thirds. In a medium bowl, using a handheld electric mixer, beat the butter with the Parmesan cheese and flour at low speed until a stiff dough forms. Divide the dough into 3 pieces, then roll each piece into a 9-inch log about 1½ inches in diameter.

**2.** Slice the logs ⅓ inch thick and arrange the slices on 2 large nonstick baking sheets. Bake the cookies for 18 minutes, or until they are golden, shifting the pans halfway through baking for even browning. Let the cookies cool for 10 minutes, then transfer them to a wire rack to cool completely. —*Marc Murphy*

## Lemon-Blueberry Muffins

**ACTIVE: 15 MIN; TOTAL: 40 MIN**
**MAKES 12 MUFFINS ● ●**

1¾ cups all-purpose flour
¾ cup plus 2 tablespoons sugar
2 teaspoons baking powder
¾ teaspoon salt
1 cup blueberries
2 large eggs
½ cup milk
¼ cup vegetable oil
Finely grated zest of 1 lemon
¼ cup fresh lemon juice

**1.** Preheat the oven to 375°. Butter a standard 12-cup muffin pan. In a medium bowl, whisk the flour with the sugar, baking powder and salt. Stir in the blueberries. In another medium bowl, whisk the eggs with the milk, oil and lemon zest, then whisk in the lemon juice. Using a rubber spatula, fold the egg mixture into the flour mixture until blended; do not overmix.

**2.** Spoon the batter into the prepared muffin cups and bake for about 20 minutes, or until a cake tester inserted in the center of a muffin comes out clean. Let the muffins stand in the pan for 5 minutes, then carefully transfer them to a rack to cool slightly. Serve the muffins warm or at room temperature. —*Diana Santospago*

## Spicy Creamed-Corn Cakes with Scallions

**TOTAL: 45 MIN**
**MAKES 18 CAKES ●**

1 cup buttermilk
1 cup heavy cream
1 cup canned creamed corn
2 large eggs
2 large egg yolks
5 tablespoons vegetable oil
2 cups stone-ground yellow cornmeal
1 cup all-purpose flour
1 tablespoon sugar
1½ teaspoons kosher salt
1 teaspoon baking powder
1 teaspoon baking soda
3 scallions, thinly sliced
1 cup corn kernels, thawed if frozen
1 jalapeño, seeded and minced
2 tablespoons unsalted butter
Softened butter and honey, for serving

**1.** Preheat the oven to 325°. In a blender, combine the buttermilk, cream, creamed corn, whole eggs, egg yolks and 2 tablespoons of the vegetable oil and puree.

**2.** In a bowl, whisk the cornmeal, flour, sugar, salt, baking powder and baking soda. Slowly stir in the wet ingredients and fold in the scallions, corn kernels and jalapeño. Do not overmix; there should be a few lumps.

**3.** Heat a large cast-iron skillet. Add ½ tablespoon of the vegetable oil and heat until shimmering. Spoon three ⅓-cup portions of the batter into the skillet and cook over moderately high heat until starting to brown around the edges, about 1 minute. Add 1 teaspoon of butter to the skillet and cook until bubbles form on the surface of the cakes, about 2 minutes. Flip the cakes and cook until browned on the second side. Transfer them to a baking sheet and keep warm in the oven. Repeat with the remaining oil, batter and butter. Serve the corn cakes hot, with butter and honey. —*Adam Perry Lang*

## Pumpkin-Walnut Praline Bars

**ACTIVE: 30 MIN; TOTAL: 2 HR**

**MAKES 16 BARS** ●

PASTRY

1½ cups all-purpose flour, plus
    more for dusting

1½ tablespoons granulated sugar

½ teaspoon salt

1 stick (4 ounces) cold
    unsalted butter,
    cut into ½-inch pieces

¼ cup ice water

FILLING

3 large eggs

⅔ cup light brown sugar

1 teaspoon cinnamon

½ teaspoon pumpkin-pie spice
    (see Note)

One 15-ounce can solid-pack
    pumpkin puree

½ cup evaporated milk

TOPPING

1 cup chopped walnuts
    (4 ounces)

¼ cup all-purpose flour

½ cup light brown sugar

1 stick (4 ounces) unsalted
    butter, softened

**1. MAKE THE PASTRY:** In a food processor, combine the 1½ cups of flour with the granulated sugar and salt. Add the pieces of cold butter and pulse just until they resemble small peas. Add the ice water and pulse just until the dough is lightly moistened. Turn the dough out onto a lightly floured work surface and knead several times, until it comes together. Flatten the dough into a disk, wrap in plastic and refrigerate until chilled, about 30 minutes.

**2.** Preheat the oven to 350°. Butter a 9-by-13-inch glass baking dish. On a lightly floured work surface, roll out the pastry to an 11-by-15-inch rectangle about ⅛ inch thick. Trim the pastry to a 10-by-14-inch rectangle. Roll the pastry around the rolling pin and carefully unroll it in the prepared baking dish, easing it into the corners.

Line the pastry with foil and fill with pie weights or dried beans. Bake the pastry for about 20 minutes, until it is lightly browned and just set. Remove the foil and weights and bake for 8 to 10 minutes longer, until the pastry is cooked through but not browned.

**3. MEANWHILE, MAKE THE FILLING:** In a medium bowl, whisk the eggs with the light brown sugar, cinnamon and pumpkin-pie spice. Add the pumpkin puree and whisk until smooth. Whisk in the evaporated milk until the filling is blended. Pour the filling into the prebaked crust and smooth the surface. Bake for about 20 minutes, or until the filling is set around the edges but very jiggly in the center.

**4. MEANWHILE, MAKE THE TOPPING:** In a bowl, toss the chopped walnuts, flour and brown sugar. Add the butter and stir until combined. Drop tablespoons of the topping onto the partially baked pumpkin. Bake the bars for about 20 minutes longer, or until the topping is sizzling and golden and the filling is barely jiggly in the center. Let cool completely, then cut into 16 bars.
—*Carrie Dove*

**NOTE** Pumpkin-pie spice is a mix of ground cinnamon, ginger, nutmeg, allspice, mace and cloves.

## Spicy Corn and Jalapeño Bars

**ACTIVE: 40 MIN; TOTAL: 2 HR**

**MAKES 16 BARS** ●

PASTRY

1 cup all-purpose flour

¼ cup cornmeal

1½ tablespoons sugar

1 teaspoon chili powder

½ teaspoon salt

½ teaspoon paprika

⅛ teaspoon cayenne pepper

⅛ teaspoon freshly ground
    black pepper

4 ounces cream cheese

4 tablespoons cold unsalted
    butter, cut into pieces

FILLING

2 tablespoons unsalted butter

2 cups fresh corn kernels
    (from 2 ears)

2 jalapeños, seeded and minced

1 tablespoon honey

½ pound fresh goat cheese
    (1 cup), softened

2 tablespoons snipped chives

Salt and freshly ground pepper

1 egg mixed with
    1 tablespoon water

**1. MAKE THE PASTRY:** In a food processor, combine the flour, cornmeal, sugar, chili powder, salt, paprika, cayenne and black pepper. Add the cream cheese and butter and pulse until a dough forms. Transfer the dough to a sheet of plastic wrap and press into a disk. Wrap and refrigerate until chilled, about 30 minutes.

**2. MEANWHILE, MAKE THE FILLING:** In a medium skillet, melt the butter. Add the corn kernels and cook over moderate heat until crisp-tender, about 3 minutes. Add the jalapeños and cook for 2 minutes longer. Stir in the honey and transfer

## ingredient
**FABULOUS HONEYS**

Drizzle the unfiltered honey from **Hamptons Honey Company** on French toast or pancakes. **DETAILS** $30 for four 16-ounce jars; hamptonshoney.com.

● FAST  ● HEALTHY  ● MAKE AHEAD  ● STAFF FAVORITE

**APRICOT, COCONUT AND ALMOND BARS**

**CURRIED CHICKEN SALAD WITH GARAM MASALA BISCUITS**

to a bowl. Add the goat cheese and stir until melted. Stir in the chives, season with salt and pepper and let the filling cool to room temperature.

**3.** Preheat the oven to 350°. Line a baking sheet with parchment. On a well-floured surface, roll out the pastry to a 12-by-15-inch rectangle. Roll the pastry around the rolling pin and carefully unroll onto the baking sheet. Refrigerate for 10 minutes.

**4.** Spread the filling on half of the pastry, leaving a ½-inch border on 3 sides. Brush the border all around with egg wash; fold the pastry over the filling. Press the edges to seal. Refrigerate for 10 minutes.

**5.** Brush the top of the pastry with the egg wash. Bake for about 20 minutes, until the pastry is golden. Transfer the baking sheet to a wire rack and let cool. Slide the parchment paper onto a work surface and cut the pastry into 16 bars. —*Carrie Dove*

## Apricot, Coconut and Almond Bars
**ACTIVE: 30 MIN; TOTAL: 1 HR 30 MIN**
**MAKES 16 BARS** ●

These oat bars, packed with fruit and nuts, are like delicious granola made to go.

- 1½  cups water
- ½  cup granulated sugar
- 1½  cups dried apricots (10 ounces), finely diced
- 1  stick (4 ounces) unsalted butter
- ⅓  cup light brown sugar
- ¼  cup honey

Pinch of salt

- 1½  cups sweetened shredded coconut (4 ounces)
- ¾  cup sliced blanched almonds (2½ ounces)
- 2½  cups old-fashioned rolled oats
- ½  cup all-purpose flour

**1.** Preheat the oven to 350°. Butter a 10-by-15-inch jelly roll pan. In a medium saucepan, combine the water, granulated sugar and apricots and bring to a boil. Simmer over moderate heat, stirring occasionally, until the apricots are tender and plump, about 15 minutes. Drain and return the apricots to the pan. Add the butter, brown sugar, honey and salt and cook just until the butter is melted. Transfer to a bowl.

**2.** Spread the coconut and almonds on separate baking sheets and toast them for 6 to 7 minutes, until they are lightly golden. Stir the coconut and almonds into the apricot mixture along with the rolled oats and flour. Spread the mixture in the jelly roll pan in an even layer. Bake for 25 minutes, or until golden. Let the bars cool on a rack, then cut into 16 bars. —*Carrie Dove*

**MAKE AHEAD** The bars can be stored in an airtight container for up to 2 days.

## Curried Chicken Salad with Garam Masala Biscuits

**ACTIVE: 30 MIN; TOTAL: 1 HR**

**8 SERVINGS** ●

Garam masala is an Indian spice mix that can include up to 12 different ingredients, such as cinnamon, clove, cardamom, cumin and fennel. San Francisco Bay Area caterer Carrie Dove uses the blend to give flaky biscuits a complex flavor and mild heat, then fills the biscuits with a curried chicken salad that contains grapes, pistachios and cilantro.

- 1 carrot, coarsely chopped
- 1 onion, coarsely chopped
- 1 teaspoon black peppercorns
- 1 bay leaf
- 4 pounds chicken breast halves, on the bone, with skin
- 1 cup mayonnaise, plus more for spreading
- 1 tablespoon curry powder
- 1 tablespoon fresh lime juice
- 3 cups red grapes (about 14 ounces), halved
- 2 celery ribs, preferably from the heart, finely diced
- 2 tablespoons coarsely chopped cilantro
- ¼ cup shelled pistachios, toasted (see Note)

Salt and freshly ground pepper

Garam Masala Biscuits (recipe follows)

**1.** Fill a large pot with 3 quarts of water. Add the chopped carrot and onion, the peppercorns and the bay leaf and bring the water to a simmer. Add the chicken breast halves and simmer them over moderate heat until the chicken is cooked through, about 30 minutes. Transfer the cooked chicken to a plate and refrigerate until it is cool enough to handle. Reserve the chicken broth for another use.

**2.** Remove and discard all of the chicken skin. Remove the chicken meat from the bones and cut into ½-inch pieces.

**3.** In a medium bowl, mix the 1 cup of mayonnaise with the curry powder and lime juice. Stir in the chicken pieces, grapes, celery, cilantro and pistachios. Season the chicken salad with salt and pepper and transfer to a serving bowl or platter. Serve the curried chicken salad with the Garam Masala Biscuits on the side. Alternatively, split the biscuits in half and spread them lightly with mayonnaise. Mound the chicken salad on the bottom halves of the biscuits and close the sandwiches. Serve the assembled sandwiches right away.
—*Carrie Dove*

**NOTE** To toast pistachios, spread them out in a pie plate and bake in a 350° oven for 5 minutes.

**MAKE AHEAD** The curried chicken salad can be refrigerated overnight. Let the salad return to room temperature before serving. Add the grapes and pistachios shortly before serving.

### GARAM MASALA BISCUITS

**ACTIVE: 20 MIN; TOTAL: 40 MIN**

**MAKES 8 BISCUITS** ●

- 2 cups all-purpose flour, plus more for dusting
- 3 tablespoons granulated sugar
- 1½ tablespoons garam masala
- 2 teaspoons baking powder
- 1 teaspoon salt
- ½ teaspoon baking soda
- 6 tablespoons cold unsalted butter, cut into ½-inch pieces
- ¾ cup buttermilk, plus more for brushing

**1.** Preheat the oven to 375°. In a medium bowl, whisk the 2 cups of all-purpose flour with the granulated sugar, garam masala, baking powder, salt and baking soda. Using a pastry blender or 2 table knives, cut the pieces of cold butter into the flour mixture until they are the size of small peas. Add the ¾ cup of buttermilk and stir until a dough forms.

**2.** Turn the dough out onto a lightly floured surface and knead it 2 or 3 times. Roll or pat the dough into a 6-by-12-inch rectangle about ¾ inch thick. Using a floured knife, cut the dough into 8 square biscuits. Brush the tops of the biscuits with buttermilk and transfer them to a baking sheet. Bake the biscuits for about 18 minutes, or until risen and golden. Transfer the biscuits to a wire rack to cool. —*C.D.*

## Cheddar-Polenta Biscuits with Ham Salad

**TOTAL: 30 MIN**

**MAKES 8 SANDWICHES** ● ● ●

- 1¼ cups all-purpose flour
- ¾ cup instant polenta
- 1 tablespoon baking powder
- 1 teaspoon sugar

Salt and freshly ground black pepper

- 6 tablespoons unsalted butter, cut into pieces
- ½ cup packed shredded sharp cheddar cheese
- 1 cup milk
- 2 scallions, white and light green parts only, chopped
- 1 small celery rib, cut into 1-inch pieces
- 1 jalapeño, seeded and quartered
- ½ pound sliced smoked ham, coarsely chopped
- ¼ cup mayonnaise
- 1 tablespoon Dijon mustard

**1.** Preheat the oven to 425°. Lightly grease a large baking sheet. In a medium bowl, combine the flour, instant polenta, baking powder, sugar and ½ teaspoon each of salt and pepper. Using 2 table knives, cut the butter into the dry ingredients until the mixture resembles coarse meal. Add the cheddar cheese, then stir in the milk until the biscuit dough is moistened.

**2.** Using 2 large soupspoons, scoop 8 mounds of the biscuit dough onto the prepared baking sheet. Lightly press down on each mound. Bake the biscuits for about 19 minutes, or until the tops are golden and the bottoms are browned. Transfer the biscuits to a wire rack to cool slightly.

**3.** In a mini food processor, pulse the chopped scallions and celery and the quartered jalapeño until the vegetables are finely chopped. Add the chopped ham to the processor and pulse just until the ham is finely chopped. Pulse in the mayonnaise and mustard, then season the ham salad lightly with salt and pepper. Slice the cheese and polenta biscuits, fill them with the ham salad and serve at once.
—*Grace Parisi*

### Cornmeal-and-Ricotta Waffles
**TOTAL: 45 MIN**
MAKES 2 DOZEN 4-INCH WAFFLES
1½ cups ricotta cheese
  2 cups milk
  6 large eggs, separated
  ½ cup sugar
  2 cups cake flour
  ½ cup fine yellow cornmeal
  1 tablespoon baking powder
  ¼ teaspoon salt
  1 stick (4 ounces) unsalted butter, melted, plus more for serving
Pure maple syrup, for serving
Crisp bacon strips, for serving

**1.** Heat an 8-inch square waffle iron and preheat the oven to 200°. In a large bowl, whisk the ricotta cheese with the milk, egg yolks and sugar. In a medium bowl, whisk the flour with the cornmeal, baking powder and salt. Whisk the dry ingredients into the ricotta mixture until combined. Stir in the melted butter.

**2.** In a large bowl, using an electric mixer, beat the egg whites until firm peaks form. Fold the beaten egg whites into the waffle batter until no streaks remain.

**3.** Coat the waffle iron with vegetable oil spray and spoon about 1½ cups of the batter onto the waffle iron. Close the waffle iron and cook until the waffles are golden and crisp. Serve the cornmeal waffles immediately or transfer them to a rack in the oven to keep warm. Serve the waffles with pure maple syrup and crisp bacon.
—*Michael Mina*

### Coconut Pancakes with Bananas and Passion Fruit Syrup
**TOTAL: 45 MIN**
4 TO 6 SERVINGS
  ½ cup passion fruit pulp
  1 cup plus 1 tablespoon sugar
  1 cup water
1¾ cups all-purpose flour
  ¾ cup finely grated unsweetened coconut
  1 teaspoon baking powder
Pinch of salt
  4 large eggs, separated
  1 cup whole milk
  1 cup unsweetened coconut milk
  3 tablespoons unsalted butter, melted
4 to 6 bananas, halved lengthwise

**1.** Preheat the oven to 300°. In a small saucepan, bring the passion fruit pulp, 1 cup of the sugar and the water to a boil. Simmer over low heat until slightly reduced, about 10 minutes. Let cool slightly.

**2.** In a bowl, mix the flour, coconut, baking powder, salt and remaining 1 tablespoon of sugar. In another bowl, whisk the egg yolks, whole milk and coconut milk. Add to the dry ingredients and stir until evenly moistened. The batter will be a little lumpy.

**3.** In a bowl, using an electric mixer, beat the egg whites at medium speed until firm peaks form. Fold the egg whites into the batter until no streaks remain.

**4.** Heat a large griddle and brush it with some of the melted butter. For each pancake, spoon a 3-tablespoon mound of batter onto the griddle and cook over moderate heat, turning once, until golden and cooked through, about 4 minutes. Transfer to a baking sheet and keep warm. Repeat with the remaining butter and batter. Transfer the pancakes to plates; serve with the bananas and passion fruit syrup. —*Bill Granger*

### Peanut Butter Crunch French Toast
**TOTAL: 30 MIN**
8 SERVINGS ● ●.
  ½ cup creamy peanut butter
Sixteen ½-inch-thick slices of brioche
  4 large eggs, beaten
  ¼ cup heavy cream
  2 teaspoons pure vanilla extract
  4 cups cornflakes, finely crushed
  4 tablespoons unsalted butter
Confectioners' sugar, for dusting
  4 cups mixed berries
Maple syrup, for serving

**1.** Preheat the oven to 250°. Line a large baking sheet with wax paper. Spread 1 tablespoon of the peanut butter on each of 8 slices of brioche and cover with the remaining 8 slices, making sandwiches.

**2.** In a pie plate, beat the eggs, cream and vanilla. In another pie plate, spread the cornflakes. Soak the sandwiches in the egg mixture, then dredge in the cornflakes, pressing to help the cornflakes adhere. Transfer to the baking sheet.

**3.** Melt 1 tablespoon of the butter in a very large skillet. Add 4 sandwiches and cook over moderate heat until golden and crisp on the bottom, 2 to 3 minutes. Transfer the half-cooked sandwiches to the baking sheet. Add another tablespoon of butter to the skillet, flip the sandwiches back into the skillet and cook until golden and crisp on the bottom, 2 minutes longer. Transfer to the baking sheet and keep warm in the oven. Wipe out the pan. Cook the remaining sandwiches in the remaining butter. Transfer to plates and dust with confectioners' sugar. Top with the berries and drizzle with maple syrup. —*Grace Parisi*

PEANUT BUTTER CRUNCH
FRENCH TOAST

In the July issue, chef Nancy Silverton fed lucky party guests a Strawberry Ice Cream Pie with Cinnamon–Black Pepper Strawberry Sauce (P. 307).

# pies & fruit desserts

**BAKED APPLE POTPIES WITH FLAKY PASTRY LIDS**

**LEMON CURD TART WITH PECAN-CITRUS SAUCE**

## Baked Apple Potpies with Flaky Pastry Lids

**ACTIVE: 1 HR; TOTAL: 2 HR**

**8 SERVINGS** ●

This delightful dessert is from Chicago pastry chef Mindy Segal, who also prepares first and main courses at her restaurant HotChocolate. Her secret is the gooey apple cider sauce that's tossed with the apple chunks. Baking the pastry lid crusts separately keeps them crisp.

**PASTRY**

- 1 large egg yolk
- 3 tablespoons ice water
- 1¾ cups all-purpose flour, plus more for dusting
- 1½ teaspoons granulated sugar
- Pinch of salt
- Pinch of cinnamon
- 1 stick plus 2 tablespoons cold unsalted butter, cut into pieces

**FILLING**

- 1 quart sparkling apple cider
- ¾ cup white dessert wine, such as Sauternes
- 6 tablespoons light brown sugar
- 2 tablespoons light corn syrup
- Salt and freshly ground pepper
- 6 Pink Lady apples (about 3 pounds)—peeled, cored and cut into ½-inch pieces
- 3 Granny Smith apples (about 1½ pounds)—peeled, cored and cut into ½-inch pieces
- 1½ tablespoons cornstarch
- 4 tablespoons cold unsalted butter, cut into 8 pieces

**1. MAKE THE PASTRY:** In a small bowl, combine the egg yolk with the ice water. In a food processor, pulse the 1¾ cups of flour with the granulated sugar, salt and cinnamon. Add the butter pieces and pulse until the mixture resembles small peas. Sprinkle on the egg yolk and water mixture and pulse just until the pastry comes together. Turn the pastry out onto a sheet of plastic wrap and pat it into a disk. Wrap the pastry and chill until firm, at least 1 hour or overnight.

**2. MEANWHILE, MAKE THE FILLING:** Preheat the oven to 375°. In a medium saucepan, boil the sparkling apple cider with the dessert wine over moderately high heat until the liquid is reduced to 1¼ cups, about 40 minutes. Remove the cider syrup from the heat. Add the brown sugar and corn syrup and season the sauce lightly with a pinch each of salt and pepper.

**3.** In a large bowl, toss the apples with the cornstarch; pour the hot cider syrup over the apples and toss again. Using a slotted spoon, transfer the apples into eight 1-cup ramekins. Pour the remaining cider syrup from the bowl over the apples and top each serving with 1 piece of the butter. Set the ramekins on a baking sheet and bake for about 45 minutes, stirring the apples occasionally, until they are browned in spots and just tender. Cover the ramekins with foil and bake the apples for 10 to 15 minutes longer, or until they are very tender.

**4** Meanwhile, line a rimmed baking sheet with parchment paper. On a lightly floured work surface, roll out the pastry to a ¼-inch thickness. Using a 4½-inch round cutter, stamp out 8 pastry rounds; if necessary, press the scraps together to stamp out more rounds. Transfer the pastry rounds to the prepared baking sheet and prick them several times with a fork. Crimp the edges of the pastry rounds decoratively and chill the pastry until it is firm, about 10 minutes.

**5.** Bake the pastry rounds for about 15 minutes, or until they are golden and crisp. Let the baked crusts cool on the baking sheet. Top each of the ramekins with a crust and bake for 5 minutes longer. Transfer the ramekins to plates and serve at once. —*Mindy Segal*

**SERVE WITH** Vanilla ice cream.

**MAKE AHEAD** The apple potpies can be made early in the day. Reheat the potpies before serving.

### Lemon Curd Tart with Pecan-Citrus Sauce

**ACTIVE: 2 HR; TOTAL: 5 HR**

10 SERVINGS ●

In this variation of Key lime pie, lemon curd replaces the lime curd and a cinnamon-pecan cookie crust stands in for the typical graham cracker crust. If you make the tart during the summer, use gooseberries from the farmers' market for a garnish.

8 large egg yolks
1 cup sugar
¾ cup fresh lemon juice
1 tablespoon plus 1 teaspoon grated lemon zest

2 sticks (8 ounces) unsalted butter, 1 stick cut into cubes
Cinnamon-Pecan Cookie Crust (recipe follows)
1 grapefruit
1 lemon
1 lime
¾ cup pecan halves (3 ounces)
¼ cup Grand Marnier
2 tablespoons sugar mixed with 2 tablespoons hot water
2 tablespoons heavy cream
Pinch of salt

**1.** In a medium heatproof bowl, whisk the egg yolks with the sugar, lemon juice and lemon zest. Fill a medium saucepan with 1 inch of water and bring to a boil. Set the bowl containing the egg yolk and lemon mixture over the boiling water, reduce the heat to moderate and cook the mixture, whisking constantly, until it is thickened, about 12 minutes. Remove the bowl from the heat and whisk in the butter cubes. Fill the chilled cookie crust with the warm lemon curd and refrigerate until the lemon curd is firm enough to cut, about 3 hours.

**2.** Using a sharp knife, peel the grapefruit, lemon and lime, removing the bitter white pith. Cut in between the membranes of the citrus fruit to release the sections into a bowl. In a medium skillet, melt the remaining stick of butter. Add the pecan halves and cook them over moderate heat, stirring, until they are golden, about 6 minutes. Remove the skillet from the heat and add the Grand Marnier. Return the skillet to the heat and carefully ignite the liquid with a long match. When the flames subside, add the sugar and water mixture and boil until thickened, about 1 minute. Add the cream and salt and boil the pecan-citrus sauce for 1 minute longer.

**3.** Just before serving, stir the citrus fruit sections into the sauce. Cut the lemon curd tart into wedges and serve with the pecan-citrus sauce. —*Michael Mina*

**CINNAMON-PECAN COOKIE CRUST**

**ACTIVE: 45 MIN; TOTAL: 1 HR 35 MIN**

MAKES ONE 9½-INCH CRUST ●

1½ sticks (6 ounces) unsalted butter, softened
¼ cup sugar
1 large egg yolk
½ teaspoon grated lemon zest
½ teaspoon pure vanilla extract
1 cup plus 2 tablespoons cake flour, plus more for dusting
¾ cup pecans (3 ounces), finely ground
¼ teaspoon baking powder
¼ teaspoon cinnamon
Pinch of salt

**1.** In a large bowl, beat 6 tablespoons of the butter with the sugar until light and fluffy. Add the egg yolk, lemon zest and vanilla and beat until combined. In a medium bowl, whisk the 1 cup plus 2 tablespoons of flour with the pecans, baking powder, cinnamon and salt. Add the dry ingredients to the wet and beat just until combined. Flatten the dough into a disk, wrap in plastic and refrigerate until firm, about 20 minutes.

**2.** Preheat the oven to 350°. On a lightly floured surface, roll out the cookie dough a scant ¼ inch thick. Cut the dough into 4 pieces and transfer to 2 baking sheets. Bake in the upper and lower thirds of the oven for 15 minutes, or until crisp; shift the pans from top to bottom and front to back for even baking. Let cool on a wire rack.

**3.** Transfer the baked cookie pieces to a sturdy, resealable plastic bag and crush gently with a rolling pin. Transfer the crumbs to a food processor, add the remaining 6 tablespoons of butter and process until moistened. Press the crumbs into a 9½-inch fluted tart pan with a removable bottom, forming an even layer all around; pack the crumbs tightly. Refrigerate the cookie crust until chilled and ready to use, about 15 minutes. —*M.M.*

**MAKE AHEAD** The crust can be kept in an airtight container for 2 days.

CITRUS GRATINS WITH
TOASTED ALMONDS

## Citrus Gratins with Toasted Almonds

**TOTAL: 25 MIN**

**4 SERVINGS** ●●

This warm citrus dessert is an updated version of the old-fashioned half grapefruit topped with brown sugar and broiled.

- 2 grapefruits
- 2 navel oranges
- 2 tangerines
- ¼ teaspoon cinnamon
- ¼ teaspoon finely grated lime zest
- ¾ cup sliced almonds
- 2 tablespoons turbinado sugar
- 2 teaspoons vegetable oil

Pinch of salt

**1.** Preheat the broiler. Set the oven rack 8 inches from the heat. Using a sharp knife, peel the grapefruits, oranges and tangerines, removing all of the bitter white pith. Working over a medium bowl, cut in between the membranes to release the sections into the bowl. Gently stir in the cinnamon and lime zest.

**2.** Spoon the citrus sections into individual gratin dishes. In a small bowl, toss the almonds with the turbinado sugar, oil and salt. Scatter the sugared almonds over the citrus fruit. Broil the gratins for about 2 minutes, rotating the dishes, until the almonds are deep golden brown. Serve the gratins at once. —*Marcia Kiesel*

**MAKE AHEAD** The recipe can be prepared through Step 1 up to 4 hours in advance.

## Grated-Apple Tartlets

**ACTIVE: 25 MIN; TOTAL: 2 HR**

**8 SERVINGS** ●

**TART SHELLS**

- 1 stick (4 ounces) unsalted butter, softened
- ¼ cup granulated sugar
- 1 large egg yolk
- 1 cup all-purpose flour, plus more for dusting

Pinch of salt

**CRUMBLE**

- ¼ cup slivered, blanched almonds
- 3 tablespoons all-purpose flour
- 2 tablespoons light brown sugar
- 2 teaspoons finely grated orange zest
- 2 tablespoons unsalted butter

**FILLING**

- 4 medium Cortland apples
- ¼ cup light brown sugar
- ¼ cup granulated sugar
- 1 teaspoon fresh lemon juice
- 1 teaspoon pure vanilla extract
- ¼ teaspoon cinnamon

**1. MAKE THE TART SHELLS:** In a bowl, beat the butter with the granulated sugar until fluffy. Beat in the egg yolk. Add the 1 cup of flour and the salt; beat until a dough just begins to form. Transfer the dough to a work surface and roll into a log. Wrap the dough in plastic and refrigerate until chilled, about 1 hour.

**2.** Preheat the oven to 375°. Cut the dough into 8 pieces. On a lightly floured surface, roll out each piece to a 3-inch round. Transfer the rounds to eight 4-inch fluted tartlet molds with removable bottoms. Press the dough into the molds and up the sides. Refrigerate until firm, about 15 minutes.

**3. MAKE THE CRUMBLE:** In a mini food processor, pulse the almonds, flour, brown sugar and zest until the nuts are coarsely chopped. Add the butter; pulse until the mixture resembles coarse meal.

**4. MAKE THE FILLING:** Coarsely grate the apples and squeeze out the excess liquid. Transfer to a bowl and stir in the sugars, lemon juice, vanilla and cinnamon.

**5.** Using a fork, fill the tart shells with the apple mixture, leaving all the excess liquid in the bowl. Top the tartlets with the crumble. Transfer to a rimmed baking sheet and bake for about 35 minutes, until the crust is lightly browned. Serve the apple tartlets at once. —*Jeremy Jackson*

**MAKE AHEAD** The tartlets can be kept at room temperature for up to 2 days.

## Temple Orange Gelées with Whipped Meringue

**TOTAL: 30 MIN PLUS 3 HR CHILLING**

**4 SERVINGS** ●●

These orange gelées don't depend on butter, cream or any other kind of fat for flavor. Instead, they get a sweet, tangy taste from temple oranges, which practically burst with juice when their thin skin is torn open.

- 2½ cups fresh temple orange juice, strained (from 4 large oranges)
- ¼ cup plus 2½ tablespoons sugar
- 1 tablespoon plus ¾ teaspoon unflavored gelatin (1½ envelopes)
- 2 teaspoons finely grated orange zest
- 2 tablespoons water
- 1 large egg white

**1.** In a small saucepan, combine the orange juice with ¼ cup plus ½ tablespoon of the sugar; stir to dissolve the sugar. Sprinkle the gelatin over the juice in an even layer. Let stand until the gelatin softens, about 5 minutes. Set the pan over moderate heat, swirling once or twice, until the juice is very warm and the gelatin has dissolved, about 2 minutes. Slowly pour the juice into glasses or glass bowls. Refrigerate until firm, at least 3 hours.

**2.** Just before serving, in a small saucepan, combine the orange zest with the water and remaining 2 tablespoons of sugar. Simmer over moderately high heat until syrupy, about 3 minutes. Meanwhile, in a small stainless steel bowl, using a hand-held mixer, beat the egg white at medium-high speed until it holds a soft peak. Beat in the hot syrup at high speed and continue to beat until firm and glossy, about 30 seconds. Dollop the meringue over the gelées and serve. —*Marcia Kiesel*

**MAKE AHEAD** The gelées can be refrigerated for up to 2 days.

## Pistachio Pavlovas with Oranges and Blood Orange Sorbet

**ACTIVE: 45 MIN; TOTAL: 3 HR**

**8 SERVINGS** ● ●

- ¾ cup unsalted pistachios
- 3 large egg whites, at room temperature
- ¾ cup superfine sugar
- 1½ teaspoons fresh lemon juice
- 1½ teaspoons cornstarch
- 1 teaspoon pure vanilla extract
- 3 navel oranges
- ½ pint blood orange sorbet

**Candied Orange Slices (recipe follows)**

**1.** Preheat the oven to 325°. Line a baking sheet with parchment paper. Spread the nuts in a pie plate. Toast for 5 minutes, until lightly browned. Cool, then finely chop.

**2.** In a medium bowl, using a handheld electric mixer, beat the egg whites at medium-high speed until soft peaks form. Add the sugar 1 tablespoon at a time, beating well between additions. Increase the speed to high and beat until the whites are stiff and glossy, 4 minutes. Beat in the lemon juice, cornstarch and vanilla. Fold in all but ¼ cup of the nuts. Spoon the meringue onto the baking sheet in 8 evenly spaced mounds. Using a small spoon or offset metal spatula, make a deep well in the center of each meringue. Sprinkle 2 tablespoons of the remaining nuts over the tops.

**3.** Bake the meringues in the center of the oven for 5 minutes. Reduce the oven temperature to 225° and bake for 1 hour. Turn the oven off, prop the door slightly ajar and leave the meringues in for 1 hour longer. They should be white, crisp on the outside and chewy on the inside.

**4.** Using a sharp knife, peel the oranges, removing all the bitter white pith. Thinly slice the oranges crosswise. Set the meringues on plates. Top with the fresh orange slices and a scoop of the sorbet. Sprinkle with the remaining 2 tablespoons of pistachios, garnish with the Candied Orange Slices and serve. —*Grace Parisi*

### CANDIED ORANGE SLICES

**TOTAL: 35 MIN**

**MAKES ABOUT 8 SLICES** ● ● ●

- 1½ cups water
- ½ cup granulated sugar
- 1 navel orange, sliced crosswise ¼ inch thick

In a medium skillet, combine the water and sugar and bring to a boil. Add the orange slices and cook over moderate heat, turning them occasionally, until the liquid is reduced to a thin syrup and the orange slices are translucent, about 20 minutes. Reduce the heat to moderately low and simmer until the syrup is thick and the slices are tender but still intact, turning occasionally, about 10 minutes. Transfer the orange slices to a rack to cool. Reserve the syrup for another use. —*G.P.*

**MAKE AHEAD** The Candied Orange Slices can be refrigerated for up to 2 weeks.

## Liqueur-Infused Oranges with Ice Cream and Custard Sauce

**ACTIVE: 30 MIN; TOTAL: 1 HR**

**8 SERVINGS**

- 3 large egg yolks
- 2 large eggs
- 1½ cups fresh orange juice
- ½ cup sugar
- 1 tablespoon cornstarch
- 8 large navel oranges
- 2 tablespoons plus 2 teaspoons orange liqueur, such as Gran Torres
- 1 pint orange ice cream, sherbet or sorbet

**1.** In a small, heavy saucepan, whisk the egg yolks with the whole eggs, orange juice, sugar and cornstarch. Cook over moderate heat, whisking constantly, until the mixture thickens and reaches 180° on a candy thermometer, about 5 minutes. Strain the custard through a fine sieve set over a bowl. Let cool to room temperature, stirring a few times. Press a sheet of plastic wrap directly on the custard and refrigerate until very cold, about 1 hour.

**2.** Meanwhile, using a sharp knife, peel the oranges, removing all of the bitter white pith. Cut in between the membranes to release the sections. Cut the orange sections into ½-inch dice.

**3.** Spoon the oranges into glasses or bowls and top each serving with 1 teaspoon of the liqueur, ¼ cup of the custard and a scoop of the ice cream. —*Sergi Millet*

## Flaugnarde with Pears

**ACTIVE: 30 MIN; TOTAL: 2 HR 30 MIN**

**6 TO 8 SERVINGS** ● ●

Flaugnarde, similar to an airy German apple pancake, can be made with rum-marinated apples, tea-soaked prunes in Armagnac syrup or, as in this recipe, pears and rum.

- 3 large eggs
- 1½ cups pastry flour

**Pinch of salt**

- 1 cup warm milk
- 1 tablespoon dark rum
- 2½ tablespoons unsalted butter, softened
- 2 ripe pears, such as Bartlett— peeled, cored and thinly sliced
- 2½ tablespoons superfine sugar

**1.** In a bowl, whisk the eggs, flour, salt and ¼ cup of the milk to a smooth paste. Whisk in the remaining ¾ cup of milk and the rum. Strain the batter through a fine sieve. Cover with plastic wrap and let stand at room temperature for 1 to 2 hours.

**2.** Preheat the oven to 450° and coat a 9-inch cake pan with half the butter. Pour the batter into the pan and gently set the pear slices on top. Dot the cake with the remaining butter and bake in the lower third of the oven for 15 minutes. Reduce the temperature to 400° and bake for 30 minutes longer, or until the cake is puffed and deeply golden. Let cool for 2 minutes, then run a knife around the edge. Set a spatula under the cake to loosen it, then slide it onto a plate. Sprinkle with the sugar and serve. —*Paula Wolfert*

ORO BLANCO

LIMEQUAT

UGLI FRUIT

SWEET LIME

ETROG

PAGE MANDARIN

MINNEOLA TANGELO

BERGAMOT

KEY LIME

POMELO

KAFFIR LIME

HEIRLOOM NAVEL

MANDARINQUAT

**Pomelo** An oversize, mildly tart, grapefruit-like citrus with a yellow-green superthick skin.
**Oro Blanco** A white-fleshed hybrid of pomelo and grapefruit with a thick rind and sweet taste.
**Ugli Fruit** A grapefruit-tangerine cross with yellow-orange rind and sweet flesh.

**Heirloom Navel** A juicy, intense-tasting orange with dense yet yielding flesh.
**Minneola Tangelo** A hybrid of grapefruit and tangerine with sweet-tart flesh.
**Page Mandarin** A Minneola-tangelo-and-clementine hybrid with red-orange flesh.
**Mandarinquat** A hybrid of mandarin orange and

kumquat with edible rind and sour flesh.
**Limequat** A cross between a lime and a kumquat. Used for pickling and preserves.
**Sweet Lime** Pale yellow flesh, low acidity, best juiced.
**Kaffir Lime** A seedy, sour lime with bumpy skin. The leaves and zest are flavorful and aromatic.

**Key Lime** One-third the size of a regular lime, with a tart, floral flavor.
**Etrog** The thick yellow-orange peel of this citrus is candied or added to salads.
**Bergamot** Rind is rich in the essential oil used to flavor Earl Grey tea. (Available from melissas.com and friedas.com.)

● FAST   ● HEALTHY   ● MAKE AHEAD   ● STAFF FAVORITE

## Chilled Strawberry Soup with Mint Cream and Vanilla Crisps

**ACTIVE: 1 HR; TOTAL: 1 HR 25 MIN**

8 SERVINGS ● ◐

Stewing strawberries over simmering water concentrates the flavor beautifully; the minty cream topping makes the soup even more elegant, as do the layered vanilla phyllo crisps. Known as *feuilles de brique* in French, they can also be used as the base for a napoleon, or as an accompaniment to a savory soup if you substitute olive oil for the butter, and salt for the vanilla sugar. They're worth the effort, but you can use store-bought tuiles instead.

> 3 **pounds strawberries, hulled,**
> **2 pounds coarsely chopped,**
> **1 pound quartered**
> 1 **cup sugar**
> 2 **whole star anise pods, broken**
> **into pieces**
> **Zest of 1 orange, removed with a**
> **vegetable peeler**
> ¾ **cup chopped mint leaves,**
> **plus 8 small sprigs for garnish**
> 2 **cups crème fraîche**
> ½ **vanilla bean, seeds scraped**
> 8 **sheets of phyllo dough**
> 1 **stick (4 ounces) unsalted**
> **butter, melted**
> **Salt**

**1.** MAKE THE STRAWBERRY SOUP: In a large saucepan, bring 1 inch of water to a simmer. Place the chopped strawberries in a stainless steel bowl. Stir in ½ cup of the sugar and cover the bowl with plastic wrap. Set the bowl over the simmering water and cook over low heat until the strawberries have exuded their juices, about 1 hour.

**2.** Prepare a large ice-water bath. Carefully remove the bowl from the pan. Discard the plastic wrap. Stir the star anise, orange zest and ¼ cup of the chopped mint into the berries. Set the bowl in the ice bath and stir the soup occasionally for 15 minutes, or until chilled. Strain through a fine sieve set over a bowl and refrigerate.

**3.** MEANWHILE, MAKE THE MINT CREAM: In a mortar, pound the remaining ½ cup of chopped mint with 3 tablespoons of the sugar until a wet paste forms, then scrape into a bowl and stir in the crème fraîche; refrigerate for 20 minutes. Strain the mint cream through a fine sieve set over a stainless steel bowl. Using a handheld mixer, beat the mint cream to firm peaks.

**4.** MAKE THE PHYLLO CRISPS: Preheat the oven to 350°. Line a large rimmed baking sheet with parchment paper. In a bowl, using your fingers, rub the vanilla bean seeds into ¼ cup of the sugar. Work with 1 sheet of phyllo at a time and keep the rest covered with plastic. Lay the phyllo on a work surface, brush lightly with melted butter and sprinkle with vanilla sugar. Top with another sheet. Repeat, layering the phyllo, butter and sugar 6 times. Use all of the vanilla sugar. Brush the final layer with butter and sprinkle lightly with salt.

**5.** Using a 3½-inch round biscuit cutter, stamp out 8 rounds from the phyllo and arrange on the parchment-lined baking sheet. Top with a second sheet of parchment paper and another large baking sheet, pressing lightly. Bake for 8 minutes, or until lightly browned and crisp. Carefully remove the top baking sheet and parchment paper and let the crisps cool.

**6.** In a large bowl, toss the quartered strawberries with the remaining 1 tablespoon of sugar; let stand for 5 minutes. Ladle the soup into shallow bowls. Top with the mint cream. Scatter the quartered strawberries over the mint cream. Garnish with the mint sprigs and serve with the crisps. —*Michael Cimarusti*

## Strawberry, Rhubarb and Rose Fool

**ACTIVE: 30 MIN; TOTAL: 1 HR**

10 SERVINGS

> 2½ **pounds rhubarb, stalks sliced**
> **crosswise ½ inch thick (8 cups)**
> 1 **cup sugar**
> ¼ **cup water**
> ¼ **cup rose syrup (optional; see Note)**
> ½ **teaspoon fresh lemon juice**
> 3 **cups heavy cream**
> 1 **pound strawberries, thinly sliced**
> **(2½ cups)**
> ½ **cup unsprayed rose petals, finely**
> **shredded (optional)**

**1.** In a large saucepan, combine the sliced rhubarb, sugar and water and bring to a boil. Cover and cook the rhubarb over moderate heat, stirring occasionally, until the fruit breaks down, about 10 minutes. Uncover the rhubarb and cook, stirring frequently, until the liquid has evaporated and the rhubarb is thick and jammy, about 10 minutes longer. Transfer the rhubarb to a bowl and refrigerate until it is chilled. Stir the rose syrup and lemon juice into the stewed rhubarb.

**2.** In a medium bowl, beat the heavy cream until soft peaks form. Spoon half of the stewed rhubarb into 10 wine or parfait glasses and top the rhubarb with half of the sliced strawberries and half of the whipped cream. Repeat with the remaining rhubarb, strawberries and cream. Garnish the fool with the rose petals and serve immediately. —*Seen Lippert*

**NOTE** Rose syrup is available at specialty food stores. The not-too-sweet Mymouné brand of rose syrup from Lebanon is available at kalustyans.com.

## Warm Sweet Grits with Strawberry Compote

**ACTIVE: 1 HR 15 MIN; TOTAL: 2 HR**

6 SERVINGS

> 2 **cups milk**
> 6 **cardamom pods, lightly crushed**
> 1 **vanilla bean, split, seeds scraped**
> ½ **cinnamon stick**
> ½ **cup plus 2 tablespoons sugar**
> 2 **pints strawberries, hulled,**
> **quartered if large**
> 1 **tablespoon framboise liqueur**
> **Zest of 1 lime, removed with a**
> **vegetable peeler**

3 tablespoons unsalted butter

1 cup stone-ground white grits (not instant)

4 cups warm water

¼ cup light brown sugar

**Vanilla ice cream, for serving**

1. In a small saucepan, combine the milk with 4 of the cardamom pods, the vanilla bean and seeds, the cinnamon stick and ¼ cup plus 2 tablespoons of sugar. Bring to a simmer, stirring until the sugar dissolves. Remove from the heat and let stand for 45 minutes. Strain the infused milk into a bowl and discard the solids.

2. Meanwhile, in a medium saucepan, combine the strawberries, framboise, lime zest and the remaining ¼ cup of sugar and 2 cardamom pods and let stand for 10 minutes. Cook over high heat, stirring occasionally, until the berries are softened, 4 to 5 minutes. Let cool slightly. Discard the lime zest and cardamom pods.

3. In a large saucepan, melt the butter. Add the grits and cook over high heat, stirring until heated through, about 5 minutes. Gradually whisk in the warm water. Reduce the heat to moderately low and cook, stirring with a wooden spoon every 2 to 3 minutes, until the water has been absorbed and the grits are thickened, about 20 minutes. Whisk in the infused milk until smooth. Cook, stirring frequently with a wooden spoon, until the grits are thickened, about 30 minutes longer. Pour the grits into a shallow 5- to 6-cup baking dish and let cool for 10 minutes.

4. Preheat the broiler and position a rack 8 inches from the heat. Sprinkle the brown sugar over the grits and lightly rub it into an even layer. Broil the grits until the sugar melts and caramelizes, about 5 minutes, shifting the dish as necessary for even browning. Alternatively, use a propane torch to caramelize the sugar. Spoon the grits into shallow bowls and top with a scoop of ice cream. Spoon the strawberry compote on the side. —*Tony Maws*

## Superquick Strawberry Ice Cream

**TOTAL: 10 MIN**

**MAKES 3 CUPS** ● ●

Spanish chef Ferran Adrià popularized savory ice creams in flavors like polenta. He shows his inventiveness here in a different way, by revealing how to make a delicious *helado* without an ice cream maker; he just purees frozen fruit in a food processor. It doesn't get much simpler.

1 pound frozen strawberries

½ cup fromage blanc or plain, low-fat yogurt

¼ cup plus 2 tablespoons sugar

In a food processor, puree the strawberries with the fromage blanc and sugar for 2 to 3 minutes, scraping down the side of the bowl occasionally. Transfer to a bowl and serve immediately. —*Ferran Adrià*

## Strawberry Ice Cream Pie

**ACTIVE: 40 MIN; TOTAL: 2 HR**

**MAKES ONE 9-INCH PIE** ●

1 cup graham cracker crumbs

½ stick unsalted butter, melted

¼ teaspoon cinnamon

**Pinch of freshly grated nutmeg**

1½ pints strawberry ice cream

**Cinnamon–Black Pepper Strawberry Sauce (recipe follows)**

1 pint strawberry sorbet

1. Preheat the oven to 325°. In a medium bowl, mix the graham cracker crumbs with the butter, cinnamon and nutmeg. Press into a 9-inch glass or ceramic pie plate to form an even crust. Bake in the center of the oven for 8 minutes, or until lightly browned. Let cool completely.

2. Let the ice cream thaw in the refrigerator for 15 minutes. Scoop the ice cream into a bowl and, using an electric mixer, beat just until very soft but not melted. Spread the softened ice cream in the pie shell. Freeze for at least 1½ hours, or until firm.

3. Cut the pie into wedges and serve with the sauce and scoops of strawberry sorbet. —*Nancy Silverton*

## CINNAMON–BLACK PEPPER STRAWBERRY SAUCE

**TOTAL: 35 MIN**

**MAKES ABOUT 1 CUP** ● ●

¼ cup plus 2 tablespoons sugar

3 tablespoons water

1 cinnamon stick

5 black peppercorns, lightly crushed

2 whole cloves

1½ cups dry red wine

1 pint strawberries, thinly sliced

1. In a saucepan, boil the sugar, water, cinnamon, peppercorns and cloves, stirring, just until the sugar dissolves. Cook over moderately high heat, without stirring, until the syrup begins to turn brown at the edge, 3 minutes. Cook, swirling the pan, until a medium-amber caramel forms, 2 to 3 minutes. Off the heat, carefully stir in the wine. Cook over moderately high heat, stirring occasionally, until the caramel is dissolved and the sauce reduced to 1 cup, 8 minutes.

2. Strain through a fine sieve into a skillet. Cook over moderately high heat until slightly syrupy and reduced to ½ cup. Add the berries and cook, stirring occasionally, until just softened and syrupy, 5 minutes. Serve warm or at room temperature. —*N.S.*

# F&W taste test

**STRAWBERRY PRESERVES**

F&W editors tasted 15 widely available strawberry preserves and jams and rated **Bonne Maman** the best. **DETAILS** $3 for 13 ounces.

## Alsatian Rhubarb Tart

ACTIVE: 45 MIN; TOTAL: 2 HR PLUS
OVERNIGHT DRAINING AND COOLING

MAKES ONE 10-INCH TART ●

FILLING

    2   pounds rhubarb stalks, cut
        into ⅓-inch dice
1⅓  cups sugar
    1   cup heavy cream
    2   large egg yolks
    3   large egg whites
Pinch of salt

PASTRY

    2   cups all-purpose flour
    1   teaspoon sugar
Pinch of salt
    1   stick (4 ounces) cold unsalted
        butter, cut into ½-inch pieces
    1   large egg
    2   tablespoons plus 1 teaspoon
        ice water

1. MAKE THE FILLING: In a medium bowl, toss the rhubarb with ½ cup of the sugar; transfer to a strainer. Set it over the bowl and refrigerate overnight to drain.

2. MAKE THE PASTRY: In a food processor, combine the flour, sugar and salt. Add the butter and pulse just until the size of peas. In a bowl, whisk the egg with the ice water. Drizzle the egg mixture over the dough and pulse just until evenly moistened; do not let it form a ball. Turn the dough out onto a work surface, gather it together and shape into a disk. Wrap in plastic and refrigerate until firm, at least 30 minutes.

3. Preheat the oven to 375°. On a lightly floured surface, roll out the pastry to a 14-inch round. Fit the pastry into a 10-inch tart pan with a removable bottom and trim the overhanging pastry.

4. Line the pastry with foil and fill with pie weights, dried beans or rice. Bake the tart shell in the lower third of the oven for about 20 minutes, or until the pastry is set. Carefully remove the foil and weights and bake for 10 minutes longer, or until the shell is cooked and the bottom is lightly golden.

5. Press on the rhubarb to extract as much liquid as possible. In a bowl, toss the rhubarb with ⅓ cup plus 1 tablespoon of the sugar. Spread the rhubarb in the shell and bake in the center of the oven for 15 minutes, or until the rhubarb is just tender.

6. In a medium bowl, whisk the cream with the egg yolks and 3 tablespoons of the sugar. Pour the custard over the rhubarb and bake in the lower third of the oven for about 20 minutes, or until set.

7. Increase the oven temperature to 425° and position a rack in the upper third of the oven. In a large bowl, using a handheld electric mixer, beat the egg whites with the salt until firm peaks form. Gradually add the remaining ¼ cup of sugar, beating until the whites are stiff and glossy. Spread the meringue over the tart all the way to the side. Bake in the upper third of the oven for 5 minutes, or just until the meringue is lightly browned. Let the tart cool, then remove the ring, slide the tart onto a cake plate and serve.
—Jean-Georges Vongerichten

## Thick Shakes with Strawberry-Mascarpone Panini

ACTIVE: 30 MIN; TOTAL: 2 HR

4 SERVINGS ●

    6   large egg yolks
½   cup granulated sugar
    2   cups milk
    1   cup heavy cream
    2   vanilla beans, split, seeds scraped
    1   pound strawberries
        (2 pints), sliced
½   cup fresh orange juice
    1   teaspoon finely grated orange zest
    1   tablespoon balsamic vinegar
Salt and freshly ground pepper
½   cup mascarpone
    8   slices of brioche (½ inch thick)
    2   tablespoons unsalted
        butter, softened
Confectioners' sugar, for dusting
    2   pints strawberry ice cream

1. Fill a large metal bowl with ice water and set another large metal bowl in it. Set a strainer in the bowl.

2. In a medium bowl, whisk the egg yolks with ¼ cup of the granulated sugar until slightly pale. In a medium saucepan, heat the milk with the cream and vanilla beans and seeds until small bubbles appear around the edge. Add the hot milk to the egg mixture in a thin stream, whisking constantly. Return the mixture to the saucepan and cook it over moderate heat, stirring constantly with a wooden spoon until it is slightly thickened, about 5 minutes. Strain the vanilla sauce into the bowl in the ice bath and let cool completely, stirring occasionally.

3. Meanwhile, in a saucepan, combine the sliced strawberries, orange juice, grated orange zest, balsamic vinegar and the remaining ¼ cup of granulated sugar; season the fruit mixture very lightly with salt and pepper. Bring the fruit to a boil and cook over moderately high heat, stirring frequently, until the mixture has become jammy, about 10 minutes. Transfer the jam to a bowl and let cool.

4. Heat a panini press or griddle over low heat. Spread the mascarpone on 4 of the brioche slices. Spoon 3 tablespoons of the jam on each of the other 4 slices and close the sandwiches. Brush the sandwiches with the butter and grill or press them until they are golden, about 5 minutes. Transfer the grilled panini to a cutting board, dust them with confectioners' sugar and cut each one in half.

5. Put 1 pint of the strawberry ice cream and half of the vanilla sauce into a blender and blend until smooth. Pour the milk shakes into 2 large glasses. Repeat with the remaining ice cream and vanilla sauce to make 2 more milk shakes. Serve the strawberry milk shakes right away, with the panini. —Rob Evans

MAKE AHEAD The vanilla sauce and jam can be refrigerated for up to 3 days.

THICK SHAKE WITH STRAWBERRY-
MASCARPONE PANINI

## Sweet Cherry Clafoutis

**ACTIVE: 30 MIN; TOTAL: 3 HR**

**6 TO 8 SERVINGS**

- 1 **pound sweet cherries, pitted and patted dry with paper towels**
- ¼ **cup granulated sugar**
- ½ **teaspoon finely grated lemon zest**
- ½ **cup all-purpose flour, plus more for dusting**

**Pinch of salt**

- 3 **large eggs, lightly beaten**
- 2 **cups milk**
- 4 **tablespoons unsalted butter, softened, plus more for the dish**
- 2 **tablespoons Cognac or brandy**
- ½ **teaspoon pure vanilla extract**

**Confectioners' sugar for dusting**

**1.** In a bowl, toss the cherries with 3 tablespoons of the granulated sugar and the lemon zest. Spread the cherries out on a baking sheet and freeze for 1½ hours.

**2.** Meanwhile, in another bowl, whisk the ½ cup of flour and the salt. Whisk in the eggs. In a small saucepan, heat ½ cup of the milk with 3 tablespoons of the butter until the butter melts. Whisk the warm milk into the flour mixture just until smooth. Whisk in the remaining 1½ cups of milk. Add the Cognac and vanilla, cover and let rest at room temperature for at least 1 hour.

**3.** Preheat the oven to 425°. Butter a 9½-inch deep-dish pie plate and dust with flour. Spread the cherries in a single layer in the pie plate, adding any sugar from the baking sheet to the cherries. Whisk the batter again and pour it evenly over the cherries.

**4.** Bake the clafoutis just above the center of the oven for 20 minutes, or until the top is just set and golden. Top with the remaining 1 tablespoon of granulated sugar and 1 tablespoon of butter. Bake for 10 to 15 minutes longer, or until a knife inserted in the center comes out clean. Transfer to a rack to cool. Dust with confectioners' sugar, cut into wedges and serve.

—*Paula Wolfert*

## Blueberry Meringue Tarts

**ACTIVE: 45 MIN; TOTAL: 2 HR**

**6 SERVINGS** ●

**PASTRY DISKS**

- 1⅓ **cups all-purpose flour, plus more for dusting**
- ¼ **cup plus 2 tablespoons cake flour**
- ¼ **cup plus 2 tablespoons cornmeal**
- ¼ **teaspoon baking powder**
- ¼ **teaspoon salt**
- 4 **ounces (½ cup) chilled cream cheese, cut into pieces**
- 1½ **sticks (6 ounces) cold unsalted butter, cut into tablespoons**
- 2 **tablespoons ice water**
- 2 **teaspoons white vinegar**
- 2 **tablespoons granulated sugar**
- 1 **tablespoon turbinado or granulated brown sugar**
- 1 **tablespoon light brown sugar**
- ¼ **teaspoon cinnamon**
- 1 **egg beaten with 1 tablespoon water**

**COMPOTE**

- ⅓ **cup light brown sugar**

**Juice and strips of zest from 2 limes**

- ¾ **cup fresh orange juice**
- 2¼ **pounds blueberries**

**MERINGUE**

- ½ **cup plus 1 tablespoon granulated sugar**
- 3 **tablespoons water**
- 3 **large egg whites**
- ½ **teaspoon cream of tartar**

**1. MAKE THE PASTRY DISKS:** In a food processor, pulse the 1⅓ cups of all-purpose flour with the cake flour, cornmeal, baking powder and salt. Add the cream cheese and pulse until the mixture resembles coarse meal. Add the butter and pulse just until the dough resembles small peas. Sprinkle on the ice water and vinegar and pulse just until a dough begins to form. Turn the dough onto a work surface and knead just until it comes together; roll into an 8-inch log, wrap in plastic and refrigerate until firm, at least 30 minutes.

**2.** Preheat the oven to 375°. In a bowl, combine the sugars; stir in the cinnamon. Cut the chilled dough into 12 slices. On a lightly floured surface, roll out each slice to a ⅛-inch thickness. Using a 4-inch round biscuit cutter, stamp out 12 rounds. Poke each round several times with a fork, then brush with the egg wash. Sprinkle the rounds with the cinnamon sugar and transfer to a large nonstick baking sheet. Bake for about 13 minutes, until golden; let cool.

**3. MEANWHILE, MAKE THE COMPOTE:** In a saucepan, bring the brown sugar, lime juice, lime zest and orange juice to a boil. Add the blueberries and cook over moderate heat, stirring occasionally, until they begin to pop, about 6 minutes. Transfer the blueberries to a bowl; let cool. Pour the berries into a strainer set over a large bowl and let stand for 30 minutes, until most of the liquid has drained off. Transfer the blueberry juice to a pitcher.

**4. MAKE THE MERINGUE:** Preheat the oven to 425°. Position a rack 6 inches from the heat source. In a saucepan, stir ½ cup of the sugar with the water over moderate heat until dissolved. Cook without stirring until the syrup reaches 243° to 245° on an instant-read candy thermometer, 8 minutes. In a bowl, beat the egg whites on medium-high until frothy. Add the cream of tartar. Beat until firm peaks form. Reduce the speed to medium-low and carefully add the syrup in a thin stream. After the syrup has been added, add the remaining 1 tablespoon of sugar. Increase the speed to high and beat until the meringue cools to room temperature, 5 minutes.

**5.** Arrange the disks on the baking sheet. Using a slotted spoon, mound the berry compote on the disks. Spoon the meringue onto 6 of the disks and, using 2 forks, pull it into long spikes. Bake all of the disks for 4 minutes, until the meringue is golden. Put the meringue-less disks on plates; place a meringue-topped disk on each and drizzle with blueberry juice. —*Nicole Krasinski*

BLUEBERRY MERINGUE TART

LEMON CUSTARDS WITH BLACKBERRIES

## Lemon Custards with Blackberries

**ACTIVE: 10 MIN; TOTAL: 1 HR PLUS
3 HR COOLING**

4 SERVINGS ● ●

- 2 cups low-fat milk
- 3 large eggs
- 1 large egg yolk
- ⅓ cup sugar

Finely grated zest of 1 lemon

- 1 teaspoon pure vanilla extract
- ½ teaspoon pure lemon extract (optional)
- ⅛ teaspoon salt
- ½ cup fresh blackberries

Mint sprigs, for garnish (optional)

**1.** Preheat the oven to 325° and position a rack in the lower third. In a saucepan, heat the milk just until small bubbles appear around the edge. Meanwhile, in a medium bowl, whisk the eggs, egg yolk, sugar, lemon zest, vanilla, lemon extract and salt. Whisk the hot milk into the egg mixture. Pour the custard into four ¾-cup ramekins and transfer to a small roasting pan. Place the pan in the oven and carefully pour enough hot water into it to reach halfway up the sides of the ramekins.

**2.** Bake the custards for 50 minutes, or until they are just set around the edge but still slightly jiggly in the center. Immediately transfer to a wire rack to cool, then refrigerate until chilled, at least 3 hours. Scatter the berries on top and garnish with mint sprigs. —*Constance Snow*

## Peaches with Basil-Lime Ice

**TOTAL: 30 MIN**

4 SERVINGS ● ●

- 1 cup loosely packed basil leaves
- ⅓ cup sugar
- 2 tablespoons fresh lime juice, plus ½ teaspoon finely grated lime zest
- 1 cup water
- 2 large freestone peaches, cut into wedges

**1.** Bring a small saucepan of water to a boil and fill a small bowl with ice water. Add the basil to the saucepan and blanch for 10 seconds. Drain and immediately transfer to the ice water to cool. Drain, gently squeezing out the excess water.

**2.** Transfer the basil to a blender. Add the sugar, lime juice, lime zest and water and puree until smooth, about 1 minute. Strain the liquid through a fine sieve and transfer to an ice cream maker. Process according to the manufacturer's instructions, about 15 to 20 minutes. Transfer the ice to a shallow dish and freeze until just firm enough to scoop, about 10 minutes.

**3.** Scoop the basil-lime ice into 4 bowls. Top with the peach wedges and serve immediately. —*Jerry Traunfeld*

CONFIT OF PEACHES WITH MINT

CARAMELIZED PEACH TATIN

### Confit of Peaches with Mint

**TOTAL: 20 MIN**

4 SERVINGS ● ● ●

There's no showy technique behind this incredibly easy, luscious dessert—you just need great ripe, slightly firm peaches to soak in a simple fruit-infused syrup. Thomas Keller, chef at the French Laundry in Yountville, California, tops the fruit with Petit Suisse, a fresh French cheese sold in small tubs at specialty food stores, and a sprinkling of toasted almonds. He prefers Marcona, the delectable Spanish nuts.

- ¼ **cup whole blanched almonds**
- 4 **medium freestone peaches**
- 1 **cup water**
- 1 **cup sugar**
- 2 **mint sprigs, plus 2 tablespoons shredded mint**
- ¼ **cup Petit Suisse, fromage blanc or crème fraîche**

**1.** Preheat the oven to 350°. Spread the blanched almonds in a pie plate and toast them for about 5 minutes, or until they are lightly golden. Let the almonds cool.

**2.** Meanwhile, using a sturdy vegetable peeler, peel the peaches; transfer the skins to a small saucepan. Add the water, sugar and mint sprigs and bring to a boil. Reduce the heat to moderately low and simmer for 10 minutes.

**3.** Cut the peaches into small wedges and transfer them to a heatproof bowl. Strain the syrup over the peach wedges and let stand for 5 minutes. Divide the peaches among 4 bowls and spoon the syrup on top. Garnish each serving with the Petit Suisse, sprinkle with the toasted almonds and shredded mint and serve immediately.
—*Thomas Keller*

**MAKE AHEAD** The peaches can be refrigerated in the syrup overnight.

### Caramelized Peach Tatin

**ACTIVE: 15 MIN; TOTAL: 45 MIN**

4 SERVINGS ●

- ¼ **cup sugar**
- 1 **tablespoon water**
- 1 **teaspoon light corn syrup**
- 3 **medium freestone peaches— peeled, halved and pitted**

**One 5-ounce sheet of frozen all-butter puff pastry, thawed but very cold**

**Vanilla ice cream, for serving**

**1.** Preheat the oven to 400°. In a small saucepan, combine the sugar, water and corn syrup and bring to a simmer over moderate heat. Simmer the syrup without stirring until an amber caramel forms, about 6 minutes. Pour the caramel into an 8-inch ovenproof skillet, tilting to coat the bottom. Set the peach halves in the caramel, cut side up.

312

**2.** On a lightly floured surface, cut the puff pastry into an 8-inch round. Set the round over the peaches in the skillet and bake until the pastry is richly browned and puffed, about 30 minutes. Remove the skillet from the oven and let stand for 5 minutes. Carefully invert the peach tart onto a cake plate and let stand until warm. Cut the tart into wedges and serve with vanilla ice cream. —*Jonathan Benno*

### Yogurt Pudding with Red and Golden Raspberries

**ACTIVE: 20 MIN; TOTAL: 1 HR 15 MIN**

**8 SERVINGS** ● ●

This delicate dessert is one of cookbook author Jeremy Jackson's favorite ways to use fresh-picked raspberries. He lays the fruit in a silky custard made with yogurt and cream, then bakes it until thick.

- 1 cup heavy cream
- ½ vanilla bean, split, seeds scraped
- 3 large eggs
- ½ cup sugar
- 1 cup plain yogurt
- 2 teaspoons framboise liqueur
- ⅓ cup all-purpose flour
- ½ pound raspberries (2 cups)

**1.** Preheat the oven to 325°. In a small saucepan, bring the cream and the vanilla bean and seeds to a simmer. Remove from the heat, cover and let steep for 15 minutes. Discard the vanilla bean.

**2.** In a medium bowl, beat the eggs with the sugar until thick and pale. Beat in the yogurt and framboise, then slowly beat in the vanilla cream. Using a whisk, beat in the flour in 3 additions until smooth.

**3.** Set a 10-inch glass pie plate in a roasting pan. Pour the pudding mixture into the pie plate and dot with the raspberries. Pour enough hot water into the roasting pan to reach halfway up the side of the pie plate. Bake the pudding for about 40 minutes, until just set and lightly browned around the edge. Remove from the water bath, let cool slightly and serve. —*Jeremy Jackson*

### Pistachio Meringues with Lemon Cream and Berries

**ACTIVE: 1 HR; TOTAL: 2 HR 45 MIN**

**8 SERVINGS**

TV chef Tyler Florence transforms the Pavlova, an Australian dessert of meringue topped with whipped cream and fresh fruit, by adding tart lemon curd, crunchy pistachios and fresh ginger.

**MERINGUES**

- 5 egg whites, at room temperature
- ⅛ teaspoon cream of tartar
- 1 cup plus 2 tablespoons sugar
- 1 teaspoon pure vanilla extract
- ½ cup unsalted pistachios, finely chopped

**LEMON CREAM AND BERRIES**

- 6 large egg yolks
- 1 cup sugar

Juice and finely grated zest of
- 4 lemons
- 1 tablespoon plus 1 teaspoon finely grated fresh ginger
- 1 stick (4 ounces) cold unsalted butter, cut into pieces
- 1 cup heavy cream
- 1 pound strawberries, hulled and sliced (3½ cups)

**1. MAKE THE MERINGUES:** Preheat the oven to 250°. Line 2 baking sheets with parchment paper and lightly spray them with vegetable oil. In a large bowl, using a handheld electric mixer, beat the egg whites with the cream of tartar until soft peaks form. Beat in the sugar, 1 tablespoon at a time, until firm peaks form. Add the vanilla and continue to beat at high speed until the meringue is thick and glossy, about 2 minutes longer.

**2.** Spoon 8 round mounds of meringue onto each of the prepared baking sheets. Using the back of a spoon, make small decorative peaks on each meringue. Sprinkle the chopped pistachios on the meringues. Bake for 1 hour and 15 minutes, rotating the sheets halfway through, until the meringues are lightly browned at the

tips. Turn the oven off and leave the door slightly open. Let the meringues cool in the oven for 1 hour.

**3. MEANWHILE, MAKE THE LEMON CREAM:** Fill a saucepan with 2 inches of water and bring to a simmer. In a medium stainless steel bowl, whisk the egg yolks with the sugar, lemon juice and zest and ginger. Set the bowl over—not in—the simmering water and whisk constantly until the curd is thick, about 20 minutes.

**4.** Remove the bowl from the heat and whisk in the butter, a few pieces at a time, until fully incorporated. Press the lemon curd through a fine strainer set over a bowl. Press a piece of plastic wrap directly onto the surface of the curd and refrigerate it until thoroughly chilled, at least 1 hour.

**5.** In a medium bowl, beat the heavy cream until stiff. Whisk one-third of the whipped cream into the lemon curd, then fold in the remaining whipped cream. Refrigerate until ready to use.

**6.** Set the meringues on plates. Spoon about ⅓ cup of the lemon cream on each, top with the sliced strawberries and serve. —*Tyler Florence*

## tool

### MULTITASKING GRATER

Cuispro's Accutec Deluxe Dual Grater cleverly combines two surfaces—one for finely **zesting** citrus and the other for coarsely **grating** hard cheese. **DETAILS** $15 from amazon.com.

## Sweet and Flaky Nectarine Tartlets

**ACTIVE: 45 MIN; TOTAL: 1 HR 30 MIN**
**MAKES 16 TARTLETS** ●
Make these rustic, superflaky tartlets with the sweetest nectarines you can find.

- ¼ cup ice water
- 1 large egg yolk
- ½ teaspoon white wine vinegar
- ¾ cup plus 2 tablespoons all-purpose flour, plus more for dusting
- 5 tablespoons cornstarch
- ½ teaspoon salt
- 1 stick (4 ounces) cold unsalted butter, cut into ½-inch pieces
- ½ cup sugar
- ½ cup water
- ½ vanilla bean, split, seeds scraped
- 2 teaspoons fresh lemon juice
- 3 nectarines (1¼ pounds), pitted and cut into ½-inch pieces

**1.** In a small bowl, combine the ice water with the egg yolk and vinegar. In a food processor, pulse the ¾ cup plus 2 tablespoons of flour with the cornstarch and salt. Add the butter and pulse until it is the size of peas. Sprinkle on the egg mixture and pulse just until a soft dough forms. Turn the pastry out onto a floured work surface and roll it into an 8-inch log. Wrap the pastry log in plastic and refrigerate until firm, about 30 minutes.

**2.** Preheat the oven to 375°. Line 2 baking sheets with parchment paper. In a saucepan, bring the sugar, water and vanilla bean and seeds to a boil, stirring until the sugar dissolves. Remove from the heat. Add the lemon juice and nectarines; let cool.

**3.** On a lightly floured work surface, cut the pastry log into sixteen ½-inch slices. Using a floured rolling pin, roll out each slice to a 3-inch round and transfer to the prepared baking sheets. Drain the nectarines and arrange them on the pastry rounds, leaving a border all around. Fold the border up and over the nectarines, pleating the edges; the tartlets should be about 2 inches wide.

**4.** Bake the tartlets for about 25 minutes, until they are golden and bubbling; shift the pans halfway through baking. Let cool and serve. —*Sherry Yard*
**MAKE AHEAD** The tartlets can be kept at room temperature for up to 2 days.

## Cold and Creamy Mango-Coconut Terrine

**ACTIVE: 45 MIN; TOTAL: 1 HR 30 MIN**
**PLUS OVERNIGHT FREEZING**
**6 TO 8 SERVINGS** ●
Lauren Chattman, author of *Icebox Desserts*, makes a creamy chilled terrine with layers of fluffy coconut mousse and sweet-tart mango sorbet, plus crunchy bits of sesame praline for a delicious contrast.

- ¾ cup sugar
- ¼ cup plus 3 tablespoons water
- ¼ cup sesame seeds
- 1 pint mango sorbet, softened slightly
- 1 envelope unflavored gelatin
- One 15-ounce can cream of coconut (such as Coco López)
- 1½ cups chilled heavy cream
- ¼ teaspoon pure coconut extract (optional)
- Diced fresh mango and fresh coconut shavings, for garnish

**1.** Butter a large rimmed baking sheet. In a small saucepan, combine the sugar with the ¼ cup of water and bring to a simmer, stirring until the sugar dissolves. Cover and simmer the syrup over moderate heat for 1 minute. Uncover and simmer over moderately high heat, without stirring, until an amber caramel forms, about 6 minutes. Remove the caramel from the heat and stir in the sesame seeds with a skewer or chopstick. Immediately pour the caramel onto the baking sheet and tilt carefully to spread it in a thin layer. Using 2 forks, pull and stretch the caramel into as thin a layer as possible. Let the caramel cool completely, about 20 minutes.

**2.** Using a spatula, pry the sesame praline from the sheet and break the candy into shards. Transfer half of the shards to a food processor and pulse them until a fine powder forms. Reserve the remaining shards for garnish.

**3.** Line a 9-by-4½-inch loaf pan with plastic wrap. Spoon the mango sorbet into the loaf pan and smooth the surface of the sorbet. Freeze the sorbet until firm, about 30 minutes.

**4.** In a medium microwavable bowl, sprinkle the unflavored gelatin over the remaining 3 tablespoons of water and let soften for 2 minutes. Microwave on high power for 10 seconds, just until melted. Whisk in the cream of coconut.

**5.** In a large bowl, using an electric mixer, beat the heavy cream with the coconut extract at high speed until firm. Add the cream of coconut mixture and beat at low speed just until combined.

**6.** Using the plastic wrap, carefully lift the frozen sorbet rectangle out of the loaf pan and return it to the freezer in the wrap. Line the loaf pan with a double sheet of plastic wrap, leaving at least 2 inches of overhang on all sides. Pour one-third of the coconut mousse into the loaf pan and sprinkle with half of the sesame praline powder. Unwrap the sorbet rectangle. Ease it into the loaf pan and sprinkle with the remaining praline powder. Using a rubber spatula, gently spread the remaining coconut mousse on top. Fold the overhanging plastic wrap over the top of the terrine and freeze until the terrine is firm, at least 6 hours or overnight.

**7.** Carefully unmold and unwrap the terrine. Using a hot knife, cut the terrine into slices. Garnish the slices with the reserved praline shards, diced mango and fresh coconut and serve. —*Lauren Chattman*
**MAKE AHEAD** The terrine can be frozen for up to 3 days. The sesame praline shards can be stored in an airtight container for up to 3 days.

COLD AND CREAMY
MANGO-COCONUT TERRINE

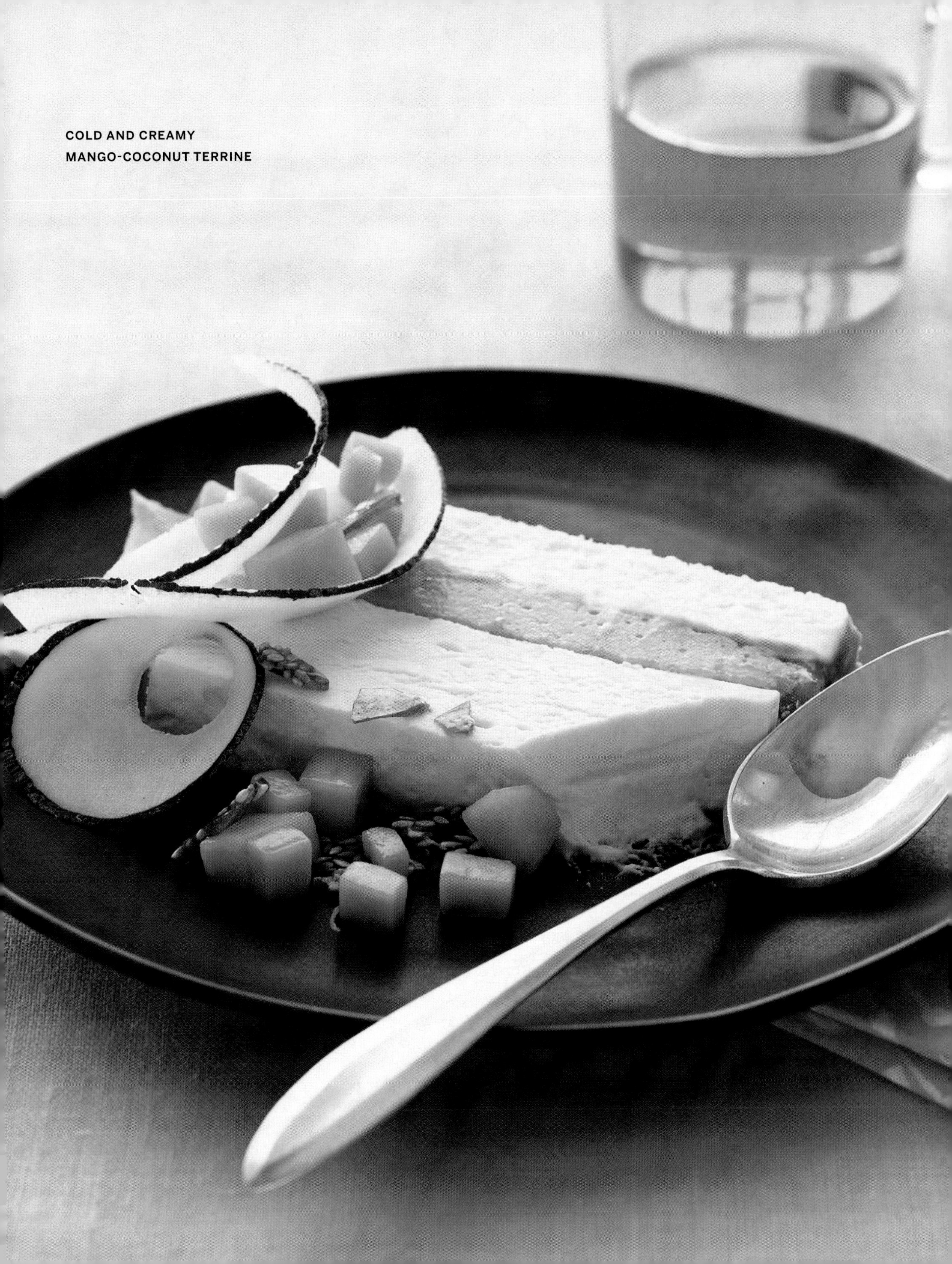

### Caramelized Fruit with Rosemary

**TOTAL: 30 MIN**

8 SERVINGS ● ●

Caramelizing pears, bananas and mangoes intensifies their sweetness. A touch of gooey caramel drizzled on the warm fruit makes it even better.

- 1 cup sugar
- 1 tablespoon fresh lemon juice
- 1 rosemary sprig
- ½ cup water
- 2 large firm but ripe Bartlett pears—peeled, cored and cut into ¾-inch cubes
- 2 mangoes, peeled and cut into 1-inch cubes
- 3 bananas, cut into 1-inch pieces

**1.** Preheat the broiler. In a small saucepan, combine ½ cup of the sugar with the lemon juice, rosemary and ¼ cup of the water and bring to a boil, stirring until the sugar dissolves. Let the rosemary syrup cool.

**2.** In another small saucepan, combine the remaining ½ cup of sugar with 2 tablespoons of the water. Cook over high heat, stirring, until the sugar dissolves. Cook without stirring until a deep amber caramel forms, about 5 minutes longer. Remove the syrup from the heat and carefully add the remaining 2 tablespoons of water. When the steam subsides, stir the caramel over moderate heat until smooth.

**3.** Thread the fruit onto 16 skewers. Set the skewers on a baking sheet and brush with the rosemary syrup; let the skewered fruit stand for 10 minutes. Broil the fruit skewers on one side only for about 3 minutes, or until the fruit is caramelized. Transfer the skewers of caramelized fruit to a large plate, drizzle with the caramel sauce and serve. —*André Soltner*

**SERVE WITH** Nonfat frozen yogurt.

**MAKE AHEAD** The rosemary syrup and caramel sauce can be kept at room temperature for up to 1 day.

### Dulce de Leche Ice Cream Pie

**ACTIVE: 20 MIN; TOTAL: 2 HR**

MAKES ONE 9-INCH PIE ●

If you don't want to make your own caramel or fudge sauce, try using high-quality jarred ones like King's Cupboard cream caramel sauce (kingscupboard.com) and Scharffen Berger chocolate sauce (scharffenberger.com).

- 1 cup graham cracker crumbs
- ½ stick unsalted butter, melted
- ¼ teaspoon cinnamon
- Pinch of freshly grated nutmeg
- 1½ pints dulce de leche ice cream
- Mocha Hot Fudge Sauce (recipe follows)
- Vanilla-Caramel Sauce (recipe follows)
- Spanish salted peanuts with skin, toasted, for serving

**1.** Preheat the oven to 325°. In a medium bowl, mix the graham cracker crumbs with the butter, cinnamon and nutmeg. Press the crumbs into a 9-inch glass or ceramic pie plate to form an even crust. Bake the crust in the center of the oven for 8 minutes, or until lightly browned. Let cool.

**2.** Let the ice cream thaw in the refrigerator for 15 minutes. Scoop the ice cream into a large bowl and, using an electric mixer, beat it just until very soft but not melted. Spread the softened ice cream into the pie shell and freeze for at least 1½ hours, or until the ice cream is firm.

**3.** Cut the pie into wedges and serve with the dessert sauces and peanuts.
—*Nancy Silverton*

**MAKE AHEAD** The pie can be frozen for up to 2 weeks.

### MOCHA HOT FUDGE SAUCE

**TOTAL: 15 MIN**

MAKES ABOUT 1½ CUPS ● ●

- ⅓ cup water
- ¼ cup light corn syrup
- ¼ cup plus 2 tablespoons unsweetened cocoa powder
- 2 tablespoons sugar
- 4 ounces bittersweet chocolate, melted and slightly cooled
- 3 tablespoons brewed coffee
- 1 tablespoon rum

In a medium saucepan, whisk the water with the corn syrup, cocoa powder and sugar until smooth. Bring to a boil. Remove from the heat and whisk in the melted chocolate. Gradually whisk in the coffee and rum. Serve warm. *N.S.*

**MAKE AHEAD** The sauce can be refrigerated for up to 2 weeks.

### VANILLA-CARAMEL SAUCE

**TOTAL: 20 MIN**

MAKES ABOUT 1½ CUPS ● ●

- ½ cup heavy cream
- 4 tablespoons unsalted butter
- ½ vanilla bean, split, seeds scraped
- 2 tablespoons light corn syrup
- ¾ cup sugar
- 2 tablespoons water

**1.** In a small saucepan, combine the heavy cream, butter and the vanilla bean with its seeds. Bring the cream to a simmer, then remove from the heat.

**2.** In a heavy, medium saucepan, cook the corn syrup over moderate heat until bubbling. Sprinkle in ¼ cup of the sugar and cook, stirring, just until the edge begins to turn a light amber, about 2 minutes. Repeat with the remaining sugar, adding ¼ cup at a time. Once all of the sugar has been added, cook the corn syrup mixture until a medium-amber caramel forms, stirring and swirling the pan, about 5 minutes.

**3.** Remove the caramel from the heat and carefully add the cream mixture. Cook the caramel over moderate heat, stirring frequently until any hardened sugar melts and the caramel is bubbling, 2 to 3 minutes. Let cool slightly, then whisk in the water. Remove the vanilla bean and serve warm or at room temperature. —*N.S.*

**MAKE AHEAD** The sauce can be refrigerated for up to 2 weeks.

**CONCORD GRAPE GRANITA**

**FRUIT MERINGUE KEBABS**

## Concord Grape Granita

**ACTIVE: 20 MIN; TOTAL: 4 HR 30 MIN**

4 SERVINGS ● ● ●

¼ cup plus 2 tablespoons sugar
¼ cup plus 2 tablespoons water
1¾ cups plus 2 tablespoons fresh
　　Concord grape juice

**1.** In a saucepan, simmer the sugar and water to dissolve the sugar. Let cool.

**2.** In a 9-inch square glass baking dish, combine the sugar syrup and the Concord grape juice. Freeze for 30 minutes. Using 2 forks, scrape any frozen crystals into the center of the dish. Continue to freeze, scraping every 30 minutes, until the mixture is totally frozen and granular, about 4 hours total. Scrape the grape granita into chilled bowls and serve.
—*Eugenia Giobbi Bone and Edward Giobbi*

**MAKE AHEAD** The granita can be frozen for up to 2 days.

## Fruit Meringue Kebabs

**TOTAL: 20 MIN**

4 SERVINGS ● ●

These fun and easy meringue-coated fruit skewers are from superstar chef Ferran Adrià of El Bulli in Rosas, Spain.

2 large egg whites, at room
　　temperature
½ cup sugar
1 large round apple, halved
　　lengthwise
8 small strawberries, hulled
**Eight 1-inch pieces of fresh pineapple**
**Eight 1-inch pieces of mango**
**Eight 1-inch-thick slices of firm,**
　　**ripe banana**

**1.** Preheat the broiler and position a rack in the lower third of the oven. In a large stainless steel bowl, using a handheld electric mixer, beat the egg whites at medium speed until soft peaks form.

Beat in the sugar, 1 tablespoon at a time, beating thoroughly between additions. Increase the speed to high and beat the whites until they are glossy and hold firm peaks, 2 to 3 minutes longer.

**2.** Arrange the apple halves cut side down on a sturdy baking sheet. Slide 2 of the strawberries and 2 pieces of the pineapple, mango and banana onto each of 4 wooden skewers.

**3.** Using a butter knife or a small offset spatula, spread the meringue evenly over the fruit in a thick layer. Stick the skewers into the apple halves to keep the kebabs upright; don't let the kebabs touch each other. Broil the kebabs for about 30 seconds, turning the pan as necessary, until the meringue is golden and caramelized in spots. Alternatively, brown the meringue with a small blowtorch. Serve the fruit kebabs right away. —*Ferran Adrià*

● FAST　● HEALTHY　● MAKE AHEAD　● STAFF FAVORITE

317

## Chocolate Pecan Pie

**ACTIVE: 45 MIN; TOTAL: 4 HR**

**MAKES ONE 9-INCH PIE ● ●**

Dark chocolate gives this classic dish a deep flavor and fudgy texture.

DOUGH

  2  **cups all-purpose flour,
      plus more for rolling**
  1  **teaspoon sugar**
  ½  **teaspoon kosher salt**
1½  **sticks (6 ounces) cold unsalted
      butter, cut into ¼-inch dice**
  ¼  **cup ice water**

FILLING

1½  **cups pecan halves**
  4  **tablespoons unsalted butter**
  6  **ounces bittersweet chocolate,
      broken into pieces**
  ½  **cup light brown sugar**
  3  **large eggs, lightly beaten**
  ¾  **cup light corn syrup**
  1  **teaspoon pure vanilla extract**
**Pinch of kosher salt**
**Unsweetened whipped cream**

**1. MAKE THE DOUGH:** In a food processor, combine the 2 cups of flour with the sugar and salt; process to mix. Add the butter and

## ingredient
**MEXICAN ICE CREAM**

**Palapa Azul** ice creams and sorbets are made from traditional Mexican recipes. F&W loved the cinnamon-laced chocolate flavor. **DETAILS** $4 for 1 pint at Whole Foods Markets.

process until the largest pieces of butter are the size of peas. With the machine on, slowly add the ice water and process just until it is incorporated. Transfer the dough to a bowl and knead a few times. Pat the dough into a 1-inch-thick disk and wrap in plastic. Refrigerate until firm, at least 1 hour or overnight.

**2.** Let the dough soften slightly. On a lightly floured work surface, roll out the dough to a round about ⅛ inch thick. Roll the dough onto the rolling pin and unroll it over a 9-inch glass pie plate. Press the dough into the pie plate, being careful not to stretch it. Using scissors, trim the overhanging dough to 1½ inches. Fold the overhang under itself and crimp decoratively. Refrigerate the pie shell until firm, at least 30 minutes.

**3.** Preheat the oven to 375°. Prick the chilled pie shell all over with the tines of a fork. Line the shell with foil and fill with dried beans or pie weights. Fold the foil over the weights so the side of the pie shell is exposed. Bake the shell for 25 minutes, or until the side and rim are golden. Carefully remove the foil and continue baking the shell until the bottom is beginning to brown, about 15 minutes longer. Reduce the oven temperature to 350°.

**4. MAKE THE FILLING:** Spread the pecans on a baking sheet and bake for 5 minutes, stirring once. Transfer the pecans to a plate. In a small microwavable glass bowl, melt the butter with the chocolate in a microwave oven. Stir until blended and smooth. Scrape the chocolate mixture into a medium bowl and add the brown sugar. Stir in the eggs, corn syrup, vanilla and salt, then stir in the pecans.

**5.** Pour the filling into the pie shell and bake for 45 to 50 minutes, or until set in the center. Let the pie cool completely. Serve with whipped cream. —*Susan Spungen*

**MAKE AHEAD** The pecan pie can be refrigerated overnight. Serve cold or bring to room temperature before serving.

## Grilled Banana Splits with Coffee Ice Cream and Mocha Sauce

**TOTAL: 50 MIN PLUS 4 HR MACERATING**

8 SERVINGS

  2  **quarts plus 1 cup water**
  1  **cup light brown sugar**
  3  **cinnamon sticks, broken**
  3  **star anise pods**
  ½  **cup dark rum**
  8  **firm, ripe bananas**
  ¾  **cup granulated sugar**
  ⅔  **cup unsweetened cocoa powder**
  3  **tablespoons instant
      espresso powder**
  1  **cup heavy cream**
  3  **ounces semisweet chocolate,
      chopped**
**Turbinado sugar, for dredging**
  3  **pints coffee ice cream**
**Whipped cream and chopped nuts,
      for serving**

**1.** In a large saucepan, combine 2 quarts of the water with the brown sugar, cinnamon sticks and star anise and bring to a boil, stirring to dissolve the sugar. Remove from the heat. Add the rum and bananas and let stand for 4 hours.

**2.** In a medium saucepan, whisk the remaining 1 cup of water with the granulated sugar, cocoa powder and espresso powder and bring to a boil. Whisk in the cream and simmer over low heat, stirring occasionally, until thickened, about 40 minutes. Stir in the chocolate until melted. Remove from the heat; keep warm.

**3.** Light a grill. Drain the bananas and pat dry with paper towels. Put the turbinado sugar in a shallow bowl. Cut each banana in half lengthwise; dip each half in the sugar to coat evenly and grill over high heat until richly caramelized, 1 minute per side.

**4.** Transfer 2 banana halves to each of 8 bowls. Place 3 scoops of ice cream in each split banana and top with ¼ cup of the mocha sauce. Dollop whipped cream over the splits, top with the nuts and serve. —*Johnny Iuzzini*

## Caramelized Banana Tartes Tatin

**ACTIVE: 30 MIN; TOTAL: 1 HR 10 MIN**

**MAKES TWO 10-INCH TARTS** ●

Traditional tarte Tatin is made with apples, but San Francisco chef Michael Mina uses bananas. Arranging the slices in the buttery caramel can be a little trickier than working with apple wedges, but don't fuss too much or the caramel will cool and harden before you're done.

1½ cups sugar

¼ cup water

4 tablespoons unsalted butter

10 firm, ripe bananas

1½ pounds cold all-butter puff pastry

1 egg yolk beaten with
   1 tablespoon water

**1.** Preheat the oven to 400°. In each of two 10-inch ovenproof skillets, stir ¾ cup of sugar with 2 tablespoons of water. Cook over moderately high heat, stirring occasionally, until a light amber caramel forms. Remove from the heat, add 2 tablespoons of butter to each and stir until combined.

**2.** Slice the bananas ½ inch thick. Carefully arrange the bananas in the skillets in overlapping concentric circles, working from the edges to the center.

**3.** On a lightly floured surface, roll out the pastry ¼ inch thick. Using a pot lid or plate as a template, cut out two 10-inch rounds. Poke the pastry all over with a fork and lay the rounds over the bananas. Lightly brush the pastry with egg wash. Bake the tarts in the upper and lower thirds of the oven for about 40 minutes, or until the pastry is golden brown and puffed and the filling is bubbling. Shift the pans from top to bottom during baking for even browning.

**4.** Run the tip of a knife around the edge of each tart to loosen the crust. Let stand for 10 minutes. Working with 1 skillet at a time, set a skillet over moderate heat for 10 seconds. Invert a plate over the skillet, then carefully flip both plate and skillet. Tap lightly, then remove the skillet. Cut the tarts into wedges; serve. —*Michael Mina*

## Apricot-Filled Dessert Gnocchi with Cinnamon-Sugar Crumbs

**ACTIVE: 45 MIN; TOTAL: 1 HR 30 MIN**

8 SERVINGS

1 pound baking potatoes, not peeled

1 large egg, lightly beaten

1 teaspoon salt

1 cup plus 2 tablespoons all-purpose flour, plus more for kneading and dusting

1 cup apricot preserves

6 tablespoons unsalted butter

1 cup plain dry bread crumbs

⅓ cup sugar

2 teaspoons cinnamon

**1.** In a medium saucepan, cover the potatoes with cold water and bring to a boil. Reduce the heat to moderate and cook until tender, 45 minutes. Drain, let cool slightly and peel, then pass through a ricer. Transfer to a plate and let cool.

**2.** Transfer the potatoes to a bowl. Make a well in the center. Add the egg and salt to the well, then stir in the potatoes. Add 1 cup of the flour; stir until a stiff dough forms. Transfer to a work surface and quickly knead in the remaining 2 tablespoons of flour until smooth and firm. Add more flour if the dough is not firm or smooth; the less you use, the softer the dough will be.

**3.** Roll the gnocchi dough into a log and cut it into 16 pieces. Flatten 1 piece of the dough into a 3-inch round in your palm. Spoon a scant tablespoon of the preserves into the center of the dough and carefully pinch the seams together, rolling and patting the dough into a ball. Pinch together any tears and transfer the ball to a large plate dusted with flour. Repeat with the remaining dough and preserves.

**4.** In a large nonstick skillet, melt 4 tablespoons of the butter. Add the bread crumbs and cook over moderate heat, stirring, until golden and very crisp, about 7 minutes. Remove from the heat and stir in the sugar and cinnamon. Transfer the crumbs to a pie plate. Wipe out the skillet.

**5.** In a large pot of boiling water, cook half of the gnocchi just until they rise to the surface, stirring once, 5 minutes. Using a slotted spoon, transfer them to a large plate and gently pat dry with paper towels. Repeat with the remaining gnocchi.

**6.** Melt the remaining 2 tablespoons of butter in the skillet. Add the gnocchi and cook over moderately high heat, turning once, until lightly browned. Add the gnocchi to the plate; roll to coat with crumbs. Transfer to plates and serve. —*Lidia Bastianich*

## Roasted Figs with Red Wine–Fig Sauce

**ACTIVE: 15 MIN; TOTAL: 40 MIN**

4 SERVINGS

20 purple figs (about 1½ pounds), stems trimmed

2 tablespoons unsalted butter, melted

¼ cup plus 1 tablespoon sugar

1 cup dry red wine

2 mint sprigs

1 cinnamon stick, broken in half

Ground allspice, for sprinkling

Vanilla ice cream, for serving

**1.** Preheat the oven to 450°. Stand 16 of the figs upright in a shallow baking dish. Using a small knife, make a cross in each one and lightly press to open the incisions slightly. Brush the tops of the figs with the melted butter and sprinkle with 1 tablespoon of the sugar. Bake in the upper third of the oven for about 25 minutes, or until the figs are tender and glazed on top.

**2.** Coarsely chop the remaining 4 figs. Transfer to a mini food processor and puree. In a medium saucepan, combine the red wine with the remaining ¼ cup of sugar, the mint sprigs and cinnamon stick and boil over high heat until reduced by half, about 5 minutes. Discard the mint and cinnamon stick and stir in the fig puree.

**3.** Spoon the sauce onto plates. Set 4 figs on each, sprinkle with allspice, add some ice cream and serve. —*Roland Chanliaud*

Two heavenly desserts: luscious Milk-Jam Éclairs (below; recipe P. 333) from the April issue and low-fat Angel Food Cupcakes with Raspberry Swirl (opposite; recipe P. 331) from January.

# cakes, cookies & more

**BANANA LAYER CAKE WITH MASCARPONE FROSTING**

**LEMON UPSIDE-DOWN CAKE**

## Banana Layer Cake with Mascarpone Frosting

**ACTIVE: 30 MIN; TOTAL: 1 HR 30 MIN**

**8 TO 10 SERVINGS** ● ●

1½ cups all-purpose flour, plus more
  for dusting
¾ teaspoon baking powder
¾ teaspoon baking soda
Scant ½ teaspoon salt
 1 stick (4 ounces) unsalted
  butter, softened
¾ cup granulated sugar
 2 large egg yolks
 1 teaspoon pure vanilla extract
¾ cup mashed ripe bananas, plus
  2 large bananas thinly sliced
¼ cup plus 2 tablespoons buttermilk
 3 large egg whites
1½ cups chilled mascarpone
  (12 ounces; see Note)
1¾ cups confectioners' sugar

**1.** Preheat the oven to 325°. Butter a 9-inch round cake pan and line it with parchment paper; butter the paper. Dust the pan with flour, tapping out any excess. In a medium bowl, whisk the 1½ cups of flour with the baking powder, baking soda and salt.

**2.** In a large bowl, using a handheld electric mixer, beat the butter and granulated sugar at medium-high speed until light and fluffy, about 3 minutes. Beat in the egg yolks and vanilla extract. Add the mashed bananas and beat until smooth. Add half of the dry ingredients and beat at low speed until moistened. Beat in half of the buttermilk, then add the remaining dry ingredients and the remaining buttermilk.

**3.** In a bowl, beat the egg whites at medium-high speed until firm peaks form. Beat one-fourth of the whites into the batter at low speed. Using a rubber spatula, fold in the rest until no streaks remain. Scrape the

batter into the prepared pan and smooth the top. Bake for 40 minutes, until the top is golden and springy and a toothpick inserted in the center comes out clean; the top will be slightly cracked. Cool in the pan for 15 minutes, then invert onto a rack to cool completely. Peel off the paper.

**4.** In a medium bowl, beat the mascarpone with the confectioners' sugar at medium speed until light and fluffy, about 2 minutes. Using a large serrated knife, cut the cake horizontally into 3 layers. Place the top layer, cut side up, on a cake plate and spread with one-third of the frosting. Arrange half of the banana slices in a single layer on the frosting. Top with the middle layer. Cover the cake with another third of the frosting and the remaining bananas. Cover with the bottom cake layer, cut side down, and frost the top. Refrigerate for at least 30 minutes. —*Lauren Dawson*

322

**NOTE** Mascarpone, a superrich, delicate and creamy Italian cheese, is blended here with confectioners' sugar to create a sublime frosting. For the best results, try to buy mascarpone that's very fresh.

**MAKE AHEAD** The baked and cooled cake, tightly wrapped in plastic, can be refrigerated for 3 days or frozen for 1 month.

## Lemon Upside-Down Cake
**ACTIVE: 30 MIN; TOTAL: 1 HR 20 MIN**
**MAKES ONE 9-INCH CAKE** ●

- 1½ sticks (6 ounces) unsalted butter, softened
- ¾ cup plus 2 tablespoons light brown sugar
- 2 thin-skinned lemons, sliced paper-thin crosswise, seeds discarded
- 1½ cups all-purpose flour
- 2 teaspoons baking powder
- ¼ teaspoon salt
- 1 cup granulated sugar
- 1 teaspoon pure vanilla extract
- 2 large eggs, separated
- ¾ cup whole milk
- ¼ teaspoon cream of tartar

Sweetened whipped cream, for serving

1. Preheat the oven to 350°. Set a 9-inch nonstick cake pan over moderate heat and add 4 tablespoons of the butter. When melted, stir in the brown sugar until dissolved, 1 minute. Remove from the heat. Arrange the lemons in the brown sugar.

2. In a medium bowl, whisk the flour with the baking powder and salt. In a large bowl, with an electric mixer, beat the remaining 8 tablespoons of butter with the granulated sugar until light and fluffy. Beat in the vanilla and the egg yolks, 1 at a time. At low speed, beat in the dry ingredients in 3 batches, alternating with the milk.

3. In a stainless steel bowl, beat the egg whites with the cream of tartar at high speed until firm peaks form. Fold one-third of the beaten whites into the batter, then fold in the rest. Scrape the batter into the prepared pan and bake for about

30 minutes, or until a toothpick inserted in the center comes out clean. Let cool in the pan for 15 minutes, then invert onto a plate. Serve warm or at room temperature with whipped cream. —*Cal Peternell*

## Red Velvet Cake with Cream Cheese Ice Cream
**TOTAL: 2 HR PLUS 8 HR CHILLING AND FREEZING**
**12 SERVINGS** ●

Southern red velvet cake is usually a tall layer cake slathered with cream cheese icing and studded with pecans. In this deconstructed version, the cake is low (like a torte), the pecans are coated in caramel and the cream cheese icing is transformed into cream cheese–flavored ice cream.

ICE CREAM
- 2 cups skim milk
- 1 cup heavy cream
- 1 pound cream cheese, cut into cubes, at room temperature
- 6 ounces white chocolate, coarsely chopped
- 12 large egg yolks
- 1 cup granulated sugar

Pinch of salt

CAKE
- 2½ cups all-purpose flour, plus more for the pan
- 1½ cups granulated sugar
- 1 tablespoon cocoa powder
- 1 teaspoon baking soda
- 1 teaspoon salt
- 1½ cups vegetable oil
- 1 cup buttermilk
- 2 large eggs
- 2 tablespoons red food coloring (four ¼-ounce bottles)
- 1 teaspoon distilled white vinegar
- 1 teaspoon pure vanilla extract

Confectioners' sugar, for serving

PECAN PRALINE
- 1 cup granulated sugar
- ¼ cup water
- 1 cup pecan halves, toasted

1. **MAKE THE ICE CREAM:** In a saucepan, warm the milk and cream. In a bowl, combine the cheese and chocolate. In a bowl, whisk the yolks, granulated sugar and salt until thick and pale. Gradually whisk the hot milk and cream into the yolks. Pour the mixture back into the saucepan and cook over moderately low heat, stirring constantly, until it coats the back of a spoon, 6 minutes; do not boil. Strain through a fine sieve over the cheese and chocolate. Let stand for 1 minute; stir until smooth. Refrigerate until chilled, 4 hours.

2. Pour the custard into an ice cream maker and churn. Transfer to an airtight container and freeze until firm, 4 hours.

3. **MAKE THE CAKE:** Preheat the oven to 350°. Butter and flour a 12-inch round cake pan. In a bowl, whisk the 2½ cups of flour with the granulated sugar, cocoa, baking soda and salt. In a medium bowl, whisk the oil with the buttermilk, eggs, food coloring, vinegar and vanilla. Whisk the liquid ingredients into the flour mixture. Pour the batter into the prepared pan and bake for 40 minutes. Transfer the cake to a rack and let it cool completely in the pan, 2 hours.

4. **MAKE THE PECAN PRALINE:** Line a baking sheet with parchment paper. In a heavy, medium saucepan, combine the granulated sugar and water. Cook over moderate heat without stirring until a deep amber caramel forms, 15 minutes. Remove the pan from the heat and stir in the pecans. Pour the praline onto the parchment-lined baking sheet and spread evenly. Let cool until hardened, then chop medium-fine and transfer to a bowl.

5. Line the baking sheet with another sheet of parchment paper. Scoop 12 balls of the cream-cheese ice cream and set them on the baking sheet. Freeze the balls.

6. Slice the cake into 12 wedges and dust with confectioners' sugar. Transfer to plates. Roll the ice cream balls in the pecan praline. Serve with the cake.
—*Allison Vines-Rushing and Slade Rushing*

# cakes, cookies & more

## Warm Pumpkin Cake

**ACTIVE: 20 MIN; TOTAL: 2 HR**

**6 SERVINGS** ●

Tom Fundaro, chef at Villa Creek Restaurant in Paso Robles, California, asked his pastry chef Susan Masch for a pumpkin dessert that "wasn't the ubiquitous crème brûlée." Masch came up with this riff on a traditional English steamed pudding. Warm, soft, spicy and simple, it's one of the best pumpkin desserts you'll ever eat.

1¼   **cups all-purpose flour**

1¼   **teaspoons baking powder**

1⅛   **teaspoons ground cinnamon**

¼   **teaspoon ground ginger**

⅛   **teaspoon ground cloves**

⅛   **teaspoon salt**

6   **tablespoons unsalted butter, softened**

1   **cup sugar**

2   **large eggs**

¾   **cup unsweetened canned pumpkin puree**

1½   **tablespoons fresh lemon juice**

3   **Medjool dates, finely chopped**

**Vanilla ice cream, for serving**

**1.** Butter a 2-quart soufflé mold. In a bowl, whisk the flour, baking powder, cinnamon, ginger, cloves and salt. In a bowl, using a handheld mixer, beat the butter and sugar until fluffy. Beat in the eggs, 1 at a time. In a bowl, mix the pumpkin puree with the lemon juice, then beat into the eggs. Add the dry ingredients and dates and beat slowly until blended. Scrape the batter into the prepared mold; smooth the top.

**2.** Cover the soufflé dish with a sheet of buttered foil, seal and transfer to a large enameled cast-iron casserole. Pour enough hot water into the casserole to reach halfway up the side of the mold; bring to a boil. Cover and simmer over moderately low heat until the cake is set, about 1 hour and 10 minutes. Remove from the casserole and let cool for 30 minutes. Remove the foil and spoon the cake onto plates. Serve with vanilla ice cream. —*Susan Masch*

## Fudgy Chocolate Layer Cake

**ACTIVE: 1 HR; TOTAL: 2 HR PLUS 1 HR COOLING**

**MAKES ONE 8-INCH THREE-LAYER CAKE** ● ●

Andrew Shotts, the owner of Garrison Confections in Providence, applies his talents here to a fudgy chocolate cake, mixing lots of buttermilk and coffee into the batter to create an incredibly moist, rich and fudgy dessert.

**CHOCOLATE CAKE**

1½   **cups sugar**

1¼   **cups all-purpose flour**

¾   **cup unsweetened cocoa powder**

2½   **teaspoons baking powder**

1½   **teaspoons baking soda**

⅛   **teaspoon salt**

1   **cup buttermilk**

3   **large eggs**

2½   **teaspoons pure vanilla extract**

6   **tablespoons unsalted butter, softened**

1   **cup hot coffee**

**FILLING AND FROSTING**

1¼   **pounds bittersweet chocolate, finely chopped**

1   **cup heavy cream**

2   **tablespoons light corn syrup**

5   **tablespoons unsalted butter, softened**

1   **tablespoon sugar**

1   **tablespoon water**

**1. MAKE THE CHOCOLATE CAKE:** Preheat the oven to 325°. Line the bottoms of three 8-inch round cake pans with rounds of parchment paper. Spray the cake pans and the parchment paper with vegetable oil cooking spray.

**2.** In a large bowl, whisk the sugar with the flour, cocoa powder, baking powder, baking soda and salt. In a small bowl, whisk the buttermilk with the eggs and the vanilla extract. In another small bowl, melt the butter in the hot coffee over moderate heat. Using an electric mixer, beat half of the buttermilk and egg mixture into the dry ingredients at low speed. Beat half of the coffee mixture into the batter, then scrape down the bowl. Beat the remaining buttermilk and coffee mixtures into the batter until they are incorporated.

**3.** Pour the batter into the prepared pans, dividing it evenly, and bake for 25 to 30 minutes, rotating the pans halfway through baking, until the cakes are springy to the touch. Let the cakes cool in the pans for 10 minutes, then turn them out onto a rack to cool completely. Peel the parchment paper off the bottom of the cakes.

**4. MEANWHILE, MAKE THE FILLING AND FROSTING:** Put the finely chopped bittersweet chocolate in a large heatproof bowl. In a small saucepan, bring the heavy cream and the light corn syrup to a boil. Immediately pour the hot cream and corn syrup over the chocolate and let the mixture stand in a warm place for 5 minutes. Gently whisk the chocolate ganache until it is smooth. Whisk the butter into the chocolate ganache until it is incorporated. Refrigerate the ganache, stirring frequently, until the mixture is thick enough to spread, about 30 minutes.

**5.** In a microwavable bowl, combine the sugar with the water and heat for 30 seconds. Stir to dissolve the sugar. Set a cake layer on a cake plate or cake cardboard and brush lightly with the sugar syrup. Spread about ¾ cup of the chocolate ganache onto the cake in an even ¼-inch layer. Repeat with the remaining cake layers, sugar syrup and chocolate frosting. Spread the remaining frosting around the side of the cake. Let the chocolate cake stand at room temperature for at least 1 hour before slicing. —*Andrew Shotts*

**MAKE AHEAD** The finished chocolate cake will stay fresh in the refrigerator for up to 3 days. Bring the cake to room temperature before slicing.

FUDGY CHOCOLATE
LAYER CAKE

CHOCOLATE AND PISTACHIO BISCOTTI

QUADRUPLE CHOCOLATE BROWNIE

## Chocolate and Pistachio Biscotti

**ACTIVE: 45 MIN; TOTAL: 2 HR**
**MAKES ABOUT 6½ DOZEN**
**BISCOTTI** ● ●

Michelle Myers, pastry chef at Sona restaurant and Boule *pâtisserie* in Los Angeles, makes a traditional but visually surprising cookie—the crispiest, crunchiest, most chocolaty biscotti, studded with bright green pistachios.

- 2 **cups all-purpose flour**
- ¾ **cup unsweetened cocoa powder, preferably Dutch-process**
- ½ **teaspoon baking soda**

Pinch of salt

- 3 **large eggs**
- 1¼ **cups light brown sugar**
- 4 **tablespoons unsalted butter, softened**
- 1 **tablespoon pure vanilla extract**
- 1 **teaspoon pure coffee extract**
- 1 **teaspoon pure almond extract**
- 7½ **ounces bittersweet chocolate, chopped, or 1½ cups bittersweet chocolate chips**
- 1 **cup unsalted, shelled pistachios (6 ounces)**

**1.** Preheat the oven to 350°. Line 2 baking sheets with parchment paper. In a large bowl, whisk the flour with the cocoa powder, baking soda and salt. Using an electric mixer, beat in the eggs at low speed until a crumbly dough forms.

**2.** In another bowl, beat the light brown sugar with the butter and the vanilla, coffee and almond extracts until combined. Scrape the mixture into the crumbly dough and beat at medium speed until a soft, sticky dough forms. Add the chopped bittersweet chocolate and shelled pistachios and beat at low speed just until they are evenly distributed.

**3.** Divide the dough into 4 clumps and transfer 2 of the clumps to each baking sheet. Form each clump into an 8-inch-long rope; pat the ropes until they are logs about 2 inches wide and ¾ inch thick. Bake the logs for about 22 minutes, until they are puffed and springy to the touch; rotate the pans halfway through baking. Carefully transfer the logs to a wire rack to cool for 10 minutes. Lower the oven temperature to 200°.

**4.** Using a sharp knife, cut the logs crosswise into scant ½-inch-thick slices; each log will yield about 20 biscotti. Return the slices to the baking sheets and bake them for about 30 minutes longer, flipping the biscotti once after 15 minutes, until they are crisp. Transfer the biscotti to racks to cool. —*Michelle Myers*

**MAKE AHEAD** The biscotti can be stored in an airtight container for up to 1 week.

## Quadruple Chocolate Brownies

**ACTIVE: 30 MIN; TOTAL: 1 HR PLUS
1 HR COOLING**

**MAKES 4 DOZEN BROWNIES ● ◉**

By swirling chunks of white, milk and bittersweet chocolate into a batter made with unsweetened chocolate, then melting and drizzling more all over the top, San Francisco chocolatier Michael Recchiuti has created a sweet with all the chocolates he likes in one brownie.

- 5 sticks (1¼ pounds) unsalted butter, softened
- 1 pound unsweetened chocolate, chopped
- 5½ cups sugar
- 16 large eggs
- 2 tablespoons pure vanilla extract
- 1½ teaspoons kosher salt
- 3¾ cups all-purpose flour
- ½ pound bittersweet chocolate, chopped into ½-inch pieces
- ½ pound white chocolate, chopped into ½-inch pieces
- ½ pound milk chocolate, chopped into ½-inch pieces

**1.** Preheat the oven to 300°. Line the bottoms of two 9-by-13-inch baking pans with parchment paper. In a large saucepan, heat the butter with the unsweetened chocolate over low heat, stirring frequently, until melted. In a large bowl, whisk the sugar with the eggs, vanilla and salt. Add the melted chocolate and whisk until smooth. Add the flour and whisk until incorporated. Stir in 5 ounces of each of the chopped chocolates. Spread the batter in the prepared pans.

**2.** Place the remaining chopped chocolates separately in 3 small microwavable bowls and melt. Using a spoon, drizzle the melted chocolates over the batter. Using a table knife, make swirls in the batter for a marbled effect. Bake the brownies for about 35 minutes, rotating the pans halfway through, until the tops are shiny and the brownies are set.

**3.** Transfer the brownies to a wire rack to cool completely before cutting into squares. —*Michael Recchiuti*

**MAKE AHEAD** The brownies can be refrigerated for up to 1 week.

## Double-Chocolate Biscotti

**ACTIVE: 25 MIN; TOTAL: 1 HR 20 MIN**

**MAKES ABOUT 32 BISCOTTI ●**

These aren't your typical dry biscotti—they're tender and flecked with chocolate-covered espresso beans.

- 2 cups all-purpose flour
- ½ cup cocoa powder
- 1½ teaspoons baking powder
- ½ teaspoon baking soda
- ½ teaspoon salt
- 1 stick (4 ounces) unsalted butter, at room temperature
- 1 cup sugar
- 2 large eggs
- ½ cup semisweet chocolate chips
- ½ cup chocolate-covered espresso beans
- 1 large egg white, lightly beaten

**1.** Preheat the oven to 325°. In a medium bowl, sift together the flour, cocoa, baking powder, baking soda and salt. In a large bowl, using an electric mixer, cream the butter with the sugar. Beat in the eggs, 1 at a time. At low speed, gradually beat in the flour mixture. Fold in the chocolate chips and chocolate-covered espresso beans.

**2.** Divide the dough in half and form each half into a 2-inch-wide log. Transfer the logs to a large baking sheet and brush with the egg white. Bake for 30 minutes, then let cool on the baking sheet for 10 minutes.

**3.** Increase the oven temperature to 350°. Using 2 large metal spatulas, transfer the logs to a work surface. Cut crosswise into ½-inch slices. Arrange the slices on 2 large baking sheets, cut side down, and bake for 15 minutes longer, until slightly dry. Let cool on the baking sheets. —*Carrie Dove*

**MAKE AHEAD** The biscotti can be stored in an airtight container for up to 1 week.

## Temptation Island Cookies

**TOTAL: 1 HR**

**MAKES ABOUT 28 COOKIES ● ◉**

- 3 cups all-purpose flour
- 2½ teaspoons baking powder
- 2 teaspoons baking soda
- ½ teaspoon salt
- 2 sticks (½ pound) unsalted butter, softened
- 2 cups light brown sugar
- ¼ cup granulated sugar
- 2 large eggs
- 2 teaspoons pure vanilla extract
- 1⅓ cups sweetened shredded coconut
- ¾ cup milk chocolate chips
- ¾ cup golden raisins
- ¾ cup macadamia nuts, chopped

**1.** Preheat the oven to 350° and position 2 racks in the lower third. In a medium bowl, whisk together the flour, baking powder, baking soda and salt. In a large bowl, using an electric mixer, beat the butter, light brown sugar and granulated sugar until the mixture is fluffy. Beat the eggs and vanilla at medium speed into the butter and sugar mixture until they are combined. Add the dry ingredients to the dough and beat at low speed until they are barely combined. Add the coconut, chocolate chips, raisins and macadamia nuts to the dough and beat until they are evenly distributed.

**2.** For each cookie, use an ice cream scoop or a large spoon to scoop 3 tablespoons of the dough onto parchment-lined or non-stick baking sheets; space them 2 inches apart. Bake the cookies for 15 minutes, until lightly browned and crisp around the edges but a little soft in the centers; shift the pans from top to bottom and front to back for even baking. Let the cookies cool for 10 minutes on the baking sheets, then transfer them to a wire rack to cool completely. —*Melissa McKinney*

**MAKE AHEAD** The cookies can be stored in an airtight container for up to 1 week.

# cakes, cookies & more

## Toasted Bread and Bittersweet Chocolate

**TOTAL: 10 MIN**

4 SERVINGS ●

Nothing could be easier than slapping a piece of chocolate on a slice of bread: Spanish children do it all the time as an after-school snack. But by sprinkling the melted chocolate with sea salt and extra-virgin olive oil, Catalan chef Ferran Adrià turns kids' food into something parents will want to try.

16   thin baguette slices

One 4-ounce bar of bittersweet chocolate, cut into 16 pieces

1   tablespoon extra-virgin olive oil

Coarse sea salt, for sprinkling

Preheat the broiler. Position a rack 8 inches from the heat. Spread the bread on a baking sheet and broil until toasted, 30 seconds. Turn the slices over and set a square of chocolate on each one. Broil until the bread is golden and the chocolate begins to melt (30 seconds). Transfer the toasts to plates and drizzle with the olive oil. Lightly sprinkle sea salt on the chocolate and serve right away. —*Ferran Adrià*

## Nut–Chocolate Chunk Cookies

**TOTAL: 50 MIN**

MAKES ABOUT 20 COOKIES ●

The secret to these perfectly chewy cookies is chilling the dough for 20 minutes. This firms the dough, which makes it easier to scoop out and less likely to spread during baking.

1   cup all-purpose flour

½   teaspoon baking soda

¼   teaspoon salt

6   tablespoons unsalted butter, softened

¾   cup light brown sugar

1   large egg

1   teaspoon pure vanilla extract

½   cup chunky unsweetened hazelnut or almond butter

1   cup semisweet chocolate chips

1. Preheat the oven to 350°. In a medium bowl, whisk the flour, baking soda and salt. In a large bowl, cream the butter and sugar. Beat in the egg and vanilla, followed by the hazelnut butter. Beat in the dry ingredients, then fold in the chocolate chips. Refrigerate the dough for 20 minutes.

2. Scoop rounded tablespoons of the dough onto 2 ungreased cookie sheets. Bake the cookies in the lower and upper thirds of the oven for 18 to 20 minutes, or until golden; for even baking, shift the sheets from top to bottom and front to back halfway through. Let cool for 5 minutes, then transfer to racks to cool completely. —*Grace Parisi*

**MAKE AHEAD** The cookies can be stored in an airtight container for up to 4 days.

## Chocolate–Brown Sugar Brownies

**TOTAL: 40 MIN PLUS 1 HR COOLING**

MAKES 2 DOZEN BROWNIES ●

2   sticks (½ pound) unsalted butter

4   ounces unsweetened chocolate, coarsely chopped

4   large eggs

1   cup granulated sugar

1   cup packed light brown sugar

1   teaspoon pure vanilla extract

¾   cup all-purpose flour, plus more for the pan

1   cup pecans, coarsely chopped

1. Preheat the oven to 350°. Butter and lightly flour a 9-by-13-inch baking dish. In the top of a double boiler, melt the butter with the chocolate; let cool.

2. In a bowl, beat the eggs with the granulated and brown sugars until thickened; beat in the vanilla. Using a rubber spatula, gently fold in the chocolate mixture until combined. Sift the ¾ cup of flour over the batter and fold it in. Fold in the pecans.

3. Pour the batter into the prepared pan and bake for about 25 minutes, or until a tester inserted in the center comes out with moist crumbs attached. Let the brownies cool in the pan for 1 hour before cutting into squares. —*Marcia Kiesel*

## Peanut Butter– Chocolate Chunk Cookies

**TOTAL: 1 HR**

MAKES ABOUT 28 COOKIES ●

2⅓   cups all-purpose flour

1½   teaspoons baking soda

1   teaspoon baking powder

1   teaspoon salt

2   sticks (½ pound) unsalted butter, softened

1   cup light brown sugar

1   cup granulated sugar

2   large eggs

1   teaspoon pure vanilla extract

1⅓   cups creamy peanut butter

½   pound bittersweet chocolate, cut into ½-inch chunks (1½ cups)

½   cup salted peanuts

1. Preheat the oven to 350° and position 2 racks in the lower third. In a medium bowl, whisk together the flour, baking soda, baking powder and salt. In a large bowl, using an electric mixer, beat the butter with the brown sugar and granulated sugar until fluffy. Add the eggs and vanilla and beat at low speed until the ingredients are blended. Add the peanut butter and beat until combined. Beat in the dry ingredients just until incorporated. Beat in the chocolate chunks and peanuts.

2. For each cookie, use an ice cream scoop or a large spoon to scoop 3 tablespoons of the dough onto parchment-lined or non-stick baking sheets. Space the cookies 2 inches apart. Bake for about 13 minutes for slightly chewy cookies and about 15 minutes for crisp cookies; about halfway through, shift the baking sheets from top to bottom and front to back for even baking. Let the cookies cool for 10 minutes on the baking sheets, then transfer them to a wire rack to cool completely. —*Melissa McKinney*

**MAKE AHEAD** The peanut butter and chocolate chunk cookies can be stored in an airtight container for up to 1 week.

## Mel's Best Brownies

**TOTAL: 2 HR 30 MIN**
**MAKES 16 BROWNIES ●**
BROWNIES

- 1 stick (4 ounces) unsalted butter
- 4 ounces unsweetened chocolate, coarsely chopped
- 1¼ cups sugar
- 2 teaspoons pure vanilla extract
- ¼ teaspoon salt
- 2 large eggs
- 1 cup all-purpose flour
- ¼ cup unsweetened cocoa powder

GLAZE

- 4 ounces bittersweet chocolate, coarsely chopped
- 5 tablespoons unsalted butter
- 1 tablespoon light corn syrup

Pinch of salt

**1. MAKE THE BROWNIES:** Preheat the oven to 350° and butter an 8-inch square baking pan. In a medium saucepan, combine the butter and unsweetened chocolate and cook over low heat, stirring frequently, until the chocolate is melted. Transfer the chocolate to a medium bowl and let cool for 5 minutes. Using a whisk, beat in the sugar, vanilla and salt. Add the eggs and whisk until the brownie batter is smooth. Add the flour and cocoa and continue whisking until smooth.

**2.** Scrape the batter into the prepared pan and bake for about 22 minutes, or until a toothpick inserted in the center comes out with a few moist crumbs attached. Transfer the brownies in their pan to a wire rack and let cool completely.

**3. MAKE THE GLAZE:** In a small saucepan, combine the bittersweet chocolate, butter, corn syrup and salt and cook over low heat, stirring frequently, just until the chocolate is melted. Pour the warm glaze over the brownies and let cool at room temperature for 30 minutes, or until the glaze is set.

Refrigerate the brownies until the glaze is firm, about 30 minutes.

**4.** Run a knife around the edge of the pan and carefully transfer the entire layer of brownies to a cutting board. Cut the brownies into 16 squares and serve at once. —*Melissa McKinney*

**MAKE AHEAD** The brownies can be stored in an airtight container for up to 1 week.

## Butternut Squash and Chocolate Brownies

**ACTIVE: 25 MIN; TOTAL: 2 HR PLUS 1 HR COOLING**
**MAKES 12 LARGE BROWNIES ●**
This recipe is by Michelle Lyon, the pastry chef at the Carneros Inn in Napa Valley, California. Mixing butternut squash puree into the batter gives these brownies a subtle earthy flavor and supermoist texture. They are great on their own and even better in an ice cream sundae.

- ½ medium butternut squash (1½ pounds)—peeled, seeded and cut into 4 pieces
- 5 ounces unsweetened chocolate
- 1 stick plus 3 tablespoons unsalted butter, cut into tablespoons
- 4 large eggs
- 2 cups sugar
- 1½ teaspoons pure vanilla extract
- ½ teaspoon kosher salt
- 1¼ cups plus 2 tablespoons all-purpose flour
- ¾ teaspoon baking powder

**1.** Preheat the oven to 375°. Pour ½ inch of water into an 8-inch square baking pan. Add the squash, cover with foil and roast for 1 hour, or until tender. Reduce the oven temperature to 350°. Drain the squash and puree it in a food processor; you should have 1½ cups.

**2.** Lightly butter a 9-by-13-inch metal baking pan and line the bottom with parchment paper; butter the paper. Bring 1 inch of water to a gentle simmer in a small

saucepan. Set a medium heatproof bowl over the saucepan and add the chocolate and butter. Let the chocolate melt, stirring frequently. Set the chocolate aside and let it cool slightly.

**3.** In a large bowl, beat the eggs, sugar, vanilla and salt at medium speed until pale and thick, about 2 minutes. Beat in the melted chocolate and the squash. At low speed, beat in the flour and baking powder. Pour the batter into the prepared baking pan and bake for 25 minutes, or until a cake tester inserted in the center comes out clean. Transfer the pan to a wire rack and let cool completely before cutting into brownies. —*Michelle Lyon*

**MAKE AHEAD** The squash and chocolate brownies can be stored in an airtight container for up to 3 days.

## ingredient
### MOOD-ENHANCING BARS

Origins and chocolate master Jacques Torres have teamed up to create **Sensory Therapy chocolate bars,** infused with essential oils to help you relax or rev up. Origins **Cocoa Therapy body products** are infused with cocoa butter too. **DETAILS** $5 at Origins stores.

# cakes, cookies & more

## Butter Cookie and Cream Stacks with Raspberries

**ACTIVE: 30 MIN; TOTAL: 1 HR PLUS 1 HR 30 MIN CHILLING**

**MAKES 4 LARGE COOKIES**

The layers of homemade butter cookies with crème fraîche and raspberries make crumbly, sweet and tangy stacks.

- ¼ cup sliced almonds
- 1¾ cups all-purpose flour, plus more for dusting
- 1¼ cups confectioners' sugar, sifted, plus more for dusting
- Pinch of salt
- 1 stick plus 2 tablespoons cold unsalted butter, cut into small pieces
- 1 large egg, beaten
- ⅛ teaspoon pure vanilla extract
- ½ cup crème fraîche
- 1½ teaspoons granulated sugar
- 1¼ cups raspberries
- 4 mint sprigs

**1.** Preheat the oven to 350°. In a food processor, finely chop the almonds. Add the 1¾ cups of flour, 1¼ cups of confectioners' sugar and the salt and process to blend. Add the butter, egg and vanilla and pulse until a soft dough forms. Transfer the dough to a work surface and knead it very gently until smooth. Press the dough into a disk, wrap it in plastic and refrigerate until thoroughly chilled, about 1½ hours.

**2.** Line a large rimmed baking sheet with parchment paper. On a lightly floured work surface, roll the dough into a round about ¼ inch thick. Using a 2½-inch round biscuit cutter, stamp out 12 rounds and transfer them to the prepared baking sheet. Bake for about 14 minutes, or until the cookies are firm but pale. Transfer to a rack and let cool on the sheet.

**3.** In a small bowl, mix the crème fraîche with the granulated sugar. To assemble the stacks, center 1 cookie on a plate and spread it with 1 tablespoon of the crème fraîche. Arrange 5 raspberries in a circle on the cookie. Set another cookie on top and repeat with another tablespoon of crème fraîche and 5 raspberries. Top with a third cookie and a raspberry. Dust with confectioners' sugar and garnish with a mint sprig. Repeat with the remaining cookies, crème fraîche, raspberries and mint sprigs and serve. —*Jane Martin*

**SERVE WITH** Raspberry sauce.

**MAKE AHEAD** The cookie dough can be refrigerated overnight or frozen for up to 1 month.

## Dark-Chocolate Bark with Walnuts and Dried Cherries

**TOTAL: 30 MIN**

**MAKES 4 DOZEN PIECES** ● ● ●

- 1½ cups walnut halves (6 ounces)
- 9 ounces bittersweet chocolate, finely chopped
- 1 cup dried sour cherries (4 ounces), coarsely chopped
- 2 tablespoons finely chopped crystallized ginger

**1.** Preheat the oven to 350°. Spread the walnuts on a baking sheet and toast for 8 minutes, or until golden and fragrant. Let cool, then coarsely chop.

**2.** Line a baking sheet with parchment or wax paper. In a glass bowl, heat two-thirds of the chocolate in a microwave oven at high power in 30-second bursts until just melted. Stir until smooth. Add the remaining chocolate and stir until melted. Stir in the walnuts, cherries and crystallized ginger until evenly coated. Scrape the mixture onto the prepared baking sheet and spread it into a 12-by-8-inch rectangle. Refrigerate for 10 minutes, or until firm enough to cut.

**3.** Cut the bark into 48 pieces (6 rows by 8 rows) and transfer to a plate. Serve cold or at room temperature. —*Grace Parisi*

**MAKE AHEAD** The bark can be kept in an airtight container at room temperature for up to 4 days or refrigerated for up to 2 weeks.

## Cranberry-Oatmeal Cookies with White-Chocolate Chips

**TOTAL: 1 HR**

**MAKES ABOUT 28 COOKIES** ●

- 2 sticks (½ pound) unsalted butter, softened
- 1½ cups light brown sugar
- 1 teaspoon baking soda
- ¼ cup warm water
- 2 large eggs
- 1 teaspoon pure vanilla extract
- Finely grated zest of 1 orange
- 1 cup plus 2 tablespoons all-purpose flour
- 1 teaspoon salt
- 3 cups old-fashioned rolled oats
- 1½ cups dried cranberries
- 1½ cups white-chocolate chips

**1.** Preheat the oven to 350° and position 2 racks in the lower third. In a large bowl, using an electric mixer, beat the butter and brown sugar until they are fluffy. In a small bowl, dissolve the baking soda in the warm water, then beat the baking soda and water into the butter and sugar mixture. Add the eggs, vanilla and orange zest to the batter and beat at low speed until they are combined. Beat the flour and salt into the dough until it is barely combined, then mix the oats, cranberries and chips into the cookie dough.

**2.** For each cookie, use an ice cream scoop or a large spoon to scoop 3 tablespoons of the dough onto parchment-lined or non-stick baking sheets; space them 2 inches apart. Bake the cookies for about 13 minutes, until lightly browned and crisp around the edges but a little soft in the centers; halfway through baking, shift the pans from top to bottom and front to back for even cooking. Let the cookies cool for 10 minutes on the baking sheets, then transfer them to a wire rack to cool completely. —*Melissa McKinney*

**MAKE AHEAD** The cranberry-oatmeal cookies can be stored in an airtight container for up to 1 week.

## Hazelnut Baklava

**ACTIVE: 1 HR; TOTAL: 2 HR 30 MIN**
**PLUS 1 HR COOLING**

**12 TO 14 SERVINGS** ●

Although baklava specialists spend years perfecting their dough-rolling technique, this incredible homemade version is easy to make with ready-made phyllo dough from the supermarket.

- **1 pound shelled hazelnuts**
- **2 cups sugar**
- **1 pound phyllo dough**
- **2 sticks (½ pound) unsalted butter, melted**
- **1½ cups water**
- **1 teaspoon fresh lemon juice**

**1.** Preheat the oven to 350°. Butter a 9-by-13-inch baking dish. Spread the hazelnuts on a rimmed baking sheet and bake until the nuts are fragrant and the skins blister, about 12 minutes. Transfer the hazelnuts to a clean kitchen towel to cool completely. Rub the nuts together in the towel to loosen the skins; don't worry if some aren't totally peeled. Transfer the peeled hazelnuts to a food processor, add ¼ cup of the sugar and pulse until finely chopped.

**2.** Set the phyllo dough on a work surface and cut the stack in half; you should have 2 stacks of 8-by-12-inch rectangles. Cover 1 stack of phyllo sheets with a lightly damp paper towel and plastic wrap. Layer the other stack of phyllo in the prepared baking dish, lightly brushing each sheet with melted butter. Spread the finely chopped hazelnuts over the top layer of phyllo in an even layer. Cover with the remaining phyllo, lightly brushing each sheet with melted butter and saving the nicest 2 or 3 sheets for the top layer. Brush the top of the baklava evenly with butter and press lightly to compact it.

**3.** Using a ruler and a sharp paring knife, cut the baklava lengthwise into 2-inch strips, then cut the strips on the diagonal to form diamonds.

**4.** Bake the baklava until golden, about 25 minutes. Turn the oven down to 300° and continue baking until the baklava is browned, about 30 minutes longer. Transfer the baking dish to a rack. Run the knife through the cuts to make sure the diamonds are separated.

**5.** In a small saucepan, combine the remaining 1¾ cups of sugar with the water and bring to a boil. Simmer for 5 minutes, stirring to dissolve the sugar. Stir the lemon juice into the syrup. Pour the hot syrup evenly over the baklava and let cool for at least 1 hour before serving.
—*Eveline Zoutendijk*

**MAKE AHEAD** The baklava can be covered with foil and kept at room temperature for up to 2 days.

## Angel Food Cupcakes with Raspberry Swirl

**ACTIVE: 30 MIN; TOTAL: 1 HR 30 MIN**
**MAKES 18 CUPCAKES** ● ●

These sweet little angel food cupcakes have a delicious jam filling made with lots of fresh raspberries.

FILLING

- **3 cups raspberries (¾ pound)**
- **¼ cup plus 2 tablespoons granulated sugar**
- **4 teaspoons cornstarch dissolved in 4 teaspoons water**

CUPCAKES

- **1 cup cake flour**
- **½ cup confectioners' sugar**
- **10 large egg whites (1¼ cups), at room temperature**
- **½ teaspoon salt**
- **1 plump vanilla bean, split lengthwise, seeds scraped**
- **1 teaspoon cream of tartar**
- **¾ cup granulated sugar**

GLAZE

- **1½ cups confectioners' sugar**
- **1½ tablespoons butter, melted**
- **1½ tablespoons water**
- **Pinch of salt**

**1.** MAKE THE FILLING: In a medium saucepan, combine 2½ cups of the raspberries with the granulated sugar and cook over moderately high heat, crushing the berries, until very soft and broken down, about 5 minutes. Strain the raspberry puree into a bowl and discard the seeds. Return the puree to the saucepan. Add the remaining ½ cup of raspberries and the dissolved cornstarch and bring to a boil. Cook, gently crushing the berries, until the raspberry filling is glossy and thickened, about 3 minutes. Let cool, then refrigerate until firm, about 1 hour.

**2.** MEANWHILE, MAKE THE CUPCAKES: Preheat the oven to 325°. Set 18 foil muffin cups on a rimmed baking sheet. In a small bowl, combine the cake flour with the confectioners' sugar. In a large bowl, combine the egg whites with the salt, vanilla seeds and cream of tartar and beat until soft peaks form. Using an electric mixture, gradually beat in the granulated sugar, 1 tablespoon at a time, until the whites are firm and glossy. Sift the flour mixture over the egg whites in 2 additions, folding gently until incorporated.

**3.** Spoon the batter into the muffin cups. Bake for 13 to 15 minutes, shifting the pan from front to back, until the cupcakes are springy and golden. Transfer the cupcakes to a rack to cool.

**4.** Using a wooden skewer, poke a ¼-inch-wide hole in the top of each of the cupcakes. Using a pastry bag fitted with a plain ¼-inch tip, pipe about 1 tablespoon of the filling into each cupcake.

**5.** MAKE THE GLAZE: In a small bowl, stir together all of the ingredients. Spoon a small bit of the glaze over the raspberry hole and let set, about 5 minutes. Drizzle and spread the remaining glaze over the cupcakes and let set, about 10 minutes. Transfer the cupcakes to a platter and serve. —*Grace Parisi*

**MAKE AHEAD** The cupcakes can be stored in an airtight container for up to 2 days.

**RASPBERRY SHORTBREAD BARS**

**DOUGHNUTS IN CARDAMOM SYRUP**

### Raspberry Shortbread Bars

**ACTIVE: 25 MIN; TOTAL: 1 HR 30 MIN PLUS CHILLING**

**MAKES 2 DOZEN BARS** ● ◐

Instead of using a rolling pin to make the flaky pastry for her delicate shortbread bars, Melissa McKinney of Criollo, a bakery in Portland, Oregon, relies on a grater. She chills the dough, grates it into a baking dish, then tops it lightly with raspberry preserves and more grated dough before baking it.

- 2 cups all-purpose flour
- 1 teaspoon baking powder
- ¼ teaspoon salt
- 2 sticks (½ pound) unsalted butter, softened
- 1 cup sugar
- 2 large egg yolks
- ½ teaspoon pure vanilla extract
- ¾ cup seedless raspberry preserves or jam (8 ounces)

Confectioners' sugar, for dusting (optional)

**1.** In a bowl, whisk together the flour, baking powder and salt. In another medium bowl, using an electric mixer, beat the butter and sugar at low speed until combined. Beat in the egg yolks and vanilla. Add the dry ingredients and beat at low speed until a soft dough forms. Halve the dough and form into logs; wrap in plastic and refrigerate until firm, at least 1 hour.

**2.** Preheat the oven to 350° and butter an 8½-by-11-inch glass baking dish. Working over the baking dish, coarsely shred 1 log of dough on the large holes of a box grater, evenly distributing the dough in the baking dish. Do not pat or press the dough. Using a spoon, dollop the preserves over the dough and gently spread in an even layer. Grate the second log of dough on top. Using a rubber spatula, tuck in any shreds of dough sticking to the sides of the baking dish to prevent them from burning.

**3.** Bake the shortbread on the bottom rack of the oven for about 35 minutes, covering it with foil halfway through baking.

The shortbread is done when the pastry is golden all over. Let cool completely, then cut into 24 bars. Dust the tops with confectioners' sugar and serve.
—*Melissa McKinney*

## Doughnuts in Cardamom Syrup

**ACTIVE: 1 HR; TOTAL: 3 HR**
**MAKES ABOUT 40 DOUGHNUTS**
These fried doughnuts dripping with syrup are a nod to Sephardic Jewish tradition.

1¾ cups warm water, plus 1 cup water
2 envelopes active dry yeast
3¾ cups all-purpose flour, sifted, plus more for dusting
2 cups plus 2 tablespoons sugar
¾ teaspoon salt
1 cup sliced almonds
2 tablespoons fresh lemon juice
2 teaspoons ground cardamom
1 teaspoon rose water
Vegetable oil, for frying

**1.** In a large bowl, combine the 1¾ cups of warm water with the yeast and let stand for 5 minutes. Using a wooden spoon, stir in the 3¾ cups of flour, 2 tablespoons of the sugar and the salt. Turn the dough out onto a lightly floured work surface. Knead lightly until the dough is silky. Oil a medium bowl and add the dough. Cover with plastic wrap and let rise until doubled in bulk, about 1½ hours. Punch down the dough, then let it rise again for another 30 minutes.

**2.** Meanwhile, preheat the oven to 350°. Spread the almonds in a pie plate and bake for 10 minutes. In a medium saucepan, combine the remaining 2 cups of sugar and 1 cup of water with the lemon juice and cardamom and simmer over moderate heat until reduced by half; strain. Let the syrup cool slightly, then stir in the rose water.

**3.** In a large saucepan, heat the vegetable oil to 325°. Meanwhile, divide the dough into quarters. Cut each quarter into 10 pieces. Using wet hands, shape into balls and poke a hole in the center of each.

Carefully add the doughnuts to the hot oil in batches and fry until browned, about 1 minute per side. Drain on paper towels.
**4.** Dip one side of each doughnut in the syrup and sprinkle with the almonds; serve. —*Rachel Klein*
**MAKE AHEAD** The recipe can be made through Step 1 and refrigerated overnight. Bring to room temperature before proceeding.

## Milk-Jam Éclairs

**TOTAL: 2 HR PLUS COOLING**
**MAKES 16 ÉCLAIRS** ● ●
French milk jam is cheap and easy to make—simply cook down whole milk with sugar and vanilla until it forms a caramel-like sauce.

2 quarts whole milk
2 cups sugar
1 plump vanilla bean, split lengthwise, seeds scraped
1 cup water
1 stick (4 ounces) unsalted butter
½ teaspoon salt
1 cup all-purpose flour
4 large eggs
1½ cups heavy cream, chilled

**1.** In a large saucepan, combine the milk, sugar and the vanilla bean and seeds and bring to a boil. Simmer over moderate heat for about 1 hour and 40 minutes, stirring frequently, until the milk jam is golden and the consistency of sour cream; the milk jam may break and separate. Discard the vanilla bean. Transfer the milk jam to a blender or food processor and process until smooth and creamy, about 1 minute. Transfer the milk jam to a heatproof container and refrigerate.
**2.** Meanwhile, preheat the oven to 400°. Line 2 large baking sheets with parchment paper. Position racks in the middle and lower third of the oven. In a medium saucepan, bring the water to a boil. Add the butter and salt and cook over moderate heat just until the butter is melted. Add

the flour all at once and stir vigorously with a wooden spoon until the dough comes together in a cohesive mass, 1 to 2 minutes. Remove from the heat and let stand for 2 minutes. Using a handheld electric mixer, beat the dough at medium speed for 1 minute. Beat in the eggs, 1 at a time, until a sticky dough forms.
**3.** Transfer the dough to a large pastry bag fitted with a 1-inch plain tip. On each baking sheet, pipe out eight 6-by-1-inch ropes. Using a moistened finger tip, smooth out any points or spikes of dough. Bake the éclairs for 25 minutes, until lightly golden and risen, shifting the pans from top to bottom and front to back halfway through.
**4.** Reduce the oven temperature to 250° and bake for 20 minutes longer, until the éclairs are crisp and golden. Carefully poke both ends of each éclair with a skewer to allow steam to escape. Turn the oven off and let the éclairs sit with the door slightly ajar for 30 minutes, until the insides are somewhat dry. Remove from the oven and let cool completely.
**5.** In a large bowl, using an electric mixer, beat the heavy cream at high speed until firm. Transfer ¾ cup of the milk jam to a medium bowl and beat in one-fourth of the whipped cream. Fold the milk-jam mixture into the remaining whipped cream until no streaks remain. Fill a pastry bag fitted with a ¼-inch plain tip with half of the milk-jam cream. Squeeze the cream into both ends of each éclair to fill. Alternatively, split each éclair horizontally, spoon the filling in and replace the tops. Transfer the filled éclairs to a platter.
**6.** Spoon about ½ cup of the milk jam into a microwavable bowl and heat until spreadable, about 20 seconds. Spread about 1½ teaspoons of the milk jam on top of each éclair and serve. —*Grace Parisi*
**MAKE AHEAD** The éclairs can be refrigerated overnight. The remaining milk jam can be refrigerated in an airtight jar for up to 2 months.

# cakes, cookies & more

## Italian Almond Tart with Champagne Sabayon and Roasted Red Grapes

**ACTIVE: 20 MIN; TOTAL: 1 HR PLUS COOLING**

12 SERVINGS ●

This rustic dessert is from the Lombardy region of Northern Italy, where it's called *shrisolona*. Chef Suzanne Goin of Lucques in Los Angeles thinks of it as a cross between biscotti and shortbread. She recommends dipping chunks of the tart into Champagne-spiked sabayon, an airy sauce made with whipped egg yolks.

- ¾ cup natural almonds (4 ounces)
- 1 large egg yolk
- 1 tablespoon finely grated orange zest
- ¼ teaspoon pure almond extract
- ¼ teaspoon pure vanilla extract
- 1 cup plus 2 tablespoons all-purpose flour
- 6 tablespoons fine cornmeal
- ½ teaspoon kosher salt
- 7 tablespoons cold unsalted butter, cut into ½-inch pieces
- ⅓ cup granulated sugar
- 3 tablespoons brown sugar

Champagne Sabayon and Roasted Red Grapes (recipes follow), for serving

**1.** Preheat the oven to 350°. Butter a 9-inch springform pan. Spread the almonds on a baking sheet and toast them for 10 minutes, until golden. Let cool slightly, then coarsely chop. Leave the oven on.

**2.** In a small bowl, mix the egg yolk with the orange zest and the almond and vanilla extracts. In a medium bowl, mix the flour, cornmeal and salt. Cut the butter into the dry ingredients with a pastry blender or rub it in with your fingers, until the mixture resembles coarse meal. Stir the granulated sugar, the brown sugar and the toasted almonds into the dough. Gently work in the egg yolk mixture with your hands; the dough should be crumbly.

**3.** Transfer the dough to the prepared pan and loosely press the crumbs; the surface should be uneven. Bake for about 40 minutes, or until the tart is deep golden brown. Transfer to a rack and let cool completely before unmolding.

**4.** Break the tart into large pieces. Pile on a platter with the Roasted Red Grapes and Champagne Sabayon. —*Suzanne Goin*

**MAKE AHEAD** The almond tart can be stored in an airtight container for 2 days.

## CHAMPAGNE SABAYON

**ACTIVE: 30 MIN; TOTAL: 50 MIN PLUS CHILLING**

12 SERVINGS ●

- 1 cup water
- 1 cup sugar
- 1 vanilla bean, split lengthwise, seeds scraped
- One 750-ml bottle brut Champagne or sparkling wine
- 1 dozen large egg yolks
- 2 cups heavy cream

**1.** In a saucepan, bring the water, sugar and vanilla bean and seeds to a boil. Reduce the heat to moderately high and cook, without stirring, to a light golden caramel, 10 minutes. Add the Champagne and simmer until reduced to 2 cups, 20 minutes.

**2.** In a large heatproof bowl, lightly beat the egg yolks. Very gradually whisk in ¼ cup of the hot Champagne caramel until blended. Slowly whisk in the remaining caramel. Set the mixture over a saucepan filled with 1 inch of simmering water. Cook over low heat, whisking constantly, until the custard thickens enough to form a ribbon when it falls from the whisk, about 10 minutes. Remove the vanilla bean. Transfer the custard to a bowl and let cool, then refrigerate until chilled.

**3.** Whip the cream just until firm. Fold into the Champagne custard and transfer to a serving bowl; serve cold. —*S.G.*

**MAKE AHEAD** The sabayon can be prepared through Step 2 up to 2 days ahead.

## ROASTED RED GRAPES

**TOTAL: 15 MIN**

12 SERVINGS ● ● ●

- 1 pound red grapes, cut into 12 bunches
- 1 tablespoon grapeseed oil

Large pinch of sugar

Pinch of salt

Preheat the oven to 450°. On a baking sheet, toss the grapes, oil, sugar and salt. Roast for 12 minutes, or until the skins are slightly blistered. Serve warm. —*S.G.*

**MAKE AHEAD** The grapes can be roasted up to 6 hours ahead.

## Gingerbread Roll with Cinnamon Cream

**TOTAL: 1 HR PLUS 3 HR CHILLING**

8 TO 10 SERVINGS ●

- 5 large eggs, separated
- ½ cup molasses
- ¼ cup plus ⅓ cup dark brown sugar
- 2 tablespoons finely grated fresh ginger
- ¾ cup cake flour
- 1 teaspoon baking powder
- 1 teaspoon ground ginger
- ¾ teaspoon ground allspice
- ½ teaspoon freshly ground black pepper
- ¼ teaspoon salt
- ¼ cup plus 2 tablespoons granulated sugar
- 1 teaspoon unflavored gelatin
- 1 tablespoon cold water
- 4 ounces cream cheese, softened
- ½ teaspoon ground cinnamon
- 12 ounces crème fraîche
- ½ cup confectioners' sugar
- 1 stick (4 ounces) unsalted butter

Two 4-inch cinnamon sticks

- 8 whole cloves
- 2 tablespoons dark rum
- 2 tablespoons apple cider

Confectioners' sugar, for dusting

Toasted pecans and dried cranberries, for garnish

**1.** MAKE THE CAKE: Preheat the oven to 325°. Line a 12-by-17-inch rimmed baking sheet with parchment paper. In a large bowl, using an electric mixer, beat the egg yolks until pale, about 2 minutes. Add the molasses, ¼ cup of the brown sugar and the fresh ginger and beat until combined. In a medium bowl, whisk the flour, baking powder, ground ginger, allspice, black pepper and salt. Beat the dry ingredients into the egg yolk mixture until combined.

**2.** In a clean bowl, using clean beaters, beat the egg whites until soft peaks form. Gradually add ¼ cup of the granulated sugar and beat until firm and glossy. Fold the egg whites into the batter until no streaks remain. Spread the batter onto the prepared baking sheet in an even layer. Bake for about 15 minutes, until lightly browned and firm to the touch. Transfer to a rack and let cool for 10 minutes.

**3.** Sprinkle the cake with the remaining 2 tablespoons of granulated sugar. Run the blade of a sharp knife around the edge of the pan. Cover the cake with a clean kitchen towel and top with a large cutting board. Holding the pan, towel and cutting board, invert the cake onto the cutting board. Remove the pan and carefully peel off the parchment paper. Cover loosely with a kitchen towel and let the gingerbread cool completely.

**4.** MAKE THE FILLING: In a small microwavable bowl, sprinkle the gelatin over the cold water; let stand until softened, about 5 minutes. Microwave at high power until the gelatin is melted, about 10 seconds. In a clean bowl, beat the cream cheese with the cinnamon and gelatin until smooth. In another bowl, whip the crème fraîche with the confectioners' sugar until stiff. Fold the cream cheese into the crème fraîche.

**5.** Spread the filling evenly over the entire surface of the cake. Starting at a short end, roll up the cake jelly-roll–style. Wrap the gingerbread roll tightly in plastic and refrigerate until firm, at least 3 hours.

**6.** MAKE THE SAUCE: In a small saucepan, melt the butter. Add the remaining ⅓ cup of dark brown sugar and bring to a boil, whisking constantly. Add the cinnamon sticks and cloves. Whisk in the rum and cider and remove from the heat. Let the butter-rum sauce steep for 1 hour. Discard the cinnamon sticks and cloves.

**7.** Unwrap the gingerbread roll and transfer it to a plate; dust lightly with confectioners' sugar. Cut into slices and bring to room temperature. Garnish the gingerbread roll with the pecans and cranberries and serve with the butter-rum sauce. —*Jennifer Giblin*

**MAKE AHEAD** The finished roll can be refrigerated overnight. The sauce can be refrigerated for up to 3 days; reheat gently before serving.

## Crackly Date and Walnut Cakes

**ACTIVE: 20 MIN; TOTAL: 50 MIN**

**6 SERVINGS** ● ●

Moroccans who serve cakes at teatime rather than as dessert tend to prefer somewhat savory versions. Dusting the buttered ramekins with sugar helps these light and tender cakes develop incredibly crackly crusts but adds hardly any sweetness.

Butter and granulated sugar,
  for coating
1  cup all-purpose flour
1½ teaspoons baking powder
1  teaspoon ground cinnamon
Pinch of salt
5  large eggs, separated
1  cup confectioners' sugar
1  cup pitted dates, chopped
1  cup chopped walnuts
  (4 ounces)
⅓  cup vegetable oil

**1.** Preheat the oven to 350°. Butter and sugar six 1-cup ramekins. In a small bowl, whisk the flour with the baking powder, cinnamon and salt. In a large bowl, whisk the egg yolks with the confectioners' sugar until dissolved. Stir in the dates, walnuts and oil, then stir in the dry ingredients.

**2.** In a large stainless steel bowl, beat the egg whites until they form firm peaks. Stir one-third of the beaten whites into the cake batter to loosen it, then fold in another third of the whites until they are incorporated. Gently fold in the remaining third of the whites until just a few white streaks remain. Neatly spoon the cake batter into the prepared ramekins.

**3.** Bake the date and walnut cakes for about 30 minutes, or until they are puffed and a toothpick inserted in the center of one of the cakes comes out clean. Let the Crackly Date and Walnut Cakes cool in the ramekins for 5 minutes. Run a thin knife around the sides to loosen the cakes and unmold them onto a rack. Serve warm or at room temperature.

—*Dar Liqama Cooking School*

**SERVE WITH** Sweetened whipped cream.

**MAKE AHEAD** The date and walnut cakes can be prepared early in the day and kept at room temperature.

# equipment
**PANINI PRESS DESSERTS**

A panini press is a very versatile piece of equipment, so don't use it just for savory sandwiches. **Grilled doughnuts** are excellent too. Try pressing sugar-cake doughnuts (above), which develop an irresistibly crispy, caramelized crust. The same technique works well with chocolate croissants and angel food cake. A grilled Nutella-filled brioche sandwich also tastes pretty good.

# cakes, cookies & more

## Classic Tiramisù
**TOTAL: 25 MIN PLUS OVERNIGHT RESTING**
**6 SERVINGS ●**

This is tiramisù at its most timeless: tender coffee-infused cookies in incredibly rich mascarpone cream with a gentle dusting of cocoa powder.

- ½ cup heavy cream
- 2 large eggs, separated
- ⅓ cup plus 1 tablespoon granulated sugar
- ½ pound mascarpone (1 cup)
- 1 cup strong brewed espresso, at room temperature
- One 7-ounce package dry ladyfingers, preferably Italian *savoiardi* (see Note)
- ¼ cup unsweetened cocoa powder, for dusting

1. In a medium bowl, whip the heavy cream until firm, then refrigerate. In a large bowl, beat the egg yolks with ⅓ cup of the sugar until light in color. In another bowl, using a whisk or handheld electric mixer, beat the egg whites until they hold soft peaks. Add the remaining 1 tablespoon of sugar to the whites and beat until firm and glossy. Using a rubber spatula, fold the whipped cream into the beaten yolk-and-sugar mixture, then fold in the mascarpone and one-third of the beaten egg whites. Gently fold in the remaining egg whites.

2. Pour the espresso into a bowl. Dip both sides of half of the ladyfingers in the espresso; use them to line the bottom of an 8-by-10 glass or ceramic baking dish. Spoon half of the mascarpone cream over the ladyfingers and spread in a smooth, even layer. Dip both sides of the remaining ladyfingers in the espresso and arrange on top. Spread the remaining mascarpone cream over the ladyfingers in an even layer. Cover and refrigerate overnight.

3. Just before serving, sift the cocoa powder over the top of the tiramisù; cut into squares and serve. —*Marco Gallotta*

**NOTE** *Savoiardi* ladyfingers can be found at Italian specialty food shops.

**MAKE AHEAD** The tiramisù can be refrigerated for up to 2 days.

## Vietnamese Profiteroles with Coffee Ice Cream
**ACTIVE: 45 MIN; TOTAL: 2 HR**
**10 SERVINGS**
PROFITEROLES

- ½ cup plus 2 tablespoons water
- ½ cup whole milk
- 1 stick (4 ounces) unsalted butter, cut into pieces
- 2 tablespoons sweetened condensed milk
- Salt
- 1 cup all-purpose flour
- 4 large eggs
- 2 large egg yolks
- Coarse sea salt
- Vietnamese Coffee Ice Cream (recipe follows)

MOCHA SAUCE
- ½ cup brewed Vietnamese coffee or strong espresso
- ¼ cup plus 2 tablespoons unsweetened cocoa powder
- ¼ cup sugar
- ¼ cup light corn syrup
- Salt
- 2 ounces semisweet chocolate, coarsely chopped
- 1 tablespoon unsalted butter
- 1½ teaspoons coffee liqueur

1. **MAKE THE PROFITEROLES:** Preheat the oven to 400°. Line 2 large baking sheets with parchment paper. In a saucepan, mix ½ cup of the water, the whole milk, butter, condensed milk and ¼ teaspoon of salt and bring to a boil. Remove from the heat and add the flour all at once; stir with a wooden spoon until a smooth mass forms. Return the saucepan to the heat and cook over moderate heat, stirring constantly, until the dough pulls away from the side of the pan and begins to dry out, 4 to 5 minutes.

2. Transfer the dough to a large bowl and beat at medium speed until slightly cooled, about 1 minute. At low speed, beat in the whole eggs 1 at a time, beating until incorporated between additions. Beat in 1 of the egg yolks until incorporated.

3. Transfer the dough to a pastry bag fitted with a ½-inch plain tip. Pipe thirty 1½-inch mounds onto the baking sheets about 1 inch apart. In a bowl, mix the remaining egg yolk and 2 tablespoons of water. Lightly brush each mound with the egg wash and sprinkle lightly with sea salt. Bake for 10 minutes, until puffed and lightly browned. Lower the oven temperature to 350° and bake the puffs for 20 minutes longer, until golden and crisp. Let cool on the sheets, then slice each puff in half horizontally.

4. Line a baking sheet with wax paper. Working with 6 puffs at a time, fill each puff with the ice cream; replace the tops. Freeze the profiteroles on the baking sheet while you fill the rest. Freeze the filled profiteroles just until firm, about 20 minutes.

5. **MAKE THE MOCHA SAUCE:** In a saucepan, combine the coffee, cocoa powder, sugar, corn syrup and ¼ teaspoon of salt; whisk until smooth. Bring to a boil, whisking constantly. Remove from the heat and whisk in the chocolate, butter and coffee liqueur. Transfer the sauce to a pitcher.

6. Transfer the profiteroles to plates, drizzle with the mocha sauce and serve. —*Pichet Ong*

### VIETNAMESE COFFEE ICE CREAM
**ACTIVE: 10 MIN; TOTAL: 40 MIN PLUS FREEZING**
MAKES ABOUT 1 QUART ●

- 2 cups whole milk
- 1 cup plus 2 tablespoons sweetened condensed milk
- ½ cup fine-ground Vietnamese coffee or dark-roast coffee
- Pinch of salt
- 6 large egg yolks

VIETNAMESE PROFITEROLES WITH COFFEE ICE CREAM

LEMON-AND-CINNAMON-SCENTED FLAN

1. In a saucepan, combine the milks, coffee and salt and bring to a simmer. Remove from the heat and let stand for 20 minutes. Strain through a fine sieve lined with several layers of moistened cheesecloth.

2. Return the steeped milk to the saucepan and bring to a simmer. In a bowl, whisk the egg yolks until slightly pale. Gradually whisk in the hot milk; refrigerate until cold. Freeze the custard in an ice cream maker. Transfer the ice cream to a container and freeze until firm enough to scoop. —*P.O.*

## Lemon-and-Cinnamon-Scented Flans

**ACTIVE: 20 MIN; TOTAL: 1 HR 10 MIN PLUS 4 HR 30 MIN COOLING**

**6 SERVINGS** ●

When adding the warm milk to the egg mixture, be sure to add it slowly, whisking constantly, so the eggs don't curdle.

2½ cups whole milk
Peel of ½ lemon
1 medium cinnamon stick, broken
1 cup sugar
¼ cup water
5 large eggs

1. Preheat the oven to 300°. Set six 5- to 6-ounce ramekins in a medium baking pan. In a medium saucepan, combine the milk, lemon peel and cinnamon stick and bring to a boil. Remove from the heat and let stand for 15 minutes; discard the lemon peel and cinnamon stick.

2. In a saucepan, cook ½ cup of the sugar with the water over moderately high heat, stirring, just until dissolved. Lower the heat to moderate and let the syrup simmer, without stirring, until a deep amber caramel forms, about 15 minutes. Immediately pour the caramel into the ramekins, tilting as necessary to evenly coat the bottoms.

3. In a large bowl, whisk the eggs with the remaining ½ cup of sugar. Slowly whisk in the warm milk, then strain the custard through a fine sieve into a large measuring cup or a large bowl. Pour the strained custard into the ramekins in the baking pan. Pour enough hot water into the baking pan to reach halfway up the sides of the ramekins. Bake the flans for about 40 minutes, until a knife inserted into one of the flans comes out clean. Transfer the ramekins to a rack and let the flans cool to room temperature. Refrigerate the flans for at least 4 hours or overnight.

4. To serve, run a thin knife around each flan. Top each flan with an inverted dessert plate and unmold, letting the caramel run over the flans. Serve at once.
—*Jeff Koehler*

**MAKE AHEAD** The flans can be refrigerated for up to 2 days in the ramekins.

## Dulce de Leche Bread Pudding

**TOTAL: 30 MIN**

**8 SERVINGS** ● ● ●

This gooey bread pudding flavored with caramel-like dulce de leche from Latin America is so much more than the sum of its parts. To add even more flavor to the dessert, throw in a handful of fresh or frozen raspberries or blueberries just before baking. The Classic Crème Anglaise that is used to soak the bread here is one of Senior Test Kitchen Associate Grace Parisi's favorite fast sauces. It's one of the master recipes from her latest cookbook, *Get Saucy*.

Classic Crème Anglaise
    (recipe follows)
½  cup dulce de leche (see Note),
    plus more for serving
4  tablespoons unsalted
    butter, melted
4  large egg whites, at room
    temperature
¾  pound crustless challah,
    cut into 1-inch cubes
    (10 cups)

**1.** Preheat the oven to 425° and butter a 2-quart shallow baking dish. In a large bowl, stir the crème anglaise with the ½ cup of dulce de leche and the butter. Whisk in the egg whites. Add the challah, stirring and gently mashing until the cubes are nearly soaked, 2 to 3 minutes. Transfer the bread mixture to the prepared baking dish and bake for about 12 minutes, until firm and bubbling around the edges.

**2.** Heat the broiler. Broil the pudding for 1 to 2 minutes, shifting the dish a few times, until browned all over. Cut the bread pudding into squares, drizzle with dulce de leche and serve. —*Grace Parisi*

**NOTE** Dulce de leche is available at most supermarkets and at specialty markets and Latin markets.

**MAKE AHEAD** The Dulce de Leche Bread Pudding can be made early in the day and reheated before serving.

## CLASSIC CRÈME ANGLAISE

**TOTAL: 10 MIN**

**MAKES ABOUT 2¼ CUPS** ● ●

The single most nerve-racking thing about preparing this simple, elegant custard sauce is making sure that it doesn't overcook and curdle. Parisi prevents this by putting together a cold water bath to stop the sauce from cooking and setting it near the stove before she even cracks an egg.

2  cups half-and-half or
    whole milk
1  whole vanilla bean,
    split lengthwise
½  cup sugar
4  large egg yolks, at room
    temperature

**1.** Set a large fine-mesh strainer over a medium bowl and set the bowl in a shallow pan of cold water. Set the prepared water bath near the stove.

**2.** In a large saucepan, combine the half-and-half and split vanilla bean and cook over moderately low heat just until small bubbles appear around the rim of the saucepan, about 5 minutes.

**3.** In another medium bowl, whisk the sugar and egg yolks just until they are combined. Whisk half of the hot half-and-half in a thin stream into the beaten egg yolks and sugar. Pour the egg yolk mixture back into the saucepan and cook the custard sauce over moderate heat, stirring it constantly with a wooden spoon, until the sauce has thickened slightly, 4 to 5 minutes. Immediately strain the custard sauce into the medium bowl in the cold water bath to stop the cooking. Remove the vanilla bean and scrape the vanilla seeds into the custard sauce. Serve the sauce right away or refrigerate until chilled. —*G.P.*

**APPLICATIONS** Serve the crème anglaise as a sauce for fresh berries or poached fruit; spoon it over pound cake or chocolate cake; or use it as a base for making ice cream.

## Krispy Kreme Bread Pudding with Espresso Whipped Cream

**ACTIVE: 30 MIN; TOTAL: 3 HR 30 MIN**

**8 TO 10 SERVINGS**

"This recipe was created over a breakfast of—what else?—Krispy Kremes," says chef Govind Armstrong of Table 8 in Los Angeles. The espresso-infused whipped cream makes a brilliant, and equally decadent, topping for the bread pudding.

18  glazed doughnuts,
    cut into sixths
1  quart heavy cream
2  cups milk
10  large egg yolks
2  large whole eggs
½  cup sweetened
    condensed milk
½  cup brewed espresso, chilled

**1.** Preheat the oven to 250°. Line 2 baking sheets with parchment paper. Spread the doughnut pieces on baking sheets and bake for about 30 minutes, until dry on the outside and semifirm inside. Raise the oven temperature to 350°.

**2.** In a large bowl, whisk 2 cups of the cream with the milk, egg yolks, whole eggs and condensed milk. Add the doughnut pieces and let soak until softened, about 1 hour; stir every 15 minutes.

**3.** Lightly butter a 9-by-13-inch baking dish. Spoon the doughnut mixture into the prepared baking dish and cover with foil. Set the dish in a roasting pan and add enough water to the pan to reach halfway up the sides of the baking dish. Bake the bread pudding for 40 minutes. Remove the foil and bake for about 20 minutes longer, or until the bread pudding is set.

**4.** Preheat the broiler. Broil the bread pudding for about 3 minutes, or until the top is lightly browned. Let cool for 30 minutes.

**5.** Meanwhile, in a medium bowl, whip the remaining 2 cups of cream to semi-soft peaks. Stir in the espresso and serve with the warm bread pudding.
—*Govind Armstrong*

# cakes, cookies & more

## Vanilla Ice Cream Sundaes with Hot Fudge and Caramel Sauces

**TOTAL: 30 MIN**

8 SERVINGS ●

HOT FUDGE SAUCE

½ pound bittersweet chocolate, coarsely chopped

1 cup water

¼ cup plus 2 tablespoons sugar

¼ cup light corn syrup

¼ cup unsweetened cocoa powder

1 tablespoon instant espresso mixed with 1 teaspoon water

CARAMEL SAUCE

1 cup sugar

1 tablespoon light corn syrup

1 cup heavy cream

2 tablespoons unsalted butter

FOR THE SUNDAES

Vanilla ice cream

½ cup chopped nuts

**1. MAKE THE HOT FUDGE SAUCE:** Melt the chocolate in a small saucepan set in a larger pan of simmering water; stir until smooth. Meanwhile, in a medium saucepan, combine the water with the sugar and corn syrup and bring to a boil over high heat. Whisk in the cocoa powder, reduce the heat to moderate and cook, stirring, until slightly thickened, about 3 minutes. Remove the pan from the heat and whisk in the melted chocolate and the espresso dissolved in water.

**2. MAKE THE CARAMEL SAUCE:** In a medium saucepan, combine the sugar with the light corn syrup and cook over moderately high heat, without stirring, until a deep-amber caramel forms, about 6 minutes. Using a wet pastry brush, wash down any crystals from the side of the pan. Remove the pan from the heat and carefully stir in the cream and butter; the sauce will bubble up. Cook the caramel sauce over moderate heat for 5 minutes, stirring occasionally.

**3. MAKE THE SUNDAES:** Spoon the ice cream into sundae glasses or bowls. Top with the hot fudge and caramel sauces, sprinkle with nuts and serve.

—*Lissa Doumani*

**MAKE AHEAD** The hot fudge and caramel sauces can be refrigerated for up to 1 week. Rewarm them before serving.

## Semolina Pudding with Saffron and Nuts

**TOTAL: 20 MIN PLUS 1 HR 30 MIN COOLING**

12 SERVINGS ● ●

6 cups plus 1 tablespoon whole milk

½ teaspoon saffron threads

½ cup blanched whole almonds

½ cup shelled unsalted pistachios

2 tablespoons unsalted butter

⅔ cup semolina

½ cup plus 2 tablespoons sugar

¾ teaspoon ground cardamom

Edible silver leaf, for garnish (optional; see Note)

**1.** Preheat the oven to 350°. In a small dish, combine 1 tablespoon of the milk with the saffron and let steep for 30 minutes.

**2.** Spread the almonds and pistachios on a rimmed baking sheet and bake for about 5 minutes, or until the almonds are pale golden brown. Let cool, then coarsely chop the almonds and pistachios.

**3.** Melt the butter in a large saucepan. Stir in the semolina and cook over moderately high heat, stirring, until fragrant and golden brown, about 4 minutes. Slowly whisk in the sugar, cardamom and remaining 6 cups of milk and bring to a boil, whisking. Reduce the heat to moderately low and cook, whisking often, until thickened, about 8 minutes. Scrape the semolina into a large, shallow serving dish and press a sheet of plastic wrap directly on the surface to prevent a skin from forming. Let cool to room temperature, about 1½ hours.

**4.** Just before serving, lightly stir the saffron milk into the semolina in quick dashes. Sprinkle with the toasted nuts, decorate with the silver leaf and serve.

—*Neelam Batra*

**NOTE** Silver leaf is a completely flavorless, microscopically thin sheet of real silver that comes between sheets of paper. It's available at Indian groceries and at qualityspices.com.

**MAKE AHEAD** The semolina pudding can be prepared through Step 3 and refrigerated overnight.

## Rice Pudding with Cinnamon

**ACTIVE: 30 MIN; TOTAL: 1 HR 20 MIN**

8 SERVINGS ●

6¼ cups whole milk

2 cinnamon sticks, plus ground cinnamon for dusting

Zest of 1 lemon, in wide strips

½ cup medium grain rice

2 large eggs, separated

3 tablespoons sugar

**1.** In a medium saucepan, combine 6 cups of the milk with the cinnamon sticks and lemon zest; bring to a boil. Add the rice and simmer over low heat, stirring often, until the rice is tender and most of the milk has been absorbed, about 1 hour. Discard the cinnamon sticks and zest. Pour the rice pudding into a serving dish.

**2.** In a small saucepan, heat the remaining ¼ cup of milk. In a medium stainless steel bowl, whisk the egg yolks with the sugar. Stir in the hot milk. Set the bowl over a saucepan of simmering water and whisk the yolks constantly until thickened and streaks appear at the bottom of the bowl as you whisk, 6 to 7 minutes. Remove the bowl from the heat and whisk the yolk mixture to cool it slightly.

**3.** In a medium stainless steel bowl, whisk the egg whites until firm peaks form. Fold the whites into the yolk mixture and spread over the rice pudding. Dust with ground cinnamon and serve. —*Victoria Amory*

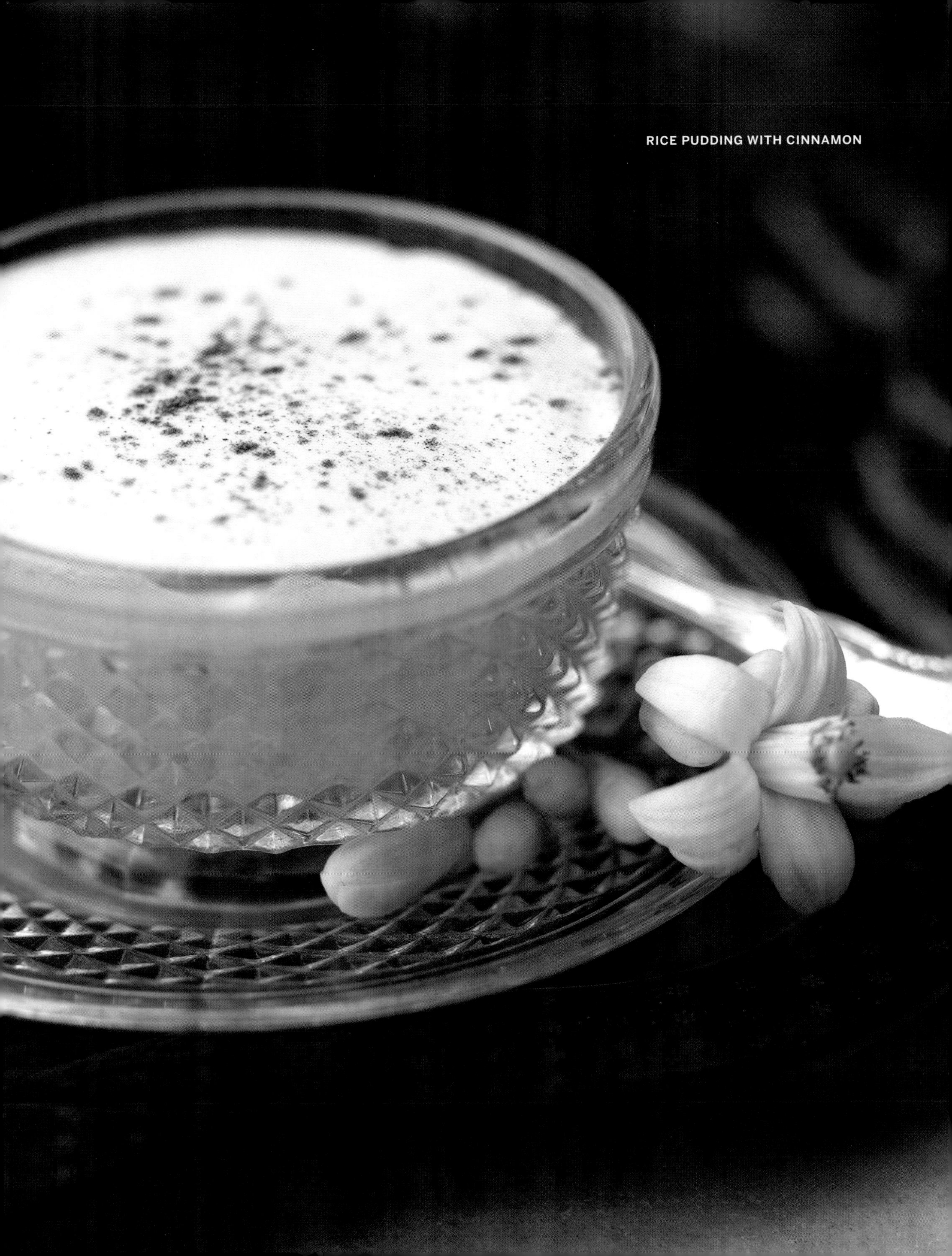

RICE PUDDING WITH CINNAMON

# cakes, cookies & more

## Warm Chocolate Pudding Cakes

**TOTAL: 30 MIN**

**8 SERVINGS** ●

The batter for these buttery little chocolate pudding cakes comes together almost effortlessly in a food processor—and the recipe is also very quick to make.

- ½ cup plus 2 tablespoons sugar
- ¼ cup sweet sherry
- 4 ounces bittersweet or semisweet chocolate chips (¾ cup)
- 1 stick (4 ounces) unsalted butter, softened
- 3 large eggs
- 1 tablespoon all-purpose flour

Vanilla ice cream, for serving

**1.** Preheat the oven to 350° and spray 8 nonstick muffin cups with vegetable oil cooking spray. In a small saucepan, combine the sugar and the sweet sherry and bring to a boil. In a food processor, pulse the bittersweet chocolate chips until they are chopped. With the machine on, pour in the sherry syrup and process until the chocolate is melted and smooth. Blend the butter into the chocolate a little bit at a time. Add the eggs, 1 at a time, then add the flour to the batter.

**2.** Spoon the pudding cake batter into the prepared muffin cups. Set the muffin pan in a roasting pan filled with 1 inch of warm water. Bake the pudding cakes for about 20 minutes, or until the cakes are risen around the edges and firm. Let the pudding cakes cool slightly in the pan.

**3.** Carefully remove the muffin pan from the roasting pan. Pat the bottom of the muffin pan dry, then invert a baking sheet lined with wax paper over the pan and the cakes. Turn over the baking sheet along with the muffin pan and turn the cakes out onto the wax paper. Using a spatula, gently transfer the pudding cakes to serving plates. Top the cakes with ice cream and serve immediately. —*Andy Nusser*

## Chocolate Mousse

**TOTAL: 40 MIN PLUS 2 HR CHILLING**

**8 SERVINGS** ● ●

Adding coffee to this recipe for chocolate mousse sets it apart from the standard and adds a great earthiness to its intense chocolate flavor.

- 12 ounces bittersweet chocolate, coarsely chopped
- 6 tablespoons unsalted butter
- 2 tablespoons pure vanilla extract
- 6 large eggs, separated
- ¾ cup plus 2 tablespoons granulated sugar
- ¼ cup plus 2 tablespoons strong brewed coffee
- ½ teaspoon cream of tartar
- 2½ cups heavy cream
- 1½ tablespoons confectioners' sugar
- 1 teaspoon instant espresso

**1.** In a medium saucepan, melt the bittersweet chocolate with the butter over moderately low heat, stirring occasionally. Remove the chocolate from the heat and stir in the vanilla.

**2.** In a medium heatproof bowl, whisk the egg yolks with ¼ cup plus 2 tablespoons of the granulated sugar and the coffee. Set the bowl over a saucepan of simmering water and whisk constantly until the yolks are frothy and an instant-read thermometer inserted into the beaten egg yolks registers 160°, about 6 minutes. Remove the egg yolks from the heat and fold in the melted chocolate.

**3.** In another medium bowl, whisk the egg whites with the cream of tartar and the remaining ½ cup of granulated sugar. Set the bowl over the saucepan of simmering water and whisk the whites constantly until an instant-read thermometer inserted in the whites registers 140°, about 5 minutes. Remove the bowl of egg whites from the saucepan and continue beating the whites until they are stiff and glossy. Fold the beaten whites into the semisweet chocolate mixture.

**4.** In a clean bowl, beat 1 cup of the heavy cream until firm. Fold the cream into the chocolate mixture until no streaks remain. Spoon the mousse into 8 serving bowls or glasses, such as martini glasses. Chill for at least 2 hours.

**5.** Just before serving the chocolate mousse, beat the remaining 1½ cups of heavy cream with the confectioners' sugar until firm. Sprinkle the instant espresso onto the whipped cream and fold it in gently so that some of the flecks and streaks remain visible. Dollop the coffee-flavored whipped cream over the Chocolate Mousse and serve immediately. —*Marc Murphy*

**MAKE AHEAD** The Chocolate Mousse can be prepared through Step 4 and refrigerated for up to 2 days.

## Butterscotch Crèmes Brûlées with Caramel Corn

**ACTIVE: 1 HR; TOTAL: 3 HR PLUS 5 HR CHILLING**

**8 SERVINGS** ● ●

In his salute to dime-store sweets, pastry chef James Foran of Arterra in San Diego tops a silky butterscotch crème brûlée with his homemade Cracker Jack. The caramel corn is also delicious on its own.

- 3 cups heavy cream
- 1 cup whole milk
- 1 cup dark brown sugar
- ¼ teaspoon salt
- 2 ounces milk chocolate, chopped
- 2 tablespoons plus 1 teaspoon pure vanilla extract
- 9 large egg yolks
- ⅓ cup granulated sugar

Caramel Corn (recipe follows)

**1.** Preheat the oven to 300°. In a medium saucepan, combine the cream with the milk, brown sugar and salt. Cook over moderate heat, stirring, until the sugar melts and small bubbles appear around the rim. Remove from the heat and whisk in the chocolate until melted. Add the vanilla. In a medium bowl, whisk the egg yolks.

**CHOCOLATE MOUSSE**

**BUTTERSCOTCH CRÈME BRÛLÉE WITH CARAMEL CORN**

Gradually whisk the hot cream mixture into the egg yolks, then strain the custard through a fine sieve into a bowl.

**2.** Set eight ½-cup ramekins in a roasting pan. Pour the custard into the ramekins and add enough hot water to the roasting pan to reach halfway up the sides of the ramekins. Cover the roasting pan with foil and bake for 35 to 40 minutes, or until the crèmes brûlées are set but still slightly jiggly in the centers. Uncover and let cool in the pan. Refrigerate until very cold and firm, at least 5 hours.

**3.** Set the ramekins in the freezer for 20 minutes, until icy cold. Preheat the broiler and position a rack 6 inches from the heat. Place 4 of the ramekins in a baking pan and fill it with ice. Sprinkle about 2 teaspoons of granulated sugar evenly over each crème brûlée and broil for about 1 minute, until the tops are caramelized. Remove the crèmes

brûlées from the ice water and refrigerate just until chilled, about 15 minutes. Repeat with the remaining crèmes brûlées. Alternatively, caramelize the sugar with a propane or brûlée torch. Top the crèmes brûlées with the Caramel Corn and serve.
—*James Foran*

**MAKE AHEAD** The crème brûlée recipe can be prepared through Step 2 and refrigerated overnight.

## CARAMEL CORN
**ACTIVE: 15 MIN; TOTAL: 45 MIN**
MAKES 3½ CUPS

- ½ **cup sugar**
- 1 **tablespoon light corn syrup**
- 2 **tablespoons water**
- 2 **tablespoons unsalted butter**
- ½ **teaspoon kosher salt**
- 2½ **cups freshly popped corn**
- ¼ **cup honey-roasted peanuts**

Line a large baking sheet with lightly buttered parchment paper or foil. In a medium saucepan, combine the sugar, light corn syrup and water and bring to a boil. Wash down the side of the saucepan with a wet pastry brush. Cook the syrup over moderate heat without stirring until a medium amber caramel forms, about 7 minutes. Remove the caramel from the heat and carefully stir in the butter and salt until the butter is melted. Add the popcorn and peanuts to the caramel syrup and carefully stir to coat all of the pieces with caramel. Pour the Caramel Corn onto the buttered sheet and spread it in an even layer. Drizzle any remaining caramel on top. Let cool for 30 minutes, then break the Caramel Corn into small pieces. —*J.F.*

**MAKE AHEAD** The Caramel Corn can be stored in an airtight container for up to 2 days.

HOMEMADE YODELS

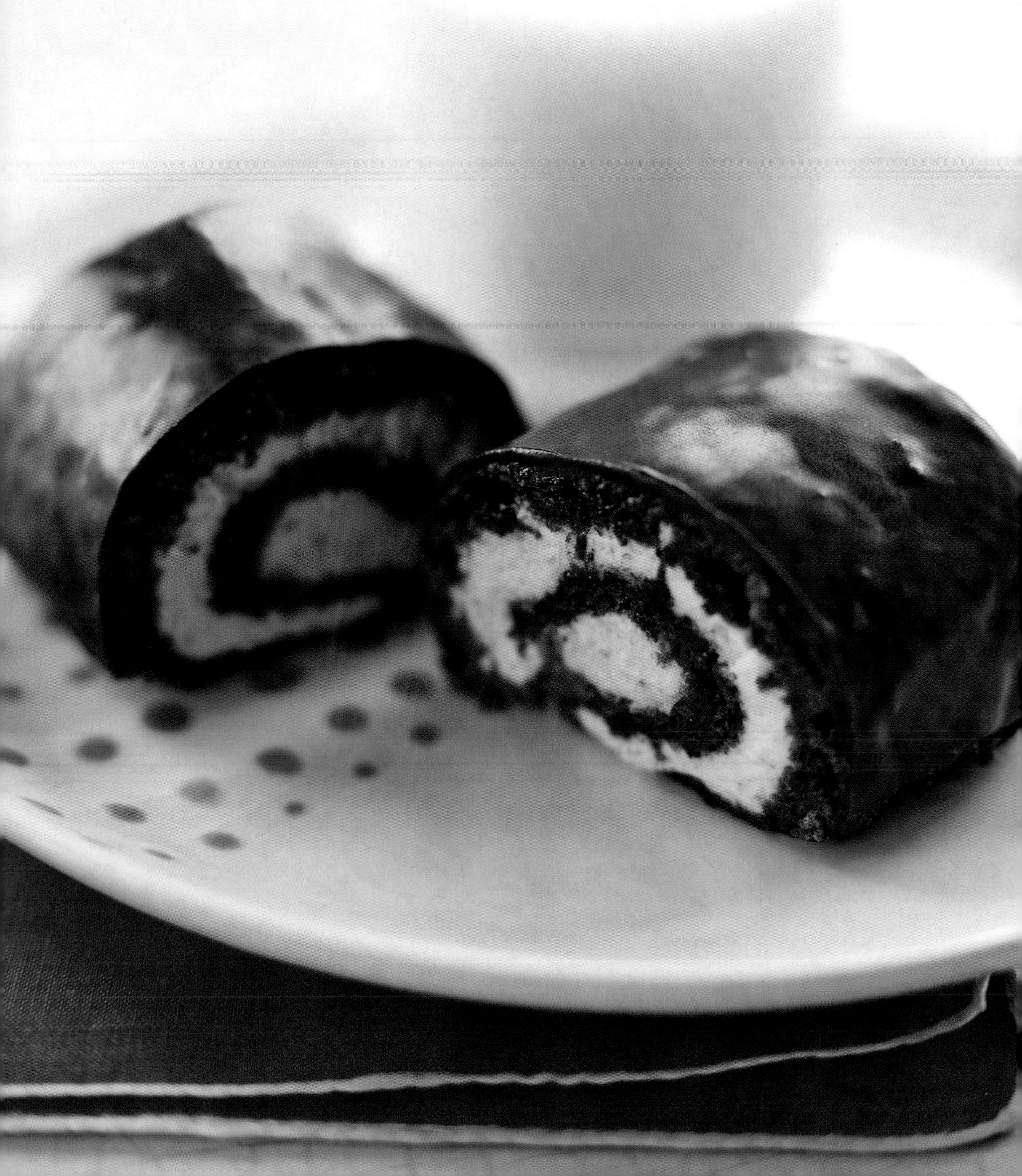

## Homemade Yodels

**TOTAL: 2 HR PLUS 2 HR FREEZING**

**MAKES 10 YODELS** ●

- 5 large eggs, separated
- ¾ teaspoon cream of tartar
- 1¼ cups confectioners' sugar
- ¼ cup all-purpose flour, plus more for dusting
- 3 tablespoons unsweetened cocoa, plus more for dusting
- 1½ teaspoons pure vanilla extract
- ½ cup plus 2 tablespoons granulated sugar
- 1¼ cups plus 2 tablespoons heavy cream
- 2 tablespoons unsalted butter
- 2 tablespoons sour cream

Pinch of salt

- 12 ounces bittersweet or semisweet chocolate, chopped
- ¼ cup vegetable oil

**1.** Preheat the oven to 325°. Lightly butter two 10½-by-15½-inch jelly-roll pans and line the bottoms with parchment paper. Butter the parchment paper. Dust the jelly-roll pans with flour, tapping out any excess.

**2.** In a large bowl, using an electric mixer, beat the egg whites with ½ teaspoon of the cream of tartar at high speed until soft peaks form. Add ½ cup of the confectioners' sugar and beat at high speed until the egg whites are stiff and glossy.

**3.** In another large bowl, beat the egg yolks until they are pale, about 2 minutes. Add the ¼ cup of flour, 3 tablespoons of cocoa, ½ cup of the confectioners' sugar and 1 teaspoon of vanilla and beat at low speed until the ingredients are combined. Beat in one-fourth of the egg whites, then fold in the remaining egg whites until no streaks remain. Pour the cake batter into the prepared jelly-roll pans and spread in a thin, even layer. Bake the chocolate cakes for 6 minutes, until they are firm and slightly puffed. Transfer the pans to a rack and let the cakes cool for 5 minutes.

**4.** Run the tip of a knife around the edges of the cakes. Dust the cakes with cocoa and cover each one with a sheet of wax paper slightly larger than the pan. Invert the cakes onto the wax paper and remove the pans. Cover the cakes with plastic wrap to keep moist.

**5.** In a small bowl, combine 2 tablespoons of very hot water with 2 tablespoons of the granulated sugar and stir until the sugar dissolves. Let the sugar syrup cool to room temperature.

**6.** In a small saucepan, combine the remaining ½ cup of granulated sugar and ¼ teaspoon of cream of tartar with 3 tablespoons of water and cook over moderately high heat, washing down the side of the pan with a wet pastry brush and gently swirling the pan, until a deep amber caramel forms, about 6 minutes. Remove from the heat. Add ¼ cup plus 2 tablespoons of the heavy cream and the butter and stir just until combined. Cook over high heat for 1 minute. Transfer the caramel sauce to a heatproof bowl and let cool completely.

**7.** In a large bowl, using an electric mixer, combine the remaining 1 cup of heavy cream, ¼ cup of confectioners' sugar and ½ teaspoon of vanilla. Beat in the sour cream and salt, then beat until firm peaks form. Fold in the cooled caramel sauce and refrigerate.

**8.** Peel the parchment paper off both cakes and brush the surfaces with the sugar syrup. Spread the caramel cream over each cake in a thin, even layer. Working with the long side nearest you, roll up each cake, using the wax paper to help you form a tight roll. Wrap the rolls in the wax paper, transfer to a baking sheet and freeze until very firm, about 2 hours.

**9.** Melt the chopped chocolate in a medium microwavable bowl. Whisk in the oil. Let the glaze cool slightly. Line a baking sheet with wax paper. Unwrap the rolls and cut each one into 5 pieces. Working quickly, dip both ends of each roll into the chocolate glaze, then dip the tops and bottoms, letting any excess glaze drip back into the bowl. Place the rolls on the prepared baking sheet and refrigerate just until the glaze is completely set. Serve the yodels cold or at room temperature. —*Sue McCown*

**MAKE AHEAD** The chilled yodels can be individually wrapped in plastic and refrigerated for up to 4 days or frozen for up to 2 weeks.

## Chocolate-Coconut S'mores

**TOTAL: 15 MIN**

**4 SERVINGS** ●

This dessert is one of TV chef Bobby Flay's favorite fast recipes. It was inspired by the journeys Flay took around the U.S. for his shows, trips that also inspired the recipes at Bar Americain, his new regional American restaurant in New York City.

- ½ cup sweetened, shredded coconut
- 8 chocolate or plain graham crackers

One 4-ounce bar bittersweet chocolate, broken into 4 rectangles

- 12 large marshmallows

**1.** Preheat the oven to 350°. Spread the shredded coconut on a pie plate and toast it for about 4 minutes, or until it is golden. Arrange four 8-inch sheets of aluminum foil on a work surface. Place 1 graham cracker on each sheet of foil and top with a piece of chocolate. Mound the coconut on top of the chocolate.

**2.** Thread 3 marshmallows on each of 4 skewers. Toast the marshmallows over a gas flame until they are golden and melted. Slide the toasted marshmallows onto the coconut and top the s'mores with the remaining graham crackers. Wrap the Coconut-Chocolate S'mores in the aluminum foil and bake them for 3 to 4 minutes, until the chocolate is just melted. Serve the s'mores at once. —*Bobby Flay*

# cakes, cookies & more

## Gingerbread Cookies with Royal Icing

**ACTIVE: 1 HR; TOTAL: 1 HR 30 MIN PLUS 4 HR CHILLING**

**MAKES 2½ DOZEN COOKIES** ●

- 3 cups all-purpose flour, plus more for dusting
- 1 teaspoon baking soda
- ¾ teaspoon ground ginger
- ½ teaspoon ground cinnamon
- ½ teaspoon ground allspice
- ½ teaspoon ground cloves
- ½ teaspoon salt
- 1 stick (4 ounces) unsalted butter
- ¼ cup vegetable shortening
- ½ cup packed light brown sugar
- ⅔ cup molasses
- 1 large egg
- 1 pound confectioners' sugar
- 2 large egg whites
- 2 tablespoons warm water

**1.** In a medium bowl, whisk the 3 cups of flour with the baking soda, ginger, cinnamon, allspice, cloves and salt. In a large bowl, using a handheld electric mixer, beat the butter with the shortening and brown sugar at medium speed until light and fluffy, about 2 minutes. Add the molasses and egg to the butter mixture and beat until smooth. At low speed, beat in the dry ingredients until combined. Scrape the dough onto a large sheet of plastic wrap and pat it into a disk. Refrigerate until very cold and firm, at least 4 hours.

**2.** Preheat the oven to 350°. Position the racks in the upper and lower thirds of the oven. Cut the dough in half; work with one piece at a time and keep the other refrigerated. On a lightly floured surface, roll out the dough ⅜ inch thick. Flour 3-inch cookie cutters to discourage the dough from sticking. Stamp out cookies as close together as possible and transfer them to baking sheets. Gather the scraps, pat them into a disk and refrigerate until firm. Bake the cookies for about 16 minutes, or until the edges are lightly browned; shift the pans from front to back and top to bottom halfway through baking. Let the cookies cool on the sheets for 10 minutes, then transfer them to wire racks to cool. Repeat with the remaining dough and scraps.

**3.** In a large bowl, whisk the confectioners' sugar with the egg whites until moistened. Add the water and whisk until smooth. Decorate the cooled cookies with the icing, using a pastry bag with a small plain tip or using an offset spatula. —*Michael Mina*

## Toffee Crunch Cake

**ACTIVE: 1 HR; TOTAL: 2 HR PLUS 2 HR 30 MIN FREEZING AND CHILLING**

**12 SERVINGS**

With its layers of tender chocolate cake and chocolaty sour cream frosting, this dessert is completely spectacular. But Patti Dellamonica-Bauler, the pastry chef at One Market in San Francisco, takes the recipe one step further by covering the cake in toasted almonds and crushed toffee candy.

**CAKE**

- 1½ cups all-purpose flour
- 1 cup unsweetened cocoa powder (not Dutch-process)
- 2 teaspoons baking powder
- 2 teaspoons baking soda
- ¼ teaspoon kosher salt
- 2 cups sugar
- 1 cup buttermilk, at room temperature
- 4 large eggs, at room temperature
- 1 cup strong brewed coffee, cooled
- 1 stick (4 ounces) unsalted butter, melted and cooled
- 2 teaspoons pure vanilla extract

**FROSTING**

- ½ pound bittersweet chocolate, coarsely chopped
- ¼ pound unsweetened chocolate, coarsely chopped
- 4 sticks (1 pound) unsalted butter, at room temperature
- ¼ teaspoon kosher salt
- 1 tablespoon dark rum
- 2 teaspoons pure vanilla extract
- 3¼ cups confectioners' sugar
- ¼ cup sour cream, at room temperature
- 1½ cups sliced almonds
- 1 cup coarsely chopped chocolate-covered toffee bars, such as Skor bars or Heath bars (four 1.4-ounce bars)

**1. MAKE THE CAKE:** Preheat the oven to 350°. Butter a 12-by-16-inch rimmed baking sheet and line the bottom with parchment paper. In a large bowl, sift the flour, cocoa, baking powder, baking soda and salt. Whisk in the sugar.

**2.** In a medium bowl, whisk the buttermilk, eggs, coffee, butter and vanilla. Whisk the wet ingredients into the dry until blended. Scrape onto the prepared baking sheet and smooth the top. Bake for 22 minutes, or until a tester inserted in the center comes out clean. Transfer to a rack, let cool for 30 minutes, then freeze until firm, 1 hour.

**3. MAKE THE FROSTING:** Bring a saucepan filled with 1 inch of water to a simmer. Combine the bittersweet and unsweetened chocolate in a heatproof bowl and set the bowl over—not in—the simmering water to melt the chocolate; let cool slightly.

**4.** In a large bowl, using an electric mixer, beat the butter and salt at medium speed until smooth. Beat in the rum, vanilla and melted chocolate until fully incorporated. Beat in the confectioners' sugar one-third at a time, scraping down the bowl between additions. Using a rubber spatula, fold in the sour cream until no white streaks remain. Refrigerate until ready to use.

**5.** Spread the almonds on a rimmed baking sheet and bake for 8 minutes, until lightly toasted. Transfer to a bowl; let cool.

**6.** Slice the frozen cake in half crosswise and transfer one half to a serving plate. Spread one-third of the frosting on the cake and top with the other half of the cake. Refrigerate for 30 minutes, until the frosting is set. Spread the remaining frosting evenly over the top and sides of the cake and refrigerate for 1 hour longer, or until the frosting is set.

**7.** An hour before serving, remove the cake from the refrigerator. Toss the toffee bars with the almonds and gently press into the top and sides of the cake. Slice and serve. —*Patti Dellamonica-Bauler*

## Latte Crèmes Brûlées

**ACTIVE: 25 MIN; TOTAL: 1 HR 30 MIN PLUS 6 HR CHILLING**

**8 SERVINGS ●**

This coffee-flavored crème brûlée is delicate and custardy, with a crackly top.

- 1 **quart half-and-half**
- 1 **cup sugar**
- 1 **vanilla bean, split lengthwise, seeds scraped**
- 10 **large egg yolks**

**Pinch of salt**

- 1 **cup strong brewed espresso**

**Boiling water**

- ¼ **cup light brown sugar**

**1.** Preheat the oven to 300°. In a medium saucepan, combine the half-and-half, sugar and the vanilla bean and seeds and bring to a simmer.

**2.** In a medium bowl, beat the egg yolks with the salt. Very gradually whisk in the hot half-and-half mixture, then whisk in the espresso.

**3.** Arrange eight 8-ounce ramekins in a roasting pan and fill them with the custard. Transfer the roasting pan to the oven and carefully add enough boiling water to the pan to reach halfway up the sides of the ramekins. Bake the custards for 1 hour, until jiggly in the centers but set around the edges. Let cool for 10 minutes in the water bath, then carefully transfer to a rack and let the custards cool slightly. Refrigerate the custards for at least 6 hours or overnight.

**4.** Preheat the broiler. Return the ramekins to the roasting pan; fill the pan with ice. Add enough cold water to the pan to reach halfway up the sides of the ramekins. Use a paper towel to blot any damp spots on the surface of each custard. Using a coarse sieve, sift about 1½ teaspoons of the light brown sugar over each custard. Broil the custards 4 inches from the heat for 20 seconds, or until the sugar is bubbling. Let cool until the sugar hardens, then serve. —*Jeanette Peabody*

**MAKE AHEAD** The recipe can be prepared through Step 3 and refrigerated for up to 2 days.

## Maple-Buttermilk Pudding Cake

**ACTIVE: 20 MIN; TOTAL: 1 HR 5 MIN**

**MAKES ONE 8-INCH SQUARE CAKE ●**

This sweet pudding cake with candied edges, a Maine favorite borrowed from neighboring Quebec, is known as *pouding aux chômeurs*—the unemployed guy's pudding. Chef Sam Hayward of Fore Street restaurant in Portland doesn't know how this dessert got its name, but its lavish amounts of maple syrup probably helped make it popular.

- 1⅓ **cups dark amber maple syrup**
- 1 **stick plus 3 tablespoons unsalted butter, at room temperature**
- 1 **cup all-purpose flour**
- 2 **teaspoons baking powder**
- ½ **teaspoon salt**

**Pinch of mace**

- 1 **large egg**
- 1 **large egg yolk**
- ⅓ **cup buttermilk**
- 2 **teaspoons pure vanilla extract**
- ⅔ **cup sugar**

**1.** Preheat the oven to 350°. Lightly butter an 8-inch square glass or ceramic baking dish. Line the bottom of the dish with a piece of parchment paper and butter the paper. In a medium saucepan, boil the maple syrup over moderate heat until reduced to 1 cup, about 6 minutes. Remove the syrup from the heat, whisk in 3 tablespoons of the butter, then pour into the prepared baking dish.

**2.** In a small bowl, whisk the flour with the baking powder, salt and mace. In another small bowl, whisk the whole egg and egg yolk with the buttermilk and vanilla. In a large bowl, beat the remaining stick of butter with the sugar at medium speed until light and fluffy, about 2 minutes. At low speed, beat in the dry ingredients in 2 batches, alternating with the liquid ingredients; beat until the batter is smooth.

**3.** Evenly dollop heaping tablespoons of the cake batter on top of the maple syrup in the prepared pan. Bake the pudding cake for 35 minutes, or until the top is nicely browned and a toothpick inserted in the center comes out clean. Let the cake stand for 10 minutes before serving. —*Sam Hayward*

**SERVE WITH** Unsweetened whipped heavy cream or crème fraîche.

**MAKE AHEAD** The pudding can be made earlier in the day and served at room temperature or reheated in a 350° oven for 10 minutes.

## superfast
### SORBET SANDWICHES

Soften mango, grapefruit or blood orange sorbet slightly, then sandwich between crunchy store-bought sugar cookies; freeze briefly and serve. The same technique works just as well with ice cream.

# cakes, cookies & more

## Spiced Chocolate Fondue

**ACTIVE: 10 MIN; TOTAL: 30 MIN**

**4 TO 6 SERVINGS** ● ●

Fragrant with crushed cinnamon sticks, whole cloves, cardamom pods, and ground ginger, this spiced chocolate fondue is from Caroline Yeh, owner of Temper Chocolates in Boston. The fondue holds up remarkably well at room temperature, which makes it good for parties. Serve it with hunks of gingerbread, apples or shortbread for dunking.

- 1½ **cups heavy cream**
- ¼ **cup whole milk**
- **Eight 4-inch cinnamon**
  **sticks, crushed**
- 2 **teaspoons whole**
  **cardamom pods**
- 1 **teaspoon whole cloves**
- 1 **teaspoon black peppercorns**
- ½ **teaspoon ground ginger**
- ½ **teaspoon freshly**
  **grated nutmeg**
- ½ **pound bittersweet chocolate,**
  **coarsely chopped**

**1.** In a small saucepan, combine the heavy cream with the whole milk, cinnamon sticks, cardamom pods, whole cloves, peppercorns, ginger and nutmeg and bring the cream to a boil. Remove the spiced cream from the heat and let it steep for 20 minutes.

**2.** Strain the spiced cream into a bowl and wipe out the saucepan. Return the cream to the saucepan and bring it back to a boil. Put the chopped bittersweet chocolate in the bowl and pour the hot spiced cream over the chocolate. Let the spiced chocolate cream stand for 3 minutes, then whisk the cream until it is smooth. Transfer the Spiced Chocolate Fondue to a bowl and serve immediately. —*Caroline Yeh*

**MAKE AHEAD** The Spiced Chocolate Fondue will stay fresh in a small glass jar in the refrigerator for up to 4 days. Reheat the fondue gently in the microwave for a few minutes before serving.

## Soft-Centered Chocolate Puddings

**TOTAL: 30 MIN**

**4 SERVINGS** ● ●

- 7 **ounces bittersweet**
  **chocolate, chopped**
- 7 **tablespoons unsalted butter**
- 2 **tablespoons all-purpose flour**
- ½ **cup sugar**
- 3 **large eggs**

**Crème fraîche, for serving**

**1.** Preheat the oven to 400°. In a saucepan, bring ½ inch of water to a simmer. Put the bittersweet chocolate and the butter in a heatproof bowl and set it over the saucepan until the chocolate is melted. Stir the chocolate, then remove it from the heat.

**2.** In a small bowl, mix the flour with the sugar. In a medium bowl, whisk the eggs. Whisk the flour and sugar into the eggs, then stir in the melted chocolate until combined. Scrape the chocolate pudding into four 1-cup ramekins. Bake the pudding for about 12 minutes, until the edges are firm and the centers are still runny. Serve the chocolate puddings at once, passing crème fraîche at the table. —*Bill Granger*

## Bittersweet Chocolate Truffles Rolled in Spices

**ACTIVE: 1 HR 30 MIN;**

**TOTAL: 2 HR 30 MIN**

**MAKES ABOUT 4 DOZEN TRUFFLES** ●

Joan Coukos of New York City's Chocolat Moderne is a self-taught chocolatier. Her bittersweet truffles are coated with a variety of flavorings, including blends of Chinese and Mexican spices.

- 1 **cup heavy cream**
- 3 **tablespoons light corn syrup**
- ¾ **pound bittersweet chocolate,**
  **finely chopped**
- 4 **tablespoons unsalted**
  **butter, softened**
- ⅓ **cup finely shredded**
  **unsweetened coconut**
- ¼ **teaspoon ground cardamom**
- **Pinch of ground cloves**
- ⅔ **cup plus 2 tablespoons sugar**
- 1 **tablespoon plus ¼ teaspoon**
  **ground cinnamon**
- 1 **teaspoon ground allspice**
- 1 **teaspoon ground**
  **chipotle powder**
- 1 **teaspoon ancho powder**
- ½ **cup unsweetened**
  **cocoa powder**
- ½ **teaspoon five-spice powder**

**1.** In a medium saucepan, bring the heavy cream and the corn syrup to a boil. Put the chopped bittersweet chocolate in a medium bowl and pour the hot cream over it. Let the chocolate stand for 2 to 3 minutes, then whisk the chocolate until smooth. Whisk the butter into the chocolate. Refrigerate the chocolate ganache until firm, at least 1 hour.

**2.** Meanwhile, in a small dry skillet, toast the coconut over moderate heat, stirring constantly, until just lightly browned, about 2 minutes. Transfer the coconut to a small bowl and let cool. Stir in the cardamom, cloves, 2 tablespoons of the sugar and ¼ teaspoon of the cinnamon. In another small bowl, whisk ⅓ cup of the sugar with the remaining 1 tablespoon of cinnamon, the allspice and the chipotle and ancho chile powders. In a third small bowl, whisk ¼ cup of the cocoa powder with the five-spice powder and the remaining ⅓ cup of sugar. Put the remaining ¼ cup of cocoa in another small bowl.

**3.** Line a baking sheet with parchment paper. Scoop up level tablespoons of the ganache and drop them onto the parchment. Place the baking sheet in the refrigerator for 10 minutes. Using your hands, roll each mound of ganache into a ball; you may have to cool your hands in ice water periodically while you work.

**4.** Roll 1 truffle at a time into 1 of the spice coatings. Return the truffles to the baking sheet, cover loosely and refrigerate until chilled. —*Joan Coukos*

BITTERSWEET CHOCOLATE
TRUFFLES ROLLED IN SPICES

For a story in the November issue, chef Govind Armstrong mixed Pomegranate Margaritas (P. 353) for a Los Angeles poolside get-together.

# drinks

**CARDAMOM LASSI**

**UPRISING SUN REFRESHERS**

## Cardamom Lassi

**TOTAL: 5 MIN**

**MAKES 4 DRINKS** ● ●

Freshly ground whole cardamom pods can add extra flavor to this frothy sweet-and-tart yogurt drink, but the preground cardamom powder called for here works perfectly well too.

1 quart plain low-fat yogurt

6 to 8 tablespoons sugar

4 large ice cubes

1 teaspoon ground cardamom

Spoon the plain low-fat yogurt into a blender, then add 6 tablespoons of the sugar. Add the ice cubes and ground cardamom and blend until the yogurt mixture is smooth and frothy. Add up to 2 more tablespoons of sugar if you want a sweeter drink. Pour the lassi into tall glasses and serve cold. —*Heather Carlucci-Rodriguez*

## Uprising Sun Refresher

**TOTAL: 10 MIN**

**MAKES 1 DRINK** ● ●

This tangy fruit drink is flavored with mint and pomegranate juice. The vibrant colors resemble those of a brilliant sunrise.

3 large mint leaves, minced

1 teaspoon sugar

1 cup pineapple juice

Ice cubes

1 tablespoon pomegranate juice (see Note)

Place the mint leaves and sugar in a tall glass and muddle together. Stir in the pineapple juice. Add enough ice cubes to fill the glass. Add the pomegranate juice and do not stir. Serve. —*Shaun Danyel Hergatt*

**NOTE** Pomegranate juice is available bottled, or make your own by cutting a pomegranate in half and using a citrus juicer; a large fruit will yield about half a cup.

## Hibiscus Apple Cider

**TOTAL: 40 MIN PLUS 3 HR CHILLING**

**MAKES 8 DRINKS** ● ●

Instead of a sports drink, San Francisco Bay Area caterer Carrie Dove opts for this refreshing blend of hibiscus tea and sweet apple cider. It's also wonderful spiked with sparkling apple cider or sparkling white grape juice.

1 quart water

6 hibiscus tea bags (Red Zinger)

1 quart apple cider

**1.** In a medium saucepan, bring the water to a boil. Add the tea bags, remove from the heat and let steep for 30 minutes.

**2.** Discard the tea bags and transfer the tea to a large pitcher. Add the apple cider and refrigerate until cold, about 3 hours. —*Carrie Dove*

**MAKE AHEAD** The drink can be refrigerated for up to 3 days.

## Watermelon and Ginger Limeade

**TOTAL: 30 MIN**

**MAKES 8 DRINKS** ● ● ●

½ cup water

¼ cup sugar

1½ tablespoons grated fresh
   ginger

8 cups seedless watermelon
   cubes, plus 8 small wedges
   for garnish (from an 8-pound
   watermelon)

½ cup fresh lime juice

Ice cubes

**1.** In a small saucepan, combine the water with the sugar and ginger and bring to a boil. Cover the saucepan and simmer the ginger syrup over low heat for 10 minutes. Strain the syrup into a small bowl.

**2.** Puree the watermelon cubes in a food processor. Strain the watermelon puree through a fine sieve set over a bowl. Stir the ginger syrup and lime juice into the watermelon puree.

**3.** Fill 8 tall glasses with ice cubes and add the limeade. Garnish the drinks with the watermelon wedges and serve.
—*Bradford Thompson*

**MAKE AHEAD** The limeade recipe can be made through Step 2 and refrigerated overnight.

## Shanghai Lily

**TOTAL: 20 MIN**

**MAKES 1 DRINK** ● ●

This cold, fragrant infusion gets most of its flavor from vitamin-C-packed lychees.

1 stalk of fresh lemongrass, tender
   inner bulb only, thinly sliced

One ½-inch piece of fresh ginger,
   peeled and thinly sliced

½ cup water

5 canned lychees in syrup,
   drained, plus ¼ cup lychee syrup
   from the can

¼ teaspoon finely grated lime zest

Ice cubes

¼ cup pineapple juice

**1.** In small saucepan, combine the sliced lemongrass with the sliced ginger and the water and bring to a boil. Cover the saucepan and simmer over low heat for 5 minutes. Let the lemongrass and ginger cool slightly, then puree in a blender. Pass the puree through a fine strainer.

**2.** Rinse out the blender. Add 4 of the lychees, the lychee syrup and the lime zest to the blender and puree. Pass the lychee puree through a coarse strainer.

**3.** Fill a highball glass with ice cubes. Add the lemongrass-ginger puree, the lychee puree and the pineapple juice and mix. Garnish the drink with the remaining lychee and serve immediately.
—*Shaun Danyel Hergatt*

## Iced Mint Aguas Frescas

**ACTIVE: 15 MIN; TOTAL: 1 HR 40 MIN**

**MAKES 8 DRINKS** ●

*Aguas frescas* are traditional Mexican drinks made with ice water, sugar and fruit. Pastry chef Sherry Yard of Spago in Los Angeles takes some liberties with her particularly invigorating version, adding fresh mint and ginger along with some lemon juice and honey. Her *aguas frescas* are also terrific with a shot of rum or vodka.

1½ cups sugar

3 tablespoons honey

2 cups water

⅓ cup fresh ginger slices
   (about 2 ounces)

2 ounces mint sprigs,
   leaves only

¼ cup plus 2 tablespoons
   fresh lemon juice, plus lemon
   slices for garnish

1½ liters chilled sparkling water
   or seltzer

Ice cubes

**1.** In a medium saucepan, combine the sugar, honey and water and bring to a boil, stirring constantly until the sugar dissolves. Remove the syrup from the heat. Add the ginger slices and half of the mint

leaves and let the syrup stand until it is cooled, about 1 hour.

**2.** Strain the cooled ginger and mint syrup into a large pitcher, pressing down hard on the ginger slices and mint leaves to extract as much of the liquid as possible; discard the solids. Refrigerate the ginger and mint syrup until it is well chilled, about 30 minutes.

**3.** Add the remaining mint leaves, the lemon juice and the lemon slices to the syrup in the pitcher. Stir in the sparkling water and serve the drinks in tall glasses over ice cubes. —*Sherry Yard*

**MAKE AHEAD** The *aguas frescas* can be prepared through Step 2 and refrigerated for up to 1 week.

## Mint and Lime Tequila Refreshers

**TOTAL: 15 MIN**

**MAKES 6 DRINKS** ●

You can replace the tequila with rum or the Brazilian sugarcane liquor cachaça. Also consider fixing a nonalcoholic version using 4 cups of club soda instead of 3.

**Leaves from 1 medium bunch of mint**

½ cup plus 1 tablespoon
   superfine sugar

½ cup plus 1 tablespoon
   fresh lime juice

1½ cups silver tequila

Ice cubes

3 cups chilled club soda

In a large cocktail shaker, muddle the mint leaves with the sugar and lime juice. Strain into a small pitcher and stir in the silver tequila. Fill 6 highball glasses with ice and pour the cocktail over the cubes. Top each drink with ½ cup of the club soda and serve. —*Marcia Kiesel*

## Pomegranate Margaritas

**TOTAL: 15 MIN**

**MAKES 8 DRINKS** ●

"I just love pomegranates," says Govind Armstrong of Table 8 in Los Angeles. He uses the tart fruit in everything from salads to sauces. "Last winter, so many farmers brought me pomegranates that I had to think of something else to do with them. So I came up with this cocktail."

**1¾ cups chilled pomegranate juice**
**Kosher salt**
**1½ cups silver tequila**
**1 cup triple sec**
**⅔ cup fresh lime juice**
**Ice cubes**
**8 lime wheels, for garnish**

**1.** Pour ¼ cup of the pomegranate juice into a saucer and spread some salt in another. Moisten the outer edge of 8 margarita glasses with the pomegranate juice, then coat with salt.

**2.** In a pitcher, stir the remaining 1½ cups of pomegranate juice with the tequila, triple

# ingredient
## COCKTAIL CHERRIES

Most maraschino cherries taste like the fake almond-flavored syrup they're soaked in—not fruit. Now Michter's, the acclaimed whiskey producer, has introduced **Small Batch Cocktail Cherries,** which are made with tart Michigan Balaton fruit. These not-too-sweet cherries have such true flavor, you might be tempted to use them in a pie as well as in a cocktail. **DETAILS** $7 for 9 ounces; hitimewine.com.

sec and lime juice. Working in batches, shake the mixture in a large ice-filled shaker, then strain into the glasses. Garnish each margarita with a lime wheel and serve. —*Govind Armstrong*

## Pomegranate–Orange Pekoe Iced Tea
**TOTAL: 1 HR PLUS 3 HR CHILLING**
**MAKES ABOUT 8 DRINKS** ● ●

**Basic Simple Syrup (recipe follows)**
**Zest of 2 oranges, removed in strips**
**8 cups cold water**
**9 orange pekoe tea bags**
**2 cups pomegranate juice**
**Ice cubes**
**1 orange, sliced into 8 rounds**

**1.** Prepare the Basic Simple Syrup as directed, adding the orange zest before bringing to a boil. Remove from the heat and let steep for 30 minutes. Strain the syrup into a large measuring cup.

**2.** In a large saucepan, bring the cold water to a boil. Remove from the heat and add the tea bags; let steep for 5 minutes. Remove the tea bags and let the tea cool to room temperature. Transfer to a bowl and refrigerate until chilled, about 3 hours.

**3.** Pour the tea and pomegranate juice into a large pitcher. Stir in ¾ cup of the orange syrup, or more to taste; refrigerate the remaining syrup for later use. Serve in tall glasses over ice cubes. Garnish each drink with an orange slice. —*Melissa Rubel*

**MAKE AHEAD** The tea can be refrigerated in a covered pitcher for up to 2 days.

## BASIC SIMPLE SYRUP
**TOTAL: 5 MIN**
**MAKES ABOUT 1½ CUPS** ●

**1 cup sugar**
**1 cup water**

In a small saucepan, bring the sugar and water to a boil. Simmer over moderate heat until the sugar dissolves. —*M.R.*

**MAKE AHEAD** The syrup can be refrigerated for up to 3 weeks.

## Pomegranate-Banana Smoothies
**TOTAL: 5 MIN**
**MAKES 6 DRINKS** ● ●

**2 cups plain nonfat yogurt, well chilled**
**2 cups pure pomegranate juice (fresh squeezed or bottled fresh), well chilled**
**2 large bananas, thickly sliced crosswise**

In a blender, combine the yogurt with the pomegranate juice. Add the banana slices and puree. Pour the smoothie into 6 tall chilled glasses and serve. —*Grace Parisi*

## Iced Green Tea with Ginger
**TOTAL: 1 HR PLUS 3 HR CHILLING**
**MAKES ABOUT 8 DRINKS** ● ●

**Basic Simple Syrup (recipe at left)**
**One 3-inch piece of fresh ginger, thinly sliced**
**8 cups cold water**
**8 green tea bags**
**Ice cubes**
**Lemon wedges, for garnish**

**1.** Prepare the Basic Simple Syrup as directed, adding half of the sliced ginger before bringing it to a boil. Remove the syrup from the heat and let steep for 30 minutes. Strain the ginger syrup into a large measuring cup.

**2.** In a large saucepan, combine the remaining sliced ginger with the cold water and bring to a boil. Remove from the heat and add the tea bags. Let steep for 6 minutes. Strain the tea into a large bowl and let cool to room temperature, then refrigerate until chilled, about 3 hours.

**3.** Pour the tea into a large pitcher and stir in 1 cup of the ginger syrup, or more to taste; refrigerate the remaining syrup for later use. Serve the tea in tall glasses over ice cubes, garnished with lemon wedges. —*Melissa Rubel*

**MAKE AHEAD** The Iced Green Tea with Ginger can be refrigerated in a covered pitcher for up to 2 days.

POMEGRANATE-BANANA
SMOOTHIES

MINTY LEMON ICED TEA

TANGY HIBISCUS-LIME ICED TEA

## Minty Lemon Iced Tea

**TOTAL: 40 MIN PLUS 3 HR CHILLING**

MAKES ABOUT 8 DRINKS ● ●

Basic Simple Syrup (p. 354)

- 1 cup mint leaves, plus 16 sprigs
- 8 cups cold water
- 8 Irish breakfast tea bags
- ¼ cup plus 1 tablespoon fresh lemon juice

Ice cubes

- 1 lemon, thinly sliced, for garnish

**1.** Prepare the Basic Simple Syrup as directed, adding 8 mint sprigs before bringing it to a boil. Remove from the heat and let cool slightly, about 10 minutes. Strain the mint syrup into a blender and puree with the 1 cup of mint leaves.

**2.** In a large saucepan, bring the cold water to a boil. Remove from the heat, add the tea bags and let steep for 5 minutes. Remove the tea bags and let the tea cool to room temperature. Transfer to a bowl and refrigerate until chilled, about 3 hours.

**3.** Pour the tea into a pitcher, add the lemon juice and stir in ¾ cup of the mint syrup, or more to taste; refrigerate the remaining syrup for later use. Serve in tall glasses over ice. Garnish each drink with a mint sprig and a lemon slice. —*Melissa Rubel*

**MAKE AHEAD** The Minty Lemon Iced Tea can be refrigerated in a covered pitcher for up to 2 days.

## Tangy Hibiscus-Lime Iced Tea

**TOTAL: 1 HR PLUS 3 HR CHILLING**

MAKES ABOUT 8 DRINKS ● ●

- 1 cup sugar
- 1 cup warm water

Zest of 4 limes, removed in strips

- 8 cups cold water
- ¾ cup dried hibiscus flowers (see Note)

Ice cubes

**1.** In a small saucepan, bring the sugar, water and lime zest to a boil. Remove from the heat and let steep for 30 minutes. Strain the syrup into a measuring cup.

**2.** In a large saucepan, bring the cold water and hibiscus flowers to a boil. Remove from the heat; let steep for 20 minutes. Refrigerate until chilled, about 3 hours.

**3.** Strain the hibiscus tea into a pitcher. Stir in ½ cup of the lime syrup, or more to taste; refrigerate the remaining syrup for later use. Serve the tea in tall glasses over ice cubes. —*Melissa Rubel*

**NOTE** Dried hibiscus flowers are available at health food stores, Latin markets and tea shops.

## Rooibos-Raspberry Iced Tea with Vanilla

**TOTAL: 1 HR PLUS 3 HR CHILLING**

**MAKES ABOUT 8 DRINKS** ● ●

Basic Simple Syrup (p. 354)

- ½ vanilla bean, split, seeds scraped
- 8 cups cold water
- 8 rooibos tea bags
- 1 cup thawed, unsweetened frozen raspberries
- ½ cup raspberry or mixed berry juice
- 1 tablespoon fresh lemon juice

Ice cubes

**1.** Prepare the Basic Simple Syrup as directed, adding the vanilla seeds and bean before bringing it to a boil. Remove the syrup from the heat and let steep for 30 minutes. Strain the vanilla syrup into a large measuring cup.

**2.** In a large saucepan, bring the cold water to boil. Remove from the heat, add the tea bags and steep for 5 minutes. Remove the tea bags and let the tea cool to room temperature, then refrigerate until chilled, about 3 hours.

**3.** In a blender, puree the raspberries. Strain the puree into a large pitcher. Add the tea, raspberry juice and lemon juice. Stir in ½ cup of the vanilla syrup, or more to taste; refrigerate the remaining syrup for later use. Serve the tea in tall glasses over ice cubes. —*Melissa Rubel*

**MAKE AHEAD** The tea can be refrigerated in a covered pitcher for up to 2 days.

## Double Lemongrass Iced Tea

**TOTAL: 2 HR PLUS 3 HR CHILLING**

**MAKES 8 DRINKS** ● ●

Basic Simple Syrup (p. 354)

- 10 lemongrass stalks, 6 stalks crushed and finely chopped, 2 stalks halved lengthwise, then crosswise
- 8 cups cold water
- 8 white tea bags

Ice cubes

**1.** Prepare the Basic Simple Syrup as directed, adding half of the chopped lemongrass before bringing it to a boil. Remove from the heat and let steep for 30 minutes. Strain the lemongrass syrup into a large measuring cup.

**2.** Meanwhile, in a large saucepan, combine the remaining chopped lemongrass with the cold water and bring to a boil. Remove from the heat and let stand for 1 hour, then bring back to a boil. Remove from the heat and add the tea bags; let steep for 5 minutes. Remove the tea bags and let the tea cool to room temperature. Transfer the tea to a bowl and refrigerate until chilled, about 3 hours.

**3.** Pour the lemongrass tea into a pitcher and stir in ½ cup of the lemongrass syrup, or more to taste; refrigerate the remaining syrup for later use. Serve in tall glasses over ice cubes. Garnish each drink with a lemongrass stalk. —*Melissa Rubel*

**MAKE AHEAD** The tea can be refrigerated in a covered pitcher for up to 2 days.

## Spiced Ginseng Iced Tea

**TOTAL: 30 MIN PLUS 3 HR CHILLING**

**MAKES ABOUT 8 DRINKS** ● ●

- 8 cups cold water
- 8 cardamom pods, crushed
- 6 whole cloves
- 2 cinnamon sticks
- 1 star anise pod
- 8 ginseng tea bags
- ¼ cup plus 1 tablespoon honey

Ice cubes

In a large saucepan, combine the cold water with the cardamom pods, whole cloves, cinnamon sticks and star anise pod and bring to a boil. Remove from the heat and add the tea bags. Let the tea steep for 5 minutes. Remove the tea bags and stir in the honey until it dissolves. Strain the tea into a pitcher and let cool to room temperature, then refrigerate until chilled, about 3 hours. Serve the tea in tall glasses over ice cubes. —*Melissa Rubel*

**MAKE AHEAD** The tea can be refrigerated in a covered pitcher for up to 2 days.

## Chocolate and Whiskey Liqueur

**TOTAL: 10 MIN PLUS OVERNIGHT CHILLING**

**MAKES ABOUT 1 QUART** ●

You can also make this recipe with vodka instead of whiskey for a more neutral flavor.

- ½ cup light corn syrup
- ¼ cup water
- 1 vanilla bean, split, seeds scraped
- 4 ounces bittersweet chocolate

One 14-ounce can sweetened condensed milk

- 1 cup half-and-half
- ½ cup heavy cream
- 1 cup Irish whiskey

## snack

**COCKTAIL PEANUTS**

Feridies big and salty peanuts are gently roasted in peanut oil. **DETAILS** $8 from feridies.com.

In a small saucepan, combine the corn syrup, water and vanilla bean seeds and bring to a boil. Add the bittersweet chocolate and whisk it into the syrup over moderate heat until it is melted. Transfer the chocolate syrup to a blender and let cool for 5 minutes. Add the condensed milk, half-and-half and cream to the chocolate syrup and blend. Pour the mixture into a bowl and stir in the whiskey. Blend the mixture in batches for 30 seconds. Pour into bottles and refrigerate overnight. —*Christopher Elbow*

**MAKE AHEAD** The liqueur will keep in the refrigerator for up to 2 weeks.

## Spice-Infused Sangria
**ACTIVE: 20 MIN; TOTAL: 1 HR PLUS OVERNIGHT CHILLING**
**MAKES ABOUT 2 QUARTS** ●
SPICE SYRUP
2   cups water
1   cup sugar
4   star anise pods
½   teaspoon black peppercorns
½   teaspoon whole cloves
Two 3-inch cinnamon sticks
One 1-inch piece of fresh ginger
SANGRIA
One 750-ml bottle dry red wine, such as Grenache, Syrah or Cabernet Sauvignon
½   cup fresh orange juice
½   cup light rum
¼   cup brandy
¼   cup Cointreau or Triple Sec
1½  cups club soda
2   navel oranges—peeled, halved, seeded and cut into large dice
1   lime—peeled, halved, seeded and cut into large dice
1   Granny Smith apple—halved, cored and cut into large dice
1   Bartlett pear—halved, cored and cut into large dice
Ice cubes

**1. MAKE THE SPICE SYRUP:** In a small saucepan, combine the water, sugar, star anise, peppercorns, cloves, cinnamon sticks and ginger. Bring to a simmer over moderately high heat, stirring to dissolve the sugar. Boil the syrup until it is slightly syrupy, about 15 minutes. Let the spice syrup cool, then strain into a glass jar.

**2. MAKE THE SANGRIA:** Pour the red wine into a 3-quart pitcher. Stir in the orange juice, rum, brandy, Cointreau, club soda and ¼ cup of the spice syrup; add more syrup if you prefer a sweeter sangria. Add the diced oranges, lime, apple and pear and refrigerate overnight. Serve the sangria in tall glasses over ice cubes.
—*Julie Taras and Tasha Garcia*

**MAKE AHEAD** The sangria can be refrigerated for up to 4 days. The spice syrup can be refrigerated for up to 2 weeks.

## Icy Lemon-Ginger Vodka Cocktails
**ACTIVE: 15 MIN; TOTAL: 30 MIN PLUS 4 HR FREEZING**
**MAKES 8 DRINKS**
These slushy, potent cocktails are easy to make in batches. They're also ideal for parties because most of the preparation can be done in advance.

One 3-inch piece of fresh ginger, peeled and thinly sliced
2   cups water
1½  cups sugar
Finely grated zest of 1 lemon
1   cup fresh lemon juice
8   cups crushed ice
2   cups vodka
8   mint sprigs, for garnish

**1.** In a small saucepan, combine the sliced ginger with the water and sugar and bring to a simmer over moderate heat. Simmer for 5 minutes, then let the ginger syrup cool slightly. Transfer the syrup to a blender and puree. Strain the syrup into a large, shallow glass dish. Stir in the lemon zest and lemon juice. Cover and freeze the lemon-ginger syrup until firm, at least 4 hours.

**2.** Remove the lemon-ginger mixture from the freezer and let stand at room temperature for 5 minutes, then chop into large pieces. Put half of the pieces into a blender, add 4 cups of the crushed ice and 1 cup of the vodka and blend until slushy. Pour the cocktail into 4 glasses, garnish each drink with a mint sprig and serve immediately. Repeat with the remaining frozen lemon-ginger mixture, crushed ice, vodka and mint sprigs. Serve the cocktails as soon as they are ready. —*Tyler Florence*

**MAKE AHEAD** The lemon-ginger mixture can be frozen for up to 1 week.

## Jasmine Spritzers
**TOTAL: 20 MIN**
**MAKES 12 DRINKS** ●
This vodka cocktail gets its incredible floral flavor from jasmine essential oil. Even a small amount is powerful.

1½  cups warm water
½   cup sugar
2   drops jasmine essential oil (see Note)
½   cup fresh lime juice
1½  cups orange vodka
1½  cups Grand Marnier
Ice cubes
3   cups chilled club soda
12  small pieces of lime peel, formed into twists (optional)

**1.** In a small pitcher, combine the water and sugar and stir well to dissolve the sugar. Gently stir the jasmine essential oil and the fresh lime juice into the sweetened water to make a jasmine syrup.

**2.** In a large pitcher, combine the vodka with the Grand Marnier and jasmine syrup. Add ice cubes and stir briskly, then strain into chilled martini glasses. Top each Jasmine Spritzer with ¼ cup of the chilled club soda and garnish each drink with a lime twist. —*Rachel Klein*

**NOTE** Pure jasmine essential oil is available at most health food stores and from essentialthree.com; 888-482-7662.

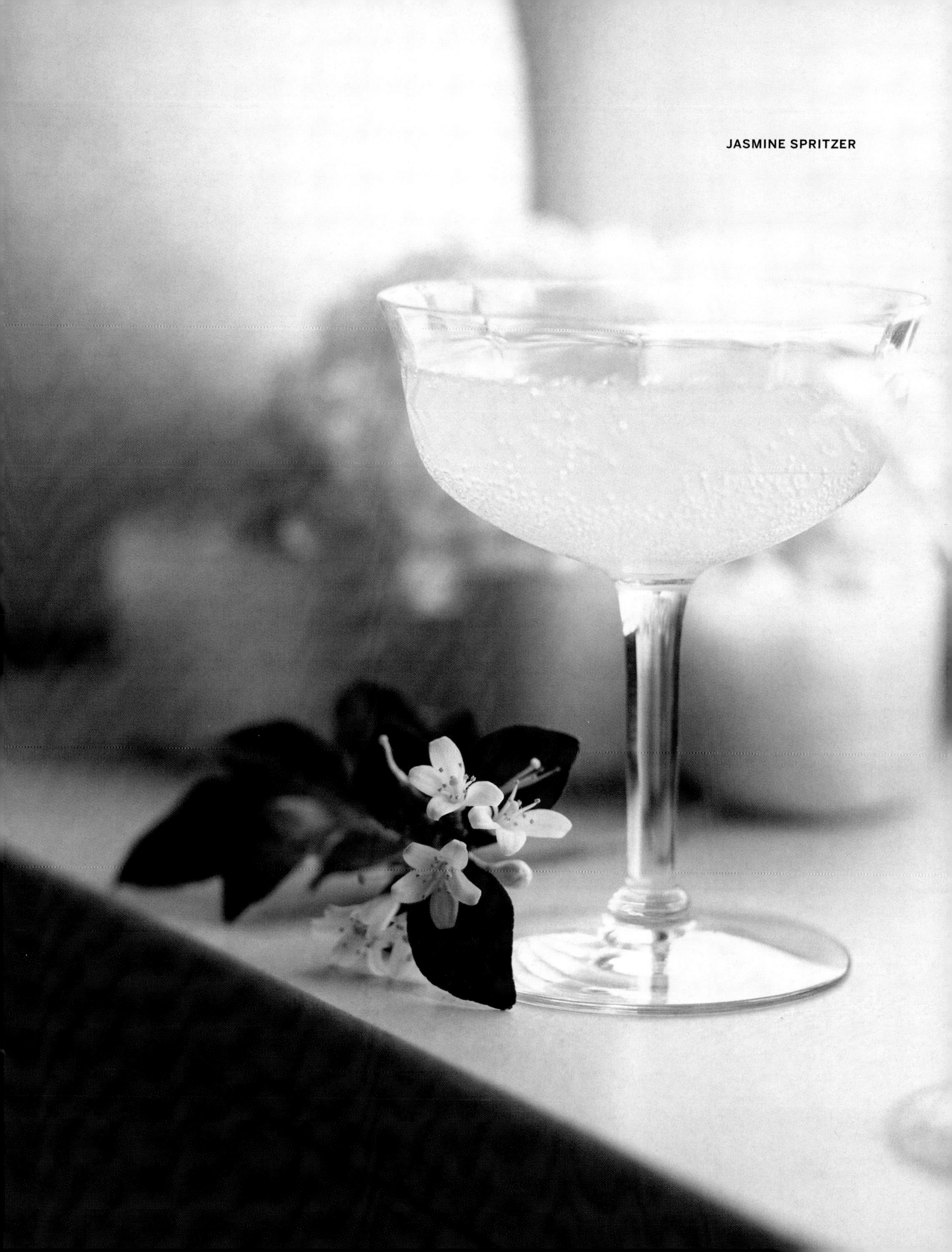

JASMINE SPRITZER

Supermodel Christy Turlington Burns was a guest at a wine-tasting party hosted by chef Marc Murphy in the April issue. She learned how to identify wine flavors like bell pepper and red cherry.

# wine pairings

# wine pairings

Ray Isle, a senior editor at FOOD & WINE, has created the ultimate user-friendly guide to pairing wine and food. The glossary here, with descriptions of key wine varieties and advice on pairing specific bottles with specific recipes, is both flexible and focused.

# champagne & sparkling wines

Champagne, which is produced only in the Champagne region of France, is the greatest sparkling wine in the world—it's effervescent and lively, at the same time offering tremendous complexity and finesse. Champagnes are usually a blend of grapes, typically Pinot Noir and Chardonnay, often with a touch of Pinot Meunier as well. They range from dry (brut) to mildly sweet (demi-sec) to very sweet (doux). Different producers, or "houses," have different styles, too, ranging from light and delicate to rich and full-flavored. Many other countries also make sparkling wines. Those from North America tend to be more fruit-forward than most Champagnes. Cava, an inexpensive sparkler from Spain, often has an earthy character. Italy's Prosecco is also affordable, and popular for its engaging foaminess and hint of sweetness on the finish. Sparkling wines make great aperitifs, but they're also good throughout the meal, especially with shellfish and salty or spicy dishes.

### DRY, LIGHT CHAMPAGNE
Perrier Jouët Grand Brut (France)
Laurent-Perrier Brut L-P (France)
Taittinger Brut La Française (France)
#### PAIRING
• Grilled Fish with Citrus Pearl Sauce, 193

### DRY, RICH CHAMPAGNE
Veuve Clicquot Brut Yellow Label (France)
Gosset Brut Excellence (France)
Bollinger Brut Special Cuvée (France)

#### PAIRINGS
• Duck Confit Cooked in a Pouch, 119
• Roasted Veal Loin with Chestnut Stuffing and Pickled Golden Raisins, 169

### DRY, FRUITY SPARKLING WINE
Zardetto Prosecco Brut (Italy)
Mionetto Prosecco (Italy)
Scharffenberger Brut (California)
Mumm Napa Brut Prestige (California)
#### PAIRING
• Silky Spaghetti with Prosciutto and Egg, 90

### DRY, EARTHY SPARKLING WINE
Freixenet Cordon Negro Brut Cava (Spain)
Gramona Gran Cuvée (Spain)
Mont Marçal Brut Reserva Cava (Spain)
#### PAIRING
• Garlicky Shrimp with Olive Oil, 206

# whites

### ALBARIÑO & VINHO VERDE
The Albariño grape produces Spain's best white wines, fresh, lively bottlings that pair especially well with seafood—no surprise, as Albariño is grown in Galicia, where the fishing industry drives the economy. Mostly made in stainless steel tanks without oak, Albariño has crisp flavors that suggest grapefruit and other citrus fruits, with a light mineral edge. Vinho Verde, or "green wine," from northern Portugal, often blends the Albariño grape (called Alvarinho there) with local varieties Loureiro and Trajadura. Bottled so young that it often has a lightly spritzy quality, Vinho Verde has a razor-sharp acidity and ocean freshness; it too is an ideal match for raw shellfish.

### ZESTY, FRESH ALBARIÑO/VINHO VERDE
Condes de Albarei Albariño (Spain)
Lusco Albariño (Spain)
Quinta da Aveleda Vinho Verde (Portugal)
#### PAIRINGS
• Toasted Spaghetti with Clams, 84
• Quail Escabèche, 120
• Cod with Basque Wine Sauce, 186

- Green Bell Peppers Stuffed with Salt Cod, 187
- Quick Curried Shrimp Salad, 203
- Saucy Clams and Shrimp with
  Wild Mushrooms, 210
- Crab, Avocado and Sorrel Salad, 214

## CHARDONNAY & WHITE BURGUNDY

Chardonnay is grown in almost every wine-producing country in the world, and it's used to create wines in a wide range of styles. It is originally from France's Burgundy region, where the best white Burgundies are powerful and rich, with complex fruit flavors and notes of earth and minerals. More affordable Chardonnays from Burgundy—for instance, those simply labeled Bourgogne Blanc—are crisp and lively, with apple and lemon flavors. Chardonnays from America, Australia and Chile tend to be ripe and full-bodied, even buttery, with higher alcohol levels and vanilla notes from oak aging. Recently, however, more and more wine regions have been experimenting with fruity, fresh Chardonnays produced with very little or even no oak aging. Pair Chardonnays in the leaner Burgundian style with roasted chicken or seafood; the more voluptuous New World Chardonnays pair well with pasta dishes made with cream or cheese, with lobster or other rich seafood and with Asian dishes that include coconut milk.

### RICH, COMPLEX WHITE BURGUNDY
Olivier Leflaive Meursault-Charmes 1er Cru
  (France)
Leroy Bourgogne Blanc (France)
Deux Montille Meursault (France)
#### PAIRINGS
- Roasted Chicken with Tarragon Jus, 95
- Lemony Chicken Fricassee with Shallots and
  Morels, 113
- Lobster and Pea Shoots with Butter-Fried Ginger
  and Garlic, 215
- Seafood Newburg, 215

### LIGHT, CRISP WHITE BURGUNDY
Labouré-Roi Mâcon-Villages Blanc (France)
Dominique Cornin Domaine de Lalande
  Mâcon Chaintré (France)
Jean-Marc Brocard Domaine Sainte Claire
  Chablis (France)

#### PAIRINGS
- Baked Four-Cheese Spaghetti, 80
- Swordfish Kebabs with Lemon and Bay Leaves, 185
- Grilled Shrimp Rolls with Sorrel, 204
- Mussels Roasted in Almond-Garlic Butter, 210

### RIPE, LUXURIOUS CHARDONNAY
Wild Horse (California)
Penfolds Thomas Hyland (Australia)
Shingleback (Australia)
Casa Lapostolle Cuvée Alexandre (Chile)
#### PAIRINGS
- Salmon Fillets with Leek Fondue, 180
- Salmon Burgers with Horseradish-Dill Sauce, 181
- Stuffed Trout with Purple-Potato Gratin, 192
- Smoky Shrimp and Cheesy Grits, 206
- Shrimp with Creamy Grits, 208
- Point Lookout Lobster Salad, 215

### FRUITY, LOW-OAK CHARDONNAY
Nozzole Le Bruniche (Italy)
Ruffino La Solatìa (Italy)
Yalumba Y Series Unwooded (Australia)
#### PAIRINGS
- Scallion-Chicken Noodles, 90
- Magnolia Chicken Jambalaya, 100
- Crispy-Skin Salmon with Vegetable Noodle Salad, 180
- Swordfish with Orzo, Pistachios and Olives, 185
- Grilled Trout with Ginger and Vinegar, 190
- Steamed Mussels with Coconut Milk and Thai Chiles, 211
- Creamy Crab Stew, 216

## CHENIN BLANC
Chenin Blanc is the star of France's Loire region, where it's used for complex Vouvrays and Savennières. Chenin has also proved to be at home in parts of California (particularly the little-known Clarksburg region), in Washington State and in South Africa, which produces some of the best-value white wines around—tart, medium-bodied whites with flavors of apple and peach. The more affordable South African, Californian and Washington versions are good with light fish or simple poultry dishes.

### FRUITY, SOFT CHENIN BLANC
Hogue (Washington State)
Vinum Cellars CNW (California)
Pecan Stream (South Africa)

# wine pairings

### PAIRINGS
- Orzo Salad with Feta, Spinach and Mushrooms, 81
- Sweet Spiced Chicken Breasts with Anisette, 101
- Grilled Pork with Curried Apricots and Napa Cabbage, 157
- Soba Salad with Tuna Tartare, 185

### COMPLEX, AROMATIC CHENIN BLANC
Domaine des Baumard Savennières (France)
Marc Brédif Vouvray (France)
### PAIRINGS
- Sweet Potato Gnocchi with Pecans and Brown Butter, 84
- Spanish Mackerel with Three Sauces, 190

## GEWÜRZTRAMINER
One of the most easily identifiable grapes—the flamboyant aroma recalls roses, lychee nuts and spices such as clove and allspice—Gewürztraminer reaches its peak in France's Alsace region, producing luxuriant, full-bodied wines ranging from dry to quite sweet, with flavors of apricot, apple and baking spices. Gewürztraminer pairs well with classic Alsace cuisine—a rich tarte flambée made with ham and Gruyère, for instance. American Gewürztraminers tend to be less dense and unctuous, though they typically have a touch of sweetness on the finish and a delicate spiciness. Pair them with Asian food of all kinds.

### RICH ALSACE GEWÜRZTRAMINER
Hugel & Fils (France)
Domaine Bott-Geyl (France)
### PAIRINGS
- Seared Tuna with Potatoes and Anchovy Vinaigrette, 182
- Shrimp and Coconut Curry, 203

### SPICY AMERICAN GEWÜRZTRAMINER
Navarro Vineyards (California)
Martin Ray Angeline (California)
### PAIRINGS
- Spicy Chicken Curry, 113
- Tuna Tacos with Onions, 182
- Flat Breads with Shrimp and Romesco Sauce, 204

## GRÜNER VELTLINER
Grüner Veltliner, from Austria, has recently become a darling of top American sommeliers, after decades of near obscurity in the United States. A refreshing, medium-bodied, peppery white wine with stone fruit flavors, it goes with everything from green salads to cold poached salmon to roasted chicken. The best Grüners can be quite expensive and have enormous aging potential.

### PEPPERY, REFRESHING GRÜNER VELTLINER
Hirsch Veltliner #1 (Austria)
Domäne Wachau Terrassen Federspiel (Austria)
### PAIRINGS
- Spaetzle with Buttery Japanese Bread Crumbs, 89
- Clay Pot Ginger Chicken, 106
- Crisp Green Beans with Pork Belly, 155
- Grilled Spot Prawns with Crispy Shaved Vegetables, 206

## MARSANNE & ROUSSANNE
These two grapes, originally from France's Rhône Valley, have recently become popular with winemakers in California's Central Coast. The flavor of Marsanne typically suggests peaches and citrus fruits; Roussanne tends to be more subtle, with a mineral backbone. In the bottle, they're often together as part of a blend—for instance, in white wines from the northern Rhône, or in many bottlings from the Santa Barbara area. Either separately or together, they're a great match for chicken dishes, particularly exotically spiced ones, as well as for fish in complex sauces.

### MINERALLY MARSANNE OR ROUSSANNE
Qupé (California)
Tablas Creek Esprit de Beaucastel Blanc (California)
M. Chapoutier Crozes-Hermitage Les Meysonniers (France)
### PAIRINGS
- Olive-Mint Pesto Meatballs with Fettuccine, 87
- Whole Grilled Chicken with Wilted Arugula, 96
- Chicken with Honey, Lemon and Oregano, 100
- Chicken Salad with Cumin-Scented Carrot Raita, 108
- Free-Form Chicken Potpie, 111
- Halibut with Walnut-Olive Relish, 188
- Maine Shrimp and Scallop Stew, 208

## PINOT BLANC & PINOT BIANCO

These are two names for the same grape; the first one is French and the second Italian. The French versions, from Alsace, are musky and creamy-textured; those from Italy have zippier acidity, with pear or even soft citrus flavors. American Pinot Blancs are usually made in the French style, as the name suggests. Pour Pinot Blancs with cheese-based dishes; Pinot Biancos go nicely with light foods like chicken breasts or flaky white fish in a simple sauce.

### ZIPPY, FRESH PINOT BIANCO
Terlan (Italy)
Alois Lageder (Italy)
**PAIRINGS**
• Pasta with Spicy Almond Pesto, 80
• Salt-and-Pepper Crab, 214

### CREAMY, SUPPLE PINOT BLANC
Domaines Schlumberger Les Princes Abbés (France)
Chalone Vineyard (California)
**PAIRINGS**
• Miso-Cured Salmon with Endive and Ginger-Pickled Shallot Salad, 180
• Roasted Shrimp with Lentils and Sun-Dried Tomatoes, 207

## PINOT GRIS & PINOT GRIGIO

Pinot Gris (from France's Alsace) and Pinot Grigio (from Italy) are the same grape variety. Italian Pinots (and others modeled on them) tend to be light, simple wines with suggestions of peach and melon. These crisp, fresh whites are ideal as an aperitif or with light seafood or chicken breast dishes. Bottlings from Alsace are richer, with strong notes of almonds, spice and sometimes honey. American versions, mainly from Oregon, often tend more toward the Alsace style, and thus are mostly labeled Pinot Gris. They go well with creamy pastas or smoked foods.

### LIGHT, FRESH PINOT GRIGIO
Alois Lageder (Italy)
Kris (Italy)
**PAIRINGS**
• Seafood Pasta with Tuscan Hot Oil, 87
• Halibut with Fresh Fennel and New Potatoes, 188
• Flounder Rolls with Pesto, 196

### FULL-BODIED, RICH PINOT GRIS
Domaine Marcel Deiss Beblenheim (France)
Trimbach Réserve (France)
King Estate (Oregon)
A to Z Wineworks (Oregon)
**PAIRINGS**
• Citrus-and-Ginger-Roasted Chicken, 98
• Almond-Crusted Chicken Wings, 107
• Duck Breasts with Mustard and Candied Kumquats, 116
• Sumac-Crusted Black Cod Salad, 186
• Roasted Halibut with Vegetables en Papillote, 188
• Sizzled Scallops, 211

## RIESLING

Riesling is one of the great white grapes, and the style of the wines it produces varies dramatically by region. German Rieslings balance impressive acidity with apple and citrus fruit flavors, and range from dry and refreshing to sweet and unctuous. Alsace and Austrian Rieslings are higher in alcohol, which makes them more full-bodied, but they are quite dry, full of mineral notes. Australia's Rieslings (the best are from the Clare Valley) are zippy and full of lime and other citrus flavors. Those from Washington State tend to split the difference, offering juicy, appley fruit and lively acidity, with a hint of sweetness. Rieslings are extraordinarily versatile with food. In general, pair lighter, crisper Rieslings with delicate (or raw) fish; more substantial Rieslings are good with Asian food, chicken, salmon and tuna.

### TART, CITRUSY RIESLING
Annie's Lane (Australia)
Mr. Riggs (Australia)
**PAIRINGS**
• Spicy Thai Pomelo Salad with Smoked Salmon, 180
• Shrimp Boil with Three-Bean Salad, 202

### VIVID, LIGHTLY SWEET RIESLING
Loosen Dr. L (Germany)
S. A. Prüm Essence (Germany)
Chateau Ste. Michelle Columbia Valley (Washington)
**PAIRINGS**
• Dan Dan Noodles with Pickled Mustard Greens, 90
• Thai Chicken Thighs with Garlic and Lime, 106
• Gingery Chicken Satay with Peanut Sauce, 108
• Fiery Grilled Beef Salad with Oranges and Crispy Shallots, 130

# wine pairings

- Sautéed German Sausages with Bacon and Apple Sauerkraut, 174
- Rio Grande Trout with Riesling, 189
- Shrimp with Bacon and Chiles, 200
- Crispy Vietnamese Crêpes with Shrimp, Pork and Bean Sprouts, 200
- Shrimp with Tangy Tomato Sauce, 202

### FULL-BODIED, MINERALLY RIESLING
Domaines Schlumberger Les Princes Abbés (France)
Weingut Bründlmayer (Austria)
**PAIRINGS**
- Baked Pasta with Shrimp, 88
- Crispy Salt-and-Pepper Squid, 194

## SAUVIGNON BLANC
Sauvignon's herbal scent and tart, citrus-driven flavors make it instantly identifiable. The best regions for Sauvignon are the Loire Valley in France, where it takes on a firm, minerally depth; New Zealand, where it recalls the tartness of gooseberries and, sometimes, an almost green, jalapeño-like note; California, where it pairs crisp grassiness and a melon-like flavor; and South Africa, particularly the Cape region, where it combines the minerality of France with the rounder fruit of California. Sauvignon Blanc teams well with light fish, shellfish, salads and green vegetables, and it's a perfect aperitif, too.

### LIVELY, TART SAUVIGNON BLANC
Geyser Peak Winery (California)
Voss Vineyards (California)
**PAIRINGS**
- Mackerel Escabèche with Asparagus and Artichoke Hearts, 190
- Steamed Tofu with Shrimp and Black Bean Sauce, 208
- Steamed Mussels with Pesto and Tomatoes, 211

### MINERALLY, COMPLEX SAUVIGNON BLANC
Morandé Terrarum Reserva (Chile)
Ladoucette Pouilly-Fumé (France)
**PAIRINGS**
- Monkfish in Tomato-Garlic Sauce, 195
- Fried Parsley-Flecked Shrimp Cakes, 203
- Citrus-Marinated Shrimp with Grilled-Onion and Orange Salad, 209

## SOAVE, VERDICCHIO & GAVI
These three light, usually inexpensive wines from Italy all match well with a wide range of foods. Soave, mostly made from the Garganega grape, is a fruity white that often has an almond note. Verdicchio, made from the grape of the same name, has a lemony zestiness. Gavi, made from a grape called Cortese, is typically tart, with an aroma that suggests fresh limes. All pair well with herby pasta sauces like pesto, white fish or vegetable dishes.

### FRESH, LIVELY SOAVE OR SIMILAR ITALIAN WHITE
Gini La Frosca Soave Classico (Italy)
Pieropan Soave Classico (Italy)
Principessa Gavia Gavi (Italy)
Fazi Battaglia Verdicchio dei Castelli di Jesi Classico (Italy)
**PAIRINGS**
- Pecorino Ravioli with Walnuts and Marjoram, 82
- Moroccan Swordfish Kebabs, 185
- Warm Seafood and Spinach Salad, 192
- Oven-Roasted Smelts with Cornichon Mayonnaise, 193
- Stir-Fried Sichuan Shrimp with Dried Red Chiles, 201
- Italian Seafood Salad with String Beans, 216

## VERMENTINO
An up-and-coming white grape from the coastal regions of Italy, Vermentino marries vivacious acidity with stony minerality. The best Vermentinos come from very different parts of Italy—from Liguria in the north and from the island of Sardinia, off the central west coast. Drink Vermentino with seafood dishes of all kinds.

### FRESH, MINERALLY VERMENTINO
Antinori (Italy)
Argiolas Costamolino (Italy)
Cecchi Litorale (Italy)
**PAIRINGS**
- Farfalle with Salsa Verde and Grilled Ricotta Salata, 81
- Tonnarelli with Pecorino and Black Pepper, 84
- Cannelloni with Ricotta, Shrimp and Leeks, 88
- Hearty Braised Chicken Legs, 107
- Seared Tuscan-Style Meat Loaf, 170
- Sea Bass with Caper Berries, Green Olives and Meyer Lemon, 194
- San Francisco Seafood Stew, 212

## VIOGNIER

Viogniers are seductive white wines, lush with peach and honeysuckle scents, a round, mouth-filling texture and little acidity. The Condrieu region in France's Rhône Valley produces the world's greatest Viogniers, and they can often be quite expensive; California and occasionally Australia have also had success with this grape. Viognier pairs well with grilled seafood; it's also a good match for most foods flavored with fruit salsas.

### LUSH, FRAGRANT VIOGNIER

Heggies Vineyard (Australia)
Jean-Luc Colombo La Violette (France)
RH Phillips EXP (California)

### PAIRINGS

- Roasted Chicken with Walnut-Arugula Pesto, 98
- Chicken Tagine with Sweet Potatoes, 101
- Snapper with Spicy Crab-and-Andouille Sauce, 196
- Grilled Shrimp with Habanero-Garlic Vinaigrette, 201

# rosés

Rosé—that is, dry rosé—may be the world's most underrated wine. Combining the light, lively freshness of white wines with the fruit and depth of reds, good rosés pair well with a remarkable range of foods, from delicate fish like sole to meats such as pork and veal. They also complement a range of ethnic cuisines—Chinese, Thai, Mexican and Greek. The best rosés, from southern France, are typically blends of grapes such as Syrah, Grenache, Cinsaut and Mourvèdre. Italy, Greece and Spain also produce terrific, refreshing rosés. American and Australian rosés, which tend to be fruitier and heavier, can also be very good.

### FRESH, FRUITY ROSÉ

Castello di Ama (Italy)
Les Domaniers de Puits Moret (France)
Château Pesquié Les Terrasses (France)
SoloRosa (California)

### PAIRINGS

- Persian Roasted Chicken with Dried Cherry–Saffron Rice, 94
- Fried Chicken Cutlets with Salsa, 98
- Baked Chicken with Potatoes, Fennel and Mint, 103

- Spicy Lemongrass Chicken, 105
- Steak Salad with Creamy Italian Dressing, 132
- Lamb Kebabs with Cool Cucumber Salad, 146
- Roasted Veal Chops with Young Garlic Vinaigrette, 166
- Sautéed Calamari with Chorizo, 194
- Shrimp, Asparagus and Eggs in Spicy Tomato Sauce, 202
- Sizzled Shrimp Provençal, 207
- Amazing Stuffed Clams, 210
- Seafood Paella with Spinach and Arugula, 214

# reds

## BARBERA

Barbera, which grows primarily in Italy's Piedmont region, mostly produces medium-bodied wines with firm acidity and flavors suggesting red cherries with a touch of spice. (Barrel-aged versions tend to be more full-bodied, as well as more expensive.) A great wine for pastas with meat- or tomato-based sauces, Barbera is also good with game and hard cheeses.

### BRIGHT, TART BARBERA

Coppo Camp du Rouss (Italy)
Damilano (Italy)
Prunotto Fiulot (Italy)

### PAIRINGS

- Pennette with Spicy Tomato Sauce, 81
- Chicken Legs Marinated in Yogurt and Spices, 106
- Sizzled Veal with Fresh-Herb Salad, 171
- Dungeness Crab Cioppino, 212

## BEAUJOLAIS & GAMAY

Gamay, the grape of France's Beaujolais region, makes wines that embody everything that region is known for: light, fruity, easy-to-drink reds, ideal for a party or a picnic. Typically they are not aged in oak barrels and are released early (Beaujolais Nouveau, which appears on shelves little more than a month after the grapes are harvested, is the extreme example). Little Gamay is grown outside of Beaujolais, but what has been planted pairs well with the same foods as Beaujolais: light chicken dishes, salads, cheeses and charcuterie.

# wine pairings

### FRUITY, LIGHT-BODIED BEAUJOLAIS/GAMAY
Patrick Brunet Domaine de Robert Fleurie (France)
Georges Duboeuf Morgon Jean Descombes
  Beaujolais (France)
Beringer Gamay Beaujolais (California)
#### PAIRINGS
• Beer Can Chicken, 96
• Crisp Spiced Chicken, 102
• Veal Milanese with Eggplant and Onions, 167
• Peppery Tuna with Dilled Potato Salad, 182
• Bacon-Wrapped Tuna Steaks with Frisée and
  Avocado Salad, 184
• Spicy Shrimp and Chorizo Kebabs, 207

### CABERNET SAUVIGNON
Arguably the most significant red wine grape, Cabernet Sauvignon has traveled far beyond its origins in France's Bordeaux—it's now widely planted in almost every wine-producing country. Depending on climate, Cabernet can make either firm, tannic wines that recall red currants with a touch of tobacco or green bell pepper (colder climates) or softer wines that recall ripe black currants or black cherries (warmer climates). It almost always has substantial tannins, which help great Cabernets age for many years. The classic pairing with Cabernet is lamb, but it goes well with almost any meat—beef, pork, venison, even rabbit.

### FIRM, COMPLEX CABERNET SAUVIGNON
Moss Wood (Australia)
Château d'Issan Margaux (France)
Robert Mondavi Winery Reserve (California)
#### PAIRINGS
• Grilled Skirt Steak with Fregola and Frying Peppers, 126
• Calf's Liver with Green Beans, 129
• Salt-and-Pepper-Crusted Prime Rib with Sage Jus, 134
• Lamb Chops with Garlic Custards, 141
• Roasted Saddle of Lamb with Anchovy-Herb
  Stuffing, 141
• Lamb Rib Chops with Vegetable Hash, 142
• Rack of Lamb with Mustard Crumbs, 144
• Roasted Rack of Lamb with Walnut Sauce, 150

### RICH, RIPE CABERNET SAUVIGNON
Beringer Napa Valley (California)
Penfolds Bin 407 (Australia)
Catena (Argentina)

#### PAIRINGS
• Grilled Rib-Eye Tagliata with Watercress and
  Potatoes, 125
• Spice-Crusted Pork-Blade Steaks, 157
• Pork in Adobo Sauce, 162

### CARMENÈRE
Carmenère has emerged as a star grape in Chile, now that its old vines are no longer mistaken for Merlot. Its origins are the same as Merlot's: France's Bordeaux region, which may account for the confusion. Carmenère tends to have more savory flavors than Merlot, though—ripe plums and berries, with notes of coffee and dark spice. It's terrific with grilled meats, spicy stews and hard cheeses.

### SAVORY, SPICY CARMENÈRE
Concha y Toro Casillero del Diablo (Chile)
Santa Rita 120 (Chile)
Apaltagua (Chile)
#### PAIRINGS
• Tomato-Basil Chicken with Spices, 105
• Chicken Wings with Sweet-and-Spicy Pantry
  Sauce, 107
• Andean Chicken and Potato Cake, 110
• Peruvian Beef and Noodle Stew, 129
• Lamb Chops Sizzled with Garlic, 142
• Baked Pork Tamale, 160

### DOLCETTO
Though Dolcetto means "little sweet one," wines from this Italian grape are dry, grapey, tart, simple reds distinguished by their vibrant purple color and ebullient berry juiciness. Dolcettos should be drunk young, with antipasti, pastas with meat sauces or roasted poultry of any kind.

### JUICY, FRESH DOLCETTO
Einaudi (Italy)
Prunotto (Italy)
Vietti (Italy)
#### PAIRINGS
• Circassian Chicken, 108
• Rolled Lamb Cutlets Stuffed with Pancetta and
  Pecorino, 138
• Curly Corn Dogs, 174
• Plank-Barbecued Salmon, 181

## GRENACHE

When made well, Grenache produces full-bodied, high-alcohol red wines that tend to be low in acidity and full of black cherry and raspberry flavors. Grenache is often blended with other grapes to make dark, powerful reds in regions such as France's Châteauneuf-du-Pape or Spain's Rioja and Priorato. On its own in Australia and the United States, it can produce deeply fruity, juicy wines that go perfectly with grilled meats, sausages and highly spiced dishes.

### JUICY, SPICY GRENACHE

Domaine les Pallières Gigondas (France)
Domaine du Cayron Gigondas (France)
Bodegas Nekeas El Chaparral deVega Sindoa
  Grenache (Spain)
Alban Vineyards (California)
d'Arenberg The Custodian (Australia)

#### PAIRINGS

- Grilled Chicken and Watercress Salad with Canadian Bacon, 102
- Smoked Paprika–Rubbed Steaks with Valdeón Butter, 125
- Braised Short Ribs with Celery-Root Pancakes, 133
- Spicy Beef with Fermented Black Beans and Scallions, 135
- Pork Chops with Sautéed Apples, 157
- Catalan-Style Braised Veal Ribs with Green Olives, 166

## MALBEC

Originally used as a blending grape in France's Bordeaux region, Malbec has found its true home in Argentina's Mendoza region. There, it produces darkly fruity wines with hints of black pepper and leather—like a traditional rustic country red, but with riper, fuller fruit. Malbecs are often very affordable, too, and go wonderfully with steaks and roasts, hearty stews and grilled sausages.

### RUSTIC, PEPPERY MALBEC

Navarro Correas (Argentina)
Trumpeter (Argentina)
Budini (Argentina)

#### PAIRINGS

- Mole Poblano Chicken, 110
- Grilled Game Hens with Four Herbs, 119
- Soy-Ginger Flank Steak with Grilled Eggplant, 129

- Beef Stew with Port and Porcini, 132
- Lamb Meatballs with Mint, 138
- Two-Day Spice-Rubbed Pork Chops, 155
- Glazed Pork Tenderloin with Cumin-Spiked Corn Sauce, 160

## MERLOT

The most widely planted grape in France's Bordeaux region isn't Cabernet Sauvignon; it's Merlot. That's because Merlot blends so well with other grapes, and also because Merlot's gentle succulence and plummy flavors have gained favor as worldwide tastes have shifted toward fruitier, easier-drinking wines. Good Merlots are made in France, Italy, Chile, the United States and Australia, and all of them tend to share supple, velvety tannins and round black cherry or plum flavors. Merlot pairs well with many foods—try it with pâtés or other charcuterie, pork or veal roasts or rich, cheesy gratins.

### LIVELY, FRUITY MERLOT

Falesco (Italy)
Columbia Crest Grand Estates (Washington)
Blackstone (California)

#### PAIRINGS

- Pad See Yew, 91
- Creole Fried Chicken, 105
- Pork Ribs with Orange and Tomato Glaze, 165
- Hot Dog Melts, 174

### DEEP, VELVETY MERLOT

Oakville Ranch Vineyards (California)
Geyser Peak Winery Shorenstein Vineyard
  (California)
La Fleur de Bouärd (France)

#### PAIRINGS

- Nori-Crusted Sirloin with Shiitake and Wasabi, 124
- BLT Burgers with Garlicky Mayonnaise, 135
- Pork Rib Roast with Sweet Onion Puree and Crisp Sage Tempura, 164

## NEBBIOLO, BAROLO & BARBARESCO

Nebbiolo is the greatest grape of Italy's Piedmont. And if you ask a farmer, it is unquestionably one of the most difficult to grow. Certainly it is formidable, with fierce tannins and acidity, but it is also gloriously scented— "tar and roses" is the classic description—and has a supple, evocative flavor that lingers on the tongue.

# wine pairings

Those flavors are more substantial and emphatic in Barolos and more delicate and filigreed in Barbarescos, the two primary wines from Piedmont. Pour good Nebbiolo with foods such as braised short ribs, beef roasts, bollito misto and anything that involves truffles.

### COMPLEX, AROMATIC NEBBIOLO
Michele Chiarlo Barolo (Italy)
Poderi Colla Barbaresco (Italy)
**PAIRINGS**
• Balsamic Steaks, 125
• Pot Roast Smothered in Bacon and Onions, 127

## PINOT NOIR & RED BURGUNDY
Pinot Noir probably inspires more rhapsodies—and disappointments—among wine lovers than any other grape. When it's good, it's ethereally aromatic, with flavors ranging from ripe red berries to sweet black cherries, and tannins that are firm but never obtrusive. (When bad, unfortunately, it's acidic, raspy and bland.) The greatest Pinot Noirs come from France's Burgundy region, age-worthy wines that are usually quite expensive. More affordable and typically more fruit-forward Pinots can be found from California and Oregon as well as New Zealand, Chile and Australia. Pinot Noir pairs well with a great range of foods—fruitier versions make a great match with salmon or other fatty fish, roasted chicken or pasta dishes; bigger, more tannic Pinots are ideal with duck and other game birds, casseroles or, of course, stews such as beef bourguignon.

### COMPLEX, ELEGANT PINOT NOIR
Louis Jadot Gevrey-Chambertin (France)
Ata Rangi (New Zealand)
St. Innocent Seven Springs Vineyard (Oregon)
**PAIRINGS**
• Roasted Guinea Hens with Cumin-Date Sauce, 120
• Roasted Goose with Crispy Skin, 121
• Stuffed Pork Chops with Onion and Shiitake, 157
• Veal Chops with Chorizo Stuffing, 171
• Salmon with Lemon Glaze and Rosemary Crumbs, 178
• Roast Salmon with Couscous Crust, 179

### RIPE, JUICY PINOT NOIR
Handley (California)
Rodney Strong Russian River Valley (California)
Meridian Reserve (California)

**PAIRINGS**
• Grilled Chicken Breasts with Spicy Pecan Butter, 101
• Chicken with Mushroom Hash, 102
• Deep-Fried Turkey Brined in Cayenne and Brown Sugar, 114
• Peking Duck Stir-Fry, 119
• Grilled Quail with Mushroom Quinoa Risotto, 121
• Meat Tacos with Mole Sauce, 160
• Salmon Rice Bowl with Ginger-Lime Sauce, 178
• Pan-Roasted Salmon with Soy-Ginger Glaze, 179
• Tuna Steaks with Currant and Fresh-Herb Salsa, 184
• Grilled Tuna with Tomato and Cucumber Salad, 184
• Seared Cod with Chile Sauce, 188

## RIOJA & TEMPRANILLO
Tempranillo, the top red grape of Spain, is best known as the main component in red Rioja, where it contributes earthy cherry flavors and firm structure. It is also used in almost every other region of Spain, and generally produces medium-bodied, firm reds suitable for meat dishes of all kinds, particularly lamb.

### EARTHY, MEDIUM-BODIED TEMPRANILLO
Finca Antigua (Spain)
Pesquera Ribera del Duero (Spain)
Bodegas Montecillo Rioja Crianza (Spain)
**PAIRINGS**
• Rotisserie Chicken with Dried Fruit and Pine Nuts, 95
• Duck with Cranberry Mostaza, 115
• Duck Breasts with Fresh Cherry Sauce and Grilled Apricots, 116
• Skirt Steak with Onion Marmalade, 126
• Pistachio-Crusted Rack of Lamb with Pancetta, 149
• Crusty Roast Leg of Lamb with British Mint Sauce, 150
• Pork Stew with Cockles and Spicy Red Pepper Sauce, 154
• Poor Man's Paella, 172

## SANGIOVESE
Sangiovese is primarily known for the principal role it plays in Tuscan wines such as Chianti, Brunello and Carmignano, though these days more and more of it is also being grown in the United States and Australia. Italian Sangioveses have vibrant acidity and substantial tannins, along with fresh cherry fruit and herbal scents.

New World versions tend toward softer acidity and fleshier fruit. Pair Sangioveses with rare steaks, roasted game birds (or wild boar), rich chicken or mushroom dishes or anything with tomato sauce.

### CHERRY-INFLECTED, EARTHY SANGIOVESE

Castellare di Castellina Chianti di Classico (Italy)
Antinori Pèppoli Chianti Classico (Italy)
Ruffino Chianti (Italy)

**PAIRINGS**
- Whole Wheat Spaghetti and Turkey Meatballs, 82
- Chicken Potpie with Cream Biscuit Topping, 111
- Garlicky Herb-Rubbed Hanger Steaks, 128
- Oven-Braised Lamb with Gremolata, 143
- Pork with Parsley and Olives, 158
- Veal Meatballs with Fried Sage Leaves, 172

## SYRAH & SHIRAZ

Probably no other grape scores higher on the intensity meter than Syrah. It's the marquee grape of France's Rhône Valley, where it makes smoky, powerful reds with hints of black pepper. It has also become the signature grape of Australia, where it's known as Shiraz, and typically produces fruitier, less tannic wines marked by sweet blackberry flavors. American Syrahs lean more toward the Australian mold, thanks to California's similarly moderate weather; there are a few very good, earthy Syrahs coming from South Africa, too. Barbecued foods with a smoky char pair nicely with Syrah, as do lamb, venison and game birds.

### INTENSE, SPICY SYRAH

Jaboulet Crozes-Hermitage (France)
Bonny Doon Domaine des Blagueurs Syrah (France)
Porcupine Ridge (South Africa)

**PAIRINGS**
- Greek Island Lamb Burgers with Grilled Feta, 136
- Jicama, Kirby and Carrot Salad with Charred Lamb, 140
- Lamb Stew with Swiss Chard and Garlic-Parsley Toasts, 144
- Grilled Leg of Lamb with Garlic and Rosemary, 146
- Braised Lamb Shanks with Trahana Pasta and Ricotta Salata, 146
- Grilled Leg of Lamb with Feta and Herb Salsa, 149
- Toulouse-Style Cassoulet, 174

### ROUND, DEEP-FLAVORED SYRAH

Qupé Central Coast (California)
Zaca Mesa (California)
Red Bicyclette (France)

**PAIRINGS**
- Skirt Steak with Shiso-Shallot Butter, 126
- Smoky Barbecued Brisket, 134
- Lamb Chops with Parsnips, 142
- Lamb Tagine with Prunes, 143
- Mahogany Glazed Spareribs, 163

### FRUITY, LUSCIOUS SHIRAZ

Woop Woop (Australia)
Tintara McLaren Vale (Australia)
Vasse Felix Adams Road (Australia)

**PAIRINGS**
- Slow-Smoked Turkey with Cane Syrup–Coffee Glaze, 115
- Beef Sukiyaki Noodles, 130
- Chile-Stuffed Cheeseburgers, 136
- Pork Chops with Nectarine Relish, 158

## ZINFANDEL

Though Zinfandel is descended from the Croatian grape Crljenak, the wine it produces is entirely Californian in character. The California wine country's warm, easygoing weather gives Zinfandel a jammy, juicy fruitiness (except when it's made into dull, lightly sweet white Zinfandel). Typically high in both alcohol and flavor—boysenberries with a touch of brambly spiciness—Zinfandel is the perfect cookout wine, great with grilled burgers, sausages or chicken, or even chips and dip.

### INTENSE, FRUITY ZINFANDEL

Three Thieves (California)
Rancho Zabaco Sonoma Heritage Vines (California)
St. Francis Old Vines (California)
Lolonis (California)

**PAIRINGS**
- Sesame Noodles with Prosciutto, 88
- Roasted Turkey with Shallot Butter and Thyme Gravy, 113
- Pan-Fried Pork Chops with Quinoa Pilaf, 156
- Pork with Strawberry-Herb Sauce, 158
- Oven-Fried Pork Carnitas with Guacamole and Orange Salsa, 162
- Barbecued Baby Back Ribs, 163
- Sausages with Grilled-Onion Chowchow, 172

# sizes & substitutions

## Cookware Sizes

When a recipe instructs you to use a small saucepan or a medium skillet, what does that really mean? Here are the pan, pot and baking dish sizes most commonly called for in recipes.

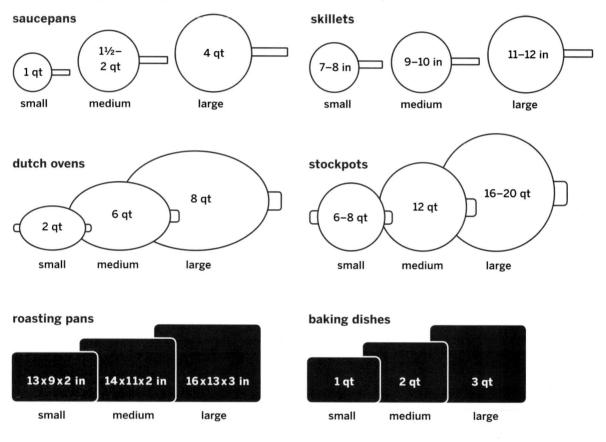

**saucepans**

1 qt — small
1½–2 qt — medium
4 qt — large

**skillets**

7–8 in — small
9–10 in — medium
11–12 in — large

**dutch ovens**

2 qt — small
6 qt — medium
8 qt — large

**stockpots**

6–8 qt — small
12 qt — medium
16–20 qt — large

**roasting pans**

13 x 9 x 2 in — small
14 x 11 x 2 in — medium
16 x 13 x 3 in — large

**baking dishes**

1 qt — small
2 qt — medium
3 qt — large

## How to Measure Cookware

When following a recipe, it is very important to know that the size of your pot, pan or baking dish matches what is called for. Manufacturers sometimes mark their cookware in inches or quarts, but often they don't. Here's what you need to know.

**DEPTH**
Measure on the inside of the dish, pot or pan from the bottom to the rim.

**VOLUME**
Fill the cookware (a baking dish, ramekin, soufflé mold, saucepan or any other piece of equipment) to the rim with water, then carefully pour the water into a measuring cup.

**WIDTH**
**BAKEWARE** Measure across the top of the pan, from inside edge to inside edge.

**FLUTED BAKING PANS OR DISHES** Measure from the inside of an outward curve to the inside of the opposite outward curve.

**SAUCEPANS AND SKILLETS** Measure across the top, usually from outside edge to outside edge.

372

# Pantry Staple Substitutions

| INGREDIENT | SUBSTITUTE |
|---|---|
| ARROWROOT | 1 teaspoon = 1 tablespoon all-purpose flour = 1½ teaspoons cornstarch |
| BAKING POWDER | 1 teaspoon = ¼ teaspoon baking soda plus ½ teaspoon cream of tartar |
| BUTTER | ½ pound (2 sticks) = ⅞ cup vegetable oil = ⅞ cup shortening |
| CHOCOLATE | **Unsweetened** 1 ounce melted = 3 tablespoons cocoa plus 1 tablespoon butter, shortening or vegetable oil<br>**Semisweet pieces** One 6-ounce package = 1 cup chopped dark chocolate |
| COCONUT MILK | 1 cup = 1 cup heavy cream |
| COGNAC | 1 tablespoon = 1 tablespoon brandy, bourbon or whiskey |
| CORNSTARCH | 1 tablespoon = 2 tablespoons all-purpose flour = 2 teaspoons arrowroot |
| CREAM | **Crème fraîche** ½ cup = ½ cup sour cream = ¼ cup sour cream plus ¼ cup heavy cream<br>**Half-and-half** 1 cup = ½ cup light cream plus ½ cup milk<br>**Light** 1 cup = ½ cup heavy cream plus ½ cup milk<br>**Sour** 1 cup = 1 cup plain yogurt |
| FISH SAUCE | 1 tablespoon = 1 tablespoon soy sauce blended with 4 mashed anchovies |
| FLOUR | **All-purpose** 1 cup = 1 cup plus 2 tablespoons cake flour<br>**Cake** 1 cup = ⅞ cup (1 cup minus 2 tablespoons) all-purpose flour<br>**Self-rising** 1 cup = 1 cup all-purpose flour plus 1¼ teaspoons baking powder and a pinch of salt |
| HORSERADISH | 1 tablespoon grated fresh = 2 tablespoons prepared |
| LEMON | **Juice** 1 teaspoon juice = ½ teaspoon vinegar<br>**Zest** 1 teaspoon grated zest = ½ teaspoon pure lemon extract |
| MADEIRA | 1 tablespoon = 1 tablespoon sherry or port |

| INGREDIENT | SUBSTITUTE |
|---|---|
| MARSALA | 1 tablespoon = 1 tablespoon sherry or port |
| MILK | **Buttermilk** 1 cup = 1 cup yogurt = 1 tablespoon vinegar or lemon juice plus enough milk to equal 1 cup, left to stand for 5 minutes<br>**Skim** 1 cup = ½ cup evaporated skim milk plus ½ cup water = ⅓ cup nonfat dry milk plus ¾ cup water<br>**Whole** 1 cup = ½ cup evaporated milk plus ½ cup water |
| MIRIN | 1 tablespoon = 1 tablespoon sweet sherry or sweet vermouth |
| MOLASSES | 1 cup = 1 cup dark corn syrup = ¾ cup brown or granulated sugar plus ¼ cup more liquid used in recipe |
| PANCETTA | Ounce for ounce, use lean bacon |
| PROSCIUTTO | Ounce for ounce, use country ham |
| SAKE | 1 tablespoon = 1 tablespoon dry sherry or vermouth |
| TAMARIND PASTE | 1 tablespoon = 1 tablespoon prune puree plus 1 tablespoon lemon juice |
| TAPIOCA, QUICK COOKING | 1 tablespoon = 1½ tablespoons all-purpose flour |
| TOMATO PUREE | 1 part tomato paste to 1 part water |
| TOMATO SAUCE | 1 part tomato paste to 2 parts water |
| VINEGAR | **Wine** 1 teaspoon = 2 teaspoons lemon juice<br>**Balsamic** 1 tablespoon = 1 tablespoon wine vinegar plus a pinch of sugar |
| WASABI | **Powdered** 1 teaspoon = 1 teaspoon hot dry mustard<br>**Prepared** 1 teaspoon = 1 teaspoon dry mustard plus ½ teaspoon vinegar plus ¼ teaspoon oil plus ⅛ teaspoon salt |
| YEAST | **Dry** 1 envelope = 1 scant teaspoon = ¼ ounce<br>**Fresh** 1 small cake (0.6 ounce) = 1 envelope dry yeast |
| YOGURT | 1 cup = 1 cup buttermilk = 1 cup sour cream |

# recipe index

## a

# recipe index

# recipe index

# recipe index

# recite index

# recipe index

# recipe index

# recipe index

# recipe index

# recipe index

# recipe index

# recipe index

# recipe index

# recipe index

# contributors

**Karen Adler** is a cooking teacher and cookbook author. Her forthcoming book, *Weeknight Grilling with the BBQ Queens,* co-written with Judith Fertig, is due out in spring 2006.

**Ferran Adrià** is the chef and owner of the avant-garde El Bulli in Rosas, Spain, and a co-creator of Fast Good, a fast-food restaurant in Madrid. He is also the author of *El Bulli: 1998–2002.*

**Victoria Amory** grew up in the Andalucía region of Spain and now writes a food and entertaining column for Florida's *Palm Beach Daily News.*

**David Ansel** created the Soup Peddler, a soup subscription service in Austin. He is the author of *The Soup Peddler's Slow & Difficult Soups.*

**Govind Armstrong** is the executive chef at Table 8 restaurants in Los Angeles and Miami and a co-owner of RokBar in Los Angeles.

**Christopher Bakken,** a poet and English professor at Allegheny College in Meadville, Pennsylvania, won the 2004 F&W Readers' Burger Contest.

**Paul Bartolotta** is a co-owner of the Bartolotta Restaurant Group based in Milwaukee and the chef at Bartolotta Ristorante di Mare in the Wynn Las Vegas Resort and Country Club.

**Lidia Bastianich** is the owner of four restaurants, including Felidia in New York City. She hosts the public television cooking show *Lidia's Family Table* and has authored several cookbooks.

**Neelam Batra** was born in New Delhi and has been teaching Indian cooking for over 20 years. She is the author of three cookbooks, including *1,000 Indian Recipes.*

**Jonathan Benno** is the *chef de cuisine* at Per Se in New York City.

**Rolando Beramendi** owns Manicaretti, an Italian foods import company, and Bellavitae restaurant, both in New York City.

**Peter Berley** is a private chef, caterer and cooking instructor who made his name at New York City's Angelica Kitchen. He is the author of *Fresh Food Fast* and *The Modern Vegetarian Kitchen.*

**Chef Bobo** (Robert Surles) is the executive chef and director of food services at the Calhoun School in New York City. He is author of *Chef Bobo's Good Food Cookbook.*

**Eugenia Giobbi Bone** is a food writer and co-author, with her father, Edward Giobbi, of *Italian Family Dining.*

**Daniel Boulud,** an F&W Best New Chef 1988, is the chef and owner of Daniel, Café Boulud and db Bistro Moderne in New York City and spinoffs in Las Vegas and Palm Beach, Florida. He is also the author of several cookbooks, including *Daniel's Dish.*

**James Boyce** is the executive chef at Studio in the Montage Resort & Spa Laguna Beach in California.

**Heather Carlucci-Rodriguez** is the chef and owner of Lassi in New York City.

**Roland Chanliaud** is the chef at Le Jardin des Ramparts in Beaune, France.

**Lauren Chattman** is a pastry chef and cookbook author. Her most recent book is *Icebox Desserts.*

**Michael Cimarusti** is the executive chef and co-owner of Providence in Los Angeles.

**Melissa Clark** is a freelance food writer who contributes regularly to F&W. She has co-authored 16 cookbooks, including *East of Paris* with David Bouley. She recently published her first solo cookbook, *Chef, Interrupted.*

**Tyson Cole,** an F&W Best New Chef 2005, is the executive chef at Uchi in Austin.

**Tom Colicchio,** an F&W Best New Chef 1991, is the chef and co-owner of Gramercy Tavern in New York City and the chef and owner of the Craft empire in New York City and Las Vegas. He is also the author of *Think Like a Chef* and *The Craft of Cooking.*

**Gennaro Contaldo** is the chef and owner of Passione in London and author of the restaurant's eponymous cookbook.

**Joan Coukos** is the owner of Chocolat Moderne in New York City.

**The Dar Liqama Cooking School,** run by the England-based Rhode School of Cuisine, teaches Moroccan cooking in a luxury villa in La Palmeraie, just outside of Marrakech.

**Seth Bixby Daugherty,** an F&W Best New Chef 2005, is the executive chef at Cosmos in Graves 601 Hotel in Minneapolis.

**Lauren Dawson** is the pastry chef at Hearth in New York City.

**Josh DeChellis** is the chef and co-owner of Sumile and the executive chef at Jovia, both in New York City.

**Patti Dellamonica-Bauler** is the pastry chef at One Market in San Francisco.

**Lissa Doumani,** an F&W Best New Chef 1991, is the pastry chef and co-owner of Terra in St. Helena, California, and Ame in San Francisco. She also co-wrote *Terra, Cooking from the Heart of the Napa Valley* with her husband, Hiro Sone.

**Carrie Dove** owns Carrie Dove Catering in San Rafael, California.

**Christopher Elbow** is the owner of Christopher Elbow Artisanal Chocolates in Kansas City, Missouri.

**Christophe Emé,** an F&W Best New Chef 2005, is the executive chef and owner of Ortolan in Los Angeles.

**Todd English,** an F&W Best New Chef 1990, is the chef and owner of Olives restaurants as well as other restaurants in cities across the United States. He is the author of several cookbooks, including *The Olives Table.*

**Corbin Evans** is the chef and co-owner of Lulu's in the Garden in New Orleans.

**Rob Evans,** an F&W Best New Chef 2004, is the chef and co-owner of Hugo's and Duckfat in Portland, Maine.

**Terese Fantasia** was the runner-up in the 2004 F&W Readers' Burger Contest.

**Efisio Farris** is the chef and owner of Arcodoro in Houston and Arcodoro & Pomodoro in Dallas. He also owns GourmetSardinia, an import company.

**Judith Fertig** is a cooking teacher and cookbook author. Her forthcoming book, *Weeknight Grilling with the BBQ Queens,* co-written with Karen Adler, is due out in spring 2006.

**Dominique Filoni** is an F&W Best New Chef 2004.

**Bobby Flay** is the chef and owner of Bolo, Mesa Grill and Bar Americain in New York City as well as Mesa Grill in Las Vegas. He also stars in several shows on the Food Network, including *BBQ with Bobby Flay* and *FoodNation,* and is the resident chef on CBS's *Early Show.* He has authored several cookbooks; his most recent is *Grilling for Life.*

**Tyler Florence** hosts several shows on the Food Network, including *Tyler's Ultimate.* He is the author of two cookbooks: *Tyler Florence's Real Kitchen* and *Eat This Book.*

**John Folse** is the owner of the New Orleans–based specialty food company Chef John Folse & Co. He has written seven cookbooks, including *The Encyclopedia of Cajun and Creole Cuisine.*

**Susanna Foo,** an F&W Best New Chef 1989, is the chef and owner of Susanna Foo Chinese Cuisine in Philadelphia and Suilan by Susanna Foo in Atlantic City. She has written two cookbooks; her most recent is *Susanna Foo Fresh Inspiration.*

**James Foran** is the pastry chef at Arterra in San Diego.

**Nobuo Fukuda,** an F&W Best New Chef 2003, is the chef and co-owner of Sea Saw in Scottsdale, Arizona.

**Tom Fundaro** is the executive chef at Villa Creek in Paso Robles, California.

**Cornelius Gallagher,** an F&W Best New Chef 2003, is the executive chef at Oceana in New York City.

**Shea Gallante,** an F&W Best New Chef 2005, is the chef at Cru in New York City.

**Marco Gallotta** is the executive chef at 'Gusto in Rome.

**Tasha Garcia** is a co-chef and co-owner, with Julie Taras, of Little Giant in New York City.

**Colby Garrelts,** an F&W Best New Chef 2005, is the executive chef and co-owner of Bluestem in Kansas City, Missouri.

**Jennifer Giblin** is the pastry chef at Blue Smoke in New York City.

**Edward Giobbi** is a co-author, with his daughter, Eugenia Giobbi Bone, of *Italian Family Dining.*

**Maggie Glezer** is the author of numerous award-winning books about bread baking, including *Artisan Baking.*

**Suzanne Goin,** an F&W Best New Chef 1999, is the chef and co-owner of Lucques and A.O.C. in Los Angeles. She is the author of the cookbook *Sunday Suppers at Lucques.*

**Kevin Graham,** an F&W Best New Chef 1991, is the chef at El Monte Sagrado Resort in Taos, New Mexico.

**Bill Granger** is the chef and owner of bills and bills 2 in Sydney. He has written three cookbooks; his most recent is *bills open kitchen.*

**Linda Greenlaw** is a former fishing boat captain featured in the book *The Perfect Storm.* She is the author of three best-selling memoirs and co-author, with her mother, Martha Greenlaw, of *Recipes from a Very Small Island.*

**Martha Greenlaw** is a co-author, with her daughter, Linda Greenlaw, of *Recipes from a Very Small Island.*

**Melissa Guerra** is a cookbook author and the owner of melisaguerra.com, an online purveyor of Mexican products.

# contributors

**Donna Hay** is an Australia-based cooking authority and creator of *Donna Hay* magazine. She has written eight cookbooks, including *The Instant Cook*.

**Gerry Hayden** is the former chef at Aureole and Amuse restaurants in New York City. He is opening a bed-and-breakfast and restaurant on Long Island.

**Sam Hayward** Is the chef and owner of Fore Street in Portland, Maine.

**Anissa Helou** is a London-based cookbook author. Her latest book is *The Fifth Quarter*.

**Shaun Danyel Hergatt** is the executive chef at The Setai resort in Miami.

**Maria Hines,** an F&W Best New Chef 2005, is the chef at Earth & Ocean in the W Hotel in Seattle.

**Gail Hobbs-Page** is the owner of Caromont Farmstead Chèvre and the executive chef of Feast! café and cheese shop in Charlottesville, Virginia.

**Ken Hom** has authored over 20 cookbooks, starred in several cooking shows and created a line of cookware called Tao. He also has his own line of Asian sauces, noodles and rice.

**Yasuhiro Honma** is the chef at En Japanese Brasserie in New York City.

**Daniel Humm,** an F&W Best New Chef 2005, is the executive chef at Campton Place in San Francisco.

**Johnny Iuzzini** is the executive pastry chef at Jean Georges in New York City.

**Jeremy Jackson** is the author of several cookbooks, including *Picnic: Simple Food that Travels Well*.

**Cheryl Alters Jamison and Bill Jamison** have written 10 cookbooks; their next one, *The Big Book of Outdoor Cooking & Entertaining,* is due out in spring 2006.

**Kimball Jones** is the executive chef at the Carneros Inn in Napa Valley and co-author of two cookbooks, *Sharing the Vineyard Table* and *The Casual Vineyard Table*.

**Maya Kaimal** is a food writer and the author of two cookbooks, *Curried Favors* and *Savoring the Spice Coast of India*. She also has her own line of Indian sauces, Maya Kaimal Fine Indian Foods.

**Pano Karatassos** is the executive chef at Kyma in Atlanta.

**Elizabeth Karmel** is the creator of GirlsattheGrill.com, a grilling and barbecue information resource, and Grill Friends, a line of ceramic serving pieces and grilling tools. She is the author of *Taming the Flame*.

**Thomas Keller** is the executive chef and owner of several restaurants: The French Laundry, Bouchon and Bouchon Bakery in Yountville, California; Bouchon in Las Vegas; and Per Se in New York City. He has written two cookbooks, *The French Laundry Cookbook* and *Bouchon*.

**Marcia Kiesel** is the F&W Test Kitchen supervisor and co-author of *The Simple Art of Vietnamese Cooking*.

**Rachel Klein** is the executive chef at Om in Cambridge, Massachusetts.

**Jeff Koehler** is an American writer and photographer living in Barcelona. He is the author of *La Paella: Deliciously Authentic Rice Dishes from Spain's Mediterranean Coast,* due out in spring 2006.

**Nicole Krasinski** is the pastry chef at Rubicon in San Francisco.

**Emeril Lagasse** stars in two shows on the Food Network: *Emeril Live* and *The Essence of Emeril*. He is the creator of his own line of food products and cookware and the author of 11 cookbooks,

including, most recently, *Emeril's Delmonico*. He is also the chef and owner of restaurants in New Orleans, Miami, Atlanta, Las Vegas and Orlando, Florida.

**Ray Lampe** (a.k.a. Dr. BBQ) is a national barbecue champion, teacher and author of *Dr. BBQ's Big Time Barbecue Cookbook*. He has his own line of barbecue sauces and rubs.

**Adam Perry Lang** is the chef and owner of Daisy May's BBQ USA in New York City.

**Cecilia Hae-Jin Lee** is a food writer and the author of *Eating Korean*.

**Austin Leslie** was the chef at New Orleans's Chez Helene and Pampy's Creole Kitchen before his death in 2005.

**Seen Lippert,** a former chef at Chez Panisse in Berkeley, is a cooking consultant and a member of the Yale Sustainable Food Project Steering Committee in New Haven, Connecticut.

**Anita Lo,** an F&W Best New Chef 2001, is the chef and owner of Anissa in New York City.

**The Lobel Family,** which includes Stanley, Leon, Mark, Evan and David Lobel, owns Lobel's Prime Meats, a butcher shop in New York City. They have written seven cookbooks.

**Michelle Lyon** is the pastry chef at the Carneros Inn in Napa Valley.

**Lachlan Mackinnon-Patterson,** an F&W Best New Chef 2005, is the chef and co-owner of Frasca Food and Wine in Boulder, Colorado.

**Jane Martin** is the chef aboard *Prosperité,* a luxury barge that runs along the Canal de Bourgogne in France.

**Daisy Martinez** is the host of the PBS program *Daisy Cooks! with Daisy Martinez* and author of the show's companion cookbook.

**Susan Masch** is the pastry chef at Villa Creek in Paso Robles, California.

**Dave Matthews** is a rock star with numerous albums, including *Stand Up*. He is the owner of Best of What's Around Farm and Blenheim Vineyards, both near Charlottesville, Virginia.

**Tony Maws,** an F&W Best New Chef 2005, is the chef at Craigie Street Bistrot in Cambridge, Massachusetts.

**Sue McCown** is the pastry chef at Earth & Ocean in the W Hotel in Seattle.

**Nancie McDermott** is a food writer and cooking teacher specializing in Southeast Asia.

**Melissa McKinney** is the pastry chef and owner of Criollo Bakery in Portland, Oregon.

**Janet Mendel** is an American-born journalist who has lived in Spain for more than 30 years. She is the author of many Spanish cookbooks, including *Food of La Mancha,* due out in 2006.

**Marc Meyer** is the executive chef and owner of Five Points and Cookshop restaurants in New York City. He is also the author of the cookbook *Brunch: 100 Recipes from Five Points Restaurant.*

**Sergi Millet** is the executive chef at Mas Rabell, a private restaurant in Catalonia, Spain, where the Torres wine family entertains.

**Michael Mina** is the executive chef of the Mina Group, which includes restaurants in San Francisco, Las Vegas and San Jose, California. The flagship is Michael Mina restaurant in San Francisco.

**Marc Murphy** is the executive chef and co-owner of Landmarc in New York City.

**Michelle Myers** is the pastry chef and co-owner of Sona restaurant and Boule *pâtisserie* in Los Angeles.

**Andy Nusser** is the executive chef and co-owner of Casa Mono in New York City.

**Nancy Oakes,** an F&W Best New Chef 1993, is the chef and co-owner of Boulevard in San Francisco and co-author of *Boulevard: The Cookbook.*

**Bradley Ogden** is a co-owner of the Lark Creek Restaurant Group, which operates several restaurants in California and Las Vegas.

**Pichet Ong** is the pastry chef at Spice Market and 66 in New York City.

**Grace Parisi** is the F&W Test Kitchen senior associate and the author of *Get Saucy.*

**Jeanette Peabody** is the *chef de cuisine* at Hamiltons' at First & Main in Charlottesville, Virginia.

**Jacques Pépin** is an F&W contributing editor, master chef, television personality and cooking teacher. He is the author of the memoir *The Apprentice: My Life in the Kitchen* and 23 cookbooks, including *Jacques Pépin: Fast Food My Way,* the companion volume to the public TV series of the same name. Personal chef to three French heads of state, including Charles de Gaulle, before moving to the United States in 1959, Pépin is a 2004 recipient of the French Legion of Honor.

**Michael "Cal" Peternell** is a chef at Chez Panisse Café in Berkeley.

**Mai Pham** is the chef and owner of Lemon Grass in Sacramento, California, and the author of two cookbooks: *The Best of Vietnamese and Thai Cooking* and *Pleasures of the Vietnamese Table.*

**Charles Phan** is the chef and owner of the Slanted Door in San Francisco.

**Emmanuel Piqueras** is the chef at Andina in Portland, Oregon.

**Wolfgang Puck** is the chef and owner of several restaurants, including Spago in Beverly Hills and Las Vegas, and of Wolfgang Puck Worldwide, a catering and events company. He stars in the Food Network show *Wolfgang Puck's Cooking Class* and has written numerous cookbooks.

**Steven Raichlen** is an award-winning author of 26 cookbooks, including *Barbecue USA: 425 Fiery Recipes from All Across America.* His PBS series, *Barbecue University with Steven Raichlen,* is based on his popular cooking school at the Greenbrier resort in White Sulfur Springs, West Virginia. He is also the creator of the Best of Barbecue line of grilling accessories.

**Alex Raij** is the executive chef at Tía Pol in New York City.

**Michael Recchiuti** is the owner of Recchiuti Confections in San Francisco and the author of *Chocolate Obsession.*

**Michael Romano,** an F&W Best New Chef 1991, is the executive chef and co-owner of Union Square Cafe. He also co-authored *The Union Square Cafe Cookbook* and *Second Helpings from Union Square Cafe.*

**Melissa Rubel** is an assistant food editor at F&W Books and the F&W Test Kitchen associate.

**Slade Rushing** is a co-chef and co-owner, with his wife, Allison Vines-Rushing, of Long Branch in Abita Springs, Louisiana.

**Aarón Sanchez** is the chef and co-owner of Paladar and Centrico restaurants in New York City and author of *La Comida del Barrio.*

**Richard Sandoval** is the chef and owner of Modern Mexican Restaurants in San Francisco, New York, Denver, Las Vegas and Washington, D.C.

# contributors

**Diana Santospago** is the innkeeper at the Inn at Isle au Haut in Maine.

**Amaryll Schwertner** is the executive chef and owner of Boulette's Larder, a specialty food shop and restaurant in San Francisco.

**Mindy Segal** is the chef and owner of HotChocolate in Chicago.

**Anoosh Shariat** is the executive chef at Park Place on Main in Louisville, Kentucky.

**Ron Shewchuk** is the chief cook of the Canadian champion barbecue team Rockin' Ronnie's Butt Shredders and author of *Barbecue Secrets*.

**Hiroko Shimbo** is a cooking teacher, food writer and the author of *The Japanese Kitchen* and *The Sushi Experience*.

**Andrew Shotts** is the owner of Garrison Confections in Providence.

**Nancy Silverton,** a Los Angeles–based chef and restaurateur, is a founder and former owner of La Brea Bakery and Campanile restaurant in Los Angeles. She is now a consultant to several restaurants in Los Angeles. She has written six cookbooks; her next is *Twist of the Wrist*.

**Constance Snow** is a cookbook author. Her most recent book is *The Rustic Table*.

**André Soltner** is the dean of classic studies at the French Culinary Institute in New York City. He was the chef and owner of New York City's Lutèce restaurant, which closed in 2004, and is a co-author of *The Lutèce Cookbook*. He won the James Beard Foundation Lifetime Achievement Award in 1993.

**Hiro Sone,** an F&W Best New Chef 1991, is chef and owner of Terra in St. Helena, California, and Ame in San Francisco. He is also a co-author of *Terra, Cooking from the Heart of the Napa Valley*.

**Katy Sparks,** an F&W Best New Chef 1998, is the culinary director and chef of Balducci's markets, based in New York City, and the author of *Sparks in the Kitchen*.

**Susan Spungen** is the former editorial director of food and entertaining at Martha Stewart Living Omnimedia. She is the author of *Recipes: A Collection for the Modern Cook*.

**Rick Stein** is the chef and owner of the Seafood Restaurant in Padstow, England. He is the author of nine cookbooks, including his most recent, *Rick Stein's Complete Seafood*.

**Mark Strausman** is the executive chef and co-owner of Coco Pazzo in New York City.

**Julie Taras** is a co-chef and co-owner, with Tasha Garcia, of Little Giant in New York City.

**Bradford Thompson,** an F&W Best New Chef 2004, is the *chef de cuisine* at Mary Elaine's in Scottsdale, Arizona.

**Laurent Tourondel,** an F&W Best New Chef 1998, is the chef and owner of BLT Steak, BLT Prime and BLT Fish in New York City. He is the author of *Go Fish*.

**Corinne Trang** is a cooking teacher, food writer and author of *Authentic Vietnamese Cooking, Essentials of Asian Cuisine* and *The Asian Grill*.

**Jerry Traunfeld** is the executive chef at The Herbfarm restaurant near Seattle. He is also the author of *The Herbfarm Cookbook* and *The Herbal Kitchen*.

**Jeff Tunks** is the chef and co-owner of Acadiana, Ceiba, DC Coast and TenPenh restaurants in Washington, D.C.

**Howie Velie** is the chef and owner of Magnolia Restaurant in Scottsville, Virginia.

**Allison Vines-Rushing** is a co-chef and co-owner, with her husband, Slade Rushing, of Long Branch in Abita Springs, Louisiana.

**Jean-Georges Vongerichten,** an F&W contributing editor, is the chef and co-owner of numerous restaurants around the world, including Jean Georges, Spice Market and Perry Street in New York City. He has co-authored *Simple Cuisine, Cooking at Home with a Four-Star Chef* and *Simple to Spectacular*.

**Aaron Whitcomb** is the executive chef at Table 6 in Denver.

**Ann Withey** is a co-founder of the food companies Smartfood and Annie's Homegrown.

**Paula Wolfert,** an F&W contributing editor, is the author of many award-winning cookbooks, including *Mediterranean Cooking, Couscous and Other Good Food from Morocco* and the recently updated *Cooking of Southwest France*.

**Sherry Yard** is the pastry chef at Spago in Beverly Hills and Las Vegas. She is the author of *The Secrets of Baking: Simple Techniques for Sophisticated Desserts*.

**Caroline Yeh** is the owner of Temper Chocolates in Boston.

**Grace Young** is the author of *The Wisdom of the Chinese Kitchen* and co-author of *The Breath of a Wok*.

**Eric Ziebold,** an F&W Best New Chef 2005, is the chef at Cityzen in the Mandarin Oriental Hotel in Washington, D.C.

**Eveline Zoutendijk** is the owner of Sarnic Hotel in Istanbul, where she also teaches cooking classes.

# photographers

**Bacon, Quentin** 19 (top), 22 (left), 27 (top), 43 (right), 72 (right), 80 (right), 83, 94 (left, right), 118, 124 (left), 147 (right), 148, 152, 153, 154 (left), 195 (bottom), 200 (right), 218, 219, 220 (right), 235, 265 (right), 297, 312 (left, right), 317 (right), 320, 322 (left), 332 (top), 343 (left), 344, 360, 361

**Baigrie, James** 41, 55 (left), 140 (left), 164 (top), 186 (left), 238 (right), 261 (right), 350, 351

**Chessum, Jake** 65 (bottom)

**C Squared Studios/Getty Images** 136 (habanero, green jalapeño)

**Davies and Starr/Getty Images** 136 (red holland chile)

**Davis, Reed** 58 (right), 156 (bottom), 356 (top, bottom)

**Doben, Brian** 265 (left)

**Gallagher, Dana** 25, 39, 72 (left), 104, 117, 145, 241, 302, 305, 309, 311 (left), 315, 321, 337 (right)

**Gentl & Hyers** 6, 47, 151, 268 (right), 300 (left), 337 (left), 341, 408

**Gissinger, Hans** 325, 326 (left, right), 349

**Halenda, Gregor** 143, 196, 329

**Heinser, Thomas** 139, 322 (right)

**Hill, Ethan** 56, 57

**Howard, Rob** 248, 249, 275, 294 (left, right)

**Ida, Akiko & Pierre Javelle** 266

**Janisch, Frances** 65 (top), 69, 109 (bottom), 122, 123, 135, 154 (right), 161 (bottom), 189 (right), 243 (bottom), 245, 250 (left, right), 255 (top), 300 (right), 343 (right)

**Kachatorian, Ray** 85

**Keller & Keller** 19 (bottom), 22 (right), 99, 198, 199, 263, 332 (bottom), 359

**Kernick, John** 8, 9, 51 (left), 34, 35, 164 (bottom), 168, 261 (left), 284 (left, right), 298, 299

**Kim, Kang** 318

**Kim, Yunhee** 52, 62, 175, 229, 257, 279, 293, 313, 357

**Ledner, Catherine** 78, 79, 128 (top), 205

**Lew, Rick** 183, 276 (right)

**Linder, Lisa** 176, 177

**McCaul, Andrew** 97, 163, 166

**McEvoy, Maura** 4, 51 (right), 91 (right), 124 (right), 256, 290

**Mentis, Anastassios** 45

**Meppem, William** 10 (right), 13, 55 (right), 140 (right), 195 (top), 200 (left), 217

**Miller, Ellie** 48, 128 (bottom), 231, 276 (left), 281

**Ngo, Ngoc Minh** 27 (bottom), 352 (right)

**Okada, Kana** 74, 131

**Prince, David** 354

**Christina Peters/Getty Images** 136 (anaheim, red jalapeño, banana, bird, and scotch bonnet chiles)

**Resen, Laura** 209 (bottom)

**Rooney, Deirdre** 77, 109 (top), 161 (top), 178 (right), 338

**Rupp, Tina** 10 (left), 36 (left), 80 (left), 86, 103 (left, right), 112, 137, 147 (left), 156 (top), 159, 173, 178 (left), 197, 209 (top), 213, 220 (left), 226 (top, bottom), 243 (top), 255 (bottom), 259, 267, 273, 289, 311 (right), 317 (left), 352 (left), 355

**Sanchez, Hector** 262, 335

**Strecker, Kirsten** 36 (right), 43 (left), 65 (bottom), 223

**Taylor, David Lewis** 89, 100

**Tinslay, Petrina** 92, 93, 238 (left), 268 (left), 282. Images from *simply bill* by Bill Granger: 91 (left), 283

**Burke Triolo Productions/ Getty Images** 120

**Webber, Wendell T.** 32, 54, 307, 347

**Williams, Anna** 14, 31, 58 (left), 61, 186 (right), 191

**Michael S. Yamashita/Corbis** 192

**Zipstein, Roy** 189 (left)